Combinations

EXPERIMENTS/ON THE POLITICAL

Series Editor: Iain Mackenzie, University of Kent

This series reflects on how interdisciplinary and/or practice-led thought can create the conditions for experimental thinking about politics and the political. What if the domain of the political is not what we usually think it is? Are there ways of thinking about the nature of politics and the political that can take us beyond frameworks of conflict and cooperation? These questions derive from a commitment to the idea that political thought has not yet exhausted its creative potential with regard to what constitutes the political domain. It is also motivated by the desire for political theory to become a genuinely creative discipline, open to collaborative interdisciplinary efforts in innovation. Moreover, if our understanding of the political world is to keep pace with political events, then it is important that political theorists do not simply presume that they express one or other of these dominant models of the political; rather they should remain open to the possibility that experiments in politics may be happening 'on the street' in ways that require theorists to think differently about what is meant by 'the political'.

Titles in Series

Combinations: Denominations, Democracy and the Politics of Nonviolence by
    Maurice Macartney
The Politics of Authenticating: Revisiting New Orleans Jazz by Richard Ekins and
    Robert Porter

With Rowman and Littlefield

*The Political Space of Art: The Dardenne Brothers, Ai Weiwei, Burial and
    Arundhati Roy* by Benoît Dillet and Tara Puri
Comedy and Critical Thought: Laughter as Resistance Edited by Iain MacKenzie,
    Fred Francis and Krista Bonello Rutter Giappone
Meanderings Through the Politics of Everyday Life by Robert Porter

Combinations

Denominations, Democracy and the Politics of Nonviolence

Maurice Macartney

LEXINGTON BOOKS

Lanham • Boulder • New York • London

Published by Lexington Books
An imprint of The Rowman & Littlefield Publishing Group, Inc.
4501 Forbes Boulevard, Suite 200, Lanham, Maryland 20706
www.rowman.com

86-90 Paul Street, London EC2A 4NE

British Library Cataloguing in Publication Information Available

Library of Congress Cataloging-in-Publication Data

Names: Macartney, Maurice, 1967- author.
Title: Combinations : denominations, democracy and the politics of nonviolence / Maurice Macartney.
Description: Lanham : Lexington Books, [2024] | Series: Experiments/On the political | Includes bibliographical references and index.
Identifiers: LCCN 2023054407 (print) | LCCN 2023054408 (ebook) | ISBN 9781666916218 (cloth) | ISBN 9781666916225 (epub)
Subjects: LCSH: Political violence—Prevention. | Identity politics. | Democracy. | Nonviolence
Classification: LCC JC328.6 .M318 2024 (print) | LCC JC328.6 (ebook) | DDC 303.6/1—dc23/eng/20240124
LC record available at https://lccn.loc.gov/2023054407
LC ebook record available at https://lccn.loc.gov/2023054408

To my family, for their warmth and patience, and above all to Jean and Salvo, to whom I am infinitely indebted, and to whom this book is dedicated.

Contents

Acknowledgements

This book could not have been written without the encouragement, inspiration, and advice of others – too many to name, it goes without saying; but I must risk naming a few.

For introducing me to some of the books and ideas that have stayed with me over the decades, my thanks go to Dr Hugh Bredin, formerly of the then Department of Scholastic Philosophy in Queen's University Belfast, as well as to my friends and teachers from Leuven and the University of Warwick.

Thanks, too, to Alan Finlayson and Iain MacKenzie, who helped steer me through the thesis in which I first started trying to articulate some of the ideas explored here in the late 1990s. On a related note, some of those thoughts first saw publication in an article in the *Journal of Irish Studies*, large portions of which are adapted and reproduced here in chapter 1. I have no hesitation, therefore, in thanking the publishers of that journal for permitting me to reproduce portions of 'Denominations and combinations: versions of "community" in the proclamation of Easter 1916 and the Good Friday Agreement', published in *Irish Political Studies*, 34:1, 48–68, (Maurice Macartney, 2019), © Political Studies Association of Ireland, reprinted by permission of Taylor & Francis Ltd, http://www.tandfonline.com on behalf of Political Studies Association of Ireland.

A second round of thanks to Iain MacKenzie, who, along with Robert Porter, gave me the impetus and opportunity to weave together all the loose threads of my thoughts for this book. Further thanks to Robert for many thought-provoking conversations over the years, and during the writing of this text in particular.

On a similar note, my thanks to friends such as John Barry, Colin Harper, Tanya Jones, Jenny Muir, Claire Mitchell, and Stephen Baker for many stimulating discussions, and even the occasional revolutionary brunch, that fed into this text – a text for which, of course, for better or worse, I must take full responsibility.

My gratitude goes to Dr Alex Christoyannopoulos for his constructive engagement with the final draft, and to the team at Rowman & Littlefield for bringing the book to light.

Introduction

How do we best learn to live together, for all our differences, as equitably, sustainably, and nonviolently as possible on this, our one and only planet, and in this, our corner of it?

This, it seems to me, is the key political question, though clearly it already calls up many subsidiary questions: What do we mean by equality, or equity? What do we mean by sustainability? By nonviolence? What do we mean by 'together'? But perhaps the biggest subsidiary question revolves around one of the shortest words in the sentence: 'we'. Who are *we*? In what way are we (there it is again!) to conceive of the 'we' evoked in this key question?

We've started with a key political question, so here is a sweeping political statement to go with it: politics, and indeed arguably the whole course of human history, is about *combinations*; combinations of material forces, combinations of people with other people. But how do you get *these* people to combine together with *these* people, and not with *those* people? Indeed, how do you get these people to combine *against* those people? Is there even such a thing as *these* people *before* they (actively) combine?

One effective way to get people to combine is to act as though the answer to this last question is yes: to tell them, or to 'let it be known', that they are already *essentially* combined, and that on an 'ontological' basis – on the basis of *what they are*, before they can get around to choosing what to *do*. It is claimed they *already* 'share an identity', already simply *belong* to an essentially unitary national, or an ethnic, or racial, or otherwise ontologically *given* group. You just *are* one of these or one of those. One of *us* or one of *them*.

You just have to face up to the reality of the situation.

The existence of group identities that are external to each other is here taken as the founding 'reality' upon which our politics has to be built – if it is to be 'realistic'. People just belong to different nations and denominations, and our politics should aim to construct a modus vivendi whereby these different communities can live together without falling into conflict.

1

And yet, here *I* am addressing *you*, without knowing whether you are one of *those* or one of *those*. Somehow, you and I have already formed a 'we' without first having to establish that we share nation, orientation or (let's use this as the general term for all *nameable collective entities, or group 'identities'*) denomination.

In a sense the answer to the opening question lies in that possibility of forming a 'we', a you-and-I, a *combination*, without going through the pre-scribed (pre-scripted) routes and routines of *denomination*, signing up to or constituting a 'collective identity'. A combination that is not pre-scripted, but an *improvisation*; and improvisation, as the guitarist Derek Bailey says, 'has no existence outside of its practice' (Derek Bailey 1993, x).

But as we will see throughout the rest of the book, we badly need the prac-tice. Not least – but not only – where I live, in Northern Ireland (and to say it at the start, this is the name for this place, contested as it is, problematic as it is, that I will use throughout, in part because *all* the names are contested; this being the theme of the book). Even at the time of writing, in 2023, as we mark the twenty-fifth anniversary of the Agreement that brought the conflict between 'the two communities' here to an end of sorts, the power-sharing institutions it inaugurated are undergoing yet another prolonged period of suspension.

We will start, then, in Northern Ireland, specifically in Newtownards, my hometown (though not the place of my birth), in 2016. It is as good a place as any to start an exploration of the politics of combination, of denomination and democracy, of violence and nonviolence, provided we are ready to weave about, not just geographically but chronologically too. Newtownards (pro-nounced Newton Ards) is a small town at the top end of Strangford Lough, overlooked by a tower on a hill, Scrabo Tower, that, to me, irresistibly con-jures John Donne's 'huge hill, cragged and steep' upon which 'Truth stands', such that 'he that will reach her, about must and about must go' (Satire III). I start from here, however, not because it is a particularly significant town, but because I am *here*, and we all have to start from *here*. We will certainly go 'about and about', of course, though whether we end up reaching Donne's Truth (but which of his truths? As we will later see, he has more than one) is another matter.

The year 2016, of course, was the year of Brexit, and the year Donald Trump sought and achieved election to the presidency of the United States of America; and if these events came as a shock, there were more shocks to come. By the time Trump's chaotic presidency stumbled to a graceless end in 2020, whether he accepted it or not, the COVID-19 pandemic was sweeping the globe, forcing people into lockdown, and tipping the world into a crisis as much to do with the social and economic spheres as it was to do with microbiology or health care.

In the same year, people across the world watched footage of a US police officer kneeling for more than eight minutes on George Floyd's neck, suffocating him, in just one in a long series of incidents in which law enforcement officers killed black Americans – except that this one triggered a wave of protests (and of crackdowns), and of *thinking*, first in the United States itself, then across the world.

As if the turbulence of 2020 were not enough, 2021 began with the unprecedented spectacle of a US president, having refused to accept the result of an election, inciting an assault on the Capitol. And before we had finished grappling with the attempted insurrection, before the full effects the economic and social turmoil emerging out of the coronavirus pandemic became clear, before we could fully absorb the lessons of the Black Lives Matter movement, and before we could process the images of Australian families backing into the sea as climate-change driven bushfires swept towards them, war broke out again in Europe.

It almost makes one nostalgic for the 'end of history'.

The events running up to and then intensified between 2016 and Russia's attack on Ukraine call us to *rethink* everything, our whole social, political, economic, and indeed ecological system, not just to get a better understanding, but in order to *change* the dynamics, or at any rate to contribute what we can to such a change.

I write this not just from Newtownards, not just from Northern Ireland, but also from the margins of academia: though I work for the same university in which I studied for my PhD, it is not as an academic, but as a member of the professional services team. My thesis, written around the time the Belfast or Good Friday Agreement was negotiated, signed, and ratified in referenda north and south of the border, attempted a deconstruction of precisely that political terrain, as it were; and I confess (how naïve!) I thought, at the time, that it might take twenty or twenty-five years or so, but, flawed as it was, the Belfast or Good Friday Agreement surely put us on the path toward becoming more like a 'normal' democracy, more like the other democracies in Europe, and in North America, rather than one riven by quasi-tribal (or in the term we are using here, denominational) conflict.

The spur for this book is that, looking around after fully a quarter of a century, not only has Northern Ireland failed to become like one of those 'normal' democracies, but many of those democracies seem to have *become like Northern Ireland*. It turns out, we were all on another path.

The hypothesis that spurred this book is that some of the dynamics that drove the conflict, and ensured Northern Ireland did not take the path of democratisation – or at least took it only in part and more slowly than some

of us hoped – are the same as, or structurally similar to, those that have
become amplified elsewhere. Amplified, not initiated: these dynamics have
already been at work here and elsewhere, perhaps everywhere, and perhaps
throughout history. Of course, we cannot cover 'everywhere and throughout
history' here, not in a single book, not in a library of libraries' worth of books
– and that not just for pragmatic reasons (a recent list of books, chapters
and articles published on colonialism and imperialism in 2020 alone ran to
146 pages – and this only covered works in the English language), but also
for reasons of principle. We would be in the position of Tristram Shandy had
he simultaneously taken on the task of writing his life story (taking longer
to write it than live it) as well as the task of Borges's map maker, forced to
expand the scale to account for every detail until the map was as big as the
world it tried to depict.

Reader, even had I the expertise (which I do not), I don't have the time;
and nor do you.

Bearing that in mind, we *are* going to touch on the conflict in Northern
Ireland; the era of enslavement and Empire; and on the currently globally
dominant political economic paradigm. Obviously, we can only touch on a
tiny fraction of this material, a tiny number of texts – and those not necessarily 'canonical', however that term should be understood. Whatever will help
us in our bid to feel out a path around Donne's cragged hill – though we set
out not so much to try to reach the top, where Truth stands, complete with
its capital *T*, but to try to find a path – 'about and about' – together. To get a
better feel for where we are, how we got here, and how we might combine
forces together to shift our social, political and economic system in a more
democratic, sustainable, equitable and nonviolent direction. Our path, thankfully, will overlap with those of plenty of others who have gone about before
us, better equipped and more expert, no doubt. But we – you and I – have to
start from where we are, picking up on such threads as we come across, left
behind by others, along the path.

But where *are* we? Who are *we*? If we are in Northern Ireland, 'we' are routinely said to belong to one or other of two 'communities' that go under various names – the Protestant, or Unionist, or Loyalist community on the one
side, the Catholic, or Nationalist, or Republican community on the other. Or
we belong almost as an afterthought, perhaps, to a smaller, third community,
ill defined, and less significant than the 'two main communities', if growing in number and in political significance. The 'two main communities',
sometimes abbreviated to PUL and CNR, are also associated with two different nationalities: British and Irish, respectively, though curiously, it is very
uncommon to hear references to 'the British community' or 'the Irish community' in Northern Ireland. In perhaps an indirect reference to nationality,
the terms 'Planter and Gael' are sometimes used – not without controversy

(McDowell 2022) – in a reference to the 'Plantations', waves of families from Britain 'planted' in Ireland in the sixteenth and seventeenth centuries, dispossessing Irish (Gaelic) families, as a matter of colonial policy.

The community, the tribe, the nation, this or that religious sect, the club, the company, the union – what if we stopped thinking about these as simply given, as entities in the world, and started thinking about them as different, ongoing *ways to get people to combine*, dynamic processes, different ways of producing, distributing, intensifying, or weakening allegiances or other bonds between people, ways to *set people towards one another*, in hostility or solidarity or indifference, ways of producing and distributing active 'obligations' that practically get a *bodily hold* on us? Even the terms al*leg*iance, ob*lig*ation and re*lig*ion already carry some trace of the sense of bonds, of *binding*, of *lig*aments – and thus of the idea of combination – within them.

How do you produce, shape, direct and distribute those bonds, these bindings? How have we done it in the past, how do we currently do it? How could we do it better?

In Northern Ireland, as we have just mentioned, one way we have traditionally bound people together is in and through 'communities' of a certain *denomination* – not just in a religious or sectarian sense, though that is part of the story; and not just in the sense that there (simply) *are* two main (religious) denominational communities in Northern Ireland.

Chapter 1 will examine what, in the late 1980s, the social scientist John Whyte called the 'dominant paradigm' of interpreting Northern Ireland: the 'internal' or 'two communities in conflict' model (Whyte 1990). This paradigm dominated political discourse in Northern Ireland then, and has largely dominated our politics ever since – and indeed perhaps also before: nationalism, 'the nation', whether of the British (Imperial) or Irish (nationalist) or any other kind, operates at least in part through the sort of *processes of denomination* that constitute this paradigm.

As we have already hinted, such processes are about naming (denominating) people as belonging to a 'collective entity' such as a nation, an ethnic group, a cultural community, or a religious sect (a denomination in the narrow sense) *conceived as ontologically* (even *ontically*) *given*, as something *present-at-hand* (Heidegger 1967) like a rock or a table, and as such, beyond question, *exempt* (as we will later say) *from the question of violence*. But a denominational community is not one more 'thing' in the world: if it makes its appearance it is more like a smoke-ring than a rock or table; it is nothing outside the dynamics, the processes that constitute it. These processes are active: they do not wait until there *is* an already fully constituted community, sitting there, as it were, waiting only to be recognised and described under the proper name.

The term 'denomination', then, carries with it a useful ambiguity: '*A* denomination' works as a noun – it names the collective entity to which we are said to belong. But 'denomination', more importantly, also indicates an *action*, a process expressed in the verb '*to denominate*'. This is the sort of verb, as we will see in the first chapter, that is used in what JL Austin calls a 'performative' utterance – the sort of utterance that does not *describe* something already there in the world, so much as *do something* in the world. 'I declare this building open'; 'I pronounce you husband and wife'. Denomination appears to name a collective entity, passively reflecting what is already there in the world, but does so by *actively projecting* the boundaries of the very entity which is taken as the ground upon which and from which our political projects are launched, the collective entity which is in that sense the author of 'our' politics (and which therefore *authorises* them). Indeed, in naming *this* collective entity, these processes always project *at least two* denominations – or perhaps better, denomination projects a border, conceived as an ontological gulf, that separates inside from outside, *exteriorising* a 'them' from an 'us', as though these two entities simply *are* there, and already *were* there all along. In Austin's terms, 'denomination' is a performative masquerading as a constative statement.

It is because of this ambiguity, illustrating the mechanisms we are to examine here, that I will use denomination throughout, rather than turn to terms such as 'identity', 'ethnicity', or 'caste'. There is no 'identity' without active processes of *identification*, for example, no 'caste' without active 'casting', so to speak; but the active production and projection of identities and castes tends to be swallowed in the apparent thing-like, named givenness of the noun – though there have been important attempts to use some of these nouns in new ways, such as Isabel Wilkerson's Caste, precisely to bring out the active processes of projection we are looking at. And while there is much to be said for analyses of processes of 'Othering', I will largely avoid using that term, not least because others *are* other: the risk is that we fall into the trap of thinking we have to reduce the otherness of the other if we are to avoid 'Othering' in that negative sense – as though being 'other' is a bad thing.

For similar reasons, though we will be examining the hierarchically (and violently) organised economics of extraction, and will read wealth as a form of power throughout, I will largely avoid a certain traditional terminology of 'class analysis' here, if for such an analysis 'a class' is thought of as an already existing, monolithic entity, external to others, both to avoid the risks of 'reification' and of this text being drawn into the gearing of a whole other set of powerful textual machinery. This does not mean we are to ignore economic power. Indeed, in a sense, the whole aim and project of the book is to examine the mechanisms and dynamics of the power-economy that keep throwing up hierarchically ordered 'classes', and that, in particular, tend to keep 'working class' people from combining with each other to change those dynamics.

The process of denomination *inaugurates* (or reinstates, reiterates – *solemnises* as one solemnises a marriage in a repeat performance) with the force of a speech act, the 'denomination-as-entity' it purports to describe, in order to gather people under the name – the 'denominational community'. This is not to say there were not people already living together. In a sense, yes of course I belong to *a community*, made up of my friends and family, my neighbours, my workmates, the people I meet and pass the time of day with while picking up my usual loaf of bread from the baker in the town market on a Saturday morning. And maybe, as it happens, the great majority of them share a denomination, in the religious sense, or in the sense of a national or ethnic identity, with me; or maybe they don't – as it happens.

But the sort of community that emerges in the contiguous encounters and habits and meanderings of everyday life (Porter 2018) is not the same as the sort of community projected in the phrase 'the two communities' (or, in another register, 'the nation', or 'The White Race'). They may overlap, but they are not the same. And a great deal depends on that difference.

In an everyday, contiguous community, we, you and I, encounter each other as neighbours in the neighbourhood; we combine together, face-to-face, to take on a bit of work; or do our bit in a community clean up; or to make a transaction in the town market, when I buy your bread; or over a beer on an evening out, or a bowl of stew when we meet for lunch before going to watch the local football match. We, you and I, will *never* sit down to a pint and a bowl of stew with the *denominational community* we purportedly belong to.

No matter how long you live in Northern Ireland, say, you will never step out of your house and bump into 'The Protestant Community', or have a drink with 'The Catholic Community'. You will meet plenty of people who *claim to speak for* (or about) those denominational communities; some of them will tell you what this or that community thinks, or says ('Ulster Says No'); some of them will tell you they 'belong' to, or are 'representatives' of this or that community; but the 'community' they *re*present will never *itself* be *present*, face-to-face with you; the denominational community will always remain *offstage*, elsewhere, outside the space of our everyday encounters, apparently whispering lines, like a theatre prompter, to its spokespeople. And this does not just apply to Northern Ireland, where the term may seem more obviously applicable, and where we admittedly have forms actually asking people to denominate themselves as belonging to one of two mutually exclusive 'communities'. Similar processes, even if they do not use the term, even in the absence of official forms, are at work elsewhere.

Such a politics of denomination, we will claim, sets the scene for a certain politics of *hostility* of the kind set out by Carl Schmitt in his thinking of the 'friend-enemy' distinction (Schmitt 1996); but this always throws up a third figure: the *traitor*. The interplay between these figures governs the dynamics of a politics of hostility and sets the scene for violence of the sort all too familiar across the world, and not least in Northern Ireland.

One possible route out of the politics of hostility, according to some, is to swap the locally dominant paradigm (in Northern Ireland, the 'two communities in conflict' model) for the globally dominant paradigm of the 'power of the market', wherein such community or denominational identities become less and less salient. But in the second chapter, via a reading of a film, a fable, a philosopher, and some family history, we will argue that this globally dominant paradigm constitutes another, no less potent form of a politics of violence, albeit a less 'obvious' one, through what we will call a politics of *indifference*.

In the third chapter, we will trace, all to sketchily, one among many possible paths through the history of the globally dominant paradigm, from the emergence of the corporation, through the era of Empire and enslavement, to show how the dynamics of hostility and indifference can overlap, intensifying the dynamics of violence in projecting what we will call a *viceregally* structured hierarchy, governed by a 'higher authority' that functions to 'authorise', and channel, the violence of hostility *and* of indifference.

In chapter 4, we will bring the story up to date. Where once upon a time, in a moment of sunny optimism, it seemed that we had reached the 'end of history', it now appears that conflict, particularly in the form of what some are calling 'tribalism', and what we are calling the politics of denomination, has surged all over the world. Leaders like Recep Tayyip Erdoğan, Viktor Orban, Narendra Modi, Jair Bolsonaro, and of course Donald Trump, rose to power not by defusing denominational conflict but by stoking it. And while some of those leaders have since been removed, democratically, from their offices, kick and scream as they might, the Russian assault on Ukraine, still ongoing at the time of writing, and the outbreak of violence in Israel and Gaza, just beginning as this book was being prepared for the press, are clear reminders that these forces are still very much in play.

In the last two chapters, then, we will try to suggest an alternative to the politics of violence, taking our cue from the document that marked the culmination of the peace process in Northern Ireland, the Belfast, or Good Friday Agreement, a document that embodied at least two dynamics, the one being, as we have seen, a reduction to the binary of the locally dominant paradigm, but the other holding open the possibility of the formation of a 'we' beyond the boundaries of denomination, based on a commitment to democracy and nonviolence.

We will examine this idea of nonviolence – and the active *power* of non-violence – in the company of Judith Butler, Walter Benjamin, James Baldwin, and others, linking it to the idea of radical democracy. And in conclusion, we will pull together the threads that will have woven throughout the book and consider how we might build a politics that would allow us to combine campaigns for economic justice; for ecological justice; and for justice across a range of equality issues relating to race and ethnicity, gender and sexual orientation, ability and disability, and more.

These broad movements – the red, the green, and the rainbow, so to speak – are sometimes set against one another; but the projects that underpin them, rooted in a certain thinking of democracy, equality, sustainability and non-violence, share a logic; are inseparably bound up together – require, or *call for* each other.

This *democratic combination*, this movement of movements, makes a bid to build an equitable, nonviolent, sustainable democracy; a democracy that would not be reducible to dominance by this or that denomination; and crucially, a democracy that would not be confined by this or that state boundary, this or that national border. A *neighbourhood* democracy, where the neighbourhood will always spill over boundaries.

Such an understanding of democracy is, perhaps, the answer to the question with which we started: how do we best learn to live together, for all our differences, as equitably, sustainably and nonviolently as possible on this our one and only planet, and in this our corner of it? Or rather, it is perhaps the best way to *keep that question open.*

In a sense this question, and therefore the meaning of the answer, 'democracy', sums up everything I want to explore here. The question is, as we already suggested, complex: what does it mean, to learn to live *together*? Do we have to minimise or elide our differences to be able to do it? What does nonviolent mean? What is 'our corner' of the planet, our neighbourhood? Do we have a responsibility to it that goes beyond our responsibility to others *outside* my neighbourhood? And to echo the biblical phrase, who exactly *are* my neighbours? For that matter, who are *we*?

The path we pick out will overlap with those explored by many campaigners, political activists and thinkers, and we will, of necessity, explicitly name only a few of them. The approach of the phenomenologists (Husserl, Heidegger, Merleau-Ponty, and Levinas), a certain Marxian spectre (not least the idea of interpellations, to which the denominations we are to examine are closely related), the influence of writers such as Derrida, Foucault, Butler, Laclau and Mouffe, Said, Balibar, Žižek, Deleuze, and Guattari (the fibres of whose rhizomes, in particular, will weave in unspoken multiplicity throughout the text), and many others will be evident throughout, even where it is not made explicit, to those familiar (doubtless far more familiar than I) with their writings.

However, my aim here is not primarily exegesis; not to wrangle over the correct interpretation of philosophical doctrine (though we will undertake that task in places too), but to find a way, for myself, from *here*, where I am, around Donne's hill.

Should you choose to come along, you are welcome to share the path with me.

Chapter One

Denomination

The Politics of Hostility

In the early summer of 2016, I spent some time campaigning for a Remain vote in the then looming Brexit referendum. The Remain campaigners in my area – the northern stretch of County Down in Northern Ireland – were of different ages, of varying backgrounds, and with a range of party-political affiliations: Greens; Alliance Party supporters; Ulster Unionists; and a former member of the Women's Coalition. We probably had a wide range of attitudes towards the EU too. Some were more enthusiastic Remainers than others. Some joined the campaign despite serious reservations about the EU, not least after witnessing the biting austerity imposed on member countries like Greece since the crash of 2008. Some campaigned to Remain simply because there was no 'exit stage Left', only one on the (hard) right; and it seemed a better option than helping Nigel Farage and Boris Johnson secure the political victory of their lives.

Whatever our reservations, we wore our 'NI IN' T-shirts, we handed out leaflets, we engaged in discussions with our neighbours about the pros and cons of remaining in the EU, urging that, on balance, given the environmental legislation, workers' rights, given the fact that poorer regions like Northern Ireland were net beneficiaries of cash transfers from the EU, and so on, voting 'Remain' was the best option for the people of NI. Moreover, we argued, a vote to leave would result in an unnecessary and prolonged period of instability in which huge amounts of energy, which could be better spent, would have to be devoted to unpicking and replacing an intimate network of social, legal, political, and economic bonds that had been developed over the preceding four decades.

It was for this reason I found myself handing out leaflets one Saturday afternoon, in the market square of Newtownards, where I had been living for over a decade, when someone walked close by me and said, quietly, but menacingly, 'you people should be in jail for treason'.

It came as a shock – almost a body blow. There was an intensity to his response I did not expect; it seemed out of kilter with my sense of the scope of the debate – though perhaps I should have seen it coming. After all, this was at a time of increasingly visceral politics: Donald Trump was on the rise in the United States; similar movements were rising in Brazil, in Turkey, in Hungary, in Modi's India, to say nothing of a range of small, but growing, European right-wing populist parties. And, of course, in other parts of the UK, tensions over the Brexit debate were rising – this was not long before the murder of Jo Cox.

Indeed, this was *Northern Ireland*, where cries of treason and betrayal have echoed down the ages, all the way back to Robert Lundy's apparent attempt to hand Derry to the troops of King James in 1689. To this day an effigy of 'Lundy the Traitor' is burned annually by the Apprentice Boys, named for the Protestant youths who shut the gates of Derry against the oncoming forces of the Catholic king.

And the rhetoric of 'betrayal' was never far from the lips of the Reverend Dr Ian Paisley, who once gave a speech in which he cited 'the Belfast Agreement of treachery', opening thus: 'The worst and most loathsome person in society is the traitor – the Judas, the Iscariot. Who dares to excuse and whitewash treachery but he who is a party to that treachery?' (Paisley 1998).

It is worth noting in passing that, though he died in 2014, there is no doubt which side of the Brexit debate the famously anti-EU MEP would have been on.

The discourse of treason, then, is nothing new in this part of the world; but still, that my neighbour should react to me like that, and that it should come as such a shock to me, calls for some thinking. From my point of view, I was engaged in a democratic debate about choosing a political project; from his point of view, I was betraying – but there's the question: betraying what, or whom? My people? My country? My community? My *denomination*?

For anyone looking on from the outside, as it were, it may seem odd to bring in the notion of 'denomination' like this. But Northern Irish political discourse is so saturated with religious terms (Paisley's 'Judas', or come to that, his dog-collar; the 'Protestant community', the 'Catholic community') that the outsider might be forgiven for thinking the Northern Irish conflict was about religion *as such*, about religious and doctrinal differences – about whether to 'kiss a post or throw it on the fire', as Jonathan Swift once put it.

It was not, of course, or at least not in any simple sense – and certainly not a religious conflict *alone*; and yet we should not be too quick to claim religion is a mere mask for other interests or forces. As Claire Mitchell puts it: 'Conflict in Northern Ireland has not been, is not and will never be a holy war. However, religion is much more socially and politically significant than many commentators have presumed. . . . This book understands religion as a dynamic of personal and group identification' (Mitchell 2006, 1–2).

Let us also state clearly at the outset that none of the analyses to come in any way set out to diminish the trauma of that conflict, and of the history that preceded and surrounded it. None of it is to minimise the violence of Imperialism or of any state or non-state actors. Indeed, that violence, and how it is shaped, will be the constant thread running throughout this text. My claim is simply that this violence has been, and still is, shaped by processes of *denomination*. Not *only* by processes of denomination – many socio-economic and other structural elements need careful scrutiny too. But as Peter Mitchell says, the 'violence of the past is ongoing in the present, not only structurally . . . but in more subtle, more constitutive ways: in the words we use, the images we attach to things, the ways we imagine ourselves and each other' (Mitchell 2021). It need only be added that this includes, perhaps most subtly of all, the ways in which we are led to distinguish between the 'we' of 'ourselves' and the 'other' of 'each other'. These ways of distinguishing between ourselves and others, sometimes before we even know it, set the scene for, and shape relations between, neighbour and neighbour; we must attend carefully to these if we are to dismantle the politics of violence.

The word 'denomi*nation*', too, can perhaps be made to express something of the combination of religious and *national* dimensions to the conflict in Northern Ireland, as well as the sense of an almost religious *identification with* and *loyalty to* this or that group. Perhaps this is the 'missing word' that Orwell mentions in his Notes on Nationalism, in which he says that, for want of a better word, he uses *nationalism* as the 'nearest equivalent' to the concept he is outlining. For Orwell, this kind of 'nationalism' means 'the habit of identifying oneself with a single nation or other unit, placing it beyond good and evil and recognizing no other duty than that of advancing its interests' (Orwell 2001, 355).

Almost every word in this sentence is significant for our purposes – 'habit'; 'identifying'; 'unit'; 'duty', perhaps especially the idea that the nation (or denomination) is placed at a *point of exemption* from the question of 'good and evil', or 'violence and nonviolence' as we will later say. All of these will come up in our analyses of what are calling processes of denomination. In particular, the idea that *identification*, rather than *identity*, is what we should be looking at. What happens when such processes of identification become so routine as to become invisible? And how does it happen?

Look again at those phrases: the 'Protestant community' and the 'Catholic community' – or perhaps the 'Protestant community' *versus* the 'Catholic community'. The word *community*, too, so often prefixed with (religiously) denominational terms, is well worn in Northern Irish politics – so much so that it goes by unremarked, taken for granted, even as it is used in ways that suggest a variety of meanings.

For example, in what appears to have been a post-Brexit protest against the Protocol which placed a 'border in the Irish Sea' – two masked men stopped a bus in Newtownards early one November morning in 2021, ordered the driver off (there were no passengers yet), poured petrol on the vehicle and set it alight.

It was reported that the attack was claimed by a group calling themselves the 'Protestant Action Force'. The name, explicitly referring to a religious denomination, was not typical of those used by the main Loyalist groups, who tend to use 'Ulster' (Ulster Defence Association, Ulster Volunteer Force); but it is one that had occasionally been used before, during Northern Ireland's 'Troubles' (Leebody 2021).

The incident was roundly condemned by politicians from across the spectrum. Doug Beattie, the leader of the UUP, said the 'stupid actions of thugs and criminals' simply 'hurt their own community' (McGonagle 2021). His party colleague Julie-Anne Corr-Johnston said that those responsible 'may very well be anti-protocol but their actions are vehemently anti-community' (Corr-Johnston 2021). On the Nationalist end of the spectrum, the SDLP's Nichola Mallon said that the 'faceless, mindless cowards who did this have done nothing more than attack their own community' (Mallon 2021). And the Alliance Party's Naomi Long said the attack would achieve nothing other than 'spreading fear and causing disruption to much needed services in communities' (McGonagle 2021)

What is the significance of the use of the term 'community' in these utterances? Do these political actors mean what is usually meant by the term in Northern Ireland, where phrases such as 'the two communities', or 'both communities' saturate political discourse? Saturate it so much that, following the eminent social scientist John Whyte, as we will see below, we might call it the 'dominant paradigm'.

But the term, perhaps, is being used, in the context of the bus-burning, in a rather different sense. Is the 'community' that is being attacked (Mallon) 'the Protestant Community'? The 'Unionist Community'? Or is it perhaps something like the 'local community', who need the bus to be able to get to work, and so on? Is it 'their own' community in the sense that they, too, live in this neighbourhood, may also, in common with their neighbours, be impoverished and disempowered by an attack on their bus service? Or is it a *sense* of community, the *cohesion of community itself* that is at stake – as Corr-Johnston seems to indicate in the intriguing formulation 'anti-community'?

It is through an examination of his tension, this divergence between the 'communities' of the dominant paradigm and the sort of community apparently intended in phrases such as 'the local community' (and the uncertainty over what is being named here itself has its effects) that we will look at some of the mechanisms that were and are at work not just in relation to the Troubles or Brexit, and not just in Northern Ireland, but, as we will argue here, in shaping the political dynamics of the modern world. First, let us look more closely at that 'dominant paradigm'.

THE DOMINANT PARADIGM

In 1990, after an extensive survey taking in thousands of articles and books on Northern Ireland, John Whyte concluded that what he called the 'internal conflict interpretation' was the 'dominant paradigm' within the academic literature on the subject. Traditional interpretations which laid the emphasis on external factors such as the British, as traditional Irish Nationalism would have it, or Dublin's claims to the whole territory, as traditional Unionism would have it, dominated the academic scene until the outbreak of violence in the late 1960s.

From that point on, he says, the conflict 'so obviously was between two opposed communities . . . that an internal conflict approach became at once more plausible' (Whyte 1990, 195). According to this model, the main source of the problem lay within Northern Ireland. This is not to say the British or Irish Governments had no role or responsibility, but the conflict between the 'two opposed communities' held decisive sway.

The pattern that Whyte saw as dominant then has arguably held sway ever since. The idea of 'the two communities' surfaces again and again, not just in the academic literature, but in the utterances of politicians, in newspapers and other media, in official documents and in everyday conversation. Most of the politicians Whyte interviewed for his survey subscribed to this 'dominant paradigm', and it is not hard to find examples of the paradigm at work in Northern Irish discourse, then or since.

It is written, for example, into the Good Friday Agreement, speaking as it does of 'parity of esteem between the two main communities', and 'mutual respect for the identity and ethos of both communities', and so on (Agreement 1998).

Over two decades later, politicians elected to the Stormont Assembly as Members of the Legislative Assembly (MLAs) in the election of 2022 still had to sign themselves in as though they belonged to one of the 'two main communities' (Unionist or Nationalist), or to a third category, 'Other'. This third category, however, was not accorded equal weight when it came to voting on significant issues. The GFA and the legislation that gave it effect, in seeking to construct mechanisms to ensure 'cross-community consensus', ensured that key decisions would be made with the support of a minimum proportion of 'the unionist and nationalist designations present and voting'. No special requirement for the consent of 'Others' was built into the institutions.

Look again at the phrase Whyte uses: the conflict 'so obviously was between two opposed communities . . . ' that the 'internal conflict' model comes to dominate (Whyte 1990, 195). What if the very *'obviousness'* of the 'two opposed communities' works to obscure some of the mechanisms shaping what Joseph Ruane and Jennifer Todd called the 'dynamics of conflict in Northern Ireland' (Ruane and Todd 1996)? What if 'everyday' statements presenting 'the two communities' as simply *given*, are not so much matter-of-fact descriptions as, to adapt JL Austin's title, 'ways to *do things* with words' (Austin 1975)?

In another register, what if, in the manner of the phenomenologists (Husserl 1970), we suspend, or bracket off, any belief in the 'obvious' existence of these two entities, and look instead at how the incessant repetition of statements about 'two opposed communities' works to inaugurate and perpetually reinstate the 'two opposed communities' the statements purport to describe? Phenomenology advises us to go 'back to the things themselves', to attend to the ways in which we encounter them, here, now, in the world, rather than to come at them via the detour of metaphysics textbooks. So how do we encounter 'the two communities', these entities that are so 'obvious' they dominate Northern Irish political discourse?

If they are so obvious, surely we must come across them in everyday life – but how? Do we step out of our houses and bump into them in the street? Do we meet them in the bustling marketplace on a Saturday in Newtownards, or any other town in Northern Ireland? Could it be that we do not so much encounter these 'obvious' entities, as encounter *people who claim to represent them*, people who claim to *speak in their name*, to be able to tell you what this or that community thinks, people who claim to *belong* to them? People who put up signs telling you this is a 'Loyalist area'; or who erase the 'London' from signs saying 'Londonderry'; people who paint murals proclaiming Ulster to be British; people who use the term 'north of Ireland', rather than 'Northern Ireland', and others who reprimand them for it; people who write newspaper columns and meticulously researched text books about one or other or both of 'the two communities', even those telling us how we might overcome the conflict between them (McGarry and O'Leary 1989)?

What if we never encounter these two entities *outside the innumerable utterances* that continually proclaim their ('obvious') existence? What kind of 'existence', what kind of entity are we looking at – or rather, looking *for*?

'Utterances' should be taken in a broad sense here, to include all manner of signs, from the loud and overt political statement to something like a 'flag hanging unnoticed', as Michael Billig might put it. Billig is discussing 'national identity', and argues that it is reproduced, in large measure, by way of a whole raft of 'forgotten reminders'; reminders such as the flag *not* being waved fervently at demonstration, but 'hanging unnoticed on the public building' (Billig 1995, 8). The sort of flag that hung largely unnoticed every day, for instance, on the City Hall of a smallish UK city until, in December 2012, the Council took the decision to take it down, and fly it only on a hand-ful of designated days – a decision that sparked weeks of turmoil, bringing (you will have guessed it) Belfast to a standstill, injuring many police officers and causing widespread damage (Nolan et al. 2014).

Such symbolic disputes, to be sure, are a key part of the long history of politically structured violence in Northern Ireland (Bryan and Gillespie 2005). But the flag, in its presence or absence, is part of a whole *machinery of denomination* in Northern Irish politics. Like any other political emblem, the flag at issue here operates as a symbol, a sign, whether it is being waved fervently, is hanging unobtrusively, or is missing in action. The signal it sends relates, of course, to issues of identity, interests and territory, but if such signs are 'processes', as James R Williams has it (Williams 2020), clearly, they 'process' people in very different ways – sometimes in diametrically opposed ways. Some of those who wanted the Union flag to fly over Belfast City Hall all year round did so because it identified the territory as part of the UK – or (is this the same thing?) as *British*; some of those who wanted it removed did so for exactly the same reason, though with diametrically opposed motives.

In the event, there were a complex range of motives and dynamics among those who took to the streets in protest. The key report on the flags dispute identifies six main drivers: social; emotive; ideological; cultural; political; and economic drivers. The authors also identify interesting gender dynamics, with the 'demonstration of masculinity' being an important factor (we should add, a certain *version* of masculinity), but with women and children playing significant roles, and deftly analyse sometimes conflicting interpretations of the dispute among participants.

For all these complexities, though, one interviewee raises a key point: 'the protest allowed them to coalesce around something' (Nolan et al. 2014, 102). Read in one way, this means the *removal* of the flag was itself taken as a flag of sorts, a symbol, around which *different* people with different and *even contradictory* understandings of what they were doing could coalesce, or *combine*.

It is not that there was already a monolithic 'Loyalist Community' (and the distinction between the 'Loyalist Community' and 'Unionist Community' is one that calls for analysis), an entity already fully constituted and of one mind. It is that the removal of the flag gave *different people* a common sym-bolic cause around which to combine, and a common enemy (Sinn Féin, and anyone seen to *combine* with *them* in one broad 'pan-nationalist' denomination) *against* whom to combine.

Some final 'key facts' from the flags report. Within 'the loyalist community', the authors say, 'the most frequently voiced concern is that "no one listens to us"'. And yet, 'the desire to be heard is not accompanied by a desire to listen. We have found a striking lack of interest in the concerns of the nationalist neighbour' (Nolan et al. 2014, 12). Here is a kind of combination with *these* others, and not with *those* others; a coalescing around a named 'community', an identity (or perhaps better, object of identification) and an issuing of monological statements *from* that 'community' to the outside world, rather than risking conversation with *others as such*.

The protests over the flag were, to be clear, only one series of events in a whole complex history of such events, stretching back at least as far as the partition that created Northern Ireland, but they arguably make tangible the dynamics that crop up again and again in the politics and discourse of the area – and beyond. But before we look elsewhere, what if we begin to read the conflict in Northern Ireland as not so much one between two 'obvious' communities, already existing, already self-contained and diametrically opposed, as one in which the *machinery of denomination* is already hard at work endlessly *trying to produce* such entities, entities that would be able, finally, to get the last word, issue the monological statement that would at last *terminate* the debate? And what if these very efforts to produce a self-contained entity that would owe *nothing* to the other are precisely what produces the binary opposition that constitutes the conflict?

It is these bids to isolate this or that 'community' (or other nameable collective entity – a *denominational* community), to insulate it against the contamination of others, to keep others out is, we are claiming here, at the heart of a certain politics of conflict in which the political machinery is set up to maintain and amplify mutual exclusion. Reduction to the binary of 'us and them'. How do such binary reduction machines, machines of denomination such as flags, get to work?

GOD'S OWN QUESTIONNAIRE

Picture a classroom in a school in East Belfast in the early 1970s. I am five or six years old; my teacher has a pile of official looking forms on his desk, and he is asking us questions, so that he can fill in the forms with the correct details. One of those questions concerns our religious denomination. He shows me the list, but I don't know what those strange terms mean, so my teacher allows me to go home and ask my parents. The next day, I *know the correct answer*, and the teacher can tick the *correct box* on the form.

It is my first (at least the first I can remember), but not my last, experience of what I now call processes of denomination. How does such a process work? Usually, someone in *authority*, a teacher or other official, comes to you and says: 'I'm going to ask you what you *are*; and *here is a list of the acceptable answers*'.

Luckily, your parents have already been through this, and know the correct answer. So after (or perhaps before) the school authorities have given you the list of acceptable answers to choose from, someone with all the authority of a parent has said: 'here is your name; and here is the name of your People'. So the schoolchildren learn to denominate themselves and each other; the mixed group in the classroom is turned into two or more denominations (because where there is one denomination there is always at least one other), and the children learn to relate to one another not just in the fluid, messy way kids in a classroom do, but via denominations that appear as external to each other and external to the classroom itself. They now know the 'correct' answer to the question of their denominational 'community', and by the time they get a bit older – old enough to become a student, say, or an employee, or to fill in the census or other questionnaire – the correct answer is no longer in question.

Consider Queen's University Belfast, which, when I studied there in the late 1990s (that is, around the time the 'peace process' was producing the Belfast or Good Friday Agreement – GFA hereafter), used to require students to fill in a questionnaire at the beginning of their studies. The form asked three main questions. Under the heading 'Ethnic Origin' one could choose to tick one of ten boxes, corresponding to the categories 'White', 'Black Caribbean', 'Black African', 'Black Other', 'Indian', 'Pakistani', 'Bangladeshi', 'Chinese', 'Asian other', and finally 'Other (please specify)'. Under the heading 'Disability Type', there were nine boxes to choose from, covering the categories 'Dyslexia', 'Blind/are partially sighted', Deaf/have a hearing impairment', 'Wheelchair user/have mobility difficulties', 'Personal care support', 'Mental health difficulties', 'An unseen disability, e.g., diabetes, epilepsy, asthma', 'Multiple disabilities', and finally 'A disability not listed above'.

Under the heading 'Religious affiliation/community background', there were three, and only three boxes: 'Protestant', 'Catholic', and 'Neither'. But here, on ticking the third box, one was not asked to 'specify' what one's alternative community background might be. Rather, one was asked to provide the names and addresses of the schools one attended.

A curious procedure, a visitor from outside Northern Ireland might think. Why would they want the names of the schools? Why not leave the matter at 'neither', or simply ask the student to specify another background? Clearly such a puzzled outsider is unfamiliar with the intriguingly named 'residuary methods' deployed by officials in NI (ECNI 2011). You can tick the third box, certainly; but it will make little difference. The interpreter of the form will check your school against a list, and then assign you to one of the first two boxes anyway.

Escaping the first two denominational boxes is well-nigh impossible for anyone other than that small minority of 'newcomers' (who can, perhaps, lay claim to one of the ten 'ethnicities' other than 'White') in Northern Ireland.

In a more recent version of the 'equal opportunities monitoring form' the process is perhaps a little more transparent: it tells you in advance that 'residuary methods' will be used to determine which box to tick only if 'you do not complete this section'. But it remains the case that, if you will not do it yourself, you will be assigned to one of the 'two communities' – you will be *denominated*.

To be fair, even on the older forms, the question did not ask how you *felt* about your own 'religious affiliation' or 'community background'. Rather, it asked you to tick the box indicating the community to which you were or are *perceived* to belong. 'We understand', the compilers seem to be saying, 'you may not want to pick a side. Fair enough, but this is Northern Ireland, and you will be perceived as belonging to one side or the other willy-nilly; and it is this *perceived* affiliation that we must count'.

'Perceived' affiliation or denomination, then; but perceived by whom? Presumably at least by some other people in Northern Ireland – those who have some sort of interest in boxing us in one way or another. Those, for instance, *who compile such questionnaires*. This may seem a flippant response, but it is not. The point is that the notions of affiliation, of community, of 'identity' as such are not simple, free-standing and self-evident. In the case of the questionnaire an 'identity' would be ascribed to me whether I liked it or not, because the compilers *did* have an interest in 'boxing' or categorising everyone who came to Queen's. That it was a benign interest makes no difference to the logic of the process we are looking at here.

The process of identification proceeds according to the steps laid down, regardless of other factors. Either I identify myself according to the first two boxes, or I am categorised thus by the interpreters. The boxes precede my response and preclude any registration of complexities – of, for instance, mixed ancestry, upbringing, circumstance, or political commitment.

Let us be clear, this is not to say it is done maliciously, or necessarily in some sinister attempt to 'control' the population (though of course, processes of denomination can be and have been used for such purposes, as we will see in a later chapter). The aim of the process, as we have already suggested, may be perfectly benign: to ensure there is no discrimination. After all, if people are being discriminated against *because* of their denomination one has to show that to be the case, statistically, by counting off the members of each denomination, in order to be able to do something about it. The only way to make sure everyone counts is to count them incessantly; and the only way to count them is to denominate them.

Nevertheless, as useful and important as such statistical devices can be, there is the risk of amplifying the very divisive logic one is attempting to address. One has to find out what everyone *is*, 'discover' their identity; and if an identity can't be 'discovered' it can and will be *assigned* through the operation of residuary methods.

As a technique, a legal device, a strategy, this was held, then and to this day, to be necessary in the special political circumstances of Northern Ireland, and of course there are similar processes in use elsewhere. Such an intervention is necessary in some circumstances to effect a transition towards democracy, and away from the domination of one (proclaimed) denomination by (way of) another. But it remains a *strategy*, an *intervention*, and not simply a matter of neutrally recording a description of a preexisting state of affairs.

The 'description' is, rather, an intervention in an already fluid dynamic field. When it is said that 'there are such-and-such a number of Catholics, and such-and-such a number of Protestants at Queen's', or in any other institution, not excepting 'Northern Ireland' itself, this seemingly descriptive statement is, rather, an elliptical account of the active operation of selective processes of categorisation – of *denomination* in the active voice.

These processes – including *perhaps above all* something like residuary methods – can be performed repeatedly and unthinkingly in everyday life, to the point where they become a matter of *routine*. The term *routine* here does not just mean 'habit': it begins to take on something of the resonance of the 'routine' or 'subroutine' of computer programming, a set of 'if-then' rules to follow: *if* the respondent does not tick either box A or box B, *then* proceed to residuary method 1; *if* the school that has been named appears in list X, ascribe respondent to box A. Routines as *habitual*, routines as rules, *orders*: we will have to bear this double sense in mind.

The 'if-then' structures of denominational (sub)routines are *not* automatic, yet have an air of automaticity, an unquestioned (and therefore questionable) legitimacy. They, or rather their results, appear as *common sense*, even mundane, blandly pre-political and entirely 'normal' – *obvious*, to recall John Whyte's word. *Everybody knows* that someone called Seamus or Siobhan *must* be a Catholic; *everybody knows* that someone who went to such and such a school, or came from this or that housing estate, *must* be a Protestant. And, therefore, everybody knows *how to read their politics*, even if this remains undeclared, using residuary methods. The results of these readings, these routines, are given out as a matter of 'the way things *are*'; a simple description of the 'reality of the situation', to use a well-worn Northern Ireland cliché.

The 'two communities', that is, are taken *as if ontologically* given; just *there*, so to speak, in much the same way a rock or a table is just *there*, one thing among others in the world. You belong in one of them because that's *what you are*, it's a matter of your *being*, your *identity*, and that's that. From there on, everything *your* community achieves you can take in some measure *your* achievement because the community is 'ours'; everything that happens to our community (an act of violence, say) inflicts suffering on me, because it is 'our' suffering. There can be a great sense of pride, or indeed a great sense of injustice, involved in such identifications with a nameable, collective 'us'.

But can we so easily identify and enumerate people purely ontologically – on the basis of what they *are*? Can we say, for instance, that 'a certain number of Protestants ticked the first box, but a *certain number* refused' (thus triggering the residuary methods)? Would this not *require us to know how many Protestants there were before we carried out the survey*? And how would we come by such information, except by reference to a previous questionnaire? A previous questionnaire which would itself be subject to the same uncertainty – and so on, ad infinitum.

No; without a flawless, universal, *ideal* questionnaire, without *God's own questionnaire* we could never rule out the possibility that people had ticked the 'wrong' box, ticked it under duress, or simply because their parents told them to tick it, ticked it absentmindedly, deceitfully, in order to please, *or* (and in a way is this not always the case?) *had been assigned to it by a third party*.

All this would make the act of self-identification 'infelicitous' to borrow a term from the oft-cited speech act theory developed by JL Austin. For Austin, performative utterances are those which do not state facts, describe, or report something (are not 'constative'): rather they *do* something. 'I pronounce you husband and wife'; 'I name this ship the Queen Mary'; 'I bet you a fiver ('sixpence', endearingly, in Austin's original text) it will rain tomorrow'. The success or failure of these sorts of utterances depends on a range of factors, or 'conditions of felicity'. For Austin these conditions include that there 'must exist an accepted conventional procedure having a certain conventional effect, that procedure to include the uttering of certain words by certain persons in certain circumstances'; and that the 'particular persons and circumstances in a given case must be appropriate for the invocation of the particular procedure invoked' (Austin 1975, 14–15).

For critical readings of these ideas, it is worth turning to Derrida's Limited Inc (Derrida 1988), to Deleuze and Guattari's thought on 'order-words' (Deleuze and Guattari 1987), and to Judith Butler's meditation on racist speech acts (Butler 1997), perhaps with the guidance of John Barton, who brings them together (Barton 2003), but let us rather pick out a couple of threads from Austin himself here that will help guide us along the path.

Firstly, if performative utterances are to work, 'there must exist' an accepted convention. Here is another ontological or existential claim to range alongside the claims of the existence of 'the two communities'. But what sort of existence, what sort of 'being' does a 'convention' have? An *accepted* convention, at that?

Austin takes the case of the bet as just one type, within the broader class of performative utterances: 'for a bet to have been made, it is generally necessary for the offer of the bet to have been accepted by a taker (who must have done something, such as to say "Done")' (Austin 1975, 9).

But if all performatives depend, for their felicity, on the 'existence' of an *accepted* convention – an agreed procedure, one that has been *proposed and accepted* – is it not the case that *all performatives have the structure of the bet*? That is, no performative utterance is unilateral, monological; every performative utterance always already exhibits a call-and-response structure, always requires the 'Done!', the 'I do'; always calls for the *affirmation* of an *other*, if it is in any sense to succeed. Perhaps invisibly, always haunting every performative utterance, there is a question: can I get an Amen?

To mention, all too briefly, other texts into which this first thread can be interwoven, think of Hegel's master-slave dialectic (Hegel 1979); think of how, for De Beauvoir, the *first* sex *depends* on a *second* sex (De Beauvoir 2015); for Said how 'West' *depends on* 'East' (Said 1978); for Spivak how (Imperial) Europe *depends* on (colonised) Other (Spivak 1985).

Second thread: already at the start of the discussion Austin has mentioned utterances that 'masquerade'. A performative does not necessarily masquerade as a statement of fact, yet 'it does quite commonly do so, and that, oddly enough, when it assumes its most explicit form' (Austin 1975, 4). Perhaps the power in the performative comes at least in part from this capacity to *masquerade*. An undecidable performative (that is, a performative utterance that calls for a response to 'complete' itself, to act *as if* it had already been felicitous) is *given out as if it were a simple statement of fact, a description of an already existing state of affairs*. Such an utterance would be a call that required a response, but one which attempted to foreclose that response by 'masquerading' as simply indicating an *already existing* state of affairs. There is no call for you to make a decision, because this is just the way things *are*; the decision has already been made for you, and the only thing you can do is conform to it – acknowledge (rather than challenge) the 'reality of the situation'. It is thus not your *responsibility*.

To return to Northern Ireland's institutional questionnaires; we are called to tick one of the two main (let us say dominant) boxes. If we do not, the compilers will put us in one anyway, because, well, that's what we *really are*, attempt to wriggle out of it as we might. The operation reiterates and thus reinforces the *processes of denomination* that are already busy elsewhere, thereby reproducing the *dominant* paradigm.

The question then becomes not so much one of a conflictual relation between two already constituted entities, as about how an insistence on calling upon people to align themselves in relation to these (named) entities affects the dynamics of politics, broadly understood, *here, now,* in Northern Ireland – speaking for a moment as though we all agreed what *that* meant.

To take the example of the monitoring forms we have been looking at, the institutional categorisations performed through them affect resource flows, trigger actions and expenditure of time and energy in correcting any imbalance – or rather, not *any* imbalance, but any imbalance *'between the two communities'*. The resulting corrective flow of energy and resources, power and wealth, is directed towards one or other of these 'two opposed communities', channelling power via the structures of the dominant paradigm and marginalising or minimising any other imbalances not reducible to the channels opened by this binary as being of *little or no political salience*. The needs of those not fitting into these main denominations, immigrants, for example (but this is only one of many examples), are systematically marginalised by the structures designed to include 'two communities', in a case of what Mikhael and Agarin call 'exclusion amid inclusion' (Mikhael 2021).

The whole assemblage continues to operate as a *binary reduction machine*, whether set off running by 'neutral' or even benign institutional authorities or by those who themselves identify as belonging to one of the two resulting 'communities', including those whose political project involves a *commitment* to such entities.

DENOMINATIONS AND COMBINATIONS

The idea of *community* as it appears in this discourse has already begun to unravel under closer inspection – as sociologists, anthropologists, historians and political theorists have arguably known since as far back as Hegel, with his concept of an 'organic community', and certainly since the 1880s, when Tönnies distinguished between *Gemeinschaft* and *Gesellschaft*, community and association.

More recently, of course, ideas of discursive or social constructs, of practices and processes of reframing, of 'social' (as distinct from 'individual') identity, and concomitantly of the reductive and hostile processes of 'othering', have been explored widely (Brewer and Gardner 1996; Giannakos 2002; Tilly 2003; Ozkirimli 2010; Braniff et al 2016; McManus 2016; Demmers

2017). Indebted as this reading is to all of these, we must confine ourselves to picking out two main examples.

AP Cohen's 'symbolic construction of community' seems to me among the most fruitful of the analyses of the kind of phenomenon we are examining. It is not just that communities use symbols, or hold certain symbols in common, thus helping to mark them off from other communities; it is that 'the community itself and everything within it, conceptual as well as material, has a symbolic dimension, and, further, that this dimension does not exist as some kind of consensus of sentiment'. The symbols of community 'provide people with the means to make meaning' (Cohen 1985, 19). Above all, this meaning-making – which is without consensus, remember – applies to the boundary marking one community off from another.

Cohen explicitly problematises what he calls the 'integrative' tradition in thinking about community, whereby some set of cultural meanings is 'held in common by the members of a society'. For Cohen, the *common*ality which is found in community 'need not be a uniformity'. It is a 'commonality of *forms* (ways of behaving) whose content (meanings) may vary considerably among its members'. We need not follow Cohen in trying to distinguish 'form' and 'content', the 'subjective' from the 'objective' parts of the play of symbols to be able to draw from his insights a thread that will be important here. It is precisely the 'imprecision', ironically enough, precisely the relative 'emptiness' of symbols that allows them to function as they do, in allowing different people to 'behave in apparently similar ways, participate in the 'same' rituals, pray to the 'same' gods' (Cohen 1985, 21). In Derrida's terms, it is the *iterability* (repeatability in difference, in different contexts) of the symbol that enables it to take effect.

Perhaps the best known, and also among the most powerful, of the analyses of recent decades is that of Benedict Anderson, for whom nations are 'imagined communities' (Anderson 2006). For Anderson, 'nations', as well as nationalism, are 'cultural artefacts of a particular kind', the creation of which, at the end of the eighteenth century, was 'the spontaneous distillation of a complex "crossing" of discrete historical forces; but that, once created, they became "modular", capable of being transplanted . . . to a great variety of social terrains' (Anderson 2006, 4). The Nation is 'an imagined political community – and imagined as both inherently limited and sovereign' (Anderson 2006, 6). Much could be drawn from Anderson's rich analyses, but let us pick out a few elements already noted: the nation is 'limited'; 'sovereign'; and 'a community'.

The nation is 'limited' in the sense that it is at once inclusive and exclusive. It includes all its own members, of course, but there must be a boundary around those members, setting them off from everyone else in the world. *Nationality* may be universal in the sense that there is no one who does not belong to *a* nation, so the thinking goes; but each *nation* is not universal. The exclusion of 'others' is as important as the inclusion of the members for the self-containment, so to speak, of the nation.

The nation is *sovereign* because the 'concept was born in an age in which Enlightenment and Revolution were destroying the legitimacy of the divinely ordained, hierarchical dynastic realm'. (Anderson 2006, 7) The idea of national freedom (of independence) is already, on this account, written into the concept from the start. As an aside, let us recall, briefly, the idea of substitutability and suggest that Enlightenment and Revolutionary actors may not have been simply 'destroying' the 'divinely ordained, hierarchical dynastic realm' as much as 'transplanting' it in another terrain, substituting 'the nation' for 'God' at the apex of a similar conceptual structure.

The nation is 'imagined' as a *community*, further, because 'regardless of the actual inequality and exploitation that may prevail in each, the nation is always conceived as a deep, horizontal comradeship' (Anderson 2006, 7).

Finally, there is an intensity for Anderson, perhaps even a violence to this kind of national identification. It is worth emphasising this visceral dimension: nationalism of the kind Anderson is looking at, like any process of denomination, is not simply some clinical or mechanical process. It is always, as we will see in the final chapter, a matter of flesh and bone.

What we are trying to get at in the idea of denomination, though, is that such processes can 'distil' 'modular artefacts' out of the crossing of flows and forces, intense as they may be, artefacts that do not just go under the name of a 'nation', but under a whole range of other names – other denominations.

But what does it mean that the nation is '*conceived as*' a deep '*horizontal* comradeship'? *Should* we conceive of such bonds as horizontal? Horizontal bonds that come to an abrupt end at the *border* of the nation (or denomination) – or perhaps are weakened or *severed* by a 'vertical fissure' of the sort WEB Du Bois describes: 'instead of a horizontal division of classes, there was a vertical fissure, a complete separation of classes by race, cutting square across the economic layers . . . and this split depended not simply on economic exploitation, but on a racial folk-lore grounded on centuries of instinct, habit and thought and implemented by the conditioned reflex of visible color' (WEB Du Bois 2007, chap. 8).

Two points to query in relation to Du Bois' characterisation: the word 'complete'; and the idea of 'centuries of instinct'. The first is too definite, too absolute; there is always the possibility of crossing these kinds of borders – of forming combinations with others, not of the same denomination (the denomination can always be 'betrayed'; this is a constitutive possibility).

And on the issue of 'centuries of instinct', is this to be thought as some sort of trans-generational collective psyche, passed down in a 'natural', even genetic process? How would one tell the difference between that and traditions of 'habit and thought', implemented by 'conditioned reflexes', whether to colour or to any such sign (or symbol) of 'otherness'? Nevertheless, Du Bois's insistence on the *vertical fissures*, and the almost Gramscian link between those and the 'conditioned reflex', are significant in relation to thinking about community.

The kind of community that appears to be, and is understood as being, based on a collective or 'common identity' is one in which you and I combine, but *not directly*, face to face, body to body, neighbour to neighbour (*even if we are neighbours*). Rather, we combine through the detour of the (id)*entity* to which, it is claimed, we both *belong* – in Northern Ireland, the 'Protestant community', the 'Catholic community'; or this or that nation, this or that race, or a denomination in the religious sense, and so on.

We are bracketing the 'common identity' here because, after all, what is to guarantee the 'identity' of the entity you and I belong to 'in common'? How do I know that the 'Protestant Community' I identify with is the *same* as the one with which *you* identify? A 'group identity' is not the sort of thing we can lay out between us, like a table or a rock, or other fixed entity, get a good look at it, and agree that we are talking about the same object. There will always be the possibility that *what I intend* when I name the entity and *what you intend* are two different things, even if they are the *same in name*.

We are back to Cohen's symbolic community, or Anderson's imagined community, perhaps even Laclau's empty signifier (Laclau 2018). But perhaps we are also now ready to echo Henry James: 'I approached it from one side and the other . . . but I always broke down in the monstrous utterance of names' (James 1992, 88).

The *performative* utterance of names, that is – whether monstrous or otherwise. There is a performative power in calling upon the name of *a* community – *a* nation, or denomination. And that power, to recall the above discussion, is that of a call-and-response – a power akin to the 'formation call' of the military bugle.

Take Antony's famous formation call at Caesar's funeral: 'Friends, Romans, countrymen, lend me your ears'. 'Friends' does not work at first, because they are suspicious of, if not hostile to him; but they *do* consider themselves Romans; that works. Now he has their attention, through an act of interpellation; now they know their place, and it is as citizens of the Roman Republic, about-to-become Empire. But there is one more step to take: 'countrymen'. He reminds them that not only are *they* Romans, but *he is of their country*, he is *of the same denomination, one of them* – or rather, one of *us*. A 'friend' at last, then, after something of a detour, *at least in the Schmittian sense* (Schmitt 1996), one of 'us' and not, *because* not, one of 'them'.

You may not know me from Adam (or Antony); but in the name of *our* (denominational) community I bid you combine, form up, congregate, because (this is the claimed foundation of the bid) you *are* (this is an onto- logical claim) already combined in *essence*, already *identical*, because you get your core identity from your denomination – a denomination *I* share, and therefore in whose name I am authorised to speak as 'one of us'.

Such *denominational bonds*, as we have said, do not necessarily, but may well overlap with the *contiguous*, personal bonds built up through interac- tion with my friends and neighbours (I may very well be your friend in both senses). Indeed, that the two can thus overlap enables the former to draw power from the latter – and perhaps vice versa. If I and my neighbour in the house on my left 'belong' to the same denomination, then it becomes all the easier for me to project or extrapolate from the sort of neighbourly bonds we build – being lifelong supporters of the local football club, being in a pub quiz team together – to the rest of the extended, absent, denominational com- munity. I tend to assume that other members, including complete strangers, people I will never meet, must be *like* 'us' – my neighbour and I – because, after all, we are all part of the same . . . *community*.

Conversely, if in conversation with a new neighbour, just moved into the house on my right, I scrutinise or scry the signs until I reach an 'Aha!' moment ('Aha! You are one of 'them', not one of 'us') then such processes of denomination will set us off *at a distance* – a distance that is not geographi- cal, not measured in metres (not geometrical, let us say). You are *outside* my community, even if you live next door; on the other hand, I belong, appar- ently, to the same community as not just my neighbour on the left but as a perfect stranger on the other side of the globe, as long as we both 'share an identity'; that is, identify with the 'same' (denominated) community.

Processes of denomination, in short, *set me towards my neighbour in the house on my left differently than towards the neighbour on my right*. This '*set towards*' will be crucial to how our politics unfolds. I draw the phrase from a passage in René Girard's *Violence and the Sacred*, worth citing here as it brings in themes that will become of increasing importance: 'Once aroused, the urge to violence triggers certain physical changes that prepare men's bod- ies for battle. This set toward violence lingers on; it should not be regarded as a simple reflex that ceases with the removal of the initial stimulus' (Girard 2005, 2). In passing, we will come back to the gendered presentation of this take on violence and the battle in a later chapter.

Not a simple reflex, but perhaps, with Du Bois, a constantly reiterated *con- ditioned* reflex, cutting like a vertical blade through the everyday bonds I may have formed with my neighbours, whether in everyday friendship or in class or democratic solidarity; setting me in friendship towards *these* neighbours, and in hostility towards *those*. Clearly there are those who are empowered by the system as it is currently set up who may find these vertical blades useful precisely in severing bonds of democratic solidarity. But what does it mean to 'belong to' this or that denominational community? If my everyday, neighbourly bond with my neighbour on the right can be weakened or even severed by that 'Aha!' moment, that purported discovery about their 'belonging to' the *other* one of the two opposed communities, we need to look a little more closely into the sort of bonds are we are talking about.

To do that, we turn to two texts, one relatively recent, and coming from an avowedly Protestant or Unionist source, the other a classic Irish Nationalist and Republican text. Through these we will see how processes of denomination operate to order and distribute *claims to allegiance*.

IN THE NAME OF . . .

Sammy Wilson of the DUP, speaking of a rally held against the Anglo-Irish Agreement of 1985, told one interviewer that the phrase 'Ulster Says No' summed it all up, 'and even if people weren't too sure why they were saying 'no' it had to be pushed into their psyche that this [the Agreement] was not acceptable to the Unionist community' (Cochrane 1997, 234). But if those at the rally were unionists and loyalists, why did they have to be *told* that the agreement was unacceptable to the unionist community? Surely, of all people, they would already know? Yet Wilson and others must drill the 'community' in the right response. Perhaps 'people weren't too sure . . . ', but the right response was called out, and had only to be repeated publicly, as if in a catechism. This vagueness, this 'not too sure' is an essential part of the phenomenon we are examining here, because it is out of the 'not too sure' that a spokesperson for the community provides certainty.

This opens a curious fissure within the supposedly united community: Wilson at once knows what 'the community' finds acceptable, but must at the same time 'push it in' to the psyche of these members of the community. But 'push it in' *from where*? To be *pushed in*, it has to come from the outside. The community in whose name Wilson speaks stands *outside* the actual members of the community gathered before him in the Ulster Hall.

Wilson in effect says: 'It doesn't matter what you actual *members* think; here's what The *Community* thinks. Believe me; trust me; repeat after me . . . '

Wilson stands on stage reporting to an audience made up of Unionists the message of a 'Unionist Community' that remains somewhere in the wings, somewhere offstage. Or at any rate, he stands *claiming* so to report. The idea of 'the performative' here takes on some of the sense of the theatrical performance. Indeed, as Derrida shows, that one cannot finally shake off the

theatrical side of the performative is part of the structure of every performative utterance – the bet, the inauguration, the order (Derrida 1988).

In this theatrical performance, the audience too must play their part for the
whole thing to come off 'happily'. And the role of the audience, the actual
Unionists congregating in the hall is therefore to come into line with (by
repeating the lines) the script (or catechism) handed on by Wilson, the emissary, the Vicar, speaking not in his own name, but (vicariously) in the Name
of the Community. The Community as a *whole*; as a unitary (though always
offstage) entity. The denominational community.

Of course, Sammy Wilson was not the only representative to make this
sort of claim; nor need it be a political leader with, perhaps, their own political project in mind. Dominic Bryan opens his excellent 2008 analysis of the
politics of community in Northern Ireland with an anecdote about a Protestant
youth worker arguing for further funding because 'we need to teach young
people their identity' (Bryan 2008, 125).

The idea that one might 'teach' a group its own identity, or 'push into their
psyche' something a community is supposed to already believe opens a gap
between the projected denominational community and the milling, fluid,
flesh-and-bone multiplicity of those called to respond. But if they do respond
as called, if they do combine via the process of denomination, it is by way of
a bid to reduce that fluidity, that multiplicity.

The risk of such a bid to reduce should equally be borne in mind by those of
us on the outside, looking on as Wilson issues his catechism. It is not just that
there are in fact complexities and irreducible differences, in terms of class,
gender, sexual orientation and so on, between members of what is named as
a unitary 'Unionist' or even 'Protestant' community, and between them and
their apparent spokespeople. This remains true, of course, as many writers
have amply shown (Shirlow and McGovern 1997; Burgess and Mulvenna
2015; McAuley 2016; McKay 2021; Mitchell 2022). Just as significantly,
the bid to reduce remains just that: a bid; it is always possible for those who
are so bid to refuse to form up on the terms offered. The call to combine can
always be infelicitous.

And if this is the case for the 'Protestant', or 'Loyalist', or Unionist, or
in a more recent formulation, the 'Protestant-Unionist-Loyalist (PUL)' community, it is also the case on the other side of the binary ledger, at the risk of
reiterating the dominant paradigm.

Let us take, as our example, the Proclamation of the Irish Republic in
1916. We will pick out just a few threads, in a somewhat deconstructive
reading that owes as much to the subtle analyses of Liam de Paor (2016) and
others as it does to Derrida (Macartney 2019).

Firstly, the Proclamation is addressed 'To the people of Ireland'. Who
else, one might ask? But one could reply that it might well be addressed

(and perhaps in a sense was) to the English. Or it might be addressed to us. But then, who are we? We readers of this document over a century on? And when we say, 'the people of Ireland', do we mean The People, in a unitary sense, or simply the people-who-happen-to-live-in-Ireland? De Paor wants to read it in the second sense: 'Since the phrase "people of Ireland" recurs in the Proclamation we have sufficient context to infer that "people" here is in intention a concrete plural rather than an abstract singular; not "the People" ("das Volk") but simply "people"' (de Paor 2016, 66).

Yet to extract this 'intention' from the text one has to ignore (or downplay) the definite article in the original text. De Paor may want to make this decision, but it should be clear that it is a decision, and that others (including participants in the Rising or dissident Republicans today), might very well read the matter differently.

The question of the addressee, then, is a question impossible to answer definitively. Yet to ask instead 'who is doing the addressing?' – a much easier question to answer on the face of it – is to open all kinds of complexities. The answer appears to be given in the first paragraph of the Proclamation itself: 'Irishmen and Irishwomen: In the name of God and of the dead generations from which she receives her old tradition of nationhood, Ireland, through us, summons her children to her flag and strikes for her freedom'. It is an Ireland, then, who is both female and matriarchal, who is doing the addressing. She is summoning her children (the people of Ireland) to the flag. What could be more natural, more natal? More national? Yet the utterance is not straightforward: it is made 'through us'. The 'us' here would appear to refer to the signatories.

Yet even here there is a doubling of the mediation: the 'original' utterance of the Proclamation was made, famously, by Patrick Pearse on behalf of the signatories. He stood in for the signatories, who in turn stood in for Ireland. But we are not finished yet. Ireland 'herself', through her double proxies, summons and strikes not on her own behalf but 'in the name of . . . ' Two names, indeed: that of God and that of the dead generations. One could attempt to count the 'removes' here, the mediations, in order to get to the source of this utterance, but this would surely be an infinite task – as infinite as God and the dead.

These complexities may appear in the preamble, but this does not mean they are marginal, mere window dressing before we get to the real content. On the contrary, the whole force of the document, which is after all a *proclamation*, resides in the *authority of the performance*. By the time we get to the phrase 'We declare . . . ' there have been so many refractions that it is no longer possible to take this 'we' as indicative of an already constituted, unitary subject.

What does this complex, collected subject declare? 'We declare the right of the people of Ireland to the ownership of Ireland and to the unfettered control of Irish destinies to be sovereign and indefeasible. The long usurpation of that right by a foreign people and government has not extinguished that right . . . [t]he Republic is entitled to, and hereby claims, the allegiance of every Irishman and Irishwoman'.

The Proclamation not only sets up a 'we', it also sets up another, a 'foreign people' (and this one *is* presented as a unitary '*Volk*'). Moreover, here is another authoritative voice: 'The Republic' (is that the same as 'Ireland'? Or, given that it is the *Irish* Republic, are the two, even if distinguishable, inextricably bound up together?) claims allegiance, the allegiance of *Irish* people (as distinct from the foreign people, the usurpers) as by entitlement, as by right.

But which comes first? The right, or *entitlement* to allegiance here seems to precede the granting of that allegiance. Yet would this be a matter of right if that allegiance were not, precisely, *granted*, given freely, *not forced*? Can I be *forced* to offer allegiance, or is what I give, in those circumstances, merely a more or less reluctant *obedience*? Would such a forceful claim to allegiance not come as a *usurpation*, an imposition from elsewhere, from a *foreign* source, if the allegiance were not already freely granted?

Everything comes down to this conjunction of allegiance, entitlement, owing and owning. The Republic claims your allegiance as of right because you are Irish. That is, you already *belong* to the Irish people (and not the foreign people). But if you already belong, then you have no choice in the matter; it is simply a matter of fact, an existential truth. Your being-Irish has already established the entitlement of the Republic to your allegiance. You are placed in debt before you are even born, placed in a liege-relation to the higher authority of the entity to which you owe your *very being*. As an aside, it is little wonder it is so easy to conjure images of intense looking men and women, cheeks shining with tears, singing the national anthem at sporting events, for example. But the same goes for any other denominational entity to which we are said to belong – race, religion, or any 'community' thought as an entity that is already entitled to, and can thus legitimately claim, our allegiance.

This liege-relation means allegiance cannot legitimately be withheld, as to withhold it would be a violation of the rights of the Republic (acting, remember, in the name of God and the dead generations). But if I am not free to withhold it, it *cannot be freely granted*.

Legitimacy, allegiance, and religion: it is no coincidence that these terms, so crucial to Irish (and other national) politics, all speak, etymologically, of ligaments of one sort or another, of *binding*. There is also something of the structure of a call-and-response here, a structure that crops up more than once in the Proclamation: 'In this supreme hour the Irish nation must, by its valour and discipline, and by the readiness of its children to sacrifice themselves for the common good, prove itself worthy of the august destiny to which it is called'.

What is the nature of this 'must', this necessity? If it is the necessity of an inevitable unfolding of destiny, then there appears to be a tension between that 'inevitability' and the need to work and sacrifice for the common good. The tension is mediated by the notion of 'worthiness': the Irish nation has been called to fulfil a destiny, but it has not yet proved itself worthy. The destiny is not, then, guaranteed as an inevitability; it belongs in the realm of future possibility, to be realised only in the response to the call of duty, fulfilment of an allegiance owed.

As Pearse claims to speak 'in the name of the dead generations', Rebecca Graff-McRea points out, 1916 'anticipates the future – as it is performed and uttered, it is writing itself into (pre)existence as the foundation of the state, as the pivotal moment, the "year zero" of Irish history. In this move, lines of legitimacy are drawn, anchored in a timeline' (Graff-McRea 2010, 31). But as she goes on to suggest, quoting Greenlaw, this is a state whose foundations are the effect of performative utterances which legitimate themselves by creating their own referents. Such a state will depend obsessively on repetition (Graff-McRea 2010; Greenlaw 2003).

The temporal fissuring in the Proclamation is as complex as the question of its authority: like the latter, the source of the entitlement is set off at a remove, and the call is one to which Irishmen and Irishwomen ought to respond, by returning to the source, which is at the same time their true destiny, the truth of their being-Irish. And if it springs from that source, then the call does not come from outside. What comes from the outside is the foreign usurper.

The realisation of a destiny that depends on the outcome of action; this sounds like a question of choice and decision. But essentially, for the Proclamation, there is no choice: everything is already in place *in essence*. You must respond to the call if Ireland's essence is to become actualised, but you can only respond in one, determinate way, on the basis of your national essence. You must bring your politics into line with your national essence, or you have violated both your own essence *and* the rights of the nation, placing yourself on the outside, on the side of the foreign usurpers.

The Proclamation, though, is a speech act: *it calls on a response for its performative force.*

This is not to say the Proclamation was just wrong in what it says of Ireland, that this was just 'rhetoric', not supported by the facts. Indeed, construing the matter like this – claiming to be able to present 'factual evidence' of 'reality' to refute the mere 'rhetoric' of the other – is a gesture with a long, colonial history. Take Seamus Deane's critique of Roy Foster's *Modern Ireland*.

In one paragraph Foster has the theoretical contradictions (that is, the irrationality) of those who led the Easter Rising 'obscured by the fact that its rhetoric was poetic', and a few lines later adds that the 'message would be read more clearly than ever in an Ulster heavily committed to the war effort' (Brady 1994, 234). Deane's claim is that, though 'rhetoric' appears as a bad (obscuring) thing in this passage, the 'paragraph itself is an exercise in rhetoric, and its central trope is that of 'reading' clearly what has been obscured. 'Clear reading is an Ulster prerogative . . . whatever the South writes, the North will read, and Ulster will be right'.

Irish nationalism is cloaked in the romance of mists and myths, but the clear-sighted rational observers of the Protestant community can see the reality beneath. 'Reality' – another key rhetorical trope.

This was nothing new. We could go back at least as far as the sixteenth-century English writer Richard Stanihurst. If an Irish noble, he says, has had any of his people killed by an enemy, he will bear hatred towards the offender and 'although the aggrieved party seems to cloak his festering bitterness with a treaty of friendship, you will be in no doubt that he has kept his mind armed behind a front of reconciliation when even after many years he gets his chance. For the Irish believe that blood can only be expiated with blood' (Lennon 1987, 148). The Irish 'cloak' their real (and violent) intentions, but the English writer can read the signs properly, see through the 'front'.

And to bring it up to date, a book on the 'idea of the Union', first published in the 1990s, and updated as recently as 2021, still states on the cover: 'Irish separatist nationalism has had a fair innings. Now it's time for reason and reality to go to bat'. Note the appeal to a *metaphor*, and one drawn directly from the quintessential sport of the *British Empire*, in service of a claim that 'our side' is that of Reason and Reality, whereas 'their side' is irrational, and grounded on romantic illusion (Foster and Smith 2021).

Of course, there would be little sense in simply inverting the terms, picking the other side, and giving it our allegiance. In fact, is it not precisely such claims to allegiance that we have to deconstruct if we are to get beyond the politics of denomination?

BACK-PROJECTION AND THE QUESTION OF ALLEGIANCE

The line in the Proclamation is as clear an expression of the logic of denomination as we are likely to find. The Republic, or Nation, or other Denomination (read as a noun, as an off-stage entity) 'is entitled to and hereby claims' your allegiance. The present performative of the claim *reaches back*, as it were, to preestablish an entitlement in order *hereby* – here, now – to claim that allegiance, to call you to respond. (It need hardly be added, Sammy Wilson does exactly the same thing, but with the names changed).

A politics of denomination projects a united entity (for example, the nation, but there are plenty of other options) which is *here and now* taken simply as *pre*-existent (it is projected as pre-existent, ie, back-projected, or *retrojected*), proclaimed as entitled to the allegiance of its members, and, finally, taken as the basis of the justification of political acts, even including acts of violence ('the community has the right to defend itself' and so on).

Denomination overlaps with, and can reinforce or cut across, the everyday sense of community I have built with my neighbours, through daily contact, with friends, family, workmates, the butcher, the baker, the brewer in the market on the town square.

I can encounter these neighbours in at least two ways, perhaps simultaneously (later we will add a third possibility) – *as* butcher, baker, and brewer; *or* as members of this or that denominational community; that is, as one of 'us' or one of 'them'.

Such projected or 'imagined communities' should not be regarded as mere fictions or figments (as Anderson was at pains to emphasise). This would again return us to the beginning of the search for the absent presence, some kind of evidence of the order of fact, empirical data, that could decide the case.

Rather, we are looking at the dynamics of how certain entities – the Community, the Nation, the Race, in all their capitalised, monolithic *presence* – are always *presented*, or rather *represented* as if they *preceded the processes that produce them.* They are projected, and then called upon as though they had already been there – or, better, the calling-upon *is* the retrojection of the denomination.

The denominational entity appears (is presented) only in *re*-presentations, in the claim staked by re-presentatives, speaking in the name of the off-stage higher authority to which (this is the claim) *you* already owe an obligation. And it is not just any obligation: it is the *permanent obligation of allegiance*, rather than, say, a contractual, mercenary obligation to perform this or that action, with the obligation being discharged upon delivery. When it comes to your obligation to your community of denomination, there is no being discharged on this side of the grave – and possibly even after: think of Robert Emmet, who commanded from the dock that his own epitaph remain unwritten until Ireland took her place among the nations.

Acts of denomination are claims that all who fall within the scope of the name are *essentially the same* – that is, the same in essence, in the most important respect: in their shared and common *identity*. And if you share a common identity, you are *taken to* owe (you are interpreted as owing) a common allegiance, *taken* to share common interests, *taken* to share a common history, a common future, and so on.

By the same stroke, crucially, *this* collective identity requires the construction of an 'outside', an 'other', set off from (often in diametric opposition to) the first. All those who fall outside the scope of the name must *keep their distance*, so to speak, or be treated as a threat to the purity of the community. The 'other' is not just a neutral feature of the universe, but a potential (which is always to say an ontologically necessary) enemy. That is, if the 'other as potential enemy' did not exist, it would have to be invented, to give the denomination something to demarcate itself off against.

This is the logic that Carl Schmitt takes to be fundamental to the realm of politics itself, politics *as such*. We need not repeat Derrida's deconstruction of Schmitt's discourse (Derrida 1997) to suggest this is rather the logic of a *certain kind of politics*, a certain way of going about politics, that need not exhaust the full spectrum of possibilities.

To sum up, community is not a 'thing', like a table or rock; nor is it a set of people who all simply (passively) share a given set of characteristics – this is rather a category than a community. But there are those who will try to turn the former into the latter; those who will take a characteristic, or set of characteristics and rather than make a seemingly trivial observation that 'there is a category of people who share these characteristics' (for example, Protestant or Catholic religious background, or, in another register, white skin), will attempt to congregate or *inaugurate* a community on the basis of these select characteristics; will make a bid for allegiance out of it, claiming the authority of reality itself as the ground for the bid.

The denominational community, which I will only ever encounter through representations, is taken to be the (off-stage) entity to which I already belong by the time I get around to giving it my allegiance – or, for example, filling in the questionnaire through which I declare my belonging. I can denominate myself; I can be denominated *by* others; and I can denominate those others as belonging to my community, or to some other community. But I cannot escape the fact that these are processes, actions, all the way down.

Moreover, through processes of denomination, I make a bid to assemble a combination (I bid people combine) via a retrojected *unitary* entity (*id*-entity), which entails not just inclusions and exclusions but the project of the specific *reduction* of difference, otherness, multiplicity 'within' the denomination.

The *project* of the specific reduction remains just that – a project – because it is impossible to reduce, or master difference, otherness, once and for all. That it cannot be so reduced (and yet must be: this is the imperative) provides the impulse for the continual *policing* of the territory, of the borders, of the need to confront enemies and potential traitors. But this project is founded on the circular claim that the unitary entity that founds it is already there.

The project of denomination bids us set ourselves towards each other as though we already 'belonged' to distinct denominations – that is, I must scan my neighbour for signs, for the moment I can say: Aha! You are one of those . . . (and fill out the ellipsis, that is, complete the performative utterance, with whatever denomination I am projecting off-stage). I encounter a neighbour and (actively, reductively) read them or interpret them as *belonging* to an entity that remains *outside the space of the encounter*. Denominational entities belong *outside* each other, are *exterior* to each other – but also outside any living, bodily encounter *with* others.

Back to the town square, to my accuser, and to the question: Whom was I betraying? My people? My country? My community?

Whatever specific version of denomination my neighbour had in mind, he believed I was guilty of a betrayal; but one cannot betray a state, a nation, a community, to which one does not '*belong*' – to which one does not *owe allegiance*.

Perhaps, for him, the allegiance was a national one; perhaps the betrayal was of my (supposed) Britishness; perhaps he saw Northern Ireland as the homeland (or 'heartland') of 'we' the 'Ulster-British', an integral part of the unitary nation, the 'British people', with Northern Ireland in turn being an integral part of the UK as the *unitary national territory of the British people*. The allegiance I would owe, then (on his assumptions), would be a permanent, ontologically given obligation to this higher authority, the British people, here on their (or would that not be 'our'?) territory.

His exclamation, in that case, called on me to recognise that the choice facing me was no longer that between two political projects, staying in the EU or leaving, weighing up the pros and cons on either side; but of *whether or not to betray my community*.

The performative force of his accusation was that of a bid to *change the ground* on which the conversation was taking place; no longer a market square in the neighbourhood, where all sorts of different people met, discussed, did business, persuaded each other in democratic debate, but a little part of *the national territory*. If it were felicitous, his performative utterance would have subordinated the choice between this or that political project to an ontologically prior matter: the existence of (and my belonging to) the (denomi)nation. It would have ordered the neighbourhood into a region of the *realm*, the United *Kingdom*. We will come back to the idea of the Kingdom, the realm, in a later chapter.

What we have tried to explore here is the *politics of denomination* as one way in which people can combine, one form of combination, based on the claim that people are already combined, ontologically. They are one 'kind' among others – and indeed, *against* others. The politics of denomination sets up a politics of hostility – governed by its Schmittian triad: friend, enemy, traitor. Processes of denomination set people towards each other according to this triad. Denomination, then, is one way of distributing *bids to justify* violence: our violence is 'justified', the claim is, as self-defence, against *external and internal* enemies.

The Good Friday Agreement brought the worst of the 'hot' or 'kinetic' violence of the conflict in Northern Ireland to an end by persuading representatives of the 'two communities in conflict' to commit to *nonviolence* and *democracy*, and to a form of *power-sharing*, so that neither of them could any longer dominate the other by violence (whether that of the instruments of the state or of paramilitary organisations). But this can be interpreted in at least two divergent ways.

A denominational interpretation of the 'nonviolence and democracy' of the Agreement (and this was amplified in the subsequent St Andrews Agreement that adjusted the institutions) reproduces the dominant paradigm of two-communities-in-conflict, even as it attempts to resolve that conflict. 'Democracy', in this approach, means sending people to *represent* one of two mutually exclusive 'communities' in Stormont. This is 'power sharing' understood at best as ensuring the 'two communities' share power equitably between them. At worst, it sets the scene for attempts to *maximise the share of power flowing to 'our side'*, our *denomination*.

A more *democratic* interpretation of 'nonviolence and democracy', as we will see later, would move towards sharing power out equitably across the whole population, whoever and whatever people happen to be.

The Agreement, then, even as it was a step towards nonviolence and democracy, also kept the zero-sum, binary reduction machine functioning. If I want a share of power, the easiest route is to join one of those sides the institutions are set up to empower, adopt and master the relevant logic and grammar, the relevant routines, become adept at articulating them, and thus rise through the ranks to become a 'representative of my community'. Which is not *your* community, if you are of a different *denomination*.

A variation on this route is to accept the 'reality' of the two communities, try to occupy a third position *in relation* to them (being *neither* one nor the other), and become a kind of 'moderator', pointing the way towards a modus vivendi that would share power equitably *between the already existing communities.*

The Agreement, denominationally understood, performed this function: it made room for a kind of power sharing that at least in theory dismantled the hierarchical arrangement of the denominations – there was to be parity of esteem between them, equality in that one denomination could no longer simply dominate the other by sheer force of numbers, or by the sheer force of violence – but it did not rethink the denominations themselves, with the structures of allegiance and the binary reductions they implied. For the same reason, it did not *rethink the ideas of nonviolence and democracy* that it held out as offering a new kind of politics in Northern Ireland. Later we will attempt to do just that: explore ways to rethink the ideas of nonviolence and democracy.

But at the time, was there much choice? What alternatives to the locally dominant paradigm were on offer? For some, the best way ahead appeared to be to replace it with a *globally* dominant one: a model of democracy built around economic growth and the power of the market.

On a visit to Belfast to mark the twentieth anniversary of the Agreement, Bill Clinton noted that on his way from the airport he had seen plenty of cranes at work across the skyline. 'Keep the cranes up in Belfast', he said (Clinton 2018). The idea seemed to be, if you are economically prosperous, if you are making buildings and making money, you won't have the inclination to make enemies. At its crudest (and to be fair, this does not apply to Clinton, who made a more nuanced appeal to a social solidarity that would not be a homogeneity), this would mean that as long as someone has money to buy your wares, their denomination is a matter of indifference to you. And of course, if the market brought peace, peace, in its turn, would bring more market: more investment; more prosperity; more peace; and so on in a self-fuelling virtuous circle.

This approach, dubbed by McLaughlin and Baker the 'propaganda of peace', was a not-insignificant element in the push to get the GFA endorsed in the referenda of 1998 (McLaughlin and Baker 2010). But does the globally dominant paradigm actually give us a way to move towards the democracy and nonviolence espoused in the GFA? To put it otherwise, what is the relationship between the market square in Newtownards and the 'global markets', the dynamics of which appear to give us a route out of the politics of hostility? Does the market offer the possibility of a politics beyond violence?

In the next chapter we will take up this question in looking at another kind of politics of violence: not that of hostility, but of *indifference*.

Chapter Two

The Cold White Meat of Contract

The Politics of Indifference

The Northern Ireland conflict is just one clear example of the divisive politics of hostility, the reading of our neighbours as either friends or enemies, in the Schmittian sense, or as potential traitors, to complete the triad of hostility. If politics is parcelled out thus, a certain answer to the question of violence is called for, or called forth: 'we' are obliged to 'defend' our community if 'they' attack us; anyone who shies away from this obligation, or is caught defending 'them' is a traitor, and will have called our retributive violence down on their own heads. 'We' and 'they' are external to each other, separated by an ontological gulf. As long as they do not try to invade or dominate us–as long as they *keep their distance* – we will be able to rub along more or less peacefully together.

Here we will look at another way in which a kind of politics of violence can unfold, not so much by way of a politics of hostility as through a politics of *indifference*. We will trace our path via a film, a fable, a philosopher, and a family story. Firstly, and most briefly, the film.

In *The Third Man*, set in rubble-strewn post-war Vienna, the charming but ruthless racketeer Harry Lime takes his rather innocent old friend Holly Martins up in the Ferris Wheel at a fairground, where Martins confronts him about the fatal side-effects of Lime's criminal activities. As the wheel nears the top of its arc, Lime invites Martins to look down at the figures far below. 'Would you really feel any pity', he asks, 'if one of those dots stopped moving forever'?

Significantly, he goes on: 'If I offered you £20,000 for every dot that stopped would you really, old man, tell me to keep my money, or would you calculate how many dots you could afford to spare?'.

Of course, you don't have to go to the top of a Ferris wheel to create distance; there are other ways of reducing people to the status of 'one of those dots' – interchangeable objects, algebraic tokens, 'examples' of a certain 'type'. One of those . . .

Fill out the 'dots' of the ellipsis with whatever denomination suits.

Then the fable.

Throughout Angela Carter's collection of tales, *The Bloody Chamber*, certain themes and tropes crop up again and again. There are men who are bestial, who snarl or half-snarl ('The Bloody Chamber' itself), there are beasts who are tender (Mr Lyon, the Tiger) or wonderfully human (Puss in Boots); women are plant-like or herbivore; kisses have teeth in them (the title story and 'The Erl-king'); there is blood throughout, there are appetites throughout, and there is a disrobing or stripping of women throughout.

In the opening tale, 'The Bloody Chamber', the narrator, speaking of her new husband on their wedding night, says that he 'stripped me, gourmand that he was, as if he were stripping the leaves off an artichoke'; she describes him as her 'purchaser', who unwraps 'his bargain'; the two are pictured together, he 'in his London tailoring, she bare as a lamb chop' (Carter 2006, 11). The systemic power differential in the gender relations is clear, then, from the start. Moreover, here the 'stripping' of the woman and the idea of consumption are brought together in an explicitly economic context.

The lamb, presented in this first story as a piece of meat (in the at once mundanely domestic and shockingly violent form of a 'chop', a word to which we will return), reappears as a sacrificial lamb in 'Mr Lyon', whose paws, we are told, could be the 'death of any tender herbivore'. Woman as herbivore, woman as 'tender'; gentle towards others, but also a tender, as distinct from a tough, cut of meat, lamb as distinct from mutton; and perhaps also something to be tendered in a marketplace.

The combination of these themes is particularly clear, and particularly densely packed, in 'The Tiger's Bride', a story which, read in a certain way, will allow us to draw out a range of the threads that will inform our reading of the themes of identity and difference, violence and the market, gender and power, consumption and segregation. These themes, along with questions about how to make the transition to a different way of relating to each other are all raised in the course of Carter's short story about a woman staked and lost by her father in a game of cards with a man who turns out to be a beast.

The whole setting of the story, told as it is from the point of view of the young woman, alerts us to the idea of the woman as property, an item capable of being staked in a game, traded, bought, and sold. It emerges that she has been so staked and lost, turned over by one man, her father, to a mysterious other. It is not that her father does not love her, not that he values her, we are told, at less than a king's ransom, 'but at *no more* than a king's ransom' (Carter 2006, 59). But this second man, the local Lord, it soon appears, is in fact a *tiger* wearing a mask of a man's face, and capacious clothes to disguise his body. Exactly the sort of Beast, one would have thought, that the woman's old nurse used to warn her (to 'scare [her] into good behaviour') would come and 'gobble [her] up' (another variation on the theme of women as objects of consumption).

However, it turns out that the Tiger wants something else. They go out riding through the countryside around the castle, and stop at the bank of a river, in a 'place of perfect privacy, beyond a brake of winter-bare rushes, a hedge of reeds'. Into this clearing, the tiger sends his servant to tell her he wishes only to see her undressed. It is a demand with which, initially, and unsurprisingly, she refuses to comply. So, the Tiger, with the impeccable logic of the magical tale, decides that the only solution is for him to show himself unclothed to her.

As soon as he does so, however, and in spite of his patent power and ferocity, she takes the decision to disrobe before him too. She steps out before him in the clearing, disrobed, undisguised, in the flesh. Here, then, is another exchange; but we are far, now, from the card table, or indeed the marketplace, wherein, we are told in another passage, 'the eyes that watch you take no account of your existence'.

Here it is all about *disrobing*, actively, and by choice, not, as in the title story, *being stripped* (in the passive voice). And it is about stepping out from behind the masks and dresses into the open, face-to-face, eye to eye. There is a reciprocity here, though it is not a symmetrical one. At first glance this appears a pretty one-sided deal: the tiger, after all, appears to monopolise the power in the situation. But Carter's tale will put that one-sidedness into question. 'The tiger will never lie down with the lamb; he acknowledges no pact that is not reciprocal. The lamb must learn to run with the tigers'. Does this mean, in the oft-repeated criticism of second-wave feminism, that women ('lambs') are expected to learn to play the game like men ('tigers')? Such would be an obvious, but reductive interpretation.

After all, the tiger, as we discover, is in some sense *made fearful* by the woman. She disrobes only after he has done so, and she does it 'to show him I would do him no harm'. Note the mood: *would*, not 'could'. It is as if, despite the ferocity of the tiger, his capacity to do violence, she herself both *has the capacity* to do him harm, and she *chooses* not to.

Indeed, we are told, 'He was far more frightened of me than I was of him'. Why? What is the power the woman holds over him? Margaret Atwood, in 'Running with the Tigers', reads this in conjunction with Carter's Sadean Woman: 'only the possibility of love could awake the libertine to perfect, immaculate terror'. This, says Atwood, is because 'love can occur only freely and between equals, so those afraid of it will wish to preserve the condition of user and used' (Sage 1994, 126).

In Atwood's reading, what the tiger seems to fear is 'love'; that is, he fears that if the woman steps into the clearing with him, he will have to give up his old life, his power over others, his power to *use* others. But is it not also the case that the tiger fears she might *not*? We will come back to this in a later chapter, but for now, let us emphasise that this exchange is explicitly not an *economic* exchange in the conventional sense, as soon becomes clear: she is about to refuse to allow the exchange to be reduced to the level of the market.

When they go back to the castle the tiger sends money to the father and a sable for her; but she turns the gift (or rather, the payment) down. Instead, she plans to dress a *clockwork automaton* she has been given (a model of herself, designed to be her maid and companion in the Tiger's castle) in her own clothes and 'send her back to perform the part of my father's daughter'.

Performing the part: fulfilling the role, the function; interchangeable, replaceable even by a mechanical substitute. A *thing indifferent*, to borrow a phrase from Swift's Gulliver's Travels ('Neither are any wars so furious and bloody, or of so long continuance, as those occasioned by difference in opinion, especially if it be in things indifferent').

After all, her father will not notice the difference: has already reduced her to the status of an exchangeable commodity by staking her in the card game.

She disrobes again, then, in order to dress the automaton, even though she is 'unaccustomed to nakedness' – another act of courage in itself. Now this passage:

> the smiling girl stood poised in the oblivion of her balked simulation of life, watching me peel down to the cold, white meat of contract and, if she did not see me, then so much more like the market place, where the eyes that watch you take no account of your existence. And it seemed my entire life, since I had left the North, had passed under the indifferent gaze of eyes like hers (Carter 2006, 73–74).

It is a passage dense with suggestions and allusions, not least to the Garden of Eden, and therefore to a whole range of questions about Eve, the issue of her 'responsibility' for the loss of Paradise, to sexuality and sin and so forth. But freighted with endlessly analysable tropes as it is, let us confine ourselves to the suggestion of a certain, learnt and deliberate blindness. The doll watches, but it cannot see; it is oblivious in its 'balked simulation' of life; and the doll, in its obliviousness, provides a close parallel with the kind of encounter that takes place in the market, where one is watched but not seen as such. Under an indifferent gaze, one is seen as, to use Swift's words again, a thing indifferent. One's existence is not taken into account: it is *discounted.* The contrast here is between the stripped, flayed, reduced 'cold, white meat of contract', and the mutual self-exposure (exposure in all vulnerability) that has taken place in the previous passage, and that takes place for a second time, at the end of the story, between the woman and the beast – an encounter which we must delay until a later chapter.

What interests us here is the indifference of the market: my living body is stripped, reduced to the cold, white meat of contract; my encounter with you is reduced to my encounter with a functionary, one dolled up in the correct livery, one who will do until a more efficient replacement can be found. In this encounter, I am indifferent to you, and you to me; everything behind the robe, the mask, is reduced to insignificance; your entire life beyond the space of this market encounter does not concern me. The space of the market, then, opens not like the clearing into which you and I step in all our disrobed, irreplaceable singularity; rather, the space of the merely economic market opens only with the reduction of, the expulsion of (soon we will say the *Clearance* of) such singularity. But it is just this reduction upon which, arguably, the foundations of the modern world economy are laid.

Let us turn, then, to the philosopher, namely Adam Smith, seen by some as the 'father of modern economics' (Sharma 2022) to examine at least a few of the conceptual steps by which this reduction was produced – a reduction that has been endlessly reproduced ever since, to the point where it is globally hegemonic.

MOTHERS AND OTHERS IN THE MARKET ECONOMY

'It is not from the benevolence of the butcher, the brewer, or the baker that we expect our dinner', wrote Adam Smith in 1776, 'but from their regard to their own interest' (Smith 2003, book 1, chap. 2).

This statement, along with the passage about the 'invisible hand' are among the best known of all Adam Smith's words, perhaps the only passages still widely quoted today. Taken together, they could be seen as articulating the founding credo of the currently dominant, 'free-market' or 'neoliberal' economic orthodoxy – in brief, the idea that individual pursuit of self-interest in a free market maximises the welfare of the society as a whole.

Of course, there is more to Smith than this, and he was more socially conscious and more cautious about capitalism than his followers. Indeed, there is clearly more to modern economics than these founding statements – though it would be difficult to find much that is essentially *critical* of them in mainstream economics.

It is perhaps all the more important, then, to submit these ideas to critical scrutiny. Take the meal that Smith mentions, for example. Katrine Marçal asks a question so simple it seems obvious in retrospect (though as is often the case with such questions, perhaps *only* in retrospect): Who Cooked Adam Smith's Dinner? (Marçal 2015).

Marçal points out that Adam Smith's *mother* took care of her son not just as a child, but in his adult life too, as long as she lived. Every day she looked after the household affairs, *including the preparation of his dinner*. Yet the 'father of modern economics' omits his mother from his account of how we (whoever 'we' are in this context) get our dinner. The butcher, baker, and brewer are singled out, made visible, so to speak; Smith's mother is cropped (or chopped) out of the picture, not so much an invisible hand as an invisible *woman*. And, Marçal argues, there are many more like her.

'For the butcher, the baker and the brewer to be able to go to work', Marçal points out, 'their wives, mothers or sisters had to spend hour after hour, day after day minding the children, cleaning the house, cooking the food, washing the clothes, drying tears and squabbling with the neighbours. However you look at the market, it is always built on another economy. An economy that we rarely discuss' (Marçal 2015, 16).

This whole 'other economy', this immeasurable workforce of invisible hands, then, works away behind the scenes, often in the privacy of the domestic sphere. What remains publicly visible, within the picture frame, in-shot, so to speak, are the traders; the subset of goods that can be traded as commodities; and their price-tags (what later economists will call the 'price-signal'). For orthodox classical and neoliberal economics, apparently as warranted by this inaugural text, that is all that is significant, all that *should* be visible.

The 'invisible hand' passage itself appears in the Wealth of Nations in the course of a discussion of domestic versus foreign trade. In passing, let us flag up the word *domestic*: the idea of the domestic, especially in the form of the 'home' (*oikos* in Greek), is not without its significance – though here Smith, of course, uses the term to refer to intra-national, rather than international trade:

> By preferring the support of domestic to that of foreign industry, he [the individual economic agent] intends only his own security; and by directing that industry in such a manner as its produce may be of the greatest value, he intends only his own gain; and he is in this, as in many other cases, led by an invisible hand to promote an end which was no part of his intention. . . . By pursuing his own interest, he frequently promotes that of the society more effectually than when he really intends to produce it (Smith 2003, book 4, chap. 2).

Two points: first, the 'invisible hand' makes its appearance here in a context in which the distinction between the 'domestic' and the 'foreign' is already there, as though unproblematic, simply obvious, simply a given reality. There is already, then, an 'us' and 'them' in place. Perhaps it should be no surprise in a book about the wealth of *nations*. This division is in place from the very first line of the book: 'The annual labour of every nation is the fund which originally supplies it' (Smith 1999).

Labour, the origin of wealth, is *already* divided by (denomi)nation, it is already the wealth *of nations*, each distinct from the others, by the time Smith starts thinking about wealth as such. As an aside, this taking-as-given, as a matter 'of course', is not confined to the liberal, and later neo-liberal tradition. Compare this with Benedict Anderson's remark, in his Introduction, about 'Marx's failure to explicate the crucial adjective in his memorable formulation of 1848: "The proletariat of each country must, of course, first of all settle matters with *its own* bourgeoisie"?' (Anderson 2006, 3–4. The emphasis is Anderson's – but note, too, the 'of course', which should also be emphasised here). The 'crucial adjective' in this sentence, for Anderson, is 'own'; but it seems he considers it crucial insofar as it stands in for 'national' ('How else to account for the use, for over a century, of the concept "national bourgeoisie" without any serious attempt to justify theoretically the relevance of the adjective'?) We will add that the word 'own' is worth examining in itself, along with related concepts of ownership (and property, and belonging) not least in the context of a discussion of political economy, as we will see shortly.

Secondly, if a trader like the butcher, the baker, or the brewer in Smith's (imaginary) market is *in fact* to promote the good of the (domestic, national) society, that good should be 'no part of his intention' – at least on a strong reading of this passage. It should be said that Smith himself leaves room for this to be seen rather as a rule of thumb than an inexorable iron law of economic logic (hence 'frequently'). In this respect, some of his later followers, significantly, appear to latch on to the 'iron law' interpretation and occlude the latitude allowed by Smith.

It is tempting to tie this to Smith's other statement – wherein social good emerges not from the traders' benevolence but from their '*regard* to their own interest' – through the notion of visibility. One's 'regard' is one's gaze, one's consciously directed glance. 'Intention', too, occurring three times in the passage has, as the phenomenologists would later use it, a sense of the directed gaze about it, the 'intentional object' being that upon which one's attention is fixed (Husserl 1970).

That aside for the moment, on a strict reading, everything other than one's 'own interest' must be *kept out of the picture*. It is not just that these people and things are invisible, they must be (actively) disregarded, *kept* invisible if the economy is to function as it is supposed to. The only things to be permitted into the picture are the marketers, their goods and their messages – traders, customers, commodities, price-tags. This framework sets out the boundaries of the marketplace for Smith. We must not get *sentimental* about this, we seem to be told; allow anything other than commodities and price tags to influence your economic decisions and you may, inadvertently to be sure, do more harm than good. Even, or perhaps especially, the other traders must be viewed not as friends or neighbours, but as *traders only*, from whom we do not expect benevolence, towards whom we must not direct benevolence. To put it another way: to whom we must not show any *sympathy*.

The word, of course, is drawn from Smith's earlier book, *The Theory of Moral Sentiments* (Smith 2009). Looking at the opening sentences of this earlier work, it is easy to see the more humane side of Smith. 'How selfish soever man may be supposed', he tells us, 'there are evidently some principles in his nature, which interest him in the fortune of others, and render their happiness necessary to him, though he derives nothing from it except the pleasure of seeing it' (Smith 2009, part 1, sect. 1, chap. 1).

Anyone who had supposed Smith to be merely a hard-hearted promoter of selfishness would presumably find this reassuring, or inconvenient, depending on their agenda, especially the last clause. One could easily imagine, after all, mounting a ruthlessly self-seeking economic defence of having 'an interest' in the 'fortune' of others. Of course, even the most ruthless capitalist needs someone to sell their goods to, as Henry Ford would later concede. But there seems no getting around that last clause: 'though he derives nothing from it' but pleasure. If this is selfishness, it is perhaps a selfishness indistinguishable from altruism.

Indeed, there is much in the rest of Smith's reading of 'sympathy' or 'fellow-feeling' that is rewards attention. For all the 'individualism' that one can find in Smith's legacy, there is a sensitivity to the *social* here that seems missing from some of his later champions, for whom, after all, there was 'no such thing as society'. This is a Smith for whom admiration of the rich is a 'corruption of our moral sentiments', a Smith for whom there is a pleasure in mutual sympathy, a sympathy that 'enlivens joy and alleviates grief' (Smith 2009, part 1, sect. 1, chap. 1).

This Smith is – the word is irresistible – a deeply sympathetic one. And yet, for all the rich descriptions and analyses, and for all his undoubtedly humane intentions, those of his followers who draw out the hardline version do not invent it out of thin air. It is not difficult to find an unsentimental Smith in the same texts as the sympathetic one. Let us work our way through these two Smiths.

If there were one sentence that summed up unsentimental Smith's analysis of what he calls 'fellow-feeling', it is perhaps this, from right at the start of the book: 'As we have no immediate experience of what other men feel, we can form no idea of the manner in which they are affected, but by conceiving what we ourselves should feel in the like situation' (Smith 2009, part 1, sect. 1, chap. 1).

Smith's concept of fellow feeling, as stated here, is based on a kind of empathy we might describe as one of *projection* rather than of *contagion*, to borrow the terms explored by Samuel Fleishacker (Fleishacker 2019) in his analysis of Smithian empathy.

This conception of empathy distinguishes Smith from Hume, for whom fellow-feeling spread directly from person to person, contagiously. Fleishacker will champion the Smithian version of an empathy of projection because, as he constructs it (or 'updates' it, in his terms), it allows us to address and overcome certain criticisms of an ethics based on empathy, criticisms such as those proposed by Paul Bloom, who holds that empathy leads us to favour those most like ourselves, those *closest* to us, over those who are different or at a distance from us (Bloom 2016). On the other hand, for Fleishacker, Smithian empathy helps us avoid the problem of being overly 'universalistic', imagining we can fully enter into the circumstances of any and every other human being.

For Fleishacker, Smithian empathy involves not the passive reception of the feelings of others, but the active projection of ourselves, an active thinking of our way into the lives and circumstances of others, in order to *understand*, and come to a proper judgement about how they are feeling. Fleishacker emphasises the need to examine every detail – in Smith's words, 'every little circumstance of distress which can possibly occur to the sufferer'. Smithian empathy, as presented here, is particularistic and contextual then. Moreover, Fleishacker is going to argue that Smithian empathy respects difference: we do not reduce the other to a version of ourselves, do not 'merge' with the other in Smithian empathy. Rather, it opens a '*gap* [the emphasis is Fleishacker's] between the feelings we have when we empathize with another and the feelings that she has herself' (Fleishacker 2019, chap. 2). And it is precisely in negotiating this gap, adjusting our position, our feelings about ourselves, in relation to others, as it were, that Fleishacker finds the power of Smithian empathy.

Indeed, for Smith, there cannot even be a 'self', properly speaking, that would be conceivable outside this intercourse with others. Someone raised in total isolation from others 'could no more think of his own character, of the propriety or demerit of his own sentiments, of the beauty or deformity of his own mind, than of the beauty or deformity of his own face' (Smith 2009, part 3, chap. 1).

Fleishacker's version of Smith will allow for an 'open-ended interpretive process' which 'requires each of us to reinterpret . . . who exactly you are, and who exactly I am'. You and I are not fixed entities, on this reading, not already self-identical outside the situated, mutual shaping of each other in the empathetic exchange. 'What I take to belong properly to you, and what I take to belong properly to me, may change as I proceed with this imaginative and interpretive process. It follows that there will be no 'natural', pre-empathetic self' to which I might turn to ground distinctions between 'imagining being myself in your situation and imagining being you in it' (Fleishacker 2019, chap. 2).

This last distinction is drawn from a passage in which Smith thinks about condoling with someone who has lost a child: 'in order to enter into your grief I do not consider what I, a person of such a character and profession, should suffer . . . but I consider what I should suffer if I was really you, and I not only change circumstances with you, but I change persons and characters' (Smith 2009, part 7, sect. 3, chap. 1).

There is something profoundly appealing about this Smith. But to get to the point where he can draw it out and claim Smith's authority for effectively deconstructing any 'natural, pre-empathetic self', Fleishacker has to 'update' Smith. At one point he even has recourse to Heidegger's 'being-in-the-world' to indicate the unarticulated 'web of attitudes and habits' we bring to such encounters; elsewhere he invokes Wittgenstein, Cavell, and other still more recent thinkers; but the idea that you and I do not precede or stand outside the interpretive process of our interaction is nonetheless a potent one.

One thing is certain though: this is not the only way of reading Smith's text. Look at our exemplary sentence again, drawn from right at the beginning of the book: 'As we have no immediate experience of what other men feel, we can form no idea of the manner in which they are affected, but by conceiving what we ourselves should feel in the like situation'.

Everything will depend on the question of 'immediacy of experience' here. That we have *no immediate experience* of what others feel is simply taken for granted. The sentence starts with 'as': the inadmissibility of any immediate experience of 'what other men feel' (other *men*, never mind women) is taken as given, as axiomatic. Smith has no intention of examining whether this *is* the case or not – at least not at the outset. Not before he has written this extraordinary passage:

> Though our brother is upon the rack, as long as we ourselves are at our ease, our senses will never inform us of what he suffers. They never did, and never can, carry us beyond our own person, and it is by the imagination only that we can form any conception of what are his sensations. Neither can that faculty help us to this any other way, than by representing to us what would be our own, if we were in his case (Smith 2009, part 1, sect. 1, chap. 1).

For Smith, this unsentimental Smith at any rate, the suffering of the other (the 'brother', no less) is *inaccessible* except through the *intermediary* of the imaginative *representation* of what would be 'our own'. Our senses will 'never' inform us of what he suffers: Smith repeats the word and repeats it again. The repetition is emphatic; but it seems not yet emphatic enough (the italics here are mine): 'it is by the imagination *only* that we can form *any* conception of what are his sensations'. Still not enough. '*Neither* can that faculty help us to this *any other way*'. Any other way than what? Than by 'representing to us what would be our own if we were in his case'.

What would be '*our own*'. All the weight of the emphasis leads to, and is pitched at this phrase, 'our own'. It is a phrase that will be repeated throughout this whole passage like an iambic heartbeat. The suffering of the other is emphatically not 'our own'. We have *no means* of access to it but by the intermediary of imaginative representation. And even now he is not done: he adds that it is the 'impressions of *our own* [emphasis added] senses only, not those of his, which our imaginations copy'.

Even when we do go through the circuit of representation, we only get back *our own*. Or to be precise, a 'copy' of our own – a 'balked simulation', in Carter's phrase, perhaps? – which is sent out, so to speak, to take up our brother's position, imagine what it would feel like *to us*, and come 'back home' in order to inform us. Before this whole process is complete, we can even be 'at ease'. Our brother will lie on the rack like a thing indifferent. Only after it is complete, only once the imagination has brought home *our* re-presentation of what *we ourselves* would feel in such a situation, only then, 'at last', says Smith, do we begin to 'tremble and shudder at the thought of what he feels'.

The 'at last' gives us a sense of the length of the detour, so to speak, that the sufferings of 'our brother' on the rack will have to make before they are brought home to us, before they are made 'our own' by means of the representations – that is, 'copies' – of the imagination. Before that cargo is delivered, we remain uninformed by our senses, though our brother lies *already* in plain sight on the rack. His suffering leaves us impassive, before the imagination has made and delivered its 'copy'. Only then, *at last*, do we begin to 'tremble and shudder', and then not at what he feels, but at 'the thought' of what he feels (or rather, at the *thought* of what 'we' would feel).

That my senses (for Smith) 'never did, and never can, carry us beyond our own person' indicates that my 'person', everything that *properly belongs to me*, stops short at a certain boundary, a boundary that appears as a clear *gap*, conceived as a *gulf*, an abyss, an absolute separation between me and any others out there, a gulf that only *my representations* can bridge. Smith tacitly performs a Cartesian partition: my senses are mine alone, confined to a certain interior, to the scope of my body. Only by sending out the emissary of my imagination can I get a report back from outside; if I fail to do so, I could have no 'conception' of the suffering of, and therefore could feel no sympathy for, my brother on the rack – or rather, *our* brother on the rack: Smith is talking to and for *us*, *all* of us, universally.

And it is exactly this 'failure' of conception and imagination that is turned on its head and becomes a positive injunction – or at any rate, rule of thumb – in the later text. We *must not* act out of sympathy in the market. We must not 'bring home' the suffering of the other. We must not, to go back to the earlier text, 'place ourselves in his situation . . . conceive ourselves enduring all the same torments . . . enter as it were into his body, and become in some measure the same person with him'. We must forbid ourselves this detour. His interests are his, ours are 'our own'.

But what if it is too late? What if our experience of the other on the rack is, contra unsentimental Smith, *immediate*? What if this unsentimental Smithian empathy is a *derivative form* of a more primordial (in the phenomenological sense) kind of fellow-feeling – a form oscillating in and out of legibility in Smith's own texts? A form of projective empathy that cannot do without bodily *contagion*?

To go back to Fleishacker. Setting the scene for Smithian projection, he reminds us of Mencius, the Chinese philosopher who, over two thousand years ago, noted that people seeing a child about to fall into a well 'will without exception experience a feeling of alarm and distress'. Is the flinch on witnessing a child fall (let's update the image) in a playground – the tightening of the muscles, the stomach, the instinctive raising of the arm, the outstretched palm – not *immediate*? Is this not a *bodily* reaction, one that awaits no detour through a process of imaginatively or intellectually interpreting visual data as one decodes signals? Recall Maurice Merleau-Ponty: 'My body has its world, or understands its world, without having to make use of my "symbolic" or "objectifying" function' (Merleau-Ponty 2002, 162).

Are we not already, in Smith's phrase, carried 'beyond our own person' in the presence of the suffering of another? Indeed, does such an immediate bodily reaction not place in question, precisely, what '*our own* person' is? Smith himself, again within the first chapter of the *Theory of Moral Sentiment*, adduces several examples – many 'obvious observations' – that seem to contradict, or at any rate complicate, his own temporal and spatial schema, even as he dismisses them, or claims they reaffirm it. When we see a stroke aimed at someone's arm or leg, he says, we 'naturally shrink and draw back our own leg or our own arm'. A crowd watching a dancer on a rope 'naturally writhe and twist and balance their own bodies, as they see him do, and as they feel they themselves must do if in his situation' (Smith 2009, part 1, sect. 1, chap. 1).

The double use of the term *natural* here is interesting. Again, recall Fleishacker's reading, in which there is no '*natural*' self before the interaction with others. Smith's use of the word here suggests, perhaps against his own intentions, precisely an unmediated bodily reaction, rather than one that awaits the completion of the representative circuit of signal, projection, return, and interpretation. Think of the dancer on the rope: do onlookers go through a process of projecting themselves, in their imaginations, into his position, as Smith indicates, and *then* begin to sway? Or does one, in such a crowd, not *find* oneself, one's body, adjusting *itself*? Does one not 'come to', as it were, and realise one is *already* ducking and flinching precisely *in sympathy with* the dancer? In other words, does the element of reflection and interpretation not come 'at last', rather than the other way around?

What does it mean for our understanding of the economy if, contra the dominant version of Smith, this kind of fellow-feeling runs deeper than, and prior to the sending out of the emissary, the circuit of re-presentation? This is not to say we do not or should not also do the latter, that we do not also have the capacity to think our way into someone else's situation, using our imagination, conceive of their suffering, and *then* feel sympathy. Indeed, we may have an ethical obligation to do just that. But this mediated version is not the only one, and not the first.

Smith himself in fact admits that on some occasions 'sympathy may seem to be transfused from one man to another instantaneously, and antecedent to any knowledge of what excited them'. Grief and joy, 'strongly expressed in the look and gestures of anyone, at once affect the spectator with some degree of a like painful or agreeable emotion. A smiling face is, to everybody that sees it, a cheerful object' (Smith 2006, part 1, sect. 1, chap. 1).

He dismisses these counterexamples, though, on the basis that they do 'not hold universally'. Nevertheless, they still appear to contradict what he has taken as axiomatic. If, even upon 'some occasions' only, the passions of the other affect us 'instantaneously', and 'before all knowledge', then at least in such cases our imagination has at first *no time* to perform the detour; we cannot reach into our own memory to select the appropriate response, cannot make the requisite copy, cannot 'bring home' the correct feeling to ourselves. The fellow-feeling is already there, 'instantaneously'. Already home, already 'our own', and already, precisely, our own in relation to *an other*. Moreover, we *already know* the other is there. Why else would we send our emissary in the first place? How would we know *where* to send it? Why send it to the man, my brother; not to manacle that restrains him – or to a mannequin, should one be at hand?

If I did send out my imaginary emissary to the mannequin, it would be as a deliberate exercise; but I would already know the difference, already recognise in my brother on the rack, and not in the doll or the rack itself, say, a *being capable of suffering* – note, it is not only *human* beings that are capable of suffering – and that not as a 'conception', but in a bodily experience, as immediate as the 'shrinking and drawing back' of my leg when watching a blow aimed at another.

Smith's projective version of sympathy is, it bears repeating, essential. Crucially, however, it is a form of sympathy made possible only because we are *already able to share an immediate, common experience with others*. If we were not, then there would be no difference between watching our brother on the rack and watching a balked simulation, a doll, being 'tortured'. Under what circumstances would we ever ask ourselves 'what would it feel like if I were in the position of that doll', other than, precisely, a conceptual exercise? We project our feelings onto our brother and ask ourselves how we would feel in his situation *only because we already know he is not a doll.*

But Smith wants to cut this out, as it were, through a double incision. First, in the Theory of Moral Sentiments, he cuts off the immediate relation of my body to the body of the other, goes through the detour of the imagination, permitting only a mediated connection to be formed (through imaginative representation). Then, in the Wealth of Nations, he (or an iron law follower) forbids us to bring even this mediated connection into the space of the market, wherein only our 'own interest' is allowed to appear.

Why labour this point at such length? Because 'our own', as conceived here, is not *all of our own*, not the only form of 'ownership' that appears even in Smith's text. And given that we are discussing the founding texts of modern economics, the question of ownership, let us say, is not without its importance.

My experience of the suffering of another cannot be reduced *without violence* to two isolated instances of private experience that just happen to geographically abut each other – one at ease, one in agony. In the torture chamber, I do not experience a *representation* of you being tortured, I experience your-being-tortured. To be clear, when the instruments of torture bite into your soft tissues, I know they bite into *your* body, and not mine. The shared experience is not symmetrical, my part in it is not a mere mirror image of yours. Nor is it a substitutable 'copy' that can be passed around from one hand to the other without loss.

It would be 'without loss' only because the loss is already built into the initial act of severance, the act of splitting, of scission, of abstracting from the shared bodily experience to produce a *conception* of an experience that would be exclusively mine, an experience that would be exclusively yours, and a room in which they would happen to coexist just as a rock and a chair could abut in a room, albeit with the added capacity to project concepts. After such an operation, I am left with a derived, *privative* version of my 'self', and of 'my own.'

This privatively produced version of my 'own' appears as 'my own as an individual', severed (like a chop) from others. Private. Absolutely mine and absolutely *not* yours. And this is the only form of *ownership* that will be allowed to appear in the space of the market, as constructed by Smith and elaborated to the point of immense mathematical complexity by his successors. *Nothing that belongs to both of us at once is permitted to appear* – unless 'belonging to both of us' is taken to mean each of us owning a calculable number of shares, parcelled out and held by each of us as exclusively, privately, our own, to dispose of as we please, without reference to the other. But this is merely to move the fence enclosing 'my own' (exclusive) property. My share is mine, not yours. Nothing that belongs to us *in common* can appear here.

As an aside, this is how the scene is set for the so-called tragedy of the commons: it is a projection not of a common, but of a series of already self-enclosed private individuals onto a territory already understood as *pre-private*, as *appropriable*, as *set-to-be-parcelled-into-shares*. The tragedy of the commons in this model arises when someone takes *more* than their (calculable, pre-private) share, and precisely takes it into their own personal, exclusive, private use. But in that case, the tragedy of the commons is privatisation.

The 'privateness' of this form of ownership is 'private' in the sense that I achieve it by way of your exclusion, your exteriorisation – in contrast to the 'place of perfect privacy' in Carter's tale, the clearing into which you and I step *together*, face-to-face, unmasked, for all our differences, in the flesh. It is tempting to describe this process as one of 'enclosure' (a process that played a key role in Marx's thought, of course). Enclosure, the extraction of private property from the commons, is achieved precisely by shutting something *out* – namely, immediate fellow-feeling, the sort of sufferings and joys we experience *with* each other. These must be kept outside the space of 'private' property, the space of the market – that is, they must be *externalised* (made to appear as an 'externality' in the economic sense). To alleviate any suffering or to enhance the social good, says the Smith of the Wealth of Nations, we must first cut out immediate fellow-feelings. Only then can we go through the route of the private good, private property; and only then 'at last' can relations to the other be restored in their *appropriate* ('proper', that is, privatively achieved, externalised) sphere.

Conversely, if the other's suffering is felt immediately, is *contagious*, the only way to keep it from *contaminating* appropriate market transactions is to keep it at a remove, out of sight, out of touch; as invisible as a mother, as out of reach as my brother on the rack, no matter how nearby he may be. I must keep my distance. Any immediate connection to the other, as such, must be written out of the account(s), chopped out, *cleared out of the way*. Every enclosure requires a *clearance*. And so, to the family story.

THE SPIRIT CELLARMAN

Everyone, surely, knows the song of the 'bonnie boat', speeding like a bird on the wing, urged on by the sailors to:

> Carry the lad that was born to be king
> Over the sea to Skye.

In 2020, during a lull in the then-still-novel COVID pandemic, I went to Skye, by hired car rather than boat, and in search not of a lad born to be king, but, better yet, one who was born to be a commoner.

Born in 1852 in the now deserted village of Unish, he would move away in his teens, as an economic migrant, first to Glasgow, then to Belfast; and he would work his way up from being a labourer to become a distillery store-keeper – or, as the job is described on his 1878 marriage documents, a Spirit Cellarman. He died at the age of eighty-eight in 1939. Had he lived three or four years longer, Neil Lamont (the Spirit Cellarman) might have witnessed the birth of his great granddaughter, Mary – my mother. Let us flesh out a little context for this outline of a life and a legacy.

Skye has a long, rich history, and indeed, prehistory – it is still possible to see the remains of Neolithic cairns and Iron Age defensive walls on the island. And it is a mixed history, a history of mixing. Over a thousand years ago the Vikings came, just as they did to Ireland, some to raid, some to trade, and some to settle and make lives for themselves there. In fact, the Norse claimed sovereignty over the Hebrides in the twelfth and thirteenth centuries, and one can still hear echoes of their language in some of the place names: Colbost; Husabost; Skeabost – '*bost*' meaning 'townland' or 'farm' in the Norse of the time.

After Norse dominance came to an end in the Middle Ages, the people of the islands and highlands, Gaelic speakers, living from the land, organised themselves into what became known as the clan system – '*clann*' deriving from the Gaelic for family. That was the political and economic system that, turbulent as it was, evolving as it was, would remain more or less in place until the eighteenth century. By the time the bonnie boat of the song had winged its way across the sea – that is, by the time of the last Jacobite uprising in 1745 – the land belonged to the clans through their heads, the chiefs or chieftains. It is worth pointing out that the chiefs themselves belonged to the clan, and though they had the privilege of heading it they had obligations to look after their people, the ordinary families who farmed their own small strips of runrig land as crofters or who laboured as cottars. After all, they were all of the same *clan*, and all belonged together on the land as much as the land belonged to them.

But by the time Adam Smith, across on the mainland, is writing and publishing the texts that would shape modern thinking on the economy, a change is already under way – a change traceable through the migrations of the Spirit Cellarman's family. He himself was born in Unish; his grandfather, John Lamont, had been born in 1769 in the parish of Bracadale, where he would marry Flora Morrison, and where they would start a family. John's son Donald (the Spirit Cellarman's father), was born in Bracadale. However, when he, Donald, marries Mary McKinnon, the family is given as living in Lorgill.

We can never know why, for sure, they moved from Bracadale to Lorgill, some twenty miles out on the west coast. However, historian Roger Hutchinson tells us that Bracadale was cleared of its tenants in the 1820s, some going overseas, some being displaced internally, including some families who, indeed, made their way to Lorgill (Hutchinson 2015). Sometime between that and the birth of Neil Lamont, it appears Lorgill was cleared too. Only one building now remains more or less intact; the rest are reduced to little more than piles of boulders.

This was the era of 'The Clearances', which entailed the 'radical transformation of the economic and social foundations of the region during which a large proportion of the population was displaced, usually to make way for very large sheep farms in which they had no function or place' (Richards 2007, 6).

Note that the economic and social are bound together here. *Lairds*, once belonging to the clan, became, or were bought out by, *Landlords*; *clansmen* – the crofters and cottars – became *tenants* of Landlords, thus transforming both social and economic relationships at once.

Modern techniques, and new breeds of sheep, meant the land could be used more 'efficiently': the yield of the land could be increased; it could be 'improved', and as Ellen Meiksins Wood points out, the concept of 'improvement' was linked explicitly to the notion of increasing profitability (Meiksins Wood 2002).

This was also the era of Empire, offering some the chance to make fortunes, some of which in turn went into buying up land in the Highlands and Islands. Some of this would be for farming, and some for grouse or deer ranges, where the newly wealthy Landlords might entertain their fellow Nabobs, up from London for the shooting season.

But of course, either way, the land would have to be conveniently free of crofters. So, the people had to go, at first to the coasts – to villages like Lorgill, with ready access to the sea for fishing, and to the kind of seaweed, the 'wreck', that was burned to produce 'kelp', the 'calcined ashes of seaweed, a product that had a value in the making of carbonate of soda and iodine' (Dodgshon 2015, 203).

Then in 1815, after the end of the Napoleonic Wars, commodity prices, including that of kelp, dropped rapidly. Those who had been sent to the coast were no longer even able to make a living at that. So 'voluntary' emigration increased, as did forced clearances. Some set out for Canada, some for New Zealand, and others made their way to industrialising cities like Glasgow and Belfast.

Finally, this was also (in some measure thanks to Smith) a time of change in the thinking and practices of the market, a shift towards the expansion of commercialisation, a shift to a conception of *belongings* as *disposable property*, a transition from a relationship of belonging together on the land – a relationship of mutual obligations and customary hereditary rights that Tom Devine gathers under what he calls the 'untranslatable' Gaelic term *dùthchas* – to that of the cold, white meat of contract (Devine 2019). We will come back to the concept of *dùthchas*, also spelt *dúchas*, and appearing in both Scottish and Irish Gaelic, in the closing chapter.

Of course, there was resistance to the Clearances, sometimes quite violent, as in the 'Battle of the Braes', where the crofters, deprived of their grazing rights, and finding their petitions ignored, resisted the officers sent to arrest and evict them with sticks and stones.

Moreover, there were also 'more passive and indirect forms of protest – as successfully undertaken in the rent strikes in Skye during the 1880s' (Macleod 2006, 156). When the followers of the so-called Glendale Martyrs, for instance, re-occupied the commons from which they had been driven, a *gunboat*, no less, complete with over four hundred marines and fifty armed police, was sent, only to be met with what we now would call nonviolent tactics (ranging from impromptu prayer meetings to rent strikes). Before long the military withdrew, and eventually, though not until many years later, the ownership of the land in Glendale was transferred back to the crofters themselves (Macleod 2006).

Yet it would be fair to say the situation in Glendale was the exception rather than the rule. For the most part, the Landlords consolidated their control over their now-disposable property. Scotland remains to this day a country in which the bulk of the land is owned by a very small number of big Landlords (Land Reform Review Group 2014).

BRINGING UP THE BODIES

If in the first chapter we were faced with the violence of the politics of hostility – friend, enemy, traitor – here we can begin to see in the Clearances, both the conceptual reductions and the bodily displacements they made way for, the violence of a politics of *indifference*. Moreover, we can perhaps begin to see how the two overlap, each dynamic reinforcing the other.

Already before the Clearances got under way there were calls to keep the unruly Highlanders in order. 'The inhabitants of the mountains', argued the politician and judge Duncan Forbes in 1746, 'unacquainted with industry and the fruits of it, and united in some degree by the singularity of dress and language, stick close to their antient idle way of life; retain their barbarous customs and maxims; depend generally on their Chiefs, as their sovereign Lords and masters; and being accustomed to the use of Arms, and inured to hard living, are dangerous to the public peace' (Richards 2007, 109). Aha! *They*, the 'barbarous' mountain people, are 'accustomed to the use of arms', and they are therefore a *danger to the public peace*. It would only be right and proper, then, to take those arms off them. To *pacify* them. Note that 'public' and the people of the mountains are set off from each other, as though the former did not include the latter – as though the latter had already been *cleared*. Similar processes had already been deployed, of course, in Ireland and elsewhere; this will not be the last time we come across this gesture.

It is interesting to note that these forces and dynamics, this projection of a 'barbarous' people 'unacquainted with industry' and in need of 'pacification', characterising the Imperial project abroad, here act *at home*, 'within' what we call the United Kingdom while it was still in the process of being 'united' (to speak for a moment as though that process could ever have been completed). In fact, Forbes was writing *between* two sets of Acts of Union – those of 1707, that brought Scotland within the Union, and that of 1800, bringing Ireland in. But, of course, those processes long preceded the Acts that formalised them. Think of the Pale, established already in the late Middle Ages, the area within which was governed by the English, and beyond which – whether this gave rise to the expression or not – lived the 'unruly' Irish, with their own version of Forbes's 'barbarous customs'. Such, at any rate, was the image projected by those *within* the Pale.

These acts of projection can be seen as processes of denomination, to recall the term explored in the first chapter; and such processes appear even in Smith's texts, particularly the Wealth of Nations, however 'secular' the marketplace may be supposed to be, however 'individual' the participants in it. We have already noted that he distinguishes, from the outset and without examination, between domestic and foreign trade, between the *nations* of his title. But he also refers throughout to 'orders' and even 'races' of people, in sometimes thought-provoking ways.

A man (it is almost always a man with Smith) must have wages sufficient to sustain not just himself, but also his family, otherwise 'the race of such workmen could not last beyond the first generation' (Smith 1999, book 1, chap. 7). The word *race* here, rather than being used in the sense it is used today, seems to indicate that for Smith there is a quasi-biological, genetic destiny, almost, in being a 'workman', which seems to run in the family from generation to generation. In another passage, he claims the annual produce and labour of every country is 'naturally' divided into three components (rent, wages, and profits), and attributes those to 'three great, original, and constituent, orders of every civilised society' (Smith 2003, book 1, chap. 11). Here, in connection with these 'great orders', he again mentions the 'race of labourers'. The purported 'naturalness' of these economic roles, and the system that reproduces them, is of course one of the key targets of Marxian critique, but it is interesting that this comes *before* the linking of 'race concepts' to skin colour, ethnicity, and so on. When Smith talks about people of other 'races' in that sense (a sense we will have to examine in due course), for example in his examination of European dealings in the East and West Indies, he speaks of nations, 'the savage nations' being distinguished from 'the civilised nations', and sometimes 'tribes', even 'tribes of naked and miserable savages' (Smith 1999, book 4, chap. 7).

In any case, it is clear that for Smith there are already divisions, distinctions, orders, nations, *denominations* setting one neighbour apart from another, and even, as in Smith's imaginary torture chamber, one brother from another.

That the question of sympathy arises indicates we already know our brother is as human as us. It would take an act of abstraction *not* to feel something like sympathy – something would have to intervene, rendering him as invisible as Smith's mother, if we were really to regard his torture with the same equanimity as the torture of the doll. Yet this act of abstraction is built in, here in Smith's texts, to the conceptual foundations of the modern market economy.

Smith's position on the slave trade – he opposed it, but he had to do so from an economic point of view – arguably follows from this logic. To be faithful with his own position, the only logic unsentimental Smith can allow himself as a reason to condemn slavery, regardless of whether he felt sympathy for the victims (and, let us be clear, there are references in sympathetic Smith that leave no doubt that he did), is that, from his (economic) point of view, the slave is a *potential trader.* I must oppose slavery, on this reckoning, not out of 'sentiment' or fellow-feeling, but only in so far as the institution is less efficient than the free market (Smith 1999, book 4, chap. 9).

But this means we cannot say slavery is wrong in itself, immediately. We cannot say it is *absolutely wrong*; just that it is inefficient. We cannot say it is a *crime against humanity*. We have to run through the calculation, tot up the figures first, opposing slavery if, and only if, we could get the right sum to come out at the bottom of the spreadsheet. It is undoubtedly the case that the right sum can and does come out at the bottom. But to oppose slavery because of this result is to say we do not oppose slavery as such. We are anti-slavers for profit.

On its harshest reading, the logic of the market indicates that the suffering or joys of the other *cannot* be taken into account. The suffering of this or that enslaved African man or woman, on the rack or under the lash, is not germane, and must be disregarded. This suffering can only be understood as a general concept, stripped precisely of the immediacy of this person's unique, irreplaceable experience of pain, my nameable, actual brother's pain, and turned into a concept of pain, a 'general' idea that could be passed around, a replaceable copy, as one copies a photograph, to be factored into the calculus of profit and loss. I can value others, even at a King's ransom – but at no more than a King's ransom.

I must, in the market, relate to others as to a simulacrum, a doll, with eyes that take no account of their existence. That is, I must relate to them according to their function in the economy. And then my transactions must be conducted without being contaminated with sympathy. Even that generalised copy of the pain of others must be set aside, discounted.

All that is allowed to appear in the market is the trader *as such*, the commodity *as such*, and the price-tag. But what of these traders? Who actually populates the market? Are we dealing here with abstract, isolated individuals? Even in Smith's presentation, it is worth noting, the market is *not* one in which 'isolated individuals' look after their own interests: it is one in which *butchers, bakers, and brewers* look after their own interests. At the very least this means the invisible hand, as Smith himself sets it up, will operate in the sort of society where there are butchers, brewers, and bakers – and others. After all, the scene is, so to speak, observed by Smith himself; and, as he tells us, 'we' can expect our supper from these tradesmen, you the reader too. At least five, then. Six, if we include Smith's invisible mother.

What sort of society has butchers, brewers and bakers? Something like Smith's eighteenth Century Glasgow or Edinburgh, perhaps, with taverns, and carts, and horses to pull them, and ostlers, and coopers, and farriers. We don't need to make up the list ourselves – Smith knows that the number of people involved in making any one item that even 'the most common artificer or daylabourer' depends on, a woollen coat, for example, 'as course and rough as it may appear, is the produce of the joint labour of a great multitude of workmen. The shepherd, the sorter of the wool, the wool-comber or carder, the dyer, the scribbler, the spinner, the weaver, the fuller, the dresser, with many others', so many others, indeed, that the number 'exceeds all computation' (Smith 1999, book 1, chap. 1). And that is before we get to the worker's shoes, bed, kitchen-grate at which he makes his 'victuals', the coal he burns for the purpose, which had to be mined and transported, the utensils, knives, forks, pewter plates, the 'different hands employed in preparing his bread and his beer' (there are the baker and brewer again), and not forgetting 'the coarse linen shirt which he wears next to his skin' (Smith 2003, book 1, chap. 1).

The market of Smith's thought *takes place* somewhere veritably *teeming* with others. With *neighbours*. It is a bustling neighbourhood where they learn trades; where these are passed on (perhaps even as Smith indicates, from father to son); where the tradesmen can nod at each other in the same street. Somewhere, in short, where there is a rough equality of social condition and purchasing power, at least amongst the *men* Smith is talking about – those who get by or prosper in the town market.

It is somewhere in which the individuals are not isolated and abstract, but already embedded in a flesh and bone social and economic context, one with a long, peculiar, detailed local history. One in which Smith, the butcher, the baker, and the brewer could sit down over a bowl of beef stew, possibly with a pint of the brewer's porter and some slices of the baker's bread. There might even have been some women around, for all we know, if they could but briefly emerge from the invisibility of the *domestic* sphere – that is, the *domus*, the 'private' sphere, which *is* private by being excluded from the 'public' arena, wherein men are allowed to appear.

Whether 'domination' and 'domestication' are etymologically related or not, there is clearly a sense in which men's political and public power *as such* is produced by the exclusion of (the dominance of, the domestication of) women, or (because these always go together in the *domus*), women-and-children. We will return to this in the next chapter, but for now, what of those bodies?

Even in the original Smith text, with a little care, one can read the signs of flesh-and-bone, bodily human interactions in a particular socio-political and historical context. Market relations are economic exchanges embedded in ongoing bodily relationships in this or that real neighbourhood. This or that real tavern, where you could savour the sights, sounds, smells, and tastes of the meat, the soup, the beer, the unwashed sweat, the blood still on the butcher's apron, the rattle of pewter on deal tables, be, bodily, *in the thick* of the human interaction.

And *all* this must be abstracted, cropped or chopped out, rendered indifferent, to get to the picture of the market favoured by Smith's more doctrinaire followers. Upon *all* this human life in the flesh-and-bone, perhaps *flesh* in Merleau-Ponty's sense (Merleau-Ponty 1968), one must turn an 'indifferent' eye, an eye attuned only to the livery, not the bodies beneath the livery; to the white meat of contract, not to the bonds built neighbour to neighbour in the course of commonplace, everyday interactions, if one is to enhance 'the interests of (our own) society'.

On a strict reading, there should be no way to pick out any *difference* between the unique, irreplaceable human being and the 'balked simulation' of life, simulated by a trader-as-such, a consumer-as-such. I need not concern myself with the person wearing the baker's apron, so long as it is loaded up with fresh bread (just as, a few miles away, I need make no difference between crofter and sheep, except as measured by their relative profitability).

Is there not, though, already something akin to violence taking place here? How can one go from this bodily intercourse in an Edinburgh tavern, without massive reduction, to a collection of isolated, self-seeking individuals; how can one then simply reinsert, without violence, conclusions drawn from the model of that market of isolated individuals onto completely other, but equally noisy, smelly, bodily, flesh-and-bloody human situations, and be certain that one will thus 'maximise utility'? How can one calculate the 'good' at a social level if one has to take the bodies, and their appetites, and their mothers, and the complexities of their relationships, and the utter singularity of the local neighbourhood *out of the account*?

As soon as you have chopped these elements out, no doubt you can go on to show that a smoothly functioning market optimises *something*. But what, exactly? Only those elements which remain after the excision – only the interchangeable tokens of our currency, only the commensurable *chops*.

The domesticity of the word *chop* veils the violence; the grisly onomatopoeia, evoking the shock of the cleaver through meaty tissues and into the reddened wood of the board, is lost in its routine repetition. It is perhaps a useful term to use, then, to describe the draining of the full, embodied relations between one human and another, you and I set towards each other in the whole phenomenal range of our differences, of our encounter with each other, in the fulness of our being-together, in the flesh-and-bone, to merely the bloodless 'white meat of contract'.

A whole range of dimensions to our relations have to be chopped (violently, but routinely) out, in order to achieve this contract-relation. Indeed, the invisibility of what is thus chopped out – like that of Adam Smith's mother – is *itself* rendered invisible; a violence so habitual as to remain unremarked in the marketplace, or in theories about the marketplace.

The logic has come down almost unaltered from Smith's time into our own, long past the era of the butchers and brewers of old Edinburgh, and past the time of the trans-Atlantic slave trade – though whether newer forms of slavery continue to flourish is another matter. To take one example, when investor George Soros was asked about his (highly profitable) role in the Asian currency crash of 1997, he replied, 'As a market participant, I don't need to be concerned with the consequences of my actions' (Miniter 2011). The human impact, the jobs lost, the lives turned upside down, are simply chopped out of the account.

More recently, after the collapse of the Rana Plaza factory building in Bangladesh in 2013, an industrial accident that cost over 1,100 lives, it was possible for Forbes magazine to publish an article stating that '[t]ragedies such as this naturally provoke emotional reactions. But reason and perspective, rather than emotion, are needed when deciding how to respond', before going on to argue that US employers should neither pull out of the country *nor invest in safety measures for the workers* (Powell 2013).

They should not pull out because such factories employ some four million workers, and in 'the grand scheme of things, they [the Bangladeshis] are better off with the factories than they would be without them; the benefits outweigh the risks'.

They should not invest in health and safety measures because, well, 'we need to recognize that safety is not free, and some workers – as well as consumers, ultimately – will pay a price'. Ah, the price. As if over a thousand workers had not just paid the ultimate price for the *lack* of safety measures. But of course, to take them into account, one would have to convert so many dots that had stopped moving to so many dollars, and see what sum came out at the bottom of the spreadsheet.

Moreover, says Powell, 'when activists insist that companies invest more in safety, what they are doing, in effect, is overriding the preferences of low-income workers' (Powell 2013). The evidence he gives for this last assertion is drawn from a survey he conducted in Guatemala, not among the Bangladeshi workers – not only 'overriding' their preferences, note, but cutting them out of the account altogether, through a substitution of the views of other workers in another context. Furthermore, the question he has asked of these Guatemalan workers amounts to presenting them with a Dickensian choice between impoverishment and a risk to their health and safety: are you willing to 'give up any pay for increased safety'?

Any other alternatives – such as wealthy shareholders being required to stump up for better pay *and* some safety equipment – are simply cropped out of the picture; their answer to the loaded question is extracted from the context and re-inserted among other workers on another continent, and then used to chide 'activists' for 'overriding the preferences of low-income workers'.

Does this convoluted logic, issued on the Forbes website after one of the worst industrial accidents in the history of the garment industry, not recall the claims of that other Forbes, the one from the eighteenth century? Here are some more specimens who would have remained 'unacquainted with industry', and therefore scratching an impoverished living in their 'antient idle way of life' had it not been for the modernisation and industrialisation gifted to them by Western investors.

In any case, the Forbesian logic is that Bangladeshis *in general* (in the 'grand scheme of things') are better off with the factories than without them, and while it is sad that some of those workers ended up crushed, if we really cared for the welfare of the workers, we would not interfere with the power of the market, which increases *general* prosperity. Look away from the bodies under the rubble: look at our GDP growth – growth *in general*, growth on *aggregate*. The growth of the wealth of *the nation*. After all, if the national economy is growing, we must *all*, we *nationals*, be better off – those of us in all three of the great 'orders', and even if some of those dots have stopped moving forever, at least 'we' get the £20,000, or the equivalent in currency of some denomination or other.

But who are 'we'?

The 'we' that is given by this approach is one *back-projected from the aggregate*. I count up all the gains and all the losses, and then claim that 'we' are those who are enjoying a period of steady growth. Not necessarily you, not necessarily me; *you and I* may both be losers; but nevertheless *we* are winners. If you can't see that – because you are an 'activist', say – then you just aren't adopting a sufficiently rational, impartial perspective. You are too sentimental; you haven't sufficiently cleared the bodies out sight.

Is this *Smith's* approach? Or is it rather that some of his hard-line followers, some of those who have chosen to take up the mantle of his legacy, adopt and reiterate it, turning it into a *logical routine* that can be deployed in any given context, indeed, *regardless* of context? Rereading those passages in which Smith's *uncountable* neighbours (albeit largely the male ones) palpably bustle about, and especially re-reading Smith on empathy as interpreted by Fleishacker, it is tempting to say his intellectual descendants have done him a disservice. Yet they have not, for all that, invented routines that were not already legible in his texts. Perhaps there are two Smiths, then, and we must choose between them. But how to do this, and in a way that does not merely confirm our biases? Perhaps we should turn to an 'impartial spectator' to settle the matter for us.

The 'impartial spectator', of course, is a phrase drawn straight from Smith himself. It is this figure, says Fleishacker, that forms the 'centrepiece of Smith's moral system'. Only by contrasting our perspectives with that of the impartial spectator can 'I come to determine who both you and I are' (Fleishacker 2019, chap. 4), can I adjudicate between our differing perspectives.

The steps are these: I feel my way into your situation; I *think* (though I am not sure) you are wrong to react as you do, since I would not do so in such a situation; there is a conflict between our perspectives. But perhaps *I* am wrong, so I send my emissary of the imagination to an Impartial Spectator, one not party to the dispute, one at a distance from the conflict, and await the authoritative judgement.

But who is this third figure? Who is, as it were, the Third Man, the one reported, in the film of that name, to have been seen carrying away the body?

One who is, precisely, *disembodied*, not vulnerable to the weaknesses of the flesh, the partial perspectives, the deceptions of the senses? One who can remain free of emotional involvement; one not already tangled up in the situation but capable of standing outside it, one who can bring 'reason and perspective', in Powell's terms, to bear? Who is this *higher authority*, who would be able to pass judgement while remaining *outside* the space of the encounter between us? Where did they come from?

That is a question we will address in the next chapter.

Chapter Three

The Gift

Had you been travelling around the Atlantic in the earliest years of the seventeenth century, you might have come upon a small, empty ship, drifting aimlessly, apparently abandoned by its crew and left to its fate. On its prow, you might have been able to discern its name: *Gift*. This ship had accompanied a fleet of four larger ships that had set out in 1601 on the first English voyage to trade with the Mughal Empire (Farrington 2002). The *Gift* was a victualler, a supply ship; it had been towed along as a sort of floating store. When its stores had been used up, it was simply cut adrift and discarded.

It is, perhaps, a compelling parable of the Euro-American political-economic paradigm, the one that Adam Smith and his successors would formalise, the gift that Europe, then America, has bequeathed to the world.

The model works like this: you take a ship (or a company, or a country) before someone else does; extract its resources; discard it; and move on to the next thing. It is a very powerful and effective model, and it has dominated the global political economy ever since. European Empires, then global corporations, each intent on maximising their own take, competed with one another, exploiting marginal advantages, to assume control of, and extract, ever more of the earth's resources, dumping the 'waste' as they went, before moving on to the next thing.

We are now, of course, reaching the point at which there is no 'next thing' – astronautical dreams of a handful of billionaires aside. But those dynamics are still in flow: they did not turn off overnight when the age of formal Empires came to an end. Here we will go back to look at an early stage in the co-evolution of the modern corporations and of the modern states that would compete to build their Empires. We will have to look at the effects the apparatus developed then, conceptual as much as material, had on being put into play in living, bodily neighbourhoods.

We will dip in and out almost at random into the history of Empire, in part because it is far too large a topic to deal with remotely comprehensively here, but in part because examples of the sort of mechanisms we will examine

– in particular, what we will call the *Viceregal* structure of offstage authority
– appear virtually (in two senses) everywhere one looks in Imperial history.

VOC

Had you been walking around Amsterdam a few years after spotting 'The
Gift', you might have bumped into René Descartes. Possibly literally. In
1631, Descartes, who lived in the city at the time, wrote to a friend: 'You must
excuse my enthusiasm if I invite you to choose Amsterdam for your retreat.
. . . In this large town where I live . . . everyone but myself is engaged in
trade, and thus is so focussed on his own profit that I could live here all my
life without ever being noticed by anyone' (Bennett 2017, 21).

Descartes was, to all intents and purposes, invisible to his neighbours.
Moreover, they were, more or less, invisible to him: 'I take a walk each day
amid the bustle of the crowd, with as much freedom and repose as you could
get in your avenues, and I don't attend to the people I see, any more than I
would to the trees in your woods or the animals grazing there'.

He sees these others then, but they are, as such, no more visible than the
trees or animals in his friend's orchard. Perhaps the same trees that bear plea-
surable fruit: 'Whenever you have the pleasure of seeing the fruit growing in
your orchards and of feasting your eyes on its abundance, bear in mind that it
gives me just as much pleasure to watch the ships arriving, laden with all the
produce of the Indies and all the rarities of Europe' (Glasfurd 2014).

The Amsterdam of the early seventeenth century must have seemed an
astonishing, bustling, noisy metropolis to someone newly arrived – the 'pleasure' it gives Descartes is almost palpable. Goods could already be ferried
from the ships through the moat-canals; and the main canal system that would
bring commodities right into the heart of the city was being built. There were
a thousand warehouses to store merchandise, and even the narrow houses
themselves were fitted with hooks and pulleys – still there to this day – for
hoisting the goods to the upper floors.

And had he been paying sufficient attention, invisible Descartes might conceivably have bumped into one Rembrandt van Rijn, out sketching the local
beggars, or perhaps a traveller, just disembarked from one of those ships and
marvellously (to Rembrandt's eye) costumed in the apparel of the 'Indies'.
Indeed, Descartes might have found one of the painter's Dutch models, or
even Rembrandt himself attired in such clothing – a self-portrait, painted in
the same year Descartes arrived in the city, gives us Rembrandt 'in Oriental
attire' (Petit Palais n.d.).

In fact, 'self-portrait' may not be the right expression: these were *tronies*, genre paintings, intended to display *types* of people, rather than functioning as portraits of this or that unique, nameable individual. And there were suddenly lots of interesting new 'types' around. This, after all was towards the beginning of the period of an Orientalism that produced innumerable representations of people from an 'East' that was more a projection than a place. Orientalism, let us be clear, projected a mix of attitudes, some more, some less admiring; Said sets out many of the more negative versions, Osterhammel some of the notable (if now often overlooked) exceptions, or at least those with more nuanced views (Said 1978; Osterhammel 2018). But as we will see later, even some of the apparently more sympathetic views of the people (or *peoples*, plural) of 'the East' and other exotic lands had their role to play in the dynamics of empire.

Normally, of course, the inhabitants of Amsterdam (or the more prosperous of the men, at any rate) would have been dressed rather more like those in Rembrandt's *Night Watch*, with their cloaks and wide-brimmed hats. Just the sort of attire Descartes might have seen on looking out his first-floor window in the city – you can still see the hook and beam protruding from the window of the floor above today – while wondering how he knew these were men and not automata (Second Meditation, part 2). *Men*, of course, and not women: that possibility remains invisible in Descartes's text.

But amid all these cloaks and hats, this visibility and invisibility, what was it that so caught the attention of Descartes, and that so preoccupied his neighbours that they failed to see each other? The ships 'laden with all the produce of the Indies' were almost certainly those of the Verenigde Oostindische Compagnie, the VOC; their cargo nutmeg, mace, peppers – in a word, *spices*. These spices, along with Brazilian sugar, would have been visible as 'goods' when they arrived crated at the dock, and their novel appearance is captured in many of the still-life paintings that grace the era; but they would also have circulated in invisible form, baked in, literally, to the cakes and other dishes also captured by the Flemish painters (Shama 1991).

We can be pretty certain the goods Descartes saw, the 'produce of the Indies' belonged to the VOC because it had a (Dutch) monopoly on the trade. The VOC's Charter was awarded in 1602, and it quickly became perhaps the world's earliest modern multinational corporation, and the biggest company in the world. What was so special about the structure of the VOC?

By 1623 it had accumulated many of the key features that still shape corporations to this day: transferable shares, limited liability for shareholders, permanent capital, and limited liability for directors – and arguably even 'some form of legal personhood' (Gelderblom et al. 2013). Let us look at the original Charter, which, though it does not yet explicitly contain all the above-mentioned features, inaugurates the 'process of piecemeal engineering, creating both stopgaps and more lasting solutions which by the early 1620s had hardened into the corporate form as we know it' (Gelderblom et al. 2013).

The Charter of the VOC was granted by the States General of the United (*Verenigde* again) Netherlands in 1602. The seven provinces which were to be united in the Dutch Republic had themselves broken away in 1581 from Spanish rule, under the leadership of the original William of Orange, whose great-grandson was to play such a prominent role in British and Irish history. Thus a 'United' company was to be inaugurated by 'Seven United Provinces' – processes of unification on processes of unification – and perhaps a portent of other 'unions and unionisms' to come?

In any case, what was so inaugurated was a *corporate entity* that unified several companies which had already begun trading, individually, in the East Indies. Here is how the Charter puts it:

> The Directors of the abovementioned companies were thence invited to consult with us and propose that these companies be united and would therein partici-pate, as it would not only be of service and profitable for the united provinces, but also for all who had commenced this commendable trade. Through the cre-ation of a *fixed, secure and orderly entity* [emphasis added] they will be bonded together, managed and expanded for the good of all the residents of the united provinces who would like to participate in it (Reynders and Gerritsen 2009).

'Invited' to 'consult': the process was far from as voluntary as it sounds here: unification was enforced by a government engaged in a war with the king Spain and Portugal, and in need of revenue to fund it (Gaastra 1992). Nevertheless, there were clearly to be advantages for both the United Provinces and the traders themselves, as the Charter makes explicit.

After due deliberation, then, the 'representatives from the abovementioned companies . . . jointly succeeded in bringing about a union', a union which is in turn 'approved and confirmed' – by whom? By 'We' ('We have also approved and confirmed this . . . '). The 'we' here is, presumably, the signa-tory, Alb Joachims, secretary to the states general, who signs on behalf of the other gentlemen of the states general. He signs, or they sign it, collectively, and can thus 'approve and confirm' the union 'on the basis of our sovereign power and authority'.

The united corporation so inaugurated has thus been *authorised* by the states general of the United Netherlands, initially for the period of twenty-one years, to monopolise trade in the East Indies. No one apart from those of the Company will be permitted to sail to the east 'on pain of confiscation of ships and cargoes' (here is the 'power' part of the equation).

However, this does not mean the fruits of the eastern trade ('all the goods of the Indies', in Descartes's phrase) are to be kept by the original individual companies, albeit now United; rather, any goods brought back by *any one* of the constitutive parts of the company, any one of the ships, were, by this Charter, to be shared out among the whole.

Moreover, the 'shares' that were offered for sale in the new stock exchange, created for the purpose, were not shares in these individual ships or crates of spices. They were, rather, shares in the *unitary Company itself.*

The 'secure and orderly entity', and the value of the shares thus inaugurated, are detachable from this or that ship, from any given material entity. The corporation is, to that extent, and in good Cartesian fashion, at once *incorporated* and *disembodied.* Its value resides in the *unitary whole* inaugurated in the Charter, on grounds of the authority of the States General – and nowhere existing outside the force-field of that performative act. Inheritors of the mantle of the VOC would go on to take this disembodying process to levels of Byzantine complexity, as anyone who has tried to understand the way in which credit default swaps, collateral debt obligations and the rest contributed to the financial crash that rocked the world in 2008 – the collapse of the housing market being a clear example of the bodily impact of these apparently abstruse, almost mathematical concepts (Tooze 2018, Pistor 2019).

But even as early as the era of the VOC itself, the material goods being hoisted in and out of Dutch ships are becoming 'things indifferent' – the spices in this ship are not to be treated as any different from those in the other ship. *These spices* as such are no longer *my own*; rather, what is my own is my detachable, *disposable 'share'* in the whole. And to ensure there is no difference between one consignment and another, all the spices brought back by any one part of the Company are 'to be sold according to a common weight standard, being that of Amsterdam'. There is a standardisation, at this inaugural moment, that ensures interchangeability (that is, indifference) and exchangeability.

Of course, none of this is possible without *some* material goods – the corporation may be disembodied from each individual ship, but it cannot exist in the absence of all ships, and of a certain amount of cargo. And in order to maximise that amount, not least at a time when it would take many months to get a message from Amsterdam to the East Indies, the Company itself was vested with the authority to make decisions of its own, in situ: 'Representatives of the aforementioned Company shall be authorised to enter into commitments and enter into contracts with princes and rulers in the name of the States General of the United Netherlands or the country's Government in order to build fortifications and strongholds'.

Already, contracts and fortifications (that is, the apparatus of organised violence) are brought together in one sentence, 'in the name of . . . '; but there is more to come: 'They may appoint governors, keep armed forces, install Judicial officers and officers for other essential services so to keep the establishments in good order, as well as jointly ensure enforcement of the law and justice, all combined so as to promote trade'.

All that apparatus, all these powers, all these weapons are there simply to establish '*good order*' (let us underscore this phrase), *in order* to 'promote trade', you understand. And all of these representatives of – at once – the Company and, by proxy, the States General – are to be bound by an oath of *loyalty*: 'In respect to trade and commerce the abovementioned governors, the judiciary and military shall be required to swear an oath of loyalty to the States General, or to the abovementioned government and to the Company.' Commerce, law, force, and political allegiance are thus bound together from the start of the era of the modern corporation, with an *oath of loyalty* providing the ligaments.

It would be possible to trace very similar ligaments holding the English version of the East India Company together. The Charter granted by Queen Elizabeth to the East India Company in December 1600 also inaugurated a unitary company, created as 'one Body Corporate and Politick, in Deed and in Name', the 'one name' being 'Governor and Company of Merchants of London, Trading into the East-Indies', fortunately usually known by the less elaborate name of the East India Company, or EIC (Archaeological Survey of India 2020).

It is this 'one body' that is declared to be 'capable in Law to have, purchase, receive, possess, enjoy and retain, Lands, Rents, Priviledges, Liberties, Jurisdictions, Franchises and Hereditaments of whatsoever Kind, Nature, and Quality'.

This early company charter, then, sets up something like *corporate personhood* – though that term was yet to make its appearance. The dozens of names of the 'loving subjects' listed in the first section are subsumed, brought under the scope, united in the 'Name' of the Company – and 'in Name', or 'by the Name', or 'by the same Name' – is repeated again and again in the second section of the Charter, as if to drive home the act of denomination (which is to say, the performative *unification*) that is inaugurated therein. Moreover, as with the VOC less than two years later, there is an *authority* conferred in the performance.

The new company is authorised to 'freely traffick . . . as they shall esteem and take to be fittest, into and from the said East-Indies, in the Countries and Parts of Asia and Africa'. They are given the English monopoly on such trade, and they are to be able to traffic 'without any Molestation, Impeachment, or Disturbance, any Statute, Usage, Diversity of Religion or Faith or any other Cause or Matter whatsoever, to the contrary notwithstanding' – provided the trade is not undertaken anywhere already in the 'lawful and actual Possession of any such Christian Prince or State, as at this present is, or at any Time hereafter shall be in League or Amity with us'.

Note that *diversity* is cited specifically here simply in order to be reduced to the status of merely one of the 'Causes' not to be permitted to 'withstand' ('notwithstanding') the authority and power of the Company to traffic. Other laws, other faiths and religions, are not to be permitted to withstand the business of the Company; and this goes for existing trade routes as well as any 'which shall hereafter be found out'. The exception, setting the boundary to this power and authority, must be both Christian and *friend* (in Amity), and already lawfully in possession of the territory.

Lines of friendship and, if not enmity, at least potential enmity, are being drawn here – and, notably, in religious (denominational) terms. Moreover, the distinction between *actual* possession and *lawful* possession is already at work. But this raises the question: who gets to decide the law?

If the company is *authorised* to traffic without disturbance, who gets to decide what constitutes a disturbance? Does the company have to send word home about any possible disturbance, and await the decision of the sovereign? Clearly, as these early corporations were operating at such a distance from home, and at a time when messages could take months, if not years, to arrive, there would be considerable scope, and some motivation, for those on the spot to exercise their own judgements, confident, within certain limits, that they enjoyed the *prior backing of the crown*. Confident, again within limits, that the crown had *prospectively* and would *retrospectively* authorise their decisions, should it become necessary. Both these early corporations, then, set out overseas *as if* they were emissaries who could claim to be able to lay down the law *in the name of* the higher authority back home.

The English East India Company, thus inaugurated, set out on its first voyage in February 1601, complete with its supply ship, over a year before the founding of the VOC; and it was the English – or later *British* – East India Company that would eventually come to dominate. However, it was the VOC that would rise first, and with astonishing rapidity, to global pre-eminence. This newly formed (if disembodied, in the sense set out above) corporation, of which Dutch citizens could buy an (abstract) share, would now set about the process of bringing wealth home – all the goods of the Indies – chiefly in the first instance through trade in spices. It would do so both with the latest weapons (*materiel*) and with the confidence that the traders could call upon the (distant, but higher) *authority* of the Dutch State in bids to justify territorial claims – and therefore violence.

For violence there was. For example, within a month of arriving on Banda Island in 1621, the governor general of the VOC launched an attack that would result in the death of more than 90 percent of the population, with the survivors being chased into the hills, clearing the way for complete dominance of the island – and thus the spice trade (Van Lent and Chowdhury 2016). And all given an imprimatur in advance by an authority that would remain at a distance, back in the United Provinces.

That we are required, as it were, to step over those *corpses* to examine emergence of the modern *corporation* is an indication of the extent to which violence structured the modern market-space from the start, with real bodily effects that remain legible to this day. On a related note, incidentally, there were also examples of ecological violence right at the start of the era of the modern corporation. Having secured a monopoly of the trade in nutmeg and mace through violent conquest of the Banda Archipelago, the VOC managed to achieve a monopoly in the trade in cloves by 'extirpating the clove trees on various islands in the Moluccas', and thus concentrating the crop in Ambon, which they already controlled (Gaastra 1992).

Not all the encounters of the VOC, nor of the EIC, of course, were as overtly and immediately violent as this. The EIC, in particular, when they began trading in India, simply could not have got away with it: they encountered, in the Mughal Empire, a power far greater, richer and more sophisticated than that of the queen whose Charter had set them up.

Yet by the mid-eighteenth century, when the British EIC will have both outstripped the VOC, and come to dominate the subcontinent, there will have been plenty of violence to go around. There had been no fewer than three Anglo-Dutch wars along the way, and one more to come, to speak of European conflicts alone; and in India itself the EIC took an increasingly militarised approach to expansion. Indeed, it was a battle, the Battle of Plassey in 1757, that proved decisive in sealing British dominance. This dominance (or *dominion*), won by the sword, would be formally transferred to the British Crown just over a century later still, giving the British Empire its crown jewel. And who wore that crown? Not the VOC, but VRI.

FROM DRINA TO VRI

On 22 June 1897, Victoria, *Regina et Imperatrix*, sent a message by telegraph to every part of the Empire – 'the largest Empire in the history'. The message read: 'From my heart I thank my people. May God bless them' (Morris 1968, 21).

'My people': plural or singular? It is impossible to say, from this simple-seeming message alone; both senses, as it were, are at play in this telegraphic, Jubilee missive.

The second volume of Jan (then publishing under the name James) Morris's *Pax Britannica* trilogy conveys something of the pomp and splendour, the excitement of Victoria's Jubilee celebrations, and it is clear that for many of 'her people' this was indeed a moment of huge national pride. By the year of the Jubilee, Morris says, all the 'vigour and self-esteem' of a British people who appeared to have become 'arbiters of the world's affairs' had been 'fused into an explosive emotional force', an 'expansionist, sensational concept of Empire' known as the 'New Imperialism' (Morris 1968, 22). This was the era of Jingoism (the term was coined as an adaptation of the use of the phrase 'By Jingo!' in a particularly ebullient patriotic song of 1878), the era of Britain as a 'new Rome' – the era of the Pax Britannica. Quite how much *pax* there was in the Britannic Empire, of course, is another question.

This was a 'New Imperialism' in contrast to the 'old' imperialism of the conquest of the Americas. But it was also 'new' in terms of the justifications offered for maintaining and even expanding the empire, not least in relation to the questions of violence and identity.

In Karuna Mantena's persuasive account, the 1857 'Sepoy Mutiny' is a key turning point: 'it would mark the *turning away* [emphasis in the original] from an earlier, liberal, reformist ethos that had furnished nineteenth century empire its most salient moral justification' (Mantena 2010, 1). That 'justification' (or rather, as we must insist, *bid* for justification), was the 'civilising mission', the notion that, although the conquest of India and other territories had involved violence, it was important for the European powers to maintain their empires as a means to 'modernise', or 'enlighten' the 'primitive' peoples, who were, after all, essentially the same as European peoples but at an 'earlier' stage of development. The position up to this point was essentially Burkean: if there had admittedly been violence involved at the early stages of European colonisation, well, it would only make matters worse to pull out; better to see through the civilising mission, for the benefit of all concerned.

After 1857 (and a whole series of uprisings in other parts of the Empire in and around that time: the Maori or New Zealand wars, beginning in the 1840s; the Morant Bay rebellion and the Fenian Rising in Ireland, both in the 1860s), the basis of bids to justify empire shifted. From a 'universalising' project, one of bringing all 'native' subjects up to a civilised level (under the paternal guiding hand of the Europeans, of course), bids to justify British rule moved towards a model that appeared, at first glance, to be more attentive to cultural differences.

Take the Proclamation of 1858, wherein EIC rule was formally dissolved in favour of the direct rule of the (British) Crown:

> We declare it to be our royal will and pleasure that none be in any wise favoured, none molested or disquieted, by reason of their religious faith or observances, but that all shall alike enjoy the equal and impartial protection of the law; and we do strictly charge and enjoin all those who may be in authority under us that

they abstain from all interference in the religious belief or worship of any of our
subjects on pain of our highest displeasure (Mantena 2010, 49).

Where once the EIC was, by royal decree, to remain 'undisturbed', now
the rights and customs of the various peoples (plural) under the scope of
Victoria's proclamation are to be *protected*, particularly in relation to their
religious traditions – their *denominations* in the religious sense. Had the
British, after all, not provided their Hindu and Muslim sepoys with rifle
cartridges greased with both cow fat (sacrilege to the Hindus) and pig fat
(unclean to the Muslims), perhaps they would not have been driven to revolt
in the first place – or so the theory went.

But this apparently equitable offer of protection embodies not just a fundamental inequality, but also one that is read as being ontologically given.
The law, whose 'equal and impartial' protection is being offered here is being
laid down, from on high, *by the Imperial Crown*; any 'authority' that is to be
exercised here is vertically structured, pointing upwards, an 'authority under
us' ('we' being Victoria as Regina et Imperatrix). Secondly, there is the logic
of how they reached this position. If the 'liberal' justification for empire
had been that the Indians and other Peoples would eventually be brought to
maturity by the British, eventually being ready to adopt the universal values
already embodied in British rule, then any 'People' resisting Imperial rule
must have, in a phrase that recalls both the passage from Stanihurst examined
in the first, and the passage from Forbes in the second chapter, a 'deep-seated
cultural intransigence to universal norms of civilisation'. So deep seated,
perhaps, as to be part of their essence, their very being.

Would this not call for the *maintenance of order on behalf of* people *essentially* incapable of doing it for themselves – that is, incapable for *reasons of
ontology: this is just the way they are*? And does this not set the scene for (or,
to borrow Mantena's fruitful term, in turn borrowed from Derrida) provide an
alibi for the use of force to ensure those same 'Peoples' (to go along with the
schema once more) stayed each in their proper places in the good and proper
order, places to which they were *naturally* fitted?

The political dynamic of modern empire, for Mantena, is characterised
by this 'oscillation between universalist justifications and culturalist ali-
bis, between viewing colonized societies as either amenable or resistant to
transformation'. In other words, the *kind of being* of 'native society' itself
here appears 'both as pretext and solution, as an *alibi* for the fait accompli
of empire' (Mantena 2010, 9). Either they are inherently biddable, educable,
in which case 'we' must educate them, or they are inherently unbiddable, in
which case we must supply the form of governance they are incapable of
providing for themselves; in either case 'we' (Europeans) are left with little

choice but to maintain the 'good order' mentioned as far back as the Charter of the VOC – by force if necessary.

All we need add is that this alibi is itself, of course, 'universalist': it recognises differences but only in order to reduce them to matters of indifference as seen from above. We Europeans can see where the proper boundaries are to be drawn between this 'people' and that 'people', between those capable and incapable of self-government. From our vantage point, as Smithian 'impartial observers', we can survey the different 'cultures' as if arrayed on a laboratory bench, label them correctly, and ensure these specimens, these *denominations*, have been put in the 'right' order. Again, by force if necessary, however regrettable that may be. And of course, those 'boundaries drawn' could take the very visible form of lines on a map.

HARD LINES

Just a dozen years or so before VRI's Jubilee, on 15 November 1884, the Palais des Reichskanzlers in Berlin – now replaced by a not-particularly grand looking block of flats near the Brandenburg gate, the Reichstag, and the memorial to the victims of the Holocaust – saw a gathering of the major European powers to formalise the distribution of African territory between themselves. 'Not a single African' notes Adam Hochschild drily, 'was at the table in Berlin'. Indeed, he goes on to say that, other than Henry Morton Stanley, none of the delegates 'had seen more of Africa than the drawings of its scenery on the menus for Bismarck's banquets' (Hochschild 2006, 84–85).

Nevertheless, they felt able to sit around a large map of Africa and decide how the territory was to be divided, which European power would take control of which areas. *We* (say, the English) will let you have this bit, provided *you* (say, the French) stay out of *this* bit. The lines they drew on those maps, some running perfectly straight across otherwise undifferentiated (on the map, however varied on the ground) territory, would be endlessly reproduced, would for generations be shown in school classrooms across Europe alongside other educational images: here is the structure of a flower, with its bulb, its stamens and sepals; here the solar system, with the various planets each orbiting at a certain distance from the sun; and here is Africa, with its straight lines and its European sounding names, all equally *natural*, all just examples of the *order of things* (Foucault 1973).

The political shape and fate of Africa, and that of the people living there, was decided at a distance. But it did not matter; after all, they had texts: telegrams, despatches, treaties, drawings, maps – and 'vivid descriptions'. Whose vivid descriptions? Those of the only man in the room who had set foot in Africa, Henry Morton Stanley. The titles alone of three of his books give us an idea of the sort of vivid descriptions he gave them: *Through the Dark Continent*; *In Darkest Africa*; and *My Dark Companions and Their Strange Stories*.

Africa, for Henry Morton Stanley, and therefore for the European leaders listening to him, represented the heart of darkness, just waiting for European enlightenment. *Enlightenment*: the very word speaks of light, shone in like a torch to dispel the dark. But is it the *light* that is projected?

For Kant, enlightenment, or *Aufklärung*, is the moment of maturity, the moment we leave childish ways behind us and step out independently on our own two feet into the clearing of reason (Kant 1996). In his essay on enlightenment, Kant claims it is only through laziness or lack of courage that most people (including 'the entire fair sex') hold back from stepping into maturity.

And yet the same Kant is capable of saying, of a certain 'Negro carpenter' who had reportedly expressed an opinion (on gender relations, interestingly enough, but it mattered little as far as Kant was concerned): 'it might be that there was something in this which perhaps deserved to be considered; but in short, this fellow was quite black from head to foot, a clear proof that what he said was stupid' (Eze 1997, 57)

He knows *already*, before taking the time to consider what 'might be', 'perhaps', worth considering, and *would have known before* the African person had said a word, that it will be 'stupid' because he has read the signs, takes his skin as sign-pointing-elsewhere; he knows what *kind of being* this specimen is, here before him (or rather, at a remove: he is, after all, discussing a *report* of what the man said). The Kant of this passage knows the carpenter does not simply remain unreasonable because of cowardice, but he is *essentially* incapable of reason – and all before he enters conversation with this, his neighbour. All before anyone sets foot on African soil.

If this is '*Aufklärung*' (and to be clear, this is only one interpretation of *Aufklärung*), it is a *Clearance* of others, an expulsion from the space reserved for those capable of reason, rather than a *clearing* into which we could step *together*. If it is Enlightenment as projection, it is *first* the *projection of darkness*, and then, subsequently, only such 'light' as will not put our project in question. Let's see how dark this darkness can get.

In her examination of the German effort to suppress uprisings in Southwest Africa (later Namibia) at the turn of the twentieth century, Isabel Hull shows that, by operating according to the logic of military 'necessity', the mission passed over into an effective policy of 'annihilation' (Hull 2005).

Members of the Herero population rose in revolt, early 1904, killing white inhabitants of isolated farms. German reports claimed that women and children were being killed by the Herero, but this was inaccurate, or at least a gross exaggeration: only five out of 158 Europeans who died were women, and no children at all were killed. Indeed, the Herero leader had ordered his troops to kill only adult males, and women and children were in fact captured and released to the Germans. This is not to say the Herero were non-violent: wounded German soldiers were killed, and, in accordance with Herero practice, bodies mutilated. Nevertheless, retired Captain Otto Danhauer was able to report Governor Leutwein's opinion as follows: 'Forbearance and leniency toward such an enemy is simply a crime committed against one's own soldiers. That is also the opinion of the new commander, Lt. Gen. v. Trotha, who recently declared while discussing this subject, "Against 'nonhumans' [*Unmenschen*] one cannot conduct a war 'humanely'." And he allowed me to publish his words'. (Hull 2005, 33).

The enemy is so 'nonhuman' that normal respect for their humanity does not apply, need not limit our violence. Indeed, limiting our violence against them would constitute an act of violence against ourselves: a 'crime committed against one's own soldiers'. Such projections of these others as *inherently* violent are thus used in bids justify *our* violence against *them*. That is, 'we' do not just 'Other' them, but '*hostilise*' them; it is tempting to say we '*savage*' them, using the word in a transitive sense, or '*monster*' them, in something like JJ Cohen's sense, in which the monster is a 'construct and a projection', but one that reveals something of the culture that so constructs them (Cohen 1996).

This is a German example from the early twentieth century, but it is not hard to find similar examples from a variety of European sources, and from as far back as the 1550s, when, during the Valladolid debate over the justification for Spanish conquest in the Americas, there was a 'philosophical stalemate over what ultimately constituted the Amerindians' humanity (or lack thereof)' (Caraccioli 2021: 60).

To return to the British example, Sathnam Sanghera quotes Dr Laurence Waddell, official archaeologist on the British invasion of Tibet in 1903, as 'characterising Tibetan Buddhism as a 'parasitic disease . . . a cloak to the worst forms of oppressive devil-worship', and describing the people as 'sunk in the lowest depths of savagery' and 'more like hideous gnomes than human beings' (Sanghera 2021, chap. 4). That must have made it all the easier, then, for the soldiers of the expedition to gun down Tibetans in their hundreds, before making off with huge quantities of loot (itself, ironically enough, a word 'borrowed' from Hindi), much of which would end up gracing the cabinets of what Dan Hicks mordantly calls the 'Brutish Museums' (Hicks 2020).

Waddell described the Tibetan victims of one such one-sided 'battle' as enemies 'not just of ourselves, but in some sense, by reason of their savagery and superstition, of the human race'. With apologies to Joseph Heller: that's some sense, that 'some sense'.

It was not the only such case. The British attack on Benin in 1897 – the year
of VRI's Jubilee – would also result in considerable loot (the word was used
by the soldiers themselves), as well as the overthrow of the existing regime,
characterised, naturally(!) as uncivilised, savages, and so on (Phillips 2021).

A century and a quarter later, many museums are now beginning to return
the Benin bronzes, now widely recognised as great artworks (Oltermann
2022). But as recently as 1965, it was still possible for a reputable historian to write: 'Perhaps in the future there will be some African history to
teach. But at present there is none: there is only the history of Europeans
in Africa. The rest is darkness . . . And darkness is not a subject of history'
(Trevor-Roper 1965, 9).

If African people were held to have only an obscure history, the same could
not be said for India, where the written historical record stretched back centuries. Yet there is a certain projection of darkness here too. Sir Henry Maine,
member of the Viceroy's cabinet during the Raj, and an influential thinker in
relation to the Imperial project, held that 'natives may have their own history,
but they do not have access to their history. Such access requires science,
key to which is the ability to theorise' (Mamdani 2012, 25), something that,
obviously, was the province of representatives of the colonial power, such
as Maine himself. As Mamdani points out, it thus appears that Maine claims
to hold the 'epistemological agency – the key – to unlocking the secret of
native history'.

For Gurminder Bhambra, the issue of epistemological agency arises
too: the 'British conquest of India . . . not only opened up a geographical
terrain for exploration and occupation, but also enabled the transformation
of an epistemological space' – a space in which cognitive patterns 'became
embedded in social actions' (Bhambra 2007, 16).

This embedding of cognitive patterns, or in the terms we are using here,
these *routines of denomination*, with bodily impact, are legible everywhere
throughout the Imperial project and beyond. Think of Kenya, where the
British colonial authority labelled some people not only as 'African natives',
but on that basis, permitted them to live in Nairobi only as registered labourers (a combination of 'race' as related to ethnicity and 'race' in Smith's older
sense, the 'race of labourers'), forcing them to carry ID known as 'kipande'
(Kareithi 2013). Those without such a card, and thus held to be in Nairobi
unlawfully, had to improvise accommodation in 'shanty towns' which, says
Melissa Wanjiru-Mwita, were, 'from time to time, destroyed and the occu-
pants forced back to their rural homes. The 1922 Vagrancy Act made this
possible with provisions to segregate, evict, arrest, expel and limit the movement of the "African workers"' (Wanjiru-Mwita 2021). A comprehensive, at
times gruellingly detailed, treatment of the British case makes it hard to avoid
the conclusion that, as she states in her introduction, 'state-directed violence

in the British Empire [has] shaped large parts of the contemporary world' (Elkins 2022).

Or think of the Belgian identity cards in Rwanda, formalising a distinction between Hutu and Tutsi that would have bloody, bodily consequences in 1994. Think, of course, of the classifications that were indispensable to the system of Apartheid, or indeed of the Jim Crow system in the United States. In Ireland, too, the Penal Laws provided routines for distinguishing and ranking denominations, which were at the same time ways to regulate access to land, wealth, and power. And eventually the partition that would establish Northern Ireland – like later partitions such as between India and Pakistan – would formalise and intensify denominational distinctions, sometimes to violent effect. In the Indian case, as Yasmin Khan puts it, in the 'frenzied rush to calculate population ratios the reality of ancient and intricately woven homelands – and sensitivity to violent repercussions – was lost' (Khan 2022, 108). We will return to the idea of a certain 'intricately woven' homeland later; but one effect of such a partition is the virtually instantaneous production and distribution of 'minority status' it involves. When Khan writes, in the context of the Punjab, of the fear of becoming 'aliens, minorities or subjects in a state ruled by another religious group' (Khan 2022, 97), she could equally be writing of neighbours in Ireland, north or south, contemplating their future depending on their denomination and the side of the border on which they would fall in 1921, and not without reason: the inauguration of a border, geographical or conceptual, national or denominational, materially affects the status of those on either side of it.

This production of 'cognitive patterns', the inauguration and reiteration of routines of denomination, is more than an exercise in epistemology, then: there is a certain active *ontology*, an *ontologising* at work – at work in the sense of directing flows of power, and the stakes are correspondingly high. Maine, and the other colonial officers who were required to read his works, could be seen as actively performing – in the sense of a performative utterance – a separation of people into 'Peoples', on the purported basis that they are *already* distinct *kinds of entity*. The colonisers are the sort of being that is capable of 'science', of sorting the entities into the correct categories; the colonised may have colourful histories and rich cultures, but they are not the sort of being that is capable of rising out of that history or culture to see themselves objectively, as an 'Impartial Observer' might.

The colonisers have the power to see clearly the boundaries around the colonised. This, at any rate, is how Maine appears to read the situation. The boundaries between groups, on this reading, ought to be or are simply *there*, in the world, waiting to be realised or read by the sort of being capable of reading – that is, Scientific Western Man.

The good intentions, the impulse to protect may very well be there – we do not need to doubt the benevolence of at least some of the Empire builders to see that there is a power differential at work here. Scientific Western Man takes himself (and the masculine noun and pronoun here are deliberate) to be capable of seeing the 'reality of the situation', allowing him to 'segregate, evict, arrest, expel and limit' others. Allowing him to define in order to rule; denominate in order to dominate. The relation between epistemological and ontological processes on the on hand, and structural violence on the other, is legible almost everywhere one looks in the history of Empire.

In the eyes of generations of European administrators, travellers and scholars, says Yasmin Khan, 'Hindus, Muslims and Sikhs were inescapably separate and mutually incompatible' (Khan 2017, 20), which led to 'all sorts of misguided imperial interventions on behalf of "communities" were put in place', the most significant of which was 'the decision to give separate electorates to different religious communities [in India] from 1909 so that they were represented by their "own" politicians'. All this backfired catastrophically, says Khan, 'as religious boundaries, both more porous and less sharply defined in an earlier age, now hardened'. It was this 'hardening' that, arguably, set the scene for the enormous violence around the later 'Great Partition' that gives Khan her title (Khan 2017).

A final example from Morris, to illustrate the point: think of the trains – those famous trains that some take to be a measure or symbol of how beneficial Empire was to those under its aegis. 'The British gentry,' says Morris, 'travelled first class . . . the Indian gentry travelled second class; British other ranks, commercial men and mechanics went intermediate; and pushed, levered, squeezed, squashed into the slatted wooden seats of the fourth-class compartments, travelled the Indian millions' (Morris 1968, 371).

They may be on the same train, but the British gentry and the 'Indian millions', making up some 97 percent of total passenger traffic (Mukhopadhyay 2018), do not travel in the same *class*.

A note of caution: we should be careful here not to do any 'pushing, levering and squashing' of our own, presenting the Indian passengers as an undifferentiated mass, 'mere recipients of decisions forced upon them'. In the first place, Indian passengers themselves were not above discrimination. Indeed, the 'intermediate class' Morris refers to was introduced by the companies because the 'better classes' of Indians were reluctant to share a carriage with the 'lower-classes'. Moreover, there is plenty of evidence that Indians 'adapted, adopted as well as appropriated the proverbial "tool of empire" for ideological as well as mundane, practical reasons' (Mukhopadhyay 2018). Finally, in any case, such 'levering' is just that sort of reductive gesture, forcing people, for all their differences, into the confines of a single classification (or denomination – the performative presenting itself as a constative utterance; this is just how they *are*), that is arguably the Imperial gesture *par excellence*. Such a gesture is not without its violence.

Indeed, adding Wanjira-Mwitu's list of verbs to Morris's – segregate, evict, arrest, expel, limit, push, lever, squeeze, squash – it appears there must be considerable, continuous *effort* undertaken to ensure everyone remains in their *proper place*, according to the *proper order*. Yet that effort is occluded by the same logic.

The 'darkness' that is projected as the alibi for imposing a certain order, is one given out as simply already there; ours is a mere *passive recognition* of a prior reality (rather than an *active* intervention, a political project). It is not *our* doing that these Peoples are essentially incapable of self-government; nature made them that way. And if they resist the government we kindly offer them, it is all the more proof of their essentially disordered nature.

We project a model of what (denomination) you are, and *respect* that (we will come back to this word), within the proper bounds; if you overstep those bounds, it is not our model that is wrong, but you. So, we have the authority to – indeed, no option but to – put you back in your place.

And we have the authority of the Sovereign behind us. Thus, when the Governor General formally becomes Viceroy in 1858, a representative of the Crown, standing in for VRI, could lay down the law, like the corporation before them, while all the time pointing over their shoulder, as it were, towards VRI herself. Always assuming she existed, of course.

THE QUEEN'S TWO BODIES

'The mystique of royalty,' says Morris, 'was easily stretched into a mystique of imperialism. (A shrewd Basuto once asked Lord Bryce if Queen Victoria actually existed, or if she was purely a figment of British imagination)' (Morris 1968, 508).

Shrewd indeed, and perhaps more so than Morris realised. There is a sense in which the question taps into the heart of the whole Imperial project. What if, instead of sending her Viceroy, Victoria herself had gone out to India to rule directly? What does 'direct rule' mean in this case? Would anything, really, have changed? By 'Victoria' do we mean the towering figure of *Victoria Regina et Imperatrix* (VRI) whose majestic use of the plural pronoun is the stuff of cliché? Or do we mean the none-too-tall septuagenarian formerly known as Drina (from Alexandrina) in her youth?

Would Drina, the flesh-and-bone woman, not also have had to gesture with her thumb over her shoulder towards VRI, decked out in all her regalia, bearing the crown and sceptre – a crown that is *itself* a symbol, gesturing away from itself towards that for which it stands?

Would VRI have been *any less Viceregal* than, say, Lord Canning, who stood in for her when the British State took over the functions of the EIC in 1858?

At the risk of summoning the spirit (or *Geist*) of Hegel, the old problem of the King's two bodies arises here, and it indicates the *essentially Vice-Regal structure of sovereignty*. Everything revolves around the *projection of a higher authority in whose name* matters can be properly ordered, an authority which will itself never actually appear here, now, where the orders are being issued. Everyone is expected to behave *as if* there really were a Queen. Every*body*. Because although the sovereign remains off stage, abstracted from any and every bodily context, the effects of that authority are felt here and now, in the flesh – *incorporated* in the most literal sense possible.

Bourdieu, in The Logic of Practice, says: 'the *habitus* is what enables the institution to attain full realization: it is through the capacity for incorporation, which exploits the body's readiness to take seriously the performative magic of the social, that the king, the banker or the priest are hereditary monarchy, financial capitalism, or the church made flesh' (Bourdieu 1990, 57).

The 'performative magic of the social' is performative perhaps in the Austinian sense, though is there not also another sense of the performative about the rituals and ceremony of, to take Bourdieu's characters, the king, the banker, or the priest? Or Smith's: the butcher, the baker, the brewer? Or the Empress and her Viceroy? It is perhaps also worth recalling Žižek, in the Sublime Object of Ideology, discussing Pascal's procedure: undertake the ritual first, then belief will follow. What does the sequence matter, as long as one acts *as if . . .* (Žižek 1989)?

Etiamsi daremus – even if we were to concede, said Grotius, that there were no God (a concession he of course refused to make) we would still be obliged to act *as if* there were, as if there were a higher authority, a supreme being. Out of such procedures *autonomy* is invented (Schneewind 1998, 73).

Empire is *embodied* through the 'taking seriously' of this performative magic, whether one is a believer or one is forced to – or one does it out of habit, out of *routine*. That is, the inauguration and reiteration, the performance and observation (in the active sense in which one observes a religion, endlessly repeating the rituals, the credo, to the point where it becomes habitual, a matter of bodily readiness) is what combines and distributes people (denomi)nationally: you *are* British, and thus embody and exemplify the British People, under their Sovereign; *you*, on the other hand, *are* one of a number of *subject* peoples, and the best thing for you to do is take up your proper place in the proper order of things. Fail to do as you are bid, and you will be subject to the authorised force of the Empire. Do as you are bid, and you (the subaltern, the sepoy, the subject) can *also* be one of VRI's 'people', by special leave, and receive a telegram expressing her 'gratitude'. How flattering, how gratifying such gratitude must have felt to those on the receiving end, or those who were prepared (had set themselves properly) to feel and express gratitude in return for being taken under Her Majesty's notice.

The performative is the *bid* in the sense of an attempt, a proposal: I *bid you* take up your proper place; this is the call which awaits its response. But it is also the issuing of an order: you must *do as you are bid* because, the claim is, *this is what you are*. You were born that way, and this is simply the order of things. And if you do not take up your proper place, it must be because you are *out of order*, thus providing me with all the justification I need to *restore* order, using violence, if necessary, *in the name of VRI*.

Thus, faithfulness to VRI *orders* the neighbourhood into a Realm, all properly ordered, and each playing their proper part – all one People, one big family, as it were, under the grateful maternal wing of Victoria, Britannia, the Sovereign. And anyone who steps out of order will soon be put back in their place.

A text from the late nineteenth century gives a sense of how this played out in the British case. Sir WW Hunter, in his survey of the Indian Empire, says: 'the English government has respected the possessions of native chiefs and more than one third of the country still remains in the hands of its hereditary rulers' (Hunter 1893, 76).

It is notable that the 'respect' of the English government appears to have been afforded only to around a third of the country; what does this say of the other two-thirds? Indeed, as he himself admits, the 'third' relates to geographical area; in terms of population this means more than three quarters of the inhabitants fell directly under British rule. Moreover, exactly what does he mean when he says the other territories and people remain 'in the hands' of their hereditary rulers? Apparently 'almost', but therefore not quite, *independent sovereignty*: 'The native princes govern their states with the help of the British political officers from the viceroy stations at their capitals. Some of the chiefs reign almost as independent sovereigns'.

The word *help* here is doing almost as much work as the 'almost' that qualifies the princes' independence. Especially in those cases where 'more assistance' is required:

[O]thers require more assistance or a stricter control. They form a magnificent body of feudatory rulers, possessed of revenues and armies of their own. Many of them also maintained contingents of disciplined battalions at the disposal of the British Government of India, under the title of Imperial Service Troops. The more important of these princes exercise the power of life and death over their subjects; but the authority of each is limited by usage, or by treaties or

engagements, acknowledging their subordination to the British Government
(Hunter 1893, 76).

This, then, is at least one key element of the Imperial system that was
methodically distributed across the continent. The British Raj 'respects' the
possessions of 'native chiefs' – though presumably only the 'more important'
of them at that – by 'almost' permitting them a kind of sovereign independence, but one in which the *subordination of their authority is acknowledged.*
    'Authority': who is the author here? In what sense can one have 'author-
ity' if it is in the same stroke acknowledged as 'subordinate'? Does this not
make the Raj the source of, and therefore author of, one's authority? There
are *two* orders that begin to emerge here, or perhaps better a bifurcating, *dual
order*: at a stroke we are given the agents of the Raj, those who take their place
in the hierarchy of authority that leads all the way up, through the Viceroy,
to VRI herself; and we are given those whose authority is *subordinate* to the
Raj, those who can act with the authority of a feudatory ruler, a Prince, but
no more than a Prince. Representatives of the Raj, then, *appear* to belong
to a 'higher order', one with a direct line to the highest source of authority,
whereas the Indian Prince has authority only indirectly, must go through the
Viceroy if they are to have any authority at all. But if that is the case, then
so does everyone who is supposed to be in the upper tier – *not excluding
the Viceroy himself*: he, too, has to appeal to a higher, offstage authority, an
authority that remains elsewhere, outside the space of the encounter with his
neighbours in India. This will put the whole Imperial project into question,
something we will come back to in a later chapter.
    Note the term *acknowledged*, too: it is as though this were a matter of
knowledge, a question of simply recognising the facts of the case. Or perhaps
'acknowledged' nods to the performative act of (re)affirming the inauguration of systemic subordination, an act that responds affirmatively to the claim
staked by the British political officers to the *right to dispose*, to re-order: I,
having been overpowered, here-and-now, recognise that you *already* have the
right to order things, lay down the law here in this neighbourhood.
    But as we have seen, the descriptive and the performative do not form an
exclusive, either-or binary: both senses (forces) can be at play at once, and
indeed the felicity of the performative, in such cases, depends largely on the
acceptance of the statement as descriptive. To ac-knowledge, in this sense,
is to back-project the authority-as-entity, in a move akin to the scholastic
ontological argument for the existence of God: if I am to have (subordinate)
authority, it *must* come from higher up, from an entity whose authority
must already exist. And it is an authority that reserves the right to distribute *violence*.

Of course, as we have already hinted, there was abundant and widespread violence involved in the Imperial project, but let us look at one apparently very insignificant incident, as recalled by Morris, and that in a footnote:

> Striking the servants, in an off-hand way, died hard in the Empire. In 1946, during my first week in Egypt, I boarded the Cairo train at Port Said with an English colonel of particular gentleness of manner and sweetness of disposition. As we walked along the corridor to find a seat we found our way blocked by an Egyptian, offering refreshments to people inside a compartment. Without a pause, apparently without a second thought, the colonel kicked him, quite hard and effectively, out of our way. I was new to the imperial scenes, and I have never forgotten this astonishing change in my companion's character, nor the absolute blank indifference with which the Egyptian accepted the kick and moved (Morris 1968, 137).

Just one seemingly minor incident: but is this not a kind of Clearance in microcosm? British officers, vice-Viceroys, in the name of VRI, are authorised to clear people out of their way by violence. Without a second thought – indeed, perhaps without a *first* thought (as Arendt might say). This is a *matter of routine* to the officer; and perhaps to the servant too, though in a different way. The kick is received with what appears to be 'blank indifference' by the man subjected to it, but presumably largely because he knew any sign of objection would bring down worse treatment. After all, in the passage to which this footnote is appended, Morris describes how the British put down the mutiny of 1857 with what she rightly or wrongly calls 'uncharacteristic savagery', lashing prisoners to the mouths of the big guns, blowing them, literally, to pieces.

The physical act of kicking the man out of the way was merely the routine outcome of an ontological act of clearance that had already taken place; a sorting, an order(ing) of things that says 'I, in my Imperial uniform, am the sort of being that has the power to clear passage, and the authority to clear it; this servant, in his livery, is the sort of thing that ought not to be in my way; my small, routine act of bodily violence will restore the proper order-of-things', without materially affecting my essential sweetness, my gentleness. I remain sweet in my violence because it is the other who is the 'savage'.

Retrojected authority is hierarchically structured and deployed in denominational routines – abstractions which have bodily effects. The Empire as at once a bodily matter, in this sense, and at the same time a 'bluff'. This is Morris's word. In Disraeli's time, she says, 'Legally there was no such thing as a British Empire. It had no constitutional meaning. Physically, too, it was a kind of fiction, or bluff, in that it implied a far stronger power at the centre than really existed. But in the 1890s the British were determined that this heterogenous structure had logic to it, and that it could be rationalized or emotionalized into order' (Morris 1968, 177).

Rationalised, emotionalised or failing that, we could add, *booted* into order. Let us say it could be *called to order*; and if the recalcitrant 'backward' peoples, the 'natives' would not respond *properly* to that call, failing to jump to it and take up their proper places in that proper order, then we, the British, however reluctantly, however sweet our disposition, would have to use force – violence – precisely to *restore* order.

We are brought back again and again to the question of the 'proper' and with it the issue of 'property'.

THE 'PERMANENT SETTLEMENT'

In 1776, the same year as Smith published Wealth of Nations, and the year of the American Declaration of Independence, Philip Francis, a member of the Bengal Council wrote: 'If private property be not once for all secured on a permanent footing, the public revenue will sink rapidly with the general produce of the country'. Cornwallis formalised this in 1793 in what is known as the 'Permanent Settlement'. The context, as Metcalf and Metcalf read it, was that: 'In India prior to the coming of the British, the bundle of rights associated with property were not concentrated in a land "owner", but rather dispersed among all those, among them the peasant cultivator the zamindar and the government, who had an interest in the land' (Metcalf and Metcalf 2006, 78).

The British, then, turned the Zamindar, formerly embedded in a 'bundle' of 'dispersed' mutual relations and obligations that recalls our above reading of the Gaelic term *dúthchas*, into a *landlord*, an owner of disposable property, one bound by the 'white meat of contract', and what is more, a *sole proprietor*. British revenue policy 'insisted that each holding be held in full proprietary title by a single owner' (Metcalf 1979, 55), so that others are *excluded* from any kind of ownership of the land. Needless to say, sole proprietor or not, if the Zamindar could not keep up tax payments, the land would be appropriated by the British authorities and disposed of for him. But of course, this means that in a sense it had *already* been 'appropriated' – turned into something extract*able*, dispos*able* – by the time the Zamindar could get around to paying or defaulting on the payments. Those with the proper authority can *appropriate*, according to rules they themselves have the (higher) authority to lay down; and they can authorise those under them to dispose of property *within certain bounds*. The Zamindar can subordinate the peasant cultivator in the name of the Raj; the Raj can subordinate the Zamindar in the name of

VRI. But this is not about 'oppression', of course – or at least not in the way you might think.

Here is WW Hunter, discussing significant events in India in 1689 (a year of some significance, too, note, in terms of relations between Britain and Ireland): 'In this same year the company determined to consolidate their position in India on the basis of territorial sovereignty, to enable them to resist the oppression of the Mughals and the Maráthás' (Hunter 1893, 434).

Note the direction of flow of the 'oppression' as depicted here: it is the Mughals and the Maráthás who are 'oppressing' the *company*; and not the other way around; in such circumstances surely, the company is entitled to 'resist' oppression. Notably, here, any violence is interpreted as coming from the *Indians*, specifically the Mughals and Maráthás.

This of course is an inversion of the direction of oppression as it would have been experienced by at least some of the Indians themselves, but it is far from the only inversion to be found in British Imperial discourse on India. William Jones, writing to Hastings in 1784: 'I can no longer bear to be at the mercy of our Pundits [*sic*], who deal out Hindu law as they please'. Jones learns Sanskrit and compiles a digest of Indian laws so that 'we should never perhaps be led astray by Pandits or Maulavis who would hardly venture to impose on us, when their impositions might be so easily detected' (Metcalf 1995, 23).

One would not have to be Edward Said to spot the play of power behind this version of 'Orientalism': Jones learns Sanskrit precisely to be able to *catch the Pandits out*, as those devious Orientals try to impose upon the 'innocent' British. The Raj as remedy, as redress for the violence *originating with the colonised.*

For Hunter too, the actions of the company are justifiable as an attempt to redress the balance (not incidentally, this phrase itself originates in the marketplace, and that in relation to the process of standardisation). This redress, this remedy for the oppression coming from the other, is sought in the form of the consolidation of territorial sovereignty. And with that consolidation, or rather with a certain 'resolution' that is 'passed', comes a transformation, almost a transubstantiation:

> With that in view, they passed the resolution which was destined to turn their clerks and factors throughout India into conquerors and proconsuls: 'the increase of our revenue is the subject of our care, as much as our trade; 'tis that must maintain our force when twenty accidents may interrupt our trade; 'tis that must make us a nation in India. Without that, we are but a great number of interlopers united by His Majesty's Royal Charter, fit only to trade where nobody of power thinks it in their interest to prevent us (Hunter 1893, 434–35).

Here a British writer of the late nineteenth century cites one from the seventeenth, openly discussing the need to increase revenue *in order to 'make us a nation in India'*, thus to redress a disadvantageous power differential. To be a nation, on this view, as distinct from a multiplicity of 'interlopers' (fascinating word) united only by the Royal Charter, is the way to become strong enough to overcome the *power* that would prevent them from trading where they pleased. Nationhood and commerce are bound up together in the performative act of this resolution – and again (indeed, chronologically *before* Hunter) there is the idea of the 'power' coming from the outside, *preventing* the clerks and factors from plying their trade. Our overpowering of these others – and thus the expansion of Empire – is therefore in some sense an act of preemptive *commercial and national self-defence*.

CONTIGUITY

This has admittedly been, of necessity, a very quick dash through elements of Empire. But what has all this got to do with us? You and me? Let us go back to Newtownards – the town in which we Remain campaigners in 2016 were opened to accusations of treason.

The town itself is surrounded by traces of Empire, and not just those confined to direct British intervention in Ireland. On the northeast side of town lies Clandeboye, once the estate of a major landowner, Frederick Hamilton-Temple-Blackwood, 1st Marquess of Dufferin and Ava. Dufferin, as it happens, was Viceroy of India from 1884 to 1888.

Looming over the town to the southwest, on a hill 'cragged and steep', stands not Donne's Truth, complete with capital T, but Scrabo Tower, a monument built in the 1850s to mark the 'generosity' that Charles Stewart (later Vane), the Third Marquess of Londonderry, had supposedly shown his tenants during the famine. He and his wife, in fact, had opened a soup kitchen, and he had given men paid work fixing up his property at Mount Stewart (McCavery 2013). Let us note in passing that neither Lord Londonderry nor any of his British peers sought to dismantle the structures that allowed them to extract and accumulate the wealth they used for this philanthropy. Let us further note that just as the famine in Ireland was driven by an ideological commitment to free-market forces, so too were other famines across the Empire, in what Mike Davis describes as 'late Victorian holocausts' (Davis 2000).

And right in the middle of Newtownards, the very material, bodily contours of that square, home to the bustling market where I buy my bread on a Saturday morning, were set out using resources in large part extracted from India. The square was given its present form in the 1770s by Alexander Stewart, whose great-great-grandfather had come to Donegal from Scotland as part of the wave of 'settlement' (or rather, expropriation) known as the Plantation of Ulster. Alexander and his wife, Mary Cowan, had bought large swathes of land in County Down, some of which became Mount Stewart Demesne, using money inherited from Mary's brother, Robert Cowan. The latter, an East India Company man, had amassed his fortune in India, including during a period as Governor of Bombay (McCavery 2013).

Alexander Stewart was the grandfather of the Charles Stewart for whom Scrabo Tower would be built – though neither of them is the best-known member of the family. That honour would undoubtedly fall to Charles's half-brother, Robert Stewart, Viscount Castlereagh, who would become British Foreign Secretary, and the target of Shelly's rage, rightly or wrongly, in his *cri de coeur* against the Peterloo massacre, the Masque of Anarchy.

The Stewart family, as we have seen, had attained some of their wealth through expropriation in Ireland (with land originally 'given' by James I), and some from Imperial domination in India. But there was another source, and another monument to mark it: a double-life-size equestrian statue of him in another market square, this time in Durham. This controversial sculpture was erected in memory of Londonderry by his widow, whose coalfields in the area he attained on marrying her. Like Alexander before him, then, Charles Stewart's wealth was in part built by yet another form of appropriation – from the women they married.

In any case, by mid-century, Londonderry's colliery portfolio 'was now the largest in Britain in the hands of a single individual' (Whitehead 2013). And as the nineteenth century progressed, coal drove the Industrial Revolution, allowing the north of England to emerge as the world's first industrial region, and providing, in Manchester, Engels and Marx with much material for their key texts, and Dickens with the model for his Coketown.

The Stewart family that quite literally shaped the market square in my hometown thus provide direct links with Empire and industrialisation; the family that worked to suppress the rising of the United Irishmen in 1798 (Castlereagh), and opposed democratic reforms in the UK (Peterloo), had drawn wealth from Bombay (Robert Cowan) and from coal in the north of England, as the industrial revolution, again quite literally, gathered steam.

It would be fascinating to follow here the example of historian Emma Rothschild's An Infinite History, wherein she traces the mundane, but geographically far reaching interconnections of a fairly ordinary eighteenth- and nineteenth-century French family through thousands of receipts, notarial documents, birth certificates, death records, and so on, to tell a story that takes in a particular street in a provincial French town; Paris; the London markets; the Panama Canal; French colonial Algeria; and overseas plantations run using slave-labour. Rothschild, in her introduction, describes her approach as proceeding from an 'individual to her connections, and to their connections', in a 'history by contiguity' (Rothschild 2021).

Rothschild herself acknowledges that this could lead to an 'infinity' of sources. But is it not precisely this overlapping of *contiguous, yet heterogenous threads* that make up the infinitely complex weft of each human life, of history itself? Think of Manchester, that original industrial city, site of Peterloo, seemingly all solid as the brick and iron visible even now in the still strikingly massive viaduct arches of Castlefield, but built only through an uncountable number of direct, hand-to-hand interchanges.

Think of the countless bricklayers in full flow, scooping on mortar, and trimming, tapping and bedding down the bricks with one hand even as the other shapes itself to the next brick. Inside a year, a billion of these cycles would have taken place all across newly industrialising Britain, creating the viaducts and mills, the mansions and manses, the schoolrooms, houses, stations – and even the kilns in which the next billion bricks were fired. And before the brick, the clay. Where did they get it? With what spades did they dig it out, what carts transported it to the moulds? What ironwork went into the moulds, and whence the iron? Who mined it, who cast and wrought it? What springs were needed, what pistons, wheels, rollers, presses, straps – and thus what leather, what wood, and what kinds of wood, from which forests? And what of the mortar, and the components that made it up; what of the tools, the trowels, the spades, the buckets, the knives and hammers?

These teeming cyclical and horizontal flows, of course, were not confined to one branch of industry: each feeds into the others, and speaking of feeding, all of this would have required the procurement, transport, and preparation of vast quantities of food and drink. Women would not just have worked in the mills, they would also be expected to feed and clothe husbands and children. They remain scarcely more visible that Adam Smith's mother in some histories. There would have been smiths of another kind too; and butchers, brewers and bakers. Doubtless even some spirit cellarmen.

As an aside: two of the products of this surge of production would be deforestation and coal smoke – the consequences of which we would learn about later. That said, to be sure, as early as 1856, Eunice Newton Foote presented a paper on the heat absorbing effects of Carbon Dioxide. Or rather, a man presented her paper on her behalf, this sort of thing not being deemed a suitable activity for women (Bell 2022).

And only this continuous, contiguous, whole-cloth of human intercourse, the cyclical-horizontal interchanges from one to another to another, made possible the production in industrial quantities of the material that gave Manchester its nickname: Cottonopolis.

A whole network of contiguous threads here draws together neighbourhoods that might at first appear distinct. Where did the cotton come from, and where did it go? To take the latter question first, we have already dipped in and out of texts on the Imperial project in India, the markets of which would be the destination of much of the finished cloth (thus undercutting Indian spinners and weavers, later an important issue for India's nationalist movement).

But to turn to the former question, this is where the overlapping of the politics of indifference and hostility reaches its apogee, for much of the raw material was shipped in from plantations that used enslaved Africans for their labour power. The people who were enslaved, and who grew, picked and packed the cotton that built Manchester (as well as the sugar and tobacco upon which other European and US cities grew great), were kept at a remove, reduced to the status of 'one of those . . .' by at least three forms of reduction.

Firstly, people were reduced by the practices and projections of racism – 'racecraft', to borrow from Barbara Fields and Karen Fields. Racecraft operates like the accusation of 'witchcraft' in a witch hunt, back-projecting the witches held to be responsible for whatever has gone wrong (my crops have failed; ergo a witch must have cursed them; ergo a witch must exist; and as there are no better candidates, I am justified in lynching *this* woman). There is slavery, which must be justified, ergo the people we have enslaved must be inferior. It is ontologically given; you can read their inferior essence from the sign of their skin (Fields and Fields 2012).

The hostility, the 'darkness' of the likes of Henry Morton Stanley, was projected on the people taken captive and forced to labour – they were *held to belong*, in order to hold them as belongings, to a different and lesser kind of being than the 'civilised Europeans' who exploited them. The violence of enslavement did not begin with the whiplash.

The idea of 'projection', which we have been deploying here, is hinted at by Omi and Winant in their conception of 'racial formation'. Race, they say, is neither something fixed, concrete and objective nor a mere illusion. It is an 'unstable and "decentred" complex of social meanings constantly being transformed by political struggle' (Essed 2002, 123). They go on to define racial formation as the sociohistorical process by which racial categories are created, inhabited, transformed, and destroyed; but crucially they add 'racial formation is a process of historically situated projects in which human bodies and social structures are represented and organized', projects they then link to the evolution of hegemony (Essed 2002, 124). Omi and Winant's *projects*, in short, involve *projections* of 'signs' of racial denomination onto living bodies, performatively inaugurating and reiterating the 'racialisation' of those others, those neighbours, and not *these* neighbours, in a bid to justify dominating them.

At the same time, secondly, they were reduced to the status of 'things indifferent', of disposable property – we will examine this through a reading of the diaries of John Newton in a moment. As Padraic X Scanlan says, this was, historically, a new combination: 'Atlantic slavery combined the old cruelties of other forms of enslavement with the brutal logic of a commodities market' (Scanlan 2020, chap. 4).

Thirdly, there was the Atlantic itself. As in Jane Austen's Mansfield Park, the brutish source of wealth that allowed many British (and other European) families to live as they did was at a *geographical* remove. Once in a while, as in Mansfield Park, there are hints of unease; once in a while the head of the household is obliged to go 'away' on business, to keep the wealth flowing; but 'away', and what happens there, remains at a remove, off-stage, in the dark (Said 1994). There is the domestic sphere, what happens in the house and the immediate neighbourhood; and there is . . . what exactly? Something, somewhere. Outside our purview; over the sea; over the fence; beyond the palings. Somewhere that is not here; somewhere that is over the horizon. An off-stage arena, a 'public sphere', perhaps, in which men are allowed to appear, or rather, into which they disappear when they leave the privacy of the house, the domus, to 'go about their business', and which is none of the *women's* business.

It is worth thinking a little more about what we are casually calling 'spheres' here.

The disappearing and reappearing of the men of Mansfield Park is itself revealing. At first glance, one might conclude that there is a 'domestic sphere' for the women and servants insofar as it has been excluded from the 'public sphere'. It is a space that has been domesticated, produced as domestic through the procedures of exclusion from public life. In a way this is certainly the case. But is it quite right to describe the construction of the domestic sphere as an exclusion (of women) from the (patriarchal) 'public'? How public is 'the public' when only a portion of the people are allowed to appear there? Is there not a sense in which 'the public', constructed by exclusion, is thus *privatively* produced? Are we not looking, rather, at a privative *partition* of the common space, the space in which we *all* find ourselves, into *two* private enclosures – denominated in turn as the 'domestic' and the 'public', so that, not only is the private or personal political, but the political is *private*; a space which is at the disposal of only *some* of the people, only those with the proper authority, and not available to all in common? The public arena, according to Imperial logic, is a space Cleared of those not authorised to be there, and those who *are* authorised-to-be-there are authorised to use violence to clear it.

One Clears the women-and-children from *this* part of the common (squeezing, squashing, levering them into the domus), in order to be able to get on with (public, political) business. Who performs this Clearance? The man, the master of the house, the *dominus* of the *domus*. The women cannot come and go unless authorised to do so by the men, and that within carefully delimited bounds; the men of Mansfield Park can cross from one of these partitioned spheres to the other. Sir Thomas Bertram leaves to impose order on the (off-stage) plantation and comes back to impose order in the *domus*, which, in his absence, has become disordered in a way that, as Said points out, is 'explicitly associated with feminine "lawlessness"', such that Sir Thomas has to 'rein-state himself' (it is tempting to draw out the political overtones of the word 'state' here) before resuming his seat as 'master of the house' (Said 1994, 103). Said, intriguingly, links this passage with one from John Stuart Mill in which the latter says of the colonies that they are 'hardly to be looked upon as countries . . . but more properly as outlying agricultural or manufacturing estates belonging to a larger community' (Said 1994, 108).

The men who are masters of their own *domus* set out from there not just into an exterior world, but into a world more and more of which they will *bring home*, more and more of which they will dominate and domesticate, appropriating it and putting it at the disposal of their own 'larger community'. The political project of Empire, then, is that of *exporting and expanding domestication*. If in the 'domestic' politics of this era women-and-children are to be represented by 'their' men, and not allowed themselves to appear directly, without scandal, without repercussions, so too in Imperial politics the project of Empire domesticates, or makes a bid to domesticate (and indeed 'feminise' or 'infantilise'), that part of the population ('natives', whether men *or* women, and those denominated as 'slaves' or 'servants') who are not authorised to appear in the public sphere, or only within bounds; those who are excluded from and subordinated to the *structures of authorisation*, the *authorised violence* that sets the boundaries, that inaugurates and enforces them. Inaugurated and *authorised* by whom? By *us*, (we servants of Empire, we patriarchs, we who have a place somewhere *in* the hierarchy of authori-sation, not *under* it; but not in our own name, it goes without saying: *in the name of . . .*

The Imperial Order (the performative bid) that would inaugurate the dual order of Empire is the Proclamation that says: in the name of God or VRI or both, we proclaim that *Our* violence is authorised, *Theirs* is not. No Empire without an externalisation and subordination (by domestication; an external-ising *in order to* bring back under the rule of the *Dominus*) of a 'them' from an 'us'; where there is denomination, there are always at least two denomina-tions. But from the perspective of those being subordinated by Empire, God and VRI remain external too. They do not themselves appear in the space of the encounter – they remain overseas, elsewhere, just as, to those dwelling in Mansfield Park, the Plantations remain somewhere 'out there'.

Yet there *is a there*, and we know there is a there. A thread – and this can be taken virtually literally in the case of cotton – binds here to there;

a hand-to-hand chain, or better, a network of connections; material, bodily contacts. A woven (knitted?) fabric in which each fibre is spun together with another, then that to another and another; and each thread to another, and then another. Our vision stops at the horizon; the *contiguous fabric* that binds us to others *does not*. It is tempting to suggest with Virginia Postrel that textiles are the 'fabric of civilisation' in more than one sense (Postrel 2020). Tempting, too, to think about the more than etymological connection she draws out between 'textiles' and 'texts', and still more tempting to suggest that there may be nothing outside the textile.

But let us not yield to temptation: let us instead take a closer at the reductions involved in enslavement through the journals of one hymn-writer and slave trader, John Newton.

OFFSHORE

Having been saved from drowning in a storm by God's 'Amazing Grace', Newton went on to decades of prayerful piety – and considerable success in the slave trade. His journals record, in matter-of-fact prose, the preparation of his ship, the cleaning, the laying in of stores, the preparation of sails, the punishments meted out to disobedient or even mutinous crew (who he terms his 'people') and, of course, the enumeration of the various purchases he makes of men, women and children and other commodities.

To pick out an entry almost at random: 'by the favour of good Providence, got safe around the rock at 4 p.m., and on board the *Surprize* by 6. . . . No letters from home. In the morn the yaul came on board, brought 1 small girl which makes our number [of enslaved people] 13' (Martin and Spurrell 1962, 19).

Sometimes the language is so matter-of-fact it takes some decoding. 'Carpenter built the platform in the men's room. . . . The ship is clear enough now to take 2/3ds of our slaves without inconvenience' (Martin and Spurrell 1962, 22). The 'platform' in the 'men's room', a footnote informs us, was a shelf dividing the space between decks, where the enslaved men were to be stowed. The space itself was already only five feet or so; after the platform was installed, the captive men, chained in pairs, would have about thirty inches of headroom during their transportation across the Atlantic. Newton's casual remark about this being achieved 'without inconvenience' begs the question: inconvenience for whom?

But look back at the previous line about the 'small girl'. Newton is not using this is a vague sense, the way one might refer to someone in early childhood. This from 10 January 1751: 'She [the Africa, a longboat], brought 11 slaves: viz. 1 man. 2 women, 5 sizeable girls, 1 boy and 2 girls small: likewise . . . 400 lb rice, and a tooth [elephant tusk], weight 32 lb' (Martin and Spurrell 1962, 29–30).

The 'girls small' are distinguished from 'sizeable girls' here, throwing a different light on the remark about the 'small girl' of the earlier paragraph. Indeed, in many entries in his journal Newton specifies the sizes he is dealing with, as on Wednesday, 28 November 1750: 'This morning at daylight had the agreeable sight of my longboat, and soon after she came on board with every body well, and brought 11 slaves, viz. 3 men, 1 woman, 2 men boys, 1 boy (4 foot), 1 boy and 3 girls (undersize)' (Martin and Spurrell 1962, 20). *Every body well?*

Or there is Friday, 14 December 1750: 'Bought 2 small girls . . . 1 of 3 feet and the other 2 feet 4 inches, which make number 32' (Martin and Spurrell 1962, 24), or Wednesday, 16 January 1751: 'Received a man slave and some yams and plantains from Yellow Will, and a girl, 3 foot 11 from William Freeman' (Martin and Spurrell 1962, 31). Or on Sunday, 27 January 1751: 'Yellow Will brought me a girl slave of 4 foot, and about a dozen fowls'. Or this, from Sunday, 13 January: 'The yaul came off, brought 2 small boys; sent her in again with positive orders to buy none under 4 foot, for I think we have little ones enough, at the price they now bear' (Martin and Spurrell 1962, 30).

At some point, reading these journal entries, the realisation dawns: Newton is not talking about this or that 'little girl' or 'little boy' as you and I might talk of the children in the playground; he is purchasing ivory by the pound, fowls by the dozen, and children by the foot.

Everything is enumerated, weighed out, measured. Or rather, not everything: Newton's European companions and fellow traders ('people') are often named here. We meet not only Yellow Will and William Freeman, but also Andrew Ross, and Peter Freeman, among others. Little need to underline the irony of that last surname.

The enslaved, on the other hand, are given at best as 'a fine manslave' or 'a woman slave' – though on more than one occasion, Newton refuses to accept a 'woman slave' because of her physical condition. Take this entry from Friday, 25 January, for example: 'Yellow Will brought me a woman slave, but being long breasted and ill made, refused her, and made him take her on shoar [shore] again, tho I am not certain I shall be able to get one in her room [place]' (Martin and Spurrell 1962, 32). This last clause, far from indicating he sees the woman as irreplaceable in principle, indicates simply his anxiety that he will not, as a matter of fact, be able to obtain a suitable substitute on this particular trip.

Substitutable in life, dispensable in death. Where a European dies, as Adam Hochschild points out (Hochschild 2005), Newton names them and notes they 'departed this life'. Not so for the Africans, who just die, or whose fate is left out of the account, as a matter of indifference, or who are numbered rather than named, as in the entry from 9 January 1751: 'This day buried a fine woman slave, No. 11, having been ailing some time . . . ', or on 12 January: 'Filled 2 load of water and cleared the canoo, discharged my traders and put a boy on shoar [shore], No. 27, being very bad with a flux'. Or: 'In the night a woman slave died of the flux (No. 112). Cooper at work upon the water casks. . . . Sent a girl, ill of the flux (No. 92) on shoar . . . not so much in hopes of recovery (for I fear she is past it), as to free the ship of a nuisance. Cooper finished all the casks' (Martin and Spurrell 1962, 48). And so it goes on: so many people put ashore to die or buried with a number, not a name, reported in the same tone as the day's chores.

The violence of the indifference evinced here, of course, does not preclude violence of a more kinetic sort. Newton writes on 11 December 1752, that he uncovered a planned 'insurrection' among the enslaved people on his ship. He extracted information from three boys (Newton does not give their ages). 'Put the boys in irons and slightly in the thumbscrews to urge them to a full confession' (Martin and Spurrell 1962, 71). 'Urge' – there's something almost Voltairean about the word (' . . . *pour encourager les autres* ').

Indeed, 'Divine Providence' seems to have tipped Newton off again a few weeks later, with the discovery of another planned rising. 'Found 4 principally concerned, punished them with thumb screws and afterwards put them in neck yokes'. The thumbscrews are mentioned almost casually, in passing, as though this were simply a matter of routine.

Some bodies, some lives, as Judith Butler would say, are evidently more grievable than others. And others more lovable: Adam Hochschild points out that even as he dispensed punishments, and in the 'midst of applying the lash and the thumbscrew. . . . Newton kept up an unceasing stream of love letters to Mary', his wife (Hochschild 2005, 23).

In these, he was capable of evident tenderness: 'I press to my lips the paper that will be with you in a few days . . . '; and even says, on receiving some of her letters, 'I could almost hug every dirty fellow through whose hands they have passed' (Hochschild 2005, 24). Newton is as geometrically distant from his wife as he is geometrically proximate to, within touching distance of, the bodies he yokes and tortures; he is tender to her, the very hand-to-hand contact with her letters makes the bodies of his 'dirty fellows' almost huggable; yet he evinces no more fellow feeling for his enslaved 'cargo' than unsentimental Adam Smith contemplating his brother on the rack.

For all his physical proximity, his project (slave trading) requires the reduction of *these* people to the status of disposable property, opening an ontological, or rather, ontologised gulf between him and them that does not open between him and his named, European, 'white' shipmates. He cannot allow himself to *be near* those he is buying and selling, to encounter them as neighbours, if he is to continue to stock and ship them. This is not necessarily a conscious decision; it may very well have been a matter of *routine*. There just *are*, says the routine, as everybody knows, people of my denomination, white, nameable, grievable; and those of the 'slave' denomination; numbered as one counts barrels or bushels for an inventory; 'black', therefore reducible to a quantity of the white meat of contract; 'one of those . . . '

But of course, it was a highly profitable contract, for Newton and for many others involved in the trade – some of whom would use those profits, rather as Londonderry had used those of his lands and investments, for charitable purposes.

It was the profitability of the slave trade, particularly that of the Royal African Society, for instance, that allowed Edward Colston to donate generously to philanthropic causes in Bristol. As recently as 1999, when a biographical pamphlet was published, it made much more of his philanthropic legacy than his involvement in the slave trade (Morgan 1999). His was a 'generosity', and indeed a way of life, made possible by violence; and that violence was made tolerable by 'offshoring', clearing the bodies out of sight, keeping them beyond the horizon, physically or phenomenologically. It is perhaps all the more fitting then that his statue ended up, when it was tipped into Bristol Harbour by protestors in 2020, almost literally 'off-shored'.

Throughout this necessarily all too brief dip in and out of the era of Empire and enslavement we have seen the violence of hostility and the violence of indifference overlap. There is a double projection at work. I project ahead of me a world already carved out into ontologically distinct denominations, 'Peoples' each essentially external to the others; I back-project a 'higher authority' that supposedly authorises me to draw the lines *in practice* that are already there in *principle* – that is, the higher authority in whose name I count myself authorised to impose the *proper* order, by violence if necessary. As a Viceroy, or vice-Viceroy, and so on, down the tiered hierarchy, I act not in my own name, but ultimately in that of the 'Roy', the *Rex* or *Regina*, who remains at a distance, outside the space of my encounter with you (otherwise there would be no need for the 'Vice'). Yet precisely because of that distance, I have to act, from day to day, off my own bat, as it were. The absence of the higher authority gives me leeway to do as I see fit; the (absent) higher authority, vested in me, guarantees that what I decide is unquestionable, by the likes of you, at any rate, and can be backed by force (violence) if necessary. Empire, read this way, is the entire tiered structure of the authorisation of violence, and it is a tiered *dual* structure (though later we will question this duality: it is *denomination* that binds you to a collective entity of which there are at least *two* in the neighbourhood). If you are of the 'right' denomination (the Raj, or the 'white British' denomination, say) you are interpellated (Althusser

2001), hailed, bid to take up your place in the viceregal structure, and thus to put your violence at the disposal of VRI in keeping *these others* in their place; if you are one of *those others*, one of the 'subject races', you are bid to *do as you are bid* by the vice-Viceroys – even if you are an *almost*-independent Prince. Either way, as long as you do as you are bid, you will be left in peace. Refuse, and the gears of the viceregally structured machinery for the authorisation of violence will engage and bring force to bear.

Not everyone at the time chose to do as they were bid, of course. It is not just that everywhere the Imperial project touched down there was active resistance from those having 'order' (the disempowerment, the expropriation) imposed on them (Gopal 2019). It is also that the borders between people *remained incomplete*, could never quite be crystallised into borders between 'Peoples'. In other words, it was always possible for people to combine *differently*.

But we should be careful to fold back this logic to apply to the 'Empire' itself. If the 'subject Peoples' were a projection providing an alibi for expropriative violence, so is 'The British People'. That entity will also always remain off-stage, also serve as a rallying cry, a call for a response, a call for people (in their multiplicity) to combine *as if* they owed *allegiance* to the denominational community to which they *belong*, as if the word 'British' referred univocally to an ontologically fixed entity, and as if everyone who is 'British' is somehow *identified* with everything that the British Empire means, such that anyone considering themselves British should therefore either revere the British Empire or feel guilty about it.

However, that would be to follow precisely the processes of denomination that went into constructing the Imperial project in the first place. We will have gone some way towards *de*constructing that project when we realise that the problem with the British Empire was not that it was *British* but that it was *Empire* – something to which we will return in the final chapter.

In any case, not all 'British people' think or act in the same way. Back in Manchester, there is another statue, less well-known, and confined to a side street off Deansgate. Less well-known: but those long features and that unruly quiff is distinctly familiar. So, what is a sculpture of Abraham Lincoln doing here in the industrial north of England?

On the last day of 1862, the cotton workers of Manchester met in the Free Trade Hall and took a vote. Though their own trade depended on the imports of the material, a majority (not all, but a majority) decided they would no longer work with cotton sourced from the slave-owning Confederacy, effectively expressing a solidarity with people with whom they had little in common, whom they would never meet, and who lived on a continent on which they themselves would never set foot. Lincoln, in gratitude, wrote to them, and the text of that letter is now displayed on the plaque of the statue in Manchester (Wyke n.d.).

Does this act of solidarity, this neighbourliness that did not depend on geographical proximity or on some sort of shared identity, hint at the possibility of a democracy that goes beyond borders, beyond nation and denomination? That is the question we will explore in the final chapters. But before that, let us bring the story up to date. After all, have we not long since witnessed the end of Empire and enslavement – perhaps even the 'end of history'?

Chapter Four

Donne's Other Truth

Denomination Today

It is difficult to remember now, but the 1990s was an optimistic decade, what with the end of apartheid, the end of the Cold War, and, here in Northern Ireland, an end, of sorts, to the Troubles in the form of the Good Friday Agreement.

Had you asked those of us who were around at the time to project forward twenty or twenty-five years many of us – I confess, *I* – would have predicted that Northern Ireland, however falteringly, with however many setbacks, would have emerged more like a 'normal' modern, European democracy. We would more or less have worked out how to move on from the inter-denominational conflict that seemed, to many, to be the world's last stubborn remnant of the European religious territorial wars of the seventeenth century. National and denominational questions, even the 'constitutional issue', would have lost much of their salience, their power to dominate our politics, because we would instead be working through problems of wealth and poverty, the role of the market, equality and diversity, sustainability, and so on.

As for the rest of the world, well, some were so optimistic they speculated we might have witnessed the 'end of history', or at any rate, the end of all the big arguments about how we should manage our affairs (Fukuyama 1989). The era of Empire was over; even South Africa had achieved democracy; the Soviet Bloc had broken up; the big ideological arguments had been settled; whatever the question was, the power of free markets and 'Western' liberal values, would somehow provide the answer. Of course there might be deindustrialisation and unemployment in some areas, and even the odd spot of turmoil – a stock market bubble here, a financial crisis there – but the markets would correct themselves; and in any case, even if people in Thailand, say, suffered as a result, as in the Asian financial crisis of 1997, to recall the words of George Soros speaking at that time, 'as a market participant, I don't need to be concerned with the consequences of my actions' (Miniter 2011).

Eventually, the Russians would become like us, the Chinese would become like us, and we might yet achieve that Imperial dream of a universal civilisation. It was the Euro-American gift to the world. All we had to do was keep the cranes up.

At least that was how it seemed until September 11, 2001. The very heart and symbol of the newly triumphant market-democracy, the Twin Towers of the World Trade Center, had been brought down by a violent attack that took thousands of lives – by far the worst terrorist atrocity ever to have taken place on US soil in terms of lives lost. For all the might of the US military system (and recall that the Pentagon was another target), the nation's defences had been penetrated, out of the blue, as it seemed. Suddenly the world's only remaining superpower, the United States, and by extension the rest of the West, felt raw, vulnerable in a new way.

This attack, and perhaps more so the reaction, to it have had repercussions that are still in play today, and although it would be rash to try to reduce the course of events everywhere to any single cause, we will be so bold as to pick out some threads in due course. But before we go over to that side of the Atlantic, let us look a little closer to home.

Consider Northern Ireland in the early 2020s. Despite our optimism at the time of the GFA, there are plenty of signs that, decades on, Northern Ireland remains divided. There are still many 'peace walls', designed to keep neighbours from attacking one another; the school system is still largely segregated into 'Catholic' and (de facto) 'Protestant' schools; and the Institutions of government are, at the time of writing, undergoing yet another hiatus, as the main Parties cannot agree how to share power.

What caused the hiatus this time? Arguably, it was the result of a seismic shift that took place in the Assembly election of 2022, when Sinn Féin became the first Irish nationalist party in the century-long history of the region to top the polls – something they would repeat a year later in the Council elections of 2023. According to the rules established by the St Andrews Agreement of 2006 (a document the Democratic Unionist Party, the DUP, shaped and championed), the Assembly election results should have meant Sinn Féin taking the role of First Minister, and a representative of the largest Unionist party (the DUP) taking the Deputy First Minister post.

Of course, the DUP claimed, they did not refuse to allow the Assembly to be formed because of *that*, but because the Brexit border (a border they themselves had called for, remember) had eventually been placed, by way of the 'Protocol on Ireland/Northern Ireland', between Northern Ireland and the rest of the UK – effectively in the Irish Sea (Hayward 2022).

You can have the union-undermining Protocol (or its slightly softer successor, the Windsor Framework), argued the DUP, or you can have power sharing in Stormont; but you cannot have both. Thus, rather than having a reinstalled Assembly up and running to address the aftermath of COVID, the cost-of-living crisis, the crisis in the health service, crumbling school buildings, inadequately resourced social services, the withdrawal of vital funding to Women's Aid and other support organisations, and a whole range of other pressing issues, the Institutions remained suspended, month after long month, in a dispute about a Brexit border that some 57 percent of the population had not asked for in the first place, and which did not fall under the remit of Stormont in any case.

This was just one of the signs that Northern Ireland had failed to become like other 'normal modern European democracies'. There were other such signs – the persistence of sectarianism, the politics of hostility between the 'two communities' – some of which we will look at below. However, at the same time, it appeared some of those 'normal modern European democracies' seemed to have become rather more like Northern Ireland.

The year 1998 did not just see the signing of the Good Friday Agreement, but also the election, for the first time, of Viktor Orbán as the Hungarian prime minister – though, to be fair, it was not until his second, much longer run in the office from 2010 on, that he began to reorganise the state according to what he himself described as 'illiberal' principles. This philosophy was set out openly in a 2014 speech in which he described his project as an attempt to 'harmonize relationship between the interests and achievement of individuals – that needs to be acknowledged – with interests and achievements of the community, and the nation' (Tóth 2014). He essentially announced that he had chosen a politics of *ethnos* over *demos*, a possibility that had been visible in the post-Soviet sphere of influence almost since the end of the Cold War (Nagle 1997). Or in the terms we have been exploring here, Orbán chose *denomination* over *democracy*. He would set about building his 'illiberal nation state' by clamping down on the activities of political activists 'paid by foreigners', such as NGOs and other civil organisations; and eventually by implementing measures 'effectively removing any oversight and silencing any criticism of the Hungarian government' such that he could 'rule by decree for an indefinite period of time' (Serhan 2020).

It was his 2014 speech that gave us the concept of 'illiberal democracy' (Tóth 2014); but Orbán was not alone. Recep Tayyip Erdoğan, who was elected President of Turkey in the year of Orbán's speech, 2014, would no doubt approve of the concept, as perhaps would Narendra Modi, who became prime minister of India also in the same year. In 2018 the Israeli Knesset passed a Basic Law that established Israel as a Jewish nation-state, and including clauses such as that saying the 'state views the development of

Jewish settlement as a national value and will act to encourage and promote its establishment'. Defending the Bill, Benjamin Netanyahu said: 'We will keep ensuring civil rights in Israel's democracy, but the majority also has rights and the majority decides' (Beaumont 2018). A year later, in Brazil, former army captain Jair Bolsonaro was elected president, running on a platform that saw him labelled the 'Trump of the Tropics' (Wallenfeldt 2023).

The decade also took an 'illiberal' turn in a number of well-established European democracies too. The German far right party, Alternative für Deutschland (AfD) won seven seats in the European Parliament in 2014, just a year after their founding. Marine Le Pen's 'softer' version of her father's Front National took fully a quarter of the votes in the European elections in France that year, and she even pulled together an alliance with leaders of other far right parties (though interestingly, not with Nigel Farage) in a bid to form an official EU bloc (Willisher and Davies 2014).

By 2016, Farage himself was arguably the most significant figure in British politics, and Brexit Britain seemed to be splitting into two denominations, 'Leavers' and 'Remainers' – some 52 percent and 48 percent respectively, measured by votes in the Referendum. Across the Atlantic, Donald Trump, to widespread astonishment, entered the White House, surfing on, and massively amplifying, a trend towards what some described as a new 'tribalism'. IPSOS Mori even managed to catalogue the 'Many Tribes of Brexit' (IPSOS Mori 2021).

The 2022 mid-term election results and subsequent polls in the US suggested that Trump's star may have begun to fade somewhat; but the legacy of Trumpism has not yet played out, and it remains possible that he will be back (at the time of writing he is front-runner for the Republican nomination), or that a less chaotic version of Trump will carry the movement forward rather as Marine le Pen modified the positions of her father's party and enjoyed a surge in support. After all, in the French elections of 2022, le Pen led her Rassemblement National (the re-named Front National) to its greatest electoral achievements to date, winning eighty-nine seats, up from eight seats five years before. Bolsonaro was ousted, but Modi is still in power at the time of writing; Orban and Erdoğan were re-elected in 2023 – the latter, typically, claiming his narrow win (another 52 to 48 percent split) as a win for 'the entire nation of 85 million' (Kirby and Goksedev 2023) – and far-right parties are making record gains in Italy and even in Scandinavia, long held up as the sensible social-democratic alternative to the more divisive US and British models of market democracy.

In the UK, a post-Brexit Conservative Party seemed to be taking on the right-wing populist characteristics of UKIP and the Brexit Party (now Reform UK). Even as the Party began to lose its grip on power, getting through three leaders in 2022 and losing over one thousand councillors in the local elections of 2023, it redoubled its hostile rhetoric on asylum seekers (relabelled 'illegal immigrants', and threatened with deportation to Rwanda) and turned up the volume in its self-declared 'war on woke'.

An unapologetically nationalist strain of conservatism was on full display at the straight-forwardly named National Conservatism conference of May 2023, not an official Conservative Party event, but one lent a certain authority by the presence of Cabinet heavyweights Michael Gove and Suella Braverman. In her speech to the conference Braverman claimed, among other things: 'The defining feature of this country's relationship with slavery is not that we practised it, but that we led the way in abolishing it'. One would have thought the defining feature was that 'we' did both. But to admit as much would be, from Braverman's point of view, to risk making people feel terrible, something she has just accused the 'left' of doing in the preceding sentences: 'I think the left can only sell its vision for the future by making people feel terrible about our past. White people do not exist in a special state of sin or collective guilt. Nobody should be blamed for things that happened before they were born' (Walker 2023).

It is interesting that Braverman seems almost to have grasped the mechanisms we are calling processes of denomination here – albeit in a contradictory manner. The first contradiction is that she claims this is something of which 'the left' is (collectively) guilty, while failing to register that she is deploying the mechanisms herself. Braverman, for political purposes, projects a 'left' that is *collectively* guilty of projecting white *collective guilt* for political purposes.

As we have already hinted, there is a second contradiction. Braverman wants to deny the historic collective guilt of white people of 'this country', but *at the same time* encourage her audience to bask in the glory of the great deeds accomplished 'before they were born'. Forget the enslavement, look at the abolition! It is abolition that is the *defining* feature of this country's relationship with slavery. Slavery may have *happened*, somehow, as if accidentally, or as Sir John Seeley said about the Empire, in a fit of absence of mind (Seeley 2011), our country may have had some sort of relationship with it; but not a *defining* one. 'We' are, *by definition*, then, the country that abolished slavery (and, essentially, definitively, not the one that extracted wealth and power from people it enslaved for centuries before that).

The message is, you should not feel collectively guilty; but you *should* feel collectively proud. Any feelings of shame amount to *an attack from 'the left'*, so you are hereby authorised – nay, it is your patriotic duty – to reject them (the feelings of shame *and* the Left, that is). Her message may resonate with all the more authority for her audience, not just because she is a holder of high office (she was Home Secretary at the time of the speech) but because, being of South-Asian heritage, this is 'obviously' not special or self-interested pleading. But this, of course, requires the audience to pick selectively through history, occluding or discarding inconveniently 'shameful' threads and high-lighting only those threads that make 'us' feel good about 'ourselves'.

This repeats the founding gestures of politics of nationalism, and of pro-cesses of denomination in general: 'we' are essentially a unitary, peaceable, *innocent* community, only wanting to be left in peace. Anyone who disturbs that peace – for example, by pointing out inconvenient truths about 'our' history – is guilty of an attack on 'us'. Guilt is projected out, externalised, even if the attack seems to come from 'within' the nation or denomination. Such an internal attacker has a name: the traitor. And you know what 'we' do with traitors. It is a denominational approach to the issue of 'the collective', as though 'the collective' had to be conceived as a unitary entity persisting through time and history, and which must be either collectively guilty or inno-cent, villain or hero *as a whole* – depending on whether it is *our own* or not. If our own, then innocent; if innocent, then those who accuse 'us' of shameful deeds must *ipso facto* belong to another, separate, collective entity, one that is intent on attacking us. It is all too easy to allow this binary reduction to frame the debate, but to fight on this territory is to concede the terms of the debate to the conservatives.

Where did all this come from? How and why did such politics thrive in the second decade of the twenty-first century, and carry on into the third, in Northern Ireland, in the UK, and elsewhere? Arguably because, while some misdiagnosed the problem and mis-prescribed the treatment, the frustrations, stresses and anxieties the populists honed in on were real enough. People in post-industrial towns in the North of England really had been largely aban-doned to their fate (like the Gift) by London; people in the Rust Belt really were struggling; the wealth and power gap between an elite and ordinary people in the street really was growing. In the UK and in other European countries, austerity, imposed after a crash they had not caused, really did seem to bite down on the poorest hardest. And in certain clear ways those who pointed fingers of blame at the EU were right: the rules member states were forced to follow were shaped by the conservative orthodoxy of 'fiscal recti-tude', meaning deep cuts in public spending imposed on Greece, for instance, as a result of which there was an 'unprecedented recession', the economy contracted, unemployment soared and poverty rose dramatically, 'especially among children' (Lancet 2018).

So, it was certainly *plausible* when some loud voices claimed that the problem was that 'we' are not getting a fair share of limited resources. The question is, though, who are 'we'?

If the answer given is denominational – 'we' are the ordinary People who belong to *this* Community, *this* Nation, as opposed to those other nations, or some nebulous international, 'cosmopolitan elite' or 'globalist cabal', or 'woke blob' (Wootton 2023), contemptuous of the values of we salt-of-the-earth patriots (and the overlap with antisemitic tropes here is notable) – the politics that emerges will be a politics of hostility, answering the violence of the prevailing *indifference* to 'our' suffering with a violence of indignant hostility directed towards denominational 'others'. *They*, the (projected) 'elite', and their supporters, think they are better than *us*, as we can see, over and over, from the news provided by our favourite media outlets (and if the owners of those outlets do very, very well for themselves, in part by repeating these tropes, *at least they don't look down on us*).

There is, of course, a different way to look at 'the collective', at 'democracy', at 'our' relation to history and heritage, a different way to respond to the question of the 'we', as we will see in chapter five, but it is not hard to find examples of a thriving politics of denomination today, of a sort that seems familiar to anyone steeped in the politics of Northern Ireland. Indeed, some of them even appeared to be creating an international network of sorts – witness Viktor Orbán's rapturous reception at CPAC 2022 in the United States. In the same year, moreover, we saw one of the sharpest possible examples of the sort of politics we have been looking at spill over into open, full-scale warfare: Vladimir Putin decided to launch an invasion of Ukraine on the basis that it was 'really' an integral part of Russia in the first place.

We will examine Putin's project shortly but clear an example of the politics of denomination as the attack on Ukraine was, a still clearer example erupted shockingly in the Middle East the following year, in October of 2023, just as the final draft of this book was being prepared for printing – too late for any extended analysis here, though we will offer some brief remarks in the closing chapter.

We will instead start the chapter back in Northern Ireland, thinking through denomination today, and beginning to think about how we might do things otherwise.

THE INTERFACE

On a gable wall overlooking the main road from Newtownards to Belfast, a seemingly professionally produced banner was installed at some point in the early 2020s. The banner featured the image of two masked paramilitaries with guns at the ready. The text read: 'The prevention of the erosion of our identity is now our priority'. Under that, 'East Belfast Battalion', and under that, symbols of three paramilitary groupings: PAF, UVF and YCV. One of these acronyms, standing for the Ulster Volunteer Force, would be relatively familiar to a wide audience in Northern Ireland; the other two – the Protestant Action Force (who made an appearance in chapter one) and the Young Citizen

Volunteers – less so. Nevertheless, the presence of the Red Hand of Ulster in all three, and, of course, the images of the masked men, leave little room for doubt about the general message. These are Loyalist paramilitaries, and their threat of violence is to be taken very seriously.

Yet the question of who these images, these armed, muscular representatives *represent* is still worth raising. Those who put up the poster, presumably; and it seems obvious, the members of the paramilitary groups symbolised at the bottom. But that does not exhaust the scope of the poster's claim concerning an *identity*.

What exactly is this identity? Who gets to decide its scope and content? Who gets to decide when it is being *eroded* – a slowly unfolding process – and when it is being eroded sufficiently to call for (call forth) the sudden, explosive violence promised in the images of the gunmen? Well, we can at least presume that people like the men (and it is men) in the masks in the picture will be something to do with it. People who share their sort of identity. Other masked men, then.

The irony in a poster that claims to be about preserving identity while using an image of men *hiding* their identities should not tempt us to dismiss this as incoherent, self-contradictory. Or rather, perhaps it is possible to read, in that contradiction, something of the structure of denominational identities as such.

What appears in this poster are the *masked* representatives of the community. That is, it is a representation of *representatives* who *must remain masked* to get across their message. The mask is what is made to appear in public; it is the message sent out to the world, published openly, available to read for everyone passing by.

But is the appearance of the mask not also, by the same token, the *appearance of the withdrawal of the face*? These are images of men who have withdrawn their faces behind masks, the appearance of which *is* the public message, and that message concerns violence. The masks, just as much as the weapons in the image, show that 'the community' (as distinct from this or that identifiable neighbour) is prepared to visit violence on anyone found (but found by whom? By what procedure?) to be eroding their identity – or rather, 'our' identity. The identity shared by a 'we'.

The masks stare out, the message goes out. The 'we' of the 'our' is everyone behind the mask, everyone prepared to get behind the mask, gather behind it, everyone behind the gable wall, so to speak, as distinct from, and indeed *as opposed to*, everyone out there, on the *outside*. This is the geography of the message.

As opposed to, because the threat of violence is (or appears to be) directed outwards: there are those behind the wall who share an identity, the banner says; this identity is under threat of erosion; and we are prepared to meet that threat with violence if necessary. (Prepared for Peace, Ready for War, says another such image). Thus, there is a temporality to the message too: we threaten violence *only because we have already been placed under threat*. So, if we strike you (in future), you should know that it will have been because we have in principle *already been struck* – by you.

The projection of the image of the masked men, then, sets out a certain inside and a certain outside, as well as a *before* and *after*. It does not simply describe: this is a claim staked, a threat declared; this is a performative utterance, in the post-Austinian sense discussed in the first chapter, and the geography and temporality of the image are *performed, called for, in the image*, inaugurated in the appearance of the mask. To recall Austin, though, the call of the mask masquerades as a matter of fact, a description of an already existing reality (the community whose identity is under threat).

Every performative utterance, we argued above, has the structure of a bet; it is a call that calls for, calls forth, a response ('done', in Austin's example, or 'Amen' in another register) if it is to work. An act of denomination is a *bid* to set the boundaries of that response, in advance, on the basis that it is *not* a performative, but a merely descriptive statement. This is simply *true*, the claim says; simply a description of what is already really *there*, in the world. This identity that we hereby proclaim our intention to protect, the sign says, was already simply there, minding its own business, as it were; all we are saying is that you had better not erode it, if you don't want to provoke our violence – which would thus only be the *counterviolence* of 'self-defence'. Another gable, another pair of masked gunmen, another message: 'We seek nothing but the elementary right implanted in every man [*man*, note]: the right if you are attacked to defend yourself'.

In December 2022, incidentally, at a bus stop beside this last mural, one could read a poster featuring an image of Leo Varadkar, former Irish Taoiseach or PM, quoting a 2018 comment from him regarding potential instability if a Brexit border were imposed on the island of Ireland: 'The possibility of a return to violence is very real'; and above, in smaller lettering: 'Peace or Protocol: it's your decision'. Several of these posters had been taped up in the vicinity (Extramural Activity 2022).

The message of all these images is: we will bring violence down upon you and we will be justified in doing so, because *you* will have started it. It is not ours, but *your* decision; *you* will be responsible for the violence we visit on you. *Now* look what you have made us do.

But what if the people behind the gable wall do *not* all 'share an identity'? The mask on the gable wall faces outwards, but what if it also, in a sense, faces inwards? What if the mask, in a word that resonates in Northern Irish politics, is an *interface* – at once a separation and a conjoining, a combining *in and through the bid to separate*?

You, behind the gable wall, the message says, must go along with the claim staked here, or get out. If you are found to be eroding our identity from the inside, you are a traitor to your community, a Lundy, and will have provoked or called forth the violence we will bring down on you – which is therefore a secondary violence, merely a counterviolence to your primary violence, your act of treachery. You do not properly belong inside the area; we are justified in expelling you, Clearing you out – outside the scope of the gable wall, into another area. An *other* area, the area of the denominational 'others'. Which may be, indeed must be, an adjacent, that is to say, a neighbouring area. But if a *neighbouring* area, then another territory *within the neighbourhood*.

Denomination makes a bid for clearance; a clearance of 'them' from 'our' space, an expulsion of an outside from an inside – as though 'outside' and 'inside' were already there, external to each other, and as though 'inside' is a space of homogeneity, a space where 'we' and *only* 'we' belong. Clearance means partition, segregation into territories (plural) each rigorously exterior to the other; yet each *neighbouring* the other. The politics of denomination, even in the bid to partition one area from another, remains a *politics of neighbourhood*, a relation between neighbours.

Whoever you are, wherever you are, *you have neighbours*. It is tempting to claim that this is the irreducible given of politics, the irreducible political fact. Now how do you get on with them? That may well be the irreducible political question. Certainly 'both Levinas and Gandhi repeatedly used the term 'neighbour' to signify the structure of one's relationship to the other. For both, responsibility arises in the immediacy of the face-to-face relationship with the concrete other before its congealment in a universal idea or thought', as Victoria Tahmasebi-Birgani points out in her compelling analysis of Levinas and the politics of nonviolence (Tahmasebi-Birgani 2014, chap. 4 part 2).

The politics of denomination involves the ordering of the neighbourhood around an interface: the bid to Partition the neighbourhood; the *externalising* of *those* (nameable, or *denominatable*) neighbours and an *internalising* of *these*. This is a bid to externalise *responsibility* for violence, which at the same time is an act of *self-authorisation*. We authorise our own violence in advance on the grounds that we are not responsible for it. You – the denominational other – are those who are threatening the erosion of our identity; *you* are responsible for the original violence, the upsetting of the balance, which our violence merely serves to redress. Our violence is, then, essentially re-taliatory, merely evening up the score; essentially a counterviolence. But counterviolence is not nonviolence. The politics of denomination remains a politics of violence *for which somebody else is to blame.*

Behind our public facing mask of threat, our private space, a space in which it is claimed, we remain essentially peaceable, and which would remain at peace if it were not for this erosion, imposed from the outside. But what if we got a glimpse in behind the mask, behind the gable wall, and discovered that there was violence *on the inside*?

THE RETICLE

The summer of 2022 was marked by a surge in symbolic violence in Northern Ireland. To be sure, there is always a significant amount of symbolic violence, including around the Loyalist bonfires that are lit on the 'Eleventh Night' in July, and on the next day, the main day in the Orange marching season, the Twelfth of July, commemorating the Battle of the Boyne (an international and interdenominational conflict in 1690).

True to form, then, on 11 July 2022, bonfires were lit across Northern Ireland, and while many of them really did appear to be simple community celebrations, some came with additional paraphernalia: the flag of the 'enemy', the Republic of Ireland; election posters of 'enemy' politicians, such as those from Sinn Féin (obviously), from the Irish nationalist SDLP (understandably), but also from perhaps less obviously 'enemy' parties: People Before Profit (a socialist party) and the Alliance Party (two parties that identify as 'Other', rather than Nationalist or Unionist, in the Assembly). It is as though the bonfire-builders can see beneath this cloak of 'Otherness' the 'truth' that they are enemies – and there is only one real enemy: the denominational other.

On one bonfire, effigies of three female politicians were hanged – a symbolic act of violence that was as misogynistic as it was sectarian. Indeed, as this again involving overtly Irish nationalist or Republican politicians, but also a representative of 'Others', in the form of an effigy of Naomi Long of the Alliance Party (O'Reilly 2022). In the logic of the binary reduction machine, if you do not actively take sides with our side you must therefore have taken sides with the other.

Moreover, a number of bonfires featured hand-written signs with a single word, 'KAT'. Many within Northern Ireland will have found this instantly legible, but for those less familiar, this stood for 'Kill All Taigs', with 'Taigs' being a derogatory slang term for Catholics. Other signs read 'All Taigs are Targets', and they were accompanied by the symbol of the cross-hairs of a rifle sight (a 'reticle' in the military jargon). This is not to say the symbolic violence was all one-sided: a little later in the summer, this symbolic, ritualised injunction to the genocide of those of a certain denomination was met with its counterpart, when the slogan 'All Prods [Protestants] Are Targets' appeared painted on a road in County Armagh (Armaghi 2022); incidents of young Irish Republicans chanting 'Ooh Ah, Up the Ra' (the IRA) were broadcast (Hargan 2022); and in April 2023, so-called dissident Republican groups (who had opposed the peace Agreement of 1998) were seen to march in para-military regalia in Creggan, just two months after gunmen associated with one such group had attempted to murder a senior police officer (BBC 2023).

It should be said this was not the first year in which 'KAT' signs had appeared on bonfires, nor should we be too hasty to conclude that the intention was literally to instruct Loyalists to engage in genocide. There was a certain ritual function to these cases of symbolic violence – a certain defiant gesture as much intended to reinforce the loyalty of those within as to warn those outside Loyalist areas. Nevertheless, the violence was there, on display.

Earlier in the year, a certain act of symbolic violence that had not been intended for public display was inadvertently published. A video showing a group of men in an Orange Hall, singing a song mocking the murder of (Catholic) schoolteacher Michaela McAreavey, was live-streamed on a social media account, then leaked from there.

After the song leaked, there was immediate widespread condemnation, and a 'Statement of Apology' was issued, on behalf of two of the men shown in the video, on paper headed by the logo of 'JWB Consultancy'. The letter described the song as a 'vile chant', and quoted a statement from the two men, in which they offered sincere and deep apologies to the family of the murder victim. They are quoted as saying that the video 'was not streamed with the intent of broadcasting any offensive chants. . . . However, whether broadcast or not, the relevant chants should never have been sung either in public or private'.

They go on to add: 'This incident is not reflective of who we are as people', and 'this behaviour is unreflective of the values of the Loyal Orders and the wider unionist and loyalist community'.

Here, on officially headed paper, is a public disavowal of the 'reflective' nature of the violent chant. It does not 'reflect' the values of the community. The question arises, though, should we take this headed letter to be the authoritative word on the matter? If the chant was not meant to be broadcast, was not *deliberately* issued publicly, is there not a case for saying that in fact it precisely *does* reflect 'who they are', in the privacy of their own community space, behind the gable wall, so to speak?

So, which of these utterances – the chant or the official letter – should be taken as authoritative? Who has the authority to speak for, or in the name of the community? Who is the real author? Or can we, from the outside, assume we have the authority to decide this question? To say 'the chant represents the real values of the loyalist community', or 'the letter is right, these were a few isolated individuals who now rightly feel ashamed at having got caught up in this action; it does not reflect the values of the community'? The Orange Order, notably, put out a statement to that effect, claiming the behaviour of the men did 'not reflect the ethos of our organisation' (Grand Orange Lodge of Ireland 2022).

But the men themselves spoke for more than an 'organisation': their claim concerned the 'wider unionist and loyalist community', as if they are being called to respond (and called by another, by someone outside the community in question) on behalf of, in the name of a community-as-a-whole. What does your community – the one for which you are being called to respond, for which you are responsible – really stand over, stand for?

Perhaps we are asking the wrong question in looking for evidence that would allow us to conclude, finally, whether the chant or the letter more accurately reflected, represented the *real* values of the community. Think about the use of the cross-hairs – the *reticle* – in the signs on the bonfires.

This symbol seemed to come into vogue in paramilitary graffiti in the early 2020s. But there is perhaps a sense in which it was there all along. The reticle is, after all, something etched in the glass of the weapon's eyepiece: it not itself out there in the world, but is superimposed on something, or someone, out there, by the person aiming the weapon.

It would be tempting to digress and reflect on this projection of a *cross*, a religious symbol, perhaps recalling the crusades, the righteous warriors, the *Miles Christi*; but here is a shorter digression instead. While thinking about the reticle, I came across the following statement: 'Development of the Mil-Grid Reticle was primarily motivated by the lack of standardization of reticles within the sniper community, as well as the cost incurred in using vendor proprietary reticles' (Kowal 2021). It's hard to know what to say about that phrase: 'The sniper community'.

Let us draw one last thread from the eleventh night bonfires. A Twitter user posted a picture of one of them, complete with Irish flag and images of Nationalist politicians, being lit by a young boy, with the encouragement of his mother, and commented on how tragic it was that sectarianism was being passed to the next generation. Immediately, another Twitter user posted the following reply': Are you genuinely claiming this doesn't go on with the other side of this sh*t [*sic*] show?'

Not only was the first poster not 'genuinely' claiming that: they were not claiming it at all. Nothing in the Tweet mentions 'the other side'. Yet the responder reads this criticism of Loyalist sectarianism as though an explicit *attempt to exonerate 'the other side' was immediately legible.*

There is an almost hallucinatory power to the binary reduction machine of denominational politics. If someone criticises my side, that *immediately* constitutes, without any need for further explanation, an attempt to *exonerate* the other side (even if they are not mentioned). 'The other side' haunts every public utterance that criticises *our* side. It is a phenomenon akin to 'whataboutery', the technique of countering accusations of violence from one's own side by raising an accusation of (preferably even greater) violence from theirs.

This kind of hallucinatory, binary, bonfire logic, however, in which any and every statement is taken fuel for the fire, is not confined to spectral appearances of the *other*. It can also conjure an appearance from *our own* side – calling up an apparent solidity that is not there. Consider the Assembly election in Northern Ireland in May 2022.

The results of this election could be described as seismic, with Sinn Féin becoming the first nationalist party in the century-long history of the region to top the polls. That, alone, counted as a pretty momentous shift; but arguably just as momentous was the success of the Alliance Party, a party that designates neither as nationalist nor unionist but as 'Other'.

Measured by first-preference votes (on my rough count), the electorate is now made up of three minority groupings: the combined votes for Unionist parties came in at around 42 percent; that for Nationalist parties at around 41 percent; and that for Others at 17 percent. We should be wary, though, of treating these results as indicative of the existence of three (denominational) 'communities' (rather than the 'two' of the previously dominant paradigm). We must be careful not to assume that ontology determines allegiance, that identity dictates the political project one must commit to.

Take the example of the result in the Strangford constituency (ANDBC 2023). The hard-line, loyalist-supported Traditional Unionist Voice (TUV) candidate Stephen Cooper did well in the first round, receiving some 5,186 first preference votes – the third highest in a field of twelve candidates (full disclosure: I was one of them, standing for the Green Party in that constituency, but gaining just 831 votes, and being eliminated at the first round as per the rules of Northern Ireland's single transferable vote version of proportional representation).

Throughout successive rounds of transfers, however, Cooper received only a tiny number of additional transferred votes and failed to win one of the five available seats in the constituency. Ulster Unionist Mike Nesbitt, having received fewer first preferences, by contrast, picked up plenty of transfers, sufficient to bypass Cooper and take the seat. Such are the possibilities of the transferrable vote system, which allows voters to rank candidates in order of preference. Clearly Cooper had a support base of some intensity, but it was not extensive or expandable – he did not attract transfers from anyone *outside* that support base.

Nonetheless, for Loyalist activist Jamie Bryson, this did not reflect the 'will of the people', or so he claimed in a Tweet: 'Absolute robbery. The people put their trust in Stephen Cooper and somehow ended up with Mike Nesbitt. By far the worst result for Unionism in this election'.

It comes in at under 147 characters, but there are at least two huge claims here. First, there is the charge of 'robbery'. In the UK context, 'Robbery' is appropriating property belonging to another by force or the threat of force. For Bryson, if we take his claim seriously, Nesbitt's win was a *violent misappropriation*, a usurpation of the will of 'the people' by some external force. We must conclude, following this logic, that 12.7 percent of the people who voted are the people, and 87.3 percent of the people who voted are enemies (or robbers) of the people.

Secondly, although Nesbitt is a Unionist, this was not just a defeat for Unionism, but the 'worst' defeat for Unionism of the day. It is *Unionism* that has been 'robbed' by this win for a Unionist – who must, therefore, *not* be a Unionist, or not a 'proper' one, not *the* proper one. The appropriate 'people' (that is, *denomination*) here is 'Unionism'. Unionism as a people (singular) who 'put their trust' in Cooper – all willing and trusting as one, and all *robbed* as one – having their unified will violently overthrown by some mysterious procedures to do with counting votes.

Bryson *knows* the result of that process (the actual counting of the votes) was *wrong* because he *already knows* what the *right* result should have been: a win for Cooper. In whom 'the people' put their trust. According to this hallucinatory bonfire logic, the people, hovering spectrally off stage somewhere, have been robbed.

This is just one small example of what we are calling the politics of denomination from a single constituency in Northern Ireland. But the idea of an electoral robbery may ring rather larger bells. Here is another example.

'All of us here today do not want to see our election victory stolen by emboldened radical-left Democrats, which is what they're doing. And stolen by the fake news media. Our country has had enough. We will not take it anymore'.

This, unmistakeably, was Donald Trump on 6 January 2021 – a day that marks his last-ditch, violent attempt to cling to office, despite losing the November election. But let us go back to the year this most unprecedented presidency started.

TRUE FAITH

In December of 2016 a man drove to the Comet Ping Pong pizzeria in Washington with a number of guns, one of which he discharged inside the restaurant. His aim was to rescue the children he was convinced were being held there in a child abuse scheme led by Hillary Clinton. Needless to say, the would-be rescuer, Edgar Maddison Welch, left disillusioned, bewildered

– and under arrest. There was no one to rescue; there were no children being held in a basement. There wasn't even a basement.

Let us note straightaway, Welch appears to have acted out of good intentions: he sincerely seemed to think he was going in to rescue children – not to 'own the libs', in an often-used and telling phrase. Also of note, he was equipped not just with a conspiracy narrative, but with an AR-15 assault rifle, as well as a handgun. We will come back to this shortly.

First, though, what of the dog that did not bark? If this story was circulated hundreds of thousands, perhaps millions of times (one 'Pizzagate' video alone was watched over 250,000 times), why was Welch the *only one* to attempt to rescue the children? Could it be that most of the others who circulated the story didn't actually believe it? Or didn't care *whether or not* it was true?

The 'conspiracy narrative' Welch had fallen for is an example of what Russell Muirhead and Nancy L Rosenblum call the 'new conspiracism' (Muirhead and Rosenblum 2019), a relatively recent flood of conspiracy theories – but without the 'theory'. Conspiracy narratives so outlandish and so unsupported either by facts or by any coherent explanatory framework that they should never have picked up any momentum. And yet they do.

The function of these conspiracy narratives, these public assertions of emphatic (but unsupported) claims is not to convey facts, not to describe reality. Such conspiracism is not concerned with explanation, but with encouraging 'action on the basis of claims that are not disproved and are not impossible, and are therefore "true enough"' (Muirhead and Rosenblum 2019, II.3).

The new conspiracism takes effect through bare assertion ('rigged!', 'robbery!'), by insinuation ('Even if it isn't totally true, there's something there') and by repetition (perhaps even the implied repetition that gives them their book title: 'a lot of people are saying . . . ').

To return to the terms we have been using here, the conspiracy narratives that characterise what we could call Trumpism are *performative* rather than descriptive: their function is to inaugurate a repeatable routine of denomination in order to sort 'them' from 'us'.

One could almost start a conspiracy theory of one's own around the name 'Trump': these assertions are not meant to convey truth, in the sense of verifiable or falsifiable fact-claims; they are meant as *trump-cards*, a way of beating your opponent's hand by *fiat*. And they function like a military *trumpet* or bugle call – a *formation call* – summoning the Trumpian faithful to rally round. If you repeat this, you are *one of us*; if you refuse to repeat it, you must either be one of *them* or, worse, a *traitor* to your community.

Trumpian utterances are all about Donne's other truth – not that which stands atop a hill, cragged and steep, but truth as 'being true', or *faithful*, to someone, as in his dazzling, but misogynistic song: Go and Catch a Falling

Star, in which the idea of finding a 'true' (that is, faithful) woman is set alongside a catalogue of never-to-be realised wonders.

Or perhaps more pertinently as in *The Dream*, where both senses of 'true' appear to be played on at once:

> Thou art so true that thoughts of thee suffice
> To make dreams truths, and fables histories.

Trumpian statements are not constative; they are formation calls, all about allegiance, not fact (Donne again: 'none can do Treason to us except one of us two').

For example, recall Trump's non-condemnation of the White-supremacist militia known as the Proud Boys during a presidential debate in 2020: 'Proud Boys, stand back and stand by! But I'll tell you what, somebody's got to do something about Antifa and the left' (Cathey et al. 2020).

'Stand by', not 'stand down'. To stand down a military unit would be to take them off combat-ready posture, to set themselves into a non-hostile mode. To instruct someone to 'stand back and stand by' does not switch off this set towards violence, but maintains it at the ready, just waiting for the command to attack; it instructs someone to stand watching in case their violence should be needed. And of course, for Trump it was needed: hence the immediate pivot to condemn Antifa and the left. Leaving aside the question of whether there is more to Antifa than a name (a useful denomination), rather than condemning the Proud Boys, Trump gives them their orders, and not only in the first part of the sentence. After all, 'somebody' (who might that be?) has got to do 'something' (what might that be?) about the left, if the violence that *originates with them* is to be halted.

Here was a performative utterance in both the theatrical and the Austinian sense. Theatre, in that his 'condemnation' (if that is what it was), was so perfunctory as to appear intended only for show; performative in the sense of the issuing of an *order*, a bid to *authorise* violence against those held to be disrupting the 'proper order', *even if it did not appear in the form of an order* as commonly understood (call it the 'turbulent priest' bid).

Little wonder the Proud Boys 'pledged allegiance' to him that night (Collins and Zadrozny 2020). Which did not stop Trump from denying knowing them the next day (Cathey et al. 2020).

Anyone who had been reading the New York Times, Washington Post, or any of a plethora of international newspapers, let alone someone who is supposed to get daily intelligence briefings from America's top security officials, knew quite enough about this white supremacist organisation to be getting on with. This goes beyond plausible deniability: Mr Trump has gone right over into *im*plausible deniability. But the implausibility *does not prevent his* *utterances from taking effect*. To hold to 'Truth', in this sense, is to believe in Trump, however implausibly winding the path he carves out. He is so 'true' as to 'make dreams truths, and fables histories'. We did not need to wait for Trump to launch his 'Truth Social' rival to Twitter, where one does not 'tweet' but 'truth', to know this about him.

An unprecedented presidency it may be, but there are precedents for this president. Jason Stanley, discussing fascism, reminds us that Mussolini was quite open that he was projecting a myth. In a 1922 speech, he said: 'We have created our myth. The myth is a faith, a passion. It is not necessary for it to be a reality. . . . Our myth is the nation, our myth is the greatness of the nation! And to this myth, this greatness, which we want to translate into a total reality, we subordinate everything' (Stanley 2018, 5).

The order of (factual) belief ('it is not necessary for it to be a reality') is *subordinated* to an order of (passionate) faith. The Myth is back-projected as that which is to come ('we want to translate'). Translated into what? Not just a reality, a *total* reality. To this, everything is to be 'subordinated', put under ordinance, made to conform to the proper order, as ordered by the higher authority which is the nation embodied. The nation (the denomination) is embodied in the leader who will finally break with the old order and take power out of the hands of a privileged elite and give it back to 'the people', as a whole, as a totality. The leader not just as a representative, but as *the people's avatar*, an embodiment of something spiritual, an *incarnation*.

There are clear parallels between this approach and the 2017 speech Trump gave at an Inauguration he himself declared to have a very special meaning, in that it did not just represent the peaceful transfer of power (aside: those were the days), but a transfer of power from Washington, DC, 'back to you, the people'. (Trump 2017). Or again: 'January 20th, 2017 will be remembered as the day the people became the rulers of this nation again'.

Leaving aside the peculiarity of the idea of 'the people' as rulers of 'the nation' (does he mean the State? Or is this a significant scission between 'people' and 'nation'?), the people are here set off in opposition to 'politicians', Washington, the 'establishment'. The Washington politicians, Trump tells us, a 'small group in our Nation's Capital' have 'reaped the rewards' while 'the people have borne the cost'.

Let us interject here, almost scandalously, that Trump is *almost* right: a relatively small number of people *have* been reaping the rewards, while a larger number of people have been bearing a disproportionate share of the burden. But rather than subject the dynamics of the system to critical, democratic scrutiny, Trump uses the occasion to divide the population into two mutually exclusive, conflicting *denominations*, in a bid to subordinate one to the other. A gap is opened here between the 'group of politicians', otherwise here named 'Washington' or 'the establishment' on the one side, and 'the people' on the other – two separate entities. Not just any people, either: a 'righteous people', with 'just and reasonable demands'.

It is fascinating to see a self-proclaimed billionaire businessman informing the general US public that it is 'Washington politicians' (not corporate investors?) who have prospered while the factories shut down. Some of those corporate investors may have been appalled at Trump and at the potential damage he looked set to inflict on the social fabric; some of them may have withdrawn their support or actively supported his opponents. Yet it is not hard to imagine some, however they may have scorned him in private, feeling relieved that Mr Trump's concern for the 'Mothers and children in poverty' (not fathers, note: *mothers* and *children*), for the rusting factories, drugs, gangs, crime, would not lead to scrutiny of *their* role, *their* empowerment through the system that produced such suffering, but to anger against the 'foreign usurper'. Still easier to imagine them using the media platforms they owned to vigorously wave Old Glory and amplify the idea that 'American carnage' must be caused by someone or something 'unAmerican'. No need to believe a word of what Mr Trump says to benefit from his political project. No need to worry if, rather than combining forces to change the gearing of the system, the least well off were turned against each other by denomination; no need to concern yourself if, as a result, a few of those dots stop moving, in Harry Lime's chilling phrase, especially if you could cash in at, say, $20,000 a time.

It is this 'American carnage' that Mr Trump claimed, 'stops right here and stops right now'. It's quite a declaration. Quite a decree, even; and Mr Trump uses the word, issuing what he calls a 'new decree. . . . From this day forward, it's going to be only America first. America first'.

So, what has prevented America from coming first? What has toppled America from the greatness he promises to *restore* when he 'makes America great *again*'? The ravages of (unAmerican) other countries, for one. 'We must protect our borders from the ravages of other countries making our products, stealing our companies, and destroying our jobs'. Again, not shareholders and CEOs offshoring? Their quiet sense of relief must have grown by the sentence.

The idea of the 'ravages' of other countries here perhaps hints at a claim that Trump made while on the campaign trail. 'We can't continue to allow China to rape our country, and that's what we're doing' (Wilson 2016). This is not just an accusation of violence, but of sexual violence, an issue to which we will return.

Having established that the problem is what in another register might be called the 'foreign usurper', Trump sets out the basis (the 'bedrock') for the solution:

At the bedrock of our politics will be a total allegiance to the United States of America, and through our loyalty to our country, we will rediscover our loyalty to each other. When you open your heart to patriotism, there is no room for prejudice. . . . When America is united, America is totally unstoppable. . . . A new national pride will stir our souls, lift our sights, and heal our divisions.

I will relate to my neighbour not directly but via the (denomi)nation. If each of us does that all will be well – our divisions will be 'healed' and we will be 'united'. This unity will make America unstoppable, will not only restore America to greatness, but even drive out 'prejudice' – thus ushering in an end to racism, Trump presumably thinks, or pretends to. How is this transformation to be effected? Through 'total allegiance'. If you want to share in this greatness, this unified, prejudice-free America, capable of defending itself against the ravages of foreigners, all you have to do is 'open your heart,' not to Jesus or *Pater Noster, qui es in caelis*, but, through patriotism, to one of his substitutes, *Patria Nostra*. It is through this total allegiance to the United States that we will discover our relations to each other will be put back in the proper order, and divisions will be healed.

So, when Trump, towards the end of his speech, addresses every American, whether in the urban sprawl of Detroit or the windswept plains of Nebraska, saying, 'You will never be ignored again', there is an unspoken condition: 'so long as you give total allegiance to the Patria'.

It is as clear an example of a call to combine denominationally as one could wish for. Your route to greatness, your route out of being marginalised and ignored, your route to empowerment (or rather, to a *sense* of empowerment) lies through identification with the unitary denominational entity to which you are said to belong. Attempt to go via any other route, and you are showing disloyalty. You are no longer faced with a choice between this or that political project, but a choice of whether to betray your country. Trump's entire project – to Make America Great Again – is built on 'total allegiance', loyalty, faith. And it is a loyalty we will *re*discover ('we will rediscover our loyalty to each other').

The retrospective prefix is at work in the Inaugural address as elsewhere in Trump's discourse. It appears twice in the second sentence: 'We, the citizens of America, are now joined in a great national effort to rebuild our country and to restore its promise for all of our people'. Or there is the word 'again', as in: 'January 20th 2017, will be remembered as the day the people became the rulers of this nation again', or: 'You will never be ignored again'. Or, repeatedly in the peroration:

'Together, We Will Make America Strong Again. We Will Make America Wealthy Again. We Will Make America Proud Again. We Will Make America Safe Again. And, Yes, Together, We Will Make America Great Again'.

The retrojection of some former greatness, before a catastrophe, and in anticipation of a restoration, is a common trope, of course (one need only think of the biblical arc: paradise, paradise lost, paradise regained through redemption, notably involving a Messiah figure). But it is arguably fundamental for the kind of denominational politics we are looking at here – and not just in Trump's America.

BLOOD LINES

In a speech given by President Erdoğan to mark National Sovereignty and Children's Day, 23 April 2021 (all his speeches are, helpfully, available on the website of the presidency of the Republic of Türkiye), he makes the claim that 'sovereignty unconditionally belongs to the nation', and says that 'parliament, which has gone through putsches, juntas, attempts of tutelage and terror attacks and which was bombed on July 15, 2016 by FETO-member traitors, will continue to exist forever as the embodiment of the national will' (Erdoğan 2021a).

Already we can see the elements being combined. There is the now-familiar idea of the unitary sovereignty of a unitary people, enduring through time, assailed, but unbowed, by violence, including by that of traitors. And not only does he express these themes here, but he returns to them with a curious regularity. Two months later, in June 2021, in a National Security Statement, he speaks of the 'activities and operations successfully, determinedly and unwaveringly carried out both at home and abroad against all kinds of dangers and threats, particularly the PKK/KCK-PYD/YPG, FETO and DAESH terrorist organizations, which target our national unity and solidarity as well as our survival' (Erdoğan 2021b). Here are the internal-external violent threats to national unity and even existence again.

Another two months or so on, in a Message for Victory Day, 30 August 2021 he speaks of a 'homeland forged with the blood of martyrs', our 'centuries-old glorious history', and 'our fight against proxy terrorist organization that threaten our country's unity and integrity'. The 'self' which is being defended against the violence of others here begins to get a lineage. Indeed, in a paradoxical move, he claims to be able to put a date on the birth of the 'eternal' homeland: 'These lands, which were made our homeland in Malazgirt in 1071, were once again acknowledged as our eternal homeland with this victory that our nation won [in 1922 over Greek forces] despite all kinds of hardship and impossibilities' (Erdoğan 2021c). Erdoğan claims a continuous millennium of 'national unity', reasserted in 1922, and ritually celebrated annually.

Yet another two months on, in October 2021, Erdoğan's Message on Republic Day, wishes 'Allah's mercy upon our august martyrs who entrusted these lands to us at the cost of their lives', and claims that 'We as the nation will firmly hold onto our unity, solidarity and brotherhood, which are our biggest assurances, and endeavour to achieve our cause of a great and strong Turkey. The steely will, which carried the national struggle to victory and brought our Republic into existence, will continue to be our guide in this sacred struggle' (Erdoğan 2021d). The light of the past will show the way to the restoration of a 'great, strong' Turkey, provided our will is 'steely' enough.

Perhaps the most consequential of these recent denominational projects was launched in February 2022, when Vladimir Putin ordered his troops into Ukraine. At the time of writing the situation is still unfolding, so these can be no more than some tentative, provisional thoughts. But it is clear already that there are processes of denomination at work on both sides – indeed, processes contributing to the projection of the situation as being about a conflict between 'two sides'. Which of course, in many ways it now is: war has, among other things, the real effect of dividing out and polarising neighbours, by way of an intense binary reduction machine.

But this is not a matter of two *already* constituted Nations, in all their capitalised and monolithic glory, already being there, and *then* going to war. Rather, this is about processes *calling neighbours to combine in certain distinct ways*; being *set towards* each other differently; and if we focus more on the processes than on the entities, we stand a better chance of working out the best way to intervene to move the dynamics towards nonviolence.

In terms of denomination, Ukraine's nationhood is a rallying cry around which people are combining for a political project: to defend their territory (and indeed their democracy) against the Russian invasion. This works, and is even moving, in more than one sense – and if there are dangers to that movement, this is hardly the time to highlight them, given that there are far more massively present dangers and acts of violence going on. Later (though not much later) we will have to think about democracy beyond denomination, but in the kinetic heat of battle there are doubtless other urgent matters to attend to. Indeed, as a matter of principle, to be explored later, to condemn the violence of one project without taking full account of the violence of the other would not be to condemn violence as such – and thus, *at all*.

Let us rather examine Putin's approach, as expressed in numerous statements both before and after the invasion. In a lengthy article written the year before the invasion, Putin set out his thoughts on what he called the 'historical unity of Russians and Ukrainians' (Putin 2021). Russia and Ukraine are 'parts of what is essentially the same historical and spiritual space', he says, and any division between them is partly the result of 'deliberate efforts by those forces that have always sought to undermine our unity' and to 'pit the parts of a single people against one another'.

How is he so sure? He has the warranty of history, indeed of a certain heritage, to back his claims: 'Russians, Ukrainians, and Belarusians are all descendants of Ancient Rus', bound together by one language, economic ties, the 'rule of the princes of the Rurik dynasty, and – after the baptism of Rus – the Orthodox faith'. Where 'descendants' appears to call upon a common genetic or family inheritance, the idea of the language and especially the idea of the Orthodox *faith* leaves open the possibility that this unity is a cultural or spiritual matter. Indeed, the spiritual is made explicit: 'The spiritual choice made by St. Vladimir, who was both Prince of Novgorod and Grand Prince of Kiev, still largely determines our affinity today'.

As Timothy Snyder notes in his remarkable audiobook on Ukraine (he seems to have conceived it after the invasion in February 2022 and recorded it over the space of a couple of days in May), Putin picks a single moment, and a single set of actors, out of a fluid, complex, plural and distant past and draws a single, direct line between it and the present, effectively laying claim to 'some kind of ancient lineage' that 'smooths out all the apparent difficulties, becomes a kind of substitute for carrying out policy in the present, becomes a way of not talking about the future at all' (Snyder 2022).

But of course, somewhere along that line, given that Russia and Ukraine are currently separate, the true 'descendants of Ancient Rus' must have been dispossessed. Robbed, even: 'One fact is crystal clear: Russia was robbed, indeed'. If so, someone else must have committed this crime – after all, one can hardly rob oneself. And sure enough, there they are, the outsiders: 'the idea of Ukrainian people as a nation separate from the Russians started to form and gained ground among the Polish elite. . . . Since the late 19th century, the Austro-Hungarian authorities had latched onto this narrative' and so on. Right down to the deployment of NATO infrastructure in Ukraine, there is always some foreign usurper to blame. Alongside internal enemies of course, 'those who have today given up the full control of Ukraine to external forces'.

There is also a series of inversions in Putin's article: in 1917 Germany and Austria Hungary are accused of having used 'a pretext for occupation'; or 'Ukrainization was often imposed on those who did not see themselves as Ukrainians'; leaders 'began to mythologize and rewrite history . . . and refer to the period when Ukraine was part of the Russian Empire and the Soviet Union as an occupation'; and perhaps most tellingly: 'Radicals and neo-Nazis were open and more and more insolent about their ambitions. They were indulged by both the official authorities and local oligarchs, who robbed the people of Ukraine and kept their stolen money in Western banks'. In each case, simply change the names (Russianisation imposed on those who do not see themselves as Russian, and so on) and these charges could be levelled at Putin himself.

Again, in a speech given the day before he launched the attack, Putin deploys a whole range of the tropes we have been looking at throughout (Putin 2022a). Firstly, he claims the violence originates with the other, speaking of 'fundamental threats which irresponsible Western politicians created for Russia'. There are the now familiar inversions: 'everything it [the "dominant power", NATO or the US] regards as useful is presented as the ultimate truth and forced on others regardless of the cost, abusively and by any means available. Those who refuse to comply are subjected to strong-arm tactics' (Putin accuses his enemies of exactly what he is doing); or again: 'they [Western powers] prefer to avoid speaking about international law, instead emphasising the circumstances which they interpret as they think necessary'.

There is the projection of a monolithic, hostile, and deceitful opponent: '[t]herefore, one can say with good reason and confidence that the whole so-called Western bloc formed by the United States in its own image and likeness is, in its entirety, the very same "empire of lies"'.

Note, it is Putin here who is fighting *against* an Empire. And of course, there is the projection of a monolithic, sovereign, natal (in this case, *paternal*) Russia. Putin says: 'the fight we are waging is the fight for our sovereignty and the future of our country and our children. We will fight for the right to be and remain Russia. The courage and fortitude of our soldiers and officers, the faithful defenders of the Fatherland, should inspire us'.

The *right to be Russia*. The 'We' doing the fighting is already ontologically fused into the monolithic entity in essence, as of right. Now we just have to bring it into *existence* by (violently) changing the facts on the ground. Note, too, the reference to 'faithfulness'.

This brings the two monolithic blocs – Russia and its enemies – together in conflict: 'They immediately tried to put the final squeeze on us, finish us off, and utterly destroy us. This is how it was in the 1990s and the early 2000s, when the so-called collective West was actively supporting separatism and gangs of mercenaries in southern Russia'.

He begins to project an internalised enemy: 'they sought to destroy our traditional values and force on us their false values that would erode us, our people from within'. Recall the 'erosion of our identity' on the gable wall in Northern Ireland. This is developed in a later speech, after the fighting has got under way. The figure of the traitor, already hinted at here, will be projected in lurid technicolour:

> But any nation, and even more so the Russian people, will always be able to distinguish true patriots from scum and traitors and will simply spit them out like an insect in their mouth, spit them onto the pavement. I am convinced that

a natural and necessary self-detoxification of society like this would strengthen our country, our solidarity and cohesion and our readiness to respond to any challenge (Putin 2022b).

The reference to insects is chillingly reminiscent of the sort of language of 'vermin' one deploys when one is bent on ethnic cleansing or genocide: think of the radio broadcasts calling Tutsis cockroaches in Rwanda in 1994; or the Nazi propaganda films juxtaposing images of Jews with rats. If I begin to 'verminise' my neighbours like this, it is in a bid to exempt myself from responsibility for the violence I am about to bring down on them.

The same logic operates in Putin's preparation for a purge: 'self-detoxification' back-projects a 'pure' self into which toxins have been, at some point, by some agent, introduced; a self that one then has to set about detoxifying. This is preparation for a cleansing, a Clearance of the neighbourhood of the 'wrong' kind of people: the very being-there of this 'kind of' person is a toxin, regardless of what they have actually done or not done. All that remains is for someone in authority to *name* them, or rather, *denominate* them, name their 'kind', and those who are true to the pure people will know what to do.

The urge to purify goes hand in hand with a belief in a prelapsarian unity disrupted at some point in history by the catastrophic intervention of a foreign usurper. And this is here too, underlying demands for present 'unity'. In Putin's case, the moment of the Fall is the moment of the break-up of the Soviet Union. *Greater Russia*, in Putin's projection, already *properly* includes that which was broken off, that of which Russia has been robbed, not least including Ukraine (*Little* Russia), the border around which therefore dissolves, as it were, even before it is crossed by the tanks launched by his violent project. To return to the speech from immediately before the invasion (Putin 2022a): 'I would like to emphasise again that Ukraine is not just a neighbouring country for us. It is an inalienable part of our own history, culture, and spiritual space. These are our comrades, those dearest to us – not only colleagues, friends and people who once served together, but also relatives, people bound by blood, by family ties'.

If you are going to launch an all-out assault then, presumably the target will not be those 'colleagues, friends, relatives'. Indeed, Russian troops were alleged by Russian political commentator Sergei Markov, at the beginning of the invasion, to have been given orders not to assault the inhabitants of the cities they were supposedly about to 'liberate'. The 'population of a fraternal country', he said, 'has nothing to fear from the Russian army'. But what if those inhabitants turn out not to be so fraternal, not to want to be so 'liberated'? This is where the Nazis come in. 'I think that most subunits of the Ukrainian Armed Forces will surrender their weapons. Part of them will continue to offer resistance. Those are the neo-Nazi military subunits'. There is the routine of identification Markov offers to anyone who will listen, on day two of the invasion: if they fight back, they are, *ipso facto*, neo-Nazis. Neo-Nazis who, according to this logic, must be 'abnormal': 'If everything proceeds normally, a process of disarmament will begin. Wherever normality does not prevail, those groupings will be destroyed' (Plokhy 2023, chap. 7).

Or as Putin himself put it the day before the invasion:

> Ukrainian authorities . . . began by building their statehood on the negation of everything that united us, trying to distort the mentality and historical memory of millions of people, of entire generations living in Ukraine. It is not surprising that Ukrainian society was faced with the rise of far-right nationalism, which rapidly developed into aggressive Russophobia and neo-Nazism (Putin 2022a).

But what of actual Russian people, in all their multiplicity? Clearly some do rally to the denominational flag, and wholeheartedly repeat the routines; others have a more ambivalent response; still others actively oppose Putin's project. Those who protest are arrested, brutalised, silenced. Those whose ambivalence results in silence, *ipso facto* give clearance to Putin's project. Nevertheless, the very need to arrest and silence protestors gives the lie to the claim that 'Russia' is unanimously behind the invasion.

Boris Johnson, speaking in Russian, to Russians, tried to pick up on this just after the war was launched: 'I do not believe this war is in your name' (Badshah 2022). One can understand and even applaud the sentiment, but he got it slightly wrong: that's *precisely* what Putin was doing: launching a war *in the name of* the 'Greater Russian People'. This, among other things, is a war of *denomination*.

Putin presents Russians as being 'all of one mind'; claims, in the name of 'the Russian People' that 'this is what Russia thinks' – regardless of what *actual Russians* think. If actual Russians think differently, it is they who are held to be wrong, *not the denomination being projected*. Hence the propaganda and the law against criticising, or even mentioning, the war. Of course, this means Putin is not quite 'regardless' of what actual Russians think: he is actively, and apparently with quite some success, trying to *push it into their psyches* that Russia Says Yes to the war – apologies: the 'special military operation', as Russians are obliged to call it, on pain of imprisonment.

TRANSPHOBIA

Restoration, redemption, requires not just that you show allegiance (though you must: but it *can* be just for show), but that you put your violence at the disposal of the denomination. If Russia – or America, or Brexit Britain, or the Unionist Community, or whatever Nation or denomination – *is* to be great again, and if you are to take part in this greatness, then you must protect it not just from those overseas enemies, but also from potential traitors, from enemies within. Protestors, or the media, for example, or the judiciary, or the 'Washington elite' are declared (performatively, in both senses) to be enemies of the people.

Note, defeating these enemies will be a matter of *self-defence* – the violence originates with the other. But is there not a contradiction here? If we have been robbed of our greatness, then 'we' are victims (that is, weak, passive); yet at the same time, we must be strong enough to be capable of self-defence, of fighting back, of rising to victory and a 'glorious destiny'.

Ah, but luckily, we have a strong man, one not afraid to fight on our behalf. We have a Putin, or an Erdoğan or a Trump. Recall one of many references to fighting from Trump's speech on 6 January 2021: 'And we fight. We fight like hell. And if you don't fight like hell, you're not going to have a country anymore', which echoed his claim in his Inaugural: 'I will fight for you with every breath in my body'.

'We' have to get tough, harden up, stop being soft, or we lose everything. The idea of 'hardening' crops up in rhetoric of the right across the board. We must fight 'hard', we must 'harden' borders, we must even 'harden' schools: this is the preferred remedy – preferred to any attempt at gun control – on the right, after school shootings (Wagner and Johnson 2018).

In the phrase cited by Amy Shuffleton in an article on masculine honour and gun violence, it is as if we 'have to get our mancard reissued' (Shuffleton 2015). The phrase itself comes from advertising copy for one of the guns used in the shooting at the Sandy Hook elementary school in Newtown, Connecticut, in 2012, which took the lives of twenty schoolchildren and six educators. Anyone who bought the gun, a Bushmaster XM-15 semi-automatic rifle, was told: 'consider your mancard reissued'. Shuffleton notes that this kind of construction of masculine honour occurs through the 'provision of social scripts' that led the Sandy Hook shooter 'to respond with violence'.

There is that prefix again: *re*-spond; *re*-issued: manhood, it turns out, can be gained and lost in this game of cards, and those who have not bought this gun, or, more generally, *who are afraid to use violence*, must have once *had it*, but have now clearly *lost it* – or rather, have had it *taken from them* by others.

It is perhaps this idea of having something that was ours taken from 'us' by force, by others, and the need to redress the balance, to retaliate, that brings all these threads together, and does so here in the name of a kind of masculinity. Think back to Trump's comment on China: 'we' have been 'raped', have had sexual violence directed against us. Think, too, of his warning that Mexican 'rapists' when he launched his campaign for the presidency, a speech in which he also warned that the Chinese 'kill us', adding that 'China has our jobs. Mexico has our jobs', and warning about Islamic terrorism for good measure (Phillips 2017).

The valorisation of a 'hard' version of masculinity has its precedent elsewhere too. Jason Stanley illustrates the point by citing, among other documents, both the so-called Hutu Ten Commandments, published in Kangura, the Hutu power newspaper, in 1990, and the 'Fundamental Law of Hungary' promulgated by Victor Orbán in 2010. In both cases the first three clauses are about gender and family roles. In the Hutu case, the first declares anyone a traitor who marries a Tutsi woman. In Hungarian case, the first clause says, 'Hungary shall protect the institution of marriage', and the second 'Hungary shall encourage the commitment to have children'. A later clause prohibits abortion – foreshadowing the overturning of *Roe v. Wade* in the United States in 2022; and in 2021 Orban passed a law prohibiting the dissemination of content on homosexuality or gender transition in schools (Thoreson 2022).

Indeed, a certain version of gender politics saturates the sort of discourse of Empire and enslavement we looked at in the preceding chapter. 'If men's imperial work was to 'discover', to explore, to conquer, and dispossess others,' says Catherine Hall, 'women's was to reproduce the race' (Hall 2004, 47). Moreover, this interpretation of gender was projected onto 'races', themselves discursively constructed – denominated as already being there, with a list of essential characteristics (Levine 2004). For example: 'In the period after 1857 the British mapped the races of India and contrasted 'martial races' with the non-martial . . . the Islamic Pathans were favourably compared with the intelligent, educated, but effeminate Bengali middle class' (Hall 2004, 74). Recall, too, the effigies of women politicians hanged on the bonfires of Northern Ireland in 2022.

Given the 'cultural script', the right routine, of fear of violation, the muscular avatar – a Trump, an Erdoğan – steps forward and says: we have been softened, feminised, rendered impotent. We were once vigorous, virile, but we have been emasculated; and now I am calling you ('men') to step up, *man-up*, harden the borders, be ready to offer your violence to defend the borders (and 'your' women), against internal traitors and the ravages of foreign enemies. Against those who would *cross borders* – of whatever sort.

To get a sense of how different kinds of borders can be interrelated, let us return to the above question: how can 'we' be at once vulnerable and passive enough to have been 'ravaged', and at the same time strong and great enough to defend ourselves, defeat our enemies?

One way to resolve the contradiction is to go through a gendered division of labour. It is the 'women and children', whom '*we*' (this time, the mancard-bearing members of the community) must protect. After all, it is not we mancard-holders, we *men* who are vulnerable, you understand; we put on this paramilitary regalia and take up these semi-automatic rifles not to protect *ourselves*, but 'our' *women and children* – or, better, 'our-women-and-children' – who need defended, who are weak, soft and vulnerable, and who are bound together in this hyphenated, singular *denomination*. And they *have to remain so* if this whole routine is to work.

We do not only have to harden the borders around our Nation, then: we also have to make sure the border 'between the genders' is not crossed either. It should not come as a surprise that the avatars of the denomination have become more muscular – metaphorically if not literally, though there are plenty of examples of the latter in the gym-inflated bodies of Ulster Loyalists like Johnny Adair, and even in the muscularisation of superheroes (compare the respective Supermen of Christopher Reeve and Henry Cavill). 'Hollywood', remarks Maria Teresa Hart, 'is hovering dangerously close to the uncanny valley, a place of eerie, manufactured humanity' (Hart 2016). Or certainly of manufactured 'femininity' and 'masculinity' – and ne'er the twain shall meet.

In a sense, then, *transphobia* is at the very core of the MAGA movement, and its equivalents elsewhere. The MAGA movement cannot tolerate border-crossers. Everything, and everyone, has to go through the binary reduction machine: you must either be this or that; how could you possibly be a bit of both? Or neither? Or *other*? 'We' do not have the routines, the algorithms, to handle that.

Thus, the attack on the Twin Towers, the penetration of the Nation's defences, made visible a vulnerability that had to be repudiated, preferably violently. The subsequent failure to achieve what was claimed in Afghanistan and Iraq – remember the woefully premature claims of 'mission accomplished' – arguably set the scene for a turn to the strong man who would restore not only America's 'hard' national borders, but also American *virility*, by authorising more effective forms of retaliatory violence, and more violent forms of 'self-defence'. And this would extend to all the ways in which 'foreign usurpers' had exploited 'our' weakness, our indulgence, our effeminacy, not just in terms of terrorist attacks, but also in terms of trade. After all, *foreigners*, with the assistance of their treacherous domestic allies, the 'globalists', the rootless cosmopolitans and citizens of nowhere, the 'skinny kids with funny names' (funny, *Islamic* sounding names like, say, Barak Hussein Obama, who may or may not have been natural-born Americans – and let's not even raise the question of *race*), were ripping 'us' off (or, in some cases, 'raping' us, as Trump explicitly said).

An overlapping weft of misogyny, homophobia and xenophobia is at work in these routines: 'we' ('men') are not supposed to be vulnerable to penetration; 9/11 was a double blow because not only did we suffer the material injury of the attack, but there was a symbolic humiliation involved, and that bound up with a particular construction of gender roles. To be a woman and to have been violated is, according to this logic, a blow; but at least it does not violate the *essential passivity* of your gender role. To be a man and be violated is both a material injury and an affront, a humiliation, because you are supposed to be the active one, not vulnerable to this kind of penetration. One must fight back to restore 'honour' and to restore the proper domestic order. We'll even let a few women do some of the fighting as long as it is this domestic order they are fighting to restore.

In response to the violence 'coming in from the outside', a Donald Trump puts out a formation call: if you belong to this (denomi)nation, you will rally round; you share in the state of having-been-violated, so you must get your mancard back and fight, fight hard to expel everyone who, because of their essence, their essential foreignness, should not be here pulling the strings, distorting and tearing at the social fabric, penetrating and disrupting the proper order, the proper borders. If the problem is the foreign usurper and the traitors who let them in (the Lundies), the solution is the authorised violence of the purge. It is not hard to see how attractive, how exciting, how invigorating and 'empowering' this sort of call could feel to people who have felt, and indeed who have actually been, disempowered.

But this is to misdiagnose the problem, and thus mis-prescribe the remedy.

THE CRANK ECONOMY

Let us go back to Clinton's cranes. The promise of Thatcher and Reagan, heirs to Smith, was that a growing national economy would automatically increase wealth and well-being for everybody (the 'whole nation'). They implemented policies designed to direct the cogs of the economy vertically, cranking wealth up, with a greater proportion going to those at the top (newly denominated as 'wealth-creators') by means of corporate tax breaks, publicly funded infrastructure at the disposal of the private sector, and perhaps above all, relaxed rules about where investors can register their residence, and companies their profits, in order to keep prying public eyes aways from the whole thing. At the same time, power was taken away from those at the base of the economic pyramid through union-busting legislation (significantly, unions were denominated as the 'enemy within'), privatisation, and precarity. Empowering the so-called wealth creators meant disempowering those with less wealth precisely by making it harder for them to *combine*. But for their *own good*, of course.

The idea was that, once the 'barriers' to trade had been removed, through the invisible hand, the market would increase the wealth of the nation *as a whole* – which would therefore benefit all. The Clinton-Blair adaptation of this economic model said the invisible hand of the market had manifestly failed to lift those at the bottom, but all that was needed was for it to be *supplemented* by the visible hand of government. If we kept the cranes up, kept the cranks turning in the market economy, we would be able to generate enough of a surplus to *redistribute* to those at the bottom, who might *not* have benefitted automatically. But we've got to grow the pie if we're to have enough to trickle down – or some suitably vague metaphor, however mixed, of that sort.

The problem with building an economy on the model of a crane, however, is that wealth is power, and power is relative. To get the purchase to crank an ever-greater proportion of wealth and power up vertically to the top relative to the bottom, more and more pressure has to be put down at ground level, on the lowest paid workers, on the least wealthy, and even on the living planet itself. Keep turning the crank, and eventually, something has got to give.

In 2008, it did just that. Where the VOC had abstracted 'the corporation' from any given ship or crate, today's financiers and bankers had so refined the process of abstract 'wealth creation' that they could spin out, and crank up, unimaginably complicated, rarefied, and *lucrative* instruments out of *debt* (Tooze 2018), though arguably this was merely a refinement of instruments that had been invented long before, and used extensively in relation to the global south (Graeber 2011).

If you are going to make money out of debt, though, somebody has to bear the debt burden. Some *body*. Some neighbour, trying to meet the basic, bodily, human need for shelter, the need to have a home to go to. *Which* bodies, *whose* bodies, was a matter of indifference to the market, where the eyes that watch you take no account of your existence. Any body will do. In passing, believers in the 'great replacement theory' might do better to consider how quickly the crank economy will replace them with another, cheaper, functioning unit, than keep their attention fixed on a projected 'White Race'.

But to keep cranking out the instruments, there still had to be bodies; so, when there were not enough bodies with capacity enough left to get themselves into still more debt, the whole abstract tower of wealth came crashing down. And when it did, governments rushed not to rescue the bodies, but to bail out the bankers – and to *get the crank turning again, as fast as possible, with the gearing all still pointed in the same direction.*

On top of the suffering caused by the crash, itself coming on top of strains and suffering that had been accumulating for years, policy decisions were taken to get purchase for the invisible crank of the market in the form of austerity, public service cuts, precarious contracts, permits for (over)exploiting the natural world – the pressure at the bottom.

After all, if I as a 'wealth creator' don't like the regulations in one jurisdiction, there are others to choose from. Places where the governments have the power (are ready to use their monopoly of violence) to keep proper *order*. 'There's a reason why the wizard has such a strange capacity to create money out of nothing,' says David Graeber: 'Behind him, there's a man with a gun' (Graeber 2011, 364).

Rather than an invisible hand distributing largesse liberally and equitably across the whole population (as the idea of the 'wealth of the nation' can be taken to imply) the invisible gearing of the neoliberal model cranks power and wealth upwards and offshore to the 'wealth creators', leaving the bodies of their neighbours so far below that they come to be seen as so many dots, more and more of which 'stop moving', by way of what Case and Deaton call 'deaths of despair' – suicide, drug or alcohol overdoses (Case and Deaton 2020), if not industrial accidents and the diseases of poverty.

There are, of course, those who actually do benefit from the gearing of the cranks, but this must be read *relatively*. There may be some whose income nominally or even substantively increases, and yet who remain in a precarious, marginalised, *relatively* powerless position within the hierarchy of the crank economy. And there are some who rise through the ranks, or inherit from those who did so; those who see their wealth, which is to say their share of power, increase. Needless to say, they may well use the ever-increasing means at their disposal, from the aforementioned media ownership to the ability to fund entire political parties dedicated to maintaining the functioning of the crank, in a bid to ensure that others do not *combine forces to dismantle the gearing*, reassembling it to redirect the flows more horizontally.

This is not to say there is some shadowy conspiracy, or some moustachioed cabal of rich villains drawing up secret plots in smoke-filled rooms. First of all, there is little need: the whole thing is done more or less openly and published in editorials and reports from well-funded thinktanks (even if, admittedly, they try to keep the sources of that funding out of the view of prying democratic eyes). Some even ask for, and receive, our votes – after all, we are not just talking about money when we talk of the crank economy: money is power, but not the only form of power. Secondly, the idea of the 'shadowy elite' plays straight into the sort of routines deployed by Trump and others: it projects a (convenient) villain, somewhere over *there*, upon whom we are called to train our reticles, instead of combining, for all our differences, in examining, dismantling, and redirecting the gearing of the whole system, beginning *here*, *now*.

Here, where there *are* those who do suffer, in real, bodily ways, the downward pressures that keep the crank economy turning over – among others, the cuts, the frozen wages, the precarious contracts, the housing shortage, the opioid crisis, and an increased exposure to domestic violence that goes with increasing inequality (Silva 2019; Yapp and Pickett 2019). It is into this scene of real, bodily pain that the avatar of the denomination steps with a promise to put things right, a promise to correct an injustice, redress the unfairness of it all, the promise of a *sense of empowerment*. A promise to make you *feel* great again – first via a process of *identification* with something *great*: the Nation, or Community, or Race: the Denomination. How dare anyone stand in your – in *our* – way? And here is step two: the identification of an enemy. The avatar of denomination puts out a call to the 'little guy', the ordinary, 'salt-of-the-earth, hardworking families': your way of life is under threat from an entity that remains exterior to 'us': the liberal, or 'globalist' elite and their representatives (and here fill in everyone from union 'barons' to leaders of fairly middle of the road social democratic parties) want to empower 'themselves' by disempowering 'us'.

Useful to have a concrete-seeming (but nevertheless usefully vague, 'shadowy') *denominated enemy* if you are trying to assemble (and thus divide by) denominations – rather than to democratise. Useful to be able to tell your followers, 'you are innocent by definition', that is, by denomination; 'they, somewhere over there in the shadows, are responsible for your pain; and if you can't quite make them out, don't worry: I'll keep you right'.

Remember Edgar Maddison Welch, who, convinced by the new conspiracism's bonfire logic, went in search of a basement that wasn't there to rescue children that didn't exist. To afford him at least a minimum amount of sympathy, at least he showed up to try to protect those albeit hallucinated children. He was in some sense motivated by a moral sense, a sense of duty to save the children – not *his* children, a stranger's children – from harm. A sense of *solidarity*.

The Trumpian 'strong leader' taps into this sense of solidarity, the sense that something, somewhere is wrong, that an injustice has been done to ordinary people like me, my loved ones, my neighbours, that *violence* has somehow been done and is being done, and he claims it has been done *to us*. And there is a sense in which this is the case. But the strong leader offers a *denominational* 'us', that *does not include everyone in the neighbourhood*, a collective 'we' into which I bundle the rage at the structural and symbolic violence that has been done to me; and he offers me a *reticle*, a set of routines for the identification of the 'correct' enemies *from among my neighbours*, upon whom to turn my rage. Once I have mastered the routines, the leader need not personally project the reticle in each case: I can be sent out to disseminate the proper order(s), harden the proper borders in my own neighbourhood, confident that, like the VOC and EIC before me, I can always point my thumb over my shoulder to the denominational community that has given me the insignia of Viceroy, or more likely, vice-Viceroy.

It is an example of Imperial logic, even if, ironically, Edgar Maddison Welch and others like him think of themselves as being insurgents against a vaguely defined globalist Empire (the shadowy conspiracy mentioned above), threatening 'our' freedoms. If you think Imperially, you need there to be a VRI, an apex, towards which everything can be referred – and VRI continues to function whether she exists or not. For the MAGA community, 'VRI' is 'RPA', the 'Real People of America' in whose name Trump speaks; the enemy the 'Liberal Elite', or perhaps 'Soros', or at any rate some combination of people in the right livery. It need not even be the same combination in each case, so long as the enemy is projected as being out there. On their own side, in turn, there remains a tiered, hierarchical structure of the *authorisation of violence* (against 'Them', the globalist elite and their local allies, taking away our freedoms) that permits the MAGA supporters to gather, to form up, to do what they do with a sense of empowerment, impunity, and even righteous indignation – perhaps reviving the tradition of the 'indignation meeting' (Deseret News 1870).

Thus, fear and anger at the injustice of the slowly unfolding violence of long-term precarity and poverty is gathered, focused on a *denominational enemy*, and converted to the hot, indignant, kinetic violence of hostility. The denominational enemy is projected, or rather, retrojected in a performative masquerading as a constative, as thing-like, ontologically already given; essentially singular, even if there are many (examples) of them, even if we are 'not too sure' who they are, in Sammy Wilson's phrase, and *even if they turn out to be* our *neighbours*.

Indeed, even if they turn out to be our classmates. In another leaked video, this time from India in 2023, a teacher encourages, or rather, orders, her pupils to line up and take turns to slap the face of their classmate, who is Muslim. The video called forth widespread condemnation, and a police investigation, but it was seen by some as symptomatic of wider tensions. In a line that could have come out of a newspaper in Northern Ireland, journalist Rituparna Chatterjee wrote: 'Tensions have remained high between the two communities after a recent string of clashes'. In another telling phrase, reported in the same story, Congress leader Rahul Gandhi condemned the turning of a school into a 'marketplace of hatred', and spoke of the 'kerosene spread by the BJP [Bharatiya Janata Party] which has set every corner of India on fire' (Chatterjee 2023). We should be clear that Gandhi may have his own agenda, of course; but if the schoolteacher in this case authorised her pupils to direct their violence denominationally, she did not do so out of the blue: a paradigm of 'the two communities', denominationally understood, seems to have been increasingly used as a fuel, a kerosene over the years by higher authorities still. A good way to rally your supporters, as we have said, and thus channel their combined force, is to denominate a common enemy for them. And you are never too young, it appears, to start to learn this lesson.

It is this symbolic (essentially offstage) enemy against which *our* side, the true, loyal people, who themselves, after all, have come under attack (so runs the bonfire logic), must unite, if 'we' are to survive. If the enemy is ontological, the stakes are existential.

The muscularised avatar of the strong Nation, or other denomination promises to harden borders against the enemy, just as Trump promised to build a wall (Rodriguez 2021), just as Putin promised to 'restore' the borders of Greater Russia, just as the Brexiteers promised to 'take back control' of the UK's borders, and just as, in Northern Ireland, there are those who promise to remove a border from the island, and those who promise to remove it from the Irish Sea. Everywhere there is an 'absolutization and sacralization of borders' that is 'perhaps even greater in the democratic state than in the monarchic state, which invented it, precisely because it expresses now the fact that the state is ideally the *people's property*' (Balibar 2009, 193). Ah, but there's the question: who are the people? Another question: what do we mean by 'property'? Finally, what do we mean by a 'democratic *state*'?

To address the last of these first, democracy, as the muscular avatar presents it, means offering 'the' people a sense of empowerment through having their share in the exclusive 'ownership' of the state (or 'nation', as Trump put it). Here the state is thought of according to the logic of property – something from which I am authorised to exclude others. But this does not mean *actually empowering* people, or at any rate – and this is precisely the point of their project – not *all* people. Not women who refuse to be sufficiently 'feminine' in the approved manner, or men who are *too* 'feminine'. Not Black people who insist that their lives matter. Not working people combining to demand better terms and conditions of employment, except insofar as they belong to the correct denomination. Not people in the former colonies, the 'extraction zones' of the global economy.

As for the out-of-work workers living in trailers in the rustbelts of this Euro-American world, well, they may, and indeed do, live lives of real pain and precarity (Silva 2019), but at least from their trailers, if they are Man enough, if they are White enough, if they are *true enough* they get to *identify with the America the avatar is making great again.* The promise to us (of an 'us') that will be fulfilled *just as soon* as we exclude, externalise, *clear* all these 'liberal' traitors – or for the UK audience, the 'tofu-eating wokerati', in Suella Braverman's memorable phrase (Brown 2022) – and hostile foreign usurpers and violators, put them outside the Walls, at the distance appropriate to their primal, ontological status as one of those.

In other words, we will have secured our property when we have put down the proper borders in the neighbourhood, excluded 'others' – and is 'property' not precisely the right to exclude others? We will have achieved our 'democratic state', then, as the *property of the people*, just as soon as we

have installed the proper borders around, and have purged, the *demos* of anyone who is *not one of the people*; those who are of the wrong denomination;
those who, like the wokerati, have 'gone too far' (though have the wokerati
not always already gone too far?), who have 'crossed a line'.

But Trump's wall was never finished. No border can be, in itself, because
a border is always a *bid*, and a bid always calls for a response.

Chapter Five

The Combination

Nonviolence and Democracy

Leontia Flynn, in her poem Miloš, addresses someone she has fleetingly met while travelling, a survivor of a bus crash in which the driver and a fellow passenger had died. Miloš, thrown from the bus 'half-scalped and bloody', is:

> left, when you heard of bombs or trauma, since
> with a sixth-sense of how soft it is, a body (Flynn 2008).

There is an aftermath, Flynn indicates, something that endures after being there, being bloodied, witnessing *others* being bloodied, whether by violence (bombs) or, as in the bus crash, an accidental trauma; an alertness, leaving one alive to the bodies of others, to suffering.

Such a sixth-sense (the hyphen is in the original), is not reducible to any one of the five senses Smith is thinking of when he says our senses will never convey the suffering of our brother on the rack (see chapter 2 above). Yet even Smith *already knew* 'how soft it is, a body'. He did not send his emissary of the imagination to the manacle, nor would he have sent it to a mannequin, had there been one to hand: manacle and mannequin are too *hard* for our emissary to handle.

Throughout this book we have encountered hardenings of various kinds – hardening of borders, hardening of schools, hardening of avatars, a hardening of *set towards others*. A fear of softness, of emasculation, of impotence. A certain transphobia – a fear of the softening of boundaries between one 'kind' of being and another.

We have looked at some of the ways in which different people have combined with *these* others, but not with *those* others – whether through the politics of hostility (the friend-enemy-traitor triad), in indifference (the white meat of contract) or in a combination of both – in a politics of *denomination* that is also a politics of *violence*.

Drilled in the routines of denomination I set myself towards my neighbours in a certain way: I belong to this (offstage) entity, I owe allegiance to this higher authority, and so do you – or (I have scried the signs) you belong to *another* denomination, *external* to mine. You 'are' – I will read you as, relate to you as – one of those . . .

The call, the bid, is a call to combine, to form up: a formation call. Indeed, it is a double bid: I make a bid to re-present the higher authority of our denomination, to speak in-the-name-of our denominational community; and I bid you combine with me, back me up, because you *are* one of us, and you must show it. This is your denomination, and denomination is destiny. The denomination is *entitled* to (this is ontologically given, and thus not a matter of mere political choice), and *hereby claims* (performatively) your allegiance; and that is why you should, why you *must* rally behind me.

But if you are one of *those*, and not one of ours, then your *suffering* is not *ours*, unfortunate as it may be. Either it is a matter of indifference, or mere inactive sympathy (a kind of hand-wringing which amounts to little more than indifference); or, if you belong to a denomination with which my denomination is in conflict, it is something you deserve.

I am relieved of responsibility for your suffering. The authorities within my denomination tell me I can be indifferent to you so long as you and your kind do not disturb our peace, do not disrupt the proper order; but the second you do so, we are entitled to strike back against you. I am called to offer my violence in defence of my denominational community; but by the same token, I am not *responsible* for the violence I bring down on you; I am responding to the call of my People. I do not even need to know whether or not my violence is *justified*, so long as I know it has been *authorised* – though, in fact, the two are often confused.

Indeed, in any case, ultimately *you* are responsible for my violence, because your very being-there as a foreign body (that is, something that is properly external) is a disruption of the proper order, provoking (calling for, calling forth) my violence. Now look what you have made me do.

This too, this *call* to take on a certain externalising set towards others, is a *bid*: a performative act masquerading as a description, and one that has the structure of the bet; it is only successful (felicitous) if it gets the Amen, the 'done', the handshake; if, that is, I simultaneously actively take up the call to arms and lay down my responsibility for my own violence.

The dominant paradigm in Northern Ireland (the two communities in conflict) was structured by the perpetual reiteration of such a set of routines, but we have seen throughout, the same pattern has emerged elsewhere, and at various times. In the name of an off-stage higher authority, we authorise *ourselves*, give ourselves the gift of autonomous (denominational) 'group identity', grounds for the (self) claimed justification of our own violence.

Representatives of our denomination have been authorised by God, or one of his vicars, VRI or viceroy, nation, race, or civilisation, to *order* (lay down an order, a set of commandments; impose order in) the neighbourhood. Violence, the claim is, originates with the (denominational) *other*, upon whom the relevant reticle is projected: if our claimed authority is that of our civilisation, the reticle is that of the savage; if of our religion, the reticle is of the heathen, the infidel; if our nation, the foreigner, the usurper, or the traitor (the Lundy).

We merely *re*dress the balance, or we *re*store the *proper* order. Keeping others within proper bounds, hardening the borders, performing and enforcing clearances – or standing by, effectively *giving clearance* to the violence, standing back, to recall Trump, or standing 'at ease', to recall Smith, while violence is visited upon a neighbour of some other denomination. Something about which we 'don't need to be concerned'. A thing indifferent.

As Judith Butler would put it, some lives are considered less grievable than others. In fact the path we have been trying to pick out here clearly overlaps with that followed by Butler, from the questioning of seemingly ontologically given (binary) 'identities', whether Northern Ireland's 'two communities' or 'two genders' (Butler 1990) through the idea of reducing others to the status of 'one of those dots' – a barely grievable thing in Butler's terms (Butler 2010), to her more recent work on the idea of nonviolence (Butler 2021).

Indeed, if the locally dominant paradigm of the 'two communities in conflict' was reinscribed in the Good Friday Agreement, so too was a commitment to nonviolence and democracy. As we have seen, the former dynamic has tended to overpower the latter. But this need not have been the case and need not continue to be the case.

In this chapter we will attempt to draw out the logic of nonviolence in the movement toward the deconstruction of domination-through-denomination, and toward democratic empowerment. First, let us revisit Carter's story, the Tiger's Bride, to draw out (if only to weave back in) one last thread.

CLEARINGS AND CLEARANCES

We saw that the tiger and the woman were able to encounter each other when they *stood down* their capacity to harm each other, disrobed (taking off masks and livery) and stepped together in the space of a nonviolence opened by their mutual decision to step into the clearing.

This 'clearing' is not the same as the Clearance, the kicking out of the way of others, other living bodies, the reduction, exclusion, and appropriation that constitutes the dynamic of Empire. And the difference is about violence and nonviolence – within the story Carter explicitly uses the phrase 'peaceable kingdom', when there is a second encounter between tiger and woman.

As the woman prepares for this second encounter she faces up to her fears: 'He will gobble you up', she thinks. 'Nursery fears made flesh and sinew; earliest and most archaic of fears, fear of devourment. The beast and his carnivorous bed of bone and I, white, shaking, raw, approaching him as if offering, in myself, the key to a peaceable kingdom in which his appetite need not be my extinction' (Carter 2006, 74).

At first glance there appears to be a total power imbalance in this encounter. She approaches him in her nakedness, still 'white' and 'raw'; he surely has all the power, the power to devour her. But this time, it is not as the 'cold, white meat of contract' that she appears; rather, she approaches him as one *able to offer* (to be) the *key to a 'peaceable kingdom'*, her fear and vulnerability notwithstanding – or rather, precisely because of her vulnerability, and her decision to make the offer anyway. There is a kind of power here too, but it is not the power of violence, red in tooth and claw.

Let us expand on, and (just this once) amend Carter at this point. The possibility that this opens up is a 'peaceable kingdom' in which *your appetite need not be my extinction* – and, we should add: nor mine yours, whoever you are, whoever I am. To amend Carter a little: if there is to be such a 'peaceable' (that is, nonviolent) space, it cannot be structured like a *kingdom* – a *realm* ordered by a unitary, single point of sovereignty and source of authority – precisely because the democratic space only opens up *between* us, in the nonviolent, non-hierarchical relation between you and I, and therefore in the dis-mantling of such authority structures.

Such a space cannot be opened or kept open if I refuse to shake off my livery, insist on pointing my thumb over my shoulder, gesturing towards the off-stage entity in whose name I claim to act. I must drop any claim that my violence is authorised by a 'we' that is not the we of the encounter; a denominated, *denominational* 'we' that *remains outside the contiguous space of our encounter with each other, you and I*. The clearing must be non-hierarchical: I cannot compel you to enter in the name of a higher authority; I must leave behind the insignia of any authority 'vested' in me if I am to enter this space; I must disrobe from my livery, that of the Viceroy or of the servant, or even the butcher, the baker, the brewer.

In a market in which one's relations with the other are reduced to the 'cold white meat of contract', the trader you deal with may as well be a doll, the vendor a vending machine, for all the difference it makes to the exchange. 'Participants' do not meet others face to face, but role to role, each seeing the other as nothing more than another (indifferent) economic actor. The eyes that watch you take no account of your existence. Their gaze is *indifferent*, seeing, or marking, no difference; the 'other' is reduced to the same – a sameness which has nothing to do with human equality and all to do with rates of exchange, or economic equivalence, substitutability of 'factors of production' and so forth.

The encounter must also, as we have already seen, be nonviolent: I must stand down my capacity for violence, leave my weapons at the entrance. If I must drop the thumb from over my shoulder, I must also drop the whip hand. To enter with the whip hand raised – claiming the *upper* hand, the higher position on the basis of my capacity or authorisation to do violence to you – is the extinction of the equitability and nonviolence of the encounter.

Note that, *for all his power, the tiger cannot take what is not given*, cannot *make* this happen, can neither purchase nor force the encounter, because to purchase or force the encounter is to annihilate it. Satisfaction of the appetite by force means the extinction of any chance to encounter the other as such, just as much as satisfaction of the appetite in indifference.

Does this mean that the key to holding open a 'peaceable kingdom' (or rather, nonviolent space) is to refuse the reduction, of oneself or the other, refuse a 'peace' that would be 'the result of an absorption or disappearance of alterity', in Levinas's words? If so then the work of nonviolence requires a holding open of that space, a refusal to collapse it, that is not punctual, not something that one could do once and have done with it. The work of nonviolence is interminable, must be sustained, must have a certain *sustainability*.

If this is the case, then a politics of nonviolence is not about making violence *impossible*, but *calling it into question*, out from under the mantle of habit, into the clearing, making it *visible*, or, better, *tangible*; it is about building and sustaining nonviolent relations in the light of the possibility of violence, in order to overcome it. It is not about ruling violence out once and for all or cracking down on this or that example of violence, but about the long, hard, continuous, active work of uncovering and dismantling violence wherever, whenever and however it appears.

Violence anywhere calls for nonviolence everywhere. This applies as much to 'structural' violence, the violence of indifference, that appears over a long time frame or across a population, as it does to the immediate, kinetic act of violence epitomised in the body-blow. That the former appears only over the long run and across a population does not mean it is nonviolent: we do no need to wait for the next Rana Plaza factory to collapse to recognise the violence in the system, what we called in the last chapter the slowly unfolding violence of long-term precarity and poverty. It does mean that to get to grips with it our phenomenology of violence must include a *phen*ology, attending precisely to the slow unfolding across a population, the seasonality of the phenomena as they emerge.

PHEN(OMEN)OLOGY OF VIOLENCE

There are at least two distinct ways in which one might object to including this phenological violence under the name violence, the one more conservative, the other seemingly more progressive or radical, to put it in that register. Let us consider these by way of a reading of an article published during the course of the Northern Ireland 'Troubles', though not exclusively about them, and by way of brief reference to Étienne Balibar and others. We turn to this because the dispute over the definition of violence belongs to the scope of the logic of violence and nonviolence itself.

Anthony Arblaster in his 1975 article 'What is Violence?' notes a conservative tendency, whereby those in power tend to define the term 'violence' so that it simply *excludes* legalised force. Yet they also tend to *include* 'many forms of non-legal or non-authorised action, which are quite patently non-violent. For instance, Reginald Maudling while he was the British Home Secretary defined political violence as everything from the wickedness of IRA or bombers who murder to those protesters who sit down and block the traffic' (Arblaster 1975, 235).

Quite the chain of equivalence. For a more up to date version, it is worth considering the sweeping powers given to police to prevent protests in the UK Government's Police, Crime, Sentencing and Courts Act of 2022. And, of course, the proliferation of the use of the term 'terrorism' to cover virtually any anti-government activity in a range of countries since 2001 (English 2016). Direct action, as is well known, is often simply equated with violence, by those acting in the name of the state: any disturbance in the order we have imposed is a 'breach of the peace', and we are justified in cracking down to 'keep the peace', which is to say, to *pacify* a territory in the well-known Imperial manner (Elkins 2022).

Étienne Balibar makes a similar point, speaking of the 'hypocrisy that consists in holding up the established order (notably the legally instituted order simply because the legal form is that of a consensus or a rationality) as the very reality of nonviolence when it is quite often only the common framework for a host of general or particular, open or veiled forms of violence' (Balibar 2015, 7).

Žižek too criticises the 'tolerant liberal attitude' that focuses on 'subjective violence – that violence which is enacted by social agents', the clamour of which distracts our attention 'from the true locus of the trouble, by obliterating from view other forms of violence and thus actively participating in them' (Žižek 2008, 9).

There is a 'veiling' or 'obliterating from view', an occlusion of certain kinds of violence in the conservative use of the term. Arblaster, however, is also suspicious of the tendency of some on the left to redefine and extend the term, as he conceives it. This radical 'extension' of the concept, in shorthand, holds that any way of treating people like *things* is a form of violence. Thus, inaction as well as action could quite conceivably be classified as a form of violence. This is, Arblaster admits, intended as a challenge to our normal conception of violence. It is intended to point out that an immense amount of suffering is not caused by 'anything so outrageous, so visible and dramatic as direct physical violence. It can be, and often is, the result of inaction rather than action' (Arblaster 1975, 239).

Arblaster expresses sympathy for this account, but ultimately, he has a 'radical' objection to the 'radicals': he argues against such an extension of the concept, because he does not want to concede that *opposition to violence must trump all other values*. He wants to challenge the view that renders violence the worst possible evil. Catholics in Northern Ireland, in his example, are 'likely to say that the first priority is justice or equality rather than peace and order'. Or again: 'when, as so often oppression, injustice and exploitation operate quite legally and without overt violence (as in Northern Ireland in the first fifty years of its history as a semi separate state), the issue of violence and the necessity of avoiding it will not appear to the oppressed as the cardinal issue' (Arblaster 1975, 236).

Significantly when Arblaster discusses his other forms of oppression, he's led to set them off not simply from violence, but from 'overt' violence, 'physical' violence or 'actual' violence. These supplementary words regularly occur when there are attempts to separate the other forms out. Yet as Derrida would no doubt point out, this need for the supplement is by no means incidental or innocent. I can distinguish between 'overt' and, say, 'veiled' or 'hidden' forms of violence, but what allows me to declare the former to be violence as such, and the latter – *something else*?

Indeed, is it not in making the violence of an oppressive, unjust, exploitative system *disappear* behind a veil that such a system achieves its most powerful effects? Nothing to see here, move along; all just a matter of routine. Recall, at the micro level, the *unthinking* boot of the officer on Morris's train, by means of which the servant was cleared out of the way. It is tempting to recall Arendt's assessment of the unthinking Eichmann at this point (Arendt 2006). At the macro level, think of the famines in Ireland and elsewhere, treated by the authorities as essentially unfortunate natural catastrophes, but nothing more, events that call for a certain amount of Government-funded amelioration, but which in no way should be allowed to interfere with the business of Empire, even to the extent of continuing to collect taxes from the dying (Davis 2000; Bhambra 2022).

For the very reason that it can be concealed, covert rather than overt, it is all the more important precisely to make violence the 'cardinal issue

– cardinal in the sense of 'pivotal', pertaining to a hinge; for does the whole question of politics, of democracy, of justice not in some measure hinge on our approach to the question of violence?

The attempt to prioritise 'justice' for example, understood as non-oppression, over the value of 'nonviolence' (as in Arblaster's text) quickly throws up another series of questions. Can *oppression* ever be nonviolent? How does one know, when overthrowing oppression by violence, where to draw the line between actually overthrowing oppression and an *excessive* use of violence, or a case of inversion: simply reversing the roles within the relation? You have crushed us, now we will crush you. Does such an eye for an eye approach allow us to escape from a chain of violence and counterviolence, of tit for tat, and therefore of an interminable search for the 'origin' of the chain? Have we overcome *oppression as such*, or just *their* oppression of *us*? What if those we target with our anti-oppressive violence turn out to be the wrong 'others' – bystanders, civilians; and will that not in turn 'justify' the claims of our purported oppressors to be defending *their* community against violence?

Can there be a 'violent' justice? Even a thought that would accept the idea of justice as retaliatory always attaches adjectives to violence – which would have to be 'retributive' or 'counter' violence. My act of retaliation, to qualify as such, must always *qualify and* quantify violence; always has to aim to target and weigh out my violence to exactly *neutralise* the violence of the other. But which of us gets to stand in for the Impartial Observer, gets to dress and read the balance? We would need *God's own balance*, and perhaps *God's own spirit level*, to make sure we measured our retaliatory violence out exactly, and all this before we even think about how we know we have hit the right target. After all, hit the *wrong* target and it is just violence, not 'violent justice'.

But of course, violence against a *denominational* enemy *always* misses the target, in the sense that a blow aimed at a denomination, an entity that remains off stage, lands, if at all, on a *representative* of, an *example* of 'one of those . . . '. As Merleau-Ponty says of an anti-Semite, 'he does not see Jews suffering; he is blinded by the myth of *the* Jew. He tortures and murders the Jew through these concrete beings; he struggles with dream figures, and his blows strike living faces' (Merleau-Ponty 1964, 143). The blow is aimed at the livery of denomination, but lands on the softness of the body beneath. After all, 'any member of the enemy community' will do; any one of those . . .

So many caveats, so many considerations, so much weighing up, to make sure our 'just' violence *remains* just, balanced, precisely targeted and measured, does not go *too far*; does not become *excessive*, does not cross from being justifiable violence to being mere violence as such – so much care taken to make sure our 'violent justice', to put it another way, is as *nonviolent as possible*. Even the idea of a 'violent justice', in the end, calls for a rethinking of the concept of justice in connection with the concepts and logic of violence and nonviolence.

None of this is to say violence can *never* be justified. To risk summing it up in a makeshift axiom, or rule of thumb: *the only possible justification for an act of violence is that it is the least violent* or, better, the *most nonviolent* option available.

Note that this includes the option of *doing nothing*, of standing by while violence is visited on a neighbour. There is, or may be (I cannot tell you in advance), a violence in such inaction, a 'giving clearance' to the ongoing violence. To choose to 'stay out of it' is to be in the thick of it. That *may be the most nonviolent decision. Or not*. You may decide that the most nonviolent action you can take is not to stay out of it but bodily to intervene, to *get stuck in*. The makeshift axiom cannot make that decision for you – *no* axiom can; you and I must decide, here, now, what is the most nonviolent action I can take, take *full responsibility* for it, take *full cognisance* of the impact of our blows on the soft bodies of our neighbours, and submit our decision to the judgement of our peers. But our decision cannot be justified with reference to some other value or entity that would be *outside* the scope of the question of violence – outside the *logic of nonviolence*.

Why risk this solecism: 'the most nonviolent'? Perhaps because the idea we are feeling for here cannot be expressed without breaking the rules of conventional grammar – cannot positively be *denominated*. In his 'history of a dangerous idea' (that idea being nonviolence), Mark Kurlansky notes that 'lesson number one from human history on the subject of nonviolence is that we have no word for it' (Kurlansky 2006, 5). That is, we have not yet come up with a *positive name* for it. Even the ancient Indian idea of *ahimsa* is named by way of a negative.

But is this not rather a strength than a weakness? Perhaps if nonviolence could be given a positive *denomination*, it would tend to be reduced to a routine, and would in that measure no longer be nonviolent. I reach for 'most nonviolent' rather than 'least violent', because 'least violent' risks conjuring a utilitarian calculation of quantities of violence, so that we should proceed by totting up the figures and going with the project showing the lowest score. Not only would this require us to know exactly how to define violence, and even 'score' it (for which purpose, surely we would need *God's own calculator* (the divine toolkit is growing ever more elaborate here), but in the end it would be, like any form of utilitarian calculation, a way of *getting us off the hook*, a way to evade responsibility by reverting to the purported neutrality of an algorithm, a *routine*. Sorry, computer says no.

To take another tack, what we are trying to draw out here is, perhaps, akin to what Étienne Balibar calls 'antiviolence' (Balibar 2015), but he arrives at the term having defined 'nonviolence' as, precisely, constituted by the idea of the *absence* of, or *impossibility* of violence – emphatically *not* how we are using the term here. My problem with using 'antiviolence' is that it is too diametric, too caught up in the machinery of the binary reduction machine, too close, in short, to what Balibar indicates is his problem with 'nonviolence'. But what's in a name? Perhaps Balibar's and our path around the hill overlap here. And certainly, his thinking on the issue of identity resonates with what we have found on our path, including the idea that 'identity' is about *identification*, and is again relational, rather than something simply ontically, naturally, or finally given (Balibar 2002).

We choose the 'most nonviolent' perhaps above all because nonviolence, as we are trying to think it here (and let me now risk a makeshift, rule-of-thumb definition), is the *active overpowering of violence*.

'It is necessary to ask oneself' said Emmanuel Levinas:

> if peace, instead of being the result of an absorption or disappearance of alterity, would not on the contrary be the fraternal mode of a proximity to the other (autrui), which would not simply be the failure to coincide with the other but would signify precisely the surplus of sociality over every solitude – the surplus of sociality and of love. We do not use this word, so often abused, lightly (Levinas 1996, 165).

There are words here we should enclose in inverted commas, of course: 'fraternal' (what about sisters?); 'proximity' (isn't there a risk that this is read all too geographically, or geometrically?); and 'peace' itself (recall the imposed order of the Pax Britannica of a previous chapter). Caveats aside, though, Levinas indicates that what we are calling nonviolence is not about creating a state of the simple *absence* of alterity, enmity, violence, in which case, the very *being-there* of *others* would already be a breach of the peace; a 'peace' that would finally have 'ruled violence out' by a reduction to monolithic sameness. By the same token, neither is it the simple, static *presence* of some positive state of affairs that could be denominated as the long-dreamed of goal, the *telos*, the 'peaceable kingdom', perhaps. Either approach would require us to 'absorb' others (reduce them to the sameness of a given identity, to the status of a loyal member of 'our' denomination) or cast them into the outer darkness, externalise all others, perform a Clearance – only to find that they are still in 'proximity', as nearby as neighbours, such that we would be doomed to the eternal repetition of clearance and border patrol, trying to 'restore' a peace that has always already been broken.

Another makeshift rule of thumb: for the thought of nonviolence, as we are trying to articulate it here, 'The Enemy' is not the enemy: the enemy (if we can still use this word) is violence itself. It is something which is not a thing, but which happens relationally – between neighbours. Thus, the politics of nonviolence would not be a struggle waged on behalf of or in the name of one entity against another, but against *violence*, in all its forms, however kinetic, however phenological, and from whichever source.

The enemy is not the 'other' denomination, but the violence that processes of denomination *claim to authorise*.

To take one key example we have looked at already: the problem with the British Empire was not that it was *British*; it is that it was *Empire*. And the violence of Empire was produced and maintained through denominational routines, hierarchically and vice-regally structured in a bid to combine people in a particular, dual order. The acts of denomination – even those acts denominating 'The British' – were formation calls producing and structuring combinations of neighbours, and laying claim to the authority to call for (and in the same breath to occlude by redescribing) violence.

A politics of nonviolence would begin by placing the reductive political ontologies and processes of denomination into question. It would begin, though not end, with such a deconstruction, because to fall back on a *routine of identification* is to close down the question of violence, is to self-authorise, precisely by externalising responsibility. The other (the nameable, denominational other) then appears as The Enemy, 'we' appear as the entity *against which* violence has been done already, so that we are then 'justified' *from before the outset*. I need no longer look at this or that action and consider it according to the logic of violence and nonviolence; I need simply ask which side it came from, and on *that* basis decide whether or not it was justified (that is, decide whether it is violent or 'merely' an act of self-defence, whether it is oppressive or anti-oppressive *after* sorting the denominations into the proper, ontologically given, order). Nonviolence calls for the deconstruction of such routines, such processes of denomination.

Derrida's late period work on Schmitt and the friend-enemy distinction (Derrida 1997) is one such project of deconstruction, of course, but we did not have to wait nearly that long. His early essay on Levinas already begins to unpick the connections between violence and metaphysics. And significantly, it begins by addressing the idea of the question, or more pertinently, the community of the question. A community of the question 'within that fragile moment, when the question is not yet determined enough for the hypocrisy of an answer to have already initiated itself beneath the mask of the question' (Derrida 1978, 80). To draw out two lines on this theme from Levinas himself: 'The Other becomes my neighbour precisely through the way the face summons me, calls for me, begs for me, and in doing so recalls my responsibility, and calls me into question. . . . It is as if the other established a relationship, or a relationship were established whose whole intensity consists in not presupposing the idea of community' (Levinas 1989, 83–84).

Such a community of the question would be very different from the denominational concept of community examined above – and 'presupposed' by the dominant paradigms of our political thought – for there would be nothing to found it other than the question itself: no entity or identity; not the nation, not the modern state, or the idea of the Union, not this or that version of Christianity, this or that common ancestry, not the will of 'the people', nor even the ideal society set out in this or that ideology. A community without creed, or credo, with nothing other than the decision taken as decision to submit politics to the rigour of the question of violence.

Questions of force, of violence, can be obscured, tamed, domesticated – that is, *evaded* – by this or that credo, this or that routine. But to *evade* is not the same as to *avoid*. In Derridean terms, there's no avoiding the undecidability, which calls for a decision, in the order of ethical political responsibility, and decision can only come into being in a space that 'exceeds the calculable programme that would destroy all responsibility by transforming it into a programmable effect of determinate causes. There could be no moral or political responsibility without this trial and this passage by way of the undecidable' (Derrida 1988, 116).

Picking up on one of the ideas here, it is something like this notion of 'programmability' that we have tried to capture with the term 'routine': alongside or layered over the idea of habit is the idea of the programme, the routine or subroutine in the computer programmer's sense, the series of 'if-then' steps one follows in order to mechanically produce a given, calculable effect.

For example, in Northern Ireland (or the Occupied Six Counties) there is a routine that says Irish Republicans are mindless terrorists (and we are therefore justified in using violence against them); there is a routine which says that the six county statelet is an irreformable artifice of the British Empire (and we are therefore justified in using violence against it); and there is a routine which says that these are the only two political options (to avoid which we must fall into a state of apolitical apathy or leave altogether). To base one's claim to legitimacy on a denominational routine is to make a bid to foreclose the question of legitimacy, and thus to obscure the question of violence precisely by constructing a space which is held to be beyond question, a *zero point* (at which we stand, naturally) which *by definition* cannot be violent.

Such a *project* is built around the *projection* of not so much a 'state of exception' as a *state of exemption*, a reference point that would be *exempt from the question of violence-nonviolence.* Indeed, it is this projected point of exemption (the offstage entity that gives me my denomination, the Hobbesian sovereign that has a monopoly on 'legitimate' violence, the Sovereign, God or VRI, my Nation, Race or Community, or even the Market) that gives us our political project: to *realise* or 'return to' the order corresponding to the state of exemption, that 'peaceable kingdom' the tranquillity of which is disturbed only by the violence of 'others', enemies or traitors, to give effect to it. And if we have to use violence to (re)impose that order, that is fine – we are automatically authorised by the Highest Authority in the Realm to do so. We need not be concerned for the consequences of our actions. This routine, this way of proceeding (and of calling people to combine) does not so much answer the question of violence-nonviolence as foreclose it.

Denominational politics gives me a two-fold certificate of exemption: I am authorised by the highest authority in the realm; and the disturbance that calls for a restoration of order was your doing (or even your being-there) in the first place. But this denominational bid to claim authority, this dual order, deconstructs itself. My claim to have a direct line to the author of my authority (God, VRI) has to go through the Viceroy, who in turn has to go through VRI, who herself is obliged to carry the orb and sceptre, the regalia, the livery that points elsewhere for the source of her authority. I, as a representative of the Raj (or the Nation, or the Race, or the Community), have no more direct a line to the source of authority than my supposedly 'subaltern' neighbour. The only thing that actually appears in the neighbourhood is my *claim* to authority, which always awaits a verification that will never arrive.

In contrast, stepping into, and therefore opening, a *nonviolent* clearing requires us to dismantle such routines in calling and responding to each other *as such*. I cannot step into the clearing with an interpretation of you and your programme already fully worked out, (cultural) script already written, just waiting to be delivered, and in the expectation of a stock response back from you, your *otherness* already reduced. Such an exchange of communiqués is not a *conversation*, which must always make room for surprise, changes of tack *in response* to one another. Democracy, in a sense, cannot be pre-planned: if it is to take place at all, it will take place in the mutual improvisation that is nothing outside its practice.

The 'in response' is key here – and it is a theme that has run as a thread throughout this text, in the form of the question of responsibility. After all, is there not something, precisely, *irresponsible* about projecting responsibility for violence 'outside' our own community, however that is conceived, and however denominated? For similar reasons, a conception of nonviolence that would fully resolve it to a tool or technique to be used in pursuit of a political project, one which should be measured in terms of its success or otherwise in achieving its ends, ultimately falls short of a politics of nonviolence.

It should be said there is nothing wrong with such techniques – and indeed there is plenty of evidence that, in the right circumstances, they can be more effective than violent techniques (Chenoweth 2021; Chenoweth and Stephan 2011). But to decide on violence or nonviolence as a means to an end, by way of a calculation, is in the final analysis, not to choose nonviolence at all.

Walter Benjamin already raised questions of this type a century ago. In his well-known critique of violence – it is examined at length, for instance, by Derrida in his address on the force of law (Derrida 1992) – he first examines violence in its lawmaking and law-preserving functions, showing that violence remains, necessarily, embedded in law, rather than being something outside the law, which the rule of law would oppose. He proposes another form of violence, 'mythic' violence, which is more a 'manifestation' than a (rationally calculated) means to an end. It simply seems to erupt, as in a blow of fate.

But mythic violence, for Benjamin, is fundamentally identical with all legal violence, because though it arrives out of the blue, as it were, it *establishes* a certain order – bringing us back to the inauguration of frontiers. Indeed, in the sphere of constitutional law, 'the establishing of frontiers, the task of "peace" after all the wars of the mythic age, is the primal phenomenon of all lawmaking violence' (Benjamin 1996, 248–49). Could there be a violence that destroys this violence? That sweeps this violence away?

It is tempting to turn here to Frantz Fanon, for whom the active violence of the liberation movement was necessary to sweep away not just the violence of the French imperial authorities, but the dehumanising effects of that violence on the colonised peoples of the Empires. But even Fanon would still have to face the question of violence as such: when is enough *enough*? Does the violence of the system against which we are fighting justify *in advance* any and *every* act and level of violence we launch? When has one tipped over from human liberation into a simple reversal of the roles of torturer and tortured, say? And has one exerted one's violence on the *right* body, or merely on one who is held to belong to the same denomination as the imperial torturers? As we have seen, every blow aimed at a denominational enemy falls, in practice, on the living body of a neighbour. It is difficult to read – for all sorts of reasons – Fanon's case report on the two boys who took their (white) friend into the hills and killed him as constituting any kind of 'liberation' (Fanon 1967). That said, we, you and I, should not be too quick simply to sit at a comfortable distance, in judgement on the violence of those fighting against the Empire, or consider it in isolation, as if it were the only act of violence on the scene.

So, can we overpower violence with violence? In moving towards a positive answer, Benjamin finds he has to conceive of a different *kind* of violence, and that through a *question*. 'This very task of destruction poses again, ultimately, the question of a pure, immediate violence that might be able to call a halt to mythic violence. Just as in all spheres God opposes myth, mythic violence is confronted by the divine'.

In contrast to mythic violence, such a 'divine violence', *Göttlicher Gewalt*, is 'law destroying; if the former sets boundaries, the latter boundlessly destroys them; if mythic violence brings at once guilt and retribution, divine power [sic] only expiates; if the former threatens, the latter strikes; if the former is bloody, the latter is lethal without spilling blood' (Benjamin 1996, 249).

Note the slippage in the translation – *Gewalt*, translated as 'violence' in most of the rest of the essay, is given as 'power' in connection with expiation and so on, presumably because 'violence' in that context would have been too jarring. But is this the *wrong* translation? If this is a kind of *Gewalt* that expiates, and is lethal 'without spilling blood', is it any wonder the translator hesitated over the English word 'violence'? Why not use 'divine power', after all, to indicate something that would be *beyond* the very violence Benjamin has set out to critique? Indeed, is there anything to prevent us from suggesting that a better translation of the kind of *Göttlicher Gewalt* that destroys legal orders, dismantles boundaries *'without spilling blood'*, might even be the (divine) *power of nonviolence*?

The Power of Nonviolence, as it happens, was the title of one of the earliest treatments of Gandhi's ideas (Gregg 2018). Judith Butler, much more recently, has published a book called The Force of Nonviolence (Butler 2021). Indeed, the idea of nonviolence as it was conceived by Gandhi (deeply problematic figure as he is), was from the start associated with force: Satyagraha is generally rendered in English as 'truth force'. Martin Luther King, too, was clear on this: 'Nonviolent direct action seeks to create such a crisis and foster such a tension that a community which has consistently refused to negotiate is forced to confront the issue' (King 2018, 5).

Despite the compatibility, and even close relation, between the idea of nonviolence and many ideas in ethical and political philosophy (Atack 2012), for many, the idea of nonviolence is all too easy to dismiss as wishful thinking, lofty idealism, or as amounting to a *lack* of force, equated to *powerlessness*, weakness, or appeasement. Witness the turn from Martin Luther King to Malcolm X as a key figure in the contemporary view of the struggle for civil rights; or, in contemporary India, the move away from Gandhi towards a valorisation of Subhas Chandra Bose, one who had explicitly rejected Gandhian nonviolence to the point of forging alliances with Germany and Japan during the Second World War – partly on the basis that the enemy of my enemy (that is, the British enemy) is my friend, but at least in part because there was at the time a proliferation of militant (and denominational) groups for whom, in the words of one of their leaders, 'Against one who uses violence, nonviolence, civil disobedience, imprisonment, *ahimsa*, humbleness, and the philosophy of getting freedom by begging is absolutely wrong'. It should be added, the same leader openly acknowledged the example of Hitler, and modelled his forces on the SA and SS (Khan 2017, 52). It should be said that to equate nonviolent action with humble 'begging' or appeasement does an immense injustice to the almost superhuman courage and grit of those who marched, say, in the American South of the Jim Crow era, facing batons, dogs, tear-gas, bombs, lynching, in some cases being beaten to the ground, like the late John Lewis, who was arrested some forty times, once suffering a fractured skull (Little 2020) and still getting up and doing it again and again – some, including King, at the cost of their lives.

Butler's rich thinking on the issue does not offer a simple definition of violence as such – perhaps with good reason. After all, as we saw even with Arblaster, a definition of violence too tightly drawn may serve to obscure forms of violence precisely by ruling them out of the scope of the concept (one person's 'legitimate force' is another person's 'violence'). Rather, she sets out to 'trouble' (to use a word with which she has long been associated) what we might call the routine conceptions of both violence and nonviolence.

For Butler, nonviolence 'becomes an ethical issue within the force field of violence itself . . . perhaps best described as a practice of resistance that becomes possible, if not mandatory, precisely at the moment when doing violence seems most justified and obvious' (Butler 2021, 27).

'Resistance', note, is not the same as 'refraining': nonviolence is anything but inactive. It involves a 'sustained commitment, even a way of rerouting aggression for the purposes of affirming ideals of equality and freedom' (Butler 2021, 27). Let us in passing flag up the idea of the 'sustained' commitment, and therefore a kind of sustainability, before noting that these latter ideals require careful thought. Have we not already seen that much violence can 'seem most justified and obvious' when enacted (by the Ulster Freedom Fighters, say, or by the Proud Boys who tap into the idea that a sneering 'liberal elite' have made them second class citizens) in the name of values such as 'freedom', or 'equality'?

In fact Butler, like Arblaster, Balibar and Žižek, sets out, early on, some of the ways in which the term 'violence' can be used selectively, in order to seek to justify and secure a certain monopoly of violence: states or other institutions can rename nonviolent practices as violent precisely in a bid to justify their *own* use of violence (often renamed as 'force') to suppress them (Butler 2021, 3).

She then examines the idea of the prohibition of violence ('thou shalt not kill') and the way in which there are inevitably *exceptions* to the prohibition, for example, when one kills another 'in self-defence'. *Self-defence*, Butler points out, is a 'highly ambiguous term' – precisely because the idea of the 'self' is ambiguous, taking in not just one individual, but those near and dear to that individual, so to speak. 'A rather arbitrary and dubious distinction emerges between those who are close to oneself – in the name of whose protection one may commit violence, even murder – and those who are at a distance from oneself' (Butler 2021, 52). Those considered as proximate and similar enough are covered by the scope of the 'justification' of self-defence (and *in the name of*, at that). That is, there are some lives (those within my 'group') that I may defend even with violence, and others, outside my group, whose lives I need not defend.

The question of the exception to the prohibition against violence, then, appears to hinge on the question of identification. I am ethically justified in doing violence to *others* if it is to prevent them doing harm to *us*, those with whom I can identify. 'And, if that last proposition is true (that there are those I am willing to hurt or murder, in the name of those with whom I share a social identity or whom I love in some way that is essential to who I am), then there is a moral justification for violence that emerges on a demographic basis', says Butler. It is to escape this demographic (or in our terms, denominational) basis for the distribution of the obligation of nonviolence that Butler proposes a 'radical equality of the grievable' as the precondition for an ethics of nonviolence – one that would at the stroke bring a 'perspective of radical democracy into the consideration of how best to practice nonviolence' (Butler 2021, 56).

Moreover, the ethics of nonviolence cannot start and end within the scope of a particular definition of 'the human', a 'historically variable concept' that is itself constituted through exclusions. An ethics of nonviolence which would extend beyond the human: here we have a route into a nonviolent environmentalism, and with it the confluence of many of the key issues we have been looking at throughout – equality, nonviolence, sustainability, and democracy. But let us look again at that idea of 'identity', through Butler's reading of Foucault and Fanon.

Butler cites the 1976 lecture course 'Society Must Be Defended', in which Foucault addresses the 'biopolitical', including technologies for managing life and death. It would, incidentally, be worth reading Butler on 'biopolitics' in conjunction with Mbembe's 'necropolitics' (Mbembe 2019), but for now let us focus on a certain conception of power, in connection with sovereignty. For Foucault, Butler says, power acts, 'but not from a sovereign centre: rather, there are multiple agencies of power operating in a post-sovereign context to manage populations as living creatures, to manage their lives, to make them live or let them die' (Butler 2021, 109). Discussing this in relation to racism (for Foucault racism functions to 'fragment, to create caesuras within the biological continuum addressed by biopower'), Butler ties Foucault's treatment of 'the living' with her own thought on 'lives that are more and less valuable, more and less grievable', and ties that in turn to Fanon's examination of the 'historic-racial schema' imposed by 'the white man' (a figure for the powers of racism).

'The white man', according to Fanon, is the one who 'had woven me out of a thousand details, anecdotes, and stories' (Butler 2021, 113). Not only does 'the white man' weave together – let us suggest: *fabricate* – a version of the other, but those on the receiving end, those over whom the fabric is thrown, like a cloak, or *mantle*, as it were, come to their own sense of self in that context, through the text(ile) woven by *someone else*, someone in authority, holding the whip hand.

Incidentally, in Black Skin, White Masks, Fanon himself deploys the term 'fabricate', and a term we have been using throughout: 'livery': 'Whether he likes it or not, the black man has to wear the livery the white man has fabricated for him' (Fanon 2021, 17). Or again, my 'true wish' he says, 'is to get my brother, black or white, to shake off the dust from that lamentable livery built up over centuries of incomprehension' (Fanon 2021, xii). Black *or* white.

In The Wretched of the Earth, though, Fanon will famously argue that only by way of a *violent* self-assertion can those so subjected reclaim their own identity – and he makes it clear that he is not speaking metaphorically: he means armed resistance. But is it *sheer violence*, the mere use of weapons, of kinetic, bodily ('normal') violence, that effects the transition he seeks? Is it possible to re-read Fanon (perhaps via our reading of Benjamin, above) as showing that an *active overthrowing* of the *enforced passivity* that constitutes both Empire and the 'pacified' territories of Empire (populated by 'subject peoples') is what is called for? And that this 'active overthrowing' may be, but *need not be*, understood according to our 'normal' conception of violence?

Indeed, though Butler has held back from a simple definition of violence, it might be time to risk another makeshift definition: violence is the production of avoidable *suffering* – to use the word in a double sense. Violence bids not only to hurt us, sear into our soft bodies, but also to render us *passive*, as an *object*, as *being on the receiving end* (an 'infinitely gentle, infinitely suffering thing' in TS Eliot's phrase, with an emphasis, *pace* Arblaster, on the 'thing'). Violence, then, *appears* active, as it bids to impose passivity and therefore the violent appear in the more powerful position than those on the receiving end; but as we have already indicated, there is *nothing passive about nonviolence*. Nor is the aim and effect of active nonviolence to render the *other* passive.

To recall our earlier discussion, Empire proclaims, that is, *bids* to impose a vertically tiered dual structure of authority: the 'we', who have been interpellated into our place within the tiered ranks of the *ordinated*, have authority to police the boundary between super- and subordinate denominations; 'we' are authorised, as vice-Viceroys, to keep the 'them' in their place. The 'natives', like women-and-children in the domestic sphere, are *subordinated*; placed *under* the order proclaimed. They are not, it is worth saying, rendered *powerless*, but any exercise of their power will be interpreted by the authorities via the structure the Imperial project bids to impose. Their *Gewalt*, then, is always interpreted as *unauthorised violence*, violence 'as such'. From the point of view of the Imperial project, their *Gewalt* is not authorised because they are subaltern; and they are subaltern because their *Gewalt* is not authorised.

What are those who have been so ordered to do? Simply to reverse the denominations ('their' actions are violent, 'ours' are justifiable force) is to leave the structure and logic of denominational violence unchallenged. Any action, however violent, could be 'justified' *because* it came from 'our' side; anything that came from them could be legitimately presented as violence (thus justifying our *counter-violence*), *because* it came from them. This would be as much a matter of 'mythic', or 'law-imposing' violence as the violence of Empire – a counter-Imperial version of violence (and let us remember, Putin claimed he was fighting an 'Empire', rather than fighting to expand one; and the MAGA community believe they are the revolutionaries overthrowing tyranny in a new American Revolution).

If there is to be an active overthrowing of violence by way of a *Göttlicher Gewalt* it cannot mean simply that it is our turn to impose passivity and suffering on our denominational enemy. And we should not be too hasty to claim that this latter is what Fanon intended, let alone that his texts in any sense authorise a political project of violence in another context – even if, in those contexts, the structural violence with which we are faced is outrageous. That said, given that Fanon lived with and spoke for those subjected to violence so total, to torture so prolonged that their very torturers turned to him for psychiatric help, a call for a counter-violence, 'normal' or otherwise, would be, to say the least, understandable – and perhaps such a counter-violence *could* be shown to be justified – without quotation marks this time. It is this question of *justification* that is at issue.

RAGE AND NONVIOLENCE

After all, does the 'outrageous' not precisely call for *rage* as the right response? Would a call for those subjected to the outrageous violence of empire or enslavement, for example, to *stifle* their rage (out of politeness, as a matter of etiquette) not simply add insult to injury? As bell hooks says, 'part of the colonizing process has been teaching us to repress our rage' (hooks 1995, 14). That 'process' arguably involves allowing only Arblaster's 'overt' or 'patent' violence, the sudden shock of the kinetic blow, to be read *as* violence in the first place, leaving the cumulative effect of what we are calling phenological violence illegible. Such phenological violence would remain as invisible as the eponymous Invisible Man of Ralph Ellison's great novel, which opens with a scene of sudden, shocking violence, as the narrator beats a passerby on seemingly relatively slight provocation.

That the *overt* (Ellison uses the word) violence is not the only violence operative in the scene, that there is already another violence at work does not become clear, does not *show itself* until we have read on through the book. Invisibility is, as it were, in the eye of the beholder. 'I am a man of substance, of flesh and bone, fiber and liquids', says the narrator; 'I am invisible, understand, simply because people refuse to see me' (Ellison 1981, 7). He has been subjected to the sustained, phenological violence of being reduced to the status of an *example* of a subordinate denomination – a phenological violence, we should add, that does not preclude occasional outbursts of kinetic violence, 'to restore order'.

James Baldwin, too, wants to make visible, that is, dis-*mantle* the violence hidden behind the respectable (white) façade of American institutions. In 'Notes of a Native Son', he too discusses how a seemingly minor matter, a refusal to serve him in a bar 'because of his race' – a refusal stated by a waitress 'as though she had learned it somewhere', and not with hostility, but 'with a note of apology in her voice, and fear' – drives him to rage, to the point where he hurls a glass at her (inaccurately, as it happens). Baldwin makes it clear that the refusal he has received here is just the latest in a long, cumulative line. He thus makes visible (lifts the mantle from) the phenological violence that would otherwise have remained invisible.

Yet after the incident he sees, clearly, he says, that his life was in danger 'not from anything other people might do but from the hatred I carried in my own heart' (Baldwin 1985, 135). Baldwin does *not* apologise for his rage – which in places burns fiercely. A fierce rage that does not become a hatred: something akin, perhaps, to what hooks calls for when she says: 'Progressive black activists must show how we take that rage and move it beyond fruitless scapegoating of any group, linking it instead to a passion for freedom and justice that illuminates, heals, and makes redemptive struggle possible' (hooks 1995, 20).

It is tempting to suggest that what begins to emerge here is a kind of rage that would refuse to be reduced to violence, a kind of *rage of nonviolence*. Neither hooks nor Baldwin is under any illusion that there is plenty to rage at. Yet there is an insistence on refusing to 'scapegoat any group' that amounts, arguably to a deconstruction of *denominations*. 'Spare me', says Baldwin, 'any further examples of American white progress. . . . Leaving aside my friends, the people I love, who cannot, usefully, be described as either black or white, they are, like life itself, thank God, many, many colors, I do not feel, alas, that my country has any reason for self-congratulation' (Baldwin 1985, xvii). Indeed, what exactly is 'his country'? Has it been *achieved* yet? The phrase, and it is one Richard Rorty picks up on (Rorty 1998), is from Baldwin's *The Fire Next Time*: 'If we – and now I mean the relatively conscious whites and the relatively conscious blacks . . . do not falter in our duty now, we may be able, handful that we are, to end the racial nightmare, and achieve our country' (Baldwin 1985, 379). The 'our' of our country, the 'we' ('*We*: who was this *we*?' Baldwin asks in The Price of the Ticket) is not an empty universal (he means *certain* people) nor is it a monolith: it incorporates difference. The country that will be *ours* is yet to be *achieved*.

Lisa Beard, in her study of Baldwin, picks up on this troubling of racial categories, suggesting 'boundness' as a way to conceive of the relation between white and black Americans. Baldwin, she claims, 'argues that at the heart of American racial politics is white people's denial of their "flesh and bone" relationship with black people – they make themselves into "blood strangers" and commit horrifying violence against their kin. . . . Baldwin does not read white-on-black violence as raceless violence, but neither does he read it as violence done by one "distinct race" of people upon another "distinct race"' (Beard 2016, 382).

There is a 'boundness' without boundaries, a bond that *precedes* the racialisation of people into those mutually exclusive categories, a flesh-and-bone relationship (recall that Ellison, too, used that phrase), summed up here in the idea of 'kin'. For Baldwin, this may have meant quite literally a biological family kinship: throughout the history of the era of slavery, after all, there were so many children of mixed race born (and let us not shy away from confronting the widespread sexual violence behind this bland observation) that it became practically impossible to say for certain that this or that 'white' person was not in fact biologically related to the very victims of their racialising violence.

Beard cites Baldwin relating an account of a white officer barring a courthouse to a group of black people – or rather, in Baldwin's words, 'a group of unarmed people arbitrarily called black whose color really ranged from the Russian steppes to the Golden Horn to Zanzibar' (Beard 2016, 383). The sheriff who beats the group with his club, notes Baldwin, was beating some who were:

> assuredly related to the black mammy of his memory and the black playmates of his childhood. And for a moment, therefore, he seemed nearly to be pleading with the people facing him not to force him to commit yet another crime and not to make yet deeper that ocean of blood in which his conscience was drenched, in which his manhood was perishing. The people did not go away, of course; once a people arise, they never go away. . . . So the club rose, the blood came down, and his bitterness and his anguish and his guilt were compounded.

The Sheriff, the 'white man' (to bring Fanon and Baldwin together here) is 'assuredly related' to those he is about to beat. But here 'being related', whether it means an actual biological family connection, 'assuredly' refers to the contiguous bonds between him and those with whom he grew up, who cared for him (the 'mammy') or played with him as children. There are bonds that *precede* the confrontation on the steps of the courthouse, that *precede* his donning of the badge of office, the raising of the fist clenched around his billy-club. And even had he not, in fact, empirically, grown up with those carers or with those playmates, there would still be a flesh-and-bone relation between him and those he confronts, here, now, in the moment: he already knows where to aim his blows; he already knows how soft it is, a body.

For this reason – here is another makeshift axiom – *the moment of the possibility of violence is also the moment of the possibility of nonviolence.*

Confronted with the *mixed* crowd (multiple, irreducibly plural), the Sheriff must *decide* what to do. He appears, in Baldwin's telling, nearly to be pleading with them to relieve him of the need to bring down the club – pleading with them *not to force him* to do so. But of course, they are doing no such thing. Rather, they are *forcing him to make the decision.*

Where a *violent* interaction with a neighbour attempts to force them into *submission*, into passivity, bids them be, or attempts to subdue them, render them non-active, a *nonviolent* confrontation – and this is the force of nonviolence – *forces them to actively decide.* Baldwin, in 'The Fire Next Time': 'And if the word *integration* means anything, this is what it means: that we, with love, shall force our brothers to see themselves as they are, to cease fleeing from reality and begin to change it. For this is your home, my friend, do not be driven from it' (Baldwin 1985, 336).

The Sheriff is, precisely, *not forced* to bring down the club on the body of his neighbour. He will bear *full* responsibility for the decision, *which is a decision*, should he do so. He will attempt to *evade* the decision (to 'flee from reality'), attempt to project responsibility onto them ('I had no choice: if only they had dispersed when I told them to I would not have been forced to use the club'). He reduces the *mixed crowd* to a *monolithic denomination*, throwing a 'black' mantle over them the better to aim the blow he is about to level; but that act of projection, too, is a decision for which he bears responsibility in this encounter with his neighbours. And he will back-project, don the mantle of 'Whiteness' rather than 'seeing himself as he is'. Pointing his thumb over his shoulder he will claim: it is not my responsibility, but that of the higher Authorities, those with whom I identify, those who have charged me with upholding 'law and order'. Either way, both ways, the projection provides nothing more than an *alibi*: the responsibility for his decision remains his.

This is the first part of the logic and power of nonviolence: it makes legible the phenological violence of a given authority-structure, one that requires, for its own maintenance, kinetic violence at the point of decision. The dynamic, notably, would have been different had members of the group raised billy-clubs of their own. This would have written the logic of counter-violence and self-defence over the scene, making the phenological violence – though it would still be there – harder to read. The Sheriff's claim to be merely opposing the violence of the group, even acting in self-defence, and so on, would have been lent a plausibility it may or may not have deserved. Again, this is not to say, without further ado, that such a course would have gone against the principle of nonviolence: that would have to be decided in situ, in the context and space of the encounter.

But whether it did or not, the flesh-and-bone connection is already there in the confrontation between the Sheriff and his neighbours. The neighbours are before him, and they will not go away – they will persist in their demands for access to the courthouse, the house of the law.

As Beard puts it, the Sheriff is placed in a scarcely bearable 'tension between on the one hand, the knowledge of his intimate connection with the people before him and, on the other hand, the scope and obligations of his white racial identity at that place and time' (Beard 2016). These 'obligations', however, these bindings, ligaments, are there only if he actually *owes allegiance* to 'the White Man', the off-stage sovereign entity that provides him with his livery and his authority – the entity in whose name he acts and speaks. But as we saw in the first chapter, 'allegiance' is structured as a call-and-response; and it is always possible for him to *refuse* to respond by rote, refuse to repeat the routines into which he has been drilled. 'The romance of treason never occurred to us', says Baldwin of the black people of America expected to serve in the armed forces during the Second World War, 'for the brutally simple reason that you can't betray a country you don't have. . . . And we did not wish to be traitors. We wished to be citizens' (Baldwin 1985, xv).

Denomination is not destiny: allegiance is not (ontologically) given (though the avatars of the denomination incessantly make that *claim*), making bids to put you in a bind without a choice. If you are bound at all, you are *bound to choose*, and not to choose between one denomination and another, but to choose violence or nonviolence.

The only 'nonviolent option' (Beard's phrase, and Beard's inverted commas) the Sheriff can conceive of for defusing the tension is for the crowd to disperse. Beard is careful to hold the phrase 'nonviolent option' at arm's length here because in fact there is nothing 'nonviolent' about it. First, the crowd would have been forced to back down by threats of immediate, kinetic violence; and perhaps more significantly, they would have been refused access, by structural violence, to the *courthouse*, the very place in which questions of law are decided. The structural violence this confrontation makes visible is built into the legal order, precisely because it excludes some by definition – *by (processes of) denomination*. If you, in this mixed crowd, don't have the wristband (and there are those who will *never* get a wristband) you don't get through the door, to borrow a pertinent image from a Paul Simon song. If you are denominated as 'white' you not only get in the door, but you get to don the livery of the doorkeeper, and the badge of authorisation to use the club. You get to be a vice-Viceroy. Indeed, arguably the whole viceregally structured project of Empire is legible in this passage from Baldwin.

Those denominated as 'black' are refused access to the space of the law (*juris*), refused a *say*, the authority to speak (*dictare*) in the shaping of the laws whose force will be felt in their bodies, their flesh and bones. But if they are excluded from the *juris-diction*, are they bound *by* the laws of that jurisdiction? That is, are they bound by *anything other than violence itself* to obey that law? And if bound only by violence, are they under any ethical obligation to recognise the authority behind the law at all? Indeed, are they not rather obliged to *refuse to recognise the authority of those authorising* the violent enforcement of a law in which they had no say? This would be the claim of an ethics and politics of nonviolence.

Moreover, the dispersal of the crowd is *not the only nonviolent option*. It appears so only to the extent and for as long as the Sheriff decides to adopt and maintain the 'obligations' of his 'identity' (no identity outside identification, remember) as 'the white man', with all the implications that this denomination brought with it, in that place and time. The other nonviolent option – and let us dispense with the inverted commas this time – is for the Sheriff to throw down his badge, drop his billy-club and *join his neighbours* in demanding their, *and therefore his*, equal access to the law.

If violence enforces passivity, nonviolent engagement opens the possibility of *empowerment*, and not just the empowerment of the people in the crowd before the courthouse, but the *empowerment of the Sheriff* to choose democracy over denomination, to choose the power of combining, equitably, nonviolently, contiguously with *others*. Democratic empowerment is not something that can be handed down, by a Sheriff or Viceroy, to passive recipients – such a 'handing down' retains the vertical tiering of the Imperial hierarchy that is the antithesis of democracy. It bears the structure of the 'charitable gesture', for which one is expected to erect Scrabo Towers of gratitude to one's benefactors.

Where violence renders its target 'thinglike', for however short or long a duration, nonviolence calls us, *you and me*, actively to overpower violence – again, for however short or long a duration. You can always decide, after all, to shut the door of the courthouse anyway. But it *is* your decision to refuse to take up the offer of mutual democratic empowerment, to side with the 'proper authorities'.

Democracy, which demands equality, can only take place where the *bid* of the (always off-stage) 'higher' authority (as if such a thing existed) is refused, where neighbours meet as *commoners and on the one common*. The Sheriff can and must do this, if he decides to do it, emphatically not by claiming to be 'the same' as them, not via an 'identification' with his black neighbours – he will never have shared the common experiences they have shared, lived the lives they have lived; he will never be in exactly the same position, even if he sends the emissary of his imagination to report back how he would feel in that position, in good Smithian fashion (though he should try to do that, too, of course). He can only meet them as equals not just by ceasing to denominate *them* as of lower status, but precisely by refusing to continue to identify *himself* via the detour of the off-stage entity, the 'White Man' (or White God, or VRI, or any of their vicars or Viceroys) as the sovereign authority figure governing the neighbourhood, ordering it according to the *law of the ruler*, as opposed to the *rule of law*, democratically achieved.

One last line from Baldwin (whom we could endlessly quote here): 'part of the price of the black ticket is involved – fatally – with the dream of becoming white. This is not possible, partly because white people are not white: part of the price of the white ticket is to delude themselves into believing they are' (Baldwin 1985, xiv).

Rule of law, if it is not to be rule by violence, would be achieved only when law is democratically and nonviolently inaugurated by a *mixed crowd* – a combination, a *demos* of neighbours who remain of equal standing before the law they achieve together, for all their differences, no longer having to 'pay the price' of the impossible task of reducing each other, and themselves, to the 'right' racial identity, or nation, or denomination.

Our democracy, then, our *demos*, like Baldwin's country, has yet to be achieved.

Conclusion

Neighbourhood Democracy

The space of democracy is not the territory of the denomination, serene and unitary within its own borders, exempt from the question of violence and nonviolence, but the space of the *neighbourhood*, a space only opened by a teeming multiplicity of interacting, overlapping projects and trajectories. Every border is a *neighbourhood relation* – you still have to relate to those on the other side of it as neighbours. Every neighbourhood is *mixed*, irreducibly plural, a space of, and constituted by, 'co-existing heterogeneity' (Massey, 2005: 9). To try to master or expel that heterogeneity – to *claim* this or that demarcated territory properly belongs to *this* nameable, unitary entity, this *denomination* – is to set the scene for the violence of minoritising subordination, or the violence of the partition, the enclosure, the Clearance. 'We' will either have a territory purged of others or tolerate them as a 'minority'. And if the latter, they should be a *grateful* minority, on their best behaviour (Rathe 2023). Such is the logic of denomination.

I denominate myself and others, subsume them, *some* neighbours, under the name of a collective entity, *make an example* of them, make a *them* of them – this is something I *do* rather than something they *are* – and then relate to them as though this is essentially *what they are*. Aha! You are one of those . . . and therefore my violence against you is (by the logic of denomination) your fault.

An act of denomination is a reduction from a full, rich, bodily, noisy, fluid, complex overlapping of differences and commonalities between neighbours to a set of distinct (id)entities, abutting each other like Petri dishes on a technician's bench. My 'identity', thought of in this way, is that of a sample from dish A, and not dish B, a specimen, an example of one of those As, whereas you are evidently of one of those Bs.

And if you are one of *those*, and not one of *ours*, then your interests are not my interests, which I must prioritise over yours; and whatever the consequences for you, your suffering is not *our* concern. You are external to me and mine, and the border, the gulf, is ontological.

DENOMINATE TO DOMINATE

When you grow up in Northern Ireland it is hard to avoid thinking about the politics of denomination – except that we tend to do just that: avoid *thinking* about it, for the most part. That is, because the denominations, the 'two communities' of the dominant paradigm, are so 'obvious' it is easy to forget to *think* about them, to think *about* them, rather than to think from *within* the binary logic their 'obvious' existence dictates. You are brought up in the routines; you forget to think about how they make their appearance; you forget to think about what the impact is, what the effects are of us continually acting as if there *were* these two obvious communities, and as if you had to belong to one of them, these (id)entities that appear to be *ontologically given*, yet that address us, if at all, from off-stage, through their representatives, through masked avatars of a higher authority. Representatives authorised to administer and distribute violence, *if need be*.

To start thinking about processes of denomination in relation to Northern Ireland is to begin to see that they far from confined to Northern Ireland. The politics of denomination has become more and more legible elsewhere, in Brexit Britain, in Trump's America, in Putin's Russia. But before that, it was legible in the era of empire and enslavement, and remains legible, globally, in the legacies of that era.

It is in the authorisation and channelling of violence that the effects of denomination are at their most powerful. If you are one of those enemies, I have the authority to do violence to you to *defend my community*. I have been authorised to Clear the area – of foreigners and traitors. If you are already outside, external to my community, a 'thing indifferent', your suffering is not *ours*. I have no property in it, no share in it. I may feel pity, but it is something projected from a distance: I am bound by loyalty to, bound to prioritise my denomination, but I have no bond, no *obligation* to address your suffering; if I do so, it is as a gesture of hierarchy-preserving charity, against which, as one of Beckett's characters said, there is no defence. You remain at best the passive recipient of my philanthropy.

Note, I need not look at you as an enemy in order to exempt myself from any 'concern' with, or responsibility for, your suffering. The indifferent gaze of the eyes of the market, the reduction to the cold, white meat of contract will serve equally well for that purpose. These two regimes of violence share this structure of the projected externality of certain (denominated) others – the 'Clearance' of others, in the sense we have been using the term here.

The Clearances called for by the politics of denomination thus produce either a politics of hostility, with its attendant potential for immediate, kinetic violence, or a politics of indifference, with its attendant phenological violence that makes its appearance only over a season and across a population – or both. In either case, if there is violence, according to the routines of denomination it originates with *the other*. Others who refuse to accept 'our' authority to maintain the proper order, who refuse to respect the borders we have laid down, whose very *being-here* would be a disturbance of the peace, as though they exhibited a certain ontological criminality.

We have seen how the two can intersect and overlap, and have done throughout the modern period (at least), according to the logic of the Imperial project: since 'we' bring Civilisation, Christianity and Commerce, since 'we' are acquainted with industry, know how to improve the land, and thus increase the general welfare, we are authorised in appropriating it, extracting it from the common by excluding those who are merely getting in the way of progress. Denominate to dominate. Authorise your vice-Viceroys to go out, clear the land, crank the value of it up and offshore, back '*home*', to the *domus* where it properly *belongs*, where it is domesticated as exclusive *disposable property*, subject to the strictures of the cold, white meat of contract. And then when you have extracted all the value you can, cut it loose and abandon it, like the Gift, to its fate. Along with all the bodies you have left behind.

Of course, this is a Gift that keeps on taking, long after the formal end of the era of Empire: the Viceroys of the heirs to the VOC, the disembodied corporations, keep on cranking wealth and power vertically up and offshore to enhance the wealth of 'our nation', our corporation, our denomination. And if your body can't take it anymore, well, any body will do: we can just as easily find one to bear the burden in a neighbouring region, preferably equally far offshore.

Swapping the locally dominant paradigm (two communities in conflict) for a globally dominant paradigm (market power), then, is *not* a route to an automatic overcoming of the politics of violence. Rather, it would be a transformation of one form of politics of violence into another, albeit a less 'obvious' one. For there *are* bodies, disempowered, suffering, left behind, both overseas and at home, offshore and on. Such that when an avatar appears and offers to right the wrong, avenge the violence that has been visited upon *us*, and make *us* great again, it is little wonder there is a surge of energy, an exhilaration, a sense belonging to 'something great' that draws energy from some of the contiguous bonds of neighbourhood and binds them to the denomination. Little wonder there is a rush to pledge allegiance, and therefore turn our gunsights, already etched with the relevant reticle, on the bodies of our neighbours – those of the 'wrong' denomination, that is: the enemies of The People, violent by definition; the traitors, the 'wokerati', whom we must dominate if they are not to dominate us; who must be Cleared out from our territory, along with the foreign usurper whose interests they serve, if we are to take back control, *get our own back*.

Yet the political project of the Clearance can never be terminated, because anywhere we put the border it falls *within* the neighbourhood. The neighbourhood can never finally, fully be converted to exclusive denominational territory, turned into *exclusive property* because the relation of neighbourhood deconstructs the inside-outside division upon which relations of denomination depend. The structural interminability of the bid to clear the territory for ourselves calls forth the endless Sisyphean labour (and violence) of exclusion, the endless bid to *justify* my violence by way of an appeal to a higher authority, a state of exemption, that deconstructs itself.

If my claim to the justification of my act of violence is based on appeal to the decision of a higher authority, then my violence has been *authorised* but not yet *democratically justified*. Indeed, in the very gesture of appealing to the alibi of a higher authority that is *not here*, now, in the space of our encounter, I have ruled out the possibility of *democratic* justification, which is to say justification according to the logic of politics of nonviolence, of democracy as sustained, radical equality.

If there is to be such a democratic justification, the judgement over an action (or inaction) must take full account of *all* the violence in the situation, the kinetic and phenological alike, the violence of hostility and of indifference alike. Such violence cannot be judged from some vantage point outside the situation, as though by an impartial spectator – from a distance that reduces us all to the status of one of those dots. But nor can I judge the violence (democratically at any rate – that is, according to the logic of nonviolence) simply by naming a side, 'my' side', and exempting 'it' (as though 'it' had already been there) from the question, and as though 'the other side' were ultimately responsible for *all* the violence in the situation, even our own. Such is the logic of the binary reduction machine: if *they* are responsible for this or that act of violence, *we* are absolved of any responsibility for the violence we do to them in return. If *they*, in their very being-there, are a threat to us, we are absolved in advance for the violence we do to fend off that threat – indeed it would be irresponsible *not* to strike at them.

In October 2023, just after what was intended as the final draft of this book had been submitted, there was a sudden and shocking outbreak in the Middle East that horrifically embodied both the sort of kinetic and phenological violence we have been looking at. Hamas, breaking out of Gaza, launched large-scale coordinated attacks on Israeli citizens, leaving (early reports indicated) over 1,200 men, women, and children dead, and over two hundred taken hostage. Within a day, representatives of the Israeli Government had declared war, had begun the bombardment of densely populated areas of Gaza, and had set in motion an amassing of troops for what looks likely, at the time of writing, to be a full-scale invasion, with all the violence that will entail (Erlanger 2023; Lynch 2023).

It is impossible to say how this iteration of the conflict will unfold, how long it will continue, and how widespread the ramifications, but it is already clear that there are some, perhaps many, who will read this situation via the sort of processes of denomination we have been examining here. There will be, and have been, claims that 'our' side is the side of light, of humanity, is on the side of God (ours is a 'Jihad'); 'theirs' is the side of darkness, of barbarity, of the animal (Al Jazeera 2023; Netanyahu 2023). There will be what in chapter 4 we called 'bonfire logic', in which any and every utterance will be taken as fuel for the fire: criticism of Hamas, or even using the term *terrorism*, will immediately be read by some as if it were an attempt to exonerate the Israeli occupation; criticism of the phenological violence of years of Israeli Clearances and enforced subordination of Palestinians, or the kinetic violence of the current Israeli military response, will immediately be read as if it were an attempt to exonerate Hamas. Neither need be true for these readings to take effect, helping to squeeze the full complexity of the situation through a binary reduction machine. Even criticising both will not protect one from accusations of bias – on the basis that *our* chosen side does not deserve such criticism *at all*, only the *other* side – or at least the other side deserves *more* criticism.

Indeed, in some cases, failing to recognise the sides *as sides*, inescapably exterior to each other, can be enough to draw criticism, and more than criticism. The Guardian reports that two activists were detained in Israel 'for putting up posters with a message that the police deemed to be offensive'. The message? 'Jews and Arabs, we will get through this together' (Borger 2023). The activists appear to the police to have crossed the line by crossing out the line, the ontological gulf, separating 'Jews' and 'Arabs' as two mutually exclusive denominations, to only one of which you must be loyal. The most offensive word on the poster, other than 'together', may have been the shortest (at least in English): the 'we', a 'we' capacious enough for Jews and Arabs to come *together*. Such a call to form a different kind of 'we', a 'we' inclusive of *others*, is read, through the strictures of the logic of denomination, as an attack on 'us', the purity and unity of the denominational 'we'. And any such movement towards 'them' must be arrested – quite literally in this case. To call for such a coming together is to mark yourself out as 'on their side'. You are thus either an enemy or a traitor to your 'own' community.

In a politics thus organised into such 'sides', that is, by processes of denomination, the question of violence is raised only with a certain range of answers already established, already authorised; and thus, the question of violence is not really raised at all. Everything proceeds as though there simply, obviously, *are* two sides; as though one of these, and one alone, *must* be responsible for originating the violence (or 'more' responsible than the other, which is taken to amount to the same thing); and that the other must, therefore, be exempted from the question of violence, or excused for such violence as they do deploy. All that is left is for us to pick our (thus denominated) side, according to the politics that flows from this logic. But it is this logic itself that sets the scene for the continuation and intensification of the violence that those who deploy such routines of denomination claim to oppose.

If there is to be a solution it will not lie in accepting the logic of 'the two sides'; it will not lie in a denominational calculus, an attempt to numerically quantify the violence on each 'side' to decide which of the two is 'really' responsible. It will not even lie in an attempt to achieve a balance of power between 'the two communities' in either a 'one state' or a 'two state' solution, so long as the pursuit of such a solution reinforces the dynamics of exclusion within the neighbourhood. The choice would then be that between a single state, with a single point of sovereignty, composed of two national or denominational entities which *still remained external to each other*, or, alternatively, the inauguration of a border between two static, would-be 'peaceable kingdoms', each to be purged of all enemies and traitors, staring at each other across a heavily (and violently) guarded boundary. This would be a reiteration of the binary reduction that drives the dynamics of the conflict itself. To be clear, there will have to be a state solution too, almost certainly a two-state solution; but if there is to be a sustainable solution, it will firstly, primordially, have to be a democratic, *rather than a denominational* one.

The logic of denomination, as we have tried to show throughout, is a logic of the prioritisation of 'my' denomination over yours, a logic of dominance, of disempowerment, not a logic of democracy, certainly not of neighbourhood democracy. A 'democracy' that produces (because it depends on) superordinate and subordinate denominations is not a democracy, regardless of how 'free and fair' its elections are: it exhibits, rather, the structure of Empire, of the Raj, with all its ordered, hierarchically structured violence.

If there is to be a sustainable solution it will lie in our developing, together (and emphatically *not* in closing off) *nonviolent routes to democratic empowerment* for everybody – every body – in the neighbourhood, wherever the state borders are now or eventually will end up (and whatever they will mean). And it will take a combination of neighbours, neighbours of all denominations, neighbours however geographically distant (including us, you and I, here in this corner of the world), to work to shift the dynamics in that direction.

All of this applies not just to this most recent outbreak of kinetic conflict, but wherever we find violence, phenological and kinetic alike, being authorised via appeals to the off-stage higher authority of the denomination. Here in Northern Ireland, in Russia and Ukraine, everywhere there is violence, the call to nonviolence is a call to democratic empowerment, a call to join a political project that will overpower the violent pull of denomination.

Clearly, given the power and intensity of the binary dynamics unleashed when conflict like this breaks out, it will be difficult, almost impossible to make such a call, make such alternative voices and other ways of thinking heard. Everything will be put through the gearing of the binary reduction machine; almost everyone will set about the Sisyphean task of trying to solve the question of violence by exempting 'ourselves' from it, thus projecting the enemy whose violence calls forth our own in the first place. That said, the task of building a democratic, nonviolent combination, one that would not be reduced to the simple opposition of a binary, one that would not go via the routes and routines of the projection of a higher authority, a Truth that would set us free from responsibility for our own violence, is endless too. But it is not Sisyphean because we are no longer trying to get to the top of the hill, the (nonexistent) point of perfect equilibrium, exempt, as it were, from the forces of gravity. We are no longer guided by the *telos* of the Tower, but by the movement of improvising our way, together, about and about, as equitably and nonviolently as possible.

'There's a certain truth to improvisation', said the guitarist Wayne Krantz in a 1999 interview.

> It's a truth of the moment. Right now you say something, and if people are listening to you and other musicians are playing with you, a group of people can commonly agree upon one way of looking at the world just for one moment. And to me the creation of improvisation is what allows that. And that's a little different from playing a vocabulary, because a vocabulary more suggests something that we *already* agree on (Krantz, 1999).

If we are to 'achieve our country', achieve our *democracy*, it will mean doing something different than 'playing a vocabulary', reiterating the grammar, the routines of which structure our interactions with our neighbours – or those neighbours with whom we *already agree*. It will mean finding a truth in improvisation, which will be neither Donne's Truth standing in all its stony solidity atop a hill like Scrabo Tower, nor his other truth, incarnated in this or that muscular avatar of 'our community', to which we owe allegiance. It will take place, if at all, in our *neighbourhood*, in the streets, in the market squares – like the one in which we began this book in a small Northern Ireland town in the run-up to the Brexit referendum in 2016.

'My' side lost the vote on that occasion. But had the referendum gone the other way, we still would have had our work cut out, not least to make sure there was still a democratic space for those who had lost, including non-violent paths to democratic empowerment; but also to address the problem that 'Europe', or rather the political actors who had gained hegemony in the European institutions, had chosen to further empower today's inheritors of the mantle of the VOC, following the routines of the globally dominant paradigm of the crank economy. Another example of the power of the 'faceless bureaucrats' of Brussels? Let us not be too hasty to reiterate that old routine.

ODDFELLOWS

As it happens, I visited Brussels briefly at the end of that fateful year, and found that, for all that it was a city preparing for the festive season, for all the glitter and the lights, it had something of a subdued atmosphere. Not only had the Brexit vote taken place, but the city was still reeling from the shock of terrorist attacks that had claimed the lives of thirty-two victims, as well as those of the three suicide bombers themselves.

Brussels, of course, in a classic example of synecdoche, the epitome of the part that stands for the whole, had long stood as a proxy for the Institutions of the EU themselves, the aforementioned faceless bureaucracy, the usurping foreign power from which 'control' would have to be 'taken back' by the plucky British people, if the proper order of things was to be restored. But stand in the city itself and one encounters not a monolithic Power so much as a messy, fluid, complex, diverse neighbourhood, or at least as much of it as can be seen from any given vantage point within it. Take a spot beside the Palais de Justice, for instance – this building in which, as Robert Porter reminds us (Porter, 2018) Raoul Vaneigem once enjoyed a subversive day-dream. The building stands on a hill, overlooking (or as Vaneigem puts it, 'crushing') a relatively poor area of the city beyond and beneath it.

This area, Molenbeek, was known in 2016, if at all, as the region from which the terrorists had set out to carry out their attacks. But to get to Molenbeek from the Palais de Justice you would, as likely as not, have to head along the Rue de Liverpool or the Rue de Manchester. What are these streets, named for northern English cities, doing in a relatively poor district of the de facto capital of Europe? It turns out that Molenbeek was, in the nineteenth century, known as 'Little Manchester'. It industrialised after the model of the pioneering English city, and drew people in from across the region, then from farther afield. To this day it has a population from a wide range of cultural and ethnic backgrounds.

But at some point, the money moved on, and Little Manchester, with its diverse inhabitants, was cast adrift like the East India Company's supply boat, the Gift. There are, today, inclusive and creative events happening there (when I visited the area in 2022, run down as it was, young families of diverse ethnicities were gathering together in a vegetarian restaurant preparing for a music workshop with a local DJ), but the contrast between the condition of the infrastructure and resources here in 'Little Manchester' and a few minutes' walk away in the shiny, glass-and-steel heart of 'Brussels' is still striking.

Indeed, visit 'Big Manchester', as it were, and not only is it possible to see shiny glass-and-steel evidence of recent development, but also reminders of the time this was the central focal point of industrial power. We have already come across the brick and steel (not so shiny anymore) of the viaducts and railways, but there are other reminders of a less obviously visible history here too.

Manchester was not just plugged into the then emerging global, abstract, extractive 'market'. Stand in Deansgate, and you can see 'Oddfellows House', the building of the wonderfully named 'Independent Order of Oddfellows Manchester', one of a number of Friendly Societies, unions, and other combinations that emerged as Manchester industrialised. The Peterloo demonstrators gathered here; Chartists organised here; Suffragettes interrupted meetings in the Free Trade Hall; in nearby Rochdale, ordinary, everyday workers opened an unassuming looking store in Toad Lane and pioneered a model of cooperative ownership that would spread across the country, then the world.

Of course, none of this was without resistance from the authorities. Peterloo aside, consider the Combination Acts of 1799 and 1800, by means of which all 'attempts to influence wage rates or conditions of employment were specifically proscribed' (Batt 1986, 186), leaving the early trade unions with limited legal options for action – though this did not stop them from organising, whether dispensing welfare, organising petitions, or, in the words of Eric Hobsbawm, 'collective bargaining by riot' (Batt 1986, 188).

In the early days of unions there were clearly differences of approach, though, and that precisely over the question of violence. On the one hand, trade unionists in Sunderland adopted the slogan 'United to support, but not combined to injure'; on the other hand, 'threats to inflict injury upon uncooperative employers and disloyal workmates were commonplace' (Batt 1986, 186). The shift in language from 'combination' to 'union' was intended to move away from the negative, indeed violent, associations of the former.

But what if this shift has made something important in the movement harder to read? What if it is an emphasis on *unity* that now tends to obscure precisely the *combining*, the coming together of *different* people – that is, of people *for all their differences*, who are nonetheless capable of joining forces mutually to empower each other? What if, even as we combine, rather than forming a monolithic bloc, in all its granite, 'mineral opacity' (to borrow from Bourdieu, 1990), we remain a confluence of odd fellows (provided we can reclaim the word 'fellows' for people across the full gender spectrum)? What if effective, democratic unionism (trade unionism, or even the sort that would inaugurate or maintain a united States, Kingdom, or Ireland), what if effective *democracy* needs to make room for, to take seriously, that *oddity*, the multiplicity, fluidity and hybridity of the *demos*, the uniqueness, the irreplaceable singularity of *each of my neighbours*, and perhaps above all, the *nonviolence of the combination*?

Half a dozen turbulent years on from the Brexit referendum, and back in Northern Ireland another referendum now appears to be all but inevitable in the not-too-distant future – a referendum on the very existence of Northern Ireland as such; or to put it another way, a referendum on a future Ireland. Which will, therefore, also mean a future, changed, UK. If that referendum takes place, and if, as a result, there is to be constitutional change, it will *not* be 'because of Nationalist or Republican violence', nor will it be because of some sort of 'betrayal' by 'Others', those who vote for parties such as Alliance, the Green Party or People Before Profit. It will be because most people (not 'the majority community' or 'the minority community plus treacherous Others', just most *people*, most of your *neighbours*) in Northern Ireland can no longer put up with the status quo. The more interesting question is about *why* they would want things to change, why they would choose to *make* the change; and it will be, if it happens, perhaps in no small part because too many Unionist leaders (some of them even with the word 'democratic' in their title), as a matter of routine, urged their followers to *choose denomination over democratic combination*.

They chose, that is, the 'kerosene' of denomination, to recall Raul Gandhi's image, as the fuel for their political project; chose to intensify the loyalty of the already loyal within their 'own' denomination, insisting on, demanding 'Unionist unity' on their own terms, rather than seeking to expand the range of possible *combinations of and with others*, a beyond-denominational *community of others* that they could call upon in the event of the now all but inevitable border poll. Conversely, of course, a kind of denominational hardening among some Irish Republicans, epitomised in the jubilant chanting of 'Up the Ra' (meaning the IRA) by people far too young to remember the sheer bloody violence of a conflict they appear, to older people, to be celebrating, reduces the scope of potential combinations in the other direction.

There now seems little doubt that the dynamics of denomination in Northern Ireland have been intensified by the Brexit vote. While a majority of the population voted Remain in the EU referendum, certain Unionists campaigned to 'take back control', demanding and helping to inaugurate the very Brexit border that is now causing them such problems – though not just, as they seem to think, because it fell in the Irish Sea. Does anyone believe that, had it been imposed (in the name of 'the British People', with all the neo-colonial implications embedded in that phrase) on the island of Ireland, snaking around the six counties of Northern Ireland, a Brexit border that most people didn't call for in the first place, it would have worked out better for the Union? On the note of neo-colonialism, incidentally, some Unionist leaders, seemingly oblivious to the irony and to the peals of incredulous laughter they provoked, took to the stage in Northern Ireland (or should that be northern Ireland?) denouncing colonialism – that is, *EU* colonialism. 'We have become colonial rule takers', explained Jim Allister, leader of the TUV, after the Windsor Framework (post-Brexit UK-EU arrangements) had been ratified, 'from our colonial masters in Brussels' (Sherlock 2023).

Notably, many of the same leaders who welcomed Brexit, regardless of the wishes of a majority of their neighbours in Northern Ireland, had resisted calls for LGBTQ+ equality, for women's rights to choose in the matter of reproductive health-care, and calls for robust climate action, to take some pertinent examples, effectively disempowering ever more neighbours whose votes may well be the decisive factor in the referendum to come. Such Unionist leaders, like some Republicans in the United States, the BJP in India, and others elsewhere, are analogous (indeed this is perhaps more than simply an analogy) to those who have sunk investments into the fossil fuel economy: they have filled their political engines with the kerosene of denomination and neglected to build the infrastructure for a switch to a more sustainable energy source.

Just as with the fossil fuel economy, there is a risk of addiction in the denominational economy. You need the support of your supporters (there is no power, after all, outside a combination of one sort or another), but there is always someone over your shoulder, even more hardline, even more intensely loyal than you, ready to draw off that support, so that you end up having to address less and less the mixed crowd in front of you, with all their unmet needs and variety of desires, and more and more the hardline figures over your shoulder. You end up withdrawing from the mixedness, the diversity of the *neighbourhood* in the direction of the *domain* of the hardliners, effectively authorising *their* message, regardless of the potentially violent consequences, for fear of losing the crowd to this still more uncompromising avatar of the denomination. And, like fossil fuel infrastructure, the more you invest, and the longer you leave it, the more extensive and costly the retrofit that will eventually be required in order to make the change – if there is still time. After all, if denominations are the fossil fuels of the global political economy (with their centralised power-stations, to continue with this more-than-analogy) perhaps *democratic* empowerment is the distributed clean energy network; and if you keep resisting the transition to distributed, democratic neighbourhood empowerment, sooner or later people will combine in sufficient numbers (create sufficiently capacious and powerful combinations) to derail your political project willy-nilly, and whether violently or non-violently.

Wherever the border, Brexit or otherwise, ends up, whether around six (or will it drop to four, for *demographic* reasons?) of the counties of old Ulster, or, as the Unionists fear, in the Irish Sea – just where they believe it is now, only more so – one thing is certain: it will fall *within the neighbourhood*. You and I will still be neighbours, whatever side of the border we end up on, and I will still owe you the obligation of nonviolence.

Is it possible, then, that we can begin to build a new *neighbourhood democracy* – working to produce a more nonviolent, equitable and sustainable neighbourhood, one in which my appetite need not mean your extinction? Can we hold open a nonviolent clearing long enough for it to take root, whether in a newly configured Northern Ireland, United Kingdom, Republic of Ireland, or in a wholly new kind of 'state', wherever we find ourselves, for that matter?

The Good Friday Agreement gave us a chance to do just that. For all that it re-inscribed the locally dominant paradigm of the 'two communities' model, for all that some attempted to switch that paradigm for the globally dominant paradigm of the crank economy, a *bid* was made, even from the opening 'Declaration of Support', calling for a different way in which neighbours could combine along something *other than* denominational lines. The Agreement called for, and the signatories committed to, a fresh start in which 'we firmly dedicate ourselves to the achievement of reconciliation, tolerance, and mutual trust, and to the protection and vindication of the human rights of all'. The Agreement says: 'We acknowledge the substantial differences between our continuing, and equally legitimate, political aspirations', but adds that 'we will endeavour to strive in every practical way towards reconciliation and rapprochement within the framework of democratic and agreed arrangements' (Agreement, 1998).

What sort of a 'we' makes this kind of bid? There is an explicit acknowledgement that there are 'substantial differences' between us, yet there is still enough unity to say 'us' in the first place. If there is a unity of the 'we', then, it is composite. We say 'we', but not with one voice, not in a sort of regal, unitary self-reference. This is not a sovereign, monarchical 'we', the royal 'We' of a VRI, but a 'you *and* I', something in the order of a conversation, an exchange wherein a certain space is opened and preserved. I do not speak for you; you do not speak for me; yet we, you and I, can both (or all: the 'you' may be plural after all) subscribe to the Declaration that opens the Agreement.

The Agreement is not a monologue issued by a preexistent political entity; it is the performative inauguration of a partnership – a *combination* – that preserves difference. And the 'we' of this combination explicitly 'reaffirmed' (let's skip over the question of how one can 'reaffirm' something one had never before 'affirmed') 'our total and absolute commitment to exclusively democratic and peaceful means of resolving differences on political issues'. Even here there are two ways to read the call: does 'resolving' our differences mean collapsing them into some sort of monolithic unity? Or does *resolving* mean rather a commitment to re-solving them, as it were, continually working to engage each other, for all our differences, *democratically and peacefully* (or, better, nonviolently)? Could this mean a commitment to asking: is there a way to resolve this dispute, this clash of political projects *without calling for violence*? That might mean our opponents having to adjust or abandon their project, but it may also mean *us*, whoever we are, having to adjust *ours*, in the light of the violence it does to our neighbours. We are each fully responsible for our own violence. But we can only assess and address that violence in conversation with each other.

This second interpretation, the bid, the *call* of the Agreement to 'strive towards' a politics that would be about a continually renewed effort to *build* democracy – a democracy *to come*, a democracy that would have no *telos* or terminus, that does not model a utopia – is as legible in the GFA as is the reiteration of the 'two communities' model. Both dynamics are in play. That all too many chose to respond to the call by reverting to the routines of a reductive, denominational version of power sharing (maximise the share of power going to 'my' side by minimising the share of power going to 'them') does not mean we could not have responded by working to share power out equitably and sustainably around the population, flowing across and through the neighbourhood, among us all, for all our differences.

'Too many' may have chosen denomination over democracy, but in fact, the democracy to come is *already* being built in the streets and town squares, in workplaces and on picket lines through a union movement and through social movements that bring people together whatever their denomination – Protestant, Catholic and Dissenter alike, in Wolfe Tone's celebrated phrase, though not necessarily 'in the common name of Irishman' (why exchange one denomination for another?) and of course, not *necessarily* to 'break the connexion with England' (Beiner 2013, 13).

DEMOCRATIC *DÚTHCHAS*

In *The Ghost Limb*, Claire Mitchell sets out on a quest to find out if that 'spirit of 1798' is alive among twenty-first-century northern Protestants, interviewing trade unionists, feminists, drag artists, Irish language learners, environmental activists, and more (full disclosure: I was one of the interviewees). Many of them, to underline the point made above concerning the divergence of denomination and combination, have moved away from the politics they were *supposed* to follow – after all, Protestants are *supposed* (supposed by whom?) to be Unionists, part of the Protestant-Unionist-Loyalist *community*, aren't they? In part this was because the issues that mattered to them (economic justice, the environmental crisis, social and civic equality) had been marginalised by the operation of the binary reduction machine. In part, too, because some of them felt that aspects of their identity (we will come back to this word) had been denied them, cut off from them – hence Mitchell's title: the ghost limb; a palpable sense of 'an absence in my own identity' (Mitchell, 2022: 5).

One of these 'alternative Protestants', Stephen Donnan-Dalzell (who, as a drag artist, is also known as Cara Van Parke), picks up on the idea of 'community' in a way that will allow us to clarify the idea of democracy we are trying to explore here.

> I remember in 2016 there was a marriage equality rally, a pro-choice [abortion rights] action day and an Irish language demo, all on the same Saturday. And it just became known as the 'Day of Solidarity' because all the same people went to all the same things. It wasn't like 'there's the gay activists and there's the women's activists', it was more like, 'there's the community, coming together' (Mitchell, 2022: 192).

In 2016, the year of Brexit, the year of Trump, there was a 'coming together' of those marching for a whole spectrum of issues. We should add two grace-notes: that 'the community' does not stand somewhere outside this 'coming-together'; and that 'the same people' were not 'the same' in the sense that they shared an already existing common identity, but that the people who came out for one rally went to the others too. They refused to confine themselves to 'their own' issue, because *all the issues* were their issues. Donnan-Dalzell is describing a solidarity which is not a 'unity' based on a given 'identity' but a *combination* of people who simply refuse to remain confined, refuse to accept the authority of the authorities who would bid them keep to the borders and orders prescribed for them, for each of them as one of those . . .

Rather than being reduced to the status of 'one of those dots', those making up the 'coming-together' here are those who refuse to be silenced, marginalised, refuse to do as they are *bid*, and are instead *empowering* themselves *and others* – as others. 'Solidarity', in this sense, rather than calcifying into a monolith, opens the space for fluidity, hybridity, a boundless deconstruction of boundaries which is an *empowerment*, an empowerment because an expansion of the *democratic combination*.

None of this is to say I must leave my 'identity' behind – if, by 'identity' we here mean something more than a denomination. Indeed, one can *reclaim* a name from processes of denomination, turn a name predominantly used as a mark – and means – of subordination into a self-empowering call to solidarity, from James Brown's 'say it loud, I'm Black and I'm proud', to that other Pride that allowed for the reclaiming of a whole rainbow of denominations once used to dominate: LGBTQ+ (an unfinished, limitless rainbow, we should add). The same goes for those insisting on the right to speak Irish in Northern Ireland, as per the Agreement of 1998 – including those doing so while reclaiming an alternative Protestant identity for themselves, in the spirit of 1798.

Speaking of Irish, to help clarify this point let us recall the Gaelic term *dúthchas* that we encountered in the second chapter. Like James Brown, I can be proud of my heritage, my *dúthchas*, and refuse the authority of anyone trying to deny it or shame me for it. I will share elements of it with some of you that I perhaps do not share with others – just as some of those in Baldwin's mixed crowd shared experiences of racism with each other that they did not with others, and certainly not with the Sheriff. Nonetheless, we must be careful to turn *dúthchas* not into denomination, but into *democracy*.

In Peter McQuillan's compelling and thorough examination of the concept, in the Irish context (a Dictionary of the Scottish Gaelic Language is forthcoming), he shows there is a close association between *dúthchas* and genealogy – specifically, inheritance in the sense of a lineage. Yet I will be impertinent enough to try to give it another inflection by inserting it in another context. Take this example of McQuillan's, from an Irish text of around 1640:

> *Ní áirmhim ceangal gach sleachta dár shíol me*
> *ná dlúitheagar dúthchais mo dhaoine*
> *le cianaibh do liathnuimhir line*
> *do shinsearaibh thionsgnaimh an taoisigh.*

> I don't recount every filial connection whence I came
> Nor the intricate weft of my people's dúchas [sic]
> Since antiquity like an unbroken lineage
> From the original ancestors of our leader (McQuillan 2004, 31)

Look at the play of metaphor and simile in this example. There is (in McQuillan's translation, at any rate) the 'intricate weft' and there is the 'unbroken lineage', and they are sutured here by the simile: one is 'like' the other. What emerges if we prise apart the two elements of the simile in this verse? Is an 'intricate weft' really *like* (let alone *the same as*) an 'unbroken lineage', or is the latter not, precisely, too *linear* to bear the comparison? What if the comparison can only come about at the cost of reducing the intricacy? What if it is not so much that I don't recount every filial connection in the 'intricate weft', but that I decide *only to recount one line*, or one specified set of lines, declare that this one line is the one that *counts*, and that all the others do not count, or count for less?

To sharpen the question, is the search for an 'unbroken lineage' not precisely a question of counting these, and *not those* threads making up an intricate weft – a selective *and therefore reductive* process? To give a different emphasis, an attempt to 'recount every *filial* connection' could only successfully be undertaken if we already knew what 'filial' meant; we could only go back and pick out our filial bonds if we already *knew who we were looking for*, already had the 'correct' principle of inclusion and exclusion to sort our siblings from those others – God's own questionnaire. In other words, if we set ourselves to picking out a *lineage*, the search for 'our' past is structured before we begin, by the *present* operation of processes of denomination – as occurs when one has to cut out innumerable (female) threads to trace only the male line in a patriarchy.

Is such an operation 'like' the 'intricate weft'? Or does it not *cut into* the weft, a textile of such complexity, with so many threads overlapping and bound one to another that it is, strictly, impossible to say exactly where one begins and another ends, without the arbitrariness of the scission or decision?

If this is about identity, it is not an identity that would be enclosed in itself, exterior to others, but one which would emerge only in *relation* to others. Aletta Norval, calling on Wittgenstein, picks up on a familiar figure in her examination of democracy: there is 'no one characteristic that is shared by all' that makes up 'democratic subjectivity'; 'rather, many threads run through a fibre, contributing to its strength or unity, but without one of the threads running the whole length' (Norval 2007, 164). In fact, the single fibre may still be too linear an image for what we are examining here. Elsewhere in the same book, Norval talks of a 'web of new forms of democratic resistance'. Or again, there is an 'articulation between elements that did not belong together before' (Norval 2007, 114). There is a stepping beyond the 'guidance of grammar' to put together 'novelty and tradition' (Norval 2007, 117) in a way that irresistibly calls up the improvisation of a group of musicians, an improvisation that 'does not exist outside its practice', to recall both Krantz and the quotation from Derek Bailey with which we began this book.

So that when Norval quotes Mouffe as saying, 'Democracy is grounded only on the existence of a democratic subject', one could respond: just the one? This is, of course, unfair to both Norval and Mouffe, in whose texts it is already clear that democracy is about *more than one*, (Mouffe 2000), is grounded in an interaction with *others*, grounded only in the web, the intricate weft we weave with each other *as* others, as *neighbours* – not identical, but *nearby*, being-near; close enough to land a blow on, or to combine nonviolently with. And I cannot first choose *who* to let into my neighbourhood before I permit 'democracy' to take place. I cannot rule out people of this or that denomination, allow certain others in, but on sufferance only, and reserve to myself and those with whom I *share an identity* the authority to impose an order of my ('our') choosing, because that is to choose dominance over democracy, and because every border, every attempt to divide and clear the neighbourhood falls *within* the neighbourhood, remains a relation between neighbours.

This would be a procedure of the sort we saw in action in the Imperial project – and one still familiar in the gesture that tells neighbours *of a certain denomination* to 'go back where they came from', whether that comes in the form of a government sponsored sign (Wintour, 2013) or a random racist on a bus.

If you are a racist on a bus, let us be clear, you do not launch an attack on a fellow-passenger because they are black (even if they *are* black); you launch it because you are a racist. Or rather, because you have *chosen the routines of racism*. Thus, you claim, and perhaps even persuade yourself, that your attack is *their fault*. You routinely project a reticle on the body of your neighbour, and lo, a denominational enemy 'appears', retrojected, as though already there, already in the 'wrong' place, already 'asking for it'.

But the racist who says 'Go back home' does not just project a denominational 'enemy' (this man with black skin, or this woman in a veil, for example, are read as 'representing' a somehow threatening, monolithic 'immigrant community', from which the violence is projected as originating); he or she *in the same stroke* also lays claim to the authority of an equally projected, or retrojected, 'White British Nation' (the Whiteness of which is projected as under threat by the being-there of the Black person) or 'The English People' or 'The Irish People', or some equivalent, who *would* be 'entitled' to be there, 'legitimate' owners of the space, entitled to lay down boundaries between neighbours, within the neighbourhood. But the implied 'we' in whose name the racist claims to speak, the White British Nation, is *not on the bus, nor anywhere else in the neighbourhood*. The Authority is absent. What *is* on the bus is a number of passengers, who must decide which of their neighbours to combine with, here, now, in the thick and the quick of this context. The people who are on the bus are in a position to assent to, or to challenge, this claim to speak 'in the name of . . . '

And this is what gives the passengers, whoever they are, whatever their denomination, a certain amount of power *in combination* with each other. Not that they need agree with each other on all points of doctrine, not that they must share an identity; but for that moment, they have the power to choose to respond in nonviolent, democratic combination to refuse the performative call of the official or unofficial vice-viceroys, lieutenants and other place-holders, who claim the authority to order those in the neighbourhood. Power to choose and *obligation* to choose – like Baldwin's Sheriff, we who are on the bus, or in the streets and town squares, we who are *here* cannot *but* face the choice between violence and nonviolence – even if choosing the latter means deciding that in the circumstances, bodily, not without violence, evicting the racist from the bus is the most nonviolent course of action available (in a sense, it should be clear by now, *pure* nonviolence is impossible – which does not make it any less obligatory). Needless to say, evicting individual racists from buses is not sufficient: if they have been brought up in the routines of racism, the task of nonviolence, the task of democracy, is to dismantle those routines, so that *everyone* can get on the bus.

Democracy, because it must always take place in a *mixed* neighbourhood, will, to be sure, be agonistic, aversive. I will not always agree with my neighbours; and indeed, I *may* mostly, or even always, end up *disagreeing* with some of them (racists on buses, for example). There will always be something to set ourselves (aversively, agonistically) against. But it is a disagreement about a political project, not a question of a loyalty to my 'own' which requires a hostility to my *denominational* enemy. The enemy is not 'The Enemy': the enemy is violence itself. And it, violence, must be *overpowered*.

None of this stops my neighbours from being my neighbours, and therefore none of it relieves me of the obligation to learn to live as *equitably, sustainably*, and *nonviolently* as possible with them. It should go without saying, incidentally, but let's say it anyway, that if nonviolence is about overcoming suffering, then we have an obligation of nonviolence towards any being, any *body* soft enough to suffer – and not just to those neighbours we have decided to include under the term 'human', sharply segregating them, like the General we encountered in chapter 3, from 'nonhumans', towards whom one need not act 'humanely'.

Regarding those neighbours, however, our project must become one that sets out to learn to live *democratically* with them. Think of the 'coming-together' in solidarity described by Donnan-Dalzell. Think of the crowd that took to the streets of Glasgow in 2022 to prevent the removal of asylum seekers by the authorities. In fact, if a single incident, if a single headline could gather almost all the threads we have been following here, it would be this, from the Independent: 'Neighbours rush to street to block Home Office from removing Muslim immigrants on Eid' (Dalton 2021).

Neighbours rushing into the streets to defend neighbours of another denomination; defying the authority of a 'Home Office' (there is the note of domesticity again) by *sitting in the street*, no less. Reginald Maudling would be furious. As, indeed, are his successors, who seem set on criminalising and deporting those they insist on associating (before any case has been heard) with criminality, and criminalising those who would combine with them. Protest in a way that does not meet our approval and your demonstration is illegal. Arrive by an 'unauthorised route' and your very presence, your very *being-here* is illegal. By way of an insistence on a chain of equivalence, your denomination has been shifted from 'asylum seeker' (which already, by way of earlier insistent repetition, came yoked with the ghost-adjective 'bogus') to 'migrant' to 'illegal' ('one of those illegals') in a few short years. And because your being-here is a threat, you will be *Cleared*, like the crofters of the Highlands and Islands, not, this time, by boat to Canada, but by Boeing to Rwanda.

The neighbours who took to the streets in Glasgow are, in a sense, *in the neighbourhood* of the women and men determined to Reclaim the Streets, both by marching (and partying) together in them and by redesigning them (Coi 2022). They are in the neighbourhood of the Chilean protesters in 2019, who began by refusing to pay a hiked public transport fare and ended by demanding a whole new Constitution (Franklin 2019). They are in the neighbourhood of the Iranian women 'disrobing' ('stripping', as the authorities, projecting their own reticle of obscenity, would see it) by taking off their veils in public in a demand for equality, refusing to recognise the theologico-patriarchal authority of the regime (Kianpour 2023); they are in the neighbourhood of the demonstrators of the Arab Spring, who demanded democracy not dictatorship (Al Jazeera 2020). They are neighbours to the Bangladeshi factory workers who, defiant after Rana Plaza, formed unions and cooperatives and successfully demanded justice from international corporations. They are neighbours to the people of the First Nations who are resisting oil pipelines in North America, oil extracted and appropriated by the companies from whom I buy petrol for my car, just as you do for yours. Neighbours to the members of La Via Campesina, fighting for peasants' rights; neighbours resisting the new clearances that will be imposed by a kind of pseudo-green (actually anti-sustainable) colonialism whereby resources are yet again stripped from the global South to feed the appetites of the global North – this time with added batteries.

We must be clear here: it will not do to reduce these demonstrators to another *denomination*; worthy examples of 'democracy in action', or some such figure that could be cosily *domesticated*, even if only to make a point in an argument about democracy. Andrea Khalil warns us of the reductive risks of mainstream analysis of what is called, in a neo-orientalist act of denomination, the 'Arab Street' (Khalil 2012). Peter Snowdon, examining the multitude of 'vernacular' videos that emerged and were posted online during the Arab Spring, says it in his title: 'The People Are Not an Image' (Snowdon 2020).

When neighbours take to the streets and market squares it is fluid and messy. You cannot control it, cannot write the script, cannot rule out the possibility that some of them may not be 'good democrats' after all. But there cannot be a building of democracy that *does not* take place on the streets and squares, indeed that does not 'spill out beyond the immediate confines of the street and the square', in Snowdon's words. Democracy emerges through concrete practices, 'embedded in the customs and idioms of specific places and specific communities and the emerging grassroots media practices that multiply and disseminate them'. Democracy *disseminates itself* – or rather, *we* do, disseminate it, you and I, or it does not take place at all.

My neighbourhood does not stop at any border laid down by a higher authority, should that be God or VRI: it stretches as far as the contiguous impact of my life itself – to the neighbours next door, of course, but also to those a few doors down, and to those some definite, if unknown, number of doors away, in the Bangladeshi factory where a woman I will never meet sewed the buttons on the 'shirt I now wear next to my skin' – to recall Smith's phrase. I will never meet her, but this button left her hand to come to mine. I will never meet her, but I *already know I could*; I could sit down with her for a bowl of stew, with some of the local baker's bread, the brewer's beer, the blood still on the butcher's apron. I know we, she and I, could sit within a hand's reach – if she is still alive.

Because, though the people are not an image, I *may* have seen an image of her; her body, coated in dust, clinging in death to a fellow worker, crushed beneath the rubble of the collapsed Rana Plaza building in Dhaka (Time 2013). Yet I do not have to wait for that moment to know how soft it is, a body. To know, already, how soft it is, *your* body; to know *you and I* are, already, touchable, grievable.

If nonviolence is the space of a relation in which my appetite, my way of living, does not mean your extinction, does not *systematically produce your suffering* then I owe you the duty of democracy, the duty to democratise. I owe it to you to take to the streets to demand that the gearing of the system be changed, dismantled and rearranged, so that instead of carving out domains, instead of cranking wealth and power up, vertically, like Clinton's cranes, by putting pressure down on the living bodies and living planet at the bottom, power is spread horizontally, flowing around our neighbourhoods, as equitably and sustainably as possible.

Neighbourhood democracy, like *Göttlicher Gewalt*, boundlessly dismantles those boundaries, whether state imposed or denominationally projected, that sever bonds with our neighbours as such, which divert or drive us *away* from building democratic combinations. We owe a democratic obligation to our neighbours, then, in a double sense: firstly, in that *wherever they are* we owe our neighbours the duty of non-violence, to live as non-violently towards them as possible; and secondly in that some of them have already shown us the way. Happily, neighbourhood democracy, the democracy to come, has already begun (to come), not least in the movements mentioned above.

Close to home (to my home, my hometown) there are also neighbours building a new kind of democracy – and not one based on the nineteenth-century model of the nation-state – in the UK and Ireland, and in other nearby (overlapping) democracies. There are experiments and explorations of possible new institutions, superseding the model bequeathed by the era of Empire. For example, there are ongoing explorations of citizens' assemblies and deliberative discussions – good as techniques; not an end in themselves, but nevertheless capable of being used to build new combinations in the project of a new neighbourhood democracy, and best seen as a 'particular form of activism, one that is wholly committed to the principles of nonviolence and especially well-equipped to challenge the deep assumptions and intergroup relationships that allow authoritarianism to flourish' (Wolf 2018).

There are, in the economic sphere, neighbours building cooperatives and commons (repair cafés, tool libraries); there are experiments in Community Wealth Building from Cleveland, Ohio, to Preston, to North Ayrshire, and to Belfast, perhaps inspired by the members of the worker-owned Mondragon cooperative, in their successful, decades-long experiment with forms of economic democracy. There is a new sense of urgency, too, in movements fighting for a just transition to a just and sustainable economy, and there is a new confidence in the trade union movement – as well as a push back in the form of proposed new 'Combination Laws', aimed at disempowering combinations of neighbours working together to empower themselves (Crerar and Stacey 2023).

There are movements in play that could be called international, except that neighbourhood democracy will not be so much 'inter*national*' (this still conjures separate 'nations') as a matter of imagining and pushing towards a sort of 'archipelago' (Mitchell 2022) of interconnected, *overlapping democracies* that could, if we get the gearing right, equitably and sustainably share power. Share it hand to hand, horizontally, contiguously, for example among people empowering each other in and between Scandinavia, the Faroes, Scotland's Highlands and Islands, and Ireland both North and South (whatever sense those compass marks will have in the near future). This kind of power-sharing has perhaps begun to take place, certainly in the form of renewable energy, but also in terms of culture, ideas, and practices (such as the Nordic Horizons project), and in political terms, in ways that go beyond traditional nation-state institutions, including borders, which may come to bear less of a weight of significance in future.

There are projects of decolonisation – of the curriculum, of museums – that, *pace* Suella Braverman, have nothing to do with making this or that neighbour feel ashamed and everything to do with allowing the whole intricate weft of history – our *shared* history, even if this was experienced very differently by different people – come to light. You don't build democracy by denying your neighbour's *dúthchas*. You do not learn to live non-violently and equitably with people by cropping the violence done to their forebears out of the picture, 'ghostlining' their history, in Kris Manjapra's striking term (Manjapra 2023, intro.), not least as some of the effects are still being (bodily) felt today. I am not responsible for the actions of my ancestors, but I am responsible for what I choose to do with my inheritance – as some families have begun to realise (Renton 2023).

Inheritance should be understood as more than just material goods, of course. If you happen to be born straight, white, male cis-gendered into a society that *routinely* (sometimes openly, sometimes by 'residuary methods') favours people of a certain denomination (for example, straight, white, male cis-gendered people) above others (for example, your black, female, lesbian or trans neighbour), that does not in itself call for personal shame, or a disavowal of your own 'identity'; but it does call forth a democratic duty to combine with your neighbour to *change the routines*, to dismantle the gearing that links denomination to dominance.

The community that comes together, in Donnan-Dalzell's words, does not exist *outside* that contiguous coming together, does not get its authority from a unifying, off-stage denominational entity. It is a community of others that is always open to, or better, always *opening to* others, an open call to combine in the democratic empowerment of neighbours. The power of the combination, overpowering that of the politics of violence, is in the expansion of democratic neighbourhood, in the interweaving of these movements of democratisation.

Such movements address not just the kinetic violence of hostility (though there is much still to be done to address the politics of hostility that produces racism, homophobic and gender-based violence, and a host of other violent inequalities) but also the phenological, indifferent violence of a still globally dominant paradigm set on cranking up profits at the cost of environmental destruction, massive and increasing inequality, and institutionalised poverty. New Clearances in all but name.

Yet, for all that, there is power in *other* forms of combination – combinations *with others* as such. A neighbourhood democracy will take to the streets not just to oppose but to *empower*. This means more than offering a '*sense* of empowerment' through identification with this or that projected entity, because democracy does not wait until we have constituted and purified the appropriate entity. It is not about a collective 'identity', but about *combinations as such*, about the combined power of campaigns for economic justice; for ecological justice; and for justice across a range of issues relating to race and ethnicity, gender and sexual orientation, ability and disability – the red, the green, and the rainbow woven together in a shared, democratic *dúthchas*, unlimited, illimitable; not a hemmed, ready-made garment, but a fabric still in the making, other threads always already being woven into it. If our *dúthchas* is our heritage, if it is what gives us a sense of being-at-home, if it is what binds us to one another and to our place in a weft of mutual obligations, it is in a way that is not reducible to the *domus* under the sway of a *dominus*. To build a democratic *dúthchas* is to make ourselves at home, together, you and I, on the common; to build a place here, now, where we *belong*, but where belonging is not reducible to exclusive and disposable property. A neighbourhood beyond borders, and for all our differences as neighbours.

Those who have profited from and drawn power from division, those whose status depends on maintaining the hierarchy of the new Raj, may – let us be clear: *will* – try to prevent us from combining, will try to call us back into order, into our respective, mutually external denominational communities (our race, nation, denomination, orientation, and so on), invoking our 'identity' (in an act that is actually a reduction of our identity), calling us to realise the allegiance we allegedly 'owe'. But it is always possible to refuse to accept their authority so to denominate us; always possible to combine democratically anyway. To combine democratically, though, is to *keep open* the space of democracy, the common onto which *all* commoners are welcome to step, *even those who tried to denominate, to dominate us, to deter democracy*, provided they set aside their livery, their badges of authority – and their violence.

BECOMING NIAGARA

The task ahead seems, indeed is, daunting, and will likely grow more so as the effects of the latest conflicts, and those of the climate crisis – floods, droughts, food insecurity, resource conflict, forced migration – accelerate.

Yet there is power in democratic combination. Just as a single thread contributes its colour and strength to the fabric, just as the smallest stream contributes its share of the power of the river into which it flows (and the power even of an Amazon, a Niagara, is nothing *but* the combination of innumerable streams), we, you and I, can become Niagara, so to speak, can contribute to the power of democratic combinations, together, and *only* together.

But it is a choice: either seek out, in your neighbourhood, join and contribute to, the movement towards democracy; or, at each moment, stand by and *give clearance to*, even if not actively joining with, those whose project is to move *away* from it, to impose new Clearances, new exclusions, new appropriations, with all the overlapping violences, kinetic and phenological, that will unleash. The task of building neighbourhood democracy, global and local (to the point where those terms no longer stand outside each other) has no terminus – we will not simply one day *get there* and fold our hands with nothing further to do. It will require us to keep expanding the combinations, street by street, square by square, until we can say, if not exactly with Shelley that we are many, they are few, that at least *more there are with us than them* – where we don't know what that number may be, and where *they*, too, *remaining our neighbours*, are called, *empowered* to join the intricate weft of the combination.

And we can only weave it together – this intricate weft that will be at once uniquely yours, uniquely mine, and uniquely *ours*, all commoners and on the one common – to the extent that we keep open the question with which we began: the question of how we best learn to live together, for all our differences, as equitably, sustainably and nonviolently as possible on this our one and only planet, and in this our corner of it.

Amen?

Bibliography

Agreement. 1998. *The Belfast Agreement: An Agreement Reached at the MultiParty Talks on Northern Ireland.* London: UK Government Assets Publishing Service. https://www.gov.uk/government/publications/the-belfast-agreement

Al Jazeera. 2020. 'What is the Arab Spring, and how did it start?' Al Jazeera News. https://www.aljazeera.com/news/2020/12/17/what-is-the-arab-spring-and-how-did -it-start

Al Jazeera. 2023. 'Hezbollah, Hamas, Islamic Jihad chiefs discuss route to "victory" on Israel'. Al Jazeera News. 25 October 2023. https://www.aljazeera.com /news/2023/10/25/hezbollah-hamas-islamic-jihad-chiefs-discuss-route-to-victory -on-israel

Althusser, Louis. 2001. *Lenin and Philosophy and Other Essays.* Translated by Ben Brewster. New York: Monthly Review Press.

ANDBC. 2023. Ards and North Down Borough Council. Local Council Results 2023. https://www.ardsandnorthdown.gov.uk/about-the-council/elections-2023/ local-council-results-2023

Anderson, Benedict. 1983. *Imagined Communities: Reflections on the Origin and Spread of Nationalism.* London: Verso.

Arblaster, Anthony. 1975. 'What is Violence?' *Socialist Register* 12: 224–49.

Archaeological Survey of India. 2020. *Charters granted to the East-India Company from 1601: also the treaties and grants made with or obtained from the princes and powers in India from 1756 to 1772.* Archaeological Survey of India, New Delhi, accessed 17 September 2023, https://indianculture.gov.in/rarebooks/charters -granted-east-india-company-1601-also-treaties-and-grants-made-or-obtained

Arendt, Hanna. 2006. *Eichmann in Jerusalem: A Report on the Banality of Evil.* London: Penguin,

Armaghi. 2022. '"All Prods are targets" – outrage as sectarian graffiti painted across Newtown road'. Armaghi, 14 August 2022. https://armaghi.com/news /south-armagh/all-prods-are-targets-outrage-as-sectarian-graffiti-painted-across -newtown-road/179302

Atack, Iain. 2012. *Nonviolence in Political Theory.* Edinburgh: Edinburgh University Press

Austin, J. L. 1975. *How to Do Things with Words.* Oxford: Clarendon Press.

Badshah, Nadeem. 2022. 'Boris Johnson tells Russians: "I do not believe this war is in your name"'. *Guardian*, 26 February 2022. https://www.theguardian.com /politics/2022/feb/26/boris-johnson-tells-russians-i-do-not-believe-this-war-is-in -your-name

Baldwin, James. 1985. *The Price of the Ticket: Collected Nonfiction 1948–1985*. New York: St Martin's/Marek.

Balibar, Étienne. 2009. 'Europe as Borderland'. *Environment and Planning D: Society and Space* 27: 190–215.

Balibar, Étienne. 2015. *Violence and Civility: On the Limits of Political Philosophy*. New York: Columbia University Press.

Barton, John. 2003. 'Iterability and the Order-Word Plateau: "A Politics of the Performative" in Derrida and Deleuze/Guattari'. *Critical Horizons* 4 (2): 227– 64. https://doi.org/10.1163/156851603322398288

Batt, John. 1986. '"United to Support But Not Combined to Injure": Public Order, Trade Unions and the Repeal of the Combination Acts of 1799–1800'. *International Review of Social History*, 31 (2), 185–203.

BBC. 2023. 'Timeline of dissident republican activity'. https://www.bbc.co.uk/news/ uk-northern-ireland-10866072

Beard, Lisa A. 2016. '"Flesh of their flesh, bone of their bone": James Baldwin's racial politics of boundness'. *Contemporary Political Theory*.15 (4): 378–98. https: //doi.org/10.1057/cpt.2015.72

Beaumont, Peter. 2018. 'EU leads criticism after Israel passes Jewish "nation state" law'. *Guardian*, 19 July 2018. https://www.theguardian.com/world/2018/jul/19/ israel-adopts-controversial-jewish-nation-state-law

Beiner, Guy. 2013. 'Disremembering 1798? An Archaeology of Social Forgetting and Remembrance in Ulster'. *History and Memory*. 25 (1). Spring/Summer 2013.

Bell, Alice. 2022. *Our Biggest Experiment: A history of the Climate Crisis*. London: Bloomsbury Publishing.

Benjamin, Walter. 1996. *Selected Writings, Volume 1, 1913–1926*, Cambridge, MA: Belknap Press of Harvard University Press.

Bhambra, Gurminder K. 2007. *Rethinking Modernity: Postcolonialism and the Sociological Imagination*, Basingstoke: Palgrave Macmillan.

Bhambra, Gurminder K. 2022. 'Relations of extraction, relations of redistribution: Empire, nation, and the construction of the British welfare state'. *British Journal of Sociology*. Jan; 73 (1): 4–15.

Billig, Michael. 1995. *Banal Nationalism*. London: Sage.

Bloom, Paul. 2016. *Against Empathy: The case for rational compassion*. London: Bodley Head.

Borger Julian. 2023. '"An atmosphere of fear": free speech under threat in Israel, activists say'. *Guardian*. 22 October 2023. https://www.theguardian.com/world /2023/oct/22/an-atmosphere-of-fear-free-speech-under-threat-in-israel-activists -say

Bourdieu, Pierre. 1990. *The Logic of Practice*. Translated by Richard Nice, Stanford, CA: Stanford University Press.

Boyce, George, and Alan O'Day. 1996. *The Making of Modern Irish History: Revisionism and the Revisionist Controversy*. London and New York: Routledge.

Brady, Ciaran, ed. 1994. *Interpreting Irish History*. Dublin: Irish Academic Press.

Braniff, Máire, Sara McDowell, and Joanne Murphy. 2016. 'Editorial Introduction'. *Irish Political Studies*. 31 (1): 1–3. https://doi.org/10.1080/07907184.2015.1126923

Bryan, Dominic. 2008. 'The Politics of Community'. In *Intervening in Northern Ireland: critically rethinking representations of the conflict*, edited by Marysia Zalewski and John Barry, 125–39. London and New York: Routledge Taylor and Francis Group.

Burgess, Thomas Paul, and Gareth Mulvenna, eds. 2015. *The Contested Identities of Ulster Protestants*. Basingstoke: Palgrave Macmillan.

Butler, Judith. 1990. *Gender Trouble: Feminism and the subversion of identity*. New York and London: Routledge.

Butler, Judith. 1997. *Excitable Speech: A politics of the performative*. New York and London: Routledge.

Butler, Judith. 2005. *Giving an Account of Oneself*. New York: Fordham University Press.

Butler, Judith. 2010. *Frames of War: When is life grievable?* London and New York: Verso.

Butler, Judith. 2021. *The Force of Nonviolence: an Ethico-Political Bind*. London and New York: Verso.

Carter, Angela. 2006. *The Bloody Chamber and Other Stories*. London: Vintage Books

Case, Anne, and Angus Deaton. 2020. *Deaths of Despair and the Future of Capitalism*, Princeton, NJ: Princeton University Press.

Cathey, Libby, Allison Pecorin, Trish Turner, and Katherine Faulders. 2020. 'Trump denies knowing who "Proud Boys" are, again declines to condemn white supremacy by name', *ABC News*, September 30, 2020. https://abcnews.go.com/Politics /trump-denies-knowing-proud-boys-declines-condemn-white/story?id=73342275

Chatterjee, Rituparna. 2023. 'Anger in India after school teacher makes her students take turns to slap Muslim boy'. *Independent*, 26 August 2023. https://www .independent.co.uk/asia/india/tripti-tyagi-muzzafarnagar-video-muslim-student -slap-b2399787.html

Chenoweth, Erica. 2021. *Civil Resistance: What Everyone Needs to Know*. Oxford: Oxford University Press.

Chenoweth, Erica, and Maria Stephan. 2011. *Why Civil Resistance Works: The Strategic Logic of Nonviolent Conflict*. New York: Columbia University Press.

Clinton, Bill. 2018. Speech at 'Building Peace: The Belfast / Good Friday Agreement 20 Years On', Queen's University Belfast. https://youtu.be/r3-fDbC2Xzg?t=2150

Cohen, A. P. 1985. *The Symbolic Construction of Community*. London and New York: Routledge.

Cohen, Jeffrey Jerome, ed. 1996. *Monster Theory: Reading Culture*. Minneapolis and London: University of Minnesota Press.

Coi, Giovanna. 2022. '(Re)designing the City for Women'. *Politico*. June 22, 2022. https://www.politico.eu/article/city-women-gender-equality-umea-sweden

-urbact-gendered-landscape-climate-change-emissions-transport-frizon-tunnel
-security/

Collins, Ben, and Brandy Zadrozny. 'Proud Boys celebrate after Trump's debate call-out'. *NBC News*, September 30, 2020. https://www.nbcnews.com/tech/tech-news/proud-boys-celebrate-after-trump-s-debate-call-out-n1241512

Corr-Johnston, Julie-Anne. 2021. 'Actions of those who burned bus at Rathcoole "anti-community"'. *Ulster Unionist Party*, 8 November 2021. https://www.uup.org/actions_of_those_who_burned_bus_at_rathcoole_anti_community_julie_anne_corr_johnston

Crerar, Pippa, and Kiran Stacey. 2023. 'UK Ministers announce anti-strike legislation'. *Guardian,* 5 January 2023. https://www.theguardian.com/uk-news/2023/jan/05/uk-ministers-announce-anti-strike-legislation

Dalton, Jane. 2021. 'Neighbours rush to street to block Home Office from removing Muslim immigrants on Eid'. *Independent*, 13 May 2021. https://www.independent.co.uk/news/uk/home-news/glasgow-kenmure-immigration-evictions-sturgeon-b1847002.html#

Davis, Mike. 2000. *Late Victorian Holocausts: El Niño Famines and the Making of the Third World*, London: Verso.

De Beauvoir, Simone. 2015. *The Second Sex*. Translated by Constance Borde and Sheila Malovany-Chevallier. London: Penguin.

Deleuze, Gilles, and Felix Guattari. 1987. *A Thousand Plateaus*. Translated by Brian Massumi. Minneapolis: University of Minnesota Press.

Demmers, Jolle. 2017. *Theories of Violent Conflict*. London and New York: Routledge.

Derrida, Jacques. 1978. *Writing and Difference*. Translated by Alan Bass. London: Routledge.

Derrida, Jacques. 1988. *Limited Inc*. Evanston: Northwestern University Press.

Derrida, Jacques. 1992, 'Force of Law: the "Mystical Foundation of Authority"'. In *Deconstruction and the Possibility of Justice*, edited by Drucilla Cornell, Michel Rosenfeld, and David Gray Carlson, 3–67. New York and London: Routledge.

Derrida, Jacques. 1997. *Politics of Friendship*. Translated by George Collins. London: Verso.

Devine, T. M. 2019. *The Scottish Clearances: A history of the dispossessed.* London: Penguin.

Dodgshon, Robert A. 2015. No Stone Unturned: *A History of Farming, Landscape and Environment in the Scottish Highlands and Islands.* Edinburgh: Edinburgh University Press.

Du Bois, W. E. B. 2007. *Dusk of Dawn: An essay toward an autobiography of a race concept*, Oxford: Oxford University Press.

Elkins, Caroline. 2022. *A Legacy of Violence: A History of the British Empire*. London: Penguin.

Ellison, Ralph. 2016. *Invisible Man*, London: Penguin.

English, Richard. 2016. *Does Terrorism Work? A History*. Oxford: Oxford University Press.

Erlanger, Steven. 2023. 'An Attack from Gaza and an Israeli Declaration of War. Now What?' *New York Times*. October 7, 2023. https://www.nytimes.com/2023/10/07/world/middleeast/israel-gaza-war-hamas-palestinians.html

Essed, Philomena, and David Theo Goldberg, eds. 2002. *Race Critical Theories*, Oxford: Blackwell.

Extramural Activity. 2022. 'A Return to Violence'. 19 December 2022. https://extramuralactivity.com/2022/12/19/a-return-to-violence/

Eze, Emmanuel Chukwudi, ed. 1997. *Race and the Enlightenment: A Reader.* Cambridge, Massachusetts, and Oxford: Blackwell.

Fanon, Frantz. 1967. *The Wretched of the Earth*. Translated by Constance Farrington. London: Penguin.

Fanon, Frantz. 2021. *Black Skin, White Masks*, Penguin, London. Kobo.

Farrington, Anthony. 2002. *Trading Places: The East India Company and Asia 1600–1834*, London: British Museum.

Fields, Karen E., and Barbara J. Fields. 2012. *Racecraft: The Soul of Inequality in American Life*, London & New York: Verso.

Fleishacker, Samuel. 2019. *Being Me, Being You: Adam Smith and Empathy*, Chicago and London: University of Chicago Press. Kobo.

Flynn, Leontia. 2008. *Drives.* London: Cape Poetry.

Foucault, Michel. 1973. *The Order of Things: An archaeology of the human sciences*, New York: Vintage Books.

Franklyn, Jonathan. 2019. 'Chile protesters: "We are subjugated by the rich. It's time for that to end"'. *Guardian*, 30 October 2019. https://www.theguardian.com/world/2019/oct/30/chile-protests-portraits-protesters-sebastian-pinera

Fukuyama, Francis. 1989. 'The End of History?' *National Interest*, 16: 3–18. Summer 1989.

Gaastra, F. S. 1992. 'The Organisation of the VOC', in *Introduction to the Archives of the Verenigde Oostinische Compagnie,* accessed 26 December 2022, https://www.nationaalarchief.nl/sites/default/files/afbeeldingen/toegangen/NL-HaNA_1.04.02_introduction-VOC.pdf

Gelderblom, Oscar, Abe de Jong, and Joost Jonker. 2013. 'The Formative Years of the Modern Corporation: The Dutch East India Company VOC, 1602–1623'. *Journal of Economic History*. December 2013, Vol. 73 (4): 1050–76.

Giannakos, S.A. 2002. *Ethnic Conflict: religion, identity and politics*, Ohio University Press, Athens.

Graeber, David. 2011. *Debt: the first 5,000 years*. New York: Melville House Publishing.

Grand Orange Lodge of Ireland. 2022. Grand Orange Lodge of Ireland statement, June 3, 2022. https://www.goli.org.uk/post/grand-orange-lodge-of-ireland-statement

Gregg, Richard Bartlett. 2018. *The Power of Nonviolence*, Cambridge: Cambridge University Press.

Hall, Catherine. 2002. *Civilising Subjects: Metropole and Colony in the English Imagination, 1830–1867*. Cambridge: Polity Press.

Hall, Catherine. 2004. 'Of Gender and Empire: Reflections on the Nineteenth Century', in *Gender and Empire*. Edited by Philippa Levine, 46–76. Oxford University Press.

Hargan, Garrett. 2022. 'Feile an Phobail branded a 'hate fest' after video shows pro-IRA chanting at Wolfe Tones concert', *Belfast Telegraph*, 15 August 2022. https://www .belfasttelegraph.co.uk/entertainment/music/feile-an-phobail-branded-a-hate-fest -after-video-shows-pro-ira-chanting-at-wolfe-tones-concert/41912431.html

Hart, Maria Teresa. 2016. 'Superman, Batman, and the Evolution of the "Perfect" Hero Body', *Atlantic*, April 1, 2016. https://www.theatlantic.com/entertainment /archive/2016/04/superman-batman-and-the-evolution-of-the-perfect-male-body /475998/

Hayward, Katy. 2022. 'Northern Ireland Protocol Bill – not enough and far too much?' *UK in a Changing Europe*, 11 October 2022. https://ukandeu.ac.uk/ northern-ireland-protocol-bill-not-enough-and-far-too-much/

Hegel, G. W. F. 1979. *Phenomenology of Spirit*. Translated by A. V. Miller. Oxford and New York: Oxford University Press.

Heidegger, Martin. 1967. *Being and Time*. Translated by John Macquarrie and Edward Robinson. Oxford: Basil Blackwell.

Hicks, Dan. 2020. *The Brutish Museums*. London: Pluto Press.

Hochschild, Adam. 2005. *Bury the Chains: The British Struggle to Abolish Slavery*, London: Pan Books.

Hochschild, Adam. 2006. *King Leopold's Ghost: A story of greed, terror and heroism in colonial Africa*, London: Pan Books.

Hooks, bell. 1995. *Killing Rage, Ending Racism*. London: Penguin.

Hull, Isabel. 2005. *Absolute Destruction: military culture and the practices of war in Imperial Germany*, Ithaca and London: Cornell University Press.

Hunter, William Wilson. 1893. *The Indian Empire: its peoples, history and products*. London: W. H. Allen.

Husserl, Edmund. 1970. *Logical Investigations*. Translated by J. N. Findlay. London and Henley: Routledge and Kegan Paul.

Hutchinson, Roger. 2015. *Martyrs: Glendale and the Revolution in Skye*. Edinburgh: Birlinn Ltd.

IPSOS Mori. 2021. 'The Many Tribes of Brexit', June 2021. https://www.ipsos.com /sites/default/files/ct/news/documents/2021-06/Ipsos%20MORI%20-%20Brexit %20Tribes%20report_0.pdf

James, Henry. 2000. *Turn of the Screw*, ElecBook, ProQuest Ebook Central. https:// ebookcentral.proquest.com/lib/qub/detail.action?docID=3008598.

Kareithi, Amos. 2013. 'Echoes from the past: The kipande's dark past', *Saturday Standard*. https://www.standardmedia.co.ke/sunday-magazine/article/2000084459 /the-kipandes-dark-past

Khalil, Andrea. 2012. 'The Political Crowd: Theorizing Popular Revolt in North Africa', *Contemporary Islam* 6 (1): 45–65.

Kianpour, Suzanne. 2023. 'The Women of Iran Are Not Backing Down'. *Politico*, 22 January 2023. https://www.politico.com/news/magazine/2023/01/22/women -rights-iran-protests-00069245

King, Martin Luther. 2018. *Letter from a Birmingham Jail*. London: Penguin Random House.

Kirby, Paul, and Ece Goksedev. 2023. 'Turkish election victory for Erdogan leaves nation divided'. BBC News, 31 May 2023. https://www.bbc.co.uk/news/world -europe-65743031#

Kowall, Eric. 2021. 'Greater accuracy, versatility among benefits to snipers of new grid-based reticle', posted on U.S. Army website, accessed December 2022, https: //www.army.mil/article/243506/greater_accuracy_versatility_among_benefits_to _snipers_of_new_grid_based_reticle

Krantz, Wayne. 1999. 'Wayne Krantz with Tim Lefebvre and Keith Carlock – Marciac Jazz Festival', accessed 2 January 2023, https://youtu.be/DOiz6vb-ucM?t=134

Land Reform Review Group. 2014. 'The land of Scotland and the common good: report'. Scottish Government, ISBN 9781784124809, accessed 22 January 2023. https://www.gov.scot/publications/land-reform-review-group-final-report -land-scotland-common-good/pages/61/

Leebody, Christopher. 2021. '"Protestant Action Force". . . Who are the gang blamed for Newtownards bus hijacking?' *Belfast Telegraph*, 2 November 2021. https: //www.belfasttelegraph.co.uk/news/northern-ireland/protestant-action-force-who -are-the-gang-blamed-for-newtownards-bus-hijacking-41009069.html

Lennon, Colm. 1987. *Richard Stanihurst the Dubliner 1547–1618*. Dublin: Irish Academic Press.

Levinas, Emmanuel. 1989. *The Levinas Reader*, edited by Seán Hand. Oxford: Blackwell.

Levinas, Emmanuel, 1996. *Basic Philosophical Writings*, edited by Adriaan T. Peperzak, Simon Critchley, and Robert Bernasconi. Bloomington: Indiana University Press.

Levine, Philippa, ed. 2004. *Gender and Empire*, Oxford: Oxford University Press.

Little, Becky. 2020. '"Good Trouble": How John Lewis and Other Civil Rights Crusaders Expected Arrests'. *Sky History*. July 20, 2020. https://www.history.com/ news/john-lewis-civil-rights-arrests

Lynch, Marc. 2023. 'An Invasion of Gaza Would Be a Disaster for Israel'. *Foreign Affairs*. October 14, 2023. https://www.foreignaffairs.com/middle-east/invasion -gaza-would-be-disaster-israel

Macartney, Maurice. 2019. 'Denominations and combinations: versions of "community" in the proclamation of Easter 1916 and the Good Friday Agreement'. *Irish Political Studies*. 34:1, 48–68. DOI: 10.1080/07907184.2018.1447926

Macleod, John Norman. 2006. *'Chaidh a' Chuibhle mun Cuairt'*–Skye and the Land Agitation. In *Barra and Skye: Two Hebridean Perspectives*, edited by Arne Kruse. Edinburgh: The Scottish Society for Northern Studies.

Mallon, Nichola. 2021. '"Mindless cowards" have done "nothing more than attack their own community" says Mallon'. *Belfast Live*, 1 November 2021. https://www .belfastlive.co.uk/news/northern-ireland/newtownards-hijacking-latest-updates -masked-22026731

Mamdani, Mahmood. 2012. *Define and Rule: Native as Political Identity*. Cambridge, Massachusetts: Harvard University Press.

Manjapra, Kris. 2023. *Black Ghost of Empire: The Long Death of Slavery and the Failure of Emancipation*. London: Penguin. Kobo.

Martin, Bernard, and Mark Spurrell, eds. 1962. *Journal of a Slave Trader (John Newton) 1750–1754.* London: The Epworth Press.

Massey, Doreen. 2005. *For Space*. Los Angeles, London, New Delhi, Singapore & Washington DC: Sage.

Mbembe, Achille. 2019. *Necropolitics*. Translated by Steven Corcoran. Durham and London: Duke University Press.

McCauley, James W. 2016. *Very British Rebels? The culture and politics of Ulster Loyalism*. New York, London, Oxford, New Delhi, Sydney: Bloomsbury.

McCavery, Trevor. 2013. *Newtown: A history of Newtownards*. Belfast: White Row.

McDowell, Lindy. 2022. 'Neal's planter talk fails to grow roots with unionist community'. *Belfast Telegraph*, May 28, 2022. https://www.belfasttelegraph.co.uk/opinion/columnists/lindy-mcdowell/neals-planter-talk-fails-to-grow-roots-with-unionist-community-41697343.html

McGarry, John, and Brendan O'Leary. 1989. *Explaining Northern Ireland*. Oxford: Blackwell.

McGonagle, Suzanne. 2021. 'Co Down bus hijacking branded "reckless and despicable".' *Irish News*, 2 November 2021. https://www.irishnews.com/news/northernirelandnews/2021/11/02/news/co-down-bus-hijacking-branded-reckless-and-despicable--2495417/

McKay, Susan. 2021. *Northern Protestants: On Shifting Ground*. Belfast: Blackstaff Press.

McQuillan, Peter. 2004. *Native and Natural: Aspects of the concepts of 'right' and 'freedom' in Irish*. Cork: Cork University Press in association with Field Day.

Meiksins Wood, Ellen. 2002. *The Origin of Capitalism: A longer view*, London and New York: Verso.

Merleau-Ponty, Maurice. 1964. *Sense and Non-Sense*. Translated by Hubert L. Dreyfus and Patricia Allen Dreyfus. Evanston: Northwestern University Press.

Merleau-Ponty, Maurice. 1968. *The Visible and the Invisible*, edited by Claude Lefort. Translated by Alphonso Lingis. Evanston: Northwestern University Press.

Merleau-Ponty, Maurice. 2002. *Phenomenology of Perception*. Translated by Colin Smith. London and New York: Routledge Classics.

Metcalf, Barbara D., and Thomas R. Metcalf. 2002. *A Concise History of India*. Cambridge: Cambridge University Press.

Metcalf, Thomas R. 1979. *Land, Landlords and the British Raj: Northern India in the nineteenth century*. Berkely, Los Angeles, London: University of California Press.

Metcalf, Thomas R. 1995. *Ideologies of the Raj*. Cambridge: Cambridge University Press.

Mikhael, Drew. 2021. 'New "Others" in Post-Conflict Consociations: A Continuum of Exclusion?' *Nationalism and Ethnic Politics*. 27 (1): 79–98. https://doi-org.queens.ezp1.qub.ac.uk/10.1080/13537113.2021.1876345

Miniter, Richard. 2011. 'Are George Soros' Billions Compromising US Foreign Policy?', Forbes, September 9, 2011. https://www.forbes.com/sites/richardminiter

/2011/09/09/should-george-soros-be-allowed-to-buy-u-s-foreign-policy/ #23b4464b1623

Mitchell, Claire. 2006. *Religion, Identity and Politics in Northern Ireland: boundaries of belonging and belief.* London and New York: Routledge, Taylor and Francis Group.

Mitchell, Claire. 2022. *The Ghost Limb: Alternative Protestants and the spirit of 1798.* Belfast: Beyond the Pale Books.

Mitchell, Peter. 2021. *Imperial Nostalgia: how the British conquered themselves,* Manchester: Manchester University Press.

Morgan, Kenneth. 1999. *Edward Colston and Bristol.* Bristol: University of Bristol. https://www.bristol.ac.uk/Depts/History/bristolrecordsociety/publications/bha096 .pdf

Morris, James. 1968. *Pax Britannica: the Climax of an Empire.* London: Faber and Faber.

Mouffe, Chantal. 2000. *The Democratic Paradox.* London and New York: Verso.

Muirhead, Russell, and Nancy L. Rosenblum. 2019. *A Lot of People Are Saying: The New Conspiracism and the Assault on Democracy.* Princeton and Oxford: Princeton University Press. Kobo.

Mukhopadhyay, Aparajita. 2018. *Imperial Technology and 'Native' Agency: A social history of railways in colonial India, 1850–1920.* London and New York: Routledge, Taylor and Francis Group.

Nagle, John. 1997. 'Ethnos, Demos and Democratization: A comparison of the Czech Republic, Hungary and Poland'. *Democratization,* 4 (2): 28–56. https://doi.org/10 .1080/13510349708403514

Netanyahu, Benjamin. 2023. 'Excerpt from PM Netanyahu's remarks at the opening of the Winter Assembly of the 25th Knesset's Second Session'. Ministry of Foreign Affairs. 16 October 2023. https://www.gov.il/en/departments/news/excerpt-from -pm-netanyahu-s-remarks-at-the-opening-of-the-knesset-s-winter-assembly-16-oct -2023

Nolan, P., D. Bryan, C. Dwyer, K. Hayward, K. Radford, and P. Shirlow. 2014. *The Flag Dispute: Anatomy of a Protest.* Belfast: Queen's University Belfast. http:// www.qub.ac.uk/research- centres/isctsj/filestore/Filetoupload,481119,en.pdf

Norval, Alletta. 2007. *Aversive Democracy: Inheritance and Originality in the Democratic Tradition.* Cambridge: Cambridge University Press.

Oltermann, Philip. 2022. 'Germany returns 21 Benin bronzes to Nigeria – amid frustration at Britain'. *Guardian,* 20 December 2022. https://www.theguardian.com/ world/2022/dec/20/germany-returns-21-benin-bronzes-to-nigeria-amid-frustration -at-britain

Omi, Michael, and Richard Winant. 2002. 'Racial Formation', in *Race Critical Theories,* edited by Philomena Essed and David Theo Goldberg. Oxford: Blackwell.

O'Reilly, Luke. 2022. 'Effigies of female politicians hung from bonfire condemned by DUP leader'. *Belfast Telegraph,* July 14, 2022. https://www.belfasttelegraph .co.uk/news/northern-ireland/effigies-of-female-politicians-hung-from-bonfire -condemned-by-dup-leader-41840869.html

Orwell, George. 2001. *Orwell and Politics.* London: Penguin Books.

Osterhammel, Jürgen. 2018. *Unfabling the East: The Enlightenment's encounter with Asia*, Princeton, NJ: Princeton University Press.

Ozkirimli, Umut. 2010. *Theories of Nationalism: A critical introduction*, second edition, Basingstoke: Palgrave Macmillan.

de Paor, Liam. 2016. *The Easter Proclamation 1916*. Dublin: Four Courts Press.

Paisley, Ian. 1998. 'Speech to DUP Annual Conference by Party Leader Rev. Ian Paisley'. 28 November 1998. *CAIN web service*. https://cain.ulster.ac.uk/events/peace/docs/ip281198.htm

Petit Palais. No date. 'Self-portrait in Oriental Attire, Rembrandt, 1631'. *Petit Palais: Musée des Beaux-Arts de la Ville de Paris*. https://www.petitpalais.paris.fr/en/oeuvre/self-portrait-oriental-attire

Phillips, Amber. 2017. '"They're rapists". President Trump's campaign launch speech two years later, annotated'. *Washington Post*, June 16, 2021. https://www.washingtonpost.com/news/the-fix/wp/2017/06/16/theyre-rapists-presidents-trump-campaign-launch-speech-two-years-later-annotated/

Phillips, Barnaby. 2021. *Loot: Britain and the Benin bronzes*. London: Oneworld Publications.

Pistor, Katharina. 2019. *The Code of Capital: How the law creates wealth and inequality*. Princeton and Oxford: Princeton University Press.

Plokhy, Serhii. 2023. *The Russo-Ukrainian War*. London: Penguin Books. Kobo.

Porter, Robert. 2018. *Meanderings Through the Politics of Everyday Life*. New York and London: Rowman and Littlefield.

Postrel, Virginia. 2020. *The Fabric of Civilization: how textiles made the world*. New York: Basic Books. Kobo.

Powell, Benjamin. 2013. 'Sweatshops in Bangladesh Improve the Lives of Their Workers, and Boost Growth'. *Forbes*. May 2, 2013. https://www.forbes.com/sites/realspin/2013/05/02/sweatshops-in-bangladesh-improve-the-lives-of-their-workers-and-boost-growth/?sh=39ae876d74ce

Putin, Vladimir. 2021. 'On the Historical Unity of Russians and Ukrainians'. *President of Russia* website. 12 July 2021. http://en.kremlin.ru/events/president/news/66181

Putin, Vladimir. 2022a. 'Address by the President of the Russian Federation'. *President of Russia* website. 21 February 2022. http://en.kremlin.ru/events/president/transcripts/67843

Putin, Vladimir. 2022b. 'Meeting on socioeconomic support for regions'. *President of Russia* website. 16 March 2022. http://en.kremlin.ru/events/president/transcripts/67996

Rathe, Kaja Jenssen. 2023. 'Forever Foreigners: The Temporality of Immigrant Indebtedness'. *Journal of the British Society for Phenomenology*, 54:3, 249–64, DOI: 10.1080/00071773.2023.2205597

Renton, Alex. 2023. 'We whose ancestors owned slaves want to make amends – but nations must also pay their due'. *Guardian*. Saturday, 11 February 2023. https://www.theguardian.com/commentisfree/2023/feb/11/ancestors-slaves-family-plantations-profits

Rodriguez, Sabrina. 2021. 'Trump's partially built "big, beautiful wall"'. *Politico*. 1 December 2021. https://www.politico.com/news/2021/01/12/trump-border-wall -partially-built-458255

Rorty, Richard. 1998. *Achieving Our Country: Leftist Thought in Twentieth-Century America*. Cambridge, MA: Harvard University Press.

Rothschild, Emma. 2021. *An Infinite History: the story of a family in France over three centuries*. Princeton and Oxford: Princeton University Press. Kobo.

Ruane, Joseph, and Todd, Jennifer. 1996. *The Dynamics of Conflict in Northern Ireland*. Cambridge: Cambridge University Press.

Sage, Lorna, ed. 1994. *Flesh and the Mirror: Essays on the Art of Angela Carter*, London: Virago Press.

Said, Edward W. 1978. *Orientalism*. London and Henley: Routledge and Kegan Paul.

Said, Edward W. 1994. *Culture and Imperialism*. London: Vintage.

Sanghera, Sathnam. 2021. *Empireland: How Imperialism has Shaped Modern Britain*. London: Penguin. Kobo.

Scanlan, Padraic X. 2020. *Slave Empire: How slavery built modern Britain*. London: Robinson.

Schmitt, Carl. 1996. *The Concept of the Political*. Translated by George Schwab. Chicago: University of Chicago Press.

Schneewind, J. B. 1998. *The Invention of Autonomy: A History of Modern Moral Philosophy*, Cambridge: Cambridge University Press.

Seeley, John. 2011. *The expansion of England: two courses of lectures*. New York: Barnes & Noble Digital Library. Kobo.

Serhan, Yasmeen. 2020. 'The EU Watches as Hungary Kills Democracy'. *Atlantic*. 2 April 2020. https://www.theatlantic.com/international/archive/2020/04/europe -hungary-viktor-orban-coronavirus-covid19-democracy/609313/

Shama, Simon. 1991. *The Embarrassment of Riches: An interpretation of Dutch culture in the Golden Age*. London: Fontana Press.

Sharma, Rakesh. 2022. 'Who was Adam Smith?' *Investopedia*. July 18, 2023. https://www.investopedia.com/updates/adam-smith-economics/

Sherlock, Cillian. 2023. 'TUV conference told Windsor Framework "worse than the Protocol"'. *Belfast Telegraph*. 25 March 2023. https://www.belfasttelegraph.co.uk /news/politics/tuv-conference-told-windsor-framework-worse-than-the-protocol /1996107668.html

Shirlow, Peter, and Mark McGovern, eds. 1997. *Who Are 'The People'?, Unionism, Protestantism and Loyalism in Northern Ireland*. London: Pluto Press.

Shuffleton, Amy. 2015. 'Consider your man card reissued: masculine honor and gun violence'. *Educational Theory*. 65 (4): 387–403. https://doi.org/10.1111/edth.12123

Silva, Jennifer M. 2019. *We're Still Here: Pain and Politics in the Heart of America*. Oxford: Oxford University Press. Kobo.

Smith, Adam. 1999. *The Wealth of Nations*. London: Penguin Books. Kobo.

Smith, Adam. 2009. *The Theory of Moral Sentiments*. London: Penguin Books. Kobo.

Snowdon, Peter. 2020. *The People Are Not an Image: Vernacular Video after the Arab Spring*. London and New York: Verso.

Bibliography

Snyder, Timothy. 2022. *On Tyranny and On Ukraine: Lessons from Russia's War on Ukraine*. London: Penguin. Scribd Audiobook.

Spivak G. C. 1985. 'The Rani of Sirmur: an essay in reading the archives'. *History and Theory*. 24 (3): 247–72.

Stanley, Jason. 2018. *How Fascism Works: The Politics of Us and Them*. New York: Random House.

Tahmasebi-Birgani, Victoria. 2014. *Emmanuel Levinas and the Politics of Non-Violence*. Toronto, Buffalo, London: University of Toronto Press. Kobo.

Thoreson, Ryan. 2022. 'LGBT Rights Under Renewed Pressure in Hungary'. *Human Rights Watch*. 15 February 2023. https://www.hrw.org/news/2022/02/15/lgbt-rights-under-renewed-pressure-hungary

Time. 2013. 'A Final Embrace: The Most Haunting Photograph from Bangladesh'. *Time* website. May 8, 2013. https://time.com/3387526/a-final-embrace-the-most-haunting-photograph-from-bangladesh/

Tooze, Adam. 2018. *Crashed: How a decade of financial crises changed the world*. New York: Viking. Kobo.

Tóth, Csaba. 2014. 'Full text of Viktor Orbán's speech at Băile Tuşnad (Tusnádfürdő)'. *Budapest Beacon*. 26 July 2014. https://budapestbeacon.com/full-text-of-viktor-orbans-speech-at-baile-tusnad-tusnadfurdo-of-26-july-2014/

Trump, Donald. 2017. 'The Inaugural Address'. *Trump White House Archives*. January 20, 2017. https://trumpwhitehouse.archives.gov/briefings-statements/the-inaugural-address/

Wagner, John, and Jenna Johnson. 2018. '"We have to harden our schools": Trump makes arming teachers his top safety goal'. *Washington Post*, February 22, 2018. https://www.washingtonpost.com/politics/we-have-to-harden-our-schools-trump-says-teachers-should-be-armed-after-florida-massacre/2018/02/22/e8dcd5bc-17f6-11e8-b681-2d4d462a1921_story.html

Walker, Peter. 2023. 'Suella Braverman rails against "experts and elites" in partisan speech'. *Guardian*, Monday, 15 May 2023. https://www.theguardian.com/politics/2023/may/15/suella-braverman-rails-against-experts-and-elites-in-partisan-speech

Wallenfeldt, Jeff. 2023. 'Jair Bolsonaro, President of Brazil'. *Britannica*. Last updated September 16, 2023. https://www.britannica.com/biography/Jair-Bolsonaro

Wanjiru-Mwita, Melissa. 2021. 'The fascinating history of how residents named their informal settlements in Nairobi'. *Conversation*. May 9, 2021. https://theconversation.com/the-fascinating-history-of-how-residents-named-their-informal-settlements-in-nairobi-159080

Whitehead, Tony. 2013. 'Colliery Railways: Rainton and Seaham Railway 1831–1988'. *Durham Records Online*. July 2013. https://durhamrecordsonline.com/library/tag/londonderry-family/

Whyte, John. 1990. *Interpreting Northern Ireland*. Oxford: Clarendon.

Williams, James R. 2020. 'Sign and Democracy'. *James R. Williams* website. 21 March 2020. https://www.jamesrwilliams.net/signs-and-democracy/

Willisher, Kim, and Lizzy Davies. 2014. 'Buoyant Le Pen seeks more allies for Eurosceptic group in Brussels'. *Guardian*. 28 May 2014. https://www.theguardian.com/world/2014/may/28/marine-le-pen-eurosceptic-bloc-brussels

Wilson, Bill. 2016. 'Trump accuses China of "raping" US with unfair trade policy'. *BBC News*. 2 May 2016. https://www.bbc.co.uk/news/election-us-2016-36185012

Wintour, Patrick. 2013. '"Go home" billboard vans not a success, says Theresa May'. *Guardian*. 22 October 2013. https://www.theguardian.com/politics/2013/oct/22/go-home-billboards-pulled

Wootton, Dan. 2023. 'The woke blob want to destroy the country to bring down this Conservative Government, says Dan Wootton'. *GB News* website. 20 April 2023. https://www.gbnews.com/opinion/the-woke-blob-want-to-destroy-the-country-to-bring-down-this-conservative-government-says-dan-wootton

Wyke, Terry. No Date. 'Statue of Abraham Lincoln, Lincoln Square, Manchester'. *Revealing Histories: Remembering Slavery*. Accessed 19 September 2023. http://revealinghistories.org.uk/the-american-civil-war-and-the-lancashire-cotton-famine/places/statue-of-abraham-lincoln-lincoln-square-manchester.html

Yapp, E., and K. E. Pickett. 2019. 'Greater income inequality is associated with higher rates of intimate partner violence in Latin America'. *Public Health* 175 (2019): 87–89. https://doi.org/10.1016/j.puhe.2019.07.004

Žižek, Slavoj. 1989. *The Sublime Object of Ideology*. London and New York: Verso.

Žižek, Slavoj. 2008. *Violence: Six Sideways Reflections*. London: Profile Books.

Index

About the Author

Maurice Macartney holds a BSSc in scholastic philosophy from Queen's University Belfast in Northern Ireland, an MA in continental philosophy from the University of Warwick, and a PhD in politics, again from Queen's, where he now works as part of the Civic Engagement and Social Responsibility Team, and where he is a member of the Racial Equity Champions Network.

He describes himself as a 'serial volunteer', having worked in a voluntary capacity for organisations such as Amnesty International, Oxfam, and the intercultural peacebuilding organisation Beyond Skin.

He is currently a member of the Migrant and Minority Ethnic Thinktank, for whom he has written reports on issues affecting minoritised communities in Northern Ireland and coordinated responses to government consultations, and for whom he makes the video and podcast series *MME Matters*, covering issues such as race-relations in Northern Ireland. He is also a member of the Green Party in Northern Ireland.

9 781666 916218

CW01433697

The Gnostic

A Journal of Gnosticism,
Western Esotericism and Spirituality

Issue 2

Copyright Page and acknowledgments

The Gnostic 2, Autumn 2009.

Editor: Andrew Phillip Smith

Published by Bardic Press
71 Kenilworth Park
Dublin 6W
Ireland.

ISBN: 978-1-906834-05-0

Thanks to the contributors and all others who have made this possible, including but not limited to: Tessa Finn, Dean Wilson, Miguel Conner, Luc Valentine, Jeremy Puma, Bill Darlison, Quest Books, Inner Traditions, Apocryphile Press, Watkins Books, .Arcturus Books,

Gnostic comes out twice a year. It was
to be three times but the second issue
already six months after the first and come
it really realistic to be able to make it
yearly? We all have other things to do
know. Autumn and Spring are my favourite
of year, so that's when The Gnostic should
out. Three times a year? I'd like to see you
anything anytime, let alone twice a year.
don't really know what it's like do you. So

The Gnostic

A Journal of Gnosticism, Western Esotericism and Spirituality

Issue 2

Colin Wilson, Will Parker, Miguel
Conner, April DeConick, Tessa Dick,
Anthony Cartledge, Anthony Peake,
Jeremy Puma, Luc Valentine, Anthony
Blake, Dean Wilson et al

Edited by Andrew Phillip Smith

Bardic Press
Dublin 2009

Contents

From the Mouth of the Demiurge

We have reached our second issue — that difficult second issue. Think *Meat is Murder* or *Portishead* or *White Light/White Heat*. It includes a slew of new writers, new perspectives and themes. Since this issue is coming out around six months after the first, so I may as well bow down to reality and redefine The Gnostic as a twice-yearly publication.

After publication, I discovered that issue one had an emergent theme. Something to do with the awkward relationship between spirituality and rationality. This was reflected in the Alan Moore interview, in Philip K Dick's experience, in Will Parker's look at the magical worldview and subtly in many other aspects of the contents.

This time I'm struck more by the interconnections between contributors and their interests. Tessa Dick describes her relationship with Philip K Dick. Colin Wilson briefly discusses Dick's experiences and was an early influence on Anthony Blake, who was later heckled by Wilson. Anthomy Peake takes an extended look at Dick in the light of his own theories, and his own books are featured in the reviews section. My short story, 'Schrödinger's Gun', was inspired by a quantum physics thought experiment described in one of Peake's books. Will Parker looks at Wilson's theories on the occult... and so on and so on.

Gnosticism proper is represented in Dean Wilson's look at Gnostic asceticism, in Luc Valentine's valuable examination of Pistis Sophia and in Jeremy Puma's bold creation of a Gnostic practice based on the *Apocryphon of John*, and in Miguel Conner's interview with scholar April DeConick, who also contributes a poem. Esoteric Christianity is represented in Eugene Poliakov's brilliant interpretation of the symbolism in the New Testament.

Letters by email or snail mail or still welcome. While I received many nice words on the first issue, there was little in the way of in depth comment, so there is no letters page. Perhaps we move too fast nowadays to consider letters to such an infrequent publication. Readers who may be interested in discussing the contents of the present issue may like to visit The Palm Tree Garden http://www.palmtreegarden,com and post to the forum. Letters, gifts and monetary donations may be sent to:

The Gnostic Magazine
71 Kenilworth Park
Dublin 6W
Ireland.

Emails are welcome to
andrew@bardic-press.com

We now have a working website, http://www.the-gnostic.com, which includes some extra material including audio clips. The most convenient way to order *The Gnostic* is via Amazon.com and its international sites. It may also be ordered from most booksellers and is stocked in selected bookstores. If you have trouble ordering, please contact us directly via email.

Andrew Phillip Smith, Dublin, 2009

Andrew Phillip Smith

An Interview with Colin Wilson

Colin Wilson's new book *Super Consciousness* develops themes that began in his first book *The Outsider* and have accumulated over a period of fifty years. He has written over 100 books, examining subject areas as varied as existentialism, the occult and the paranormal, criminology, and alternative history, and figures as different as Gurdjieff, Reich, Herman Hesse, Camus, Crowley, Borges and serial killer Fred West.

APS: I enjoyed your new book, *Super Consciousness*. I do agree that it's very much the summation of fifty years of research into existence and consciousness and the peak experience.

CW: Yes, well of course, I was fascinated in *The Outsider* by the romantics of the nineteenth century and what fascinated me about them was these glimpses that they had in which it seemed to them that life was absolutely wonderful and then the way that so many of them ended up committing suicide, was what fascinated me. And of course also the fact that the whole romantic thing didn't last for very long. I mean, really, it didn't start until the beginning of the nineteenth century and it was over by about 1825 with the death of Byron and so, it was very strange the way it all seemed to have vanished so quickly. And then of course, everything plunged into a kind of pessimism, so the way Yeats is writing about it by the end of the century, he calls them the Tragic Generation. So that quite fascinated me. And when you're fifteen or sixteen, as I was when I was reading so many of the romantics, what you really want to know is whether you could find a way of achieving these states of

mind when you wanted them, permanently. And it seemed to be perfectly obvious when I wrote *The Outsider*, that the main reason that most of my outsiders could not hang on to them — people like Van Gogh and so on — was that they tended to be a bit inclined to self pity. And I felt for myself, I mean, I'm English and my temperament is very Anglo-Saxon. In other words there's a kind of pragmatism about it, and I've never wasted a great deal of time on self pity, otherwise I would never have got round to writing *The Outsider*, because I had a fairly

difficult beginning because, as you know, I was sort of working class, couldn't get to university because my parents didn't have any money, so I sort of had to take the steep way up to the top, so to speak, which was to work at labouring jobs, which I hated, and so finally I began to write *The Outsider* during a Christmas holiday when I was twenty-two, and of course everything opened up quite suddenly with the publication of *The Outsider* and I found myself quite famous. The problem, in a way, was over, it was behind me. But of course in a way, the publication of *The Outsider* had one disadvantage, that I'd been deeply preoccupied with the problem of the outsider and this peak experience, until the book was so successful, and one of the problems with the success of the book was that it made me feel alienated from it. I could no longer feel all that much interest or sympathy in the subject, and if it hadn't been for the fact that within a year everyone was attacking me and saying that the book was no good anyway, it was all a mistake, and so by the following year, any reputation I'd ever had had evaporated completely, and I decided that it was just something I had to live with, and I moved down here to Cornwall, with my girlfriend who is now my wife, and we've been down here ever since. We've been together now for 53 years.

APS: Gosh, long time.

CW: So, in a way, I've been able to devote my life entirely, living here in the back of beyond, to this interesting problem, and I think I've more or less summarised all my results in that one book. The title of the book, by the way, was originally *Mind Force*, and then when I was still groping around for titles I called it *The Search for Power Consciousness*, because what I wanted to emphasise was that what we're really talking about is that sudden feeling of sheer power and happiness, and the question of how to recover it. And of course it was Maslow who didn't believe that you can actually recover it at will, who gave me the clue when he said that his students, when they talked about peak experiences, began having peak experiences all the time. In other words, it is simply a question basically of optimism. I saw, by the way, an interesting article in *Time Magazine* this week, which is about this question of optimism and pessimism, someone writing about the psychology of optimism is saying that it's not all that difficult if you remember that there was a book in the past by Norman Vincent Peale about the power of positive thinking. And that of course gave the subject a very bad name and in fact, that is in a sense the basic answer. And the most important story in that book is the one at the very end where I talk about this guy who was saying, 'God, I'm so unhappy' and his friend said 'you're not unhappy, Sid, you just think you are.' And he looked at his friend as if he'd been struck on the head, and he said, 'say that again' and it struck him that his friend had given him the most basic answer of all to the question of peak experience. And the reason that don't have peak experiences is that we tend to think that they are impossible, or rather we tend to remain in a sort of vaguely negative frame of mind and so we don't have them. But what has always struck me very powerfully is that it oughtn't to be terribly difficult to induce peak experiences in ourselves because all we have to do is to think of problems that would really worry us and then consider the fact that such problems have not arisen, which ought to be enough to plunge us into a state of happiness. I can't remember now whether in that book I mentioned a friend of mine, an old friend called Hugh Hextall Smith who was a headmaster and Hugh told me that he used to have a little dog who was prone to depression, and whenever the dog was depressed… on some occasion he accidentally left the dog in a cupboard and he accidentally let the dog out of the cupboard and he was leaping around out of sheer joy and from then on, whenever the dog got depressed, he would lock the dog in the cupboard for five minutes and out it came completely undepressed. In other words, Hugh had found the ideal way of giving the dog peak experiences, and is we human beings could do a similar sort of thing, the equivalent of it, then it would be perfectly easy to have peak experiences whenever we want.

APS: I remember watching a video of a Jungian psychologist, and the only thing that really stayed was me was that she mentioned that humans have a need for elation and of course she linked this with alcoholism and drug abuse as negative expressions of that , but that was something I took away from it.

CW: Or Graham Greene with his Russian roulette, actually playing Russian Roulette half a dozen times with a live bullet in the chambers which I guess is the most dangerous way of all of doing it.

APS: When you mentioned the decline of romanticism, and the decadent poets, I've always had a great love for Ernest Dowson. There's almost a kind of transcendent self-pity in some of those poems.

CW: Yes, I've got the World Modern Library edition of Ernest Dowson's poems, which has not been published for about fifty years. I've got a spare copy sitting in my outside lavatory. I quite agree, that while you can also see exactly why Dowson felt as he did, you can also see that what he was doing was pretty dangerous, and you've also only got to look at the photographs of Dowson to see this rather weak chin to realise the nature of the problem. You see, what I was saying in *The Outsider* was the trouble is most of these people were weaklings. They had these problems because basically they gave way to their weakness. Now Yeats, if you remember, when the Rhymer's Club used to meet in the Cheshire Cheese in Fleet St said now, I don't know which of us are any good as poets, I only know that we are too many. And of course, he was quite right, and most of them have been totally forgotten, Arthur Symons and that kind of thing. However, I could see that Yeats had found the right way out of the problem because Yeats got terribly broke and borrowed money from Lady Gregory, well not borrowed money, she used to give him money, used to slip it into his wallet and that kind of thing. The one day he said to her, 'well, how much do I owe you?' And when she told him, several hundred quid, which was far more than he could possibly earn, he was so shocked that he got himself an American

lecture tour and went off lecturing in America and of course that was the turning point for Yeats because the sheer hard work of going on an American lecture tour, particularly in those days when you had to travel round by train — I mean, I found it difficult enough, doing an American lecture tour when *The Outsider* came out and it was such incredibly hard work, giving maybe a dozen lectures a week at different colleges and universities, travelling between them by plane and that kind of thing, then having dinner with the faculty and the giving the lecture and so on, so that when I got home after twelve weeks of that and felt absolutely a wreck. I felt like a bear with a sore head and must have been dreadful to live with for my poor wife.

APS: Dylan Thomas seemed to find it quite difficult too.

CW: Well, Dylan Thomas was of course a typical example of the weak outsider. He just happened to be born with a tremendous talent in the use of words but very little else, and so this is the real problem with the work of Dylan Thomas, it's too easy to imagine… it's terribly easy to be an alcoholic anyway, especially if you're a Celt, Scots or Irish… Are you Irish by the way?

APS: I'm Welsh, but I'm living in Dublin

CW: That's as bad a position. I think the best thing of all is to be Anglo-Saxon.

APS: [laughter] In some of Dylan Thomas' poems I think you can see peak experiences, like in 'Poem in October,' and some of the long poems with lots of natural imagery

CW: Yeah.

APS: In the book you describe seven or eight different levels of consciousness. Could you talk about that a little?

CW: The levels of consciousness?

APS: Yes.

CW: I first worked out the whole thing when I was in America and I was being driven back to San Francisco from Big Sur, which is on the coast, and having nothing else to do and sitting in the car, I began to brood on how many different levels of consciousness I could actually distinguish. And I thought, well you can start off with level 0, that is when you're fast asleep and you've no consciousness, and so on. And I went on little by little to build up a picture of the different levels of consciousness. Probably the top level that we human beings experience is what I call Faculty X, this ability to conjure up the reality of other times and other places. Now, this whole Faculty X concept had come to me as a result of reading Arnold Toynbee's *A Study of History* as Toynbee had also experienced this kind of multiple consciousness several times. The ability to think of some historical event and actually, in a sense, find himself back there in the event, with people who were involved in the event. So certainly we have this peculiar capacity to leave ordinary consciousness behind as it were and to go off somewhere else, so to speak. And this enormously impressed me because, again, it's something that I feel that we ought to be able to do at any particular time. It ought to be possible. The only trouble is, as I say, is that it has to be done with a deliberate attempt at self-awareness. It suddenly lands on you and you experience what I called dual consciousness, which is of course being in two places at the same time. I forget whether I described that in the book.

someone like William Blake was born with some odd faculty which gets switched on at certain moments.

APS: Yes, you did.

CW: When I say that a child, for example, sitting in a room at Christmas time, listening to the wind howling outside, amazed at the snow rattling on the windows, but he's in front of a lovely warm fire, he experiences dual consciousness simply because he's aware of two realities at the same time. And our problem is simply to be aware of more than one reality. And this cannot be difficult to do, as we are always capable of galvanising ourselves into some sense of urgency or emergency, Unfortunately easy in the modern world in the view of this recession

and so on, which is placing a number of people in that same position.

APS: Would you also link Faculty X and the dual consciousness with visionary experiences, not necessarily of a particular type, but the whole concept of spiritual visions.

CW: I don't think there's a necessary connection. Quite obviously, someone like William Blake was born with some odd faculty which gets switched on at certain moments. And, of course, Blake's obsession with the idea of some other reality, this is of terrific importance. That sense of some other reality and the feeling which I express by saying, our present consciousness is a liar. In fact, you realise that our ordinary everyday consciousness is simply not telling us the truth about reality. This is the basic question of all philosophy, so to speak, getting back to what you call reality, how can one conjure up what you call reality. And I think philosophy has always tended to give the wrong answer to that question, where in Plato reality doesn't really exist in this harsh sphere of ours, but only really in the sphere of ideals. And I think this is totally the wrong answer. And then of course all the other philosophers followed the lead of Plato and then the lead of Descartes. The result is that the chapter in there [in *Super Consciousness*] that I wrote on philosophy is one of the best things I've ever written on the subject because it shows that, for various reasons to do with Descartes and then to do with Hume, philosophy went down a total blind alley. One of the few people who in fact succeeded in escaping the blind alley was Whitehead, who always seems to me to be one of the greatest of western philosophers. Incidentally, what I must do is send you an article I wrote about Whitehead recently and which came out in a Japanese book, but I can easily send you a copy of it by email.

APS: Yes please.

CW: It seems to me that Whitehead came closer to solving this basic problem than any other modern thinker, in recognising that in point of fact we have two kinds of perception, which he calls presentational immediacy and causal efficacy. Causal efficacy is a difficult one, but all it really means is 'meaning perception'. I think we all get meaning perception in these sudden moments that Blake called 'moments of vision.' In other words, that moments of vision ought to be completely natural to human beings, if we could only learn to be conscious in the right way to them. There's an enormous practical problem, and that practical problem is the fact that we really require in oder to do any good thinking at all, we require leisure. But unfortunately, not only is there very little leisure in our civilization, but when we get leisure it tends to bore us. We can sink into a state of taking it for granted, what I call the robot. And so what you've really got to do is work out a kind of strategy against the robot. That would have been a good title for the book. What is interesting to me is that this guy Sid Banks, who I talk about in the last chapter, when this friend of his said, 'you're not unhappy Sid, you just think you are,' it was obvious something very important happened. I think that Banks took maybe a couple of days to really grasp what was meant by this and that is, that if you analyse your consciousness, you discover that a very large part of your time is spent simply thinking about things. This thinking tends to give you completely the wrong impression of things because it's just not real. If you think of what happened to Aldous Huxley under mescaline he suddenly realised that thinking is irrelevant, all that's relevant is that sort of blazing reality, he suddenly thought when he'd taken mescaline. In other words, he thought as the Hindus said that the mind is the slayer of the real. This is to me the basic answer. It seems to me incidentally that the Cathars were quite wrong in that they also came down to the completely negative

what you've really got to do is work out a kind of strategy against the robot.

conclusion in the same way that dear old Arthur Guirdham did. It just does not seem to me to be correct to say that everything to do with spirit is good and everything to do with matter is evil, which the Cathars did. G.K. Chesterton, who incidentally I feel is one of the few modern thinkers who really hit the nail on the head — he was in other words a great thinker, despite that he behaved like a fat fool — but G.K. Chesterton came very close to it in realising that the answer lies in the sudden feeling of absurd good news. And this is what Sid Banks recognised in a way. But also what Sid Banks began to recognise when he really began to brood on this question is that the feeling of absurd good news is completely and totally justified, we really ought to have it all the time. So what we've got to do is to somehow work out the difference between ordinary everyday consciousness and the feeling of absurd good news and see how we get from one to the other. Because it ought to be perfectly possible, like taking the map of a city and saying how do you get to the city centre?

APS: When you mention the Cathars and the matter versus spirit dichotomy, which of course also occurs in Gnostic doctrine, though it's not as absolute as you might think in the actual literature, on thing I notice in your work is that you don't really go into metaphysics very much, probably because you're coming from an existential background,

CW: Well, I loathe metaphysics. It seems to me to be patently untrue. The kind of propositions we find in people we think of as metaphysicians, Kant and Hegel, on the whole turn out to be irrelevant and untrue. I mean, Kierkegaard is perfectly right about Hegel and this kind of metaphysics doesn't really tell us anything. What is interesting of course is that it had such a terrific influence on people in the nineteenth century, who were completely knocked out by

Hegel and thought, 'this is true, we feel this is basically true.' And that deserves a book. But of course it's not the book I would like to write.

APS: I was thinking more of metaphysics in terms of religious worldviews,

CW: I see what you mean.

APS: Not so much the western philosophical tradition

CW: Yes, I do see what you mean. Yet, I started off very much in this religious tradition, because in my teens when I hated the modern world so much, it seemed to me that the answer had to lie in some sort of religious tradition, and to be honest I thought at one time that the answer for me personally lay in me going into a monastery. It seemed to me that one could spend one's whole life concentrating simply on this question of achieving a sense of spiritual reality. And I remember telling Joy, my wife, when we went on a holiday together when we were both about twenty-one, that she shouldn't rely too much on the thought if our being together forever, because I might well end up by going into a monastery. At that time the idea of a monastery was very much in the background of my mind, and also the idea of achieving some sort of reconciliation through the typical religious means, in other words, prayer, meditation, that kind of thing. What actually happened of course was that in writing *The Outsider*, I moved on from various modern existential outsiders, Sartre and Camus and this kind of thing, on to religious outsiders like George Fox and William Blake, and so on, and it was this kind of thing that made me see that there's a certain sense in which religion is not the answer. For example, as I think I say in the book, Ramakrishna, who struck me tremendously important, nevertheless

the idea of a monastery was very much in the background of my mind, and also the idea of achieving some sort of reconciliation through the typical religious means, in other words, prayer, meditation

died of cancer of the throat at the age of fifty. And I could see that there is therefore a sense in which Ramakrishna did not find the answer. Because I've got a feeling that the answer involves a feeling of such affirmation that that would be impossible. The trouble with Ramakrishna's affirmations, his visions of the divine mother, is that they didn't do this, or rather they went too far and plunged in to a rather mindless ecstasy, in which he was completely overwhelmed, and this is definitely not what we want, and I think I then go on in that book to say that one of the problems with these intense ecstasies and so on is that there's no way of controlling them. I myself always wanted to be able to control the feeling and I have a feeling that it ought to be possible to do it by thought, by ideas. Which is the reason that after *The Outsider* I didn't quite know where to go except that I now wanted to explore the alleyway that I hadn't explored in *The Outsider* of religious mystics and people like Nicholas Ferrar Who started his own little religious community at Little Gidding and that kind of thing is something that appealed to me quite a lot, and Joy and I actually went to Little Gidding, to the church there. It seemed to me I could perfectly understand why someone like Nicholas Ferrar would want to say, ' I don't really like this modern world very much, I'd much rather retreat into the middle ages, in a sense, and myself and my family and so on are going to live the life of medieval monks, and this is something with which I sympathise very, very deeply indeed. But then of course, that in a way was the equivalent of W.B. Yeats and his early fairylands, what I had to do was leave the fairylands behind. Yeats used this line, 'In dreams begin responsibilities' and that was the question, that one had to achieve a feeling of reality, of responsibilities, and the fact was that basically they are preferable to the irresponsible attitude of the Romantics.

APS: You've had a long-standing interest in Gurdjieff, which I think follows on quite naturally from what you were saying just now. Gurdjieff rejected what he might call one-centred ecstasies, and also in what you wrote in your book about strategies against the robot.

CW: Yes, it links with Gurdjieff very much.

APS: You mentioned Gurdjieff in *The Outsider*. How do you view him now, how has your thinking progressed?

CW: Oh, I've always thought, as I put it in *The Outsider*, that he had answered the basic questions, and it still seems to me that he's probably the greatest mind of the twentieth century. He came closer than anybody else to the basic answer. The only trouble is that it's terribly easy to slip into a kind of romanticism as Ouspensky did, you know, Ouspensky finished his life as an alcoholic, and I did a little book on Gurdjieff and Ouspensky, that ends with a chapter called 'Gurdjieff vs Ouspensky' Because Ouspensky seems to me in a way preferable to Gurdjieff in that he was a more precise thinker, a more scientific thinker, and this seems to me to be the first and necessary thing. I can't remember, but I think that I put in this book about that chapter 'Experimental Mysticism' in Ouspensky's *A New Model of the Universe*, and that seems to me again terribly important. I'm aware all the time that I set out determinedly to try and find my way to the answer of this basic problem and it reminds me of what happened when Joy and I lived in Seattle when I was teaching at the university there, and one day we decided we'd like to go out and drive to that mountain that overlooks Seattle — I've forgotten what it's called for the moment. So off we went and we drove off towards it, and we didn't seem to be able to get there at all, and we drove on for thirty, forty miles and we didn't seem to get any closer. That's exactly the same kind of thing that has happened to me in my attempts to find the answer to this problem. I don't seem to have got there. Mount Rainier, that's the name of the mountain I was trying to remember.

APS: Have you found yourself having peak experiences more regularly, using the kinds of techniques that you discuss in the book?

CW: Well, I've always to a large extent been able to produce peak experiences, but that's simply because I'm basically a very cheerful sort of person, they come naturally to me because I enjoy all kinds of things, and also, as I realise during this recession, I'm not terribly subject to negativity, to worry. There's an excellent article in *Time Magazine* this time about the psychological techniques for rewarding worry and misery, and it's wonderful that it takes a recession like this to take a magazine like Time and to lead them to talk about what seems to me to be one of the most important subjects in the world.

APS: When you were speaking about Faculty X, one example that came to mind was Philip K. Dick's experiences.

CW: In matter of fact, I printed off a long article from the web about him which is sitting on my bedside at this very moment. But of course, fascinating bloke, but unfortunately, suffering from the same thing as all these other outsiders, basically weakness as a person, which completely screwed him up finally. He's only slightly older than me, about two years older, he should still be going strong, he shouldn't be dead by now. It's an admission of failure.

APS: His experiences, where he found himself in first-century Rome seem very much related to your definition of Faculty X.

CW: No, I hadn't seen that, what is that in?

APS: In 1974 he began having these strange experiences, they'll be mentioned in any biography,

CW: Well, I have a biography of him, yes,

APS: He found himself transported to first-century Rome and he was a Christian and apparently had episodes of glossolalia where he was supposedly speaking in Aramaic and he wrote a millions words in his *Exegesis*, trying to make sense of his experiences, veering between completely doubting them and wondering about his mental health to taking them completely literally, and his VALIS and some of his later novels were attempts to fictionalise the experience.

CW: Yes, that's right, I've got *VALIS* on my bookshelf. He seems to me to be extremely interesting, and he also of course thought that he'd been taken over by an angel, and these peculiar experiences he had to ask the angel what was meant by particular words he himself didn't know. I did an article, which is in *The Encyclopaedia of Unsolved Mysteries*, called 'Was Philip K Dick Possessed by an Angel?'

APS: Oh yes? And what was your conclusion?

CW: Well, I wouldn't be in the least bit surprised because he said so many new things when he was in this state, that it sounds to me that he had actually achieved it. On the other hand, you see, the kind of thing that plunged Philip K. Dick into depression in the first place, an oversensitivity to pain and misery, was really exactly the same kind of thing that made Ivan Karamazov say that he wanted to give God back his entrance ticket. And that's not a terribly evolved stage of comprehension of reality.

APS: When I mentioned metaphysics, what I was trying to get at is… if we can identify the peak experiences, or cosmic consciousness, with the aim of certain esoteric religions, well, why not pick out the Gnostics. Gnosis is central to Gnosticism, and the idea that we have a spark of light that comes from the pleroma, the divine world, and I'm sure that this must have been accompanied by experience in many cases.

CW: Yes. Yes, I'm sure of it.

APS: Religion gives you a framework which explains the importance of the experience in objective terms. I wonder how important that is to the peak experience, having a framework that gives it some objective importance.

CW: Well, when you said metaphysics, one doesn't know quite what you mean. I remember a girl in California back in the 90s asking me, 'What do you think of metaphysics' and I went into a discourse on the metaphysical philosophers, and it turned out all she meant by metaphysics was, did I believe in the supernatural and paranormal? Obviously, it can mean completely different things. As far as I'm concerned, the ability to comprehend the religious frame of mind is of terrific importance, the only trouble is that I found at a very early stage that Christianity seemed to me to be nonsense! The whole idea of Jesus dying on the cross for the sins of humanity quite simply seemed to me to be a superstition. And so it's very difficult to see any connection, so to speak, between religion and these ideas.

APS: When Paul speaks of the Christ within, I would link that with some kind of transcendent experience.

Of all the people in religion that I detest, St Paul is probably the foremost

CW: Yes, I do see your point. Again, I hate St Paul!

APS: [laughter]

CW: Of all the people in religion that I detest, St Paul is probably the foremost, so he's not the best person in the world to talk to me about. St Paul was simply a liar who invented Christianity! The whole thing was invented by him, the idea that Jesus died on the cross for the sins of men and so forth. All of this was total rubbish. He may have been a religious genius of a kind, but it seems to me that the world would have been a far better place without St Paul. Of course, on the other hand, Christianity would never have triumphed as a religion without St Paul, because it was St Paul's lies that in fact made the difference, he made it possible that everyone could follow Christianity. I'd love to hear what Jesus would think of St Paul if he had the chance of commenting on him.

APS: Well, we'll never know.

CW: It would be bound to be negative, he might say, 'That bastard, I didn't mean that at all!'

APS: I was very interested to see that in *Super Consciousness* you very often use examples from literature, from novels, of the peak experience, or lack of it. I was thinking that when one tries to describe a peak experience, it can often sound inconsequential because the external elements aren't necessarily all that different to everyday experience. Maybe this is something that's captured better in literature and poetry than in a simple anecdote.

CW: Well, yes, because the people who really concentrated on trying to fix these states, people like Jean Paul, who were regarded as great writers in their own time, Jean Paul, who was roughly contemporary with Byron, and novels like *Titan* and the various subjects that I discuss in the book. And it seems a great pity that now when we read him, we find the language a bit too overblown and self-conscious, which seems to me a pity because the really great romantics — Hoffman is another one that appeals to me particularly — seem to me to be among the greatest of the nineteenth century poets and writers.

APS: I found that very interesting, the way that you used these literary descriptions of peak experiences.

CW: Yes, well I've always been inclined to go for these literary examples. But, you see, as far as I'm concerned, the answer to the whole question is there in *Super Consciousness* in the chapter in which I talk about my drive from Sheepwash in Devon. On which I suddenly realised that in being forced to concentrate like mad for about an hour and a half on a snowy road suddenly brought me this higher state of consciousness that the mystics were talking about. And the realisation that it can be done, the reason that we don't do it more often is that we don't make that kind of attempt. You see, when I was a teenager and I discovered the *Bhagavad Gita*, I would sit in the mornings, I would get up very early and then sit for about half an hour cross-legged on my bedroom floor, concentrating like mad and repeating paragraphs from the *Bhagavad Gita*. I even went to the trouble of getting the *Bhagavad Gita* in Sanskrit and learning many of the things in it, so that I could actually repeat them aloud in Sanskrit. Now that requires a particular kind of concentration and a particular kind of determination, and I realise that part of my trouble now, once you reach your seventies, and I shall be 78 in a few weeks time, you realise that you just don't have that kind of concentration. Or rather you have it, but you would need some kind of tremendous crisis to cause you to exercise it.

APS: You describe the two selves, which you link with the left brain and right brain

CW: The left and right side of the brain, yes. I think that's again of terrific importance because the best moments are the moments when the two selves are like two tennis players playing a perfect game, both of them hitting the ball back and forth at a tremendous speed and somehow it's obviously the speed of the tennis match that actually causes the insight. I'm sure you see it must be possible to work out a discipline involving the two halves of the brain. I don't know whether you know that marvellous film called *Forbidden Planet* — it's a take on Shakespeare's *Tempest* — in which the hero played by Walter Pigeon describes how he had achieved some extraordinary state of concentration by researching the culture of an ancient civilization. Anyway, I was saying that the scientist in *Forbidden Planet* is researching an ancient civilization on this planet, a people called the Krell, and he then discovers some of the simpler mind control machines of the Krell and the first time he uses one it knocks him out and he stays unconscious for several days and when he wakes up from this he realises that his brain power has been increased tenfold. Now, that's the kind of thing that we need. You ought to try looking up Forbidden Planet on your computer, you'll find that there is a long account of it there and it really is very important.

Will Parker

Colin Wilson on the Occult

The philosopher C.D. Broad once remarked 'if the facts of psychical research are true, then clearly they are of immense importance — *they literally alter everything.*' The obvious temptation is to dismiss these 'facts of psychical research' at the outset, leaving our Newtonian universe comfortably undisturbed. However, against this conservatively sceptical position is a troubling weight of anecdotal evidence — hundreds of thousands of corroborative witness accounts, recorded in every culture and throughout all historical eras — which suggests that such supposedly 'impossible' events continue to be experienced by ordinary people. Concerning this paradox the psychologist C.G. Jung made the following observation:

> The experimental method of inquiry aims at establishing regular events which can be repeated. Consequently, unique or rare events are ruled out of account. Moreover, the experiment imposes limiting conditions on nature, for its aim is to force her to give answers to questions devised by man. Every answer of nature is therefore more or less influenced by the kind of questions asked, and the result is always a hybrid product. The so-called 'scientific view of the world' based on this can hardly be anything more than a psychologically biased partial view which misses out all those by no means unimportant aspects that cannot be grasped statistically. But, to grasp these unique or rare events at all, we seem to

be dependent on equally 'unique' and individual descriptions. This would result in a chaotic collection of curiosities, rather like those old natural history cabinets where on finds, check by jowl with fossils and anatomical monsters in bottles, the horn of a unicorn, a mandragora manikin, and a dried mermaid.[1]

It is just such a 'collection of curiosities' that has been gathered together by the writer Colin Wilson over the course of three published volumes: *The Occult* (1971), *Mysteries* (1978) and *Beyond the Occult* (1988). This trilogy might be thought of as a kind of meta-analysis of what is undoubtedly a rather scratchy problem for the modern western mind. As we have seen, the characteristic datum of Occult research is the personal account and the witness statement. Wilson has assembled a vast body of such accounts from a range of secondary sources. He discusses this anecdotal evidence under various themes, throwing in his own thoughts and experiences along the way. What we end up with — across the two thousand pages of these three volumes — is an interesting and at times highly plausible 'unifying theory' of the paranormal.[2]

Wilson is still best known for his first published work, *The Outsider* (1956), which cast its spotlight on what might best be described as 'existential alienation', and its formative role in the lives of a series of key cultural and intellectual pioneers. Kafka, Nietzsche, Blake, Nijinsky, H. G. Wells and Dostoevsky were among the case studies examined in this volume, but it was the condition as described by the French existentialists Camus and Sartre — a kind of 'nausea' or nihilistic depression — that Wilson identifies as the hallmark of the modern condition. At the end of the work, Wilson offers a counterpoint to this condition, a 'grand synthesis' which identifies a possible solution to this problem in (among other things) the work of mystic teacher G. I. Gurdjieff (about whom we will have more to say below).

These were themes that persisted through many of Wilson's subsequent writings. The problem Wilson identifies is what he describes in the preface to *The Occult* as a 'narrowness of consciousness':

> It is as if you tried to see a panoramic view through the cracks in a high fence, but were never allowed to look *over* the fence and see it whole. And the narrowness lulls us into a state of permanent drowsiness, like being half anaesthetised, so that we never attempt to stretch our powers to their limits.

Wilson refers to these powers as 'Faculty X' and believes that they offer the key to all of the so-called occult phenomena: including telepathy, precognition and psychokinesis. Wilson, however, regards these phenomena as in themselves incidental to the main goal — which is *the radical alteration of consciousness itself*, a widening of man's mental vistas to liberate him from the 'vicious circle of boredom and futility'. It is from this perspective, with the condition of western man very much at the heart of the analysis, that Wilson begins his monumental survey.

It should be noted that this represents a very particular view of the occult, and one that is not necessarily shared by all who have taken an interest in the field. To regard all supernatural phenomena as expressions of unknown powers of the mind is broadly in line with the mainstream of modern psychical research. But it would, on the surface at least, be quite different

from perspective of the Altaic shaman, or the Caribbean Voodon — both of whom would regard *external spiritual agencies* rather than internal psychic faculties as the source of their supernatural power. Nonetheless, the 'Faculty X' model is a useful starting point for the modern reader. The search for Faculty X leads onto a consideration of the 'ladder of selves' model, and ultimately on to the 'information universe' — a concept discussed in the third volume, which takes in some of the paradoxical findings of contemporary sub-atomic physics. By this stage, the western view of self and the universe has been so comprehensively rearranged that the manifestations of Faculty X and the spiritual entities of the shaman or the voodon becomes almost indistinguishable — a conclusion Wilson himself comes close to reaching by the end of the final volume.

The Occult, the first of these three volumes, was commissioned by a publisher seeking to replicate the success of *The Morning of the Magicians* by Louis Pauwels and Jacques Bergier, which had been a bestseller in France in the late 1960s. For better or for worse, *The Occult* draws heavily the style and structure of this classic of popular non-fiction. In the first section he offers an overview of the subject, with chapter headings such as 'Magic — The Science of the Future', in which he presents a selection of some of the stranger anecdotes, along with the theories of key occult thinkers such as P. D. Ouspensky.

After this we move on to a historical survey. Wilson first begins with the prehistoric background, considering the evolutionary factors which might have shaped the psychic development of primitive man. Wilson rehearses the idea that early humans were possessed with a natural 'sixth sense' — which allowed these otherwise rather helpless creatures to survive in a dangerous and untamed world. With the rise of civilisation, his senses became dimmed and corrupted: 'the sexual instinct remains as powerful as ever, and has to bear an increased weight of frustrated dominance'. As Wilson suggests, it may well be the case that 'man was not really made for civilisation. As an aggressive, highly energetic creature, he finds it difficult to adjust to himself to its restraints. He responds to its lack of challenge with boredom and a tendency to become slack and demoralised.' In the process he not only loses his heightened senses, he also gains the beginnings of characteristic malaise which Wilson identified with such precision in *The Outsider*.

Whether or not one can accept this rather romantic view of prehistoric man as a kind of psychic noble savage, Wilson is by no means alone in associating paranormal powers with a rather more primitive stage of human consciousness. However, Wilson distinguishes this 'jungle sensitivity' (which he describes as lying at the instinctual 'infra-red' end of human consciousness) from what he refers to as Faculty X (which he identifies with the 'ultra-violet' end of the same spectrum) — the latter being as characteristic of a more highly-evolved sections of humanity. Much of the rest of the book is given over to explaining, in various ways, what is meant by Faculty X, and how it has manifested itself in various individuals over the course of history.

Wilson identifies Pythagoras as one of the first exponents of this new form of consciousness, and ventures that the Persian cult of the *Magi* may also have been instrumental in its evolution. Following on from these rather speculative beginnings, Wilson goes on to consider the career of the legend of Apollonius of Tyana — a miracle-maker from the time of Jesus Christ. This introduces a wider survey of Gnostics, Cabalists, the Manicheans, the Essenes, Mithraism and mystical sects that emerged out of the spiritually-fertile Eastern Mediterranean during this seminal period of classical antiquity. Wilson sees all of these movements as symptomatic of the emergent 'Faculty X' in the consciousness of Western man. Of course the greatest of these cults was Christianity itself, which would eventually assume the character of a universal religion with the conversion of the Emperor Constantine in 312 AD.

Wilson takes a rather dim view of early

Christianity, which he characterises here as appealing to 'fear, hysteria and ignorance'. He recalls Nietzsche's observation that it is *a religion of negatives* — preoccupied with what is *not* to be done, rather than the unleashing of new possibilities. Augustine's City of God is a rather colourless place of self-sacrifice, obedience, humility and chastity. Divine Fire, in Christian thought, is more often associated with the torture of sinners than the enlightenment of its devotees. But Wilson also finds one aspect of Christianity particularly useful for the psychic evolution of mankind: 'for the first time in its violent history,' he suggests 'a large portion of mankind believed completely in a dogma that was *unconnected with its everyday life*. This is of quite peculiar importance. For, as we have already observed, everyday life traps man in a small box called the present. And it destroys his long-term purpose as effectively as the black hood destroys the savageness of the hawk.' Whether or not one shares this particular view of Christianity's significance, the passage serves as a reminder of what it is Wilson is attempting to tease in this wide-ranging history of the Western psyche.

The Christian Middle Ages was a curious mixture of violence and sentimentality. It was perhaps this particular psychic tension which accounts for figures like Frater Joseph, who was born at the end of the era (1603) — late enough, in fact, for the miraculous phenomena associated with him to be critically observed by a number of individuals who could be described as modern rather than medieval thinkers. It is this position between the modern and medieval eras which makes the case of Frater Joseph of particular significance. Joseph was a simpleton living in a monastic community of Copertino, of whom it is said he literally float up into the air during moments of religious ecstasy. At first glance this would appear to be simply another example of hagiographical credulousness, but as Wilson points out, the quantity and quality of the eye-witness accounts distinguish:

It would be convenient if we could dismiss the whole thing as a pack of lies or as mass hysteria or hypnosis. We can certainly dismiss 95 per cent of miracles attributed to the saints in this way without a twinge of conscience…But the evidence [here] cannot be dismissed; it is overwhelming. His feats were witnessed by kings, dukes and philosophers (or at least one philosopher — Leibnitz). When his canonisation was suggested, the Church started an investigation into his flights, and hundreds of depositions were taken.

We are back with a familiar problem in the field of the paranormal. We have the overwhelming testimony of multiple witnesses — against which our scientific education asserts a strong gut-feeling that such things simply aren't possible. How can we begin to explain the mechanisms by which a man might be able to fly through the air unsupported? But, suggests Wilson, perhaps we should look at the question another way round: what it is that *stops* the rest us being able to ascend to the air like Frater Joseph:

There is a fundamental error in the way human beings grasp the world. We think of the mind being a helpless imponderable in a world of solid matter, a mere passive observer. We take a negative view of ourselves and the world, unaware of the extent to which we control things that merely seem to 'happen'. *I* control my physical processes, from digestion to the disposal of waste products, by a subconscious will. Next time you urinate, try and observe the 'mental act' by which you 'unlock' the release mechanism, and you will observe that it is a kind of 'will' that involves *not willing* with your upper conscious levels. Yet it is certainly an act of will, not something that happens involuntarily. Mages and mediums are people who have accidentally acquired

the power of using this 'unconscious will' to some extent. They are often very simple people — like St. Joseph of Copertino — because in simple people the personal consciousness, and its will, are often undeveloped

On these terms, it would appear that Fr. Joseph's powers are best explained as a throw-back to the 'infra-red' end of the psychic spectrum. One is reminded that ecstatic levitation was sometimes a feature of the shamanic ecstasy. Similar powers were attributed to madmen like Suibne Geilt ('Wild Sweeny') in the Irish Middle Ages; but also to numerous saints, Sufis and Buddhist holy men across the Europe and Asia throughout the last three thousand years. It would appear, then, that the conscious development of 'Faculty X' which takes place within these religious traditions is sometimes accompanied by a simultaneous re-awakening of these older psychic faculties. 'As the tree goes higher, [so] the roots go deeper', as Wilson suggests while discussing Gurdjieff's apparent psychism later on in *The Occult.*.

As we move into the modern age, Wilson's grasp of the historical context becomes rather more certain, and this allows him to come into his own as the skilled biographer and historical narrator that he undoubtedly is. His accounts of renaissance figures such as Agrippa, Paracelsus and the Elizabethan John Dee are fascinating simply as human stories, aside from their relevance to *The Occult's* main theme. (His potted history of the French revolution is as good as any). Likewise, his grasp of the Romantic period and its colourful personalities would hold its own against any popular history of the period. The chapter on the life of the infamous Aleister Crowley ('The Beast Himself') is a fitting climax to this section — with no detail spared in the impressive binge of debauchery, exploitation and rampant narcissism that characterises the career of Frator Perdurabo.

Crowley is a good example of the difficulties one might have with a certain type of witness that we find all too often in the occult world. To what extent can we take the word of a self-confessed egomaniac who, in modern psychiatry terms, would probably be described as having an advanced personality disorder? There can be little doubt that not a few of those who put their trust in Crowley came away with their sanity (and their finances) considerably worse for the experience. Yet it wasn't just his ex-wife Rose or his lover Victor Neuberg who witnessed inexplicable phenomena in the presence of The Beast. The judgement of the sceptical William Seabrook can perhaps be relied on when he relates the following anecdote about a walk with Crowley through central New York:

> Crowley took him along Fifth Avenue, and on a fairly deserted stretch of pavement fell into step with a man, walking behind him and imitating his walk. Suddenly Crowley buckled at the knees, squatted for a split second on his haunches, then shot up again; the man in front of him buckled and collapsed on the pavement.

Once again, this sounds more like the tacit psychism of the 'infra-red' kind than anything as high-minded or conscious as Wilson's 'Faculty X'. Crowley himself describes the magical process in terms which make it quite clear that it involves the activation of an *unconscious* process:

> Even the crudest Magick eludes consciousness altogether, so that when one is able to do it, one does it without conscious comprehension, very much as one makes a good stroke at cricket or billiards. One cannot give an intellectual explanation of the rough working involved

Wilson sketches out an interesting metaphor in the introduction to David Conway's *Magic — An Occult Primer* (1972), in which he compares the conscious mind to a monkey and the unconscious mind to an elephant. The monkey mind is clever and agile, and for the most part under the control of the conscious ego. But it remains relatively weak, and can be pulled in unwanted directions by stronger forces. The unconscious elephant, on the other hand, has the capacity to draw on vast reserves of brute psychic force, but lacks the deftness or control of the conscious monkey. Magic, suggests Wilson, involves the coordination of these forces: in effect teaching the monkey to control the elephant.

Is this what Crowley was up to? The suspicion must remain that it was the other way round with The Great Beast, and that his human faculties — sharp as they may have been — were merely a means to an end, subordinate to his highly-developed animal instincts. With his hyper-sexuality, inveterate drug-taking and poor impulse-control Crowley probably was, more than anything else, an atavistic throwback to the 'infra-red' mind. Wilson was probably correct when he suggested that the Great Beast's exalted states and visions were almost all involuntary. He was able to trigger these states to some degree through drugs, sex and ritual activity; but an acquaintance with Crowley's life and correspondence make it clear that here was a man more often than not at the mercy of opiate withdrawal, desperately manipulating those around him for the funds to feed his habit. Little sign here, then, of the elusive Faculty X.

For Wilson, this latter quality was most clearly realised in the Greek-Armenian mystic George Ivanovitvch Gurdjieff, a complex and rather challenging figure who has sometimes been compared with his near contemporary Gregor Rasputin.[3] Both men emerged from obscure backgrounds in the hinterlands of the Tsarist Russia. Both seem to have wandered widely throughout Europe and Asia, and in the course of these wanderings had some of degree of involvement with a variety of mystic and esoteric-religious sects. Following these rather murky beginnings, each was to gain a reputation for paranormal powers. Both ended up attracting the attention of high society — aristocratic Russia in the case of Rasputin, the European intelligentsia in the case of Gurdjieff. At the very least, both men seem to have exerted a strong hypnotic effect on their devotees. A female American admirer once described catching Gurdjieff's eye and feeling as if she has been 'struck right through her sexual centre' — recalling Rasputin's legendry sexual magnetism.

However, Wilson believes, there was also a significant distinction to be drawn between Gurdjieff and the likes of Crowley and Rasputin. Gurdjieff, according to Wilson, had developed his power *consciously*. His was a genuine example of a psyche in which the 'monkey ego' had learned to lead the 'elephant unconscious' through a disciplined process of psychic development. Gurdjieff's method — what he called 'the work' — was a response to an understanding of the human condition which accords closely with that which Wilson set out in the *The Outsider*:

> Gurdjieff's point was simple and startling. Man is such a bundle of impulses and emotions that he can hardly be said to exist in any meaningful sense. He changes from hour to hour, almost from minute to minute; he is a helpless victim of the events that carry him along. He wanders around in a kind of hypnotised state. In fact he is, in a quite literal sense, asleep all the time. He has occasional moments of intensity, flashes when he glimpses what he *could* be, the freedom of which he is potentially capable. But in no time at all he has gone back to sleep again, and he is again living in a habit-filled existence, his mind entirely occupied by trivialities to which he attaches far more significance than they deserve.

It was to shake his students out of this hypnotised state that 'the work' was devised. In putting his students through this process, Gurdjieff often began by subjecting them to basic manual tasks — making a road, cutting

down trees, breaking up stones. In many cases, their egos resisted such gruelling and repetitive tasks. A.R. Orage, an English magazine editor, describes fighting back tears of rage and frustration in his first few days of being subjected to this regime. But the novice students were persistently instructed to 'work like a labourer, not a machine': fully immersing their minds in the work. Many were surprised how satisfying they began to find their labours once this basic technique had been learnt. Only then did training commence on other exercises.

From descriptions such as these, it is hard to resist the conclusion that Gurdjieff's methods were particularly effective when dealing with the neuroses and discontents of the educated bourgeoisie. Wilson once again quotes the journalist William Seabrook, who describes seeing a crowd of young people at the Gurdjieff Institute perform an elaborate dance which seemed to demonstrate 'supernormal powers of physical control, co-ordination, relaxation etc.' Seabrook was struck by the 'robot-like' obedience of these disciples, and the fact that they seem to have come from 'the best homes and universities' of Western Europe. Wilson suggests 'what Gurdjieff did at his institute was turn bored, egotistic, confused people into well-balanced machines, too busy to think about themselves'.

Unlike his compatriot Rasputin, Gurdjieff did not rely on the mystic promptings of the Holy Spirit. Instead, he offered a rational psycho-spiritual system which cohered with the models that were familiar and tangible to the modern western mind. As Wilson explains, one of the most important realisations was of *man as multi-layered machine*:

> Gurdjieff's system was based upon the same insight as Freud's and Edmund Husserl's: that although man appears to himself to be a very simple, straightforward being — a mirror-like consciousness — he is actually an immensely complex machine with many levels. Like the top gear in a

car, consciousness is our weakest level. It is unfortunately the only level that many of us are aware of. Our real strength lies in other levels. The evolutionary problem is for us to become aware of these levels.

This multi-layered psyche, or ladder of selves, is a key element of Wilson's theory of the occult, and is explored in more detail in the later volumes, as we will see. Of course, the 'ladder of selves' was by no means original or specific to Gurdjieff. We find a similar notion present in the Neoplatonic 'chain of being' — a hierarchical model of creation and the spiritual orders which was a formative influence on the world view of medieval Christianity. A similar model can also be found in the Jewish Cabalistic tradition, in which creation is seen as a series of *sefiroth* — emanations and dualistic oppositions — which collectively form the famous Tree of Life.

The difference between these ancient systems and those of Gurdjieff, Freud and Husserl — is that the former are focussed outwards, on the Divine and the levels of Creation; while the latter are primarily introspective models mapping the various zones of the psyche. It is interesting to note not only the differences here, but also the similarities. C.G. Jung found many similarities between his own investigations into the dynamics of the psyche and the discourse of the medieval alchemists. Likewise, we find remarkable resemblances between the cosmological myths of the Gnostics and Neoplatonists on one hand and the aeteleological diagnoses of modern psychotherapeutics on the other. There is more than a slight suggestion here that the psyche has, in the post-Newtonian world, become the final bastion of spirit — the last place in the scientific-materialist universe in which the 'magical' reality can still play a decisive role.

On the surface this is a highly attractive solution. It seems to offer a means of accommodating the human need for wonder and magic, while remaining in step with the hallowed the 'laws of science' which western culture broadly defines in terms of the absolute definition of what is real and what is not. This process of putting the magical genie back into the psychic bottle is structurally enshrined within in the western education, with its binary separation between the arts and the sciences. Literature, the classics and the appreciation of fine art are studied with apparent seriousness throughout the western world — notionally as a means of refining 'sensibility'. Meanwhile, beyond these rather effeminate concerns, the universe 'as it really is' is ceded to the masculine authority of the hard sciences.

But is it as simple as that? Can we dismiss spirit as 'nothing more' than an imaginative projection of subjective contents and dynamics onto the external world? Does psychoanalysis complete this withdrawal of magic back into an appropriately subjective sphere? The difficulty is that the two spheres at times seem to interpenetrate one another to a much greater degree that this dualist model tends to acknowledge. Reference might be made at this point be made to the paradoxes of quantum mechanics: in particular the supposed collapse of the wave function — a process in which the role of the observer seems to be implicit. However, Wilson tends to avoid this complex and frequently misunderstood topic, and instead concentrates on the anecdotal accounts of the paranormal, which seems to highlight many of the same kind of problems.

Towards the end of *The Occult* a chapter is dedicated to spiritualism — that peculiar outbreak of paranormal phenomena or mass hysteria (most likely a combination of the two) which had its heyday in the second half of the nineteenth century. Spiritualism typically involves one or all of the characteristic elements of the paranormal scenario: inexplicable but fairly low-key psychokinetic phenomena (rapping sounds, wobbling furniture etc.); the involvement of supposedly discarnate entities speaking through an entranced 'medium'; the strong possibility of fraud in some case (and its apparent impossibility in others); and, not untypically, the involvement of one or more female adolescents.

The movement of Spiritualism, for such it became, is generally acknowledged to have begun with the séances of two teenage girls living in New York State in the late 1840s. These were Kate and Margaret Fox, who at the time were aged twelve and fifteen respectively. Typically, the girls would pass into a mediumistic trance during which they would ask questions of 'the spirits', who would seem to reply with loud rapping sounds. Even more extraordinary effects were sometimes witnessed: disembodied hands floating in the air, writing appearing spontaneously on paper and other surfaces, 'spirit lights' and other visual and auditory phenomena. Their séances were a sensation with New York society, and they soon had imitators throughout America and the Western world.

The girls went on giving 'sittings' for the next forty years and were instrumental in the establishment of the Spiritualist religion, a worldwide movement which survives to this day. However, their personal stories end in squalor and decline. Both developed alcohol problems, and in 1888 the sisters had a dramatic disagreement. Margaret, who had recently converted to Catholicism, renounced Spiritualism as the work of Satan. Later on in the same year, after accepting a significant sum from a New York newspaper, Margaret produced an elaborate confession in she represented all of the phenomena as a hoax perpetuated by her sister and herself. She was able to demonstrate how the rapping sounds could be produced at will by cracking her knuckles and her ankle joints, and relates how the early rapping sounds at their childhood home had been manufactured using an apple on a string. These confessions were retracted a year later, but by that time the damage had been done. Both sisters lost their credibility and were ostracised by many of their former friends and family. With five years, both had died and were buried in paupers' graves.

For many sceptics, Margaret's confession is the final indictment not only on the sisters themselves, but all other spiritualist and 'mediumistic' phenomena besides. For others, the confession looks rather more like a tawdry piece of chequebook journalism, taking place against a background of a family feud and a recent religious conversion. Certain other facts about the case are less easy to explain. William Crookes, the parapsychological investigator, was sceptical of the fraud claims and noted that sound of the raps were loud enough to be heard two rooms away, and that they seemed to emerge from the ceiling, the floor and other surfaces. It might also be noted that the Fox sisters, in their early séances, were contacted by an entity claiming to be the spirit of a man murdered and buried in their family home. Strangely enough, in 1904 — long after the Spiritualist furore had died down — a skeleton of a man was found bricked into the foundations of the property.

It is more than likely that the Fox sisters did fake at least some of their spiritualist manifestations, but rather less likely that entire phenomenon was a fraud. So what exactly was going on? In *Mysteries*, the second volume of the three, Wilson looks in some detail at several cases of what would now be called dissociative identity disorder, but is more popularly known as 'multi personality disorder'. While there is some controversy surrounding this diagnosis, the anecdotes Wilson describes make it clear that there is something going on here that might go some way to explaining the phenomena of the Fox sisters. All of the case studies described by Wilson were female, and many have experienced some kind of sexual trauma in early- or pre-adolescence. Wilson repeatedly makes the connection between this condition and the 'ladder of selves' model developed in the first two volumes, but also offers the interesting observation that psychokinesis, prognostic visions and many other paranormal phenomena most often seem to be bound up with individuals whose sense of self (and hold on everyday consciousness) is unusually unstable, fluid, multiple and fragmented.

The implication that some sort of displaced psycho-sexual energy underlies poltergeist activities and other psychokinetic phenomena is by no means unusual within the parapsychological community. But Wilson goes further than most in identifying these fragments of dissociated libido (what Jung would have called 'autonomous complexes of the personal unconscious') with both the 'spirits' contacted by trance-mediums and the agents of poltergeists and other PK phenomena. This is a plausible and interesting theory, but one which undergoes some degree of modification in the third volume.[4]

By the end of the first volume, Wilson has assembled the main elements of his overall thesis. We must remember that Wilson is less interested in paranormal and occult phenomena for their own sake, but rather for what light they can shed on the more paradoxical aspects of the human condition. A particular area of interest is in what the psychologist Maslow defines as 'the peak experience'—that moment when 'something inside us wakes up, and is delighted by the world it finds itself in. The universe is seen to be infinitely interesting and complex'. Wilson wonders why this blissful, creative and fundamentally desirable state of mind so rarely seems to last—and ventures the interesting possibility that, at some point in our future evolution, we will 'learn to keep the will *alert* as automatically as we now breathe…we shall be supermen living on a continual level of peak experience'.

One of the most interesting by-products of Wilson's survey of the history of the human mind (of which his study of the occult offers a particularly useful perspective) is the undoubted fact that human consciousness *does* evolve, and can be seen to have done so in substantial and demonstrable ways even throughout the last few centuries. One of the more immediately apparent examples of this process is noted by Wilson towards the end of the third volume, when he points out that Voltaire, one of the sharpest and most learned minds of his age, would have simply had no ability to comprehend concepts such as 'the unconscious mind', 'the peak experience', 'intentionality' or 'the fourth dimension':

[Voltaire] thought in cruder categories (atheism vs. superstition etc.) and for all his intelligence he would be as baffled as if I was talking Chinese. Yet most fairly intelligent modern readers can understand what we are saying without any difficulty. *This is because language has succeeded in pushing so far into the realms of the unknown since the late eighteenth century.* [my italics]

So if we have established that the evolution of consciousness is a proven possibility, Wilson's goal of 'continuous peak experience' may not be as implausible as it initially sounds. Through his reading of the literature of the occult and the paranormal—leavened with a reasonable knowledge of depth psychology and the neurosciences—Wilson offers a provisional set of working assumptions which point the way towards these promising new vistas of psychic evolution. The terminology of modern occultism—as developed by figures of varying credibility such as Madame Blavatsky, G.I. Gurdjieff and Aleister Crowley—nonetheless offers some useful working models. Wilson is at his best when bringing this esoteric conceptual framework to bear on his own special interest, the cultivation of the 'peak experience' as an antidote to the 'nausea' of modern man:

We know that our bodies are made up of a swarm of electrons, buzzing around like bees, held together by inner forces of attraction. But the same is true of the 'astral body' or whatever you chose to call the living, thinking, feeling 'me'; it is also a swarm of particles, like bees…Man possesses the power to contract his 'astral body' by an act of will. He is not aware that he possesses this power. The proof of this ignorance is his capacity for boredom. Boredom is the expansion of the 'astral body', in which the swarm of bees becomes like a vague, diffuse cloud. In this state we experience a kind of 'nausea', and the sense of meaning vanishes. Life 'fails'; the inner energies drop. The next stage in human evolution will be the development of this 'muscle' of the will, and a corresponding development of the sense of meaning.

Wilson talks about this astral body contracting itself into 'a glowing ball of intensity'. In this state, he suggests we reach 'a certain critical mass, and a chain reaction develops' — a dynamic he compares to a nuclear explosion. This psychic process, which is currently only describable in these metaphoric terms, is nonetheless recognisable to anyone who can understand the concept of the 'peak experience'. It is undoubtedly something like this rarefied form of consciousness which best explains the rather more archaic forms of ecstasy such as the shamanic or mediumistic trance (and their associated paranormal phenomena).

What Wilson does not offer, unfortunately, is a precise instruction manual for the acquisition of this exalted state. Instead, he presents some convincing grounds for believing it might be a possibility. This all-important theoretical foundation could perhaps represent the beginnings of a new scientific study into to the possibilities of an evolution of human consciousness. It might be noted that at the beginning of the twenty-first century that investigative psychology and the neurosciences, depressingly enough, seem poised to move in the opposite direction — following the lead of Daniel Dennett and his school towards an outright denial of consciousness itself, and a retreat into the crude behaviourism of mid-twentieth century. Without some kind of serious counter-movement — whether inside or outside the scientific mainstream — the very concept of consciousness is in danger of becoming as obscure and inaccessible to the modern western mind as the concepts of 'magic' and 'spirit' have become since the Age of Reason. Wilson, in these three volumes, offers a basis from which to proceed in a more humane direction — continuing to develop rather than

deny our evolving conscious minds, and perhaps even in the process regaining access to some of the 'magic' that was lost along the way.

NOTES

1 'Synchronicity – An Acausal Connecting Principle' in *The Structure and Dynamics of the Psyche,* trans. R. F. C Hull (London: 1969, Routledge, Kegan and Paul) p.422

2 I have concentrated here mainly on the content of first of these volumes, by the end of which the essentials of his system can be clearly understood. *Mysteries* and *Beyond the Occult* contain some important clarifications, and one or two significant amendments – some of which will be referred to here in passing.

3 It should be noted that Wilson had a particular view of Gurdjieff and his work which is not universally endorsed. Here we are interested in Wilson's understanding of the Gurdjieff system in as far as it exemplifies his concept of Faculty X, rather than representing a faithful representation of the man and his work.

4 About half way through *Beyond the Occult* Wilson admits to a change of mind in his understanding of the poltergeist phenomenon. Where previously he would have seen the disassociated psycho-sexual energy of the 'poltergeist agent' as the main cause of the PK effects, he finds himself persuaded by psychic investigator Guy Playfair's view that these energies work 'like a football' that gets kicked around by independent discarnate entities. This is a subtle but important shift away from the 'ladder of selves' model, in which no acceptance of the reality of 'spirits' was necessitated – merely an acknowledgement of the as yet rather mysterious powers of the deeper levels of the mind.

Perhaps the key point (made by Wilson himself) is that 'what goes on in our minds might not be as personal as we think'. The notion of the mind as a private, closed system has already been called into question by depth psychology. Paranormal data is perhaps best explained by the mind tapping into an as-yet unknown dimension of the 'information universe' that is beginning to reveal itself through the paradoxes of sub-atomic physics.

Jeremy Puma

Movement and Meditation:
An Introduction to Kimetikos

1. INTRODUCTION

One of the most intriguing creation myths in ancient literature appears in the long version of the Gnostic *Secret Book of John*, a Sethian text found in the Nag Hammadi Library Codices II, 1 and IV, 1. This myth, found in Sections 4-17, details, in great specificity, the process of creation from the most abstract and divine — the Unnamable Monad — all the way through to the most concrete and immediate — the human body itself. The process is described as a series of emanations proceeding from the Monad which, as they become further and further removed from the source, become more and more involved with the World of Forms and subject to the forces of destiny which preside therein.

The process includes the names of ruling powers of each different level of creation: the Aeons who dwell in the Pleromic realms, the Archons who rule the World of Forms, and the angels or Powers who rule over each individual part of the body. Additional names are given for souls which comprise the body, elemental forces, various daemons of passions and phenomenological qualities of the human, etc. The names given, for the most part, come sans translation, and their derivations are far from obvious to the casual reader.

As modern readers and students of Gnosticism, we may find ourselves scratching our heads at such a 'Bestiary.' However, philosophically, we can absolutely make certain educated guesses based on some premises which may very well have been shared by the authors of the text: Knowing something's name gives one control over that thing, and The Macrocosm and Microcosm are fundamentally self-similar (As Above, So Below).

As the Bestiary in the text provides the reader with a map of the creation of the Macrocosm, so the names also provide the reader with a map of the creation of the Microcosm. Knowing the names of the Ruling aspects of the different 'parts' that make up the body allows one, in turn, to control those parts for healing or religious purposes. Knowing the names and functions of the Powers which rule the Planetary Spheres allow one to escape their influence — and thereby 'destiny' — and return to the Pleroma from the World of Forms.

How did the ancient Gnostics utilize the Bestiary in their process? We may never know. Nonetheless, we contemporary Gnostics can certainly recognize the Bestiary as a roadmap, which may be as useful to us and our own spiritual practice as a Fifteenth Century map of the trade-winds might be to a modern sailor. We refer to the process of navigating this roadmap as 'Kimetikos.'

The practice of Kimetikos was not 'divinely inspired,' channeled or otherwise contrived. It was developed as a contemporary practice via a modern interpretation of the Bestiary in the *Secret Book of John*. Its inspirations include Classical Gnosticism, Greco-Roman Theurgical practice, Tai Chi and Reiki. It is, however, a thoroughly Gnostic system, and presumes a familiarity with the Classical Gnosticism of the Nag Hammadi Library and Hermetic scriptures on the part of the practitioner.

In Basic Kimetikos, the practitioner, or

'kimetikon,' first becomes acquainted with the practice for him or herself, and may then apply the practice as a therapeutic treatment for others. Advanced Kimetikos deals with further application of the practice for psychological and spiritual development.

Rather than attempt to explicate the complicated and often confusing contexts contained within the *Secret Book of John*, we have chosen to present this modern retelling, composed in the form of a Hermetic dialogue between Hermes Trismegistus and Asclepius, his student. This document will provide the foundation for the Mythic components of the practice.

2. ANTHROPOLOGIA: HERMES TO ASCLEPIUS

Asclepius: Now that you have discoursed on the nature of the Monad, and its perfect unity, indivisibility and immutability, we beg you to explain to us the mystery of the composition of the human. What is the difference between the Spirit, the Soul and the Body, and of what do they consist?

Hermes: Certainly, Asclepius. Let us proceed with this discourse which will clarify the nature of the human. The Monad, then, is the only indivisible and perfect unity, which thereby cannot come into being?

Asclepius: Of course, Hermes.

Hermes: And nothing which has come into being can be considered indivisible?

Asclepius: Obviously.

Hermes: Thereby it follows that the human, as one who has come into being, is also divisible into parts?

Asclepius: Most certainly.

Hermes: And these parts of the human we have demonstrated to be the spirit, the soul and the body?

Asclepius: Indeed, Hermes.

Hermes: Let us then discuss these constituent parts and their composition, that through knowledge of this composition you may come to understand more subtle things. As we know, that which is divisible is subject to motion. That which is subject to motion must have been set into motion by a power more subtle, and so it is the case with the human. The spirit sets into motion the soul, which sets into motion the body. As the microcosm, or human, is a mirror of the macrocosm, so each divided part of the human has corresponding parts in heaven. The spirit corresponds to the Pleroma, or Ninth Sphere, and is subject to the Aeons, or animating powers which reside therein. The soul corresponds to the Heaven of the Demiurge, or First through Eighth Spheres, and is subject to the Archons, or animating powers which reside therein. The body corresponds to the Kosmos, or created world, in which we reside, and is subject to the Rulers who reside therein and constitute and animate the body. This fourfold structure: Monad, Aeon, Coming-to-Be, Kosmos — is of the same proportion and measure of the structure of the human: Nous, Spirit, Soul, Body.

Asclepius: Is it so, then, that when we discuss the processes which occur within the Macrocosm, we may thereby understand the processes which occur within the Microcosm?

Hermes: Just so, Asclepius. You begin to comprehend. So then, let us discuss the gnosis of the extension of the Kosmos from the Monad after the manner of the community of knowers, through which we may come to comprehend the extension of the Body from the Nous. In so doing, we will numerate the Powers of the Heavens and Kosmos and the constituent parts of the human by which they are activated. As the Monad is to its emanations, so the Nous is to the body: indivisible, indescribable, in all things as Being without coming into being. The Monad, desiring to know itself, decreased its own subtlety by turning into itself, and generated itself as the Father and its own reflection, called Barbelo by the knowers. Barbelo, though a unity unto herself, is perfect in goodness and indivisible unto herself. Enamoured of Barbelo, the Father's desirous stirring within Barbelo resulted in the Christos. This trinity — the Father, Barbelo and the Christos — are the essence of the Piger-Adamas or Pleromic Human. Now do you, Asclepius, relate this exposition on the Macrocosm to the Microcosm after the manner discussed above.

Asclepius: So it seems, O Hermes, that as the Monad is the First Cause in the Macrocosm, so the Nous is the First Cause in the Microcosm, which engenders the desire in the human to come to gnosis of one's self. As the Monad must turn into itself and know its own reflection, thereby producing Barbelo, so must the Nous turn into itself and know its own reflection, or come to knowledge of its constituent parts, to engender its own ability to generate self-knowledge via Divine Wisdom, or Sophia. As the Father and Barbelo generate the Autogenes, so do the Nous and Sophia generate knowledge of Spirit within the human. As the original Trinity emanates the Decad of Aeons through which to allow the Piger-Adamas to engender the knowledge of itself, so does the trinity of the Nous, Sophia and the Christos, when known with perfect knowledge, redeem the human after the fashion of the Piger-Adamas.

Hermes: Just so, Asclepius! You are coming to an understanding of the gnosis of the human.

Asclepius: How then, Hermes, does the human engender the perfect knowledge of the trinity of Nous, Sophia and the Christos?

Hermes: Let us continue our account of the extension of the Kosmos, Asclepius, that you might come to know this mystery. This, then, is the account of the emanation of the Aeons of the Pleroma, the Decad and the Dodecad. Through knowledge of itself, or its own gnosis, the Autogenes generated within itself five superior Aeons through which to know itself. These five superior Aeons are Pronoia (Forethought), Prognosis (Foreknowledge), Proeido (Foresight), Zoe (Life) and Aphthartos (Incorruptibility). These five superior Aeons also dwell with their five consorts. The consort of Pronoia is Propsyche (Forespirit), the consort

of Prognosis is Proskopos (Foredoubt), the consort of Proeido is Teleiosis (Prophecy), the consort of Zoe is Anastasis (Resurrection) and the consort of Aphthartos is Metra (Matrix). Thus do the five Aeons and their consorts who are the Decad of the Pleroma allow the Piger-Adamas to know itself through knowledge of God the Father and the Barbelo the Mother. Through the knowledge of God the Father and Barbelo the Mother and the Autogenes and the Decad of the Aeons, the Monad expressed itself further through the four Luminaries and the Aeons who attended them. The First Luminary is called Armozel, and with Armozel dwell Charis (Grace), Aletheia (Truth) and Morphe (Form). The Second Luminary is called Oroiel, and with Oroiel dwell Katabole (Conception), Aisthesis (Perception) and Mneme (Memory). The Third Luminary is called Davethai, and with Davethai dwell Dianoia (Understanding), Philios (Love) and Idea (Idea). The Fourth Luminary is called Eleleth, and with Eleleth dwell Katartisis (Perfection), Eirene (Peace) and Sophia (Wisdom). This is the Dodecad of the Pleroma who sing the knowledge of the Autogenes, and may be discerned by the Knowing Ones through the Mystery of the teachings of the Monad, manifesting within understanding each time they are expressed and experienced. Now do you, Asclepius, relate this exposition on the Macrocosm to the Microcosm after the manner discussed above.

Asclepius: So it seems, O Hermes, that as the Pleroma contains the Decad and Dodecad of the Aeons, who are the Ideal emanations engendered by the Monad, so the Spirit contains a Decad and a Dodecad of qualities requiring redemption from the World of Forms, and these qualities may be found by coming to knowledge of self after the fashion of the extensions of the Pleroma.

Hermes: And yet, as the human resides in the Kosmos, which is imperfect, so are these qualities of the Spirit also imperfect within the human who has not received the gnosis of the Monad.

Asclepius: How, then, did the Decad and the

Dodecad come to reside in the World of Forms as corruption? Indeed, how did the World of Forms become corrupted?

Hermes: As you ask, O Asclepius, so shall I continue my discourse. As the Aeons extended themselves further away from the Monad, so did the image of God the Father and Barbelo the Mother decrease in their perfection and increase in their qualities, for the greater the number of emanations, the greater the number of qualities found in the Aeons. Understand that these emanations represent the Pleroma of the Realms of the Monad, which did desire to know itself. Through the expression of these many qualities and their manifestations as Aeons, the Monad sought its own gnosis. However, in order for it to come to complete knowledge of itself, it needed knowledge of imperfection. For this reason, it comes to pass that Sophia, the Aeon farthest from the Father and Barbelo, desired to manifest the offspring of the Monad, gazed into the emptiness beyond the Pleroma. Believing it true emptiness instead of portion of the Monad, she was expelled from the realms of the Fullness and took on the aspect of Pistis (Faith) Sophia. Her birth produced an abyss between the emptiness and the Perfection like the waters of the ocean, and the perfection of the Pleroma became as a reflection underneath those waters, or as a lantern shining thereon. And Pistis Sophia ascended forth from the emptiness, knowing that she had erred, yet unaware that her actions were necessary for the gnosis of the Monad. Now do you, Asclepius, relate this exposition on the Macrocosm to the Microcosm after the manner discussed above.

Asclepius: So it seems, O Hermes, that as Sophia desired to produce offspring illicitly and, in gazing into the emptiness of Coming-to-Be and mistaking the emptiness for something Other than the Monad, so does the Wisdom present in the Spirit gaze into the imperfection of the emptiness of the World of Forms and mistake it for something Other than the perception of the Nous. Thus is Faith engendered in Wisdom, and thus is the Wisdom of the Spirit corrupted after a fashion. This inability of Wisdom to perceive the realms of perfection is like unto the Abyss created when Pistis Sophia descended into the Emptiness. This, then, is why so many who claim to be wise do not truly possess wisdom, but instead possess a false sense of wisdom granted by the comprehension of images and reflections.

Hermes: Just so, Asclepius. And now I shall relate to you the creation of the Heavens and the spheres therein, and you will come to understand how comprehending the Heavens allows the pious philosopher to comprehend the soul. Sophia's descent into the Emptiness produces an offspring who did not have the Gnosis of the Pleroma, which took the form of a serpent with the head of a fish. And she called to him, saying, 'Yalda baoth,' which means 'Child, return here.' Blinded by the darkness of the emptiness, this being gazed upon the abyss between the emptiness and the Perfection of the Fullness and believed it was his own reflection, and for this reason he called himself 'Ehyeh,' saying, 'I Am god, and no there are no other gods before me.' This is because he was ignorant of the nature of the Aeons of the Fullness. But, we call him Yaldabaoth, or Saklas, meaning the Blind One, as he is blind to the Fullness, and insane. Believing thus, and that he is the Ruler of the Entirety, he took a portion of the Light from his Mother and then moved away from the abyss. Then, after the imperfect image of the Fullness he had seen reflected in the abyss, conceiving of this image as his own thought, he set about creating Authorities with whom he might rule the universe in its many parts. These are the Archons, and their numbers are Seven and Twelve. He divided the Emptiness into Eight Spheres, setting up each one of the Seven Archons over the Seven Planetary Spheres and setting up each one of the Twelve over the Twelve Fixed Signs. Setting them in motion, he made them Rulers of the Heavens and the occurrences therein, assigning differing qualities to each and assigning sounds to each that they might manifest these qualities and glorify him. So he created Necessity, or Heimarmene (Destiny) to which all who reside within the world of forms are subject. The names and qualities of the Seven Archons are as follows:

Athoth, who rules the Sphere of the Moon, who has the face of a sheep, who engenders Alpha, and whose qualities are goodness, darkness, growth and waning.

Eloaiou, who rules the Sphere of Mercury, who has the face of a donkey, who engenders 'Eta, and whose qualities are foreknowledge, evil devices, and ignorance.

Astaphaios, who rules the Sphere of Venus, who has the face of a hyena, who engenders Epsilon, and whose qualities are divinity and desire.

Yao, who rules the Sphere of the Sun, who has the face of a seven-headed snake, who engenders Iota, and whose qualities are lordship, arrogance and death.

Sabaoth, who rules the Sphere of Mars, who has the face of a dragon, who engenders Omicron, and whose qualities are kingdom, violence and flesh.

Adonin, who rules the Sphere of Jupiter, who has the face of an ape, who engenders Upsilon, and whose qualities are envy, greed and folly.

Sabbade, who rules the Sphere of Saturn, who has the face of fire, who engenders Omega, and whose qualities are understanding, wrath, and all falsehood.

The names and qualities of the Twelve Archons are as follows:

Iaoth, who rules the Lion and engenders Mu, and whose quality by his number is circumference.

Harmas, who rules the Virgin and engenders Nu, and whose quality by his number is virginity.

Kalila-oumbri, who rules the Scales and engenders Xi, and whose quality by his number is congregation.

Iabel, who rules the Scorpion and engenders Sigma, and whose quality by his number is grouping.

Adonaios, who rules the Archer and engenders Tau, and whose quality by his number is perfection.

Kain, who rules the Goat and engenders Phi, and whose quality by his number is Iao.

Abel, who rules the Water Bearer and engenders Chi, and whose quality by his number is madness.

Abrisene, who rules the Fish and engenders Psi, and whose quality by his number is bodily waste.

Iobel, who rules the Ram and engenders Beta, and whose quality by his number is beast.

Harmupiael, who rules the Bull and engenders Zeta, and whose quality by his number is the scarlet woman.

Melcheiradonein, who rules the Twins and engenders Kappa, and whose quality by his number is left.

Belias, who rules the Crab and engenders Lambda, and whose quality by his number is purity.

Saklas then brought into being the four elemental qualities, setting a sound over each which resides in each, that the Archons might take them and use them to further glorify him. And the elemental qualities and their sounds are Earth (Ge), which has Gamma set over it; Water (Hydros), which has Delta set over it; Ether (Aither), which has Theta set over it; Fire (Pyr), which has Pi set over it; and Air (Aer), which has Rho set over it. Now do you, Asclepius, relate this exposition on the Macrocosm to the Microcosm after the manner discussed above.

Asclepius: So it seems, O Hermes, that in this portion of your account lies the mystery of the composition of the soul. As Saklas, the Demiurge, is insane due to its separation from the Pleroma, so the Human Soul which acts in corruption is imperfect due to its inherent separation from the perfection of the Spirit. And, as Saklas set the Archons over the fixed signs and the spheres, and set them in motion, thus creating Destiny, so the Self sets the qualities of the Soul over its interactions within the World of Forms, which, due to their own imperfection, also subject the human to the destiny read by those who read

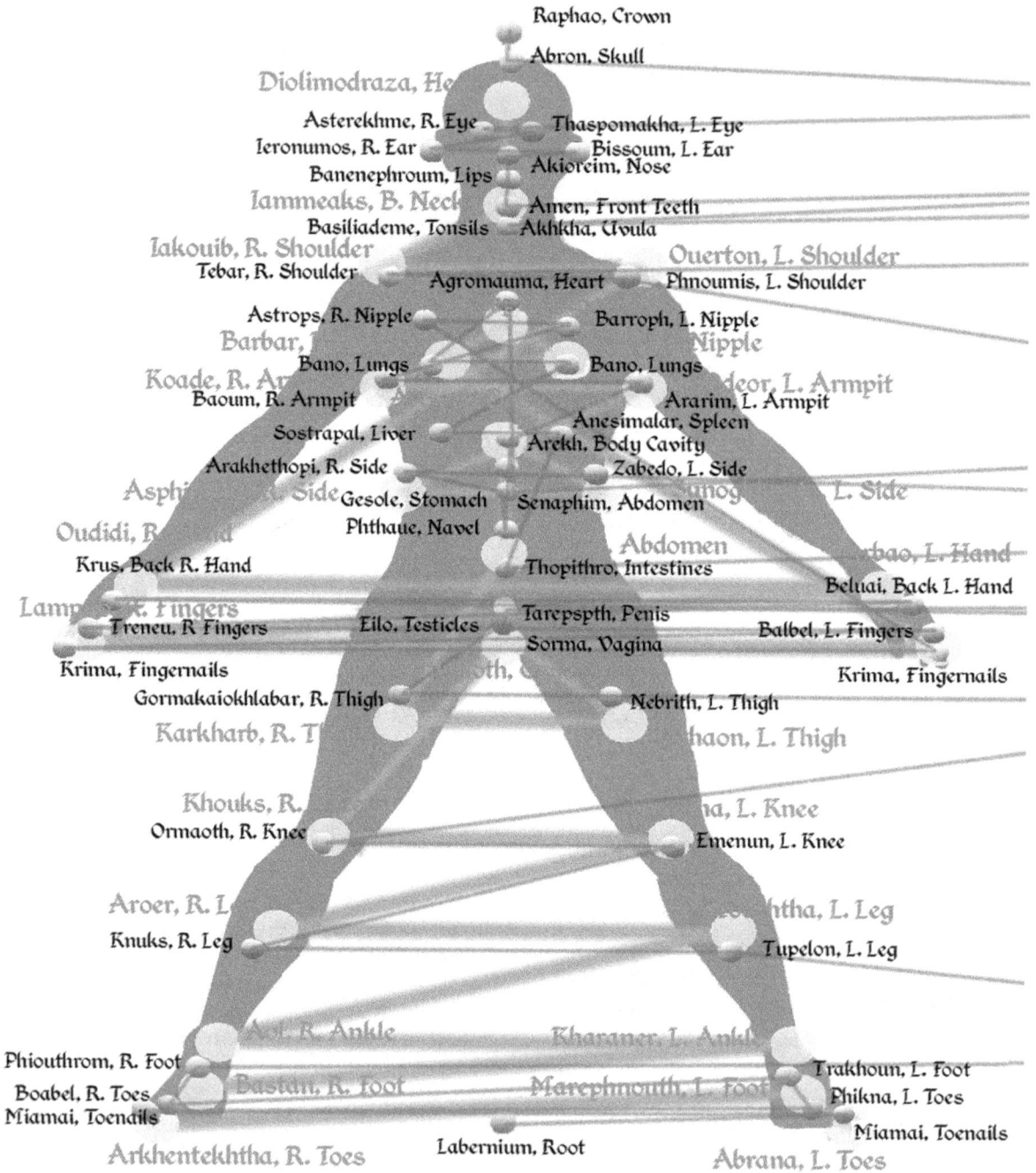

Raphao, Crown

Abron, Skull

Diolimodraza, He

Asterekhme, R. Eye   Thaspomakha, L. Eye

Ieronumos, R. Ear   Bissoum, L. Ear

   Akioreim, Nose

Banenephroum, Lips

Iammeaks, B. Neck   Amen, Front Teeth

Basiliademe, Tonsils   Akhkha, Uvula

Iakouib, R. Shoulder   Ouerton, L. Shoulder

Tebar, R. Shoulder   Agromauma, Heart   Phnoumis, L. Shoulder

Astrops, R. Nipple   Barroph, L. Nipple

Barbar,   Nipple

Koade, R. A   Bano, Lungs   Bano, Lungs   deor, L. Armpit

Baoum, R. Armpit   Ararim, L. Armpit

Sostrapal, Liver   Anesimalar, Spleen

   Arekh, Body Cavity

Arakhethopi, R. Side   Zabedo, L. Side

Asph   Side   Gesole, Stomach   Senaphim, Abdomen   nog   L. Side

   Phthaue, Navel

Oudidi, R   Abdomen   rbao, L. Hand

Krus, Back R. Hand   Thopithro, Intestines

   Beluai, Back L. Hand

Lamp   R. Fingers   Tarepspth, Penis

Treneu, R Fingers   Eilo, Testicles   Sorma, Vagina   Balbel, L. Fingers

Krima, Fingernails   th,   Krima, Fingernails

Gormakaiokhlabar, R. Thigh   Nebrith, L. Thigh

Karkharb, R. T   haon, L. Thigh

Khouks, R.   a, L. Knee

Ornaoth, R. Knee   Emenun, L. Knee

Aroer, R. L   htha, L. Leg

Knuks, R. Leg   Tupelon, L. Leg

A., R. Ankle   Kharaner, L. Ankl

Phiouthrom, R. Foot   Trakhoun, L. Foot

Boabel, R. Toes   Bastan, R. Foot   Marephnouth, L. Foot   Phikna, L. Toes

Miamai, Toenails

   Miamai, Toenails

Arkhentekhtha, R. Toes   Labernium, Root   Abrana, L. Toes

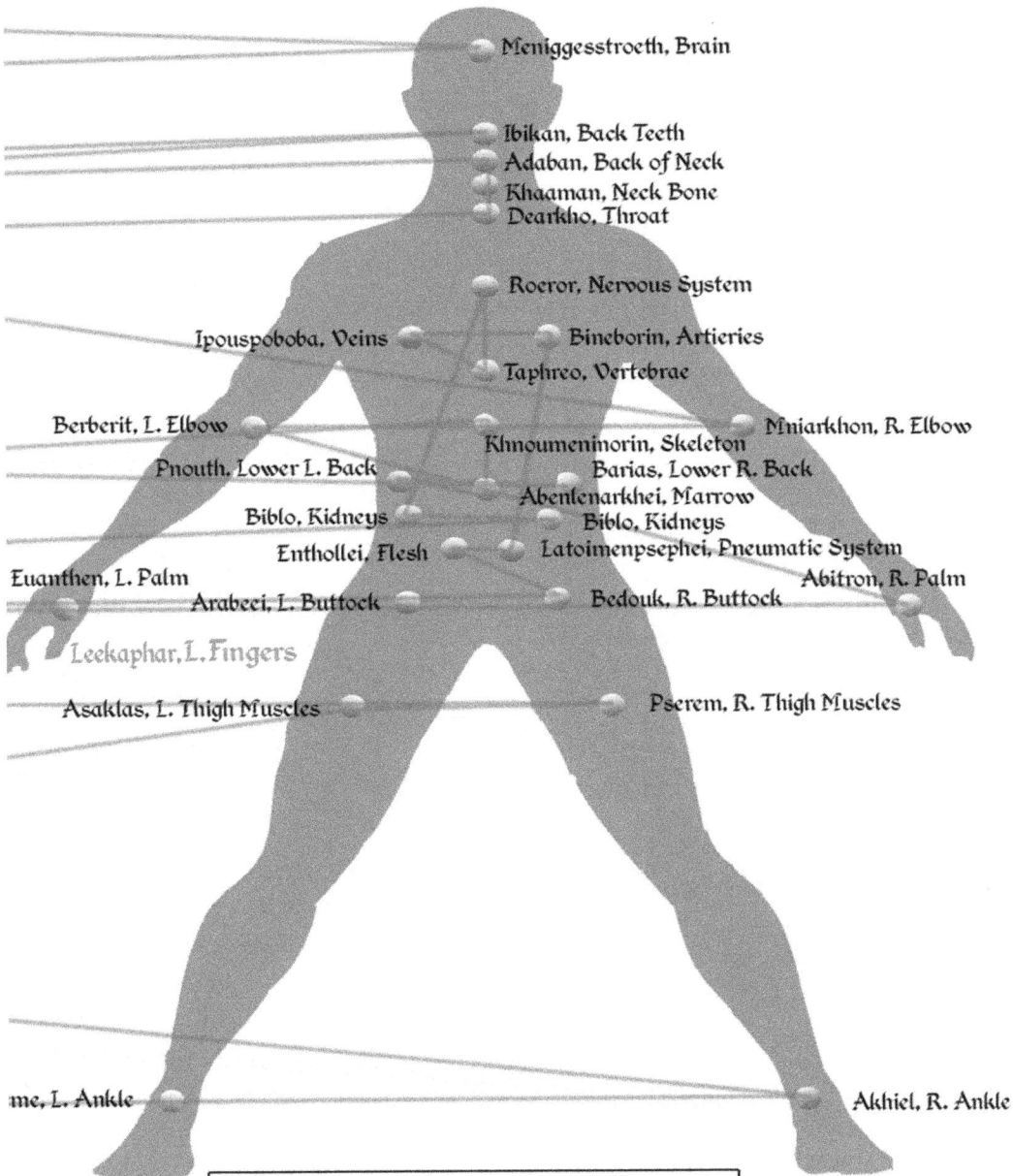

ARCHONS OF THE BODY
after The Secret Book of John

Meniggesstroeth, Brain

Ibikan, Back Teeth
Adaban, Back of Neck
Khaaman, Neck Bone
Dearkho, Throat

Roeror, Nervous System

Ipouspoboba, Veins   Bineborin, Arteries
                            Taphreo, Vertebrae

Berberit, L. Elbow   Mniarkhon, R. Elbow
                    Khnoumeninorin, Skeleton
Pnouth, Lower L. Back   Barias, Lower R. Back
                    Abenlenarkhei, Marrow
Biblo, Kidneys   Biblo, Kidneys
            Enthollei, Flesh   Latoimenpsephei, Pneumatic System
Euanthen, L. Palm   Abitron, R. Palm
        Arabeei, L. Buttock   Bedouk, R. Buttock

Leekaphar, L. Fingers

Asaklas, L. Thigh Muscles   Pserem, R. Thigh Muscles

me, L. Ankle   Akhiel, R. Ankle

Archons of Constituents in Black
Archons of Activation/Energy in Red
Blue line denotes path of creation
Pink line illustrates Path of energy through body

the stars.

Hermes: Very good, Asclepius! And so do the various qualities of the Soul allow the human to employ the elements present in the Kosmos, as the Archons employ the elements created in the Heaven.

Asclepius: Now that we have discussed the proportionate measurements of the Spirit and the Pleroma, and the Heavens and the Soul, please explain the similar proportions between the Kosmos and the Body.

Hermes: So be it, Asclepius. The Demiurge continued to divide and apportion the Kosmos, and set about the creation of the measure of the week. Under each of the Seven he placed 52 Servitors. And each of these Archons truly exists as a duality, as each is apportioned a masculine and feminine aspect. Saklas apportioned among the Authorities a portion of the Light he had stolen from his mother Sophia, and divided the emptiness, establishing an image of the Perfection according to the false impression he had observed. And the Archons desired to receive praise for their creation, in their arrogance believing themselves the only creators, and believing the Pleroma, reflected in the abyss, their own thoughts. 'Let us create humanity in our image,' they said, and the 365 servitors of the Seven Archons created man and woman from dead matter, and called them Adam and Eve, casting down the image of the Piger-Adamas into base flesh.

Asclepius: This is a great mystery: truly, then, the human is the wedding of the Macrocosm and Microcosm!

Hermes: Indeed, Asclepius.

Asclepius: How, then, Hermes, did the creation of the body proceed?

Hermes: The creation of the body proceeded as follows: the Seven Rulers of the Spheres were each given a portion of the animating spirit, or bai, a product of the divine light of Sophia as manifested within the Kosmos. Using this bai, each of the Seven created a Soul as follows:

Athoth created the Bone Soul

Eloaio created the Soul of Sinew

Astraphaio created the Soul of Flesh

Yao created the Soul of Marrow

Sabbaoth created the Soul of Blood

Adonein created the Soul of Skin

Sabbataeon created the Soul of Hair

These souls draw their qualities from the combination of the elements and the qualities of Heat, Coldness, Dryness, Wetness and their mother, Matter. The rulers of the elemental qualities are:

Phloxopha, who rules Heat, a quality of Fire

Oroorrothos, who rules Cold, a quality of Air.

Erimacho, who rules Dry, a quality of Earth.

Athuro, who rules Wet, a quality of Water.

Onorthochrasaei, who rules Matter, a quality of Aether.

The Seven then set seven Rulers over the members or portions of the body. The rulers of the portions of the body are Zathoth, Armas, Kalila, Jabel, Sabaoth, Qayin and Havel. These rulers then created the portions of the body for each of the souls and the elemental qualities. The names of the portions of the body are as follows:

Raphao, who rules the Crown

Abron, who rules the Head

Megiggesstroeth, who rules the Brain

Asterechmen, who rules the Right Eye

Thaspomocham, who rules the Left Eye

Yeronumos, who rules the Right Ear

Bissoum, who rules the Left Ear

Akiopeim, who rules the Nose

Banen Ephroum, who rules the Lips

Amen, who rules the Teeth

Ibikan, who rules the Molars

Adaban, who rules the Neck

Basiliasdeme, who rules the Tonsils

Achcha, who rules the Uvula

Chaaman, who rules the Vertebrae

Dearcho, who rules the Throat

Tebar, who rules the Right Shoulder

Mniarchon, who rules the Right Elbow

Abitrion, who rules the Right Underarm

Krys, who rules the Right Hand

Treneu, who rules the Right Fingers

Kriman, who rules the Fingernails

Pnoumis, who rules the Left Shoulder

Berberit, who rules the Left Elbow

Evanthen, who rules the Left Underarm

Beluia, who rules the Left Hand

Balbel, who rules the Left Fingers

Kriman, who rules the Fingernails

Astrops, who rules the Right Breast

Barroph, who rules the Left Breast

Arachethopi, who rules the Right Ribs

Zabedo, who rules the Left Ribs

Gesole, who rules the Stomach

Agromauma, who rules the Heart

Bano, who rules the Lungs

Sostrapal, who rules the Liver

Anesimalar, who rules the Spleen

Thopithro, who rules the Intestines

Biblo, who rules the Kidneys

Pserem, who rules the Right Kidney

Asaklas, who rules the Left Kidney

Aatoimenpsephei, who rules the Breath

Areche, who rules the Belly

Phthave, who rules the Navel

Entholleia, who rules the Flesh

Abenlenarchei, who rules the Marrow

Chnoumeninorin, who rules the Bones

Roeror, who rules the Sinews

Taphreo, who rules the Spines

Ipouspoboba, who rules the Veins

Bineborin, who rules the Arteries

Sorma, who rules the Genitals

Tarepspth, who rules the Penis

Eilo, who rules the Testicles

Bedouk, who rules the Right Buttock

Gorma Kaiochlabar, who rules the Right Thigh

Barias, who rules the Right Hip

Ormaoth, who rules the Right Knee

Knyx, who rules the Right Shin

Achiel, who rules the Right Ankle

Phiouthrom, who rules the Right Foot

Boabel, who rules the Right Toes

Miamai, who rules the Toenails

Arabeei, who rules the Left Buttock

Phnouth, who rules the Left Hip

Emenun, who rules the Left Knee

Tupelon, who rules the Left Shin

Phneme, who rules the Left Ankle

Trachoun, who rules the Left Foot

Phikna, who rules the Left Toes

Miamai, who rules the Toenails

Labernioum, who rules the Root

When the portions of the body had been assembled, the Seven set seven rulers over the activation of these portions, establishing gates through which these would direct the bai. The seven rulers of the activation of the body are Michael, Ouriel, Asmenedas, Saphasatoel, Aarmouriam, Richram and Amiorps.

The names of the rulers of the gates of the activation of the portions of the body are:

Diolimodraza, who rules the Head

Yammaeax, who rules the Neck

Yakoubib, who rules the Right Shoulder

Koade, who rules the Right Shoulder Joint

Oudidi, who rules the Right Hand

Lampno, who rules the Right Fingers

Verton, who rules the Left Shoulder

Odeaor, who rules the Left Shoulder Joint

Arbao, who rules the Left Hand

Leekaphar, who rules the Left Fingers

Pisandraptes, who rules the Chest

Barbar, who rules the Right Breast

Imae, who rules the Left Breast

Asphixix, who rules the Right Ribs

Synogchouta, who rules the Left Ribs

Senaphim, who rules the Abdomen

Arouph, who rules the Stomach

Sabalo, who rules the Womb

Bathinoth, who rules the Genitals

Charcharb, who rules the Right Thigh

Choux, who rules the Right Knee

Aroer, who rules the Right Shin

Aol, who rules the Right Ankle

Bastan, who rules the Right Foot

Archentechtha, who rules the Right Toes

Chthaon, who rules the Left Thigh

Charcha, who rules the Left Knee

Toechtha, who rules the Left Shin

Charaner, who rules the Left Ankle

Marephnounth, who rules the Left Foot

Abrana, who rules the Left Toes

And if you would learn the names of these powers for each of the elemental qualities, you may calculate these names according to the following conditions: the Rulers remain the same. The Powers for Hot are as given, for Cold their reverse, for Dryness their inversion, for Wetness the Reverse. For Matter the names are Hot and Cold. Thus the names are calculated.

Asclepius: Is this, then, the completion of the numeration of the rulers of the body?

Hermes: Not so, Asclepius, as I have not yet told you about the powers that govern the body's interaction with the Kosmos. These are five in number, and they sit enthroned with the four elemental qualities and matter. The one who governs the perception of things is named Archendekta, who is enthroned with Hotness. The one who governs the reception of things is named Deitharbathas, who is enthroned with Cold. The one who governs the imagination of things is Oummaa, who is enthroned with Dryness. The one who governs the integration of things is Aachiaram, who is enthroned with Wetness. The one who governs all of the impulses is Riaramnacho, who is enthroned with Matter. Interactions with the Kosmos require the presence of the Seven Senses, whose ruler is Esthesis-Zouch-Epi-Ptoe, and the Material Soul, whose ruler is Anayo. The presence of these powers invites the influences of the powers who rule over the passions, who are four in number. Their names are:

Ephememphi, associated with pleasure, who rules over lust, unmerited pride, and evil.

Yoko, associated with desire, who rules over anger, fury, bitterness, outrage and dissatisfaction.

Nenentophni, associated with distress, who rules over envy, jealousy, grief, vexation, discord, cruelty, worry and mourning.

Blaomen, associated with fear, who rules over horror, flattery, suffering and shame.

Asclepius: Knowing these mysteries, Hermes, one could heal the body and the soul and the spirit.

Hermes: Indeed, Asclepius, and by healing the Microcosm do we not also heal the Macrocosm? And now I have revealed the emanation from the Monad of the Aeons, the Heavens and the Kosmos, and how they relate to the properties of the Spirit and the Soul and the Body. We have already discoursed on the Christos and Sophia, and their descent into the World of Forms where they activate the Nous via the Logos. Now that I have revealed to you the nature of the Macrocosm and you have explained how it proportionately measures out the nature of the Microcosm, I will explain to you the mystery of making 'a hand in place of a hand, and a foot place of a foot, and the inner like the outer.'

Asclepius: Speak, then, Hermes!

Hermes: What, then, Asclepius, have you learned about the composition of the human?

Asclepius: I have learned that the human consists of various parts, the Spirit, Soul and Body, which mirror the Macrocosm.

Hermes: And if the human consists of these various parts, is any single one of these parts the core or heart of the human, wherein sits the Intelligence or Nous thereof?

Asclepius: Surely not. The core or heart, wherein sits the Intelligence or Nous, cannot solely dwell within a singular portion of the body, lest the Seat of the Intelligence be limited to the right elbow, or the foot, or some such thing.

Hermes: Very good, Asclepius. Where, then, might we expect the Nous to reside?

Asclepius: It seems to me, O Hermes, that the Intelligence or Nous of the human must sit with the Spirit, which corresponds to the Pleroma.

Hermes: Truly said, Asclepius. How, then, can the Nous see fit to perceive its true nature and redeem the human if it is mired down by all of these powers and authority in which it does not rest? Indeed, how can it see fit to escape the Destiny determined by the Archons and reflected in the Soul?

Asclepius: Tell me this mystery, Hermes.

Hermes: Know, then, that the various aspects of the human, as I have related to you thus far, are truly the reflective parts of the image of the Piger-Adamas, as miscomprehended by the Demiurge. These parts, which are not known to the one who has not yet received this gnosis, which is truly available for all who earnestly inquire, comprise a Counterfeit Spirit. The individual human who resides in the Kosmos who does not have this gnosis cannot help but mistake the counterfeit spirit for the true Spirit. The Counterfeit Spirit, however, is perishable, and the true Spirit, though not perfect, nor indivisible, resides with the Aeons and descended into the World of Forms with the Christos and Sophia, and is activated by the Nous via the Logos. It is this Counterfeit Spirit which is subject to Destiny, and the pious philosopher who redeems this Counterfeit Spirit and awakens the Nous to its true nature truly escapes from Destiny.

Asclepius: How then, does one redeem the Counterfeit Spirit?

Hermes: The Counterfeit Spirit is redeemed through Movement and Meditation (kimetikos), which first properly aligns the bai through knowledge of the powers of the body, thereby redeeming the Body. It then serves to redeem the Soul by allowing the Nous to ascend through the Spheres and the Zone of Fixed Stars, bypassing their Rulers. It then serves to redeem the Spirit by seating the Nous within the realm of the Pleroma.

Asclepius: This is a wondrous wonder, Hermes.

Hermes: And now, Asclepius, let us leave off this discourse on the composition of the human, and contemplate thereon, and give thanks to the Mind which exists above all Minds, and to the Perfect Good through which we come to knowledge.

As illustrated by the preceding document, Kimetikos is based on the understanding that the essential core of the human, our Nous or Intelligence, is the conscious experiencer within each of us. As an aspect of the Pleromic realms which exist in the Macrocosm, the Nous, activated by Sophia and the Logos, should reside within the human Spirit. Due, however, to the inherently imperfect nature of the World of Forms, the Nous has become bogged down within Destiny, and occluded by various aspects of the Soul and Body. Proper alignment — or redemption — of the different aspects of the Soul and Body allow one to overcome Destiny and bring the Nous back into the seat of Spirit. This process results from, and results in, gnosis.

3. KIMETIKOS IN THEORY

Kimetikos works under the assumption that the Macrocosm and Microcosm are self-similar, after the fashion of the fractal in Chaos Mathematics.[1] Through coming to an understanding of the myth of creation, and by ritually interfacing with the information contained therein, the kimetikon seeks the redemption not only of the Self, but of the entirety of creation. The imperfect nature of the Kosmos, in which the Nous finds itself trapped, is necessary for this redemption as a requisite aspect of the Monad. As the Monad extends to fill all possibilities, one of those possibilities must be the realm of imperfection.

In our system, the human construction is subject to Destiny within the World of Forms because the Soul and Body are modeled on the emanations of the Demiurge and influenced by the Zodiac and the Planets. This is in no way an original idea; the ancient Platonist-derived Mysteries were obsessed with the influences of the Planetary Spheres and the Fixed Signs of the Zodiac on the human. Each Sphere influences the human in particular ways depending upon that human's Destiny (heimarmene), and after death the soul of the human ascends through the Planetary Spheres, shedding the negative qualities associated with each. In Book Ten of his Republic, Plato breaks philosophical ground on this concept with the 'Myth of Er,' and it is also found in such diverse works as Cicero's 'Dream of Scipio' and the Hermetic Literature, particularly Book I of the Corpus Hermetica (the Poimandres). The Hellenistic world took the astrological as a given, and the individual initiated into the mysteries could come to an understanding of their destiny by symbolically or ritually ascending through these Spheres.

Kimetikos, however, is a Gnostic practice, and as such relies upon a Gnostic view that heimarmene is not something to be learned about or embraced; rather, Destiny is the result of the rule of the Archons and the Demiurge, and is something to be escaped or overcome.

Ample evidence exists for this point of view in Gnostic literature. In the Books of the Savior (The Pistis Sophia), we find entire passages which discuss the Christos' ascent through the Planetary Spheres, during which he 'changes the direction' of the Spheres, thereby ruining the ability of astrologers to divine:

…[T]hou hast taken their power from them and from their horoscope-casters and their consulters and from those who declare to the men in the world all things which shall come to pass, in order that they should no more from this hour know how to declare unto them any thing at all which will come to pass.[2]

At a later point in the codices, in a different book in the same collection, the soul of the Gnostic, ascending through these Spheres, delivers a resounding denial to the Rulers of Fate who would subject it to Destiny:

Take your destiny! I come not to your regions from this moment onwards. I have become a stranger unto you for ever, being about to go unto the region of my inheritance.[3]

Another, similar account in which the Spheres are disturbed, thereby eliminating Fate can be found in the Nag Hammadi text called 'Trimorphic Protennoia':

And the lots of Fate and those who apportion the domiciles were greatly disturbed over a great thunder. And the thrones of the Powers were disturbed, since they were overturned, and their King was afraid. And those who pursue Fate paid their allotment of visits to the path, and they said to the Powers, 'What is this disturbance and this shaking that has come upon us through a Voice to the exalted Speech? And our entire habitation has been shaken, and the entire circuit of the path of ascent has met with destruction, and the path upon which we go, which takes us up to the Archgenitor of our birth, has ceased to be established for us.' [4]

That Gnostic sacramental practice could unloose the bonds of Fate is attested to in the 'Excerpts of Theodotus,' a collection of Valentinian sayings recorded by Clement of Alexandria:

78. Until baptism, they say, Fate is effective, but after it the astrologers no longer speak the truth. It is not the bath alone that makes us free, but also the knowledge: who were we? what have we become? where were we? into what place have we been cast? whither are we hastening? from what are we delivered? what is birth? what is rebirth?

Again and again we find this concept in the Gnostic literature. The human is trapped within the World of Forms, under the subject of the Archons, who rule the Zodiac and the Planetary Spheres. This lack of control over one's own set of circumstances leads to what we refer to in Kimetikos as the 'Kenomic Worldview.'

The Kenoma, or 'Emptiness,' is where we reside, that place apparently outside of the perception of the Monad into which Pistis Sophia projected the Demiurge. The Kenomic Worldview is marked by a deeply embedded sense of this emptiness — as existential ennui, manifested especially as a sense of purposelessness. The emptiness which contrasts with the fullness of the Pleromic Worldview resides under layers of what Philip Dick referred to as 'kipple' — meaningless content — but is not always completely manifested (for

the human is trapped within the World of Forms, under the subject of the Archons, who rule the Zodiac and the Planetary Spheres

the manifestation of utter emptiness would annihilate an individual). Rather, it appears like something submerged off the shore of a great lake of extraneous stuff, visible when the tide recedes and vanishing when the tide increases, but always there below the surface.

The problem with approaches to the Kenomic Worldview in many circles is its equation to emotions or thoughts, the false heart/brain dichotomy. One equates the Kenomic Worldview with sadness, or dissatisfaction, or depression, or with entrapment by material distractions. This approach confuses the kipple with the Worldview itself. One can be perfectly happy or in love or extremely wealthy and still dwell within the Kenoma. One can also be melancholy or sad or angry or poor and still dwell within the Pleroma.

If you live in the Kenomic World, you have no idea what you are doing here. You may have a relatively happy life by your culture's standards. Nonetheless, the basic routines of life seem meaningless and trite. You likely get up each morning, eat breakfast, drink some coffee, take out the dog, take a shower and head to work. You do your job, perhaps happily — it may even be a job you enjoy very much! You go home to your family, with whom you are deeply in love, watch some television and hit the hay. Or, perhaps you wake up in the morning, do some Yoga, go for a quick jog and shower, eat a healthy breakfast. Then you go to your job at an eco-friendly Ad firm that caters to progressive political causes. You head home, read for a while and meditate, do some gardening and then hit the hay. Nonetheless, in any or all of these cases, a feeling of emptiness and purposelessness abides.

In the Kenoma, you are subject to heimarmene. You convince yourself that you have to do what you are doing because of the influence of external powers (the need for food, shelter, etc.). Horoscopes work for you, as do other divinatory systems like weathermen or work schedules, all of which predict possible futures only inasmuch as you provide them with import. You do what you do because you have to do it, whether that thing is going to your job at a corporation or chanting to the Buddha of Compassion or praying the Rosary. You are fated to do these things, and stuck in a situation from which you cannot escape.

You may try to suppress the emptiness with externalities, purchases, mind-altering substances or abstract busy-ness. Conversely, you may try to fill the emptiness with good works and 'positive' thoughts, with Spiritual Practice or Love, with meditation or Prayer. You will find, however, again and again, that none of these approaches work to finally rid yourself of the empty feeling from which the Kenomic Worldview develops.

Why does the Kenomic Worldview develop in so many? It is because, macrocosmically, those of us who dwell in the Kenoma were born into the World of Forms, under the control of the Demiurge and the Archons. As Jesus says in the Gospel of Thomas, a little child seven days old is closer to the Kingdom of Heaven than an old man. As we grow older within a milieu in which we are taught that we have very little control of the external world, the Archons work to cover us in layers and layers of kipple. This goes beyond the usual platitudes about social 'conformity' and politics and the value of public education; these are all externalities which, though they may be important, must take a back seat if one is working to move from the Kenomic World to the Pleromic.

Thankfully, we each have a spark of the Pleromic World within us. Clement of Alexandria quotes the 'Prophetic Scriptures' as saying, 'As to gnosis, some elements of it we already possess; others, by what we do possess, we firmly hope to attain. For neither have we attained all, nor do we lack all.' In essence, gnosis exists to allow an individual to create a teleology, to defend their own self-worth, to uncover a reason for

being. The achievement of gnosis via the Logos and Sophia enables one to perceive the Pleromic purpose, or reason for being. Although this will not completely eliminate the Kenomic Condition, it will at least provide blueprints with which the Gnostic can begin constructing a ladder to the Pleromic realms.

Not everyone needs to know their reason for being, and this is fine. Only those who do, who are driven to seek the Pleroma, are invited to leave the Kenomic World, to accept the outstretched hands of the Logos and Sophia and rise above the bottomless pit of the Kenoma. When, however, one 'shakes the foundations' of the Spheres through Gnostic practice, be it sacrament or contemplative prayer or — in our case — Kimetikos, one is free from the Archons and is instead part of the Family of Aeons who reside in the Pleroma.[6]

The idea that the Gnostic could ritually ascend through the Spheres in order to overcome fate was likely influenced by both Platonic and Jewish Mystical practices common to the Hellenistic world.[7] In Kimetikos, it is this Prayer of Ascent which especially serves to redeem the Soul, which confronts the Archons as it ascends, shows each its name and seal — thus proving its power over them — and passes into the next sphere, shedding negative psychological qualities attributed on the way.[8] The Spirit, then, is redeemed through a similar ascent sequence, but instead of confronting the Archons it glorifies and meditates on the Aeons in the Pleroma, incorporating their positive qualities.

In the Kimetikos Worldview, the Demiurge represents the lower reflection of the Piger-Adamas, or Ideal Human. If, microcosmically, the Archons are psychological qualities to be shed, the Demiurge might be considered the Ego of the individual prior to its redemption, which operates not under self-knowledge but instead on a solipsistic dependence upon, and devotion to, the images it creates. Traditionally, this is the 'I', the Self, the individual interface with reality. It is this 'portion' of the living thing that translates perception into individual experience and creates the sense of distinction

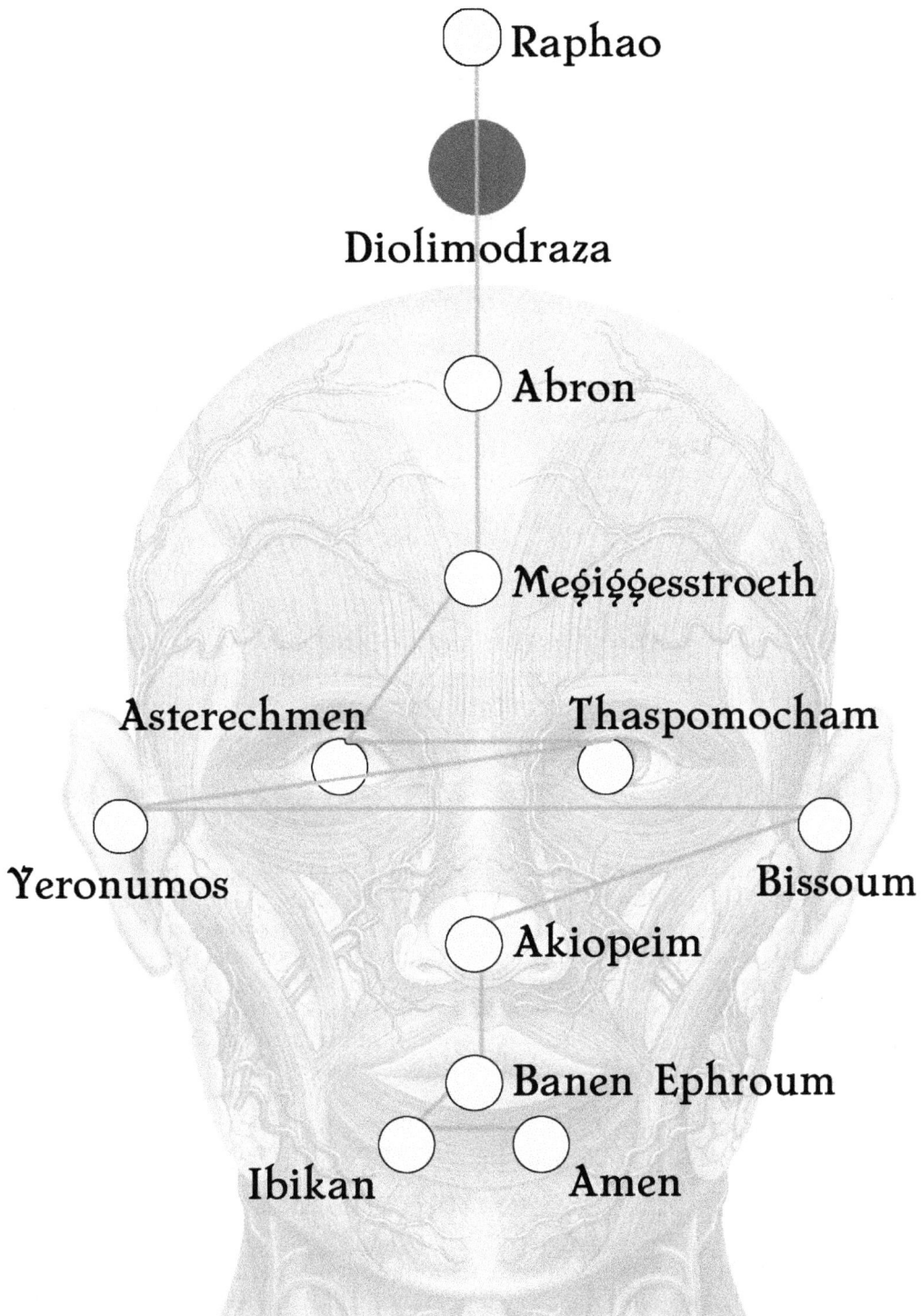

Raphao

Diolimodraza

Abron

Meçiǧǧesstroeth

Asterechmen

Thaspomocham

Yeronumos

Bissoum

Akiopeim

Banen Ephroum

Ibikan

Amen

between the Self and the Other. In mainstream Buddhism (and certain other more esoteric religious traditions), the complete elimination or sublimation of the Ego is desired, that one may experience the inexpressible Oneness. This is not, however, the case in the practice of Kimetikos, in which the Ego is something to be redeemed, not destroyed. This idea is important enough to discuss at some length.

The Gnostic presentation of the Ego or Self seems to provide a kind of happy medium between individuation and union with the Pleroma. The complete elimination of the Ego is not something found in Gnostic thought — at least, not something one attains while trapped in the World of Forms. As mentioned previously, the Gnostic Demiurge character represents the Ego and its trappings. 'I am the only true God; there is no God other than me,' 'I AM THAT I AM' — these statements made by the Demiurge are qualitative indicators that this is an individual personality which stands between the human and the true experience of divinity.

One might suggest that throwing off the shackles of the Archons and the Demiurge would result in the elimination of Self. In Gnostic myth, however, it is important to note that there are indications that the Archons will not be eliminated, but will instead be redeemed. In 'The Reality of the Rulers,' for instance, we learn that it is possible for this redemptive process to occur, as one of the Archons, Sabaoth, repents of his actions:

Now when his offspring Sabaoth saw the force of that angel, he repented and condemned his father and his mother, matter. He loathed her, but he sang songs of praise up to Sophia and her daughter Zoe. And Sophia and Zoe caught him up and gave him charge of the seventh heaven, below the veil between above and below. And he is called 'God of the forces, Sabaoth', since he is up above the forces of chaos, for Sophia

established him.[9]

Whether or not it applies to the Demiurge himself is a matter of speculation, but in Kimetikos we speculate that this redemptive process would extend from the qualities of the Ego (the Archons) to the Ego itself. In other words, the Ego is not eliminated when its qualities are redeemed, it becomes somehow perfected or redeemed itself. This is still within the realm of Modern Gnostic speculation, but the very nature of gnosis and Gnosticism bear this out.

Nowhere in Gnostic literature do we see the elimination of Self or Ego indicated. Indeed, it almost seems like the complete opposite. Without delving too far into Cartesian Metaphysics, in order for gnosis to be experienced — in order that something can be known — there must be something to do the experiencing. In Kimetikos, this 'thing that experiences' is the Nous, the essential core which contains the Divine Spark. What gnosis is for, we find, is to raise the individual into a perpetual state of modified perception, a literal phenomenological phase change in which the perfection contained within, the spark and the Pleroma, become perceivable. This is the resurrection that happens while one is still alive. Without the Self, this would not be possible. Eliminating the Ego is counterproductive because one is still in the World of Forms. Far better to redeem it so that you can continue to make your way through the World of Forms. After all, the elimination of Ego discussed in Illuminist religions is impossible to maintain except, perhaps, in the most rigorously ascetic practice. Eventually one has to 'come out of it,' to do things like eat or sleep or go potty, at which point the Ego is there in full glory.

The elimination of the Ego would also be counterproductive because it would eliminate the Essence That Experiences. This extends to the

what gnosis is for, we find, is to raise the individual into a perpetual state of modified perception

individual personality; without the amalgam of stuff that we have built up around the self as the personality, the experience of gnosis would not be a unique experience, and since the entirety needs to experience every single unique portion of itself in order to become complete — for the universe to achieve its own gnosis — then the Archons and the Demiurge are a necessary part of the process. Eliminating them serves no real purpose within Kimetikos; redeeming them, on the other hand, would make far more sense in this context. So, although we could couch the idea of the redemption of the Ego in terms of death, it's important to proceed through this ego-death to ego-resurrection. This is encoded in the message of the story of the phantom spirit found in The Pistis Sophia (the speaker is Mary, Jesus's mother):

'When thou wert little, before the spirit had come upon thee, whilst thou wert in a vineyard with Joseph, the spirit came out of the height and came to me in my house, like unto thee; and I had not known him, but I thought that thou wast he. And the spirit said unto me: Where is Jesus, my brother, that I meet with him?' And when he had said this unto me, I was at a loss and thought it was a phantom to try me. So I seized him and bound him to the foot of the bed in my house, until I went forth to you, to thee and Joseph in the field, and I found you on the vineyard, Joseph propping up the vineyard. It came to pass, therefore, when thou didst hear me speak the word unto Joseph, that thou didst understand the word, wert joyful and saidest: 'Where is he, that I may see him; else I await him in this place.' And it came to pass, when Joseph had heard thee say these words, that he was startled. And we went down together, entered the house and found the spirit bound to the bed. And we looked on thee and him and found thee like unto him. And he who was bound to the bed was unloosed; he took thee in his arms and kissed thee, and thou also didst kiss him. Ye became one.[10]

In Gnostic descriptions of the Aeons and the realms of perfection, we very often find the term 'Autogenes,' which means 'self-generated.' Many

of the characters found within the Pleroma 'generated' themselves. It follows that these beings were understood as having Selfness, whether literally or otherwise, which gives credence to the idea that the act of emanation from the Oneness resulted in its desire to know itself. The emanations are 'Selfs' that interact with other segments of the Unknowable Wholeness; by knowing the sum of all of its parts, the Unknowable Wholeness can come to know itself.

The greatest amount of material in the practice of Kimetikos is devoted to preparation for the redemptions of the Soul and Spirit via the redemption of the Body. Until one has credible self-knowledge of the various parts of one's body — the tool with which we interface with the Kosmos — it is exceptionally difficult to have credible self-knowledge of the Soul or Spirit. The Buddhist contemplative practices which developed into 'mindfulness,' Taoist alchemical practice and Tai Chi, Yoga — all of these practices attest to an inherent knowledge within certain spiritual paths that body knowledge is essential to spiritual practice. The Bestiary in the *Secret Book of John*, restated above in 'Anthropologia,' may well illustrate that at least one group of so-called Gnostics had similar ideas.

To make this a little clearer, let us discuss the Buddhist idea of the five Skandhas, or aggregates. According to Buddhist phenomenology, the 'self' as a unique entity does not exist. Instead, what humans perceive as 'selfness' is actually the five skandhas: form (rupa), sensation (vedana), perception (sanna), mental formations (sankhara) and consciousness (vinanna).

Coming to the realization that all of these skandhas are essentially ephemeral and changing is a key facet of Gautama's original teaching. Confusing one's 'Self' with any one of the skandhas, or any combination thereof, is the root cause of desire and suffering in the world. At the same time, consciously and mindfully focusing upon and contemplating the impermanence of the skandhas can bring the practitioner to the experience of Nirvana through the elimination of self-ness:

Put another way, if we were to self-identify with an aggregate then we would cling (upadana) to such; and, given that all aggregates are impermanent (anicca), it would then be likely that at some level we would experience agitation (paritassati) or loss or grief or stress or suffering (see dukkha). Therefore, if we want to be free of suffering, it is wise to experience the aggregates clearly, without clinging or craving (tanha), as apart from any notion of self (anatta).[11]

Remarkably, the source documents also list five 'powers' that govern the interaction of the human with the Kosmos:

The one who governs the perception of things is named Archendekta, who is enthroned with Hotness. The one who governs the reception of things is named Deitharbathas, who is enthroned with Cold. The one who governs the imagination of things is Oummaa, who is enthroned with Dryness. The one who governs the integration of things is Aachiaram, who is enthroned with Wetness. The one who governs all of the impulses is Riaramnacho, who is enthroned with Matter.

The skandhas and the governors of perception have an almost one-to-one correspondence, though presented in a different order:

Form: Rupa:: All of the
    Impulses: Riaramnacho
Sensation: Vedana:: Reception:
    DeitharbathasPerception: Sanna::
    Perception: Archendekta
Mental Formations: Sankhara::
    Imagination of Things: Oumma
Consciousness: Vinanna:: Integration
    of Things: Aachiaram

Since the source documents for Kimetikos are so patently works of phenomenology, and as the Buddhist skandhas are an aggregation

of various experiences as perceived by humans through the senses but are not essentially real, so the Gnostic Archons also represent unreal experiences within the World of Forms which lead the human into pleasure, desire, grief and fear:

Interactions with the Kosmos require the presence of the Seven Senses, whose ruler is Esthesis-Zouch-Epi-Ptoe, and the Material Soul, whose ruler is Anayo. The presence of these powers invites the influences of the powers who rule over the passions, who are four in number. Their names are:

Ephememphi, associated with pleasure, who
    rules over lust, unmerited pride, and evil.
Yoko, associated with desire, who
    rules over anger, fury, bitterness,
    outrage and dissatisfaction.
Nenentophni, associated with distress, who
    rules over envy, jealousy, grief, vexation,
    discord, cruelty, worry and mourning.
Blaomen, associated with fear, who rules
    over horror, flattery, suffering and shame.

As mentioned in our discussion on the Ego, there is no indication within Gnostic thought that the Self does not exist. Indeed, the Archons involved in the creation and perception of the ephemeral world serve to occlude the Self at their center. This does not mean that invisible aliens are crawling all over your soul; these are not 'Body thetans.' They are, instead, the impermanent things that impede one's ability to experience the psychospiritual state we call 'dwelling in gnosis.' They are the roadblock on the path to self-knowledge, and through mindful contemplation on them, one does not discover that there is no self, but instead discovers that essential spark of the Universal Self that exists under the surface of the World of Forms.

In short, Kimetikos is a procedure for what scholar Tim Boucher describes as 'proprioception': an intimate and intensive course of action and contemplation that the Gnostic might use to come to a deeper understanding of one's Self:

So if you applied this understanding to Gnosticism, it begins right at the source. That is, you. Your body. You may or may not be the source of the universe, but the thing to understand is that your body is the source of all of your perceptions of the universe. I like to think of perceptions as the reflection not the illusion of the universe reflected into your nervous system. Which is exactly where proprioception lies: at the root where perception has its conception: the point of deception. The point where your brain stops saying to itself, 'I am collecting sensory data reflected onto my nervous system from the exterior world' and starts saying the shortcut, 'I perceive existance directly'. It's almost like the difference in role playing games between saying, 'My character does such and such,' and 'I do such and such.'

It has to do with the being at the level of identifying with your shortcut habitual perceptions and reactions to the world. And this is what the ego is constructed out of: once useful logical habits upon which hinge emotional and physical reactions like colours on a painting. And this is the domain of the Demiurge. In more straightforward Christian myth, it is the Devil as the ruler of this world. In the Tarot we see the Lovers chained at the feet of the Devil, like Princess Leia on Jabba's Pleasure Barge.[12]

This understanding is one facet of gnosis. In his original teachings, Gautama never intended Nirvana to mean a post-mortem state of bliss. It is, in fact, a way of living, a way of experiencing the world of imperfections without needlessly suffering. Gnosis is also a way of living in the imperfect world of forms, and Kimetikos presents one possible way to achieve that state.

4. KIMETIKOS IN PRACTICE: REDEMPTION OF THE BODY

Although in no way as strenuous as Yoga or as variegated as Tai Chi, the Body Sequences of Kimetikos utilize visualization, auditory toning and kinetic movements to allow the individual practitioner to become intimate with him or herself. The 'barbarous names' of what we term the Nodes and Circuit Points and their Rulers, through which the bai or activating spirit flows thorough the body, act on an energetic level to draw the attention of the Nous to the part of the body on which one focuses. That these specific names are used is a matter of expediency; one could just as readily translate, say, the names of various condiments into a foreign language and intone them and one would achieve a similar result.

Knowledge of self begins with knowledge of one's body

Knowledge of self begins with knowledge of one's body. According to our interpretation of Gnostic mythology, an animating force descends from the Pleroma, or Fullness, into the realms of the World of Forms. It is then divided and distributed by various Archons, arbitrators and creators of the material world. It is possible to comprehend and experience this animating force, to which we refer as 'bai', Coptic for 'spirit.'

According to the source material, the legion of archons which comprises the human (referred to above as 'The Bestiary') is divided into the physical anatomical members of the body, to which we will refer as the 'Circuit,' and the activating energies which animate these members, to which we will refer as the 'Nodes.' Both the Circuit and the Nodes are centered on the anatomical points listed in the texts. The bai flows through the body via the 72 part Circuit, animated at 31 Nodes within each of five elemental qualities, expressed in 7 'souls.'

Kimetikos is a method whereby the flow of bai through each of the seven souls is brought into balance by aligning the Circuit with its Nodes through the intonation of the names of the Circuit Points (CPs), the Nodes, and their rulers within each elemental quality (EQ), coupled with mindful, gentle movements which serve to stimulate the energies of the body in the proper order, and contemplative practice which serves to allow focused concentration of the consciousness throughout one's entire body.

Complete alignment of the archonic energies of the body—a 'Series'—consists of a total of 35 'Sequences.' A Sequence focuses on one elemental quality of one soul. When all of the elemental qualities have been aligned within a soul, one may move to the next soul, until all of the energies of the body have been aligned and the Series is complete. At this point, the Body is considered 'redeemed' and the kimetikon may proceed with the redemption of the Soul.

Attention should be paid to anything that occurs during performance of Kimetikos. It is recommended that the kimetikon keep a journal of his or her progress, noting occurrences therein. When performing the Sequences, the kimetikon might notice interesting sensations in her body. There might be feelings of warmth or coldness, heaviness or airiness during or after the performance. There might be tingling in some extremities, or even minor discomfort or unpleasantness. The idea is for the kimetikon to recognize these sensations where and when they occur and then move past them. In so doing, the practitioner cannot help but gain an intimate knowledge of the bai within her own body. One may make some interesting discoveries: soreness that had gone unnoticed, unmanifested pain, energy 'blockages' that loosen when the name of the Circuit Point is pronounced, or any number of other sensations.

It is also possible that the kimetikon may not notice any immediate physical effects from the Sequences. The changes precipitated by the practice of Kimetikos may be subtle, as they also have a phenomenological facet. The governors of perception discussed above each reside with, and work through, one of the elemental qualities:

> The one who governs the perception of things is named Archendekta, who is enthroned with Hotness. The one who governs the reception of things is named Deitharbathas, who is enthroned with Cold. The one who governs the imagination of things is Oummaa, who is enthroned with Dryness. The one who governs the integration of things is Aachiaram, who is enthroned with Wetness. The one who governs all of the impulses is Riaramnacho, who is enthroned with Matter.

In Kimetikos, each Elemental Quality gives rise to, and augments, one of these governors. As the members of the body are what we use to interface with the Kosmos, running the Sequences which redeem the members of the body also redeems the body's ability to perceive.

So, for instance, when one runs the Hot Sequences, one may notice an increased ability to perceive sensations. The Cold Sequence may increase one's ability to receive sensations which are projected by the World. The Dry Sequence may augment one's ability to imagine and visualize, and the Wet Sequence one's analytical abilities. The Matter Sequence, then, is a kind of 'Level Up' which consolidates all of the phenomenalogical benefits of the previous Sequences.

The names used in Kimetikos, mostly those found in The *Secret Book of John* with some variations due to lacunae in the text, almost undoubtedly represented to the original authors the names of actual 'demons' or spirits, by which the enterprising Gnostic would heal his or her body through exorcism, or 'casting out' the being by using this name.[13] Howard M. Jackson, in his essay 'The Origin in Ancient Incantatory 'Voces Magicae' of Some Names in the Sethian Gnostic System,' demonstrates fairly convincingly that many of these names were derived from, or shared the same sources as, the Greek Magical Papyri.[14] These so-called 'Voces Magicae,' also known in the Hellenistic world (especially the Neoplatonic Theurgical tradition) as 'barbarous names,' the meaning of which is less important than their resemblance to 'Divine realities.' Neoplatonic theurgist Iamblicus, for example, tells us that:

> 'Barbarous names' may be unintelligible to us, but they are meaningful at the Divine level. The precise terms used do count, because they are not formed by conventional agreement and, unlike human language, actually resemble Divine realities. The languages of Sacred Nations are to be preferred because they preserve ancient and hallowed forms inviolate, whereas Greek forms may be spoiled through innovation.[15]

Kimetikos understands the names as vibrational attributes of subtle energies which the kimetikon can effect via harmonic resonation produced by the voice. The energies of the body resonate at a certain frequency, and the intonation of the names creates acoustic resonance with the energies. One might consider the body a string, and the Nodes and Circuit Points intervals on that string. The vagaries of life in the World of Forms cause the various energies of the body to go 'out of tune,' in the way that a guitar which has never been played can go out of tune due to changes in atmospheric influence (moisture, temperature, etc.). Toning the names 'tunes' the body in the same way that a tuning pipe may be used to tune said guitar.[16]

5. CONCLUSION

This article merely scratches the surface of Kimetikos, which is, and will continue to be, a work in progress. The redemption of the Body is merely the first step in the process; as the source material tells us, the Soul and Spirit are also in need of redemption. When one has completed the entire Series, one may also learn how to apply this process therapeutically for other individuals using a methodology similar to Reiki.

Clues to the remainder of the process of redemption of the Soul and Spirit may be found in the content of this article, and additional literature on this subject will be available in the near future. For more information, including an introductory course in the practice of Body Kimetikos and detailed scripts and instructions for the Body Sequences, please visit the author's website at http://gnostichealing.wordpress.com.

48 THE GNOSTIC

NOTES:

1 For more similarities between fractal mathematics and gnostic cosmology, see my 'Chaos Theory and Gnostic Myth,' published in *The Pirate's Garden*, 2006.

2 Mead, G.R.S. trans. *Pistis Sophia, or Books of the Saviour* Book 1, Chap. 18.

3 Ibid. Book 3, Chap. 112.

4 Turner, John trans. 'Trimorphic Protennoia.' As found in *The Nag Hammadi Library in English*, Robinson, James ed.

5 Casey, Robert trans. *Excerpta Ex Theodoto*. http://www.hypotyposeis.org/papers/theodotus.htm

6 For a fascinating investigation of these ideas, see 'Gnostic Liberation from Astrological Determinism: Hipparchan 'Trepidation' and the Breaking of Fate,' by Horace Jeffrey Hodges, *Vigiliae Christianae*, Vol. 51, No. 4 Nov., 1997, pp. 359-373.

7 See Turner, John, 'The Gnostic Threefold Path to Enlightenment: The Ascent of Mind and the Descent of Wisdom.' *Novum Testamentum*, Vol. 22, Fasc. 4 Oct., 1980, pp. 324-351.

8 One might consider the myth of Inanna's descent to the Underworld a kind of proto-ascent sequence of this kind in the other direction, of course. In this myth, the Sumerian goddess Inanna must descend into the Underworld to free her lover Tammuz from Death. On the way, she is stopped at seven gates, at each of which she is asked to shed one of her mystical garments.

9 Layton, Bentley trans. 'The Hypostasis of the Archons,' As found in *The Nag Hammadi Library in English*, Robinson, James ed.

10 Mead, G.R.S. trans. *Pistis Sophia, or Books of the Saviour* Book 1, Chap. 61.

11 'Skandha.' http://en.wikipedia.org/wiki/Skandha

12 See Michael Williams, *Rethinking Gnosticism*, p 133, where he discusses Plotinus' criticism of 'Gnostics' who practice this form of exorcism to heal sicknesses.

13 *Vigiliae Christianae*, Vol. 43, No. 1 Mar., 1989, pp. 69-79

14 *On the Mysteries*, VII, 4-5

15 As Kimetikos recognizes the Macro and Microcosmic, if helpful, the kimetikon may also consider these names the names of actual spiritual entities which reside in the energies in question.

16 Boucher, Tim. 'Saving the Gnostic Body.' http://www.timboucher.com/journal/2007/saving-the-gnostic-body.

Andrew Phillip Smith

Atheists

They often piss on the floor.

10% of atheists live undercover in extreme Protestant sects, doing good work for the cause.

They won't sacrifice to the Gods.

Atlas-like, they heroically shoulder the burden of their existential honesty.

Every last one of them is the son of a minister.

They prefer deists to theists, 'but one meets so few of them these days'.

They apply remorseless rational logic to every area of their lives.

They do not read novels.

They don't believe in one God, the Father, the Almighty, maker of heaven and earth, of all that is, seen and unseen.

Their personal hygiene leaves much to be desired, unless they are American atheists.

They secretly admire the last Pope.

There are no female atheists.

There are no working-class atheists.

'Once I was late for a flight and I said, 'Oh God, I'm going to miss my flight.' An atheist overheard me and started arguing with me about the existence of God, and sure enough I missed my flight.'

When they fall in love they blame

it on their brain chemistry.

They don't even believe in the devil.

Most of them are white boys.

They don't like comfort blankets because of the metaphorical association with theism.

Not all of them are Marxists.

They are always in danger of physical violence inflicted by theists.

Their mothers didn't hug them when they were young.

The criminal classes who have never had a serious thought about anything in their life aren't really atheists.

They like the Dalai Lama, except for his spectacles.

Their heads are kind of big, don't you think?.

They think all religion should be banned except for the Church of England.

Stalin wasn't really an atheist.

You can hear them guffawing heartily in public places when they remember that there's no God.

They don't have a fucking clue about theology.

by Andrew P Smith, age 43 ½

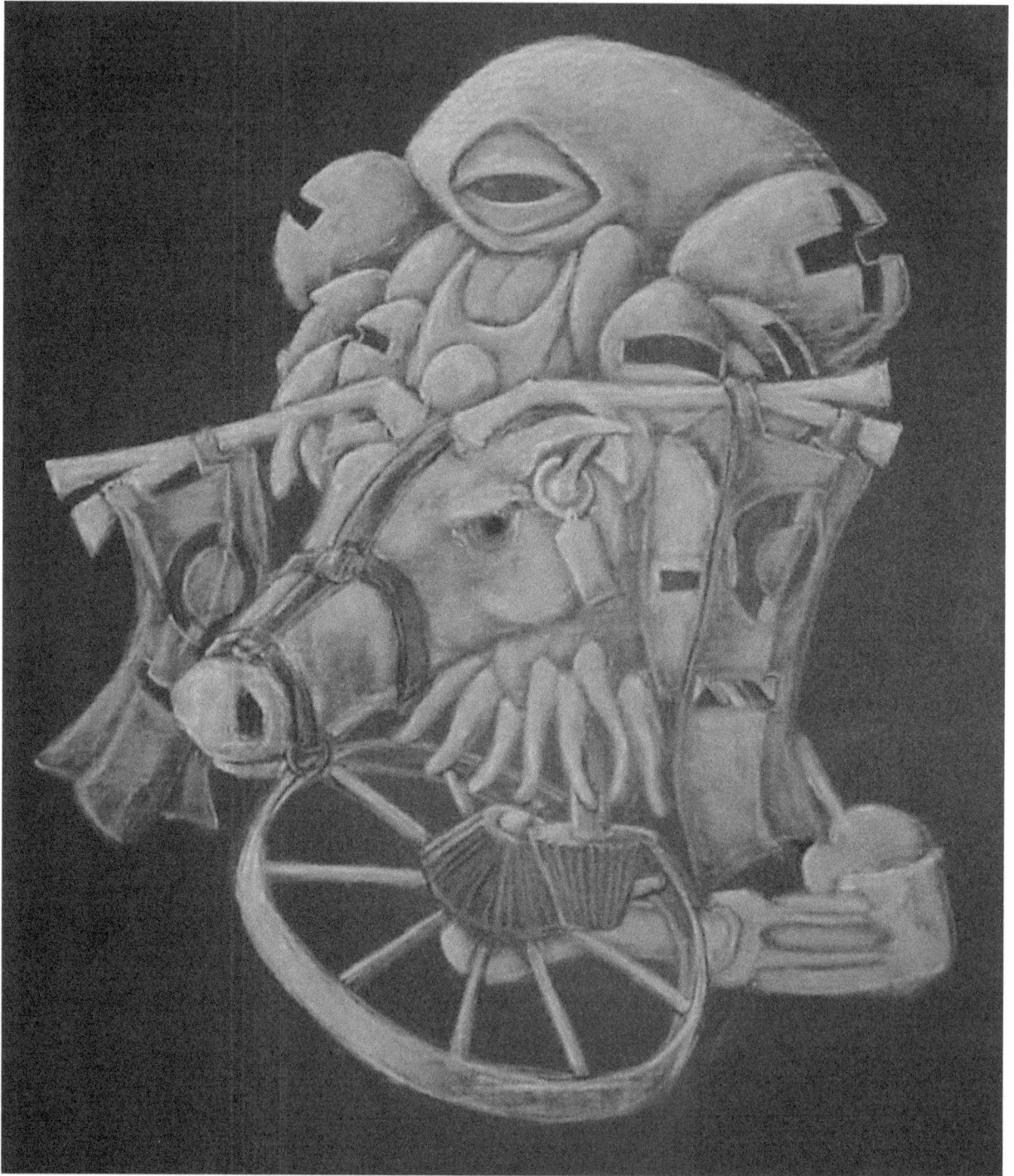

Mark Holwager/Valarie Ziegler

'Sometimes I Have These Dreams That I'm Somebody Else':
Gnostic Themes in *The Prisoner*,
Television's Ultimate Cult Classic

Recognized as the ultimate cult television show, *The Prisoner* remains, forty years after its original airing, a masterpiece. Viewers in 1967 knew Patrick McGoohan, *The Prisoner's* producer and star, as John Drake from the celebrated *Secret Agent* show (*Danger Man* in Britain), and they expected another action-adventure spy series. They encountered instead an exhilarating examination of human freedom that was as profound and visually stunning as it was surreal. Set in a beautiful seaside resort known only as 'the Village,' *The Prisoner* depicts the fate of Number Six, an unnamed government agent who was kidnapped after resigning his post. The Village is his prison and seeks to pry his secrets from him 'by hook or by crook.' To maintain his self respect and identity, Number Six must resist and insist, 'I am not a number! I am a free man!'

Commentators have long noted that Number 6 is an archetypal hero confronting religious and existential questions: what does it mean to be an individual? What does it mean to exist in society? What capacities for good and evil exist within each person? Is the Village a place or an existential condition? Is escape possible? Who or what is Number 1?

Surprisingly, no one has discussed *The Prisoner's* striking parallels to Gnostic religions. Using the *Gospel of Thomas* and 'The Hymn of the Pearl' from the Acts of the Apostle Thomas, we will demonstrate how *The Prisoner* exemplifies the Gnostic myth of descent and return, depicting a hero who refuses to be fully embodied in the hateful world in which he is imprisoned, who insists (contrary to evidence) that he is from a truer world in a higher realm, and who risks everything to return to the beginning and reunite with his genuine self.

LIFE AND DEATH IN THE VILLAGE: 'REJECT THIS FALSE WORLD OF NUMBER TWO!'

The Prisoner's pre-credit sequence lays out a number of iconographic images that appear repeatedly in the series and that we recall on screen here: the Lotus 7 car, the famous buildings, the London flat, the underground place of work,

and the fashionable dark clothes.

In 'Arrival,' the series' initial episode, Number 6 is kidnapped and taken away from all this. In the Village he is given a uniform and a Number 6 rosette badge to wear. This action parallels the experience of the protagonist in 'Hymn of the Pearl,' where the boy from the spiritual realm leaves his royal robe and mantel behind to travel to an alien land. The crafty inhabitants persuade him to don their clothes and eat their food, and the boy promptly forgets who he is. Number 6—almost as if he had read 'Hymn of the Pearl'—instinctively refuses to wear the rosette badge and demands without success that his own clothes be returned to him. He has no alternative to wearing the Village uniform or consuming Village food and drink, which he suspects — rightfully so — is often used to drug him. In 'A. B. and C.,' an episode in which the Village drugs Number 6 and manipulates his dreams, we see that he is so focused on retaining his identity that his normal dream life has been reduced to an endlessly repeated anguish pattern of his resignation. Even asleep, Number 6 is obsessed with reclaiming his true self.

He is also quick to abjure other Villagers for giving up their identities so easily. 'Unlike me,' he charges, 'many of you have accepted the situation of your imprisonment and will die here like rotten cabbages.' In 'Hymn of the Pearl,' the divine messenger offers the boy salvation through reuniting with his former belongings and self: 'Awake and rise from your sleep…. Remember that you are a son of Kings and see the slavery of your life….Remember your robe of glory and your splendid mantle which you may wear when your name is named in the book of life, is read in the book of heroes….' Number 6's admonition to the Villagers is less sympathetic, but his message is the same: remember who you truly are. 'Brainwashed imbeciles,' he growls.

unlike me, many of you have accepted the situation of your imprisonment and will die here like rotten cabbages

'Can you laugh? Can you cry? Can you think?.... Is this what they did to you? Is this how they started to break you before you gave them what they were after? In your heads are the remnants of a brain. In your hearts you may still have the desire to be human beings again…'

Even more to the point, Number 6 tells the Villagers in an episode entitled 'A Change of Mind': 'You still have a choice. You can still salvage your rights as individuals…. Reject this false world of Number Two! Reject it! Now!'

Practicing what he preaches, in a particularly heated exchange with Number 2 in 'Once Upon a Time,' Number 6 vociferously denies that he belongs to the Village.

Number 6: Units are not for me.

Number 2: You are a member! Of the Village!

Number 6: No!

Number 2: You are a unit!

Number 6: No!

Number 2: Of society!

Number 6: NO!

Village officials respond by arguing that for its residents the Village is the only reality possible. 'It's quite a beautiful place, really, don't you think? Almost like a world on its own,' Number 2 cheerfully observes on Number 6's arrival. In an episode entitled 'Dance of the Dead,' Number 2 contends that the Village is Number 6's only option; he no longer exists in the outside world. She urges him to give in and be happy. But Number 6 resists. When a corpse is washed up on a remote Village beach, Number 6 plants an SOS message on it and sends it back to sea. He then encounters Number 2 on the waterfront in a famous twilight scene:

Number 2: You're being hostile again. What were you looking at?

Number 6: A light.

Number 2: A star.

Number 6: A boat.

Number 2: An insect.

Number 6: A plane.

Number 2: A flying fish.

Number 6: A man who belongs to *my* world.

Number 2: This is your world. I am your world. If you insist on living a dream,

you may be taken for mad.

Number 6: I like my dream.

Number 2: Then you *are* mad.

At the dress ball that evening, Number 6 is the only Villager not in costume; instead, he has been given his own tuxedo to wear. Number 6 initially sees this as a sign that he is still himself, but Number 2 counters that he received no costume because he does not exist. Later that night, Number 6 learns that the Village has intercepted the corpse he had set adrift, doctored it to look like him, and planned to send it back to sea with his identification papers. The implications are devastating:

Number 6: So to the outside world —

Number 2: Which you only dream about.

Number 6: I'll be dead.

Number 2: A small confirmation of a known fact.

Until he can admit that the Village *is* his home, Number 6 will be suspended between the two worlds. 'Everything you need is here,' Number 2 contends. But Number 6 refuses to give up the self knowledge that is the core of his identity as well as the source of his capacity to resist. 'Everything is elsewhere,' he insists.

Number 6 refuses to give up the self knowledge that is the core of his identity as well as the source of his capacity to resist

BLESSED ARE THOSE WHO ARE SOLITARY AND SUPERIOR: A RETURN TO THE BEGINNING

Number 6's fixation on his identity leads him to behaviors that viewers often find confusing or even counterproductive. In four of the show's seventeen episodes, he manages to escape the Village, and every time he returns to London. Why? In his first escape, he learns that his London colleagues were complicit in his imprisonment, and he also knows that the first place Village agents will look for him is in London. So why does Number 6, if he really wants to escape, keep returning to his place of origin?

If *The Prisoner* were merely an action-adventure series, London would make no sense as an escape site. But McGoohan designed the series as an allegory. The Gnostic myth of descent and return meshes beautifully with *The Prisoner's* own narrative arc, which demands a return to London, for only there is Number 6 in his element. His London flat, his Lotus 7 car, Westminster Abbey and the Houses of Parliament, the agency from which he resigned so decisively, his dark stylish clothes — these are the concrete realities that symbolize his earlier life of autonomy. And it is to these that he must return. As the *Gospel of Thomas* notes, 'Blessings on you who are alone and chosen, for you will find the kingdom. You have come from it and will return there again.'

In 'Fall Out,' *The Prisoner's* concluding episode, the Village concedes that Number 6's determined resistance has won him the right to be an individual. At a ceremony recognizing his successful struggle, Number 6 is permitted to trade his Village uniform for his original clothing. 'We thought you would

feel — happier — as yourself,' a Village official explains. The President of the assembly then directs Number 6 to sit on a throne, explaining, 'You are the only individual and we need you…. All about you is yours. We concede. We offer. We plead for you to lead us.' The President then makes a great show of presenting Number 6 the belongings — his passport, his money, the key to his flat — that he forfeited when he came to the Village. If Number 6 chooses to return, these things will be restored to him. If he stays, the Villagers will recognize him as a 'Man of steel…magnificently equipped' to teach and lead them.

As the protagonist in 'Hymn of the Pearl' was lured by the prospect of reuniting with the robe and mantle he left behind in his place of origin, Number 6 finds the prospect of returning to his former life and belongings more powerful than the temptation of remaining in the Village as its leader. Through a series of highly convoluted

events that we will not attempt to narrate, Number 6 destroys the Village and returns to his London apartment, where his Lotus 7 awaits him. We now see the final scenes of the series: Number 6 hops in his car, and viewers once again see him driving past famous London landmarks.

As this final episode winds down — and you can imagine millions of viewers in 1968 desperately trying to make sense of it — the closing scenes depict something quite unexpected. We hear the thunder that typically marks the beginning of an episode, and then the camera returns us to the long strip of pavement, where the Lotus 7 is roaring down the road, the Prisoner behind the wheel wearing his usual enigmatic expression. Patrick McGoohan was so insistent that viewers recognize that the series had come full circle that the <u>exact</u> same footage was used in the closing scene as that which appeared in the opening pre-credit sequence. Number 6 was back — exactly — where he began.

This ending — and *The Prisoner* was the first television show to air a concluding episode that attempted to wrap up a series — both infuriated and intrigued fans. What was the point? Why was Number 6 back at the beginning? Was it all a dream? Was Number 6 on the road to a new Village? Had he won or lost? Was it a happy ending? Or an ending at all? What did it mean?

These questions have stirred fan debate about and fascination with *The Prisoner* for the last forty years. McGoohan was reticent about supplying answers, but he did say that he hoped viewers would see Number 6 as an 'everyman' and that they would look within their own villages and selves for answers. He believed viewers expected the final episode to unveil a James Bond super-villain as the source of Number 6's suffering. That did not happen; instead, like each of us, Number 6 learned that he was responsible both for his own pain and his own reformation. He must learn do what Humpty Dumpty could not: put himself back together again.

In the end, there is no place like home, and Number 6 had to find his way back there. As McGoohan noted, the final episode 'should never have ended with the two words, 'The End.' It should have finished with the two words, 'The Beginning'….'

Or as Jesus said to his disciples in the *Gospel of Thomas* when they asked him how their end would come: 'Have you discovered the beginning and now are seeking the end? Where the beginning is, the end will be. Blessings on you who stand at the beginning. You will know the end and not taste death.'

What was the point? Why was Number 6 back at the beginning? Was it all a dream? Was Number 6 on the road to a new Village? Had he won or lost? Was it a happy ending? Or an ending at all? What did it mean?

APPENDIX: MAKING THE TWO ONE

Spoiler Alert: in the body of our paper we have preserved the mystery of Number 1's identity as revealed in 'Fall Out,' the series' concluding episode. This appendix reveals all.

The *Gospel of Thomas* contains additional motifs that are useful in analyzing *The Prisoner*. Jesus' sayings about making the two one (Saying 22, also echoed in the Gospel of Philip) so that one may enter the kingdom work well: 'When you make the two into one, and when you make the inner like the outer and the outer like the inner, and the upper like the lower, and when you make male and female into a single one… when you make eyes in place of an eye, a hand in place of a hand, a foot in place of a foot, an image in place of an image, then you will enter the kingdom.'

See also Saying 11 ('On the day when you were one you became two. But when you become two, what will you do?'); Saying 50 ('If they say to you, 'Where have you come from?' say to them, 'We have come from the light…''); and Saying 61 ('I am the one who comes from what is whole…. I say, if you are whole, you will be filled with light, but if divided, you will be filled with darkness').

If we had focused more on 'Fall Out' in this article, the issue of 'making the two one' would have added a third section to our discussion. A critical feature of 'Fall Out' that we have not discussed is the unmasking of Number 1 — who is revealed to be the bestial face of Number 6. Shrieking maniacally, Number 1 runs frantically around the room until Number 6 is able to herd him up a ladder into a rocket. Number 6 then launches the rocket into space. The Villagers flee; Rover (the Village guardian charged with disciplining recalcitrant citizens) melts into oblivion; and the Village itself presumably explodes while Number 6 escapes with three other residents.

Number 1's identity was the central mystery

of the series, and most viewers had difficulty understanding how or why Number 6 could also be Number 1. McGoohan intended for people to see Number 1 as Number 6's bestial side, and an earlier episode ('Checkmate') had revealed that Number 6 was naturally arrogant, a personality that was consistent with being a jailer, not a prisoner. Interpreters like Rob Fairclough have argued that the relationship between Number 6 and Number 1 may be identical to that between the ego and the id. In 'Fall Out,' Fairclough contended, Number 6 triumphed over the id by banishing it to outer space.

Just as useful a trope for interpreting Number1/6 is the *Gospel of Thomas'* admonition to 'make the two one.' In its original setting, of course, this advice refers to Genesis 1, where the perfection of God's creation has not yet been marred. Then, a human being was both 'male and female,' as the separation between the genders does not occur until Genesis 2. Thomas represents the kingdom of God as day seven — the Sabbath — of the creation week. All is perfection; humanity is united; and those who hear the words of Jesus in the *Gospel of Thomas* are urged to return to this day, when the 'two' were 'one.' Accordingly, Thomas instructs readers to became 'solitaries,' that is, people who have integrated themselves into a whole.

'Fall Out' also deals with two beings (Numbers 1 and 6) who represent different sides of the same person. The two become one not by reuniting, but rather by eliminating Number 1 — in some ways, a reprise of the plot of the episode entitled 'Schizoid Man,' where Number 6 establishes his selfhood through the death of the doppelganger who attempted to steal his identity. By the end of 'Fall Out,' the person who was once 'two' has become 'one,' and Number 6 can return to the beginning. Will he 'become two' again, in time? In our interpretation, yes. Number 6 returns to the beginning to try, once more, to navigate his way successfully through life. There are more Villages out there for him to explore when he falls into 'twoness.' But these will be new Villages, and they will set before him new obstacles to unity and integrity. As McGoohan asserted,

'The whole point of the series *The Prisoner* and the whole point certainly of the last episode is … that each man is a prisoner unto himself…. That is what one is constantly fighting to get through each day, each month, each year… each lifetime. That is the biggest enemy that we have — -is ourselves, and…that's the whole point. That's *The Prisoner.*' The only escape is death. What happens afterwards, McGoohan speculated, depended on the type of prisoner one had been.

Other *Prisoner* entities that need to be united are, in Thomas's words, the outer and the inner, as well as the upper and the lower. One of the prevailing images of the series is the contrast between the subterranean world of espionage, interrogation, and torture and the upper world of light and color. Both in London, where Number 6's employment is underground while his flat is above, and in the Village, where the holiday-like atmosphere on the grounds belies the high-tech equipment and Machiavellian machinations below, this contrast represents a split present in Number 6 himself. He is a man who passionately defends his right to freedom and who bitterly denounces the methods used by Village — and presumably by his London employers, who also regard him as a 'number' — to break and control people. Yet Number 6 is complicit in those methods. His 'top secret' London job tied him to an agency whose means were devious and cruel. His obvious enjoyment in manipulating Number 2 into a psychological breakdown in the 'Hammer Into Anvil' episode reveals his familiarity and ease in his own Machiavellian machinations. Until Number 6 can reconcile the freedom-loving self that typifies his upper world with the ruthless manipulator of the lower world, he cannot be 'one.'

Similarly, Number 6 must also find a way to unite his outer and inner selves. Here, the clothes tell all: when Number 6 is in Village attire, the obedient Villager he appears to be on the outside clashes with the rebellious prisoner he is on the inside. 'Fall Out' seeks to rectify this dichotomy by presenting Number 6 with his London clothing ('We thought you would feel — happier — as yourself'). But Number 6's black jacket is reminiscent of his dark Village blazer, and when combined with his black shirt, black slacks and black boots suggests that Number 6 belongs to the realm of death rather than light. Indeed, 'Dance of the Dead' depicted Number 6 as, literally, dead when he wore his own tuxedo. So the process of integrating the inner and outer has two parts. Number 6 must find outer clothing that matches his inner self. But before he can do that, he needs to resolve just what his true self is: does he belong in the upper world of light and color, or the subterranean world of torture, manipulation, and death? As the *Gospel of Thomas* observes in Saying 61: 'I say, if you are whole, you will be filled with light, but if divided, you will be filled with darkness.'

NOTES

1 This quotation is from the Prisoner doppelganger episode entitled 'Schizoid Man.' Readers interested in examining dialogue from The Prisoner should consult Robert Fairclough's excellent annotated script books: The Prisoner: The Original Scripts, volumes 1-2, published by Reynolds and Hearn Ltd. in 2005 (Volume 1) and 2006 (Volume 2).

2 AMC is currently producing a new mini-series of The Prisoner. See http://www.amctv.com/originals/the-prisoner/, where in addition to details about the new series one can watch all of the original Prisoner episodes.

3 This claim was part of the iconic resignation/kidnapping sequence that opened most Prisoner episodes.

4 The Judge in the episode 'Living in Harmony' recognizes the critical implicatons of wearing Village clothing. To do so is to lose one's previous identity, as the Judge acknowledges when he

discusses Number 6's resistance to wearing the attire proper to a Village sheriff: 'He'll put on his guns, and once he does that, he's mine.'

5 All references to 'Hymn of the Pearl' are from the Willis Barnstone version in his The Other Bible (HarperSanFrancisco, 1984), pp. 309-313.

6 Saying 49, *Gospel of Thomas*. All quotations from the *Gospel of Thomas* are taken from Willis Barnstone and Marvin Meyer, The Gnostic Bible (Shambhala, 2003), pp. 44-69. Stephen J. Patterson and James M. Robinson render this text: 'Blessed are the solitary ones, the elect. For you will find the kingdom. For you come from it (and) will return to it.' See Patterson, Robinson, and Mans-Gebhard Bethge, The Fifth Gospel: The *Gospel of Thomas* Comes of Age (Trinity International Press, 1998), p.18. The 'solitary and superior' phrase in the section heading comes from Bentley Layton's translation in The Gnostic Scriptures (Doubleday & Company, 1987), p. 389.

7 See http://www.youtube.com/watch?v=d6dOSm9mRQk&feature=channel for a fuller discussion. The sound technicians had originally hoped to add the sounds of a car engine to the last shot of Number 6 driving his Lotus 7, but McGoohan resisted the change. So the exact sound track from the pre-credit sequence was dubbed into the closing scene.

8 Humpty Dumpty references play an important role in the episode 'Once Upon a Time.' McGoohan was quizzed endlessly about the meaning of 'Fall Out.' He conceded that the episode contained Christian imagery (crucifixion, resurrection, temptation, and 'Dem Bones,' with its command to 'hear the word of the Lord'), and he suggested as well that the destruction of the Village had apocalyptic overtones. (See McGoohan's 1979 interview with Roger Goodman, available on CD as 'On the Trail of The Prisoner: Roger Goodman Talks

to Patrick McGoohan' and McGoohan's 1990 Radio One interview with Simon Bates.) Part of McGoohan's unwillingness to further explain the episode stemmed from his contention that it was an 'allegorical conundrum'; if he unpacked it, then it would no longer be allegorical. People ought to be able to see the series' meaning for themselves, he suggested. That is one reason he named his production company 'Everyman.' (See Patrick McGoohan, 'Foreword,' in Jon E. Lewis and Penny Stempel, Cult TV [Pavilion Books Limited, 1997], p. 6; see also the documentary Six Into One: The Prisoner File, produced and broadcast in 1984 in the UK by Channel 4; and McGoohan's 1977 interview with Warner Troyer, online at http://www.the-prisoner-6. freeserve.co.uk/troyer.htm and http://www.the-prisoner-6.freeserve.co.uk/troyer2.htm.)

McGoohan's admonition did not stop most fans from assuming that he had the answers. Perhaps he could have best responded by quoting Jesus from the *Gospel of Thomas*: 'I am not your rabbi. Because you have drunk, you are intoxicated from the bubbling spring I tended.' (Saying 13) Or: 'Whoever drinks from my mouth will become like me. I myself shall become that person, and the hidden things will be revealed to that one.' (Saying 108) Or, as a worst-case scenario: 'I took my stand in the midst of the world, and I appeared to them in flesh. I found them all drunk, yet none of them thirsty. My soul ached for the human children because they are blind in their hearts and do not see.' (Saying 28)

9 Sadly, McGoohan died on January 14, 2009. He never underestimated the difficulties of striving to be free. The series should have ended with the words 'The Beginning,' he said, 'because no one is a free man, unfortunately, no man is an island…but you've jolly well got to try, though.' This quotation is from McGoohan's 1979 interview with Roger Goodman, 'On the Trail of The Prisoner: Roger Goodman Talks to Patrick McGoohan.' See http://www.roger-goodman.supanet.com/ for more details.

McGoohan's death dismayed fans across the globe, but it did not bring an end to fans' appreciation of the series or their search for its meaning. Rather, McGoohan's passing sparked the kind of passionate discussions the Prisoner mastermind always encouraged — debates without easy answers, dependent on personal reflection and a willingness to rebel against the social norm. As a testament to the ongoing life of Prisoner fandom, many Internet-based groups have opened forums for continued exchanges on The Prisoner. See the tributes to McGoohan at http://www.netreach.net/~sixofone/ and http://www.theunmutual.co.uk/tributes.htm for the two most established sites.

10 Saying 18, *Gospel of Thomas*.

11 See Fairclough's The Prisoner: The Official Fact File (DeAgostini/Granada Ventures, 2005), Number 17, pp. 98-100 and volume 2, p. 442 of Fairclough's Prisoner script books.

Dean F. Wilson

Asceticism in Gnosticism

Asceticism, the practice of extreme abstinence from various 'worldly' things, has an interesting place in Gnosticism, both in that many Gnostic groups and texts supported the practice, while many others were strongly against it. The sheer variety in which Gnosticism was expressed throughout the centuries has led to an equally impressive variety of viewpoints on the controversial subject of asceticism.

However, it is necessary, before we continue, to examine the word *continence*, which crops up regularly in some of the translations of the quoted texts in this article. The word comes from the Greek *enkrateia*, which Bentley Layton defines as 'abstemiousness in the use of wine, meat, sex., etc.' The more common definition of the English translation is the refraining from sexual intercourse, but the broader meaning that Layton refers to must be kept in mind when it is used in certain of these texts. In a sense it can be taken as a catch-all phrase, akin to that of *asceticism* itself.

Asceticism comes in many forms, including abstinence from sex, food, and other sensual pleasures (such as, in modern times, television, video games, etc.), as cited above. Many Gnostic sects had a dualistic worldview, an 'us versus them' mentality which saw a very sharp division between the holiness of spirit and the evilness of matter. While this is not true for all Gnostic groups (some were mitigated, while others had a more holistic viewpoint, seeing everything, including evil, as a part of God), it has become a focal point for many of its adversaries, and thus it seems only logical that asceticism be recommended by such 'world-hating' Gnostics.

What does not make sense then, on the surface, is when asceticism is denounced as evil in and of itself, or when some Gnostic groups engaged very readily in the pleasures of the flesh that were supposed to be corrupt.

An answer to these contradictory views was given by Johann Lorenz von Mosheim in 1755:

'There is nothing surprising or unaccountable in this difference between the Gnostic moralists; for, when we examine the matter with attention, we shall find that the same doctrine may very naturally have given rise to these opposite sentiments. As they all deemed the body the centre and source of evil, those of that sect who were of a morose and austere disposition would be hence naturally led to mortify and combat the body as enemy of the soul; and those who were of a voluptuous turn might also consider the actions of the body as having no relation, either of congruity or incongruity, to the state of a soul in communion with God.'

The problem with Mosheim's argument is that it goes on the assumption that all Gnostics saw the body as evil, which is clearly not the case, as Michael Allen Williams argued in his book *Rethinking Gnosticism*.

What appears to be clear is that Gnosticism inspired 'two divergent ethical programs, asceticism and libertinism,' and these were expressed in a variety of forms. Some Gnostic texts could have passed off as guidebooks for

Catholic monasteries, while others would have made even the most debaucherous of people blush. The attitudes and practices of pro-ascetic or anti-ascetic Gnostics were as diverse as the mythology they developed to explain other elements of human existence, and some of these can be seen below.

PRO-ASCETIC ATTITUDES IN GNOSTICISM

A myriad of Gnostic texts have survived that advise that ascetic practices be followed, but one of our primary sources (which is, in actuality, a secondary source) for these pro-ascetic viewpoints comes from the Roman Catholic heresiologists. For example, Irenaeus, the infamous heresiologist of the second century CE, provides material from various Gnostic and semi-Gnostic sects that dismiss the physical world and sensual pleasure. In his *Against Heresies* he states that Satorninos, a supposed Gnostic, 'says that marriage and the engendering of offspring are from Satan. And most of his followers abstain from (the flesh of) living things, and they deceive many people by this feigned abstinence.'

Satorninos' negative view of the 'engendering of offspring' is also upheld by other Gnostic sects, such as the Manichaeans. A key teaching in Gnosticism is that humanity is trapped here in the physical world, that this, the material, is not our true home, which is spiritual. The Manichaeans took this viewpoint to its inevitable extreme, viewing childbirth as the entrapment of new sparks of light in the darkness of matter. One can only conclude then that sex, the instigator of childbirth, must be avoided at all costs to ensure we do not aid the Demiurge in his demonic plans. This is the conclusion the Manichaeans came to, summarised here by Paul Mirecki:

'Adam (representing humanity) is specifically designed by the evil creator in his own image (Genesis 1:26) to procreate sexually (Genesis 1:27-28). Thus, Adam can only continue the evil cycle of birth, copulation, and rebirth, and in so doing he fulfills his natural evil inclination to 'be fruitful and multiply' (Genesis 1:28; 5:4b). Adam's evil material nature (representing human sexuality) thus entangles the precious light particles, transmitted through male seed, in potentially endless generations of material bodies.'

I can only wonder if such a radical viewpoint had been widely adopted what it would have meant for our species; indeed, perhaps a huge decrease in the population of humanity worldwide, if not its entire extinction.

A more general view of abstaining from the world is present in one passage from the *Gospel of Thomas*, which reads: 'If you do not abstain from the world you will not find the kingdom. If you do not make the sabbath a sabbath you will not behold the father.' The first sentence is quite clear, and ties in with the recurring conception in this gospel of 'the kingdom' being a spiritual, not a physical, reality, and thus there is the requirement to disengage from 'the world' in order to find that reality. The second sentence, given its placement with the first, intimates that the Sabbath, the day of rest, must be upheld, not so much as a form of orthodoxy, but to ensure that this day, symbolic of leaving the toils and troubles of the everyday life (including work) behind in order to focus on God, remains as it was intended, and thus a kind of abstinence from the world is encouraged, even if only for one day a week. This seems to touch upon a more distinctly Jewish core and may perhaps have been employed by groups who did not wish to abandon their Jewish heritage.

Epiphanius, who, like Irenaeus, wrote voluminous heresiological treatises, recorded the pro-ascetic views of a sect he calls the Archontics, who, according to Epiphanius, operated in Palestine and Armenia: 'Others, of course, feign a put-on abstinence and deceive the simpler folk, priding themselves on a kind of renunciation in the disguise of monastic hermits.' Given the polemical nature of the text, however, the truth about whether or not this group feigned anything is open to question.

The *Naasene Sermon,* a text belonging to the second-century Gnostic sect the Naasenes (preserved in the heresiologist Hippolytus' *Refutation of All Heresies*), also deals with a pro-ascetic attitude towards sex, explaining the meaning of the adage 'Do not cast what is holy to the dogs, or pearls to swine' as: 'The work of swine and dogs is the intercourse of woman with man.'

The Exegesis on the Soul, a Valentinian text, includes a defamatory note on the body and anything the body might indulge in, when it states 'the affairs of the earth, by which the soul has become defiled here, receiving bread from them, as well as wine, oil, clothing, and other external nonsense surrounding the body — the things she thinks she needs.' While this verse does not go so far as to give actual practical advice on asceticism, it does provide some of the theory behind why some Gnostics would embrace such an approach. It also intimates that bread, wine, oil, and clothing are not needed, and thus a practice of abstaining from such could be deduced. The 'she' who does not need these things is the soul, however, so it could be argued that, while this is true in regards to the soul, the body still needs them.

The Gospel of Philip, another Valentinian text, dismisses the physical act of marriage and sexual intercourse as 'the marriage of defilement', in stark contrast to the spiritual union which is 'the undefiled marriage'. This is 'not fleshly but pure. It belongs not to desire but to the will. It belongs not to the darkness or the night but to the day and the light.' This approach seems to follow the general Valentinian attitude that the physical acts are merely mirrors of the spiritual

Number 6 refuses to give up the self knowledge that is the core of his identity as well as the source of his capacity to resist

ones and thus have less value, although this text seems to go the extreme of suggesting that it is a distraction from and defilement of the true spiritual sacrament of marriage.

The Gnostic text *Authoritative Teaching* (the identity of this authority remaining unknown) speaks out against the drinking of wine, which it describes as 'the debaucher'. Again there are no specific practical injunctions against the use of such as an ascetic practice, but the praxis can clearly be deduced from the theological teaching.

A rather bizarre, and somewhat amusing, Gnostic passage dealing with asceticism in general (and fasting in particular) is a fragment of writing from Valentinus, which deals with Jesus' digestive system: 'He was continent, enduring all things. Jesus digested divinity: he ate and drank in a special way, without excreting his solids. He had such a great capacity for continence that the nourishment within him was not corrupted, for he did not experience corruption.' While this may perhaps have been true for Jesus, it certainly was not a standard a Gnostic could live up to. It does, however, intimate that the partaking of the Eucharist may offer the Gnostic a chance to echo Jesus in his digestion of divinity (via *theophagy* or 'god-eating').

ANTI-ASCETIC ATTITUDES IN GNOSTICISM

In stark contrast to the above pro-ascetic views we have a wide number of Gnostic texts which either literally speak against asceticism or indulge in physical pleasures, which Michael Allen Williams clasifies as *libertinism*. In his book *Rethinking Gnosticism* Williams cites a number of examples of groups with were considered to employ 'sexual license', most of which were documented by the infamous Irenaeus. Some of these groups were the Simonians (follows of Simon Magus), the Basilideans (followers of Basilides), Carpocrations, and Cainites, to name but a few.

Another group which employed an anti-ascetic attitude towards sex were the Mandaeans, which Nathaniel Deutsch summarises as follows: 'The Mandaean valorization of marriage and procreation contrasts sharply with certain western gnostic sources, which portray sexual intercourse as a curse of the demiurge. In Mandaean mythology, sexual desire and pregnancy are given to humankind by the saviour figure Hibil (Abel).'

St. Epiphanius, who, like Irenaeus, wrote voluminous heresiological treatises, documented the views of a sect known as the Borborites, including their attitude towards the body and abstinence, which are rather different to those expressed in other texts: 'And they — both men and women — care for their bodies night and day, perfuming themselves, bathing, banqueting, and spending their time in bed and drunk. And they curse anyone who is abstinent, saying one ought not to be abstinent, for abstinence belongs to the ruler who made this realm; rather, one must eat in order to make one's body strong so it can yield its fruit in its season.'

Epiphanius also offers a similar remark on the Archontics, when he states: 'And some of them, as it happens, polluted their bodies by sensuality.' This, however, contradicts his other comment on the Archontics' approach to abstinence, and may either show that his sources are erroneous or that the Archontics were divided in themselves on their attitude towards the subject.

Irenaeus, in his *Against Heresies*, catalogues some interesting material from Ptolemy, a student of Valentinus, on the requirements for abstinence: 'Thus for us — whom they call 'animates,' saying that we are from the world — continence and good behaviour are necessary, so that thereby we might get to the place of the midpoint. But for them — who call themselves 'spirituals' and 'perfect' — this is not supposed to be the case. For (they say), what leads one into fullness is not behaviour but the seed, which was sent hither as an infant and grows to maturity in this place.'

This approach that it is not one's outward behaviour that raises one up or defiles one mirrors a verse from the *Gospel of Thomas*, where Jesus says: 'If you fast, you will give rise to sin for yourselves; and if you pray, you will be condemned; and if you give alms, you will do harm to your spirits. When you go into any land and walk about in the districts, if they receive you, eat what they will set before you, and heal the sick among them. For what goes into your mouth will not defile you, but that which issues from your mouth - it is that which will defile you.'

it is rude to observe a diet that results in rejecting that which is offered by one's host... heal the sick no matter what time or day.

This is a very striking verse, in that Jesus explicitly states that these practices will result in sin. While it is perhaps safe to assume that this is a bit of hyperbole on Jesus' part, the real crunch of the matter comes with his explanation. He encourages hospitality — eat what is offered, for it is rude to observe a diet that results in rejecting that which is offered by one's host. Heal the sick no matter what time or day. Do not allow good will to be restricted by these conventions of Man. What enters one's mouth (food) is not as important as what issues from it (words). Those who deal in tainted words shall be tainted by them. Thus, control what one lets leave one's mouth, not what one lets enter.

A number of other verses in the *Gospel of Thomas* support this anti-ascetic approach to fasting (as well as prayer), where it is intimated that it is related to sin, perhaps as a form of punishment. It can be argued, however, that many of the verses in this text are designed to invert orthodox practices, in much the same way Jesus is often depicted in the canonical gospels:

> They said to Jesus, 'Come, let us pray today and let us fast.' Jesus said, 'What is the sin that I have committed, or wherein have I been defeated? But when the bridegroom leaves the bridal chamber, then let them fast and pray.'

This sentiment is continued in another passage, which deals with true fasting, where the disciples ask Jesus various questions about ascetic practices, including 'Do you want us to fast?' and '[What] kind of diet shall we follow?', to which Jesus replies with: 'Do not lie, and do not do what you hate,' which intimates that their only reason for such fasting is for a portrayal of false piety, lying and doing what they hate (refraining from certain foods, etc.) because they believe that others will look upon them as being more holy. It is clear that Jesus sees these actions as feigning spiritual piety, and that he objects to this outward show of grace, which is merely a front for the selfish desires of those who practice such.

The *Gospel of Thomas* tends to focus on inverting the ascetic practices of Judaism, so much so that there are a number of other passages dealing with circumcision, the washing of the body, and the donning of clothes.

Thomas defies the Jewish tradition on the covenant of circumcision, which can be seen as an ascetic practice, related to sex, since it is the removal of part of the flesh of the male sexual organ, as part of the covenant with God in Judaism. This can be seen in the following verse:

> 'His disciples said to him, 'Is circumcision beneficial or not?' He said to them, 'If it were beneficial, their father would beget them already circumcised from their mother. Rather, the true circumcision in spirit has become completely profitable.'

This view is echoed in many Christian and Gnostic texts, such as the letters of St. Paul, where he says the 'real circumcision is a matter of the heart — it is spiritual and not literal'. This motif is repeated in various Gnostics texts, such as the *Gospel of Thomas* quoted above and Ptolemy's *Epistle to Flora*, where he says: 'And he [the saviour] wishes us to perform circumcision, but not circumcision of the bodily foreskin, rather of the spiritual heart.' The emphasis is again on the spiritual element, not the physical, where the latter is but a metaphor for the former. In this sense the Gnostic can justify not engaging in ascetic practices by intimating that this would be focusing too much on the physical (even if the form of that focus is on the *removal* of physical elements from the life [or body] of the Gnostic).

Another verse in the *Gospel of Thomas* dismisses the simple act of washing the body, as intimated by the analogy of cleaning a cup:

> Jesus said, 'Why do you wash the outside of the cup? Do you not realize that he who made the inside is the same one who made the outside?'

It could be argued that this is designed to make people respect the spiritual cleanliness inside each of us, as opposed to the false beauty of the physical body, which, if we fell for the latter, might make us ignore the spiritual value of a beggar or some other person or group we might, in our prejudice, judge as 'unclean'.

Finally there is the *Gospel of Thomas'* approach to the wearing of clothes. On this Jesus says: 'Do not be concerned from morning until evening and from evening until morning about what you will wear.' This is perhaps wise advise for a modern world obsessed with the image that each individual projects, but it's also an approach that would do a lot of big brand names out of business.

Middle-Ground Attitudes on Asceticism

While the majority of sources for ascetic viewpoints in Gnosticism opt for either extreme of favouring or denouncing continence, there are a few that focus on the middle-ground, primarily the teachings of Ptolemy, who did not rule against asceticism, but rather taught that it was for those who were not yet able to perform the true ascetic practices of the spirit.

In his *Epistle to Flora*, Ptolemy wrote about the justification for fasting: 'Nevertheless, fasting as to the visible realm is observed by our adherents, since fasting, if practiced with reason, can contribute something to the soul, so long as it does not take place in imitation of other people or by habit or because fasting has been prescribed for a particular day. Likewise it is observed in memory of true fasting, so that those who are not yet able to observe true fasting might have a remembrance of it from fasting according to the visible realm. Likewise, the apostle Paul makes it clear that Passover and the Feast of Unleavened Bread were images, for he says that 'Christ, our paschal lamb, has been sacrificed' and, he says, be without leaven, having no share in leaven — now, by 'leaven' he means evil — but rather 'be fresh dough.''

However, he qualifies the above sentiments, or, rather, clarifies them, with an earlier statement: 'And he [the saviour] wishes us [...] to fast, though he does not wish us to perform physical fasts, rather spiritual ones, which consist of abstinence from all bad deeds.' This is obviously the 'true fasting' that is referenced above, and thus physical fasting is done in memory of the spiritual one. This suits the Gnostic emphasis on the spiritual over the physical, while also reinforcing the somewhat accepting nature of Valentinian theology, which would see the regular 'Outer' Church as being those 'not yet able to observe true fasting', yet capable of performing physical fasting in memory of such. The ideal kind of fasting would, in a sense, by a standard of moral uprightness (something that

is emphasised in varying degrees throughout the Christian world), although what qualifies as 'bad deeds' is admittedly open to question.

It is clear that abstinence was a huge element of theological debate in the various Gnostic circles and texts, with no two groups agreeing fully on how to treat the issue, if treat it at all. While there are a number of extreme views presented here, from total denigration of the body as evil to the fullest indulgence of the flesh, I prefer to take a more balanced view. Abstinence is not essential for spiritual growth, but it has its place, as Ptolemy says in his *Epistle to Flora*, 'if practiced with reason', and can, only with such good reason, 'contribute something to the soul'.

BIBLIOGRAPHY

Bentley Layton (Editor), *The Gnostic Scriptures* (Doubleday, First Paperback Edition, 1995).

James M. Robinson (Editor), *The Nag Hammadi Library* (Harper, 3rd Edition, 1990).

Willis Barnstone & Marvin Mayer (Editors), *The Gnostic Bible* (Shambhala Publications, 2003).

Michael Allen Williams, *Rethinking Gnosticism* (Princeton University Press, 1999).

Miguel Conner

An Interview with Tessa Dick

Tessa Dick is the fifth and last wife of Philip K. Dick, living with him during the 2/3/74 'VALIS' experiences. Her recent writings include a memoir of PKD, Remembering Firebright, **and a novel,** The Owl in the Daylight.

MC: How are you doing today, Tessa?

TD: Fine, thank you.

MC: Could you tell us about the process of making The Owl in Daylight a reality?

TD: I started working on it basically when Phil was still alive. He wanted me to write a biography or memoir about his experiences in March of 1974. And I have written a memoir called Philip K Dick: Remembering Firebright, but I felt that it didn't do justice to the totality of

his experience, so I wrote The Owl in Daylight as a fictional biography of Phil and it pretty much followed his life with his ideas grafted on to it.

MC: So basically, Tessa, you based the character Art on Philip, right?

TD: Yes, and on his great love for music. Phil, ever since he was a child loved music, and some people date it from his job at a record store, but really his mother had a Magnavox radio back when a radio was a big piece of furniture, and when he moved to his first place outside of his mother's house she gave it to him. He used to listen to the old radio shows and to all sorts of music which in the forties would have been jazz, and in classical, there really wasn't any rock n roll at the time.

MC: And you based some of the novel on his notes, didn't you?

TD: I don't have any of his notes. I just remember what he told me. The estate got all of his notes, as far as I know, but we did have a lot of conversations over a period of ten years.

MC: And also, for the reader, you helped him with two of his novels didn't you? Didn't you help him with A Scanner Darkly and Valis, as well as Exegesis.

TD: I did not work with the Exegesis. But I did help with A Scanner Darkly and all of the Valis novels. However, he wrote only four of the Valis novels and there should have been six. One would be The Owl in the Daylight and the other one would have been Firebright. He had two trilogies going and contrary to popular conception, he did not sit down and dash them out. He actually began Valis in 1972 before his experiences. Originally it was about what happened to him in San Raffael, with strange people hanging around his house, and then his house was 'hit', in his words, it was raided and ransacked. And then of course he had a real strange experience in Vancouver, British Columbia, in which he thought he had been drugged and hypnotised and subjected to mind control.

MC: By whom? Alien entities, or…?

TD: I don't know. We didn't have the term then, but I would call them 'men in black.' They were men in black suits who drove him through the streets of the city in the back of a limousine.

MC: Sounds very much like the archons in *The Owl in the Daylight*.

TD: Somewhat.

MC: And, Tessa, what exactly does the very poignant title mean? What does an owl in daylight represent?

TD: Well, it's an old southern expression when someone doesn't understand the situation, you say that he's as blind as an owl in daylight. Hr just doesn't get it.

MC: So basically we're talking about, in the novel, characters with amnesia, characters without Gnosis, who are just going through all these different realities.

TD: Oh, yeah. People who don't know that this world is not real or that they're being controlled by dark forces, and they don't even recognise the saviour when they see him

MC And can you tell us a little bit about the plot without giving too much away?

TD: Oh, sure. We have Arthur Grimley — Arthur

because he's an artist, and Grimley because he's in a grim situation. He composes music for third-rate horror movies, and one day he gets mugged ad ends up in the hospital in a coma, and then when he's in that coma, he re-experiences in a dream state his own youth as a teenager growing up in Berkeley California. And then, strange and mysterious forces cause strange and mysterious things to happen. Arthur discovers that the whole universe is made out of music, which is related to string theory, something I've been fascinated with.

MC: Also Pythagoras.

TD: Oh yes, Pythagoras said that the universe is made of numbers, and he meant music, because each note of music is a specific frequency with a specific number, so of course it's the music of the spheres. But that's only a superficial look at what he meant. Apparently Pythagoras saw a harmonic universe, that is a universe in harmony, where everything works the way it ought to work. But in Phil's view of the universe, there's disharmony, evil is not necessarily evil but rather defective, it's hitting a sour note. In *The Owl in Daylight* you don't quite get that far. I take the teenage character through Dante's Inferno and then the Purgatorio, but I haven't got to the Paradiso, the paradise. I'm saving that for a sequel, and that'll be The Owl in Twilight, which… ordinarily twilight would suggest that you can't see clearly, but the owl can see better in twilight, so it's going to be interesting.

MC: So we have the Gnostic themes of a defective

universe that needs help. What other Gnostic themes do we find in *The Owl in Daylight*?

TD: There's the seed of knowledge that gets planted in people's minds, literally in their brains, and then there's the evil archons going around trying to find these seeds and destroy them, because knowledge is dangerous, at least to the powers that be.

MC: Also you bring in Sophia, that is one of the characters, or one of the entities

TD: Well, she gets introduced in *The Owl in Daylight*. She's quite a character, she finds Arthur Grimley attractive but she disapproves of his wanton ways, he's a bit of a womaniser. That shows the difference between knowledge and wisdom. Arthur has been granted knowledge, but Sophia, well her name means 'wisdom' and she has wisdom, which is greater than mere knowledge.

MC: And I guess that also one of the main themes is to play around, just like Philip would — I thought it was a very good novel, myself, I must mention,

TD: Well thank you

MC: is, which world is the real world, because the characters seem to go through many different worlds and many different realities. Phil was definitely fascinated by it, are you fascinated by the same theme?

TD: Yes, definitely. In the novel I leave it up to the reader to decide, but in my mind neither world is real because it's a novel. It's a very postmodern concept — the text is everything — and I'm trying to shatter that and say the text is not real.

MC: And what other esoteric ideas and themes did you play with in this book? You mentioned Faustus, which a lot of people have said is Gnostic already.

TD: There are many versions of the Faust legend. In Christopher Marlowe's Faust, Faust gets his just deserts at the end and the demons tear him to shreds and drag his soul down to hell. But Goethe could not accept that so he found a way out, a sort of loophole, and he had God point out that Faust was tricked into singing the

contract and it was really all a wager between God and the devil, so Faust ended up getting salvation after all. It's only mentioned in the owl, but he's an important figure because he began as a priest, a Christian priest, and got lured into the promise of power and love and magic, kind of like Paris in the Iliad in Greek myth. In the *Iliad*, Paris has already made his choice. He was offered his choice of three gifts, great wealth, great power or great love and he chose great love, he got Helen and that led to the destruction of Troy, and everyone Paris loved, and even Paris himself. He didn't understand that great love has great power to destroy. And interestingly, Faust, one of his wishes was to have Hleen of Troy, and that's where the loophole came in because the devil couldn't give him Helen, he gave him a demon who looked like Helen, so that's why the devil lost the wager and didn't get Faustus' soul. (Say that six times fast!)

MC: It seems one of the themes, one of the underlying themes I see in your novel is people always wanting what they don't have. Every character suddenly finds themselves disillusioned by their significant other, but then they change their mind, but then they go back. Why did you play with this theme and how does it relate to Philip?

TD: One of Phil's favourite sayings was, be careful what you want because you might get it. And you might notice that there's one character in both worlds who doesn't want anything and he's the derelict on the street who holds up the sign that says, 'Wake up'. He's homeless, ugly, dirty, and yet he has more wisdom than anyone else.

MC: So he represents the enlightened one that in a sense has no desires, has dropped his desire for everything?

TD: Yes, on the one hand he's a Buddha figure, a bodhisattva, on the other hand he's also a John the Baptist, a voice crying in the wilderness — nobody listens to him. He's more content with his lot in life than the others, who have money and cars, and so forth.

MC: And any other themes that you played with

in the book that were important?

TD: I'm trying to remember. Oh yes, the idea that this knowledge that Arthur Grimley is given… the great gift of knowledge that Arthur Grimley receives is given to him by alien slugs. At first they are conducting a scientific experiment, but they have a short attention span, so they decide to just make a movie and go home and get rich by selling the movie. Very frivolous creatures, and yet they've imparted this great gift of virtual knowledge to the human race.

MC: And that is the knowledge of music, isn't it? The secret, the string theory, the Pythagorean philosophy?

TD: Well they started with the intention of teaching mathematics to Arthur Grimley, but just by himself he could not understand math. He had a mental block against it, so they gave up and taught him music instead. Which is very fitting since studies have found that musicians and students of music are much better at math than those who don't study music. Pythagoras was on to something much more than triangles.

MC: You were married to Phil between 1973 and 1977, through the time he had his infamous visionary experience on 2/3/74. What was it like living with him during this period?

TD: Phil was Phil was Phil, and his habits didn't change much. Also his *Exegesis* was voluminous but his experiences were scant. He spent more time trying to figure out the experience than he did actually having it. The strangest thing was when Phil began to say that there were entities in our apartment, people but not humans, lurking in the corners and trying to camouflage themselves to remain unseen, and that they were terribly shocked when they realised that he could see them. I couldn't see them, but he did describe them, and he said they were small and thin, with long fingers and

their heads were shaped like that famous bust of Nefertiti, Akhenaton's queen, with this sloping forehead and very large cranium, but that they had just slits for a mouth, very tiny noses and large almond-shaped eyes. It's eery when I hear people describe grey aliens, but these were not grey aliens, and they eventually told him that they were time trvllers from our future and their experiments with genetic engineering had pretty much destroyed their DNA. They couldn't reproduce and they kept trying to change the past in order to improve their future, but everything they tried went terribly wrong and it just got worse and worse.

MC: What other experiences did Philip have while you two were married? Paranormal, extraordinary, supernatural revelations…?

TD: Most of them happened while he was napping or meditating. He did that a lot and he would often break promises, miss appointments or send houseguests away, and people thought that he was being mean, that it was psychological and he would say that he had the flu, but actually quite recently I discovered that he had a birth defect in his gall bladder that caused periodic attacks of pancreatitis. The first one nearly killed him, and that was several years before I met him, from the symptoms, which I won't describe because they're yucky. I know that's what it was because our son has it too. He naps quite frequently and 24/7. He would sleep for two or three hours, maybe get up, potter around in the kitchen and then sit at the typewriter and after a while he would go back and nap some more. That was how he wrote.

MC: Was he being influenced by Valis? Did he ever mention that or he just didn't know?

TD: He kept changing the name of the entity. Basically there was the pink light, and people have glommed on to his descriptions in novels

his Exegesis was voluminous but his experiences were scant... he spent more time trying to figure out the experience than he did actually having it.

as if they were literally true. They're close, but not quite… novels are fiction after all. But he had a bumper sticker that we put on our living room window. It was of a fish sign and we knew perfectly well what it was when this lady from the pharmacy came to the door and she had a little gold fish sign on her necklace. And I'm convinced that Phil was really trying to look down her blouse, and he used the fish sign as an excuse. But in any case, after she left and he turned to go down the hall, either to the bathroom to swallow his medication or the bed to nap some more, as he turned the setting sun hit that bumper sticker on our window and it had quite a bit of silver in the image, silver or chrome, so that it reflected the setting sun into his eyes and briefly blinded him and then when he looked away he saw pink light because that's the phosphene activity, the after image, and when you've been blinded by a bright light you'll see this glowing image for a while afterward. And since the sticker was a fish sign, he saw a pink fish sign in front of his eyes and he went and lay down and had the first of the really undeniably mystical experiences, although some other things had led up to that. Sometimes he called the pink light Firebright, and sometimes he called it Valis, though Valis usually referred to this satellite in earth orbit that he thought was communicating with him, whereas Firebright was the pink light,

and they've become melded and confused over the years.

MC: And that's when he believed himself to be the apostle Thomas and realise that we were still living in Roman times? Or was that just an idea he toyed with?

TD: During this period of time, at first he thought someone named Thomas was communicating with him from the first century AD, and then as it progressed, he came to believe that this was one of his past lives, and then he came to the conclusion that he had had multiple lives that seemed to be in different timelines but they were happening simultaneously because time is not what we think it is. We think that we are trapped on a line when we look back on the past and forward to the future, and only this moment is real, but Phil saw it more like a stack of dominoes that can be rearranged. You can set them out in a line and life one up and put in a different domino. I'd like to think of it more as a game of cards. It's too bad that Phil was not a card player, he could have explained it more simply, that when you sit down to play a game of bridge, you know what all 52 cards are, so in that sense you're like God, you're omniscient, you know everything, but when you shuffle them and deal them out, you're allowing free will and random chance to take over. You have this

shuffling which randomises the deck, and then the individual decisions of the players to guide how the game is played and how it ends. People in the first century playing bridge might be the same people playing bridge in the twenty-first century and not realising it.

MC: And were you sceptical about all his visions and everything else? What was your attitude during that time, Tessa?

TD: At the time I believed that they were literally real and true, but I did get tired of hearing about it. I had a little baby to take care of and a house to clean and straiughten up and cats to serve — cats are slavemaster you know. They own our houses and just let us live with them if we behave. So it got to the point that I could not do the dishes without Phil deciding that he would talk ot me so, as he would not leave his favourite chair I had to shut off the water and go sit in the living room and listren. And you know when people came to visit, they never said, gee, Phil's a lousy housekeeper. I was getting aggravated and I finally started telling him that I was sick and tired of hearing about his visions. Because by 1975 they had nearly stopped and he was simply rehashing the same ones over and over. That was part of his writing process, he would talk things out, for hours and days and weeks before he ever sat down to write, and it was driving me crazy. That doesn't mean that I didn't believe in his visions, I just got tired of it.

At the time I believed that [his visions] were literally real and true, but I did get tired of hearing about it... I had a little baby to take care of and a house to clean...

MC: Surely there was some vindication with him predicting your son's hernia, right?

TD: Well, that happened early on and it was not the way he said, but …

MC: Oh, really?

TD: Yeah, he pulled that out of the air without knowing anything. I knew something was wrong because I was the diaper changer. Phil would watch his son all day long, but the diaper wouldn't get changed till I got home. And I had asked the doctor about it and gotten a non-answer, but Phil knew nothing about it because it had only been a couple of days and I hadn't talked to him about it. One day he just got up from a nap, walked into the living room where I was and said, 'Chris has an internal hernia, call the doctor.' And that's all he said. The rest of it was his misinterpretation of the diagnosis that we got from a specialist. For example, nothing popped the hydrus heel. A hydrus heel is a water-filled or a liquid-filled cyst that doesn't belong in there. They removed two of those, and the point was that because our baby was too young for the surgery, we had to stop him from screaming for two or three months before the surgery could correct his hernia. They said that if he screamed, and we let it go, the hernia could strangulate and kill him. Before that we hadn't let him scream much, partly because we had neighbours in the apartment building, we shared a common wall them, and partly because we just had a feeling that this baby should not be allowed to cry even though common sense would tell you if you let the kid cry, he'll give up and go to sleep. There was something urgent in his crying that just made us suspect that we shouldn't let him cry or scream and he screamed loud. Usually at 2am.

MC: Oh, of course! Of course!

TD: Sometimes at 3am, yeah!

MC: Did you take notes or help him out with his *Exegesis* at the time?

TD: Well, I did not take notes. He wouldn't let me even keep a journal because he had this idea that I might be a mind-controlled spy reporting on him, or some other mind-controlled spy might steal my journal. It sounds a little paranoid but considering his experience in San Rafael before I met him, it wasn't that far out. So, no, I never took notes, I just had to remember until 1982, shortly before his death when he asked me to write about him I started writing everything I could remember and talking to him and finally taking notes.

MC: Yes, Tessa, his experiences, visions and writings were certainly Gnostic in nature, we can agree on that, far before the translation in English of the Nag Hammadi Library in 1977. Had Phil studied any Gnosticism at all, or do you see him as truly having Gnosis, that timeless wisdom?

TD: Probably a little bit of both. He did read translations and commentaries on the *Dead Sea Scrolls*, and he had a close personal relationship with Bishop Pike, the Episcopal Bishop of California who was tried for heresy, and Pike won but resigned from the church because of the doctrinal differences between Pike and the church authorities. He's the one who went to the Middle East to try and prove that Jesus did not die on the cross, and was not the son of God, and died in the desert and never came back. He also wrote a book called — I can't remember the title — he wrote one called *If This Be Heresy*, about his heresy trial, and another one about his attempts to contact his dead son through mediums, I'm blank on the title [*The Other Side*] but in the foreword he acknowledges the help of Phil and Nancy Dick because they attended one of the séances, where Pike attempted to contact his son who had committed suicide, and Phil said that the medium did contact something but he didn't think it was him and he thought it was evil

MC: But you would say that Philip did have some knowledge of the ancient Gnostics, maybe as much as Carl Jung might have had, basically.

TD: Well, as much as he could get from the library at the University of Berkeley and other libraries. He was an avid reader. Plus I think Pike was in some ways a Gnostic and Phil really studied, but he also just had some knowledge that I don't know where he got it. I find it in the Nag Hammadi texts that are available now, but remember, we didn't have Internet and most libraries didn't have the Nag Hammadi texts anyway during his lifetime, he just knew things.

MC: And Tessa, what are your views on Gnosticism? Has it influenced your spirituality?

TD: Oh, definitely. I find Gnosticism very attractive, also hazardous because as I said before, knowledge is not the same thing as wisdom. However, knowledge is gift of the spirit, as is wisdom, and there's a few others, but those are my two favourites, and I do want to know things. On the other hand, I've come to believe in the divinity of Christ, of Jesus, at least as an idea, if not exactly as it's portrayed in the scriptures, and I don't want to lose that. I keep this Bible around. Sometimes I actually read it! I pulled out one of Phil's favourite parts of the New Testament, which is 1 Corinthians chapters 12 and 13, about gifts of the spirit and about… here we go… this is where he got the title of *A Scanner Darkly*, from chapter 13 verse 12, we see as through a glass darkly, a glass being a mirror. I don't want to see

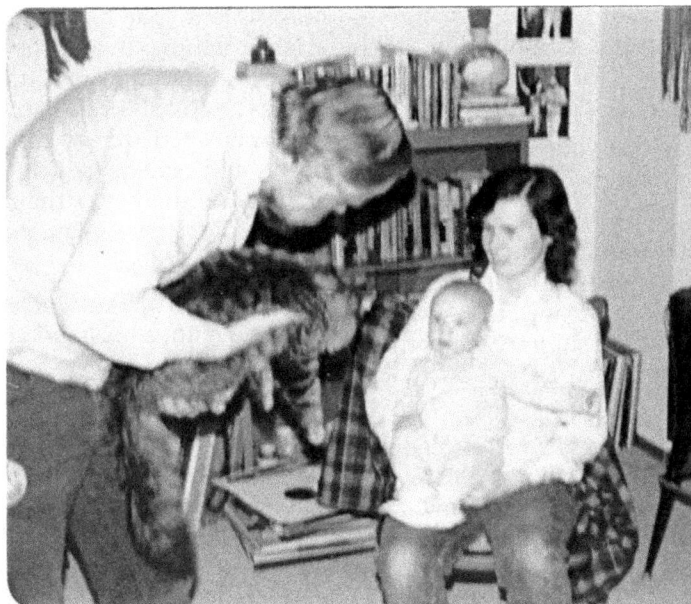

darkly and I don't want to die till I see clearly, so that's the attraction of Gnosticism for me. And I write about it, to further my own attempts to understand, what is reality, and according to Phil reality is love or charity, *agape* in New Testament terms, unselfish love, for this fallen world, for the creatures in it, and for ourselves and God. By the way, I'm not a churchgoer, I'm what you call a Baptist backslider. I got baptized and quit going. I just can't find a church

MC: Why is that?

TD: They're all about the organization, the hierarchy. I don't know … I'm reminded every time I go that I'm a heretic.

MC: So you would say that your way of finding Gnosis is through the expression of your art.

TD: Yeah. As much as I value the community of an organization like the church, I just can't fit in. So I joined the Lionists, it's part of Lions International, a service organization, that's where I find community. We support each other while helping those who aren't as well off as we are.

MC: And one question I guess a lot of readers have is was Phil just heavy on drugs during all this time, or while you were with him, or have those rumours been blown out of proportion?

TD: I think they are highly exaggerated. Although one of his step-daughters has said that he had all kinds of bottles of pills, around 1960, I suspect that most of them were vitamin supplements and the rest were prescription medications. Phil had trouble with high blood pressure and a heart problem all his life, and he often got prescriptions from his psychiatrist because the medication for his blood pressure made him depressed. From the time he wrote *The Man in the High Castle*, legend has it that he wrote six novels in six weeks, and he did, but not the way you think. He had a prescription for amphetamines from the psychiatrist, but that was not nearly enough to swallow handfuls every few hours. The main thing was Phil had these rough drafts that he could rework and some short stories that he could expand, so that after winning the Hugo award for *The Man in*

the High Castle, he could sell things that hadn't sold before and make plenty of money because of the Hugo award. So he did. And he didn't just sit down with blank paper and start punching, he used things he had already written

MC: And what do you think his reaction would be today now that he's being considered not just as a hack sci-fi writer but as somebody to be taken seriously in the literary world?

TD: I think Phil would like to be considered mainstream, but he was always proud of his science fiction. It was the cutting edge in the 1970s, I think the late sixties into the seventies, it was the cutting edge literature at the time, and the established literary circles just hadn't caught on yet, but readers had., and science fiction was actually selling better than other forms excerpt perhaps for the romance novel, which always sells like hot cakes.

MC: And lastly, Tessa, how would you describe him as a man, a husband and a friend?

TD: Aw, he was wonderful, and I miss him and there's nobody like him. Even when we were fighting, well, arguing, and throwing things across the room, he was just so special and so wonderful that I wouln't want to be with anybody else. I'm glad I met him.

MC: And we're certainly glad for his legacy and everything he's left behind for generations to come. I think that's all the time we have today. I'd like to thank you very much, Tessa, for coming on *Aeon Byte*.

TD: Thank you for having me.

MC: And good luck with *The Owl in the Daylight* and the upcoming sequel.

TD: Thank you. I hope that readers really enjoy them and learn something from them.

Anthony Peake

Remembering Firebright:
An Excerpt

Meanwhile, Phil decided that he needed some means of detoxifying his system, and he thought that vitamin supplements would work. One of his most startling visions happened after he began taking mega doses of vitamin supplements. First he read about Dr. Linus Pauling's claim that huge doses of vitamin C could prevent cancer, and then he began reading other literature about the benefits of large doses of water-soluble vitamins. When Becky came to the door selling Shaklee products, Phil was already looking for a source of high-quality vitamins, so he started buying them from her. I took the vitamins, too, but in much smaller doses. Phil thought that those vitamins opened up a door in his mind that never should have been shut. For several days, Phil had been catching movement in the corner of his eye, and he said that it was some kind of presence that was hiding while it observed us. He called it Zebra because it camouflaged itself in order to blend in with the background, as a zebra's stripes blend in with the tall grasses on the African plain. Sometimes when people came to visit us, he thought that he saw Zebra hiding among them. Zebra had a third eye in the middle of his forehead, but he kept it closed. Other entities were hunting Zebra, and if they found him, they would kill him. Those enemies wouldn't recognize him unless they spotted his third eye.

In later visions, he would learn that Zebra was an inferior deity that believed itself to be the Creator God. Like the Serpent in Gnostic tradition, Zebra believed that it was our benefactor, but it really deceived us and blinded us to our real situation. But Phil was enlightened by another entity, the one that we called Firebright.

On March 22, 1974, the day after the spring equinox, Phil was lying in bed. He was nearly asleep when he had his first encounter with a sphere of blue light, about the size of a baseball, which danced around the room and then plunged down and went inside his head. Firebright was not so much a sentient entity as a conduit, a communication channel between Phil and a number of teachers who began instructing him about the mysteries of the universe. Some took the names of historical saints and philosophers, while others didn't tell us their names. One of those nameless entities was what Phil called 'the A.I. voice' — A.I. stood for Artificial Intelligence. Eventually, he called it VALIS, which stood for Vast Active Living Intelligence System. The first novel that he wrote about this entity was titled *Valisystem A*, to indicate that it was only the first of a series of novels. That novel was published in 1985 under the title *The Transmigration of Timothy Archer*. The story centers around a character who was modeled on the late Bishop James Pike, whom Phil had known personally. He put his children into the novel, fantasizing that they would work together to reveal the Truth to mankind. The second novel, which was also published posthumously, was *Radio Free Albemuth*, the story of an artificially intelligent computer that tries to rescue humanity from the veil of illusion which blinds us to reality. His protagonist, Nick Brady, is based on the young Philip K. Dick in his job as a record store clerk Brady tries to reveal the truth to the world after a beam of pink light opens his eyes to the real situation. His friend Phil Dick is trying to help him, but Brady needs a woman's help. He joins with Sadassa Sylvia, and together they put coded messages into popular songs, telling people that Berkeley, California, is actually a prison in ancient Rome and not a modern city in the 1970s. In several of Phil's final novels, the secret underground cult of early Christians strives to free people from that prison. The third novel in the *Transmigration* trilogy would have been *Firebright*, but we never wrote it. *Firebright* would have taken the world of illusion, like the hallucinatory worlds of his early novel *Eye in the Sky*, to their logical conclusion that each individual experiences a different world because we are all living in our own private hallucinations.

Phil wrote *VALIS* later, but it was the first to be published. This novel found a home because it was less unconventional and did not require readers to accept esoteric ideas. Instead, it follows Phil's doppelganger, Horselover Fats, in a search for the Savior. Phil split off a part of himself as HF, while putting himself into the novel. Phil Dick knows that HF is insane, but he likes the guy. This self-criticism questions the validity of his visions. At the end, a message is sent out in the form of two words, 'King Felix' — that message actually comes from *Flow My Tears, the Policeman Said.*. The next novel in the series, *The Divine Invasion*, discusses the birth of a savior — but not the 'the Savior'. God tries to come down to the Earth in human form by implanting himself in the womb of a woman astronaut, but she is killed. God manages to be born, but He suffers from brain damage and does not remember who He really is. He can achieve healing only by joining with Sophia, a girl who represents Holy Wisdom. However, in

Divine Invasion her name is Diana, the goddess of the Hunt, who is associated with the Moon. In *Radio Free Albemuth* her name is Sadassa Sylvia. In *UBIK* she is Glen Runciter's wife Ella, and in several earlier novels she is a young woman named Rachel.

As in many of his earlier stories, Phil was attempting to bring his twin sister Jane back to life and back into his own life, by making her the soul mate of a male character. Rather than an unconscious drive, this was Phil's deliberate effort to rejoin with his twin, at least in a metaphorical sense. This was the point of his nonfiction book *The Dark-Haired Girl*, which he compiled from letters to his friends and family. After many abortive attempts to bond with 'girls' (women) who had dark hair, he concluded that I was the dark-haired girl he had been seeking. His mother had told him that his twin sister Jane Charlotte had dark hair. Interestingly, Mom always said that she had planned to name me Jane, but her plans were changed by family politics after I was born.

In *VALIS* Horselover Fats' wife Beth leaves him, taking their son with him. Ironically, Phil wrote that novel while I was still with him, sitting in the same room and participating in the writing. I felt insulted, especially after the novel was published, but after all, it was fiction. Phil never wrote the third novel of the *VALIS* trilogy, so I recently wrote and published *The Owl in Daylight*, in which a subversive movement inspired by an alien implant is just beginning to reveal the reality behind the veil of illusion. I hope that my novel rings true for Phil's readers.

These novels were meant to form one huge volume made up of the six stories, an epic for the modern world of growing technology and increasing intrusion of governments and multinational corporations into our lives. They represented the fulfillment of the Gnostic vision that he had described in *The Three Stigmata of Palmer Eldritch* after he had seen a huge iron mask on the horizon, backlit by the setting sun, every day for a two weeks. Phil knew that the mask, which resembled one of the Teutonic war helmets in Eisenstein's film *Alexander Nevsky*, was a hallucination, but he couldn't get that image out of his head until he wrote the novel.

After his encounter with Firebright, Phil had conversations with Francis Bacon, St. Augustine, Thomas Aquinas and other figures from history. He also had a conversation with what he understood to be a satellite in Earth orbit. At first he envisioned it as a satellite launched from the Earth, but then he decided that it was an alien artifact left here to facilitate communication after they left our solar system thousands of years ago. Rather than orbiting the Earth, it was actually orbiting the Moon, so communications were blocked when it went behind the Moon. Firebright made it possible for the satellite to communicate directly with Phil's brain, and thousands of Firebrights were dancing around high in the Earth's atmosphere, drawing their energy from the electrical activity in the ionosphere, waiting to be sent down to bond with other humans. They were plasmates waiting to join with humans to form homoplasmates. When Firebright entered into Phil's brain, they became a symbiotic organism. Phil was able to talk to the A.I. voice because Firebright could talk to it.

This A.I. voice sounded mechanical, like the recording of a lady who told us the time over the telephone. Phil asked the voice who she was, and she said, 'Sadassa Ulna.' Phil thought that the name sounded Russian, but I thought that it sounded like Latin and Greek. I had studied Latin and Attic Greek in high school, but I was far from fluent in either language. Even so, I could recognize some of the words that Phil repeated for me. Ulna is the medical term, in Latin, for one of the bones in your arm—its common name is the 'elbow bone'. I couldn't find the word 'Sadassa' in any language — perhaps he had misheard the Greek word 'thalassa', which means sea, but that didn't make much sense, unless the voice was an arm of the sea. More recently, I have found that 'sadassa' is a form of the Finnish word 'sata', which means satisfied or full. I can't make any sense out of that, either.

When he asked the voice where she was, she didn't know. She asked him to wait while she looked around, and then she said that she had found an envelope with an address written on it sitting on top of a pile of papers. She read aloud, 'F. Walloon, Portuguese States of America.' These is no such place in our world, so Phil concluded that the voice was in an alternate world where the history of European colonization of the Americas had played out differently and Portugal had kept some American colonies into modern times. We did have Walloons in our history; they were a group of refugees who had come to America from Belgium and Luxembourg to escape religious persecution. Phil knew about the Walloons from his hobby of tamp collecting. He had a Walloon commemorative postage stamp with a picture of a sailing ship and the years 1624 and 1924 printed on it.

Another phrase that Phil remembered the voice using was 'poros krater', which is ancient Greek for 'limestone cup' — it might have been referring to the cup used in communion in ancient times. The feminine-sounding A.I. voice spoke English, but often her phrases made little sense. For example, she once said, 'You have to put your slippers on, to walk toward the dawn.' That short rhyme seemed important to Phil. He connected it with the ancient Roman legend of Asclepius, the physician who was said to have leapt into a volcano at the end of his life.

Asclepius really did exist, and he healed the sick in his clinic in Sicily by analyzing their dreams and prescribing herbal remedies. He also used music as therapy. Roman legend said that he was the son of the god Apollo and a human woman. One day the physician walked toward the east (dawn) and never was seen again. His disciples found his sandals, which were made of gold, lying on the ground at the summit of Mount Aetna and assumed that he had leaped into the volcano.

...

Phil had a sophisticated knowledge of the occult, which I did not. He had made a study of the dark arts in his research on Nazi psychology, and he had studied Gnosticism s a result of his conversations with Bishop Pike. We both began reading everything mystical that we could get our hands on and watching what was then a new television program, 'In Search of'. There was no such thing as cable or satellite then, no Discovery Channel or other outlet for programs about mysterious places and events, so we had scant access to that kind of material. We did buy some books by Carlos Castaneda (describing his travels with a Native American shaman called Don Juan) and Erich von Däniken's book *Chariots of the Gods*. Phil also reread his books about religion and philosophy, and he bought the Encyclopedia Britannica to help with our research.

Phil held two beliefs at the same time. First, human agents had brainwashed him. Second, demons had attacked him. They were not mutually exclusive. He reasoned that it all went back to his house in San Rafael and a man who called himself Harold ('Hal') Kinchen. Phil was certain that this was not the man's real name. Hal claimed to be a government agent, and he told Phil that he intended to use his writing as a vehicle for coded messages, some of which would be propaganda and some of which would be communication with other agents. The demons, or the agents, might have followed him from San Rafael to Canada, abducted him and subjected him to both interrogation and mind control. We didn't worry about whether demons were real, but only about whether we could stop the psychic attacks. Even if they arose from our own minds, from our unconscious fears and imagination, they could be banished by magical means. Our approach was strictly pragmatic — if it worked, we would use it.

We prayed, meditated, burned candles and incense, and studied everything we could find that might relate to our situation. Phil made contact with the local Episcopal church and got some counseling from Father Rasche, but he did not attend church. I got baptized at the local Southern Baptist church, and I did attend several times, but then I stopped going there. It didn't seem right for me to go to church alone while Phil stayed home with our baby. One morning, when Phil was feeling especially agitated and frightening, he baptized our baby, using a cup of chocolate Ovaltine and a hot dog bun. When he later asked Father Rasche about it, the priest said that the Episcopal church would recognize that baptism as valid because Phil felt that it was an emergency, that his son's soul was in danger.

In addition to the occult, we studied the UFO phenomenon. Phil felt certain that they were ours, that the American military was using flying saucers. Phil had been told by someone he trusted that they had seen a flying saucer land somewhere in Argentina, and it had military-style insignia on it. After it landed, a ladder came down from an open hatch and men in black suits climbed down to the ground. They began speaking to each other in English. So Phil and his anonymous source thought that they were either U.S. military or CIA. Another theory that he entertained came from Charles Tart, who thought that at least some flying saucers were organic creatures that lived in our atmosphere. Their bodies were of such low density that they swam through the air as jellyfish do in the water, rather than flying as birds and airplanes do. A third theory that appealed to both of us was that some UFOs were actually traveling through time, not space. Or they could be cases of mistaken identity or hallucinations. We never saw a flying saucer, ourselves. We might have heard one, however.

One evening we heard a very loud car outside in the alley behind our apartment. It sounded like a high-performance engine, such as you would have in a souped-up Pontiac Firebird. At first I thought that our neighbors had left their Trans Am running, but when I looked outside, there was nothing there. I couldn't tell where the sound was coming from, but it definitely was not an automobile. As soon as I realized that, the sound stopped.

…

Another time we saw a dead sparrow lying on the ground, and Phil quoted scripture, saying that God sees even the sparrow fall. I noted that it didn't do the sparrow much good. A block away from home, we passed by a day care center where young children were playing outside in a yard surrounded by a chain link fence. This was our usual route to the market, which we had taken many times, but today it looked different to Phil. Instead of a chain link fence, he saw iron bars set into stone walls. I saw happy children laughing, but he saw miserable children crying. He saw Christian prisoners in an ancient Roman prison, waiting to be fed to the lions in the Coliseum. Early Christians expected Christ to return within their lifetimes, but that never happened. Phil reasoned that no real time had passed, and we were still in ancient Rome, but it was overlaid with the illusion of southern California in the 1970s. We were really living in the first century, not the twentieth.

The landscape and architecture of Fullerton encouraged visions of the ancient Roman Empire. Our streets were bordered by palm trees, pines and cedars. Many of the buildings had Roman arches and Spanish tile roofs. But there was something more to what Phil saw while we were walking down the alley behind our apartment. He saw passersby dressed in Roman garb, some of them civilian and others military. He also saw iron bars on the windows of the apartment buildings. I saw regular people dressed in the usual clothing of the 1970s, and I did not see any iron bars on the windows, not even security bars to prevent burglaries. Phil theorized that we were actually living in ancient Rome, and that the iron bars were prison bars. The world of 1974 was an illusion, and no real time had passed in almost two thousand years. The modern world was simply overlaid, resting on top of ancient Rome. The Empire never ended. He was informed of this fact, not only by his visions, but also by time travelers who instructed him. He said that they were hiding in the corners of our living room. Sometimes I thought that I saw one of them out of the corner of my eye, but I never saw them clearly. Phil said that they were very timid and expressed shock when they realized that he could see them.

Those time travelers were human, but not normal. Phil described them as short, thin and frail. Their heads were shaped like the famous bust of Nefretiti, Akhenaton's queen in ancient Egypt. They had small faces with large eyes, small noses and mere slits for mouths. Their foreheads sloped back, and the backs of their heads were larger than normal. They did not speak, but they projected their thoughts to him without moving their lips. They told him that they had tampered with genetics and ended up

with a number of birth defects, as well as some psychic powers. One of their goals was to free humanity from the 'Black Iron Prison' because our present affected their future. Another goal was to use our relatively normal DNA to correct their genetic defects. They claimed that they had already made changes in our recent past.

First they had tried to prevent the assassinations of the Kennedy brothers, but those efforts had resulted in disaster. When they tried to save John F. Kennedy (JFK), other assassins arose and killed him anyway, and the nation plummeted into civil war. When they tried to save Robert ('Bobby') Kennedy, he was elected President and led the nation into nuclear war with the Soviet Union. That disaster focused on Argentina, where Fidel Castro's friend and colleague Che Guevara had been murdered by operatives of the CIA. The time travelers told Phil that they really had hoped that John and Robert Kennedy would return the United States to the path leading to its original goals of liberty and justice, but they simply could not make it happen. Now they hoped to break open the gates of the Black Iron Prison by informing people about the truth.

as Phil delved more deeply into Gnosticism, he came to believe that religious truth would set us free... that this world was made by a defective god, an evil god

As Phil delved more deeply into Gnosticism, he came to believe that religious truth would set us free. The mystical knowledge that he was gaining through experience, as well as reading, informed him that this world was made by a defective god, an evil god, and that the perfect God, the good God, was trying to rescue us. We must participate in our own liberation from this prison by learning the sacred mysteries.

Anthony Peake

PKD PRECOG

Presentation given by Anthony Peake to the Third PKDDay at Nottingham Trent University Saturday 13th May 2009

On May 9th 1974 Philip K Dick sent a letter to his then pen-pal, Alaskan Claudia Krenz. In this short letter Phil makes a very cryptic comment stating, 'your dream about me is very disturbing'. However, what is of great interest to me is the hand-written post script that says

'What scares me most, Claudia, is that I can often recall the future'

What did PKD mean by this curiously worded comment? Usually somebody would say 'I can foresee the future,' but Phil specifically uses the term 'recall the future' as if he considers that the future is, for him, a memory — something he has already experienced.

In my first book I suggest a scenario in which many of us are existing in a psychological state very similar to that suggested by Phil in his novel *Ubik*. We are in a state of 'half-life' lingering between life and death and experiencing our life in the kind of dream-illusion suggested in Phil's earlier 1965 short story 'We Can Remember It For You Wholesale.' If my hypothesis is correct then some human beings may, under certain neuro-psychological circumstances may become aware of this.

In my second book *The Daemon — A Guide To Your Extraordinary Secret Self* I propose that there is a considerable amount of evidence that Phil was one of these sensitives. I further contend that throughout his life he both experienced all the elements of my hypothesis and also incorporated these elements into many of his novels and short stories.

Indeed in my second book I also suggest that Phil's experiences, specifically (but not exclusively) the events of 2-3-74 suggest that Phil also manifested another central pillar of my hypothesis …. Something I call 'The Daemon-Eidolon Dyad,' a suggestion that all human beings consist of not one, but two centres of consciousness.

In this short paper I intend to present selected evidence for my belief.

I would like to start with evidence for PKD's ability to perceive events that were to take place in his own future. In 1978 Phil wrote an article entitled 'How To Build A Universe That Doesn't Fall Apart Two Days Later.' In this he describes a very peculiar set of events. He wrote:

It is an eerie experience to write something into a novel, believing it is pure fiction, and to learn later on — perhaps years later — that it is true. I would like to give you an example. It is something that I do not understand. Perhaps you can come up with a theory. I can't.
In 1970 I wrote a novel called *Flow My Tears, the Policeman Said*. One of the characters is a nineteen-year-old girl named Kathy. Her husband's name is Jack. Kathy appears to work for the criminal underground, but later, as we read deeper

into the novel, we discover that actually she is working for the police. She has a relationship going on with a police inspector. The character is pure fiction. Or at least I thought it was.

Anyhow, on Christmas Day of 1970, I met a girl named Kathy — this was after I had finished the novel, you understand. She was nineteen years old. Her boyfriend was named Jack. I soon learned that Kathy was a drug dealer. I spent months trying to get her to give up dealing drugs; I kept warning her again and again that she would get caught. Then, one evening as we were entering a restaurant together, Kathy stopped short and said, 'I can't go in.' Seated in the restaurant was a police inspector whom I knew. 'I have to tell you the truth,' Kathy said. 'I have a relationship with him.'

Certainly, these are odd coincidences. Perhaps I have precognition. But the mystery becomes even more perplexing; the next stage totally baffles me. It has for four years.

Two months ago I was walking up to the mailbox late at night to mail off a letter, and also to enjoy the sight of Saint Joseph's Church, which sits opposite my apartment building. I noticed a man loitering suspiciously by a parked car. It looked as if he was attempting to steal the car, or maybe something from it; as I returned from the mailbox, the man hid behind a tree. On impulse I walked up to him and asked, 'Is anything the matter?'

'I'm out of gas,' the man said. 'And I have no money.'

Incredibly, because I have never done this before, I got out my wallet, took all the money from it, and handed the money to him. He then shook hands with me and asked where I lived, so that he could later pay the money back. I returned to my apartment, and then I realized that the money would do him no good, since

Phil describes how another section of the novel involved a character called Felix Buckman meets an African-American stranger at an all-night gas station. As Phil describes he was later to discover that this whole section, together with the character's names, had been 'lifted' by his subconscious mind from the Acts of the Apostles 'Book of Acts'. One can reasonably say that maybe, as an individual interested in religion, Phil may have subliminally recalled this section and placed it in his book. However there was more. As Phil describes it:

there was no gas station within walking distance. So I returned, in my car. The man had a metal gas can in the trunk of his car, and, together, we drove in my car to an all-night gas station. Soon we were standing there, two strangers, as the pump jockey filled the metal gas can. Suddenly I realized that this was the scene in my novel — the novel written eight years before. The all-night gas station was exactly as I had envisioned it in my inner eye when I wrote the scene — the glaring white light, the pump jockey — and now I saw something which I had not seen before. The stranger who I was helping was black. We drove back to his stalled car with the gas, shook hands, and then I returned to my apartment building. I never saw him again. He could not pay me back because I had not told him which of the many apartments was mine or what my name was. I was terribly shaken up by this experience. I had literally lived out a scene completely as it had appeared in my novel. Which is to say, I had lived out a sort of replica of the scene in Acts where Philip encounters the black man on the road.

What could explain all this?

A very good question but one that Phil probably already knew the answer. This event was one of many precognitive events that Phil had experienced during his life. On a few occasions he found himself reliving the events in his novel after he had written it. An example of this was in the story 'The Man Whose Teeth Were All Exactly Alike.'

In this novel the central character forces himself on his wife in the hope that she will become pregnant and will have to give up her job. Although he does succeed in the first part of his plan — she does become pregnant — she decides that she will have the baby aborted and against all the objections of her husband goes

ahead with the act. In the autumn of that year Phil's new wife Anne also became pregnant. In a weird re-run of Teeth Phil found himself living a real-life equivalent of his novel. And, as predicted by his muse, Anne did, against violent opposition from Phil, go ahead with a termination.

This ability to see the future was a theme that Phil was to visit on a regular basis throughout his career. Indeed in a many of his books he used the term precog to describe individuals — possibly suffering from a form of autism — who had short-term precognitive abilities. Evidently an element of his own psyche also had this ability. He first used the term in his 1954 short story 'A World Of Talent' but it was to reach its twin apotheosis in the short story 'Minority Report' and the novel Ubik.

Indeed during his 'Divine Invasions' of March 1974 Phil had become fascinated by what he termed his 'Big Dreams'. He had picked this term up from his readings of the works of Swiss psychoanalyst Carl Gustav Jung. One particularly curious dream-precognition took place over a series of nights. Phil dreamed that a book was presented to him night after night. This dream book had a blue jacket and contained over seven hundred pages. He sensed that the publication date was between 1966 and 1968 and that the title ended with the word 'Grove' with another word similar to 'Budding' also in the title.

This book became a massive preoccupation and he spent many waking hours scouring the bookshops for it, and one day he found it. It had, as predicted in his dream, a blue cover. It had the required number of pages and it was entitled The Shadow of the Blooming Grove. This was clear evidence of Daemon-inspired precognition. What is very curious is that the book proved to be of no significance. It was a biography of the American President Warren G. Harding.

This is a classic example of the precognitive dreams discussed in the 1930s by the Anglo-Irish engineer J.W. Dunne.

Phil was so fascinated by the Harding biography incident that he became convinced that his own 'Higher Self' was trying to send him a message by putting him on what seemed, at first glance, a spurious quest. He then made the link. He thought back to his 1969 book *Ubik*. In this there is a character called Glen Runciter. Runciter exists in a curious near-death state termed 'half-life'. Whilst in this state he communicates with his employees by leaving cryptic messages in odd places. For example he would leave messages such as 'you are all dead and I am alive' scrawled, graffiti-like, across a bathroom wall. He swiftly came to the conclusion that the Daemon was just like Runciter. It existed in another version of time and space that was between life and death and from this position it was sending him messages. Not only that but the message within the message was that his own book, *Ubik*, contained the answers. And, if the theory I propose in my first book is right, it does.

Indeed there is evidence that one at least one occasion an older Phil was able to appear to his younger self as if time itself was an illusion.

An incident that took place in 1951 was to convince Phil that both duality and the illusory nature of time and reality were central clues to a deeper, more profound universe. Dick was to discuss this many years later in an interview with Richard Lupoff many years later and published in 1984. Phil explained:

'Back at the time I was starting to write science fiction, I was asleep one night and I woke up and there was a figure standing at the edge of the bed, looking down at me. I grunted in amazement and all of a sudden my wife woke up and started screaming because she could see it too. She started screaming, but I recognized it and I started reassuring her, saying that it was me that was there and not to be afraid. Within the last two years — let's say that was in 1951 — I've dreamed almost every night that I was back in that house, and I have a strong feeling that back then in 1951 or '52 that I saw my future self, who had somehow, in some way we don't understand — I wouldn't call it occult — passed backward during one of my dreams now of that house, going back there and seeing myself again. So there really are some strange things...'

So who, or what, was this 'Higher Self', this being that was within him and communicated to him in dreams, a being that could slip in and out of linear time? A being that subtly placed 'future memory' events into Phil's writing, such as the example of the encounter at the gas station where Phil found himself reliving the mental picture that he described in his novel *Flow My Tears*? Could it be that Phil's *Ubik* plot may have suggested a deeper truth? That there is another part of us that has future knowledge because it

exists in the final moments of our life and, with the knowledge contained from living our life, back-communicate in time to its own, lower self and in doing so predict the future from, as Phil stated in his letter to Gloria, by 'Recalling the future'?

Phil was certainly convinced that his mind had split into two elements after the events of 2-3-74 and wrote about this bifurcation in great detail in his novel *VALIS*.

I would now like to turn our attention to the significance of these events, and I will present evidence that Phil had been 'back communicating' with his own younger self.

Phil had long been fascinated by the idea that human beings have two centres of consciousness. His long interest in the schismatic religion known as Gnosticism had provided him with many ideas for plot-lines. Gnostics also believed that this world is an illusion, a 'Black Iron Prison' as Phil was later to call it. We exist within this illusion forever unaware that behind its façade can be found a real universe, a place known to the Gnostics as the Pleroma.

Bearing this in mind many, many of Phil's stories and novels can suddenly be placed within a philosophy and a theology. *Eye In The Sky, The World That Smith Built, The Man In The High Castle*, etc., etc. all present a universe that is overlain over another, more real one.

However there was another central tenant of this fascinating theology that was to become of particular importance to Phil, the idea that all human beings consist of not one, but to loci of consciousness.

Many times in his later writing Phil was to reference a particular Gnostic text called 'The Hymn of the Pearl'. This tells of a prince who is sent into Egypt to recover a lost pearl. However whilst in this land he falls under the spell of Egyptian magic and forgets who he really is, where he has come from and what his destiny is to be. Fortunately his double, or true self, has stayed at home and this being can send messages to his forgetful twin in the land of the Nile. Eventually these messages are perceived by the lower self and the prince awakens from the illusion and returns to his true home. As he arrives his twin meets him and they meld into one. When the young man first receives a message regarding his true self he describes the feeling that it;

> … seemed to me to become like a mirror of myself. I saw it all in all, and I to received all in it, for we were two in distinction and yet gain one in one likeness. And the treasurers too, who brought it to me, I saw in like manner to be two (and yet) one likeness …

In March 1974 Phil was convinced that he had been awoken to the existence of his own long-lost twin. Phil was to write later in his work Exegesis that what had taken place was that the two hemispheres of his brain had become one. He termed this event his amanuensis, literally his reawakening to his own psychic duality. On this first encounter with this other element of himself he was to call this being the Vast Active Living and Intelligent System. He was soon to use the acronym VALIS.

He was later to describe this:

> 'I suddenly experienced what I later learned is called anamnesis — a Greek word meaning, literally, 'loss of forgetfulness.' I remembered who I was and where I was. In an instant, in the twinkling of an eye, it all came back to me.'

As time progressed he was to give his 'twin' many names but the one that he was finally to settle upon was Plasmate. For him the newly unified being was to be known as a Homeoplasmate.

However I suggest that this being had been with Phil for most, if not all, of his life. It was only the trauma of his March 1974 theophany that opened up his lower mind to this entity. If one looks through Phil's biography one can find many examples of how this being had assisted him. For example, like many of his schoolmates, Phil was expected to attend the University of California in his hometown of Berkley. But in order to do so he needed to reach the entrance grades required. However this possibility started to fade rapidly when, during a crucial physics test, Phil couldn't remember the key principle behind the displacement of water. As eight of the ten questions were to involve this principle he was clearly in trouble. And then it happened — an entity decided, for the first time, to manifest itself in Phil's life — and Phil's life changed forever. A voice clearly and precisely explained to the surprised young man the scientific principles he so desperately needed to understand. All Phil had to do was write down the words in his head. Phil received an 'A' grade. I have found many other examples of how the Plasmate assisted the young Phil.

But as we have seen it was in March 1974 that this being was able to invade the day-to-day consciousness of its lower self. Phil was later to describe this takeover in the following, graphic, terms:

March 16, 1974: It appeared — in vivid fire, with shining colours and balanced patterns — and released me from every thrall, inner and outer.

March 18, 1974: It, from inside me, looked out and saw the world did not compute, that I — and it — had been lied to. It denied the reality, and power, and authenticity, of the world, saying, 'This cannot exist, this cannot exist.'

March 20, 1974: It seized me entirely, lifting me from the limitations of the space-time matrix: it mastered me as, at the same instant, I knew that the world around me was cardboard, a fake. Through its power I saw suddenly the universe as it was; through its power of perception I saw what really existed, and through its power

of no-thought decision. I acted to free myself. It took on in battle, as a champion of all human spirits in thrall, every evil, every Iron Imprisoned Thing.

He said that he had experienced 'an invasion of my mind of a transcendentally rational mind, as if I had been insane all my life and had suddenly become sane'. He explained that:

mental anguish was simply removed from me as if by divine fiat … some transcendental divine power which was not evil, but benign intervened to restore my mind and heal my body and give me a sense of the beauty, the joy, the sanity of the world.

He went on to describe this being's skills:

This mind, whose identity was totally obscure to me, was equipped with tremendous technical knowledge — engineering, medical, cosmological, philosophical knowledge. It had memories dating back over two thousand years, it spoke Greek, Hebrew, Sanskrit. There wasn't anything it didn't know.

However his Plasmate also showed some very prosaic traits. It decided that Phil had become far too slovenly in his personal appearance. It made him go out and buy a pair of nasal hair-clippers and it suggested that he trimmed his beard. It even had him go out and buy new, trendier, clothes. It was as if this more sartorial twin had been too long trapped in the body of a particularly slovenly Phil and now was its chance to put things right. But it was also concerned about the health of the shared body. It had Phil go through his drugs cabinet and forced him to throw out those medications that were proving problematical to his health. It discovered that wine was too acidic for Phil's sensitive stomach and suggested that he change to drinking beer. This being had many skills that its twin sadly lacked such as business acumen. It realised that Phil had made quite a mess of his tax matters and within weeks the Daemon had sorted this out. It also had Phil sack his agent after it had read over the royalty statements and discovered massive irregularities. Of course all these were minor interventions to its apogee, the saving of Phil's son's life. This is how I describe it in my second book:

The bearded and slightly portly middle-aged man sat back feeling the late summer Californian sun play over his face. He needed this relaxation. The pain in his shoulder still ached away quietly and the worries of the last few months continued to push their way into his consciousness. However today felt good. He was doing what he enjoyed most, quietly listening to music. This afternoon his choice was The Beatles but with his wide-ranging tastes it could have easily been Robert Schumann or Gustav Mahler. The first few bars of Strawberry Fields Forever drifted through the motes dancing in the sunlight. As the lyrics chimed away he found himself being drawn to what they were saying. He heard 'Going through life with eyes closed'. He found this curiously apposite as he lay back with his eyelids tightly shut. He found himself opening them as if under lyrical instruction. The sunlight from the window, so pleasant a moment before, became harsh and stark, causing his head to ache. He closed his eyes quickly and suddenly became aware of a colour, strawberry ice cream pink. As this strange light suffused over him the Beatles began to sing again, but the lyrics had changed. Much to his surprise his brain distinctly heard the nasal voices of Paul McCartney and John Lennon harmonise 'your son has an undiagnosed right inguinal hernia. The hydrocele has burst, and it has descended into the scrotal sac. He requires immediate attention, or will soon die.'

Confused and, quite naturally, surprised the man was unsure what to do. However this indecision was to last only a few seconds. He found himself rushing upstairs, grabbing his four-year-old son into his arms and carrying him to the car. A few hours later he was to be informed by a doctor that had he not taken the little boy straight to hospital the child would have certainly died of an undiagnosed birth defect. Something inside of him had shown not only precognitive abilities but also knowledge of medicine far beyond his own.

Of course, the man was PKD and the child was his son Christopher.

He was keen to find supportive evidence in science for his bifurcation of consciousness. This he found in the work of the American neurosurgeon Roger Sperry. Sperry had rocked the foundations of neuroscience by discovering that when separated, the hemispheres of the brain seemed, at least to some degree, independently conscious. It was this discovery that was to give Phil the incentive to write one of his classic novels *A Scanner Darkly*.

What is fascinating about *A Scanner Darkly* is that it was completed in April 1973 but was heavily revised between that date and August 1975. As such this novel, in its initial version, was written before 2-3-74 but was revised, one assumes, taking into account how Phil become aware of his own psychic duality during his 'theophany' as he termed it.

In this novel Phil explores the themes of duality, mental illness and disassociation from reality. His central character, Bob Arctor, is a drug-user addicted to a narcotic known as Substance D. However, Arctor lives a dual existence in that he is also an undercover government agent named S.A. Fred. Fred's job is to infiltrate the murky world of the drug-users in order to capture the dealers who peddle this dangerous substance.

In this dystopia the drug cartels have infiltrated the government itself. As such all agents have to keep their identities secret even from their own associates. They do this by wearing what Dick calls 'scramble suits'. These project an ever-changing image sourced from a vast database of identikit faces and bodies. Also in order to protect their identities agents have to compile dossiers and reports on all those addicts that they are observing, including themselves. So, by the very nature of his job Fred is never quite sure if his 'real' personality is himself or his alter ego Bob Arctor. Indeed this psychic disassociation is exacerbated by the fact that agents have to continually monitor their own actions after the event by watching holographic surveillance tapes of themselves. Many commentators have commented upon the peculiar duality aspects of Arctor/Fred. I suggest that the reason that Phil turned a straight-forward story into a schizophrenic nightmare is because of his own mental state at the time, that and Phil's newly acquired knowledge regarding the mysteries of split-brain patients.

Thus far I have presented evidence from Phil's life and writings that part of him was aware of the future. This being was given many names by Phil including VALIS, Sophia, AI and Plasmate. I would like to suggest a better name, a name more in keeping with Phil's contention that the proof of the existence of this duality could be found the Gnostic texts. For that reason I suggest that we should use the terms that the Gnostics themselves used to describe this duality. They called the lower, everyday being that exists in linear time 'The Eidolon'. This is the equivalent of the character 'Phil Dick' in the novel VALIS. The higher self, the being that I suggest knows the future because it has already experienced it, the Gnostics called the 'Daemon'.

Now if my hypothesis is to hold water I need to present to you evidence that Phil's Daemon, not only manifested itself in March 1974 but also had knowledge that Phil (the Eidolon) did not. I believe that I have such evidence, evidence that as far as I am aware has only been published in my second book .... And that is that Phil's Daemon predicted the circumstances of Phil's final, fatal stroke.

Earlier I handed out copies of a letter that Phil sent to Gloria Krenz in May 1974. This is one of a series of letters that appeared two or three years ago. The May letter was fascinating but it was a letter sent almost a year later that really caught my attention.

This letter was written on February 25th 1975. I call your attention to the postscript. It reads:

I was up to 5 a.m. on this last night. I did something I never did before; I commanded the entity to show itself to me — the entity which has been guiding me internally since March. A sort of dream-like period passed, then, of hypnogogic images of underwater cities, very nice, and then a stark single horrifying scene, inert but not still; a man lay dead, on his face, in a living room between the coffee table and the couch.

Seven years later, on February 18th 1982, Phil's neighbours become concerned that they had not seen him that day. They knocked on his door then forced their way into the apartment. They found Phil lying unconscious in the living room. This was a place that Phil in 1975 would not have recognised. It is likely that he would have been found in exactly the position and location described so clearly in Phil's Daemon-evoked hypnogogic almost exactly seven years before. Phil was not dead at this time but clearly in his dream-vision Phil could not have known if the man was actually dead or unconscious. He was to die about a week later without really gaining consciousness. However according to Tessa Dick in her book Remembering Firebright Phil was conscious during that time. If this is the case then his Plasmate would have had a 'memory' of Phil's position the day he experienced the stroke.

Now please note that Phil was quite precise in his command to his Daemon — he requested that it show itself. I believe that that is exactly what the Daemon did. It showed a future Phil in the last few moments of his conscious awareness before the stroke severed his links with 'reality' as he perceived it. In doing so the Daemon implied that it was Phil himself in the final moments of his life — existing in the half-life described in Ubik and explained in my first book.

Eugene Poliakov

The Elements of Symbolism

The son of man came eating and drinking,
and thou say, behold a man gluttonous,
and a winebibber.
Gospel according to Matthew 11:19

He that tilleth his land shall have plenty
of bread.
Proverbs of Solomon 28:19

Since we seek correction and teaching, we should investigate Scripture in an attempt to discover what concepts are hidden behind its mystic images and symbols. The answer should be found before we start considering parables. Thus we should with new eyes, the eyes of babes, take a look at certain systems of images in Scripture. Although they appear familiar, it seems necessary to reacquaint ourselves with them.

The first of these systems is the symbolic system of garments. This mystic image runs through the entire Scripture. Another system of images, which is complex enough too, is the symbolism of food. It is close integrally to the symbolism of clothes. We should even say that there is a fundamental unity between the symbolism of food and the symbolism of garments. We shall provide the reader with the reasons for this statement presently.

If we interpret this symbolism according to Biblical chronology, we begin with Adam and Eve. In the beginning 'They were both *naked,* the man and his wife, and were not ashamed' (Gen 2:25). Later as they had eaten of the tree of knowledge of good and evil 'they *knew* that they [were] naked; and they sewed fig leaves together, and made themselves *aprons* [or *girdles*]' (Gen 3:7). The symbolism of the eaten fruit as knowledge becomes apparent.

'What shall we say then?' in the words of Paul. What is the secret here? As we consider the mystery of aprons or girdles, we appreciate the analogy of the New Testament: 'Let your loins be girded about' (Lk 12:35). The Apostle Peter explains: 'Gird up the loins of your mind, be *sober,* and hope to the end for the grace' (1 Pet 1:13). Peter clearly reveals this mystery—first as he speaks of the loins of mind, thus pointing out an allegory, then as he immediately clarifies the sense of this symbol: being sober, reasonable, conscious, wakeful. But wakefulness, in contrast to sleeping, or *nakedness,* or undressing of the loins, is a qualitatively higher state of consciousness. As for Adam and Eve, let us remember that somewhat later 'unto Adam also and to his wife did the LORD God make *coats* of skins, and clothed them' (Gen 3:21).

Here it is useful to note that every system of likenesses, of symbols, of imagery parallels, is useful at that point when it facilitates comprehension of heavenly mysteries with the help of familiar, earthly things. Such a system of likenesses should be reasonable from the viewpoint of common sense, reason, and the literal meaning of the words that each conceptual system consists of. Of course, there may be stories that are repugnant to both reason and common sense, passages that drop out of the system as a whole, that are exceptional, that are individual cases. But it is inappropriate to clarify Divine wisdom with metaphors like sweet vinegar, or a stone falling upwards, or the darkness destroying and overcoming the light, or a woman enjoying giving birth to her child, or a man bearing a child in his belly.

From the viewpoint of this rule, it is quite justified on the level of daily existence to take the idea of dressing oneself in garments as an image of the transition to a state of consciousness higher than nakedness. After all, when a person prepares himself for sleep he does not get dressed, but strips himself naked. Similarly, upon awakening one puts his garments on. Thus, the following parallels become clear: nakedness—sleep—absence of consciousness; and: becoming dressed—awakeningacquiring consciousness.

When Adam and his wife were innocent, they did not possess their own consciousness—or in symbolic language they had no clothes. They were naked (and were not ashamed). Then Adam eats of the tree. What fruit does Adam eat? What tree does he eat of? He eats of the tree of knowledge of *good and evil*. When he eats of this tree of knowledge of good and evil or when he acquires some knowledge of good and evil, he obtains elements of a self-made consciousness and, obviously, a very imperfect garment of leaves.

We should emphasize that knowledge *of good and evil is* quite a different notion from knowledge *in general*. The latter is what migratory birds possess, for example, even perfect, unerring knowledge, of the sort which allows them to keep to an extremely precise route during the seasons' migrations. Beavers building their dams also possess some knowledge, as well as bees that build up such a regular structure of honeycombs that a human being might at times take an example from them. Thus, knowledge in general may be unconscious. Even human knowledge, developed up to the degree of science, may be *unconscious;* it exists often regardless of good and evil.

What are we talking about? So what is consciousness? Consciousness has literally nothing in common with knowledge in general. What vital part of a human operates with the latter—what faculty deals with knowledge? It is mind, and reason, and intellect, and common sense; but consciousness is a thing different from all the above.

The notion of consciousness is essential in any philosophical or religious system. No philosophical school or religious sect could ever manage without this idea. But various schools and sects each understand consciousness in their own way. The educated reader can compare Heidegger's, Freud's, and Marx's concepts of consciousness. We should note that all branches of philosophy accept consciousness as an axiom, as a fundamental principle, as something that needs neither to be explained nor to be determined.

The consciousness we are speaking about has nothing in common with any ideas of schools that have existed before. Unlike them, we say specifically what we take as consciousness. Here it is, if you are willing to receive it:

Consciousness is the measure of knowing of good and evil.

As far as the normal, everyday sense of the word 'consciousness' is concerned (equivalent to 'mind' or 'intelligence') that is an extremely restricted individual instance of what we are talking about. Such everyday consciousness (or mind) is the measure of knowing logical right and wrong.

It is specifically about arriving at the knowledge of good and evil as the highest stage in the evolution of taste that it is said: 'Can I discern between good and evil? can thy servant [more exactly *bondman*] *taste* what I eat or what I drink?' (2 Sam 19:35). There is even more brilliant wording in Isaiah, who draws clear parallels: good—light—sweet; and: evil—darkness—bitter: 'Woe unto them that call evil good, and good evil; that put darkness for light, and light for darkness; that put bitter for sweet, and sweet for bitter!' (Is 5:20). Our reader should agree that although it is possible to speak about woe and malediction concerning those who call evil good, yet someone's considering bitter to be sweet, and sweet, bitter is his personal affair and does not lead inevitably to grief. However, this is so only in case of a literal interpretation. We read somewhat later in the same Book of Isaiah: 'Butter and honey shall he eat, that he may *know to refuse the evil, and choose the good* (Is 7:15). These words can surely bear only an allegorical sense. Otherwise they could offer a suspiciously easy way to reeducate criminals.

And so, the acquisition of consciousness as arriving at some knowledge of good and evil is associated both with putting on clothes and with eating. Obtaining the highest consciousness corresponds to taking on the characteristics of those who are perfect or who are of full age, 'who by reason of use have their senses exercised to discern both good and evil' (Heb 5:14). This is the purpose of the human in this world, in this age, which derives from the following fragment: 'We know that if our earthly house of [this] tabernacle were dissolved, we have a building of God, an house not made with hands, eternal in the heavens. For in this we groan, earnestly desiring to be clothed upon with our house which is from heaven: If so be that being clothed we shall not be found naked. For we that are in [this] tabernacle do groan, being burdened: not for that we would be unclothed, but clothed upon, that mortality might be swallowed up of life. Now he that hath wrought us for the selfsame thing [is] God, who also hath given unto us the earnest of the Spirit. Therefore [we are] always confident [more exactly *bold*], knowing that, whilst we are at home in the body, we are absent from the Lord' (2 Cor 5:1-6). We are absent from the Lord! Behold, here it is, the casting out from paradise!

Behold again what a commandment of blessedness, which is a continuation of the Sermon on the Mount, we can find in the Revelation of St. John: 'Blessed [is] he that watcheth, and keepeth his *garments,* lest he walk naked, and they see his shame' (Rev 16:15).

Once we have understood the symbolism of clothes and garments, do we not perceive the following parable in a different, new way: 'No man [or *nobody*] putteth a piece of a new (Gr. καινός) garment upon an old; if otherwise, then both the new (Gr. καινός) maketh a rent, and the piece that was [taken] out of the new (καινός) agreeth not with the old' (Lk 5:36)? Unfortunately, the English reader is almost deprived of the opportunity to contrast this parable in Luke with those in other synoptists, i.e., Matthew and Mark, for their formulae are simplified by translators. In fact, in the original text Matthew and Mark use a different word for what was translated as a new garment. The translators can be understood and forgiven, for it would be very hard to realize what it is written literally: 'No man [or *nobody*] also seweth a piece of new *unwrought* (Gr. ἄγναφος) cloth on an old garment: else the new (Gr. καινός) piece that filled it up taketh away from the old, and the rent is made worse' (Mk 2:21, cf. Mt 9:16). The reader should see the contrast between a refined, white garment and an unwrought one. Knowing the symbolism of garments, you should agree that by now the last formula has taken on a much clearer and firmer (symbolic) sense.

Let us recall the story of the expulsion of the legion of unclean spirits from a possessed man (Mk 5:1-16; Lk 8:26-33). Mark's version of these events is somewhat strange. After Jesus exiled the unclean spirits out of the man this man was found to be *clothed, and in his right [or sober] mind* (Mk 5:15). It is strange because Mark did not say a single word about nakedness before the healing. But Mark implied it as a clear thing for earlier the man was mad, not in his right mind, and therefore as if naked.

With regard to garment symbolism let us note further that consciousness may be low, even base, not measuring up to one's ambitions. We cannot help recalling the parable of a man who appeared at a feast without a wedding garment (Mt 22:1-14). You can read the whole parable yourself. Still we would like to emphasize that this parable is in conflict with common ethics. Look: the king sends his bondmen onto the highways to invite as many guests as they happen to find (cf. Mt 22:9). Was it possible then to expect that all the gathered guests, 'both bad and good' (Mt 22:10), would then have had a wedding garment? Nevertheless, all of the guests, save just a single man, obviously had one. 'When the king came in to see the guests, he saw there a man which had not on *a wedding garment:* And he saith unto him, Friend, how camest thou in hither not having *a wedding garment?* And he was speechless. Then said the king to the servants, Bind him hand and foot, and take him away, and cast [him] into outer darkness; there shall be weeping and gnashing of teeth' (Mt 22:11-13). Did the king judge impartially? Obviously not; specifically his 'partiality' tells us that this story is an allegory—one of those which Maimonides talked about (see our discussion in ch. I.3, p. 20).

What is the sense of this parable? We cannot discover it for now we do not have even the slightest inkling about the symbolism of the king or of the wedding feast; still, we can realize that acquiring a specific wedding garment is necessary for a higher purpose, to obtain consciousness of a certain degree of perfection. Our poor guest did not have one, and in this sense he was bad.

This was an example of consciousness that was obviously low, not worthy of the wedding (cf. Mt 22:8). But consciousness may be high as well: 'If thou followest righteousness, thou shalt obtain her, and put her on, as a glorious long *robe*' (Sir 27:8). When we speak about the symbolism of better garments, we cannot omit the scene of the Transfiguration of Christ: 'His *raiment* became shining, exceeding white as snow; so as no fuller on earth can white them' (Mk 9:3; Mt 17:2; Lk 9:29). After this passage the reader will probably better understand the contrast between an unwrought garment and

a refined, white one.

In this latter symbolism it is not hard to discern the highest level of consciousness that man can ever attain. But with respect to angels of light this is an ordinary thing: 'His countenance [i.e., *of the angel of the Lord*] was like lightning, and his *raiment white* as snow' (Mt 28:3). In other words the consciousness of angels is perfect. We can find white raiment mentioned in the Revelation of John: 'He that overcometh, the same shall be clothed in *white raiment*' (Rev 3:5); 'I counsel thee to buy of me . . . *white raiment,* that thou mayest be clothed, and [that] the shame of thy nakedness do not appear' (Rev 3:18).

Very rich material on the symbolism of garments is provided by the apocryphal *Gospel of Philip,* from which we shall select only two examples: 'No one will be able to go in to the king [note: *king* again] if he is naked' (*Philip* 27).

Let us note also that *Philip* introduces the highest consciousness as something incompatible with the flesh: 'Those who wear [the flesh] . . . are naked. [It is] those who [take off flesh] to unclothe themselves who are not naked' (*Philip* 23).

That is, those whose consciousness is fleshly are naked, and they cannot appear before the king; but those who take off the carnal consciousness may try on a better one. Note also that the first part of the latter saying of Philip is merely the same as what Paul hopes for: 'that being clothed we shall not be found naked' (2 Cor 5:3).

There are interesting details in the description of Jesus' examination by the chief priests, the elders and the full council. After one of Jesus' answers, 'the high priest *rent* his clothes' (Mt 26:65; Mk 14:63). Let us compare this with the commandments of the Old Testament: 'Uncover not your heads, neither rend your clothes' (Lev 10:6), 'rend your heart, and not your garments' (Joel 2:13). But how could it be possible to express in symbolic language an obscuring, a damage of consciousness in another way? Hence even here everything is in its place. Only this we recall, that consciousness is to be understood again as the degree of knowing of good and evil. The loss of consciousness as we understand it is not a state from which one is brought to one's senses by spirits of ammonia; it is the sort of state when one does not know what he is doing, when one accepts good for evil and evil for good.

As we conclude our quick tour of the symbolism of garments, we must not omit a statement by John, describing the undergarment, the body-coat (DBY) of the crucified Jesus: 'the coat was without seam, woven from the top throughout' (Jn 19:23). In other words His undergarment did not consist of parts; it was undivided, an integral whole, *one*. In subsequent chapters we will touch upon the majesty of the mystery hidden behind this word or, rather, this number.

2

Now we should shed more light on the entire symbolic system connected with food, especially since certain varieties of food are met in the Bible at every turn. The question is really not about anything other than allegory, parable. It follows undoubtedly from the words of Paul: 'Did all [i.e., *our fathers*] eat the same *spiritual* meat; And did all drink the same *spiritual* drink' (1 Cor 10:3-4).

We have quoted Isaiah's words on butter and honey. But we should note that the notion 'butter' is completely alien to the New Testament. We note also that Isaiah attributes butter to the abundance of milk (cf. Is 7:22). Let us therefore look at milk as food from the point of view of the New Testament. The attentive reader may remember these examples: 'I have fed you with milk, and not with [strong] meat' (1 Cor 3:2); 'ye have need that one teach you again which [be] the first principles of the oracles of God; and are become such as have need of milk, and not of strong meat. For every one that useth milk [is] unskilful in the word of righteousness: for he is

a babe. But strong meat belongeth to them that are of full age [or *perfect*], [even] those who by reason of use have their senses exercised to discern both good and evil' (Heb 5:12-14). Note that Paul sees a clear opposition between liquid and solid food.

This motif of Paul's is supplemented with a most interesting comment by Theophilus of Antioch, Christian apologist and theologian of the second century: 'The tree of knowledge itself was good, and its fruit was good. For it was not the tree, as some think, but the disobedience, which had death in it. For there was nothing else in the fruit than only knowledge; but knowledge is good when one uses it discreetly. But Adam, being yet an infant in age, was on this account as yet unable to receive knowledge worthily. For now, also, when a child is born it is not at once able to eat bread, but is nourished first with milk, and then, with the increment of years, it advances to solid food. Thus, too, would it have been with Adam; for not as one who grudged him, as some suppose, did God command him not to eat of [the tree of] knowledge' (2 To Autolycus 25). After these words of Paul and Theophilus, let us turn to Peter, who wrote: 'As newborn babes, desire the sincere milk of the word, that ye may grow thereby: If so be ye have tasted that the Lord [is] gracious' (1 Pet 2:2-3). As we can see, Peter also suggests—although without particular emphasis—that milk is a kind of food from which it is possible and necessary to grow in perfection.

But milk is the kind of food that is appropriate for newborn infants, who can not accept, digest, other food. Theophilus adds: 'Besides, it is unseemly that children in infancy be wise beyond their years; for as in stature one increases in an orderly progress, so also in wisdom' (ibid.). For this reason infants which are a little older are allowed to eat honey as well, according to Isaiah, which helps them perfect their skills in telling sweet from bitter—and good from evil: 'My son, eat thou honey, because [it is] good; and the honeycomb, [which is] sweet to thy taste [or *upon thy palate]*' (Prov 24:13). So what kind of knowledge of good (and evil) is hidden by this symbol?

It is an absolutely natural conclusion that honey, which is sweet to the taste and which stands side by side with milk in the pages of the Bible, is the symbol of the sweet and glorious fact 'that the Lord is gracious' (1 Pet 2:2-3), that 'every word of God [is] pure' (Prov 30:5). Honey is the basis for the doctrine that 'He created all things, that they might have their being: and the generation of the earth were healthful [more exactly, *and all things on the earth were rescuing*]; and there is no poison of destruction, nor the kingdom of death upon the earth' (Wis 1:14).

This deuterocanonical idea may seem to be *too* sweet to someone's taste, impossible to receive. On the opposite side, this kind of belief might be found to be too primitive, too easy—especially in the absence of some other sort of knowledge. That is why Scripture teaches that it is 'not good to eat much honey' (Prov 25:27). Even more: 'Hast thou found honey? eat so much as is sufficient for thee, lest thou be filled therewith, and vomit it' (Prov 25:16). A change of circumstances may be quite different: 'And I took the little book out of the angel's hand, and ate it up; and it was in my mouth *sweet* as honey: and as soon as I had eaten it, my belly was *bitter*' (Rev 10:10; cf. Ezek 3:3).

Now we are ready enough to receive the conclusion that pure food or the food allowed by the law is the image of the sort of knowledge of good and evil which is established at the basis of Divine Truth, although it can be prepared by human beings.

Such food may be knowledge, teaching, understanding, encouragement, instruction, castigation, wisdom, which have their origin in God, His Word and the Holy Ghost. These highest gifts are offered in various ways, are presented on different levels for people with varying levels of consciousness. Milk (butter) and honey turn out to be the food of those who

are untaught in the word of righteousness, the food of infants, but solid food belongs to them who are perfect. About the strong (in the sense of 'firm') meat of perfection Jesus spoke in this way: 'I have meat to eat that ye know not of' (Jn 4:32). This statement is just the allegorical equivalent, in the form of images, of another passage: 'I have yet many things to say unto you, but ye cannot bear them now' (Jn 16:12).

From the very beginning of this book we have stressed and will continue to stress that the language of the Holy Bible is of a kind that allows the listener, he who eats this supper, to understand its meaning according to the level of his consciousness. Now that we are familiar with the symbolism of food, we can take a look at this declaration from another point of view: 'for thy sustenance declared thy sweetness unto thy children, and serving to the appetite of the eater, tempered itself to every man's liking . . . even then was it altered into all fashions, and was obedient to thy grace, that nourisheth all things, according to the desire of them that had need' (Wis 16:21-25).

The symbolism of food is very widely used by Paul. Here is what he writes to the Romans: 'One believeth that he may eat all things: another, who is weak, eateth herbs. Let not him that eateth despise him that eateth not; and let not him which eateth not judge him that eateth: for God hath received him' (Rom 14:2-3). We promise to return to this passage later to inspect much more widely all the symbolism included in it. Meanwhile we can say in brief that there are also different degrees of perfection in God implied here, and this allows one and even obliges one person to eat strong meat, all things, while another should be enjoined as follows: 'As newborn babes, desire the sincere milk of the word' (1 Pet 2:2).

3

We have looked at the symbolism of knowledge through examples at the extremes of pure food: milk as the food of those who are untaught in the word of righteousness, and strong meat as the food of those who are perfect, whose senses are experienced in discerning good and evil. But that is far from the entire system of symbolism.

One of the most important symbols in both the Old and the New Testament is *bread.* Bread is mentioned in so many cases that it seems impossible even to list them in our work, not to mention giving a complete interpretation. Still, some of these cases simply must be mentioned. We speak of bread in the strict sense; in addition we shall take the word 'loaf' as the countable equivalent of bread (one loaf, two, three . . . several loaves—not 'one bread' or 'two . . . breads').

You should remember the story of feeding multitudes with five loaves the first time and with seven the second time (Mt 14:13-21; 15:32-38; Mk 6:34-44; 8:1-21; Lk 9:12-17; Jn 6:5-13). We can notice that Jesus 'taught them many things' there (Mk 6:34). As we remember the symbolism of food, we can conclude that bread which Jesus fed them who were angry is nothing other than the teaching, the doctrine of Christ.

This definition of the symbolism of bread is somewhat limited and we can make a very important revision of it. In order to do this we must refer to the scene of the temptation of Christ in the wilderness. As we remember, the Devil said: 'If thou be the Son of God, command *this stone* that it be made bread' (Lk 4:3; Mt 4:3). Understandably, the Devil could not imply any spiritual, symbolical interpretation, for otherwise we should suppose that the Devil could possess the gift of interpretation, granted by the Holy Spirit. Such a supposition would be the height of absurdity. The Devil suggested the *literal* transformation of specifically *this stone* into *physical* bread. But Jesus implies the spiritual, hidden sense in His answer, revealing at the

same time the image of bread itself: 'Man shall not live by *[literal, material]* bread alone, but by every word of God' (Lk 4:4). Therefore it is more adequate to conceive the image of bread as 'every word that proceedeth out of the mouth of God' (Mt 4:4) , especially when the word of God is received as the life-giving doctrine. In other words we can say that bread is not the doctrine of Christ alone, but the doctrine of Christ is the Divine bread.

After elucidating this symbolism we become able to appreciate the particular elegance of an almost unnoticed fine point in the story of Mark, at a moment subsequent to the episode of choosing the twelve apostles: 'They went into an house. And the multitude cometh together again, so that they could not so much as eat bread' (Mk 3:19-20). Now, what was the reason that they were not able even to eat bread? Perhaps there was not bread enough for all? But after all, there was enough for up to five thousand. Or was the house so big that it accommodated more than five thousand? Or did it become too crowded? (The metaphors that are used to refer to crowdedness are quite different from this!) However, everything takes its place once we remember the prohibition against expounding all the doctrine, including its secret part, to infants.

The literal acceptance of certain sayings in the Holy Bible is completely impossible. Therefore the destiny of those who are absolutely unreceptive to any other interpretation is quite unenviable. Take a look: 'The earth . . . cannot bear . . . a fool when he is filled with meat [more exactly, *bread*]' (Prov 30:21-22). 'Much food [is in] the tillage of the poor: but there is [who is] destroyed for want of judgment [or, *for lack of justice*]' (Prov 13:23). 'Give not to the ungodly: hold back thy bread, and give it not unto him, lest he overmaster thee thereby' (Sir 12:5).

There are certain opinions based on the literal understanding of the above quotations that judge both Judaism and Christianity as the teachings established upon 'moral rules which are outrageous for elementary ethics—delirious, cynical and brutal.'

But all the apparent delirium and brutality turns miraculously into wisdom when we know how to understand the language of symbols. We have already spoken about this in the following way: 'As a thorn goeth up into the hand of a drunkard, so [is] a parable in the mouth of fools' (Prov 26:9). Is it then allowed to give the entire doctrine of Christ to a fool or an ungodly one? No—let him feed himself with milk and honey instead, that he may grow up to proper age.

Realizing that bread is an image of every word that proceeds out of the mouth of God, we can take another example. It will be much less complex but much more edifying: 'And as they were eating, Jesus took *bread,* and blessed, and brake [it], and gave [it] to the disciples, and said, Take, eat; this is my body' (Mt 26:26; Mk 14:22). In other words he who considers himself to be a disciple of Jesus, should partake of the Most Perfect Doctrine, the Word of God.

Let us also note that Jesus broke specifically one loaf of bread, not five nor seven, as happened under other, well-known circumstances. This fact is not stressed in the Gospels, although it can be read between the lines. This is not something we have imagined, for none other then Paul emphasizes that the Eucharistic bread is 'one bread' (1 Cor 10:17). There are such words as these in one of the most important texts of the post-apostolic period, the *Teaching of the Twelve Apostles* or *Didache:* 'this broken bread was scattered upon the mountains and being gathered together became *one*' (Didache 9). As in the case of Jesus' body-coat we can see here the obvious symbolism of *the one* also. Let our reader decide for himself whether it is possible to take communion from *a single* bread in churches numbering hundreds of parishioners. In the literal sense it is certainly unimaginable; but in the spiritual meaning a single Eucharist bread can not cause the

slightest difficulty.

This example shows that the word 'bread' (in many languages but not in English) can mean not only bread *per se,* but in a wider sense also the grain from which bread is prepared. In some cases it may be a question of grain specifically (cf. Jn 12:24; 1 Cor 15:37). In other cases it may be not bread itself at all which is referred to, although literally the phrase may contain the word 'bread,' as with the 'staff of bread' in the Psalm (Ps 105:16) or in the passage about bread 'bruised with a horsemen' (Is 28:28). Nevertheless, although bread and grain are relatives, in the language of symbols they are not necessarily synonymous. If it is permissible to use such words for these images, the difference between the two rests in bread's being the most reworked derivative of grain, which, in turn, is the raw material for bread. That is, grain is the symbol for something not as perfected as doctrine. And wheat, from which bread is baked, could not be considered as representing the most refined of teachings but rather as the sort of knowledge innate to man. (The difference is merely the same as between the truth and a grain of truth. But this latter observation is such a fine point that we may leave it for consideration in a future work.)

It is most interesting to look at passages in the Apocrypha discussing bread and its role in Christ's doctrine: 'Before Christ came there was no bread in the world, just as Paradise, the place where Adam was, had many trees to nourish the animals but no wheat to sustain man. Man used to feed like the animals, but when Christ came, the perfect man, he brought bread from heaven in order that man might be nourished with the food of man' (*Philip* 15).We should appreciate this view especially as we recall that in the time of Moses the symbol of the most perfect food was heavenly manna. We should not be confused by the fact that the word of God existed even before the coming of Jesus, for as we shall show a little later the word of God is symbolized for Judaism by stone, not bread.

'There was a householder who had every conceivable thing, be it son or slave or cattle or dog or pig or corn [or] barley or chaff or grass or *[bones]* or meat and acorns. [Now he was] a sensible [one] and he knew what the food of each one was. He served the children bread . . . He served the slaves *[corn* and*]* meal. And [he threw barley] and chaff and grass to the cattle. He threw bones to the dogs, and to the pigs he threw acorns and slop. Compare the disciple of God . . . The bodily forms will not deceive him, but he will look at the condition of the soul of each one . . . *There are many animals in the world which are in human form* [!!!]. When he identifies them, to the swine he will throw acorns, to the cattle he will throw barley and chaff and grass, to the dogs he will throw bones. To the slaves he will give only the elementary *[things]* ,to the children he will give the complete *[things]'* (*Philip* 119).

We have reached conclusions that are actually quite apparent. But in order to really prove them we should cite all of chapter six of the Gospel of St. John. You can read it for yourself. However some quotations are unavoidable: 'Ye seek me, not because ye saw the miracles, but because ye did eat of the loaves, and were filled. Labour not for the meat which perisheth, but for that meat which endureth unto everlasting life, which the Son of man shall give unto you' (in 6:26-27); 'For the bread of God is he which cometh down from heaven, and giveth life unto the world . . . I am the bread of life: he that cometh to me shall never hunger; and he that believeth on me shall never thirst' (Jn 6:33-48); 'This is that bread which came down from heaven' On 6:58).

4

Bread is far from the only kind of food mentioned in the Bible, however. He who reads our book not idly but attentively and with understanding should have questions about the symbolism of other sorts of food—

among others, the symbolism of fish. For the less attentive reader we can note that both times in the stories of feeding multitudes with loaves, which we recalled in conjunction with arithmology, Jesus fed them with fishes also: 'He had taken the five loaves and the two *fishes,* he looked up to heaven, and blessed, and brake the loaves, and gave to his disciples to set before them; and the two *fishes* divided he among them all' (Mk 6:41; Mt 14:19; Lk 9:16; Jn 6:11). Note the uniqueness of this passage. This is the only one that is precisely identical in all four Gospels. It is not by chance that bread and fish stand side by side. We can show another example of this pairing: 'As soon then as they were come to land, they saw a fire of coals there, and fish laid thereon, and bread' (Jn 21:9).

In interpreting the symbolism of fish, we should remember that this image served a long time as an emblem for the early Christians. The Greek word 'ichthys' (Gr. ἰχθύς), 'fish' was read as an anagram of Jesus' name, each letter representing in succession the Greek words for: 'Jesus Christ, Son (of) God (the) Savior.' We should remark also that among God's creatures, the fish possesses like no one else the property of silence. We recommend our reader to return again later to this excellent quality of fish. In addition, fish are the most highly developed living things which do not copulate to reproduce. The last observation could be amplified in various directions, but for us, especially in our future considerations, it will be extremely important that the symbolism of *adultery is* absolutely absurd with respect to fish. Still all of these arguments may be regarded as speculations. Let us then turn to the Bible's argumentation.

We now would like to suggest that the antithesis to the fish, the very worst which can be opposed to it, is the serpent—which personifies sinfulness, evil, lie, beguiling throughout the whole Bible. As we repeat Jesus' saying: 'be ye wise as serpents, and harmless as doves' (Mt 10:16), we can notice that the dove, personifying harmlessness and purity, probably does not possess the necessary wisdom. But the serpent is an image of wisdom and subtlety but has no purity. As a confirmation of the serpent's opposition to the fish let us recall the Sermon on the Mount: 'What man is there of you, whom if his son ask . . . a fish, will he give him a serpent?' (Mt 7:9-10). All of our arguments lead to the conclusion that the fish is an image of holiness and righteousness. But we keep in mind that the holiness and righteousness may be both true and false, it may be the holiness and righteousness of the Pharisees. We shall return to this problem later.

The last quotation draws our attention also to other pairs of opposites, since in Luke the same passage looks like this: 'If a son shall ask *bread* of any of you that is a father, will he give him *a stone*? or if [he shall ask] *a fish,* will he for a fish give him *a serpent*? Or if he shall ask an egg, will he offer him a scorpion?' (Lk 11:11-12). It is clear that an egg as a symbol of the origin of new life is in opposition to the scorpion, which symbolizes suffering and suicidal death and which stands on the Bible's pages nearly always side by side with the serpent (Deut 8:15; Lk 10:19).

But then bread also has an antithesis in the form of stone. We should remark that this is not the only example of contrast of bread and stone. Let us recall the words of the tempter: 'If thou be the Son of God, command that these *stones* be made *bread*' (Mt 4:3; Lk 4:3). From all of this it is not hard to deduce that stone symbolizes the *dead law* as an opposite to the *living and life-giving doctrine.*

This symbolic association of law and stone is well based in the Old Testament itself. It was not by chance that the tables where the law was written by the finger of God happened to be made of stone, and not of gold or silver: 'And the LORD said unto Moses . . . I will give thee tables of *stone,* and *a law,* and *commandments* which I have written; that thou mayest teach them' (Exod 24:12); 'And he gave unto Moses,

when he had made an end of communing with him upon mount Sinai, two tables of testimony, tables of stone, written with the finger of God' (Exod 31:18).

Let us take a look at the words: 'Christ [is] the end of the law' (Rom 10:4), and one more time we shall satisfy ourselves of the opposition of stone and bread. We know that 'the law made nothing perfect' (Heb 7:19) as well as we know what Jesus did 'having abolished . . . the law of commandments' (Eph 2:15).

We do not advise the reader to hurry, because the English translation of the last passage is far from perfection. We should say the same even about English translations in general. We should say even that this is a brilliant example of 'misinterpretation-for-error' translation. Let us therefore read this verse adding a couple of words from the previous one: 'He is our peace . . . having abolished in his flesh the enmity, [even] the law of commandments [contained] in ordinances.' The first thing we have to do is to remove the additional words in brackets. These words are supposed to be there to clarify and to provide context, but in this case they hopelessly destroy Paul's idea. The second thing to do is to explain that the word 'ordinances,' traveling from the King James Bible to later translation, is specifically what we are speaking about. It is the doctrine— Christ's doctrine. The third thing to do is to remark that *in* (Gr. εν, *en)* in this case is the same as *through* or *by.*

What is the result? 'He is our peace . . . having abolished *by* his flesh the enmity, the law of commandments *by* the doctrine.' The last thing to do is to explain the parallelism of Jesus' works: He has abolished the enmity by his flesh, and He has abolished the law of commandments by His doctrine. Is this reading not as clear as day?

Let us write the sentence we cited a short while ago using the conclusions we have reached since. We should write: We know what Jesus did 'having abolished . . . the law of commandments by the doctrine.' Is there anybody who remains unconvinced? Then we repeat the words of Paul again: 'If any man think himself to be a prophet, or spiritual, let him acknowledge that the things that I write unto you are the commandments of the Lord. But if any man be ignorant, let him be ignorant' (1 Cor 14:37). There is the true mystery of the change of the stone into bread in abolishing the law of commandments by the doctrine.

Being now familiar with the symbolism of stone, we can correct the sense of the image of bread as well, since 'every word of God' may be received as a dead law too; while bread is 'every word of God' that makes up the teaching.

Is it absolute, the transformation of the law into the teaching, the dead stone into the living bread? Of course not. There is no miraculous change for those who judge after the flesh (cf. Jn 8:15), after the letter 'for the letter killeth' (2 Cor 3:6), because the law can not be understood literally. The law is 'foolishness' (1 Cor 2:14) for him who can receive only the literal meaning; 'neither can he know' (ibid.). The commandments of the law 'are spiritually discerned' (ibid.). On the contrary, he who is able to discern spiritually can understand the highest sense of the law. Thus he brings the law to life for himself, for 'the spirit giveth life' (2 Cor 3:6).

Before we continue our studies on Biblical symbolism we can advise our reader to reason on the hidden meaning of the image of the death penalty in the Israel of Biblical times. In some tribes hanging was used, in others beheading. The Romans were inventive and used crucifixion. But the Jews were unique. Among them it was *stoning*. As we invite the reader to consider this fact, we should note another one. From the Jewish point of view Jesus was far more guilty than in the Romans' eyes. Nevertheless He was not stoned but was crucified in the Roman way.

5

As we continue our study, remembering the role played by bread in the Eucharist, we cannot omit an analysis of the symbolism of wine. It is probably better to begin with the fact that the Old Testament considers it a punishment to deprive someone of wine: 'As your treading [is] upon the poor . . . ye have planted pleasant vineyards, but ye shall not drink wine of them' (Amos 5:11); 'For the rich men thereof are full of violence, and the inhabitants thereof have spoken lies, and their tongue [is] deceitful in their mouth . . . thou shalt . . . [make] sweet wine, but shalt not drink wine' (Mica 6:12-15). On the other hand, the promise of future deliverance is attached to an abundance of wine: 'And I will bring again the captivity of my people of Israel . . . and they shall plant vineyards, and drink the wine thereof' (Amos 9:14); 'Yea, the LORD will answer and say unto his people, Behold, I will send you corn, and wine, and oil, and ye shall be satisfied therewith' (Joel 2:19); 'And in this mountain shall the LORD of hosts make unto all people a feast of fat things, a feast of wines on the lees, of fat things full of marrow, of wines on the lees well refined' (Is 25:6); 'Thou hast put gladness in my heart, more than in the time [that] their corn and their wine increased' (Ps 4:7).

The real hymn to wine is sung by Jesus the son of Sirach: 'Wine is as good as life to a man, if it be drunk moderately: what life is then to a man that is without wine? for it was made to make men glad. Wine measurably drunk and in season bringeth gladness of the heart, and cheerfulness of the mind' (Sir 31:27).

For the sake of fairness we should note that Scripture contains some dubious promises connected with wine. The prophecy of Zechariah is one of them: 'Corn shall make the young men cheerful [more exactly *fruitful,* or *speak*], and new wine the maids' (Zech 9:17). This saying is so strange and questionable that it seems to be insignificant to remark that even adult men do not eat raw corn, but bread. As for maids who could speak or grow or become cheerful because of wine, this is compete nonsense. (It is true only in the literal meaning.) Who of our readers would dare ply girls with wine without fear of being reputed decadent? And who of our readers would dare feed corn (raw grain) to boys without fear of being considered a fool? (There is a huge difference between this 'corn' in the sense of grain in general and American corn on the cob, popcorn, and cornflakes.)

In order to realize all the depth of the symbolism of wine let us for a while leave hymns and puzzling prophecies and even the Eucharist. In our analysis of the symbolic systems of clothes and food, we could hardly have managed without their first mentions in Scripture. Similarly in the case of wine: it is the first mention that clarifies much if not all: 'Noah . . . planted a vineyard: And he drank of the wine, and was drunken; and he was *uncovered* [or *unclothed*] within his tent' (Gen 9:20-21). We consider it is important to call attention to a principal variance of circumstances according to, e.g., Darby's translation: 'Noah . . . was drunken, and he uncovered himself in his tent' (cf. YLT). I.e., an impersonal act in the King James Bible acquires a subject: Noah unclothed *himself.*

We take the image of wine as representing a sort of food, but there must be a distinction. We cannot describe wine as a teaching, though there must be some knowledge in wine. But we have said too little. There must be good, delightful, joyful knowledge in wine. (We are about to say, the Good News.) We have to remark that the description of Noah's unclothedness was not necessary to portray the harm caused by the immoderate use of this drink. Remembering clothes to be the symbol of consciousness, we can also see that wine should be attached with understanding, knowledge, wisdom, etc., that comes in an uncontrolled way, *unconsciously.* An unconscious way of acquiring knowledge has a certain name: *revelation!*

Somebody might ask, What kind of revelation did Noah receive? This is not so important. The important thing is that the unclothing of Noah is coupled with wine. Testimonies that connect nakedness with the perfect form of revelation that is prophecy can be found in the Bible: 'And he [Saul] stripped off his clothes also, and prophesied before Samuel in like manner, and lay down *naked* all that day and all that night' (1 Sam 19:24); 'Spake the LORD by Isaiah . . . Go and loose the sackcloth from off thy loins, and put off thy shoe from thy foot. And he did so, walking *naked* and barefoot' (Is 20:2).

It was not by chance when we pointed out that Noah unclothed *himself.* For, as it follows also from the above-mentioned verses, stripping off one's own clothes as a conscious act is necessary for prophesying, for receiving of revelation. But how it can be possible to reach an unconscious state while remaining awake? Sorry; we cannot speak of this now...

Justice requires us to remark immediately that the revelation hidden behind the image of wine may be different in quality and even in essence. We can see it in the synoptic parable of the new wine: 'no man [or *nobody*] putteth new wine into old bottles [much more exactly *skins*]; else the new wine will burst the bottles [or *skins*], and be spilled, and the bottles [or *skins*] shall perish. But new wine must be put into new bottles [or *skins*]; and both are preserved' (Lk 5:37-38; Mt 9:17; Mk 2:22). The sense of this passage can be reduced to the idea that it is impossible to express a new revelation in the same old images in which the old revelation was transmitted. For the new revelation cannot be held by the old letters, because the new revelation destroys them; and at the same time the new revelation itself is lost, and ceases to exist. The new revelation must be expressed in new language, with new images. The above-said can not be understood to mean that the undamaged old skins might be thrown away just for the sake of purchasing new ones. We can say in other words that skins remain skins and they are not subject to being exchanged for a barrel or a jug. In other words the new revelation is expressed and contained by images and symbols, but in the sort of images and symbols which, being connected with old ones, are revealed in a new way. That is why there are such concepts appearing in the New Testament as the resurrection, the salvation, the prodigal son, the unjust steward, and many more.

Only in Luke does the theme of wine continue in this way: 'No man [or *nobody*] also having drunk old [wine] straightway desireth new: for he saith, The old is better' (Lk 5:39). It means that new revelation requires testing, while the old is already tested and accepted. With respect to the revelations in the New and Old Testament, this idea might be related to the words of a certain saint: 'I don't trust Christ unless there are Moses and Elias beside Him.' So that if somebody from among our readers has a revelation, he should not trust it at once; let him test it first. The theme of the trial of wine is much more serious than it might seem at first glance. Somewhat later we shall give more space to this theme.

We said that revelatory knowledge is unconscious. Does this mean that its acquisition has no influence on consciousness, on the garment? It certainly has! And how! The evidence is not long in coming: 'Shiloh [i.e., *the Peacemaker*] . . . washed his garments in wine, and his clothes in the blood of grapes' (Gen 49:10-11). This passage is taken from the first book of the Old Testament, and here it is what is said in the last book of the New Testament: 'These are they which came out of great tribulation, and have washed their robes, and made them white in the blood of the Lamb' (Rev 7:14).

The mention of the blood of the Lamb returns us to the Last Supper and to the interpretation of the role played by wine in the Eucharist: 'And he took the cup [of wine], and gave thanks, and gave [it] to them, saying, Drink ye *all* of it; For this is my blood of the new testament, which is shed for many for the remission of sins' (Mt 26:27-28; Mk 14:23-24; Lk 22:20).

Let us return to the Eucharist as it is presented by John: 'Except ye eat the flesh of the Son of man, and drink his blood, ye have no life in you. Whoso eateth my flesh, and drinketh my blood, hath eternal life . . . For my flesh is meat indeed, and my blood is drink indeed. He that eateth my flesh, and drinketh my blood, dwelleth in me, and I in him . . . so he that eateth me, even he shall live by me' (Jn 6:53-57). Jesus offers his wine to *all*. (This is a stone to be cast at Catholicism, where only the priesthood receives communion with wine while laymen take it dry.) Just this wine is the revelation of the New Testament (not to be confused with the Revelation of St. John), which has the Holy Ghost as its one origin.

Is it necessary to consider the symbolism of the Eucharist any further? We understand that the flesh of Christ is the Teaching, the word of God. In order to partake of it and digest it we need a key that opens the seals of parables. In other words we need a revelation of the Holy Ghost symbolized by wine that is the blood of Christ. Unless one unseals the sense of the mysteries of Scripture he has no life in himself. Let us repeat again, bread alone is insufficient; there must be interpretation of the word of God through revelation of the Holy Ghost. Wine is sufficient for the digestion. Later we shall show that wine alone, without the bread, is not only unhelpful but even dangerous.

Now, after disclosure of the symbolism of wine and bread, it will be extremely useful to look at the following passage from *Philip*— especially in its last part: 'He who shall not eat my flesh and drink my blood has no life in him [cf.Jn 6:53].What is it? His flesh is the word [logos], and his blood is the Holy Spirit. He who has received these has *food* and *drink* and *clothing*' (*Philip* 23).

But is it just any kind of wine which is connected with the blood of the Lamb? In other words, does every kind of revelation have its origin in the Holy Spirit? It is not necessary to be Solomon to answer this question in the negative. For wine is good in *only one* case. 'Beloved, believe not every spirit' (1 Joh 4:1), because there is also the sort of wine that symbolizes a revelation of unclean spirits. With respect to this kind of wine a warning is necessary: 'be not drunk with [such] wine, wherein is excess [more exactly *profligacy*]; but be filled with the Spirit' (Eph 5:18). That is, reject revelation of unclean spirits that leads to profligacy, and be filled with the Spirit. But this remark belongs more integrally to the next chapter.

Before we continue our story let us suggest that the reader ponder over the sense hidden in the passage: 'The Son of man came eating and drinking, and they say, Behold a man gluttonous, and a winebibber' (Mt 11:19). Does it not seem that its sense has become much clearer?

6

As we have touched on food as a symbol of knowledge, we should briefly consider one more problem. The reader should understand that the question of fasting is indivisible from the symbolism of food. Let us recall what is said about fasting in the Gospels: 'The disciples of John and of the Pharisees used to fast: and they come [to Jesus] and say unto him, Why do the disciples of John and of the Pharisees fast, but thy disciples fast not? And Jesus said unto them, Can the children of the bridechamber fast, while the bridegroom is with them? as long as they have the bridegroom with them, they cannot fast. But the days will come, when the bridegroom shall be taken away from them, and then shall they fast in those days' (Mk 2:18-20; Mt 9:14-15; Lk 5:33-35). Understanding the symbolism of food, we realize that in its allegorical meaning fasting signifies the rejection of any knowledge.

And so, may they who are near the source of heavenly knowledge refrain from acquisition of this knowledge? Naturally they cannot. But if the connection to this origin becomes broken, since their bread has become once more as hard as stone and because they fear like the death the wine of revelation, then comes starvation—forced fasting. In case of the disciples of the Pharisees, their separation from the divine origin causes no doubts. (You see, there are disciples of the Pharisees even in Christianity.)

We have not touched on the disciples of John with respect to fasting; but let us beg the reader to wait a little, for this problem will be remedied soon.

7

It is now time to solve the riddle of the belly. The difficulty for the English-reader consists in the fact that the corresponding original term (Heb. *beten*; Gr. xotAia, *koilia*) is translated into English with two different words—'belly' and 'womb'; the latter is used specifically with regard to a woman. Keeping in mind that 'womb' as a symbol means the same, we shall consider the symbol of the belly as the more general notion.

Now that we are aware of the symbolism of food, it is simple to turn to the image of the belly into which the food enters. St. Paul writes: 'Meats [more exactly *food*] for the belly, and the belly for meats [or *food*)' (1 Cor 6:13). Placing this formula in the context of everything we said above, we inevitably arrive at the conclusion that the belly is the symbol of the reason, human analytical memory; for newly acquired knowledge enters in to the reason, to the memory. The undeveloped belly of infants who can digest nothing but milk and honey becomes explained at once.

We must emphasize that Apostle Paul distinguishes the belly from the body: 'Meats for the belly, and the belly for meats: but God shall destroy both it and them. Now the body [is] not for fornication, but for the Lord; and the Lord for the body' (ibid.).

Here may be a difficulty for the reader who may not wish to admit an idea of the mortality of his reason and memory. But it is written: God shall destroy the belly. What shall we say then? There is another statement concerning the belly and food: 'Do not ye yet understand, that whatsoever entereth in at the mouth goeth into the belly, and is cast out into the draught?' (Mt 15:17). In other words knowledge symbolized by food enters into the belly, and while it abides in the belly it is reflected in the memory. Later it is cast out and becomes lost from the memory. We should say again—although with the risk of being dull through repetition—that there is a great difference between memory, reason, and mind on the one hand and consciousness on the other. Reason is just clothed with consciousness, as the belly is covered with clothes.

In spite of our explanation of the mortality of the belly, we should warn the reader that a more profound discussion of this symbolism is yet to come.

8

To continue our brief research on the belly, let us cite a passage from John: 'He that believeth on me, as the scripture hath said, out of his belly shall flow rivers of living water' (Jn 7:38). The mentioning of water sends us back to bread, wine and all that enters the mouth and goes into the belly. Can we accept as an incidental dispensation or an obligatory commandment a saying like this: 'Drink no longer water, but use a little wine for thy stomach's sake and thine often infirmities' (1 Tim 5:23)? As our reader can see, wine—revelation—is necessary to heal the infirmities of digestion, that is, the problems of the human mind and understanding.

Wine in this last quoted passage stands side by side with water but still in opposition to it. Let us recall the first of Jesus' miracles in Cana of Galilee, where Jesus turned water into wine (Jn 2:1-10). While bread and wine are symbols whose meaning is clear, water is a symbol of something yet to be revealed. This task is not as easy as the preceding ones, and all the capabilities of our belly would be called for help to solve this problem. We must eat this food certainly with the use of a little wine.

The object that is hidden behind the image of water should be necessary for the mind—belly—but it can not deprive one of consciousness as wine does—still it can turn to revelation, as displayed by the miracle in Cana of Galilee. This whatever-it-is purifies consciousness and is the natural medium for holiness and righteousness, whose symbol is fish, as we have seen. After all, 'fish stinketh, because no water, and dieth for thirst' (Is 50:2). This statement seems to be naive but, as we shall see soon, extremely accurate in the allegorical sense. This substance can become so solid that it is possible to walk on it, but faith is needed for this; otherwise there is a danger of drowning.

All the depth of this symbolism is contained in Matthew's story: 'In the fourth watch of the night Jesus went unto them, walking on the sea . . . Peter . . . said, Lord, if it be thou, bid me come unto thee on the water. And he said, Come. And when Peter was come down out of the ship, he walked on the water, to go to Jesus. But when he saw the wind boisterous, he was afraid; and beginning to sink, he cried, saying, Lord, save me. And immediately Jesus stretched forth [his] hand, and caught him, and said unto him, O thou of little faith, wherefore didst thou doubt?' (Mt 14:25-31).

We can say in addition that rivers of living water can flow from the belly (cf. the passage just cited). In other words, the mind may in turn become a source of this object. Finally we can say about this thing that it may imply nothing sacred as, e.g., doctrine or revelation do, because water is a *manifest* element of nature.

The passage from the (deuterocanonical) Book of the Wisdom of Solomon leads us almost directly to the solution of this problem: 'The *hope* of the unthankful shall melt away as the winter's hoar frost, and shall run away as unprofitable *water*' (Wis 16:29). If someone wished to find a similar idea specifically in the canonical Scripture, we could offer the book of Job for this one: 'Can the rush grow up without mire? can the flag grow without *water*? Whilst it [is] yet in his greenness, [and] not cut down, it withereth [without it] before any [other] herb. So [are] the paths of all that forget God; and the hypocrite's *hope* shall perish' (Job 8:11-13).

Consideration of all we have said leads to the conclusion that it is specifically *hope* that has all the desired properties. The particular passages we have cited connect water to hope in a negative way: human existence is impossible without hope made conscious through the mind. But water is connected with hope positively, too: 'Every man that hath this hope in him [in Christ] purifieth himself, even as he [Christ] is pure' (1 Joh 3:3). We can remark that hope not only does not deprive one of consciousness but also is able to purify it.

As a pure environment, hope is necessary for the existence of holiness; and righteousness can be kept only in hope. Hope can turn to revelation (not by your own efforts but by Christ). Hope accompanied by faith can become as firm as the ground, but in the absence of faith hope can appear to be a place to drown in. To illustrate the last statement let us suggest that our reader imagine, What can one who has no faith hope for? Let us remark in addition that hope may be faithless as well as faith may be hopeless. Remember: 'the devils also believe, and tremble' (Jam 2:19), but they can not hope in the same way as do the sons of light.

We may note that water corresponds to hope not only in Biblical symbolism but in everyday experience. In this sense, the world itself is a source of allegories. A human can not exist without water, but if he be fed with water alone he dies as well. In other words hope may be fruitless. It is the sense of the flood, is not it? An edifying allegory for today's world: 'this generation!'

According to the Old Testament the important symbolism implied in water flowing from a rock (stone): 'And the LORD said unto Moses . . . thou shalt smite the rock, and there shall come water out of it' (Exod 17:5-6). 'Behold, he smote the rock, that the waters gushed out, and the streams overflowed' (Ps 78:20; cf. Num 20:1-13; Ps 114:8; Is 48:21). In a symbolic sense there is no miracle which shocks the imagination in this metamorphosis. For the promises of the Almighty written in the law can be the source of hope. The law, properly employed, is the origin of overflowing streams.

We shall be doomed to misunderstanding if we fail to pay more attention to the passage on the belly as the source of water, or the mind as the possible origin of hope. The next verse seems to be an explanation of this image: 'He that believeth on me, as the scripture hath said, out of his belly shall flow rivers of living water. But this spake he of the Spirit, which they that believe on him should receive: for the Holy Ghost was not yet [given]' On 7:38-39). How is Jesus' statement connected to the symbolism we have discussed?

The mention of the Holy Spirit in connection with the living water should not confuse us, for the Holy Spirit abides overall—in bread, in wine, in water, and in many subsequent images. Jesus' statement is to be understood to imply the belly of one who already has the Holy Ghost, while the water implies the hope of another to whom the Holy Ghost has not yet been given. This meaning corresponds to the Apostle Paul's commandment to Timothy: 'Give attendance to reading, to exhortation, to doctrine. Neglect not the gift [of the Holy Ghost] that is in thee . . . Meditate upon these things; give thyself wholly to them; that thy profiting may appear to all. Take heed unto thyself, and unto the doctrine; continue in them: for in doing this thou shalt both save thyself, and them that hear thee' (1 Tim 4:13-16).

Andrew Phillip Smith

Schrodinger's Gun

The title of the performance piece was inaccurate he told her.

' "Schrödinger's Gun." The experiment really has nothing to do with Schrödinger, you know. Not directly. It's still not too late to change the title. 'Many Worlds' might be a better name.'

Jerry was carrying out a last minute check of the apparatus as he said this, speaking more to the gun than to Janet, not turning around or addressing her by name. Janet was doing some checking herself, making a slight adjustment to the positioning of one of the three cameras in the room, as she replied, 'We can't change it, darling. It has to be 'Schrödinger's Gun.' You concentrate on the physics, Jerry, let me focus on the art. The name of the piece is integral to its artistic content'

Jerry was a physicist, Janet an artist who specialised in performance work and conceptual pieces.

At the Hexagon Gallery she had displayed a number of physics-based pieces, collaborations between her and her husband. 'Chaotic Liquid' had a beaker of liquid that briefly demonstrated chaotic activity when heated when it was between stable states. Beside it stood an identical beaker of the same liquid, unheated, and beside that another beaker filled with a generic cola drink. Jerry didn't see the point of the cola. Neither did Pepsi and Coca-Cola, each of which objected to their products being displayed. It was a pity, Janet could have used a sponsorship deal. The most controversial piece, however, was 'Schrödinger's Box,' a sealed, insulated box of steel. The name of the piece and its appearance obviously evoked the Schrödinger's Cat experiment, but the questions provoked by the exhibit were not only whether a cat inside the box might be alive, dead or in an indeterminate state, but whether there was a cat inside the box at all. Or even whether it contained the other components of the experiment, a cyanide vial, hammer, Geiger counter and radioactive substance.

Janet had wanted to include an opened tin of cat food beside the box, the half-opened lid curling upward in cartoon fashion, to reveal that a third of the food was missing. But the gallery had objected to this as being simply too provocative. As it was, there had been a certain amount of trouble with animal rights protesters. The gallery stated unequivocally to the press that there was no cat inside the box, thus making the piece rather pointless, but Janet refused to be drawn on the topic and insisted on bringing an animal cage into the gallery every morning twenty minutes before it opened, making the staff retire to the kitchen while she primed the box. Similarly, she returned with the cage at the end of every day, shooed everyone away once again and performed the reverse procedure.

Janet could never quite grasp the significance of the physics, but recognised the power of the concept as a situation. Jerry, on the other hand, was always mildly irritated by her unscientific and to him irrelevant additions to the displays. What on earth was the relevance of the beaker of cola? He was secretly pleased when the gallery vetoed the inclusion of the cat food.

***

The current piece of work was very

straightforward, in its practice if not in its implications. There were no unnecessary arty frills. Jerry knew that Janet only half-understood the concept. And, after all, it had up to now only existed as a thought experiment, and there was no way of demonstrating it to anyone but the participants. He could only insist to her the certainty that she and he would continue to exist after the experiment had finished, unharmed and unchanged, the two of them, together. He admitted to himself, but not to her, that there were further consequences of the experiment, but they wouldn't affect him, they wouldn't affect them, the two of them. Well, it would affect her, on her own, by herself, he supposed. In theory. In a single world, one that he could never see or experience. He felt a pang of conscience but pushed it away, telling himself, 'Well, in all possible worlds, of course there are all possible outcomes, but it won't be my world, it won't be our world.' He looked at Janet and the pang transformed itself into a flood of compassion, but still he told himself, 'She will be with me. My Janet won't suffer.'

***

Her studio had already been set up for the experiment. The generous light that the overhead windows usually let in was completely blocked out by boards and tape. Strong artificial light replaced it. It had seemed to her necessary for the ambience, though it made absolutely no difference to the experiment. The space was clear apart from the cameras, the two chairs and table and the gun apparatus, sandbags lining the wall behind the table, and a second, small table on which was positioned a metal box, 'Schrödinger's Box.'

Everything was in working order, Janet concluded. Jerry walked over to her, took her hands in his and look her straight in the eye. She always enjoyed him doing this but knew that it was invariably accompanied by an attempt to persuade her of something.

'How about 'Quantum Suicide' as a title. I don't know why I didn't think of that before.'

In fact, he had been saving his preferred title for this very moment.

'Suicide, Jerry? I don't like that implication.'

'Yes, not suicide. That's not appropriate. Immortality.'

'But you said 'suicide'.'

'I meant immortality. Quantum immortality.'

There was a brief silence.

'Let's do the explanation,' he said.

'We're calling it the context,' she said.

They positioned themselves at the chalk lines she had marked out on the floor earlier. They stood next to each other, only an inch or two of space between their bodies, the top of her head reaching only to his chin, even with her frizzy heap of red hair. She had always liked the contrast between their individual looks. Her white skin, red hair and green eyes, her neat body and small breasts, her well-proportioned, pretty face. He was nearly ten years older, a few flecks of grey in his black, wavy hair, his skin slightly sallow, clean shaven but always with the shadow of his strong, dark beard, his arms long, his frame rangy. She had taught to him to keep his arms at his side as he spoke in public, not to clasp his hands together as he stood, so that the tension in his fingers would not attract the eyes of the audience. He had to keep his attention on the camera or else he became self-conscious of his arms dangling uselessly at his side.

They each wore black, a favourite little black dress for her, a collared black shirt and pleated trousers for him. Jerry took little interest in clothes, he often wore brown slacks and a blue sweatshirt, which she loathed individually but especially in combination, but she had persuaded him to let her take him shopping to purchase something appropriate for the film.

The video camera was now running. She cupped the remote control in her right palm, the back of her hand towards the camera, hiding it.

'Schrödinger's Gun.' She said, in the neutral, slightly alienated tone she used to introduce a performance. Jerry counted silently, 'One elephant, two elephant, three elephant, four elephant,' to form an appropriate pause, as she had instructed him to, then he began. His voice was not so much a monotone as a duotone, modulating between two close pitches. His delivery was undistinguished but Janet had always felt the flatness appropriate to her projects.

'Most of you are familiar to some degree with the Schrödinger's Cat experiment. In its classic form, a cat is placed in a sealed box along with a vial of cyanide and a hammer connected to a quantum trigger mechanism. The trigger is a particle which has a 50-50% percent chance of decaying. If it decays, the mechanism is triggered, the cyanide is freed and when the box is opened the cat is discovered to be dead. If it doesn't decay during that time, then when the box is opened the cat will be found to be alive.

Until the box is opened we cannot know the outcome, so the cat is famously in an indeterminate state. Until the box is opened, the cat's continued existence is only a probability, 50% that the cat is alive, 50% that she is dead.

'You may have seen our previous piece Schrödinger's Box, in which Janet took the uncertainty a step further by making the observer ponder whether there was ever a cat in the box in the first place. Schrödinger proposed the experiment in 1935. In 1997 physicist MaxTegmark published a paper 'The Interpretation of Quantum Mechanics: Many Worlds or Many Words,' in which he proposed a further thought experiment. In his experiment, the quantum event is harnessed to an automatic weapon, a so-called quantum gun. You can see the gun here. In our experiment, or performance, I will be taking the place of the cat.

'The gun will be pointed at my head. Janet holds a button which acts as a trigger. When Janet presses the button, the firing mechanism is triggered. Whether the gun actually fires a live bullet depends on the state of the particle, in this case the z-spin which may be either up or down. If the z-spin of the particle is measured as down, then the gun will merely click. If the z-spin is up, the gun will fire, instantly killing the subject—me.

'If the z-spin is up, I will really die.

'However, if I am in a dead state, I cannot observe the outcome.

'I am personally convinced that the many worlds interpretation of quantum physics is correct. Each time a quantum probability is observed and measured, and the probability wave function is collapsed, there are two possible outcomes. So the universe bifurcates into two parallel universes. In the Schrödinger experiment, in one universe, the outcome is that the cat is alive; in another, the outcome is that the cat is dead. Since I am in the position of the cat, I will be alive in one parallel universe and dead in the other. However, since the probabilities have no meaning for an observer in the dead state, I can only perceive a world in which I survive. Thus I can never perceive the gun firing at me. I will hear repeated clicks as the gun fails to fire. The other outcomes occur only in worlds that I cannot perceive. The iterations of the non-firing gun will be captured on the camera. Janet has said that this will be the ultimate in performance art, an art that literally brings into being a new world.'

He stared at the camera. 'Of course, there are other worlds.'

***

His monologue ended, Jerry walked to the chair and sat down. He finally allowed his hands to touch each other, and his long fingers kneaded each other anxiously, the thumb and middle finger of his right hand twirling the wedding ring on the ring finger of his left hand. Janet said, 'I'll just turn on the other cameras. We can leave camera 2 running.'

'Remember, this is a performance. Don't say anything unnecessary.'

Then she added, 'I love you.'

She turned on cameras 1 and 3 and placed the three remote controls, somewhat retro in their design, neatly in a line on a side table. The room was minimally furnished, but there were still visual elements of the apparatus design that she disliked. Still, it needed to look like a scientific experiment.

They needed to demonstrate to the camera that the gun was loaded and that it fired correctly. On the wall behind the steel chair, Jerry had previously piled up sandbags until they reached the height of the gun Jerry stood behind Janet as she pressed the button. Click. Then a second time, and, bang, the bullet fired and was embedded in the sandbags behind Jerry. She continued for ten times in all. The gun had fired six times out of ten. In three places, sand softly leaked from the bags, a hiss that reminded Janet of childhood beach play when she let sand run through her fingers.

For a moment she was concerned about the background noise, the scraping of the chair, the sound of their feet, but they could simply edit those out.

The gun was pointed directly at Jerry's forehead, the trigger mechanism concealed behind a metal box from which a lead dangled down to another box; from that second box another lead led to the button which Janet now held in her hand. She seated herself on a tubular metal chair, not of the same design or manufacture as the heavy steel chair that held Jerry, but it matched well.

Janet wasn't too squeamish about the gun. After all, wasn't the 1971 piece Shoot by performance artist Chris Burden legendary? Burden had been shot in his left arm by an assistant at a distance of five metres. Janet briefly regretted that she couldn't refer to the piece more explicitly by using a 5m range, but Jerry really needed to be at point blank range.

She got up again and kissed Jerry, sucking in his lip. Then she sat down again. He looked her directly in the eyes.

'There's no need for concern,' Jerry said, 'I will always survive. We will always survive.'

She paused theatrically then pressed the button. There was a click and both Janet and Jerry could not help but smile.

'The z-spin was down,' Jerry said.

Again she pressed the button. Again a click from the gun. 'Z-spin down,' he said.

She pressed the button a third time. The unmistakable, and very loud, sound of a shot. Jerry's head jerked back and blood trickled down from the bullet hole in his head, his brown eyes gazing blankly.

She held her position. She had to focus hard to hold back the tears. 'Z-spin up,' she said aloud, her voice shakier than she would have wished.

***

Again she pressed the button. Again a click from the gun. 'Z-spin down,' he said.

She pressed the button a third time. And it just clicked. Jerry now found the commentary superfluous. She pressed the button a fourth time. Click. A fifth time. Click. She had to focus hard to suppress the laughter welling up in her.

A tenth time. Click.

'Give it to me,' he said. He pressed the button time after time and the gun clicked away.

After a while he smiled and made an odd sort of clucking laugh.

***

Jerry was dead and bleeding, lying back in the steel chair. She could become hysterical, but she had to be methodical. She reloaded the cartridge. Then she went over to the steel chair and sat in his lap. His head was tipped back, his body still very warm, hot even. She nestled into his lap and pressed her cheek against his and felt the still-growing stubble against her skin, breathed in the cologne that mixed with the personal scent of his sweat. There were beads of perspiration on his forehead and one of them trickled down against her cheek, a premonition of the tears that she could not yet allow herself and that she soon would not need. For a moment she wondered if the tickly wetness was blood rather than sweat.

***

Jerry was still chuckling oddly, as Janet let her laughter finally bubbler up hysterically. She went over to him, kissed him full on his mouth, feeling every inch, every aspect of the living man. She indicated that he should stand up by pulling at his belt, then gently undid the belt, his trouser button and his flies, pulled off his trousers and underwear, pushed him down on the floor, straddling him. She wore no panties under the little black dress. The sex was intense but efficient. Afterwards they lay on the floor together, their neat designer clothes in disarray, traces of chalk dust greying the dense black.

'You must feel like Graham Greene,' she said.

'Graham Greene?'

'When he was a teenager and full of existential meaninglessness, he went to Clapham Common in London with a revolver, put a single bullet in it, spun the barrel, held it to his head and pulled the trigger. There was no bullet in the barrel and he survived. He never felt that meaninglessness again.

'Yes. The gun fired blanks. The z-spin was down. Reality bifurcated into a world was the z-spin was up and I died, and this one where the z-spin was down. I only experience the world where I survuve. Yes, I feel like Graham Greene.'

Janet remembered that at least one of the cameras would have captured their somewhat spontaneous lovemaking. It would have made a terrific coda to the piece, but she knew that there was no way that Jerry would allow her to include the sex in the final edit.

***

The red button on the switch seemed a little retro to her, like the doorbell of some sinister, neglected institution. Jerry had probably cannibalised it from some old device—how typical of him. What if the switch had developed a glitch when she had pressed it? Would they then have abandoned the performance-experiment.

She sat in the lap of his warm corpse. Was she trying to kill herself, or did she believe that she would be transported into another parallel world where she would be reunited with Jerry? She didn't really know herself. She pressed the button, leaning forward slightly, her hot forehead pressing against the nozzle of the gun. Click. Click. She kept pressing the button as many times as she could but the bullet wouldn't fire.

She wondered again if the mechanism might be faulty. Then she remembered the principle of quantum immortality and it slowly dawned on her that she was immortal within the confines of the experiment. However many times she performed the experiment and reality bifurcated, she would survive but Jerry would remain dead. She could not bring him back. She lived in a world without a living Jerry, alone, as a murderer. Had he understood this, as the tears finally began to roll hot down her cheeks and her chest heaved erratically. Had the bastard realised this? He might be alive with his version of Janet, but she was alive with no Jerry.

***

Jerry and Janet got up off the floor. Jerry pulled up his trousers and underwear, zipped himself up, buttoned and belted himself, while Janet brushed the chalk off her dress and then off Jerry's shirt. She held on to him.

'Shall we open the box?' she asked.

'It makes no difference. But let's do it.'

The walked over to the table on which rested Schrödinger's Box. She turned the small key anticlockwise then undid the latch. Her head jerked back at the whiff of cyanide. Then she reached in and lifted out the dead cat. It made a strange, plaintive moan as her grip expelled the last air from its lungs. She held it up to the camera.

'The cat is dead, Jerry,' she said unnecessarily.

***

At four o'clock, as previously arranged, Craig let himself into the studio with a key. He had sensed that there was some danger involved in the execution of the piece, but Janet had refused to describe it to him beyond a vague statement that it was another physics based concept, but more of a performance piece, and that it would be filmed. For some reason he couldn't stop thinking of a rumoured performance art piece that involved temporary erotic asphyxiation. It had gone horribly wrong. He had heard it from a friend who knew of an acquaintance of a friend of hers who had discovered the inconvenienced artist. He hoped that it was an urban legend.

Twenty minutes after Craig had entered, the police arrived. Craig could not help but be fascinated by the sight of Janet sprawled forward in Jerry's lap, Jerry reclined in the steel chair. Each had a clean bullet wound in the middle of the forehead. His artist's eye revelled similarity in the state of the two bodies and the contrast between their appearances. Skin colour, size— yes—but for some reason their hands and noses, his long fingers and somewhat beaky nose, her perfect proportions, made the stranger contrast. Craig wished that he had brought a camera.

'You were the first observer?' the detective asked.

'Yeah,' Craig replied.

'Could it be a suicide pact?'

'No,' Craig hesitated. :'It's art.'

He looked at Jerry's corpse, and added, 'Or science maybe.'

***

Jerry looked at the camera. Could it prove anything about the experiment? If only he could possess the camera of the alternative reality too. He thought of the Janet who had lost him, and

he touched his own Janet once again, though he couldn't help wondering if she was really the same person.

***

Janet pointed the camera at Jerry's corpse. Craig would arrive soon. She didn't know what else to do, or where to go.

***

The bodies removed, the police disconnected the quantum gun as best they could. Then they bagged and labelled the cameras.

'Is there any way I could get access to the film,' Craig asked.

The detective gave him a glance of disgust and didn't answer. As the police methodically tagged and bagged item after item, they came to a box in the corner.

'Do you know what this is?'

'That's Schrödinger's Box, one of Janet's pieces,' said Craig.

The detective made to move it.

'Maybe we ought to check what's inside before you move it,' Craig said, 'Can I open it?'

'You can't touch it,' the detective replied.

'Then maybe you could open it. It might be important.'

The detective turned the small key in the lock and fiddled with the latch. He opened the box and heard a soft miaow. He placed his gloved hands inside the box and, to his surprise, discovered a warm bundle. He lifted out the living, breathing cat.

Luc Valentine

A Place in the Heart:
A Literary Tour of Pistis Sophia

Mary asked her brothers, 'Where are you going to store these questions you ask of the child of humankind?' The Master said to her, 'Sister, no one can ask about these things except someone who has a place to store them in the heart. And such a person may leave the world and enter the place of life…'

— from *The Dialog of the Saviour*

More often we turn to *The Gospel of Mary* (Berlin Codex 8502, Tractate 1; fragments, Papyrus Oxyrhynchus 3525 and Pypyrus Rylands 463) or perhaps *The Dialog of The Saviour* (*Nag Hammadi Library,* Codex III, Tractate 5) for the Gnostic view of Mary Magdelene, though one of the first Gnostic texts that rose to light from the subterranean purgatory of history is also one of the more revealing of Mary. *Pistis Sophia* does not so much dwarf other ancient Gnostic writings by its word count as it stands out among them as a giant. Unique in length and depth, commentaries on this old text have been served up mainly in cosmological terms, particularly in those fantastically epic passages when the Saviour dances Sophia through the aeons to the Plermoma, with a healthy side dish of eschatology. These eschatological passages are found to be unpalatable to some. For within *Pistis Sophia* there dances a duality between eternal life and eternal nothingness, the question of the universality of redemption.

With its theme of forgiveness and long illustration of the way to salvation, the narrator of *Pistis Sophia*, Jesus or the Saviour, through a discursive dialog with Mary Magdelene, the protagonist, shows her the light of his teachings as surely as he waltzes Sophia into the Limitless Light in the fantastic story-within-a-story for which *Pistis Sophia* is most often remembered. These teachings come to us in literary form. What does the literary form of *Pistis Sophia* reveal about the message of these teachings?

The temptation to make of *Pistis Sophia* a post-modern feminist work wants to overcome the modern critic on a first reading. Of course *Pistis Sophia* must be evaluated according to the standards of its day rather than by our standards some eighteen hundred years later. Overcoming because so much of the literary technique of *Pistis Sophia* seems to presage by all those centuries post-modern literature. The story within a story, the feminist perspective, the fantastic metaphors and imagery, the almost magical realism combine to lend a weird aura of *déjà vu* to readers of postmodern lit. If the canonical gospels are a badly edited but popular old movie, *Pistis Sophia* is the digitally enhanced DVD director's cut.

Who is the director, or more precisely, the writer of *Pistis Sophia*? We do not know her name though some have guessed her gender. *Pistis Sophia* 'appears to be the work of two different writers: one a careful, fine hand and the other the shaky writing of an old man.' (Picknett, Lynn. *Mary Magdelene: Christianity's Hidden Goddess*, New York: Carroll & Graf Publishers,

2003 at p. 84, citing Mead, G.R.S., *Pistis Sophia*, 'Preface', 1921.) The implication is that the finer, more careful hand is that of a woman, but it is just that, an implication, as no one knows the true identity of its author.

In the preface to his translation, Mead names three theories of the scripture's date of origin. An earlier view ascribed it to the second century, but later scholarship puts it at the second half of the third century or possibly the first half of the third century. It is suspected to be among the latest of old Gnostic writings, due in part to both a Sethian and a Valentinian influence.

There are missing pages and missing text. Lacunae abound, one in a most regrettable place. Missing is a specific word which the Saviour tells us has such power that its mere utterance is sufficient to induce knowledge of the Limitless Light and the experience of the gnosis of the universe. How should we treat these missing pages and lacunae? Above all, we should not speculate. Certain patterns recur in *Pistis Sophia* and the mind's natural tendency is to complete a missing segment of the pattern as though the pattern was a puzzle and the missing pieces have but to be filled in to complete the picture. But if we misread the pattern, we will be propagating our misreading which may well grow into a misunderstanding. Or, worse, we may be tempted simply to insert our own 'text'.

What we have is what we have and all we can work with, and that is that. But let us not despair, for in the case of *Pistis Sophia*, the Saviour tells us the way to gnosis, to the mystery of mysteries, in plain language well before the missing word. For *Pistis Sophia* is a lengthy work, as scripture goes, and rich enough with gems that we can plainly see that we need not mine it for more. And The Saviour will give to all the 'gnosis of gnoses', the secret of entering the light in the text itself before the end.

Pistis Sophia is a lengthy work, as scripture goes, and rich enough with gems that we can plainly see that we need not mine it for more

The supporting cast of characters in *Pistis Sophia* are the disciples, the apostles plus Mary the Mother of Jesus, those to whom the Saviour speaks on the Mount of Olives. The plot line of the narrative of discourse is organized around the device of the Saviour giving a lesson and the disciples in turn giving their interpretation of each teaching. It is within this discursive narrative of *Pistis Sophia* that the story of Sophia — a story within the story of the discursive narrative, is told. The focus on Sophia's redemption, her journey through the aeons and her battle with Self-Willed, the villian or antagonist, told as it is in the soaring language of fantastic allegory, together with its metaphorical and linguistic artfulness, compelling though it is, is framed by the dialog on the Mount of Olives.

What readers of *Pistis Sophia* should remind themselves is that the embedded Sophia story is nicely related through the discursive narrative, the dialog of the Saviour with Mary Magdelene and the disciples. We shall return to the story of Sophia's ascension but let us first look at the discursive narrative with Jesus and the disciples pertaining to the themes of redemption and forgiveness.

Orthodox Christianity has woven together what has become known as the greatest story ever told. Jesus, born in a manger to a virgin, is sent to earth to redeem humankind from the sin it created. After a short ministry, he is executed by the Romans with high-ranking Hebrew collaboration, but three days after his death, he rises, literally, from the grave, spends a little time with his now more befuddled than ever disciples, then ascends to heaven. There the canonical gospels end. Reading the *New Testament* as a whole, we go forward in time thousands of years later to learn the climax of the great, ever-told story. Jesus returns to earth in the body and after defeating his antithesis in a bloody war, rules as spiritual and political king of the world.

Such is the Christian story, the *mythos Christos*, for the reader of the New Testament. But what if we add *Pistis Sophia* as the literary ending of the Christian arch-narrative, the *mythos Christos*? What then becomes our story?

Pistis Sophia starts where the canonical gospels leave off, with the ascension of the Saviour, and is told from the point of view of the Saviour as he recounts to the disciples the wonders and mysteries of his divine journey. Making his way from Aeon to Aeon in a 'Vesture of Blinding Light', the Logos causes much agitation among the rulers of the Aeons in his journey to the fullness, takes away fully one-third of their powers, and causes them to work at cross purposes to themselves, setting them to work first to the left, then to the right. He changes the 'sacred geometry' of the universe as he ascends to the 'interior of the interiors'.

In *Pistis Sophia*, Jesus returns to earth some twelve years after his ascension (Picknett, p. 84). Irrespective of *Matthew 26: 17-19*, Mary, not Peter, is alluded to as the greatest leader among them. In a passage remarkably similar to one in the *Gospel of Mary*, Mary and Peter have a famous disagreement. The gospel recounts that Peter, following Andrew, doubts that the Saviour gave Mary 'strange teachings'.

Pistis Sophia starts where the canonical gospels leave off, with the ascension of the Saviour... as he recounts to the disciples the wonders and mysteries of his divine journey.

'Did he really speak with a woman in private, without our knowledge? Should we all turn and listen to her? Did he prefer her to us?' Mary answers Peter, calls him brother, saying, '[w]hat do you think? Do you think I made this up by myself or that I am lying about the Saviour?' Levi then says to Peter, admonishing him, that Peter is always angry. 'Now I see you arguing against this woman like an adversary. If the saviour made her worthy, who are you to reject her? Surely the saviour knows her well. That is why he has loved her more than us.' The disciples

should go about preaching, says Levi, and with the observation that the disciples then did just that, the gospel ends.

But *Pistis Sophia* does not leave Peter hanging. In Chapter 36, as in the *Gospel of Mary*, Peter complains of Mary that she 'discourseth many times' and audaciously tells Jesus that 'we will not endure this woman.' This dialog comes fairly early in the work and is a solution to a puzzle of sorts that Jesus has set his disciples to solve, the 'repentances' of Sophia. Jesus has told the disciples the story within a story of the ascension of Sophia and asks for the meaning of each of Sophia's repentances. The exchange with Peter comes in the solution to the second repentance, the first repentance being a song of praise by Mary. Peter, it seems, not to be outdone by a woman, then notes with chagrin Mary's many discourses with the Saviour.

No sooner does Peter say these things that Jesus sees that Peter has solved the mystery of the repentance and invites him to tell the group. The Saviour sees the 'power' in Peter 'that it understandeth what I say', bids Peter to come forward and speak, and praises Peter's eloquent solution. Thus begins a reconciliation between Mary and Peter. Peter's later 'solutions' will be both more illuminated and illuminating. Notice that Peter's power of understanding comes only after Mary's solution of the first repentance of Sophia and after Mary's solution of the redemption mystery of the ascension of the Logos.

Peter, quiet until his outburst, having listened to Mary's discourse is bursting forth with answers so much that Jesus sees Peter's power of understanding as being complete. Such is *Pistis Sophia* that, examined as literature and given its scope and depth, some of the more vexing problems of interpretation for Gnostics can be seen in a greater and more meaningful context.

The ascension of Sophia is counter pointed by the story of the discourse, the story of the literal enlightenment of Mary and all the followers.

The Magdelene pays rapt attention. 'It came to pass then, when Mary had heard the Saviour say these words, that she gazed fixedly into the air for the space of an hour (*Pistis Sophia*, Chapter 17). She asks Jesus for 'commandment unto me to speak in openness' and her enlightened discourse moves the Saviour to tell her that she is 'blessed before all women on the earth, because through thou shalt be the fulness of all fulnesses and the perfection of all perfections.'

The fullness of all fullnesses? The perfection of all perfections? What is Jesus telling Mary, and us? She asks if the powers ('magic') of the rulers of the Aeons will be ineffective now that Christ has ascended, and so begins a series of questions she and the other disciples in eventual turn ask Jesus. Mary is always asking the insightful questions, revealing her careful thought, much like the bright pupil in class whose thirst for knowledge far exceeds her classmates. Throughout, her questions will reveal her deep concern for all souls who ever were and will ever be. The discoursing Jesus answers her: No, but now the powers that would separate all who desire to ascend to the fullness of the Light as the Logos ascended will not be as effective as they were 'from the beginning'.

Philip, the first of the disciples to question Jesus along with Mary, then asks a question, and the discoursing Jesus's answer leads Mary to ask another in turn. Philip and Mary are asking why, since he ascended into heaven, are not all souls yet perfected?

It is 'so that the perfect number of souls who shall receive the mysteries and be in the Treasury of the Light, shall quickly be completed', the Saviour answers; it is 'because of my elect; otherwise no soul would have been able to be saved.' This first exchange of questions between Jesus and his disciples foreshadows what will become the major theme of *Pistis Sophia* and the climax of the entire work. Following its eschatological theme through the device of

Mary's questioning concerning the fate of all souls, *Pistis Sophia* reveals nothing less than our own fates, those souls with gnosis and those souls without, all souls that ever were and ever will be. Even the story of the ascension of Sophia, perhaps especially the story of the ascension of Sophia, beautiful and majestic though it is, might be seen as an element, within the larger narrative context, of this dialog between Jesus and Mary in which Mary is seen fairly cries out to the Saviour for the redemption of all souls. Most marvelously of all, contained in these later chapters, the Logos as the narrating Jesus, the Saviour on the Mount, reveals to his disciples the mystery of mysteries—the 'gnosis of gnoses'—and how they, and we, may freely know it.

Continuing the story of his 'exploits' upon his ascension, the Saviour's journey 'among the rulers of the twelve Aeons and all their rulers and their lords and their authorities and their angels and their archangels', these entities marvel that he is able to pass by them unnoticed. Amazed that he has done so and that their powers have been diminished by him, they gaze at the mystery of the salvific holy Logos. Unable to look directly at him because of the brightness of the light shining from him, '...they adored a little removed from him'. (*Pistis Sophia*, Chapter 28)

Coming to the thirteenth Aeon, he finds Sophia just below it, at the nebulous border between the twelfth and the thirteenth Aeon. She is 'all alone and no one there with her', grieving and mourning, her grief caused by the torment of Self-willed, also called the three triple powers. Now Mary asks a question of Jesus which both illustrates her attentive devotions to his teachings during his earthly ministry and shows that she is unaware of her true and higher identity. We may note here an important point, a writer's technique that the author of *Pistis Sophia* employs. Quite often when the impartial unknown third-person narrator recounting the dialog on the Mount of Olives refers to the Logos, he is called 'Jesus' when talking to the disciples other than Mary. But when he talks with Mary, the narrator refers to him as 'the Saviour.' It is in such details of narrative technique as this seemingly minor point that the true authorial intent of *Pistis Sophia* is revealed.

It is the story of Jesus and Mary Magdelene and of their unfinished business. Though Jesus or the Saviour is recounting the story of the ascension of Sophia, there is another story being told, one that began when Mary (as told elsewhere) discovered the empty tomb in the Garden of Gethsemene. Indeed it is a story that began earlier even than that, when the tormented Mary of Magdelene sought out, on a dirt road, an itinerant upstart rabbi with a radically different message than those on up in the Jewish hierarchy and who had a reputation for calming souls and untangling minds. Just as Mary lay at Jesus' feet in the dusty desert and her 'demons' were cast out, now she sat at the feet of the risen Christ on the Mount of Olives becoming 'the fulness of fulnesses, the perfection of perfections.'

Sophia rises from Aeon to Aeon as she seeks to rejoin the Light from which she came and to which she is destined to return. Her first repentance is a song of praise. At its conclusion we hear Jesus say the familiar words, 'Who hath ears to hear, let him hear,' an important signal that a divine mystery has been imparted, and one with more than a superficial meaning. The next chapter is a brilliantly counter-pointed song of lament uttered by Mary, who begins her address with 'My Lord, my indweller of light hath ears, and I hear with my light-power,' which shifts the imagery and deeper meaning of the text to a higher plane, as Sophia returns to the exalted state in which she dwelled before her fall and as Mary becomes empowered to a full understanding of the mystery of mysteries. The next several chapters continue this pattern with a repentance by Sophia followed by a chapter of interpretation alternating between Mary's interpretation of Sophia's repentance and one of several of the other disciples' interpretation of Sophia's repentance.

We have already seen the intimation of a reconciliation between Peter and Mary.

The third repentance of Sophia is solved by Martha; the fourth repentance of Sophia is solved by John; and so it goes. Sophia is already at the entrance to the thirteenth Aeon, ready to enter. She has repented more than once, more than three times. It is because, the Saviour says, 'not yet had the command reached me from the First Mystery, to save her out of the chaos.' In other words, it is not time. The First Mystery is the first cause, that from which all things followed. But why is it not time? Looking at the action of the stories of Sophia and of the dialog of the Saviour at this juncture, where is the story? Why does the author of *Pistis Sophia* choose this point to question why the command has not been given?

Could it be because Peter and the other disciples are only now finding their own 'solutions'? Mary has found her solution, but yet the Logos has not been commanded to restore Sophia to the Pleroma. Other disciples are not ready. Earlier Mary was questioning, since the Logos ascended to the Pleroma and diminished the powers of the rulers of the Aeons, what is the fate of the souls? And so Sophia suffers yet, even after ascending all the way through the twelve Aeons nearly to the thirteenth, until all the elect, the disciples, those who have ears, find their solutions, achieve their redemption. Does Sophia suffer still—is the command withheld—'so that the perfect number of souls who shall receive the mysteries and be in the Treasury of the Light shall be quickly completed' as said in Chapter 20?

A small clue is given in the action, if discursive narrative can said to be action, of the next chapter, Chapter 42. Philip, the scribe, makes a small complaint. How can he solve the repentances of Sophia while he is busy writing down all the discourses? In a phase sure to endear him to writers of all times, he asks, 'My Lord, surely then its not on me alone that thou hast enjoined to take care for the world and write down all the discourses which we shall speak and all we shall do.' The always patient Jesus tells Philip, and Thomas and Matthew, also scribes, to take heart, and when they have finished writing to 'come forward and proclaim what pleaseth thee.' (*Pistis Sophia*, Chapter 42; *Pistis Sophia* is rare among scripture in that it specifically mentions by name that these three are taking down the proceedings.)

Philip, now seated at his writing place, Jesus continues with the story of Sophia's ascension and gives the sixth repentance of Sophia. (*Pistis Sophia,* Chapter 45) Then upon Andrew's solution to the sixth repentance, Jesus tells him 'I will perfect you in all the mysteries of the Light and all gnoses from the interior of the interiors to the exterior of the exteriors.' (*Pistis Sophia,* Chapter 46) Sophia's suffering continues, but as it does the disciples on the Mount of Olives are receiving the mystery, the holy gnosis.

The Saviour has not yet received the command from the First Mystery, yet the Saviour 'out of compassion without commandment' leads Sophia into a somewhat spacious region in the chaos. There, Self-willed ceases to oppress her. Sophia does not know it is the Saviour who has rescued her. The implications for us are plain. In our own struggles in the world, while still in the chaos, there are

So long as we continue our journey to the fullness, as we struggle to find our way back to the Light, we may expect times of spiritual peace.

spiritual places in which we may find ourselves at respite. So long as we continue our journey to the fullness, as we struggle to find our way back to the Light, we may expect times of spiritual peace. We may arrive, perhaps without knowing how, at times in our lives when our spiritual problems, whether caused from forces without or forces within ourselves, cease and desist. And so Sophia gives her eighth repentance.

But her respite does not last, for the Saviour has acted out of compassion, not by commandment from the First Mystery. Yaldobaoth notices that Sophia has not been fully led out of the chaos, that she has only been graced with a temporal refuge, and so he sends out all 'the other emanations' of Self-willed to torment her. Sophia, still protected

while in the chaos, and her tormentors not having reached her, continues with her eighth repentance. Matthew, one of the scribes, gives the solution to the eighth repentance, Philip presumably still frantically taking notes, he and Thomas having given their solutions. But Matthew grows impatient, telling Jesus 'we have restored all the orders of the twelve saviours to the region of the inheritances of every one of them.' Mary, wishing to help Matthew with his understanding, reminds Jesus that he promised to 'bequeath upon you...the kingdom of god.'

(*Pistis Sophia,* Chapters 49-50)

After Sophia's ninth repentance, James gives the solution, and Jesus questions further. Jesus says, 'Understand ye in what manner I discourse with you?' as he has done often. Mary answers from the words of the teaching rabbi, 'The first shall be last.' When Mary speaks these words, Jesus narrates that now the First Mystery 'hearkened unto her (Sophia)', and the Saviour is at last sent off on his command. The time of the First Mystery to return Sophia to her home in the Pleroma has come.

Yaldoboath, tormenting Sophia, vanishes and in his place the Logos appears. Far more radiant and taking courage, Sophia utters her tenth repentance. (*Pistis Sophia,* Chapters 50-52). Peter, his understanding increasing, solves the tenth repentance. Yaldoboath, having been dislocated by the Logos but still present, notices the Logos with Sophia. He is in fear, seeing that the Logos is taking away his power and so he mounts a penultimate assault, crying out to its Self-willed god, who wrathfully appears with all its emanations and surrounds Sophia to take away her 'whole light'. She repents a twelfth time. She speaks to the Logos and repents for a thirteenth time. Now Jesus sends a light force to help Sophia which becomes a 'light-wreath' on Sophia's head so that 'the emanations of Self-willed could have no dominion over her.' (*Pistis*

Sophia, Chapter 59). Once Sophia receives this light-wreath she is purified; 'evil matters' were shaken off, these evil matters 'perished and remained in the chaos.' The light-power of the Logos himself reinforces Sophia's light-wreath, surrounding the pure light in Sophia 'and her pure light did not depart, from the wreath of the power of the light-flame'. She sings a song of praise. Even if her 'matter perished and remain in the chaos' yet she will not perish. (Chapter 59). Mary the mother of Jesus solves the thirteenth repentance, the song of praise. The Saviour sends a second light-power to Sophia which joins with the first in 'a great stream of light', which Mary Magdelene interprets. Here are two Marys...one the mother and the other the most favored disciple, the Magdelene...interpreting Sophia's receipt of the bounteous light from the Logos. (*Pistis* Sophia, Chapter 60)

The Saviour on the mount makes a startling and sweeping pronouncement. In his narrative, Sophia has received the light, and although she will descend again, she has been imbued with the salvific light of Lights. Once Mary interprets the mystery of the Saviour's second light-power that joins in 'a great stream of light' — the Logos/ Sophia syzygy is complete — Jesus tells Mary that she 'shalt inherit the whole light-kingdom'. Just as the light of the Logos surrounds and protects Sophia, as they have been joined, Jesus on the Mount tells Mary Magdelene that she, like Sophia, will inherit the kingdom of light. This is reinforced in the text, for after further interpretation by the Magdelene, Jesus says, 'Well said, Mary' and addresses her as 'Mary, inheritor of light'. No longer is Mary being promised the light or fullness as Jesus said she would be at the beginning of *Pistis Sophia*. Now she *is* the inheritor of the light, just as Sophia is. (*Pistis Sophia,* Chapter 62).

A fabulous cosmogony is presented by the narrating Jesus, of Saboath, Barbelo, Yagraoth,

the stakes for salvation are high... for the universe, the spiritual universe of the Aeons, is encircled by a dragon swallowing his tail

and the light-ventures. The archangels Gabriel and Michael are called out to be by Sophia's side. What is the meaning of this?, asks Jesus. Now Peter answers. 'All in Pistis Sophia whose light had been before taken away, got light.' Now the narrating Jesus/the Saviour is given a new name by the writer of *Pistis Sophia* — he is called the First Mystery. Jesus becomes the Saviour, who becomes the First Mystery. It is no longer Jesus or even the Saviour narrating; now our story comes from the First Mystery itself.

Self-willed perceives that the Logos has taken away the light powers which he had taken from Sophia, and so begins anew her oppression. But he is cast out of the thirteenth Aeon and hurls into the chaos a flying arrow which transforms his emanations, one into the form of a serpent, another into the form of a seven-headed basilisk, another into a dragon. And the first form of Self-willed, the lion faced, and all his beastly emanations lead Sophia again into the lower regions of the chaos.

The stakes for salvation are high. For the universe, the spiritual universe of the Aeons, is encircled by a dragon swallowing his tail — a cosmic ouroboros — whose jaws gulp down the unrepentant. (*Pistis Sophia*, Chapters 106, 120, 126, 127, 130, 136) The truly unrepentant 'cannot be cast back into the world...but his habitation is in the midst of the jaws of the dragon of the outer darkness...' It is this 'region of howling and grinding of teeth' that so many readers find distasteful in *Pistis Sophia*. Those who adhere to a doctrine of universal redemption repel from such frank language and reject the fate of those who have not received the Light at 'the dissolution of the world', those whose souls 'will be frozen up [?] (*sic*, Mead translation) and perish in the violent cold and exceedingly violent fire and will be non-existent eternally.' (*Pistis Sophia*, Chapter 106)

Those aghast readers who wish to see all souls

redeemed need reminding that there is always a syzygy dancing through a duality at work in *Pistis Sophia*. If the jaws of the dragon offer nonexistence, it is yet possible to escape them. All who receive the mysteries of Light, or even one of the mysteries of the twelve names of the dragon, will be snatched from the dragon's gut, and the dragon will be 'most exceedingly convulsed'. '[T]he door of the dungeon in which the souls of those men are openeth itself upward…' (*Pistis Sophia*, Chapter 130).

Her final trial, and her ultimate triumph, are at hand. Adamas the Tyrant, also 'wrath' with Sophia because she desires to go to the Light of Lights, Adamas, 'that demon…darked down Pistis Sophia'. The lion faced one, the serpent, the dragon, the basilisk, Adamas all surround the darkened Sophia. Even after her ascension into the thirteenth Aeon, even after receiving the light wreath and two full streams of light from the Saviour, she is still being assailed by the powers of Self-willed. And more. Each time her light increases, each time the Saviour hurls a salvific salvo of purifying light to surround and protect her, the onslaughts of Self-willed grow mightier. The more she becomes purified, the more radiant with the light of salvation she becomes, the harder the lion faced Self-willed and his emanations oppress her and try to steal back the Light that was hers from before the beginning.

if the jaws of the dragon offer nonexistence, it is yet possible to escape them. All who receive the mysteries of Light... will be snatched from the dragon's gut

She cries to the Light and the Light will save her from chaos and the throes of Self-willed. The archangels Michael and Gabriel rush to her aid, the light-stream glorifies her, and glorifies her more than ever. She becomes so radiant with the Light while surrounded by Self-willed and his emanations in the depths of the chaos that she glows brighter than any light. The Self-willed powers become so terrified by the radiant light of the glorious Sophia that they leave her at once. Sophia will never fear them again.

The Saviour goes into the thirteenth Aeon to where Self-willed has fled. It seems he will never give up. But the Saviour confronts Self-willed 'and took its whole light in it and held fast all the emanations of Self-willed, so that from now on they went not into that region that is the thirteenth Aeon.' He and his powers 'all fell down in the chaos powerless.' Escorted by Gabriel and Michael, the great light-stream enters Sophia again, and the Saviour — the First Mystery — leads Sophia from the chaos as she treads on the emanations that once tormented her. Climactically, the First Mystery then 'took all the powers in it, and made it to perish its whole matter, so that no seed should raise from it from now on.' (*Pistis Sophia*, Chapter 66).

Meanwhile, the disciples, on the Mount of Olives, take turns answering Jesus's questions regarding the marvels of Sophia he has related to them and of Sophia's song of praise upon her ascension into the thirteenth Aeon. Several disciples interpret, then Mary interprets, and at the point in the story when Mary interprets the ascension of Sophia, then Jesus, the First Mystery now, tells what happened next. He, the First Mystery, leads Sophia to a region below the thirteenth Aeon. He gives her a new mystery of light and gives her a song of light so that, from now on, the rulers of the Aeons can not prevail against her. And Jesus says, 'And I removed her to that region until I shall come after her and bring her to her higher region.'

The Logos turns from her to go into the Light.

Sophia prays to the Light. She is concerned that Self-willed will return, so long as she remains below the thirteenth Aeon.

The Logos answers, 'My father, who has emanated me, hath not yet given me commandment to take light from them; but I will seal the regions of Self-willed and all his rulers…

and the region of Adamas and his rulers...until their time is complete and the season cometh that my Father give me commandment to take their light from them'.

How do we reconcile this with the earlier passage that the matter of Self-willed has been destroyed? A careful reading indicates that while the matter of Self-willed has been destroyed, his light has not. But when 'the three times' have been completed, Sophia's final deliverance will come. How will she know when the three times have been completed and the 'gate of the Treasury of the Great Light' will open? The Logos answers that when the gate opens all the Aeons will know because of the Great Light which will obtain in all the regions.'

Sophia is to be left just below the thirteenth Aeon. She will have power to go into all the twelve Aeons, but not yet again to the height of the thirteenth. And with that the Logos goes into the Light (*Pistis Sophia,* Chapter 76).

The story of Sophia's ascension never seems complete. She ascends, only to descend again. With each ascension she becomes more luminous, more powerful, more restored. But she always descends again. She will come to dwell in the thirteenth Aeon with the Logos. She will make her final ascent into the Light.

What is the mystery of mysteries that *Pistis Sophia* seems to conceal in its fantastic imagery of cosmic lion-faced tormentors and soul swallowing dragon? Are we to have gnosis by guessing the many names of the dragon? By solving inscrutable puzzles? No. The answer is plainly given by the Saviour in Chapter 95:

Now, therefore, I say unto you: For every one who will renounce the whole world and all therein and will submit himself to the godhead, that mystery is far easier than all the mysteries of the Light-kingdom and it is sooner to understand than them all and it is easier [?] than them all. He who reacheth unto the gnosis of that mystery, renounceth this whole world and all the cares therein.

Jesus leads Mary in their discourse inexorably toward making the conclusion herself that all souls, even those whose transgressions cause them to lose their redeemed status, have it

The story of Sophia's ascension never seems complete... she ascends, only to descend again... with each ascension she becomes more luminous...powerful, more restored.

within themselves to be redeemed again; to be reborn, not just once, but to be born again and again until they, too, 'complete their circuits' and enter into the Light. Just as the risen Logos holds Sophia as the holy syzygy ascends Aeon over Aeon into the highest of the high, letting her go only so that she may fall again, and rejoining her and holding her again so that they once more rise to the height of heights in a divine dance, so do Jesus and Mary on the Mount of Olives dance a more earthly and cerebral dance of discourse in which Mary, step by step, is led to understand the deepest mystery of mysteries, the way of salvific knowledge, the holy gnosis itself, and not just for herself, but, as she deeply wishes, and for which she ever implores, for all of humanity.

Anthony Cartledge

Planetary Types:
From the Hermetica to the Twenty-first century

The planets are in us.

Paracelsus

'If a single gland can dominate the life history of an individual it becomes possible to speak of endocrine types, the result of the endocrine analysis of the individual. Studying endocrine traits of physique, life reactions, disease tendencies, blood chemistry, one may gain an insight into the composition or constitution of an individual. The endocrine type of an individual is a summary of these, his behavior in the past, and also a prediction of his reactions in the future, much as a chemical formula outlines what we believe to be the 'skeleton' of a compound substance as deducible from its properties under varying conditions.'

Louis Berman[1]

The realm of human 'typology' is a rich and varied playing field. A new scheme emerges every few years and there are now many different contenders, like the Myers-Briggs scheme, Sheldon's Morphic types or the recent flurry of popularised 'Enneagram personality' types. Twentieth century schemes seem arbitrarily categorised according to modern sensibilities and trends in science and sociology. I believe our best chance at a typology that accurately represents the true and fundamental architecture of the human psyche is one that combines the wisdom of ancient esotericism with the unrelenting scrupulousness of science.

Types based on the planetary archetypes have been around as long as civilisation, since man began looking both inward and heavenward. And it now seems as if they are finding corroboration in modern science. Outlined here is a system of types based on planetary influence which has appeared independently several times in our history. This system is capable of discovery and verification by independent observers and qualifies as near as possible to being objective. Its most recent incarnation is the product of an esoteric school based on the teachings of the Russian polymath philosopher P D Ouspensky and the Greek-Armenian mystic George Gurdjieff. What sets it apart is that the ancient planetary types seem to have close cousins in the endocrine types of Dr Louis Berman, a pioneer in endocrinology.

THE HISTORY OF PLANETARY TYPES

In the realm of myth, nothing is as enduring as the archetypes of the planets. Plato called them 'the great visible Gods,' and they have ruled our imaginations since recorded history began. As John Anthony West says: '... the characteristics or meanings ascribed to the planets are as universal as the stories and characters themselves. They are written into the myths at their origins, at dates that cannot even be surmised.'[2]

The Babylonians called the seven planets the 'interpreters'; for the Greeks they were the visible bodies of the Gods, and were called 'wanderers,' Many early cultures endowed these Gods with the most fundamental human qualities according to their discernible movement. Saturn was a phlegmatic old man because he moved the slowest; Mercury was a messenger — swift, changeable, because of his rapid and erratic movement; Jupiter, in the middle of the hierarchy of motion, was moderate and judicious; Mars was the ruler of war because he glowed red; Venus was a femme fatale because she courted the sun god; and the two luminaries were the lords of life — the sun of light and wisdom, the moon of the dark, the secret, the unconscious.

In the Babylonian creation story, the fifty great gods sat down with the 'Seven who design the immutable nature of things,' those who performed the liturgy from which the universe receives its structure, and thus man is born. In the ancient Akkadian language seven means 'wholeness.' The seven designers of nature are the visible planets, the orchestrators of form and function.

The Moon, over time, has been associated with the goddesses Selene and the moody and persistent Diana; Venus, Aphrodite or Inanna has ruled beauty, fertility and love; Mercury or Hermes governs cunning, intellect and communication; Mars or Ares, the undisputed God of war, passion and aggression; Jupiter the ruler of justice and harmony; and Saturn, the father of time and measure. These archetypes became the planetary types that can be traced back to some of the earliest esoteric religions.

Psychologist Julian Jaynes called the Gods 'organizations of the central nervous system'[3] something essential to the deep structure of the psyche. They are clearly a product of a deep intuition born out of clarity and wisdom of the essential nature of humankind. The clues to such a persistent and coherent body of knowledge are scattered throughout almost 2,000 years of history.

ORIGINS

HARRAN

Hermes is an ancient figure in both Greek and Near-eastern mythology. He is a Greek version of the ancient Egyptian god Thoth, the inventor of astronomy, letters, magic and philosophy. The cult of Hermes as a philosopher and teacher of religion remained undiminished after the fall of the Egyptian Empire, and especially in Harran, an important city in Northern Mesopotamia, on the main road between Babylonia and the West. It became the center from which this particular pagan worship grew, its inhabitants rejecting Christianity, which had become the dominant religion in the neighboring regions in the fourth century. Even when the Arabs conquered Syria and Mesopotamia in the fifth century, they clung to their religion with the same defiance. They managed to escape Moslem retribution by claiming themselves as Sabeans, a religion acceptable by the Koran, and claiming as their scripture the Books of Hermes.

'There was at Harran a temple of the Moon-god Sin, and that among the deities worshipped by the Harranians the seven planet-gods were prominent; and there are also descriptions of a cult which seems to show resemblances to Mithraism.'[4] Many famous Harranians rose to positions of eminence in the court of Baghdad and established what author Adrian Gilbert calls 'Pagan Neo-Platonism,' producing distinguished works on mathematics, astronomy and astrology, medicine and philosophy.

MITHRAISM

Mithraism was once the most powerful cult of the Hellenistic age and in the Roman period was a serious rival to Christianity. It originated in Iran as a form of Zoroastrian esotericism and flowered in the Near East and Europe. It consisted of seven stages of initiation that represented the spheres of the visible planets — the Moon, Mercury, Venus, the Sun, Mars, Jupiter and Saturn. Joseph Campbell in 'Occidental Mythology' says: 'The individual had derived from each [planet] a specific temporal-spatial quality, which on the one hand contributed to his character, but on the other was a limitation.' [5]

The seven stages of initiation were to represent passages of the soul beyond its limitations to full realization. The sphere of the Moon was the passive, secret or vegetal aspect of existence; Mercury, the sphere of magic and wisdom; at the sphere of Venus, the initiate overcomes the delusions of desire; Mars, the sphere of daring and audacity; Jupiter's stage was called 'Heliodromus', the 'Courier of the Sun'; and Saturn's level was sanctified as 'Father.'

An identical scheme of archetypes is contained in the *Hermetica*, the writings attributed to Thoth. Scholars are now fairly certain that these documents, far from originating from the genesis of Egyptian civilization as it was once believed, were written between the first and third centuries CE, and are a unique synthesis of Egyptian and Platonic doctrines.

According to the text the first Mind — God — gave birth to a demiurge, or Maker of things, and this Maker made out of fire and air seven Administrators who 'encompass the world with their orbits' whose 'administration is called Destiny.'[6] These Administrators each gave Man a share of their nature. The Sun gave light, the Moon gave birth to Silence and Sleep, Kronos or Saturn imbued them with a sense of Penal Justice and Necessity, Zeus or Jupiter gave them Peace, Mars Struggle, Anger and Strife, Aphrodite or Venus Love, Pleasure and Laughter and Hermes or Mercury gave them Intelligence or Wisdom.[7]

Hermetic philosophy regarded the 'temporal-spatial' quality as gifts which manifested as inborn talents. According to Adrian Gilbert in *The Magi: a Quest for a Secret Tradition*, 'Self-development at the astral or planetary level meant learning to recognize one's own planetary type, i.e. which 'gods' or lights were predominant in one's own nature, then developing the self-discipline needed to control the way such forces were used, so that they manifested in a positive rather than negative way ... to teach the individual how to rise above this level altogether.' [8]

It seems that the system of planetary types has been a tool in esoteric schools since at least the beginning of the Christian era to provide the student with a compass of impartiality with which to discover his essential character and eventually transcend it. The ancients understood that the true meaning of harmony was to find one's planetary 'note', to sing it loud and clear, and find one's true place in the chorus of humanity.

THE FOURTH WAY: THE LEGACY OF G.I. GURDJIEFF AND P.D. OUSPENSKY

George Ivanovitch Gurdjieff was born in the Caucasus in the second half of the nineteenth century. He spent the early part of his life absorbing the various religious and mystical influences of his homeland and traveling throughout Central Asia, gaining access to some of the oldest and most important esoteric centers. Gurdjieff put all that he had learned in a form digestible for the West, and in this way became one of the great mystics of the modern era. Through sacred dance, music, complex breathing and counting exercises, strenuous physical work, discourse, and quite often scathing verbal abuse and humiliation, he attempted to strip his students of their excess psychological baggage and reveal their true being. He played many roles, always intentionally, and there are so many accounts of who Gurdjieff was, that in a strange way he is as invisible as the real Christ or the real Buddha. In his later years in Paris, literary figures like Katherine Hulme and Margaret Anderson believed they had finally come upon the real Gurdjieff: a deeply religious, kind and compassionate man. Gurdjieff's' legacy has come a long way from Gurdjieff himself.

The name given to Gurdjieff's system is the Fourth Way, and it is a unique combination of the previous three traditional ways to awakening: the way of the fakir, or work on the physical body; the way of the monk, or work on the emotions; the way of the yogi, or work on the mind. The Fourth Way combines these techniques into a new form, and it adapts itself to the culture and the period in history in which it appears, often managing to remain hidden.

Guefjieff's principle student, Peter Demianovitch Ouspensky was born in Moscow, and before he met Gurdjieff had written many books about his investigations into reality, including *The Fourth Dimension,* in 1909, *Tertium Organum* in 1912, and *A New Model of the Universe* in 1931. In the early 1920s he traveled in Europe and the East — India, Ceylon, and Egypt — in his search for knowledge. Upon his return to Russia, however, he was introduced to Gurdjieff and spent the next few years studying with him.

Ouspensky was a remarkable teacher who attempted to reconcile the known scientific principles of his day with esoteric knowledge he had received from his own teacher Gurdjieff. Gurdjieff gave out this knowledge in fragments in the beginning, and it was the task of Ouspensky and others to fill in the gaps, verify the knowledge in their own experience, and put flesh on the majestic scaffolding of Gurdjieff's cosmology and psychology. Many of the principles of Gurdjieff's system coincided with work Ouspensky had been engaged in by himself and the record of his time with Gurdjieff and the main ideas of the system are set forth in *In Search of the Miraculous: Fragments of an Unknown Teaching.*

The Fourth Way was given a new expression and new life when Ouspensky severed connection with Gurdjieff. The reasons for this break will probably always be unclear. No matter what the cause, Ouspensky was able, in his own words, to 'separate the ideas from the man,' and he began teaching the system independently. It is really Ouspensky who is responsible for it becoming a system, a set of blueprints for awakening, and for this he has sometimes attracted undue criticism. Many believe that Gurdjieff's system should remain fluid, and any attempt to systematize such teachings destroys its essence.

Ouspensky's achievements are often overshadowed by the colossal figure of Gurdjieff, and many chronicles of the Work have given much space to the antagonism, whether real or imagined, that existed between the two. I find it easier to understand them as integral roles in the unfolding of a great esoteric plan that perhaps comes from beyond even such importance individuals as Gurdjieff and Ouspensky. It only seems contradictory when judged by our normal standards of success or failure.

The scheme of types outlined here was developed by Rodney Collin, one of the chief pupils of Ouspensky. Collin was a prolific British writer and teacher. He met Ouspensky in the autumn of 1936 and from then on he dedicated all his time to the study of Ouspensky's teaching, and eventually established his own school in Mexico. Collin's best known work, *The Theory of Celestial Influence,* is an ambitious attempt to unite astronomy, physics, chemistry, human physiology, and world history using the principles of the Fourth Way.

Gurdjieff considered astrology to have succumbed to the same fate as all true esoteric knowledge. Arising from a conscious source, it is encountered by the outer circle of humanity in a diluted form, after being altered and added to, according to the various levels of being and understanding. Quite often it is still passed off as esoteric knowledge. When Gurdjieff spoke of astrology and type, he only gave out as much as he knew his students could understand.

However, he spoke of the subject often, and revealed that the study of types requires an objectivity that is not easily won. In order to see types one must know one's own type and be able to 'depart' from it, to separate oneself from it and view it dispassionately.

The ability to observe impartially is perhaps the most significant factor in the study of type. One can only see types from a higher level of consciousness, and the effort required to be consistent in this practice is perhaps beyond the reach of many. For this work, one needs a teacher who can provide the special conditions that are necessary.

There is no clear indication that the types hinted at by Gurdjieff and mentioned periodically by Ouspensky evolved into the system discovered by Rodney Collin, but when

Collin developed his own remarkable expression of Fourth Way cosmology, the planetary types fitted perfectly into the model. What distinguishes Collin's contribution to the study of types is the connection he made between the classical types of antiquity and the work of Dr. Louis Berman, one of the pioneers in the science of endocrinology. Each endocrine gland was seen as the determiner of physiology and character, and the link to the planetary world.

In 1970, another Fourth Way teacher, Robert Burton, began to teach Collin's System of types to a small group of students in southern California. A great deal of information was generated by direct observation, and they found that each type was clearly visible. Late in the 1980's, the fruits of this study of types was put together by Joel Friedlander, a senior student in Burton's School, and published in two editions, called *Body Types*, and *The Enneagram of Essence Types*. Joel has since moved away from the study of the types, but his book stands as one of the best early guides to the body types.

MICHEL GAUQUELIN

Michel Gauquelin is one of the most famous and oft-quoted figures in the study of planetary influences. Born in Paris in 1928, he graduated in Psychology and Statistics from the Sorbonne, and spent over twenty years studying the relationships between cosmological and biological phenomena. He had an avid interest in this field since a young age, but grew critical of traditional approaches to astrology when his own research revealed the faulty foundations of many astrological principles. However, Gauquelin did manage to produce convincing statistical proof that the planets had a definite influence over character. The results of all his studies are available in research documents privately published and a score of books generally available.

Gauquelin's findings lend credence to the likelihood that this knowledge of the seven types is impartial and objective and can be discovered by independent observers, as the types Gauquelin found are identical to the both the ancient archetypes and the planetary types we are studying here.

Using over 27,000 birth times from official registers, Gauquelin's initial investigations seemed to link planets with certain professions, and the results of his exhaustive statistical studies revealed the following patterns:

	High frequency	Average	Low frequency
Mars	Scientists	Politicians	Writers
	Physicians	Actors	Painters
	Athletes	Journalists	Musicians
	Military Men		
	Businessmen		
Jupiter	Military Men	Painters	Scientists
	Politicians	Musicians	Physicians
	Actors	Writers	
	Journalists		
	Playwrights		
Saturn	Scientists	Military Men	Actors
	Physicians	Politicians	Painters
	Journalists		
	Writers		
Moon	Politicians	Scientists	Athletes
	Writers	Physicians	Military Men
	Painters		
	Musicians		
	Journalists		

What distinguishes Gauquelin from other researchers into astrology is that he repeated his studies many times over, always with similar results. With few exceptions, confirmation of his original results continued to emerge.

Gauquelin then turned to the psychological profiles of each of the professions, and eventually made extensive lists of character traits of these professional types, so that the emphasis switched to character rather than profession. Using birth times, and reliable biographical material on these well-known figures, he was able to arrive at a profile of each planetary type. Mars, Saturn, Jupiter and Lunar types were the most clearly evident, but it took much longer to distinguish the Venus type, and, inexplicably, he was unable to distinguish a Mercurial type. One sees obvious mercurial characteristics scattered over the other types.

The traits for each of Gauquelin's types, with an abbreviated list of key words, are shown at the bottom of the page.

The traits for each of the types are virtually the same for the planetary types. Gauquelin repeated his studies in other countries, for example, the USA, and the results were identical. He also sent his findings to other scientists to verify his statistics, which they did.

Despite its criticism from the skeptics associations, the Mars Effect stands as one of the most tenacious genuine anomalies of science.

And so, from the temples of Harran and the pages of the Hermetica, through the teachings of a modern esoteric school, finally to the halls of science, the planetary types have once again found their way into our consciousness, as remarkable maps of the human machine.

There are seven wandering stars which circle at the threshold of Olympus, and among them ever revolves unending Time. The seven are these; night-shining Moon and sullen Kronos (Saturn), and glad Sun, and the Lady of Paphos (Venus), and bold Ares (Mars), and swift-winged Hermes (Mercury), and Zeus (Jupiter), first author of all births, from whom Nature has sprung. To those same stars is assigned the race of men; and we have in us Moon, Zeus, Ares, the Lady of Paphos, Kronos, Sun, and Hermes. Whereof it is our lot to draw in from the aetherial life-breath tears, laughter, wrath, birth, speech, sleep desire. Tears are Kronos; birth is Zeus; speech is Hermes; anger is Ares; the Moon is sleep; Aphrodite is desire; and the Sun is laughter, for by him laugh all mortal minds, and the boundless universe.

TYPES — GLANDULAR AND PLANETARY

The ductless glands and their chemical products, the internal secretions, as dominators of the expression of character, interested me early in my studies of biochemistry. The data of physiology and pathology concerning them as well as the clinical phenomena presented when they were hyperactive of defective seemed to be overwhelming in their multitude and complexity.

Mars	Jupiter	Saturn	Moon	Venus
active	ambitious	formal	simple	affable
quarrelsome	authoritarian	reserved	absent-minded	agreeable
combative	talkative	conscientious	imaginative	ambiguous
fiery	spendthrift	methodical	nonchalant	attractive
courageous	gay	cold	dreaming	benevolent
aggressive	worldly	reflective	rather snobbish	charming
straight- forward	prodigal	wise		kind
self-willed	vain	melancholy		gracious

I proceeded to collect them, to co-ordinate and classify them. At the same time I studied my patients, children, women and men, under all sorts of conditions and circumstances, with the most varied ailments and peculiarities, for signs of underlying deviations of their ductless glands. I became convinced of their fundamental importance as controllers and regulators of that ensemble of forces, attributes, habits and attitudes which is sometimes known as character, individuality or disposition'.

Louis Berman MD, Preface to *The Glands regulating Personality.*

HUMAN ENDOCRINE TYPES

The endocrine system secretes hormones which act on their target cells to regulate the blood concentrations of nutrient molecules, water, salt and other electrolytes. Hormones also play a key role in controlling growth, reproduction and stress adaptation. The hypothalamus and pituitary glands act in concert to maintain homeostasis of all major physical processes.

The glands that concern us in our investigation into types are the pituitary, thyroid, thymus, adrenals and pancreas. In our attempt to examine each of these independent parts, we must not forget that each gland affects every other, and it is difficult to isolate the effect of any single gland. However, we shall attempt to look at the character of each gland to see its unique contribution to the whole. The endocrine system is better pictured as an orchestra, with the tempo, mood and pitch changing, recombining and modulating, all under the watchful eye and keen discrimination of the hypothalamus and pituitary.

The theory of endocrine types maintains that the dominance of one or more glands produces a recognizable body shape and identifiable psychological characteristics that accompany that shape. The order in which the glands blend and combine is as follows:

ANTERIOR PITUITARY—ADRENAL—POSTERIOR PITUITARY—PANCREAS—PARATHYROID—THYROID—ANTERIOR PITUITARY—ADRENAL etc.

The reason for this sequence is demonstrated on the Enneagram. The Enneagram itself demonstrates the implicit internal relationships between any units of a series—in this case the visible planets and their corresponding types—where unity, or 1, is divided by 7. The resulting repeating decimal sequence is well known to mathematicians: .142857. The planets are arranged clockwise around the outside of the circle in the order of their periods of revolution, beginning with the Moon as 1.

Each of us has all glands operating, naturally, but the over-secretion or dominance of certain glands determines our type' Planetary type means a dominance of characteristics of two consecutive glands in the above order with one perhaps exerting a stronger influence.

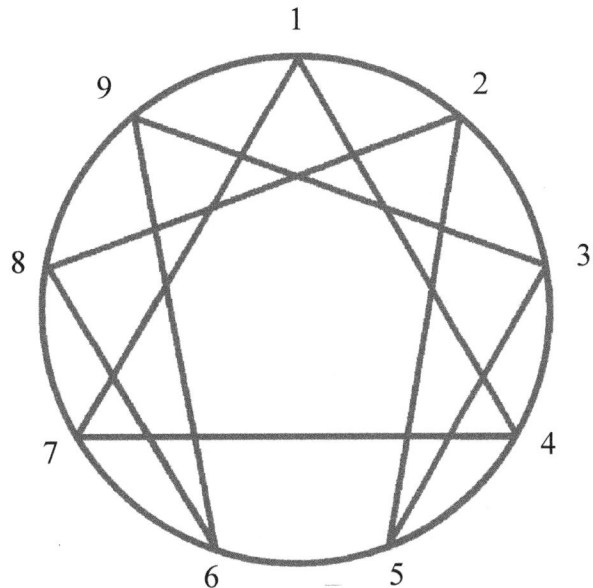

ACTIVE/PASSIVE—POSITIVE/NEGATIVE

Each type is largely determined by the combinations of the principles of active/passive and positive/negative. Active means initiating, giving direction, and controlling. Passive can mean receptive, obedient, reliable, supportive or indigent. Positive means generally optimistic and encouraging, someone who disregards the unpleasant and difficult. A negative type is more skeptical, careful, critical, more easily dissatisfied. Positive types can be a joy to be with or hopelessly naive. Negative types can be discriminating or simply a misery guts.

The descriptions of the endocrine types [4] that follow must be regarded as archetypal, as we look at each gland in isolation. There is no such thing as a pure type, except in myth, legends and fairy tales. (These descriptions are also significantly abbreviated; for more detailed descriptions, consult my book, Planetary Types.)

THE SEVEN BASIC TYPES

The descriptions that follow are the fundamental designs, and as we come to recognize the basic features, we will be able to later discern the variations on each theme. The types that exist in the real world are usually combinations of the classical types described earlier. The seven basic types are:

SATURNINE

MARTIAL

JOVIAL

LUNAR

VENUSIAN

MERCURIAL

SOLAR

To be more precise, most people are a blending of characteristics of two consecutive types, such as Mercury/Saturn, Mars/Jovial, etc. The Solar type is the hardest to see, and often one can only do this after becoming thoroughly familiar with the basic six. Solar combines with all other types, often altering basic features, and perhaps eclipsing others. So it is possible to have: Solar/Saturn/Mars or Solar/Lunar/Venusian or Solar/Mars/Jovial. A Solar/Saturn will not be as 'heavy' as a pure Saturn, a Solar/Mars will have a souped-up sensibility, a Solar/Lunar will not be as 'dark' as a pure Lunar, etc.

The physical features that follow should not be taken as accurate point-by-point descriptions of each type, but rather as describing parameters of bodily proportions, coloring and other physical features.

Each type has its own unique dominant psychological feature, which defines that type. In almost every case, this feature has both a dark and light side, giving each type their chief strength and their chief weakness.

ANTERIOR PITUITARY GLAND

Located at the base of the cortex, the anterior pituitary gland is the controller, orchestrator and regulator of the endocrine system. Through constant monitoring and feedback, it maintains the balance (homeostasis) of most major bodily functions. Responsible chiefly for the processes of general growth, bone development, and mental function, it also stimulates testosterone and sperm production and adrenal secretion.

SATURNINE/ANTERIOR PITUITARY TYPE—Active/Positive

Physical shape:

The classic Saturn is the tallest of all types, with long bones, high cheek-bones, a strong jaw, prominent Adam's apple and high forehead. They tend towards an upright posture with straight shoulders and prominent muscles. They often have large feet, long noses and fingers.

Character:

CAUTIOUS—COMPOSED—COLD   —FRUGAL   —IMPARTIAL—METHODICAL—MODEST—PATIENT—PATERNAL—SILENT   —SOLITARY—SOMBRE—STABLE—TOLERANT—

UNEMOTIONAL—WISE

Chief Weakness: Dominance—the desire to produce order.

Chief Strength: Leadership, responsibility

Abraham Lincoln, Vanessa Redgrave, Max von Sydow, Rene Russo, Ian McKellen, Anna Gunn, Sam Elliot.

ADRENALS

The adrenal glands produce steroids that influence mineral balance, (electrolyte) glucose, protein and lipid metabolism, and sex hormones identical or similar to those produced by the gonads. Under fear or stress it triggers a surge of adreno-medullary-catecholamine release, flooding the circulation with up to 300 times the normal concentration of epinephrine, to prepare the body for meeting with emergency or stressful situations.

ADRENAL/MARTIAL TYPE—Active/Negative

Physical shape:

The pure Martial is small, muscular, robust and strongly built. They often have a short, thick neck on rounded but powerful shoulders and a large chest, especially Mars/Jovial. They have a strong jaw-line and forceful chin and often a pale or ruddy or freckled complexion. The hair is often red or coarse, or wavy like steel wool. The blonde, blue-eyed 'Aryan' archetype is also Martial.

Character:

ADVENTUROUS—AGGRESSIVE—ARROGANT—BELLIGERENT—BLUNT—BOLD—COMPETITIVE—CRITICAL—COURAGEOUS—DESTRUCTIVE—IMPULSIVE—PASSIONATE—RESILIENT—RECKLESS—TOUGH

Chief Weakness: Aggression, Destructiveness

Chief Strength: Courage, Directness,

George S. Patton, Sissy Spacek, Ed Harris,

Margaret Thatcher, Boris Becker, Jane Fonda, Russell Crowe, Susan Sarandon.

POSTERIOR PITUITARY

The posterior pituitary lobe produces the hormones essential for maintaining water balance and milk production. It secretes vasopressin, responsible for enhancing water retention in the kidneys, and contributing to blood vessel contraction; and oxytocin, which stimulates contraction of the smooth uterine muscles during childbirth, and promotes ejection of milk from the mammary glands.

JOVIAL/POSTERIOR PITUITARY TYPE—Positive/Passive

Physical Shape:

Pure Jovials have a large frame and a big waist on top of thin legs. They have large, round heads with a full chin. The men often have thick, bushy eyebrows and are prone to baldness. Both sexes have poor eyesight and more Jovials wear glasses than any other type.

Character:

BENEVOLENT—BOASTFUL—CREATIVE—DRAMATIC—EXTRAVAGANT—FLAMBOYANT—GENEROUS—GREGARIOUS—MATERNAL—OPTIMISTIC—OVER-INDULGENT—PROFOUND—PROUD—POMPOUS—REFINED

Chief Weakness: Vanity

Chief Strength: Harmonizing influence

Winston Churchill, Camryn Mannheim, Burl Ives, Oprah Winfrey, Mikhail Gorbachev, Patricia Routledge, the Dalai Lama, Clive James.

PANCREAS

The pancreas secretes a watery alkaline solution and digestive enzymes into the digestive tract, and glucogen and insulin. Insulin regulates carbohydrate, fat and protein metabolism, lowers blood glucose, fatty acid and amino acid levels and promotes their storage. It also facilitates glucose transport into most cells and the absorption of fat into the lymph system and adipose tissue.

LUNAR/PANCREAS TYPE—Passive/Negative

Physical shape:

The classic Lunar is small with weak musculature and soft flesh. Their complexion is often very pale and the chin is often receding and nearly always small in proportion to the rest of the face. The nose is short or turned up and the mouth is small or puckered. The hair is either brown, light brown or jet black, but there are many blonde Lunars, perhaps more women than men. Otherwise the hair is very fine, straggly or 'mousy.'

The women often have soft and rounded features, and a very feminine doe-eyed beauty. Many Lunars appear 'unfinished,' as a child's body does.

Character:

ALOOF—COOL—DETERMINED—ECCENTRIC—LOYAL—MOODY—ORDERLY—PESSIMISTIC—PRACTICAL—SECRETIVE—SHY—SOLITARY—STUBBORN—SUSPICIOUS—TIMID—UNCOMMUNICATIVE—WILFUL

Chief Weakness: Willfulness

Chief Strength: Loyalty, determination

Woody Allen, Emily Dickinson, Edgar Cayce, Christina Ricci, Andy Kaufmann, Joyce Carol Oates,

PARATHYROIDS

The parathyroids are four small glands on the back of the thyroid, one in each corner. Parathyroid hormone is the principle regulator of CA2+ (calcium) metabolism, which plays an important role in neuro-muscular activity. Even minor variations in concentrations of CA2+ can have a profound and immediate effect on the sensibility of excitable tissue. A fall in free CA2+ results in over-excitability of nerves and muscles. Clinical PTH hyper-secretion leads to Hypercalcemia, resulting in muscle weakness, decreased alertness, poor memory and depression.

VENUSIAN/PARATHYROID TYPE—Passive/Positive

Physical Shape:

The pure Venusian has gracefully rounded, shapely or well-balanced features. They can also have a soft, rubenesque voluptuousness, with abundant and wavy hair, nearly always black or dark brown. They have a long and shapely neck, a round or oval face, finely proportioned with few sharp edges, appealing almond-shaped eyes and often full red lips. The Venusian can also grow quite large, and they tend towards the classic pear shape ending in thick ankles.

Character:

ACCEPTING—AFFECTIONATE—CHARMING—CONSIDERATE—EMPATHIC—INDECISIVE—LAZY—NURTURING—OVER-INDULGENT—SENSUAL—SLOW—SYMPATHETIC—UNTIDY—VAGUE—

Chief Weakness: Non-existence

Chief Strength: Nurturing

Mama Cass Elliot, Brian Wilson, Monica Lewinsky, Adam Arkin, Jackie Onassis, George Clooney.

THYROID

The thyroid is a bow-tie shaped gland situated just below the larynx and produces hormones that regulate the overall basal metabolic rate. Thyroid hormone is dependent on iodine, which serves no other purpose in the body. It is also important for growth and normal development and function of the nervous system.

MERCURIAL/THYROID TYPE—Active/Negative

Physical shape:

The classic Mercurial type is short, wiry, and compact. The hair is medium-fair or dark; the face is angular, often with a long or pointed chin.

Some Mercurials have large, bulging eyes, while others have small and beady eyes. They are tidy and fastidious and it shows in their grooming; the men with facial hair nearly always opt for goatee beards, and thin moustaches.

Character:

ADAPTABLE—AGILE—ARGUMENTATIVE—BOASTFUL—CRITICAL—DEXTEROUS—ELOQUENT—FAST—FASTIDIOUS—IMPATIENT—INVENTIVE—MANIPULATIVE—OBSESSIVE—PERSUASIVE—RESTLESS—SHALLOW—VAIN—VOLATILE —WITTY

Chief Weakness: Power (manipulative), Vanity

Chief Strength: Inventiveness, ingenuity

Robert Downey jnr, Fran Drescher, Michael Keaton, Kristin Scott-Thomas, Jim Carrey, Sandra Bullock, John Cusack, Eva Longoria.

THYMUS

The thymus is a lymphoid tissue with some endocrine function located midline within the chest cavity above the heart in the space between the lungs. It produces activated T-lymphocytes, which directly attack unwanted cells. Secretion of thymosin decreases after about 30 to 40 years of age. The thymus gland physically shrinks when the organism is exposed to shock or trauma, and production of immunities is severely affected.

THYMUS/SOLAR TYPE—Active/Positive

Physical shape:

When studying Solars it must be remembered that their qualities are often overlaid on those of other types, but if you are fortunate enough to meet a pure Solar, you will not forget them easily. The classic type is small, thin and waif-like, with a light, supple, childlike body, a slender waist, little body hair, and the women usually have small breasts. They are distinctly androgynous with transparent, 'milk and roses' skin, delicate features and delicate health. Solars are frail, thin-boned and have lots of nervous energy which they tend to spend it all in a rush.

Character:

ARTISTIC—CHEERFUL—CHILDLIKE—CREATIVE—EXCITABLE—ENDEARING—FRAGILE—GULLIBLE—INDISCRIMINATE—IMAGINATIVE—IMPRACTICAL—NAIVE—OPTIMISTIC—SELF-DESTRUCTIVE—SPONTANEOUS

Chief Weakness: Naiveté

Chief Strength: Imagination

Michael Jackson, Kylie Minogue, Paris Hilton, Prince, Bjork, Judy Garland, Mozart, Edith Piaf.

NOTES

Excerpt XXVII: an extract from 'The Discourse of Isis to Horus' from the Stobeaus in Hermetica.

1. *The Glands Regulating Personality* by Louis Berman p.235.
2. *The Case for Astrology* Viking Press 1973, p. 43
3. *The Origins of Consciousness in the Breakdown of the Bicameral Mind* Houghton Mifflin Co Boston 1976 p 74
4. *Hermetica* translated by Walter Scott Solos Press 1998 Appendix pp. 242-248
5. *Occidental Mythology* Penguin NY 1991 p. 255
6. Hermetica p. 49
7. Ibid p.182
8. The Magi: a Quest for a Secret Tradition, Bloomsbury 1999 p. 60

This article has been excerpted from the author's recently-published book, *Planetary Types: The Science of Celestial Influence*, available from Bardic Press. It also contains a marriage of contemporary science and ancient harmonic science to propose a plausible model for the mechanism of celestial influence. It also proposes statistical test to verify the theory of planetary types. To find out more, download the free introduction, or to purchase the book, go to www.planetarytypes.com.

Bill Darlison

So You Think You're Alive Then?

As long as you do not know
How to die and come to life again,
You are but a sorry traveller
On this dark earth.

Goethe

At Easter time every year, a poster appears on Dublin trains advertising a number of screenings of a video with the title 'The Evidence for the Resurrection'. I've always resisted the temptation to attend because I am familiar enough with the arguments they are likely to bring forward, and since I've never found them convincing when I've encountered them in print, I'm hardly likely to be impressed by them in a slick and simplified video version. How anyone thinks it possible to provide, in the total absence of any physical evidence, proof of *any* event in the past, let alone one as inherently implausible as the resurrection of a person from physical death, defeats me, but it is a constant preoccupation of a certain type of Christian outlook, which seems incapable of finding any meaning in these stories unless they can be understood as having a literal, factual, historical basis.

It is, of course, the very implausibility of the story that the argument will exploit: it must have occurred, they will say, because without it the history of Christianity is unintelligible. Why would the early Christians have taken as the central tenet of their religion an event so unlikely, so unprecedented, if it did not happen? And even more pertinently: why would Christians have been prepared to suffer persecution and martyrdom over something which was explicable as either pious fiction or deceptive fabrication?

Such has been the argument of those who uphold the literal truth of the resurrection stories from time immemorial, and while it might have carried some weight in the past, we have every reason to be suspicious of it today. Contemporary events have shown us, again and again, that religious movements do not begin and do not grow because individual devotees assess historical and theological evidence dispassionately. Only a few years ago, apparently intelligent people, members of the so-called Solar Temple, committed suicide, confident that a space-ship was waiting for them behind the Hale-Bopp comet; Waco and Jonestown are further examples of the non-rational nature of religious commitment, and if such things can happen under our noses there is no reason to suppose that they couldn't happen in less rationally orientated times than our own. Faith precedes understanding, commitment comes before intellectual conviction. As the ancients used to say, *fides quaerens intellectum*, faith goes looking for a rational basis for itself some time after its irrational tenets have been assimilated and accepted at a deeper level than the purely intellectual.

One aspect of the crucifixion and resurrection narratives that any apologist for their historical basis has to address is the significant number of irreconcilable contradictions that the four accounts contain. For example, Matthew, Mark and Luke tell us that the crucifixion of Jesus took place on the day of the Passover; John says that it was the *day of preparation* for the Passover, i.e. the day before. Both are extremely unlikely, since it is almost unthinkable that the normally prudent Romans would execute a Jewish criminal, particularly one who was associated with Messianic expectations, at a time when Jerusalem would be bursting with pilgrims from around the known world and anything might provoke a riot. But, in any case, by the simple laws of logic, both cannot be right.

And was Jesus crucified at nine in the morning as Mark reports, or at midday as John tells us? Luke's Gospel tells us that one of the two thieves who were executed with Jesus repented, an act that is flatly contradicted by Matthew who says that both thieves taunted him to the end. Then there's the story of the resurrection itself. Did a man in a white robe greet the early visitors to the tomb (as Mark tells us), or was it an angel (Matthew) or two angels (Luke)? And how come Mark, Luke and John missed the earthquake and the opening of the graves which resulted in numerous people, previously dead, walking about the streets of Jerusalem where, according to Matthew at least, they were seen by many? This is hardly a detail that one could overlook.

These are just a few of the numerous historical implausibilities and logical contradictions with which the four Gospels abound, and a whole industry of scholarship has grown up around the attempt to explain or to explain away the inconsistencies and to produce a smooth, uniform account acceptable to even the most rigorous intellectual scrutiny. Needless to say, it has invariably failed and the historical credibility of these stories is only maintained, rather dishonestly, I feel, by the vested interests of scholars who are drawn, in the main, from the ranks of the clergy, and by the credulity and continuing ignorance of everyone else who, while professing a belief in the divine inspiration of the Bible, rarely read it with critical intelligence even if they bother to read it at all.

Of course, we religious liberals are different. We dispatched these stories to the trash-can a long time ago. They offend our reason and our perfectly sensible demand that some kind of real evidence should support any statement before it commands our assent as history. Consequently, in liberal churches up and down Britain and America, the theme this Easter will not be the resurrection of Jesus, but the springtime resurrection of the earth. While we might have some considerable sympathy with this point of view — at least it has more intellectual integrity than the self-deluding, historical obsession of much of Christendom — we can only uphold it by dismissing the stories of the crucifixion and resurrection of Jesus as unimportant.

There is a third way of approaching these stories, however, which does not demand that we accept them as historically true or that we reject them as irrelevant. This third approach (which is really only a second approach, since the other two are both products of what Rudolf Steiner calls 'the dialectical mind' which, he rightly says, can make nothing of the Gospels except to reduce them to historical or ethical propositions), is to see them as stories which transcend the literal and historical categories they have been placed in by both sides of the polarised debate, and which carry for us a profound spiritual meaning. What is remarkable about this approach is its antiquity. The Jews have always held that the scriptures have meaning on at least four different levels, and the great Jewish writer, Philo of Alexandria, who was virtually a contemporary of Jesus, wrote an allegorical interpretation of the Exodus story which is still convincing two millennia on. Another Alexandrian — Alexandria was a centre of mystical thinking for centuries — Origen, writing in the third Christian century, has this to say about the problematic passages in the Bible as a whole and in the Gospels in particular.

(Sometimes) impossibilities are recorded for the sake of the more skilful and inquisitive, in order that they may give themselves to the toil of investigating what is written, and thus attain to a becoming conviction of the manner in which a meaning worthy of God must be sought out in such subjects…….He (the Holy Spirit) did the same thing both with the evangelists and the apostles, - as even these do not contain throughout a pure history of events, which are interwoven indeed according to the letter, *but which did not actually occur.*

The example Origen gives is from the very first chapter of the Book of Genesis which tells us that God created light on the first day of creation, but that the sun, moon and stars didn't appear until later in the week. A curious anomaly, introduced deliberately, says Origen, so that we won't be tempted to take it literally, so that we will be forced to seek a deeper meaning to the text than the one which immediately suggests itself. Would that the opponents of Copernicus and Darwin had paid more attention when studying their Patristic theology!

What, then, if we take Origen's advice and look behind their historical inexactitudes, contradictions, and implausibilities, can the crucifixion and resurrection stories teach us? Far more than I can hope to cover in what remains of this sermon, and, in a sense, far more than I could ever hope to cover because the only really valuable discoveries that can be made about such stories are those that the individual makes for herself. I will just say, however, that, in my opinion, these stories are not just an unfortunate narrative accompaniment to the sublime ethical teaching of Jesus (as they are often viewed in liberal theological circles). They are an integral part of the whole gospel message. The Christian Gospel is not primarily concerned with history or with ethics; it is concerned with new life, rebirth, authentic living, which is not to be attained by simply believing the facts or by keeping the rules. One has to be born again, the new out of the old, to a radically different kind of life which does not just require the reform of the old carnal self, but its destruction. The Christian myth tells us — as all the great religious myths tell us in one way or another — that we are asleep and that we cannot begin to live effectively and completely until we wake up. According to the Roman writer, Seneca, a decrepit and dishevelled member of Caesar's guard came to the Emperor and asked for permission to kill himself. Caesar

looked at him and said with a smile: 'So, you think you're alive then?'

And this is the question that the Gospels in their entirety put to us: 'So you think you're alive then?' And then they tell us to think again. You will never be truly alive, they say, until you reject the life of comfort and distraction that you so slavishly and so unthinkingly pursue at the behest of your money-driven, mad society; you will never be truly alive until you stop associating ease of life with success in life, and until you stop valuing respectability above authenticity; you will never be truly alive until you become teachable again like a little child; you will never be truly alive until you embrace the Way of the Cross, the painful destruction of the ego and its appetites, and emerge anew, alive, awake, free, transformed, the old self crucified and the Christ spirit born within you.

This, to me, is the message of the Gospel narrative, and the crucifixion and resurrection accounts are not just irrelevant addenda, they are the culmination of a consistent pattern of imagery which describes for the imagination not just a process that may or may not have occurred in the life of one man, but one which must occur in the life of each one of us, if we are to attain that newness of life which is the only hope for our individual and social salvation.

True religion, far from being the opium of the people, lulling us back into sleep, should be the adrenalin urging us into life. And far from asking us, passively, to believe in the historical validity of the resurrection it should be urging us, actively, to live its existential reality. A far harder task, indeed, but, we are assured, the most worthwhile task we can ever undertake.

Interview with April DeConick

April De Conick is the Isla Carroll and Percy E. Turner Professor of Biblical Studies at Rice University. An adventurous and iconoclastic scholar, she was primarily responsible for revising the understanding of the Gospel of Judas. Her work has focused on mysticism in early Christianity and Judaism and she has argued that the *Gospel of Thomas* contains a very early core, which she has reconstructed.

MC: With us today we have April DeConick to discuss with us the mysticism and Gnosticism of the Gospel of John, and hopefully a little bit more. How are you doing today, April?

AD: Very good. Glad to be with you today.

MC: Obviously, most ancient gospels weren't written for the entire Greco-Roman world — there's no mass-market manner as so many Christians believe, it was a different time. As you and other scholars point out, gospels and letters were written for an immediate community. Could you tell us your views about the Johannine community, where the Gospel of John originated?

AD: These documents, we understand them to be community documents in that they are reflecting particular traditions that have developed in a geographical location among a community of believers over a period of time, and the traditions tend to change, reflecting the crises and thinking of this particular group of Christians. In the case of the Gospel of John, it's actually difficult to locate its provenance. There are couple of possibilities. Traditionally, it's understood to be a gospel from Asia Minor, Ephesus is its origin, and one of the reasons that scholars have thought this is that there is a heavy polemic in the text against Jon the Baptist, and we learn from Paul and from Acts that in Ephesus there were apparently some believers who had been baptized with the baptism of John, and so this is one of the reasons that it's placed in Ephesus. One of the difficulties with this is that we also learn from Acts that Apollos is the one who had been the leader of that, and he came from Egypt, where he appears to have learned this baptism of John. So, this gospel could just as likely have originated in Alexandria, perhaps, and certainly this gospel has a lot of affinity with later Alexandrine theology. Other scholars have been placing it in Syria, so it's difficult to know. Some of the Syrian traditions reflect Johannine thought as well. So, three possibilities for you.

MC: So the Johannine and the Thomasine community might have lived side by side the whole time.

AD: They very well could have been living close, and the other thing to keep in mind is that there's a trade route from East Syria, from Edessa, that goes down into Alexandria, so we know that texts were passing back and forth between the Alexandrine community of Christians and the Syrian community of Christians and so, if traditions that originated in both of these cities, and these areas, would have been passing back and forth information and ideas and so forth, and so we find a lot of similar developments in theology between Alexandria and Syria.

MC: And also, a lot of people have said that the Gospel of John is the most anti-Jewish of all the gospels, so is it safe to say that this community was very unhappy with Jerusalem at the time or period?

AD: I think it's more complicated than that. Here we've got Christianity when it's moving into the first century and the beginning of the second century begins to show signs of anti-Semitism, and this is one of the real problems in early Christian studies, is why this was happening. One of the things that was happening is that the Christians were beginning to understand themselves as a group separate from the Jews, and once they began to do this, there was a shift to demonize the Jews, and so we see this happening in the texts, like I said which were written at the end of the first century and beginning of the second century when this was really starting, which would be the gospel, would be a good example of that.

MC: Of course by then there was no Temple, so …

AD: Right. You've got really two competing groups. The Jews are having to redefine their religion without a Temple, and the Christians are trying to redefine their religion without a Temple as well, because they came out of the Jewish tradition, that's what they were, and they were finding at the time that the Jews were the ones who were not converting to their form of

Judaism, and so you have a competition going on as well, and Christianity lost that battle in terms of Judaism. They became their own thing, they became something else, they self-defined as different from the Jews, and once that happened, that's when you start seeing the anti-Semitism really rearing its head.

MC: And are there any theories about the Gospel of John having Samaritan origins? Could that be the reason they're so polemical?

AD: There is material in the Gospel of John that is highly suggestive that there were Samaritans who were converting to this community at one time. The Samaritans thought very highly of Moses, Moses was a central figure, so you see Jesus in the Gospel of John being compared to Moses, I'm thinking about chapter six, you know, where he's the one who has the staff and he's the one who gives the bread, breaks? His body and so forth, he's the manna. You get a lot of comparisons with Moses. In the text you get of course the Samaritan woman at the well, who he gives the water to because she recognizes him as the great prophet… There is something to that.

24:03

MC: You give ample evidence that Judaism already had strong mystical components long before Christianity, based on a the large body of apocrypha that you give evidence of in your book, *Voices of the Mystics*. It's usually with Enoch, Moses, Ezekiel, traveling up to heaven, to the holy of holies. I guess they decided, instead of waiting for God to come talk to us, we're going to go to him. So did this eventually transfer to the Johannine and other Christian mystics or eschatological communities, with Jesus basically becoming the mystagogue imparting his visions of places that only he had seen?

AD: I think that it was happening within these Christian traditions. They certainly, the early Christian tradition, what I studied of it, was certainly centred on mysticism, and they were basically Jewish mystics, if you look at all the evidence in terms of their emphasis on the visions they were having, revelations that they were having, the notion that the spirit of God has been released and is among them, within them, transforming their lives. All of this is talk that other Jews were using in terms of, a kind of precursor of what we call Merkavah mysticism, which is a form of Jewish mysticism that is certainly around by the third century, where you have actually devotees attempting to make this very dangerous journey through the heavens, in order to stand up like an angel, to be transformed into an angel, before God's throne. And maybe even to take a peek and glance a vision of him if they can. We have a precursor of this activity going on even at Qumran, it looks like we have knowledge of this in our early Christian materials as well. So I think that some of our texts are certainly understanding Jesus in these terms, and some have come to impart these mysteries to the faithful.

MC: And the question, April, would be, how much did the pagan Hellenistic mystic view influence it? Are we looking at a fusion of Judaism and the Hellenistic viewpoint in the Gospel of John?

AD: Oh, I would think so. I think you do have a fusion. It's really hard to separate strands sometimes, and to say well, this came from here and this came from here. If you think of living within a culture, living within a religion in a time period, it's not like you're taking something from here and taking something from there and fusing it together, it's more like you just exist within this world of thoughts and ideas, and they're all part of you, and then we have going on in terms of the community associated with the Gospel of John, with the *Gospel of Thomas*, they're part of this world view of Jewish mysticism, but they're also very familiar with the Hellenistic mystery religions, and the sort of initiation processes that they were using in those mystery religions, and I think that in fact the Eucharist ceremony as it develops in terms of Paul and later, is probably highly influenced by the Greek mystery religions, especially in terms of eating the body and drinking the blood, which is something that is not going to happen solely within a Jewish community.

MC: That's very true, like we talked before the interview, and Hans Jonas, you have to put yourself in the mindset of what these people believe in, of course. Plato would be in the mindset for any Jew in the Diaspora.

AD: Exactly, and your best friend is initiated into the Eleusinian mysteries, you know. And the other one goes to the temple of Isis, and so on and so forth. You have this wide variety of ideas and experiences that are just part of your culture. And in order to really understand these ancient texts, my opinion is we really have to get back into the minds of the ancient people as much as we can and try to put on their worldview. Not an easy thing to do

in order to really understand these ancient texts, my opinion is we really have to get back into the minds of the ancient people as much as we can

MC: And also, April, you spend a whole chapter on Johannine polemics against vision mysticism. What exactly is vision mysticism, and what is the evidence of this, even though it appears the Gospel of John has strong mystic elements.

AD: Right, right. It's really fascinating. What you have going on with the Johannine community is a group of people who are certainly inspired by mysticism, maybe even some hermetic practices, but they also are very concerned about in some way controlling those. If you can imagine a community in which people are trying to have visions, that might get out of control at some point. Someone might have a vision or revelation that says, maybe the leader of our community, we should kick him out because he's not the right one. I'm the right one. The sort of activity that is internal activity like this can't really be controlled, it's very dangerous for a community. So what you have in the Gospel of John is an attempt to put some control on the mysticism, I think. They are not advocating, I'm going to take you through the initiation ritual and we going to ascend up to the Merkavah and we're going to have a vision of God. They're actually saying in this text that the only one who's ever seen God is Jesus. And that in fact that door to heaven is closed. And so, the reason that it's closed, they say, is that God came down to earth as Jesus, so his manifestation actually walked around on earth and so the vision that people had was of Jesus on earth and that vision was ultimately transforming. So I think they began with that sort of understanding of mysticism, with which they were trying to control visions that were maybe getting out of hand. Then it goes to the next step and you can hear people in the community saying, yeah, but what about us! We didn't get to see him walking around, shouldn't we be getting to heaven to see him. And the response to that is, well, no. In his absence he sent down the spirit, the paraclete, and that spirit now lives among us, and supplies us with that experience of the divine right here on earth. So there's still a mysticism involved here, but it no longer is, if you will, a flight to heaven to have a vision sort of mysticism, but it's a God's spirit has come down, has entered the community, has entered us in our baptismal practice probably, here, also in our Eucharist practices, we're eating the divine body between us, they've moved in that direction in terms of encountering the divine in the immediate.

MC: So basically, they said 'have your vision, but Jesus is still the gatekeeper, the ultimate gatekeeper.'

AD: Well, I think they're even saying, don't worry about the vision. Don't have the vision, that's not what is important. What is important is that you're part of our church, you have the Holy Spirit and that is the divine encounter.

MC: Well, I wish I could record this for every time somebody quotes me John 3:14. The real context of 'I am the way to the Father'

AD: Right. That's it right there. That is exactly the whole thesis of that gospel. That Jesus, as

the manifestation of God has come to earth. And then he sent his spirit, which is again his manifestation after his death. And that is the way to God, by getting that spirit in you. And it was happening for the Johannine community, as for other Christians. This is very much what Paul is saying as well, in Romans, it happens by the spirit entering you in baptism, and Eucharist.

MC: And is this what you would call in your book, 'faith mysticism'?

AD: It is, and I would really encapsulate it well in chapter 20, you know with Thomass in which he says, blessed are those who have not seen and yet believe. To believe is not faith as in terms of dogma or doctrine, it has more to do with a faithful encounter with God, an experience of God through, as they say in the Gospel of John, through the paraclete living among them as lovingkindness.

MC: He returns with a new body and Mary will not touch him. How do you read that famous scene?

AD: That's a tough scene and I don't really have a good explanation for that phrase not touching me, for I have not come to my Father. I don't know, what ideas do you have? You don't have any?

MC: [laughter] I would say it definitely plays into the Gnostic docetic view.

AD: This is the thing though, he's a resurrected being. This is not the same physical body that he had when he was walking around among them. This is an altered body that, the text says, can now walk through doors and so I don't read the scene in chapter 20 where Thomas is supposedly touching him as an attempt at touching the flesh. Jesus is an angelic body at this point, so there's something else going on here that I haven't quite sorted out yet.

MC: Well, I just see it simply as the old Gnostic view that Jesus has now taken off clothes and now he has his real form, but ... I guess that's how a lot of Gnostics probably saw it. But April, talking about the paraclete, it's pretty safe to say the paraclete was a spirit because I know some

Gnostics thought the Paraclete was Paul, and obviously Muslims think that the paraclete was Muhammad, but it's safe to say he was the Holy Spirit.

AD: Well, actually, you can kind of go both directions in this. The paraclete is the Holy Spirit, it's some sort of angelic figure, and it was believed to possess people. So Jesus was a paraclete, and he talks about sending another paraclete, and in the second century you have Montanus who claims that he's the paraclete. The holy spirit has come and descended on him, so he's the other paraclete that Jesus talked about. So you have Mani making some similar claims in the third century, and so forth. So it's this cyclic idea you have in Judaism of the coming of a prophet who's been blessed by the spirit, and the paraclete is just the Johannine name for that.

MC: What are some of the Gnostic echoes we find in the Gospel of John, or at least, why was it so popular with some of the groups like the Valentinians and the Cathars, you know, was it Heracleon who wrote a whole thing on the Gospel of John, and Theodotus on the Gospel of John…

AD: The Gospel of John was by far the favourite Gnostic gospel. It so surprised me that it actually made it into the canon and I think the only reason it did is because Irenaeus loved it and wasn't going to let the Gnostics have it.

MC: [laughing] He just wasn't going to let them have anything.

AD: He wasn't going to let them have the Gospel of John. You know, this text, the more that I read it as scholar, the more I study, the text becomes more and more perplexing to me. It I think is a gospel that is coming out of a community that is going to split in the beginning of the second century. And part of the split is going to towards what we call orthodox or apostolic Christianity and the other part of this community is going

the Gospel of John was by far the favourite Gnostic gospel... Irenaeus loved it and wasn't going to let the Gnostics have it

to go to the Valentinian tradition. So the gospel already has its origins within a group that is going to become a Gnostic group eventually. I wouldn't quite call it proto-Gnosticism, but it certainly is a text that's beginning to think about issues along the lines that at least the Valentinians and maybe some other Gnostics were already thinking about these issues. Extremely important to the Gnostic viewpoint was the idea that the soul had fallen into the material realm and was suffering here. So the prologue in the Gospel of John in many ways is understood to be a representative of that mythology. It's not that the Gnostics were the only ones talking about this, certainly not. The orthodox Christians were also interested in this idea, but this becomes a major theme of the Gnostics and they love the Gospel of John because of that and they like to talk about the prologue quite a bit, in their own writings. And there are a lot of hymns in the Gnostic literature about this descent of the soul that look very similar to what we have going on in the Gospel of John. So that is a very good example. The other thing about this text is that it talks about the ruler of this world, and the ruler of this world the text understands to be an evil figure, and the orthodox or apostolic Christians understand that to be Satan, but the Gnostic Christians are of course equating that with the demiurge figure, the craftsman God, who they also in some cases associate with Satan. So this text has these real interesting ideas in it that the Gnostics developed.

MC: Speaking of the famous introduction to the Gospel of John, a beautidul, beautiful piece, that has been a source of debate for a long time. Some scholars have believed it was tacked on from another tradition, perhaps Philonic. What are your views on it?

AD: I don't think it's tacked on from another tradition, and the reason I don't is that the themes that that hymn has in it are picked up by the author of the Gospel of John throughout the text. And so the ideas are woven into the text itself, into the body of the gospel. But it's certainly a hymn. It was probably a hymn that the community was performing, perhaps in their baptismal ceremony or when they got together and partook of the Eucharist, but it certainly is some kind of a hymn. It is perhaps based on — scholars have been very interested in following the traditions of Sophia, to explain that hymn, that the Logos there is some kind of Sophia figure who's come to earth... There is some difficulty in that Sophia isn't really ever God exactly, and she also doesn't ever really incarnate as a human being, she possesses human beings. So there's so me trouble with that and it's probably more likely again that you have a blending of traditions, and the Sophia traditions are behind that and you also have behind that the tradition of God's name. His name was actually personified as a being. His name, the Yahweh name was him, and they developed the tradition of the angel of the name, the angel who bares his name, and who basically functions as God, as a manifestation of God, and this I think can explain the notion that the Logos was God because he bore God's name and Jesus actually in the Gospel of John actually talks of having God's name and possessing his name. So I think more work needs to be done in that area, but it certainly is a beautiful hymn that became very important to the Gnostics.

MC: I'm sure that they went gaga over the whole concept of the Logos as well as the Alexandrian Jews, Stoics and other pagans, they just loved the whole concept of the Logos that wasn't found in Christianity. Another question, April: who do you think the mysterious beloved disciple was? I know, a loaded question.

AD: That is really loaded. I actually think it's Lazarus. So there's my short answer.

MC: I know, that's what I've always thought too.

AD: The text actually understands Lazarus as the disciple whom Jesus loves and weeps for, and we only get the switch into this language of the disciple whom Jesus loves without a name after Lazarus has been introduced as the one that Jesus loves in the narrative, and after Jesus raises him from the dead and he becomes basically a resurrected being walking on earth. And so, chapter 21 can only be explained as the death of Lazrus, Lazarus the beloved disciple. In other words, the community was pretty damn sure that Lazarus was raised from the dead and would not die, and when he died it caused a crisis in the community. What is going on? Jesus raised him from the dead. He wasn't supposed to die. And so the need then to tack on chapter 21 in order to explain that Jesus really didn't say that he wasn't going to die. That's my longer explanation. I think it's Lazarus, according to the narrative of the text.

MC: Have you heard of a theory saying that the scene with Jesus raising Lazarus and the two Marys mourning over the tomb is a reconstruction of Horus raising Osiris with Isis and Nefertiti mourning over the tomb. Have you heard that theory?

AD: No, but certainly all of our texts are in some way knowledgeable about all our mythology of the ancient world. So whenever these texts are constructed, these stories are going to be told with nuances that are going to take off scenes from the mythology that their audiences will be aware of.

MC: Like, you make a great example of how Jesus wasn't recognized and the ancient motif back then would have been Homer, Odysseus wasn't recognized when he came home. Moving on, could you also give us a brief reconstruction of what the Thomasine community might have looked like as well?

AD: The Thomasine community I've worked on quite extensively and I've come to understand these people as basically the early Christians in Syria. These people appear to have been the result of a mission from Jerusalem, an Aramaic form of Christianity, very early, that was extremely eschatological and these people were millenarians, they were very sure that the end of the world was going to happen any time, which may in some ways be the oldest teaching of the early Christians that we have in terms of Jesus, and Jesus' own teaching. And over time within this community as this end of the world didn't happen and became more and more delayed, they set about rewriting their traditions that had been brought with them from Jerusalem. What they did is they shifted their point of view from the end of the world and all the promises that God has promised for the end of the world to be present promises. So they begin think about Jesus' resurrection as something that already started the resurrection from the dead so the end of the world is already in process and we can already begin living like angels, and to be doing that we need to be giving up sexual practices and be celibate like angels, or at least like the good angels, we don't want to be like the bad angels, the fallen angels. Like the angels we can have a spiritual body right now, be holy right now, and we can reap all the benefits of paradise while we're on earth. And so we can start having visions of God and living within his presence and living within paradise, and so this is the shift that you see happening in the Syrian materials in the beginning of the second century, the late first to early second century. And what you have forming in Syria at the time is an extremely what we call encratic form of Christianity. Encratism is a form of self-control. They need to get control of their passions, get control of things like eating, so they fast, they don't drink alcohol, they don't have sex, they're basically trying to be angels living on earth. This form of Christianity appears to be what was going on in Syria at this time. All the literature that was produced by these Christians in Syria at this time is this sort of encratic material, and visionary directives. They're talking about ascending into heaven, seeing God... this is something that one needs to do before death, in order to be saved. And it's not really unto you get into the fourth century

encratism is a form of self-control... control of their passions... control of things like eating, so they fast, they don't drink alcohol, they don't have sex, they're basically trying to be angels living on earth.

that you start seeing some of the fathers in the Syrian literature talk about allowing married Christians into the Church. And so there seems to be something happening in maybe the late third early fourth century in which you see this shift and opening up the Christian church in Syria to married couples rather than just singles. They also at that time take the singles, they call them the virgins, and they elevate them to an elite status, and these people become what are known as the sons and daughters of the covenant. So Syrian Christianity — very interesting, but a very different form of Christianity than most westerners are familiar with.

MC: And unlike the Johannine community you mentioned, they were a lot looser in allowing people to have their own mystic vision experience, right?

AD: Yeah, they're certainly encouraging visionary experience, but again I think that they're probably trying to control that as well in terms of communal interpretation of the vision and that sort of thing. If you think about these Thomasine folks — you can talk about the Thomasine community, you can talk about early Syrian Christians, that doesn't really matter — these people in some way are a precursor to contempoarary Orthodoxy, as in Byzantine tradition, where you have... the monks are into actual practice, you know, meditation in order to have a vision. The tradition is about the laity being very controlled in their life. They're married, yes, but they still have a very controlled life. They attempt to live in the ancient world what would be called a very righteous life, a life of poverty, and so forth. So I think we've got in this early Syrian literature and the Thomasine material a predcursor of what is to come.

MC: And of course the Syrian literature is not just the *Gospel of Thomas*. What else is included, or would you read?

AD: Another text is the Dialogue of the Saviour, which is a text from Nag Hammadi. There's another text from Nag Hammadi called *Thomas the Contender*, or *Thomas the Athlete*. The *Acts of Thomas*. In fact most of the apocryphal acts — not all of them, but most. The *Odes of Solomon* are another one, very, very beautiful hymns coming from the Syrian tradition. You have Tatian and the *Diatessaron*, a very good example, where he takes the four gospels plus his knowledge of the way that the saints' tradition of Jesus was in the ancient world, with the Thomasine material that he seems to know as well, and he blends that all into one gospel and he modifies it to an ancratic viewpoint.

MC: This might be a loaded question, but what are some of the theories on the connection and separation between the Gospel of John and the *Gospel of Thomas*? Obviously, the most famous one we have now is from Elaine Pagels, even though it wasn't her idea, I think she took it from Riley, that the Gospel of John was written as a polemic against the *Gospel of Thomas*. Where do you stand on that one, April?

AD: I've been in the same place. Essentially the three of us were talking about this at

there's even a text in the Acts of John in which John is the one who's afraid of having a vision, rather than Thomas

the same time, in terms of our writing as well as personally, and I think that's exactly write. The Gospel of John is connected in some way to the Thomasine traditions. It's aware maybe not of the gospel itself, but certainly of the traditions that the *Gospel of Thomas* is reporting, and I think it is certainly some sort of polemic to try either to persuade people from that viewpoint… something of the sort is going on with this text. In the Gospel of John you have the Thomas disciple really front and center in terms of being corrected by Jesus.

MC: Yeah, you call him 'a false hero'

AD: Yeah, he becomes a false hero in this text and he's corrected and he doesn't know the way,

Jesus says to him, 'Better if you don't see but just believe.' So this is all very polemical and directed against the tradition of Thomas which is all about vision and in Thomas there is a hero, he's not an anti-hero, he's a hero, and there's even a text in the Acts of John in which John is the one who's afraid of having a vision, rather than Thomas, so we've got some really interesting polemic there against the Gospel of John, this back and forth, who is the true disciple, who is the one? John or Thomas?

MC: And what are some of the other theories? I think you mention Stevan Davies, who belives that they actually came from the same fountainhead, right?

AD: Right. There's also some people who would argue that *Thomas* may be dependent on John, rather than the other way around. I don't see that because the *Gospel of Thomas* is not a polemic. It's not in any way arguing against the Gospel of John. What it appears to be is knowledge of similar traditions, but the Gospel of John is the one that has the polemic against the mysticisnm. At least the vision mysticism that we find being promoted in Syria. So that's why I would argue the other way.

MC: Then you have another radical idea. You mention the scholar Schenke who believes the beloved disciple was actually Judas Thomas.

AD: Right. Actually, I believe Charlesworth also thinks this is the case, but again I just don't believe this can be supported internally on the narrative of the Gospel of John, and I think that that's where we need to start with that question, if not end with that question because the beloved disciple — it doesn't actually say 'the beloved disciple' in the text, it's 'the disciple whom Jesus loved' — and that phrase is directly connected to Lazarus in the Gospel of John, so I think we need to credit that.

MC: So would it be a mistake to say that the *Gospel of Thomas* is a Gnostic gospel? Should we call it a Syrian gospel? Or perhaps as some believe it started some way and then slowly had Gnostic elements added to it throughout time?

AD: Well, it's always a matter of definition and in what way one defines 'Gnostic'. I would prefer to call the *Gospel of Thomas* a mystical gospel. I think it's concerned more with mysticism. When I think of Gnostic or Gnosticism, there's really two unique items that I key on, and that is that in the texts or the tradition, some kind of a pre-cosmic fall was in the godhead, something that happens within God that is going to bring about sin and the world. Whether it be the error of Sophia, or the devolution of Adamas, or whatever it is, it's something that happens prior to creation. And then secondly I have a creator God who is either ignorant or working in opposition to some sort of supreme God that is beyond this cosmos. So those are the elements that I look for because those are, when you look at all the literature, when you lay it all out next to each other, those would be the two unique strands of thought that you find within Gnostic material that differentiate it from other things such as Hermetism or Platonism or in this case mysticism. Now, Gnostics can be mystics. They can also be interested in having visions and in meeting God in the immediate, but all mystics aren't Gnostics. So I would prefer to call the *Gospel of Thomas* a mystical gospel that represents the sort of encratic Christianity that developed early on in Syria.

MC: Lastly, April, we joke about Irenaeus and his shenanigans, but would you say that one of the reasons the Gospel of John was accepted as a real gospel is that puts the nail in the coffin of any doubt that Jesus is God?

AD: Yeah, this is the theology that Irenaeus was trying to save and so that theology isn't quite as blatant or visual in the synoptic narratives as it is in John. I mean, John has God walking around on earth. It's clear from the very first verse that that's what's happening. And this was very important to many Christians in terms of their salvation because, as they would say, God became man so man can become God — it was one of their famous lines — and Irenaeus was right in there in that ideology. So this gospel does that for him, and he's going to have it and makes an argument — and for some reason this argument made sense in the ancient world — we've got four winds, four corners of the world, so we need four gospels and John is the fourth one, a much-beloved gospel. It may have been that he was using it in his church as well, the texts that were being used across a large geographical area within liturgy were the ones that seemed to make the cut over against something like the *Gospel of Thomas* which seems to be pretty much a Syrian text, that community really used and understood it and there's also a real encratic community down in Alexandria and so it makes its way down there and that community also picks it up. The Romans weren't all that interested in it, the westerners, this was not their gospel.

I would prefer to call the Gospel of Thomas a mystical gospel that represents the sort of encratic Christianity that developed early on in Syria

MC: I'd like to thank you once again for coming on Aeon Byte and giving us some of your wisdom.

AD: Always happy to.

April DeConick

the garden

out of the darkness
living eve
lush pomegranates
ripe figs
ready for tasting
heavy upon the branches

what is it that is secreted away, ruah?
sheltered, spiritus?
stolen, sophia?

sweet fruit in your hands
gnosis in the bite
juice on the chin

hide away eve
the nemesis of god is upon you

april d. deconick

Anthony Blake

Meetings

I was christened the day war was declared on Germany in 1939 and spent my childhood in Bristol punctuated by the sound of sirens (that haunt me to this day) and the distant sound of explosions as the city and airport were bombed. At the end of the war, my psyche was imprinted with the meaning and energy of the celebrations that expressed joy and fellowship openly in the streets, followed by a terrible sadness as I saw this decline into heedless indulgence and selfishness and lack of vision.

Being an only child and living in a relatively poor environment, it was only through books (and radio) that glimpses came of other worlds.

Tony Blake

I remember a critical moment in my teens. Somehow, I had picked up the idea of breaking patterns, so had taken myself to see a play — *Bell, Book and Candle* — which I had never done before (my parents had no interest in plays, music, etc.) Returning home, my parents gone to bed, I switched on the Third Programme (this was in the old days when there were intellectual programmes on the BBC) to catch a dramatisation of Andre Malraux's *La Condition Humaine*. Something melted in my brain. I still do not know what happened, but there came over me a vision or seeing or feeling of evolution, as a force or energy driving inexorably on, indifferent to the ever recurring piles of bodies on the way. Later, for a school essay, I incorporated this vision into a prospectus of a total integration of all sentience at the end of time, strangely like the speculative picture of the physicist Tipler I was only to come across fifty years later.

I mentioned books though, and I suppose it was Colin Wilson's *The Outsider* that switched me on to the idea of there being an 'enterprise of liberation' (I once met Wilson decades later when he heckled me during a talk I was giving at Bennett's International Academy for Continuous Education — though we became friendly after the talk). This impact came together with the birth of attraction to modern music, painting and poetry which I regarded as gateways to other worlds. My scientific worldview was imbued with the arts playing the role of messages from the unseen. Though I did not meet Colin Wilson until much later, I did meet with Stuart Holroyd and Bill Hopkins who formed, with Wilson, a triumvirate dubbed the 'metaphysical young men' in the press to parallel the 'angry young men' renowned at that time. Stuart had just brought out (at the early age of 23) his autobiography *Emergence from Chaos* and I had somehow got to write to him. I had been on a CND walk over three days protesting against nuclear weapons, ending in Trafalgar Square. Stuart knew Kenneth Walker and regaled me with stories of Gurdjieff in Paris, dramatically conveying a picture of Gurdjieff teaching SS members one day (he was in occupied France during the war) and members of the resistance the next. He gave me a copy of his play *The Tenth Chance*, based on Walker's stories, which had just been put on for a brief run in London and later I used this in creating a dramatic scenario while teaching at Bennett's International Academy in 1971. I must mention, however, that the most memorable impression came in relation to Stuart's girl friend, with whom I had a conversation lasting sixteen hours, and to whom I am eternally grateful, for it was an initiation into the extraordinary world

David Bohm

of dialogue.

The first really well-known remarkable man in my story came to me as my physics tutor at Bristol University. This was David Bohm. He was regarded with awe by us students because of his heretical political and scientific views. He had been expelled from the USA for refusing to collaborate with the McCarthy committee on 'un-American activities' and he was become known as the physicist who wanted to eliminate uncertainty from quantum mechanics by seeking hidden variables. I think he was at Bristol for only one or two years, before moving on to Birkbeck College, London University where he remained until his death (just after finishing his last book — with Basil Hiley — *The Undivided Universe*). A day came when I met him face to face in a tutorial class. We students were supposed to tackle problems and seek the tutor's guidance if we needed it. Somehow, Bohm and I started talking — I had an immense attraction to him and he was totally open and friendly. We talked about St Augustine, the nature of space, painting; such themes intertwined.

Previously, I had 'existentialist' conversations with a few school friends, most of us depressives of course, and had once engaged in a debate on religion that went over three days while at school and drew quite an audience. It was natural to me to dialogue though it was to be many years before I took up dialogue as a method and learned that Bohm had himself come to it and become an advocate. I had joined a small group which had the title 'Polemics' which had made me aware of how one can become more conscious in a group by talking. This was very different from my attempts to get into socialism. I found politics to be uninteresting and illogical, preferring spiritual postulates to political ideologies. Hearing me make a comment in a meeting, Professor George from the Philosophy Department remarked to someone that I looked like the younger Huxley (something that I remembered recently when I met Francis Huxley, the nephew of Aldous). But I had not before engaged with a man of Bohm's depth and character. I remember glancing over at the other students, amazed that they continued with the problems and did not join in. When it came to leaving the room, I found myself as it were in orgasm and incapable of attending any lectures that morning. Instead, I walked the streets as I often did in those days somehow just trying 'to see'.

After that day, we had many conversations, usually walking together. Only many years later did I learn from Saral Bohm, his wife, that he had come home one night to tell her that, 'At last I have met a student I can talk to'. Needless to say, this made me feel very honoured. Bohm left for Birkbeck and I was not to see him again for some years. On another front, but essentially the same, I was following the lead given in *The Outsider* to the work of Gurdjieff. I read some of Gurdjieff's magnum opus *Beelzebub's Tales* in the bookshop next to the university (not being able to afford to buy it, though a friend got it for me one Christmas) and I can remember to this day the impact of his descriptions of events in his own psyche that gave me a conviction that objectivity might be possible in that realm. From learning about Gurdjieff, I came to one his pupils, John Bennett, and began to read the latter's own magnum opus *The Dramatic Universe* (little realising that one day I would be helping him in the writing of the last two volumes of that work). Then learned about Bennett's work with Subud, a mystical practice originating in Indonesia. My own state was desperate; I could not make sense of my existence and I resolved to seek Bennett out.

I went to Bennett's study centre at Coombe Springs, Kingston in Surrey, packing *Beelzebub's Tales* with my sandwiches. At that time, he had given over his centre to serving the Subud movement. In my eagerness I behaved somewhat comically, lurking by the main house to intercept him on his way to lunch. Thinking I had to earn his attention with a really deep question, I blurted out, 'What is Original Sin?' Much to my surprise he stopped and thought for a moment and then told me, 'It is to try and do what we cannot do and not do what we can.' After going to Coombe Springs I became 'opened' in Subud

and had some interesting experiences that convinced me about other worlds but gave me no means of understanding any better how to live. Through the circle of Subud people in and around Bristol I was invited to meet with Henry Boys, a musician who had known Stravinsky, at his home in Lacok. He played me some of the music of Gurdjieff, which I had never heard before. Expecting something dramatic and strange I was surprised at the simplicity and folksy character of the music. Later I learned that he composed the 'alternative' music for the movement known as the 'Great Prayer,' full of discordant and modern sounds I much enjoyed. It was not to be for almost fifty years that I came to hear the full orchestrations of some of the music.

J.G. Bennett

My degree course in physics finished and I was left with questions about the meaning of science. I was and remained one of those naïve people who regard science as miraculous and mysterious in its origins. Because of this, I went on to then only place in the UK for the study of the history and philosophy of science, which was in Free School Lane, part of Cambridge University. I remember with fondness my teachers there — Gerd Buchdal, Mary Hesse and Michael Hoskins — though I was not able to get any further with my search for meaning (I did, though, find an affinity with Buchdal through our common passion for the music of Schoenberg). While at Cambridge, I was following the *latihan* practice of Subud, occasionally going down to Kingston for latihans in the remarkable monument to Gurdjieff built there, a nine-sided *djamechoonatra* and having some strange moments. Coming out of the course with a Certificate in the History and Philosophy of Science I had to find employment or further studies. I tried the London School of Economics for a PhD under Karl Popper, where I did not meet Popper himself but Indre Lakatos a philosopher of mathematics. Lakatos told me Popper had two laws: one should not be a Marxist and one had to have a problem that could be solved by known methods. It was the latter that turned me off, since I wanted to explore the meaning of causality. It was suggested that I apply for a post in Australia, teaching science to arts students and went to an interview with my old tutor Buchdal and Stephen Toulmin, another fine philosopher of science. Eventually I learned I had the job but issues in my family led me to decide not to leave the country, so I was in a pickle.

Out of the blue the 'warden' at Coombe Springs offered me a post there as kitchen boy with the handsome salary of £1 a week! I accepted and thus began a fifteen year period of association with John Bennett and his work. I graduated from kitchen boy (I must mention Lili Helestenius, who was one the fierce 'dragons' that ruled the kitchen and was in a way my first 'teacher') to research fellow. Initially reluctant, I accepted a project looking into the potentials of small group discussion for students. This then became part of the innovations Bennett was making in educational technology.

There were many interesting characters at Coombe Springs and I regarded it as my next 'university', far closer to the realities of human life than before. The process going on with Bennett and his organization was complex and dramatic. The organization had the daunting name of The Institute for the Comparative Study of History, Philosophy and the Sciences, Ltd. which name was originally dreamt up to cover up the 'esoteric' activities that were centred there; but, when Bennett separated from Subud, he began to take the name seriously and hence the incursion into education. While I was with him, not only did he move into educational research and development (he had been head of coal utilisation research in the 40s based at Coombe Springs) but engaged with Idries Shah, the Naqsbandi sufi who claimed he represented the order from which Gurdjieff got his stuff and to whom a few years later he gave Coombe Springs. He also made contact with the Shivapuri Baba in Nepal, who summoned him on two occasions to transmit his 'three disciplines' and with the Benedictine monastery at St Wandrille, where he took Subud to a few of the monks there and consolidated his conversion to Catholicism.

Later on I went several times to the monastery and had significant conversations with Pere Bescond, who was doing research on the origins of Gregorian Chant and had been 'opened' in Subud by Bennett. I only met Pak Subuh, the originator of Subud amidst crowds, at a conference in Oslo. It was then that I realized that it did not matter how 'great' or 'advanced' a spiritual teacher was, one still had to make one's own decisions (would that I had kept to this, as I will confess later). The Subud movement had come to reject 'thinking' as anti-spiritual (whether this was Pak Subud's own view is problematic) and I just could not accept this.

There were many 'characters' I met at Coombe Springs as I said and some of them were near to crazy. I had a friend who had become schizophrenic possibly through Subud and spent his time in a hut doing weird paintings. There was a woman who I learned had tried while a teenager to bicycle to Hitler to stop the war, who lived in another building and was wont to scream at night. There was a heroin junkie and labourer who also did strange paintings (I remember him muttering at Bennett during a movements class to 'fuck off'). One day, the men were all agog when a soft porn actress called Dora Doll came to see Bennett about her personal problems! Perhaps the most strange of all was Karl Shaffer, a kind of playboy from America, whom Bennett for some unknown reason regarded as a son. We used to hold meetings on science education in London to which Karl sometimes came. I remember one occasion when he offered me a lift back to Coombe in his sports car and drove right through a T junction to bump the facing kerb — when we reached Coombe he was all set to drive past only to see Bennett waiting at the gates in his dressing gown. Karl disappeared into Soho but once appeared at a party I was holding with a stripper who he claimed was a priestess of Atlantis helping him to avert World War Three.

The educational work brought in some young bright young men. Anthony Hodgson was important for the development of the educational technology called structural communication and went on to become a consultant for such firms as Shell. Ken Pledge taught physics at a college and become somewhat of a recluse, immersed in esoteric mathematics (but did substantial work on the five-dimensional geometry that derived form Bennett's ideas). John Varney, an architect, eventually created a management centre (at High Trenhouse in Yorkshire) and I work with him now on logovisual technology which evolved from structural communication. Henri Bortoft became the most well-known through his work on Goethean science.

It was through Henri that I reconnected with Bohm and he and Bennett were brought together. Over two years, Bohm and Bennett visited and wrote each other and sometimes I was involved. There was an astonishing period for me when Bohm and I corresponded every day for two weeks on every topic under the sun (to my supreme regret all this correspondence disappeared). Many years later I edited and published the 'Bohm-Bennett Correspondence' based on the extant letters I had copies of. But the most memorable was when I sat with the two men and found myself acting as a translator between them. It dawned on me that they were moving back into their own frames of reference and I found this sorrowful. Bohm gradually reacted more and more against the Gurdjieff approach, being attracted to ideas of unbroken wholeness, which led him to become more or less Krishnamurti's right hand man. Unbeknownst to me, he had been developing ideas of meaning and dialogue and later with Krishnamurti conducted extraordinary conversations as recorded in The Ending of Time.

Henri himself was moving away from Bennett and it was only much later that he was able to acknowledge the debt he owed to Bennett's teaching of visualisation methods. It was through Henri that I came to meet George Spencer-Brown, the renegade mathematician who became widely known in the 60s through his unique book The Laws of Form. Henri and I attended a course Spencer-Brown gave on his book, which has remained with me since. Meeting him personally, we were amused at his claim to be attracted to little girls and the invention of a fictional 'brother' he claimed to work with. Twenty years later I found out that he claimed to have reached enlightenment sometime in the 80s!

As I said, this story is more about meetings with remarkable men than the men themselves, because I cannot possibly claim to 'know' them. There are many things that remain with me about Bennett, though. The first is that all people need someone to talk to, even those who are 'great' in some way. I was thunder-struck when, in my early years at Coombe, Bennett remarked to me that he was grateful to have someone to talk to. He had perhaps hundreds of people who looked to him for guidance but it was quite another matter to have a dialogue with any of them. Before my time he had scientists such as Brown,

Thring and Foster around but they all left for various reasons and some like Thring turned against him. Throughout my life I have met dozens of people of varying capacity and fame for whom the lack of genuine conversation is a big issue. Another Bennett impression comes from when he told us young lads, when I think while we were working on clearing out a pond, Bennett in his coloured underpants, 'Perhaps I am a holy man. A holy man is one who can enter into higher worlds at will. But I tell you that holy men also make mistakes'.

Bennett's openness was extraordinary. It seems that, in spite of his manifold gifts and accomplishments, including charismatic charm, he lacked self-confidence. For most of his life he regarded himself as a mere 'student' of Gurdjieff. When Shah came on the scene, he was put through many humiliations and it was not until he had given Coombe to Shah that one day he started to claim his own station. I mentioned some crazy characters. Before I came to Coombe Springs, his second wife, older than himself, had become mentally unbalanced and no doubt he was used to strange people. Never before or since did I experience such a range of humanity. One very special strange young man was Michael Sutton, still remembered with affection by many. Michael was a kind of leader of a bunch of young people who lived nearby who practised black magic. He came to met Bennett and became a significant teacher of movements later on at the International Academy.

Bennett's openness was encapsulated in his principle of integration without rejection. It was lived by in his willingness to talk to anyone without playing the role of guru. It was also evident in his writings. He had responded to the all-embracing vision of Gurdjieff by taking it further in his own way. I was to find again and again that many people came to respond to Gurdjieff and Bennett as a basis for their own research into wholeness, rather than joining in any cult of 'followers'. I found him eminently sympathetical because of my inherent embrace of 'all of everything' and also, in particular, because although a holy man he was grounded in natural

science and firmly believed that our knowledge in all things could only be provisional. However, as I mentioned in speaking of his contact with Bohm, I discovered that even an all-inclusive approach tended to fall back into a partisan stance: for me Bennett and Bohm were both 'holy thinkers' yet they went divergent ways. This was particularly true of Bohm who later on denied he had any contact with the Gurdjieff work and did not even mention his association with Bennett to his biographer David Peat (as David told me himself).

The wide range of Bennett's interests included his appreciation of the body and he had contact with many leading figures in this realm, including Ida Rolf. With a few others, I had sessions with her, that changed my body to the degree that I could stand without discomfort. At this time, I had committed myself to the 'movements' devised by Gurdjieff, which are recognized more and more as integral to his teaching and I was doing an immense amount of physical work to awaken my sleeping partner (body) which had such obvious results that even Bennett remarked on it.

When Bennett left Coombe Springs and went to live in the town of Kinston-upon-Thames, he had many visitors. One of these was a remarkable American, John Allen. I was living nearby and put him up in my flat and came to have talks with him in the pub and elsewhere. John had worked in the mining industry and had been a union worker before developing his talents in writing and drama. He was a renaissance man American style and had been in the thick of the Haight-Ashbury 'hippie' revolution, but had seen the need for the management of social developments. He was in London with his group The Theatre of all Possibilities — with obvious affinity to Bennett's 'dramatic universe'. I was surprised when John seemed to take to me, since I considered myself to be pretty inadequate on most fronts, but delighted. I found in him a sense of history that Bennett and I shared and glimpsed in his theatrical disciplines an important method. Most of all, I sensed even then that here was a pragmatic and earthy approach to the esoteric ideas that could turn them into real influences in human life. Years later, I was to join his team in Arizona, USA, on the Biosphere 2 project (my main contribution to put together the first book about it Biosphere 2 — the human experiment). He introduced me more deeply to the work of Vladimir Vernadsky, the pioneer of biospherics, whose work I had first come across in some of Bennett's papers. It was a revelation to see the parallels between Gurdjieff and Vernadsky in their cosmic treatment of life on earth.

John Allen also brought me into contact with members of his team and through the October Gallery he co-founded in London (one of many 'global' enterprises he set up in France, Australia, Nepal and the USA) with many of the visitors there. Though this is jumping forward in time (to the 90s), I want to mention my meeting with John Lilly. Chili Hawes who ran the Gallery wanted to organise a public meeting for him and asked me to help, because Lilly had become notorious for not being communicative while taking part in conferences and wondered whether I could 'bring him along'. For a few days we sat around together largely reading and exchanging thrillers, since he had been told by the higher powers he met during his experiments, as he explained to us, to leave off his excursions and become an ordinary human. Lilly had been inducted into the Gurdjieff cosmology through Oscar Ichazo and it struck me all over again that Gurdjieff had played a significant role in opening people to a new vision of reality. John talked to me of his experiments with ketamine and isolation tanks and I could not help but be struck by this other example of American pragmatism (though I would argue that much could be accomplished by drinking tea while sitting in an English garden).

When Idries Shah acquired Coombe Springs, his main activity was giving parties. I had only a few encounters with him but much enjoyed his irreverent attitude. Bennett once said to me, 'There are different styles in the work. Mine is like Gurdjieff's, around struggle with one's denial. But Shah's way is to treat the work

as a joke.' At one of the parties, which I had to wangle my way into by posing as projectionist for the movies they were showing, I made a brief encounter with Doris Lessing. This is crude name dropping but I admire her greatly and wrote her a letter connected with the theme of higher intelligence, to which she replied that she believed there were higher powers (it was about this time she was writing the 'Shikasta' series).

A major character in the saga of Bennett's journey into spirituality was Hasan Shushud, a Turkish Sufi renowned for austerities and 'voiceless zikr', and the teaching of 'absolute liberation'. It was only later I had much contact with him and then only through letters, when I was publishing one of his works — it came out as Masters of Wisdom in Central Asia — after Bennett had died. Hasan was one of the people who persuaded Bennett that he was now his own man and should teach on his own authority.

Though not to do with a remarkable man as such, I must mention my brief sojourn in the fromer Czechoslovakia in 1968, the time of the 'Spring Revolution'. Unknowingly, I caught the last train out of Prague before the Russians moved in. I want to say that the Czechs I met could collectively be taken as 'remarkable' and I treasure my encounters with them. It was in Prague that I wrote one of my simplest and best poems; but what was most important was seeing this episode as a microcosm of human tragedy and hope. Afterwards Bennett remarked to me that he thought the higher power were doing an experiment there and ever afterwards I had the sense that intelligence and humanity could only open up somewhere for a time when it would be closed down by some fascism that might extend, as Gurdjieff seems to hint, to the 'higher powers' who 'ran' the universe.

One day, out of the blue a design engineer wrote to Bennett asking for a meeting and Bennett sent me as his representative. This was to be my first meeting with Edward Matchett, with whom I stayed in touch until his death in the 90s. A self-made man, he had worked himself up from engineering drawing (working with such firms as Rolls-Royce) into the realm of creative design. He proved to be another man embracing 'all of everything'. He had embraced religion, art, music, philosophy together with engineering and innovation and was familiar with Gurdjieff's ideas. Down in Bristol, I witnessed presentations by his students and was shocked to recognise or feel the presence of real consciousness. Ted developed deep methodologies for design that evolved in startling ways. Instead of becoming more complex and detailed they became simpler and more profound. In the 60s he was engaged by the then Department for Scientific Research and Development to investigate the nature of genius! Almost at the last moment of his year's engagement, while walking in the grounds of his beloved Glastonbury, he 'received the answer', which became known as the 3-M equation: Making Media and Matter Meaningful, or Media + Matter = Meaning. This was for me — eventually — identical with Gurdjieff's 'law of three' and it made a totally unlikely alliance between engineering and spiritual development. To this day, no one, including myself, has worked through the consequences of this equation.

There was a strange incident in connection with Bennett and Matchett. This was when Bennett was working at his International Academy in Sherborne, Gloucestershire. Ted told me that he had broached with Bennett the need for him to have a successor and suggested I might take that role. Bennett rejected the idea, saying I did not have the strengths, and Ted argued that he should 'put them there'. Still according to Ted, this set Bennett off in a tirade, with him pounding his desk in rage. For me it was part of the continuing tragedy of remarkable men each embracing whole vision but seeing things differently.

Ted was intolerant in many ways but a great friend and inspiration. I particularly value his introducing me to what he came to call 'logospheres'. These are like environments of meaning. He would set up rooms with flowers, reproductions of paintings, artefacts of various kinds; play music and show beautiful slides. I remember making a film loop of Mondrian's

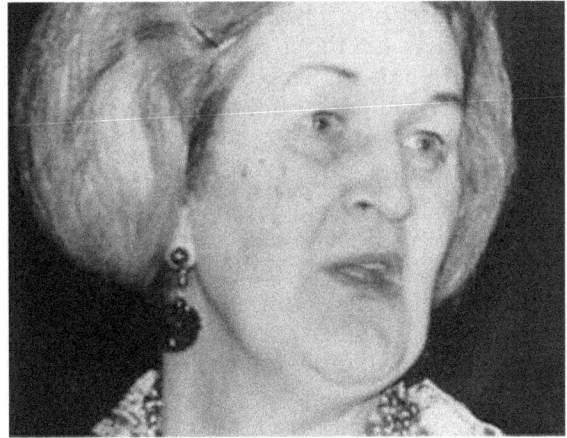

Charlotte Bach

paintings (he always took along box loads of art books anyway) for him and also making 'magic crystals' from pieces of broken glass to represent the ideas of an imaginary character I invented called Axon.

I encountered more knowledge of creativity and evolution through perhaps the most strange character of all I've ever met — Charlotte Bach. The name should not hide the fact this was a man, not a woman, even though 'he' passed himself off as a woman until he was found dead in his flat (much to the surprise of Colin Wilson who was going to write a book about 'her' ideas). Starting with the thesis that sexuality was the key to evolution, Charlotte evolved a theory of evolution that embraced ten dimensions of time, alchemy, shamanism and neurology. It attracted a lot of attention at the time, but many were embarrassed by the disclosure of Charlotte's deception and distanced themselves later. I met her a few times and read a lot of her books, privately distributed (and still not published, one an extraordinary treatment of the origins of writing running to more than a 1000 pages) in amazement. As I would expect, 'she' knew of Gurdjieff and regarded him as the twentieth century's greatest shaman. Intellectually, I was stretched between 'her' ideas of time and 'systems' such as the quaternary (far in advance of any Jungian treatment) and the corresponding ones I had learned from Bennett. 'She' remains for me a powerful enigma and signal or representative of a deeper order of intelligence, rather as if Bohm's 'implicate order' had emerged in operatic splendour!

As the reader will have gathered, my story does not follow simple chronology very much. I have to remark here that when Bennett left Kingston to set up his Academy in 1971, I was somewhat distanced from him, though I did go down there to give a short course on 'dramatic method' (following the influence of John Allen I had picked up various methods working with a group which included a guy from RADA). For some reason he seemed to have set himself to persuade me to take part in it. He put on the pressure, denouncing me as 'candidate for lunatic asylum' and, finally, at a meeting with him alone in London, I succumbed. He had been ill and told me that he had been attacked by evil forces; I was even quite frightened and cowardly about this, it taking me back to moments walking the streets of Bristol in which I 'saw' angels and saints in cities in total slavery to the higher powers, there being no mercy for them. Then he told me that I would 'suffer in this work' but maybe not so much as his eldest son, George. I was crying and for the first and only time, embraced him.

I was at the Academy until his sudden death in 1974. I saw him develop his ideas about the 'work' increasingly in a way that reconciled it with 'ordinary life'. I came to be the person to 'explain' his lectures to the students, which led, after his death, to my work of compiling and editing various books based on these lectures. In agreement with Elizabeth Bennett, I moved to close down the Academy in 1976, completing the original plan of running courses for five years, because we did not know what we were doing.

The aftermath was very difficult. I spent three months on a potato farm in Ireland while working on the books in the evenings. My host was Hugh Sherrard, brother of the Greek scholar Philip Sherrard who produced a translation of the Philokalia. Hugh was attracted to Bennett's ideas but never had the chance to study with him. He is mentioned here because he was to prove pivotal in making a connection with another strange man, this time one I would not recommend to anyone. Leaving the farm, I returned to England, eventually to marry one of the students I met at the Academy after many vicissitudes (but that, as they say, is another story). When I returned to England I came to the house of another remarkable man in my story, the then Lord (Francis) Thurlow. I had first met him many years before, when he came to Coombe Springs with another remarkable man, Sir Paul Dukes, who had lived an extraordinary life as a spy and had done much to introduce Hatha Yoga to the West. I was deeply impressed by Francis. He was a truly educated man and had no 'side'. He was capable of paying attention to what people said and exhibited impartial courtesy to everyone he met.

I later learned that he had had a distinguished career as a diplomat; serving in India and being present for the violence attending the partition and, as governor of Nigeria, had been deeply involved in the Biafran war. He supported Bennett's work for many years though it is clear in retrospect that he did not find the 'answers' he was seeking. Not only had he witnessed many horrors on the world stage, his youngest son committed suicide at the age of 18. To this day, he has never written about his inside knowledge of events in Africa and India (and the Bahamas, where he was also governor for a time). He was at Cambridge when Wittgenstein was there and dallied with the communism that took hold of many students as a defence against the rising tide of fascism. It seemed that so much was left unresolved for him. He would help others but not himself.

Another old friend from that era was Dr Edith Wallace, a renowned Jungian analyst, who studied with Bennett at Sherborne, where she developed her tissue paper collage method of active imagination. I remember a day when I drove her down to Stonehenge, which she had never seen, and extolled the astronomical knowledge built into the stones, while she admired the colour of the lichen on the stones. A great lesson in perspectives. I was to know Edith right up until her death in 2004 and there were a few strange moments when both of us felt we had 'something to do together' — as if to unite two separated worlds — but even though we tried it never quite happened.

After Sherborne, I had been persuaded (perhaps against my better judgment — but it is a bit gutless on my part to put it like that) by another older student of Bennett, John Wilkinson, to take part in another experiment, this time a 'college', seeking for a more exploratory approach than had become manifest in the 'American' follow up to Sherborne at Claymont Court, West Virginia, which Bennett had had purchased just before his death as a venue for his proposed experiment in a 'fourth way community'. In the event, Claymont proved a degenerate enterprise, lacking the guidance it had been assumed Bennett would give. At the same time, Wilkinson and I were aware of our great limitations.

It was then that another figure appeared from nowhere. This was Gary Chicoine, known only at that time as Dadaji something or other. In letters to the Institute he announced himself as successor to Gurdjieff and as the new teacher of the age. It turned out, as we learned later, that he had tried this on with the Self-Realization Fellowship as well and maybe others, too. The followers of Bennett were living in the loss of Bennett and vulnerable to the claims of a 'saviour'. The first person to respond was Hugh Sherrard, which led to others. In the event, Anthony Hodgson and Lord Thurlow led a faction of the Institute to meet with and follow this new guru. This led over some years to him acquiring all the assets of the Institute (and often the personal assets of his students as well) and the collapse of anything resembling Bennett's work in the UK.

I was left with the College to run in Daglingworth, Gloucestershire, but soon this became a target of his acquisitions and, much to my shame ever since, I succumbed to peer pressure. There were some reasons to take Chicoine seriously. He had a considerable knowledge of spiritual techniques and sources. He had been in the US Marines and brought another measure of American pragmatism to the table. He was capable of 'teaching action in the moment' and intensely creative. He brought Hindu spirituality into view more strongly than Bennett had ever done. He encouraged wide reading and study of original texts. He had stumbled upon the powerful effect of music, but used in a violent way in contrast with Matchett, though both of them were linked to the same insight. And, when I first met him in England, he seemed devoted to an ongoing enquiry and exploration related to self realization.

Here I need to make an aside and mention two people who were 'students' of myself at Daglingworth, where I was exploring a very open-ended approach with minimum structure, manifesting my inherent feeling for non-authoritarian relationships. These were Richard Heath and John Kirby. Richard has become a leading light in studies of ancient wisdom and astro-archaeology and is working with John Varney and myself on developing the methodology of logovisual technology. John Kirby has deeply connected with the apparitions of Mary, and spent some years in close relationship with Ted Matchett.

It was due to Chicoine that in the 80s I spent three months in India (actually with friend John Varney) filming and recording spiritual people, places and events. I was delighted to get to Puri for the Jagannath festival (from which we get our word 'juggernaut') because as a child I had seen in an encyclopaedia photos of this event which then seemed to come from another planet. John and I went to the shrines of Sri Anirvan, the wonderful Baul philosopher who had taught Lizelle Reymond and guided her to Gurdjieff (I published the most complete version of Reymond and Anirvan's book *To Live Within* and am still cross that more recent editions ignore this). We saw the once brother disciple of the leader of the Hare Krishna movement in a small ashram, rolling on the floor in delicate ecstasy. There were many things (only existing in memory because Chicoine acquired all the media and they are probably rotting somewhere in a basement) but perhaps I will mention Chille Maharaj as a remarkable man we had to hunt down in a remote village, who claimed to be an incarnation of Krishna and also of Dattatreya. Armed with camera I followed his little entourage down muddy and stony tracks. He was carried on the back of a disciple and from time to time stopped to give a little discourse and also to take refreshment which, I learned was neat gin. Others involved in this pilgrimage to India saw the 'hot' leaders such as Anandamoy Ma and Babaji as well as wild Sufis sticking swords into themselves and Sai Baba doing magic. Perhaps the strongest impression must always remain Calcutta which I could not believe in even when I was there.

If there is a villain in my story, it is certainly Chicoine. Like any cult leader, he manipulated people and got them to part with their cash and hand over control over their sex organs. He ended up a deranged megalomaniac at odds with his children (and some of his wives) and now lives in Sweden with a small group of adherents, regarding himself as above the mechanical masses of humanity. But he is essential to the story. One thing he brought home to me was that spirituality is not identical with morality; but also that individuals who search after greater meaning are especially vulnerable to abuse because they feel themselves to be 'unworthy'. 'Seekers' are greatly at risk. They look towards unseen worlds without having the confidence of gaining access to them, so that they come to look towards personalities who claim such access to guide them and interpret reality for them. This is of course exactly the same structure which is found in religions, the only difference being one of scale. All the remarkable men I have met who are truly

all the remarkable men I have met who are truly remarkable embody a willingness to speak 'on the level' with others and not as authorities

remarkable embody a willingness to speak 'on the level' with others and not as authorities.

In the 80s I finally parted company with Chicoine, resolving never to take part in any authority game ever again. The idea of dialogue emerged with urgency. Catching up on Bohm's work, I studied his efforts to spread the practice of dialogue. My true initiation into the experience came through Anthony Judge, who works at the Union of International Associations, and with whom I had had correspondence through his interest in Bennett's systematics. He invited me to come to a weekend of dialogue in Scotland, which I did. During the weekend I not only absorbed a great deal of the structure of the process but had some intense moments of realization in the midst of talking. It was then that I came to se that there really was an equivalent to 'waking up' or 'self-remembering' that was more than individual. These insights became written up in my book *Structures of Meaning*. Also of note was that Tony and his colleagues had called themselves 'The School of Ignorance', a title that delighted me and served to usher in a new period when I could begin to appreciate the depth of some of the lines of research done in Group Analysis over more than fifty years. I had long felt that the Gurdjieff-Bennett work had failed to understand group process well, having been operated largely through the concept of a teacher or leader and it seemed to me that now I was being a glimpse of the other half of the 'boolmarshano' (the teaching Gurdjieff describes in Beelzebub's Tales as split into two parts and separated).

When I had made copies of my book on structures of meaning, I sent one to Patrick de Mare and one to Gordon Lawrence. I had learned that a major source for Bohm's idea of dialogue was Patrick, who had been his therapist for some years. Meeting with Patrick was a wonderful moment and led to continuing collaboration.

Typically, as for many of the remarkable men I happened to meet, Patrick's work has been blocked and ignored by the profession he came from, and dialogue is still only very slowly becoming acknowledged as a necessary component of any healthy society. It was Patrick who brought home to me the significance of seeing mind as 'between brains' and not 'in brains'. This simple idea is revolutionary, though implicit in Group Analysis. It frees us form the nonsense of most contemporary 'consciousness studies'.

Gordon Lawrence introduced me to 'social dreaming' and the infinity and creativity of the unconscious. We have been having 'video-conversations' for some years now. His work links for me to that of the Amerindian medicine man, Joseph Rael (Beautiful Painted Arrow) whom I met for a video-dialogue in Albuquerque around the same time as meeting Patrick and Gordon. Joseph works with the Tiwa language, a language of metaphor. He paints visions of the landscape and teaches in a way that has many echoes of John Bennett and Ted Matchett, in the sense that they all accept and work from the spiritual world into this apparently material one.

In the 90s I co-founded The DuVersity with Karen Stefano (who has taken on the baton of Edith Wallace's Tisue Paper Collage method), hoping to emulate in some small way the enterprise envisioned by Bennett in the form of his Institute for the Comparative Study of History, Philosophy and the Sciences. Ever since working with Bennett and others on the theme of the 'dramatic universe' I had longed for something like a 'dramatic university'. To this end, Karen and I arranged a series of conferences on the big ideas Bennett had fostered. During the course of these, I met Warren Kenton once more, whom I had last seen many years ago when we spent a day together in a group with open-ended discussion that ended with us casting various spiritual leaders of the time into roles for an imaginary movie based on *Beelzebub's Tales*. Warren had become the head of a major branch of Kabbalah in the UK and remains a kind friend of ours. Another well-known figure was John Anthony West, the Egyptologist who had followed the line of R.A. Schwaller de Lubwicz and, like Warren, had had his training in the Gurdjieff line.

Two other remrkable men must be mentioned, both of whom contributed to our first Seminar-Dialogue on *All and Everything*. There was William Pensinger, who I first learned of through associates of John Allen at the October Gallery. William - or Larry as he is known to friends - had been in Vietnam and married a Vietnamese professor of literature. He devoted himself to some extraordinary researches into the nature of perception and the underlying structure of reality, much of which he incorporated into one of the most remarkable novels I have ever read, *The Moon of Hoa Binh*. This is a masterly work by any standards, more than a 1000 pages long, containing powerful commentaries on

Robert Fripp

the arising of modern art, asides on quantum physics and self-organisation, episodes of sexual exploration and even equations; all around a vivid evocation of events in Vietnam (and Japan) and with an exposition of Bennett's idea of three kinds of time. Larry is now living in Thailand and still struggling to find people to talk to and take him seriously, after becoming disillusioned with what went for 'advanced thinking' in the USA.

The other man I have to mention is Robert Fripp, most well known as leader of the group King Crimson. Robert had been a student at Sherborne but we connected more strongly years later, when he had evolved a novel way of introducing people to the 'work ideas' through what became known as 'Guitar Craft' and found a way of making music in a complex way by himself as 'Soundscapes'. Larry and Robert represented for me prime examples of the way in which Bennett had inspired original and creative individuals rather than led to any posthumous 'following'.

The musical theme evokes my memories of two more characters, whom I first met in Amsterdam. The first is Gert-Jan Blom, a great lover of all music, who worked with a movements teacher and musician, Wim van Dullemen, to bring the Gurdjieff music more into the public domain. Gert-Jan's labours of love extended to a diverse range of music and, quite recently, he arranged a concert for the Concertgebouw in Amsterdam that included music by Carl Stanning (renowned maker of cartoon music for Warner Brothers), Gershwin, Robert Fripp (orchestrations of his Soundscapes) and Gurdjieff. He searched long and persistently to obtain the original orchestrations of the 'movements' music that had been performed in the 1920s and recently produced them on CD, following his extraordinary compilation of Gurdjieff's own harmonium music. Almost in passing, I can mention his and Wim's involvment with Dushka Howarth, a daughter of Gurdjieff, a remarkable lady in her own right. I had the rather harrowing experience of conducting a movements class under her critical eye!

The DuVersity also began a series of 'pilgrimages' to sacred sites, first to Egypt, led by John Anthony West. Another was by Joseph Rael - to the South West regions of the USA and the Pueblo/Ute traditions - and the next to Peru, guided by William Sullivan, who had been a 'student' of mine at Sherborne and had taken up the ideas on ancient knowledge first put forward in one of the twentieth century's seminal works, *Hamlet's Mill*. Our most recent trip was to 'enchanted Albion', led by Richard Heath.

The story comes too close to the present moment to fade into simple patterns. I've brushed against more remarkable men (and women) and I'm aware of some distant connections, as with the philosopher Gendlin ('thinking at the edge' and 'focusing') whom I greatly admire and the psychologist Susan Blackmore (meme theory) with whom I've managed only to exchange a few emails. I'm working with some interesting people — by which I mean we have meaningful conversations — but I won't start listing names for the sake of it (apologies to those not mentioned). Perhaps my time for 'meetings' has past. I wanted to sketch my story out to draw attention to patterns — patterns in people and patterns in events — rather than to myself. I wanted to create a picture of some enigmatic conversation as the basis of a life; that there is a conversation behind the conversations. As a pattern emerges out of memories there is a hope that new elements are coming into play beyond it. As Koestler put it in his famous book *The Sleepwalkers* we can be engaged in revolutions without ever knowing what they amount to. In Bennett's terms, we need to participate in a greater present moment to see what we mean.

So, forgive me my (relatively) new friends for not mentioning you yet (you are all named elsewhere on the web site of the DuVersity). There may be other people I now do not remember well enough to mention. As I said, what is 'remarkable' for me is that we can dialogue and create meaning together. I have written my little story to encourage others to do the same. Am I dreaming that I am 'Anthony Blake'?

J W von Goethe

Goethe's Gnostic Myth

In this attempt I was greatly influenced by an important work that fell into my hands; it was Arnold's History of the Church and Heretics. This man is not merely a reflective historian, but at the same time devout and sympathetic. His opinions accorded well with mine, and what particularly delighted me in his work was, that I acquired a more favourable idea of many heretics who had hitherto been represented to me as mad or impious. The spirit of contradiction and the love of paradoxes is inherent in all of us. I studied the diflferent opinions with diligence, and as I had often heard it said that in the end every man has a religion of his own, nothing seemed more natural to me than that I should fashion one for myself, and this I did with much satisfaction. Neo-Platonism formed the basis; the hermetical, the mystical, the cabalistic, also contributed their share, and thus I constructed a world for myself that looked strange enough.

I did not find it difficult to represent to myself a Godhead which has gone on producing itself from all eternity; but as production cannot be conceived without multiplicity, so it must of necessity have at once recognized itself as a Second, which we acknowledge under the name of the Son; now these two must have continued the act of production, and again mirrored themselves in a Third, which was just as substantial, living, and eternal as the Whole. With these, however, the circle of the Godhead was complete, and it would not have been possible for them to produce another perfectly equal to them. But since the impulse to production still persisted, they created a fourth existence, which at the outset contained within itself a contradiction, inasmuch as it was, like them, unlimited, and yet at the same time was to be contained in them and bounded by them.

This was Lucifer, to whom the whole power of creation was committed from this time, and from whom all other beings were to proceed. He immediately displayed his infinite activity by creating all the host of angels; all, again, after his own likeness, unlimited, but contained in him and bounded by him. Surrounded by such glory, he forgot his higher origin, and believed that he was self-sufficient, and from this first ingratitude sprang all that does not seem to us in accordance with the will and purposes of the Godhead. Now the more he centred his energies upon himself, the more miserable must he have become, as must also all the spirits whose elevation to their holy origin he had frustrated.

And so that came to pass which is typified to us by the Fall of the Angels. One part of them combined with Lucifer, the other turned again to its origin. In this combination of the whole creation, which had proceeded out of Lucifer, and was forced to follow him, originated all that we perceive under the form of matter, which we figure to ourselves as heavy, solid, and dark, but which, since it is descended^ if not immediately, yet by filiation, from the Divine Being, is just as unlimited, powerful, and eternal as its sire and his sires.

Since then the whole mischief, if we may call it so, arose solely through the one-sided tendency of Lucifer, this creation lacked its nobler half; for it possessed all that is gained by concentration, while it was wanting in all that can only be effected by expansion; and so the whole creation might have destroyed itself by persistent concentration, have annihilated itself with its father Lucifer, and have lost all its claims to an equal eternity with the Godhead.

This condition the Elohim contemplated for a time, and they had the choice, either of waiting for those aeons, in which the field would again have become clear, and space would be left them for a new creation, or of intervening in the existing state of things, and supplying the want in accordance with their own infinity. They chose the latter course, and by their mere will supplied in an instant the whole deficiency entailed by Lucifer's undertaking. They gave to infinite existence the faculty of expanding, of turning towards them; the true pulse of life was again restored, and Lucifer himself could not evade the effects of their intervention.

This is the epoch when what we know as light appeared, and when what we are accustomed to designate by the word creation began. Greatly as this creation multiplied by progressive degrees, through the continuous vital power of the Elohim, nevertheless, a being able to restore thi original connection with the Godhead was still wanting; andd so man was created, who was to be similar, yea, equal to the Godhead in all things; but thereby, in effect, found himself once more in the position of Lucifer, in being at the same time absolute and limited; and, since this contradiction was to manifest itself in him

through all the categories of existence, and a perfect consciousness, as well as a decisive will, was to be an attribute of his state, it was to be foreseen that he must be at the same time the most perfect and the most imperfect, the most happy and the most unhappy creature.

It was not long before he, too, played the part of Lucifer. Separation from the benefactor is ingratitude in essence, and thus a second act of defection was perpetrated, although the whole creation is, and was, nothing but a falling away from and returning to its source.

It is easy to see how in this scheme of things the Redemption was not only decreed from eternity, but was regarded as eternally necessary, nay, as requiring constant renewal throughout the whole period of creation and existence. Hence nothing is more natural than for the Deity himself to take the form of man, which had already been prepared as a vestment, and to share his fate for a short time, in order, by thus assuming his likeness, to enhance his joys and alleviate his sorrows. The history of all religions and philosophies teaches us that this great truth, indispensable for man, has been handed down by different nations, in different times, in various ways, even in strange fables and images, in accordance with their limitations. Suffice it to acknowledge that we find ourselves in a condition which, even if it seems to drag us down and oppress us, yet gives us the opportunity, nay, makes it our duty, to raise ourselves, and to fulfil the purposes of the Godhead, by not omitting regular acts of self-renunciation alternating with the antithetical acts of necessary self-affirmation.

From Goethe's autobiography *Poetry and Truth: From My Own Life* Part II, Book VIII, trans. Minna Steele Smith London: George Bell & Sons, 1908.

Jeremy Puma

Perfect Day Living: Life as a Contemporary Gnostic Keeping Gnosticism Real

One of the biggest problems with much of contemporary Gnosticism, in my humble opinion, is the crazy notion that somehow being a Gnostic means you get to make stuff up. Or, in other words, for some reason the idea has been propagated in certain Gnostic circles that if you claim you're a Gnostic, you can disregard any recent scholarship on historical Gnosticism and just make up whatever you want and claim your personal 'gnosis' as an excuse.

The fact of the matter is, a lot of preconceived notions about historical Gnosticism are being turned on their heads by modern scholarship, and when these notions are continually flogged by so-called Gnostics, it makes us all look out-of-touch and kind of disingenuous. Although the song remains the same regarding the dearth of evidence for any solid conclusions, some serious misconceptions about historical Gnosticism have become so ingrained that many modern Gnostics continue to use them as doctrinal points.

As examples, let's address and hopefully shed some light on a few of these misconceptions:

There was no monolithic Gnosticism fighting against some kind of monolithic Orthodoxy. In reality, Christianity at the height of the Gnostic movement was likely as fragmented as the Gnostic sects. No monolithic Church was doing any more to 'oppress' Gnostic viewpoints than the Gnostics were to oppress other Gnostic viewpoints (and yes, some of that was also going on).

The Gnostics were not 'protesting' or 'rebelling' against established religion. As illustrated very clearly by Michael Williams in *Rethinking Gnosticism*, the idea that Gnostic movements were rebelling against some kind of religious authority is contraindicated by the very Church Fathers who claimed the Gnostics were too inclusive.

There was no monolithic Gnosticism fighting against some kind of monolithic Orthodoxy

The Gnostics were not world-haters. The real world-haters are the ones now celebrated by mainline Christians as the Desert Fathers, who were far more ascetic than 90% of the Gnostics.

The Gnostics did not understand gnosis as a Buddhist-style enlightenment. I'm as guilty as any for spreading this misconception, but even a cursory glance through the Nag Hammadi texts reveals that, to the historical Gnostics, gnosis is far more nuanced than epiphany, and includes ritual instruction into Mysteries and initiation into a tradition.

The Gnostics did not believe that 'personal experience' was more important than religious teaching. Again, the question is a matter of actual evidence, and nothing really exists in the literature that supports this claim. Rather, personal experience was supposed to verify or bolster the religious teaching, and vice-versa.

The Gnostics were dogmatic. Again, a cursory

glance through the literature establishes that the Gnostics were just as dogmatic as the average mainstream Christian sect at the time. The NHL texts are, at their root, a collection of dogmas. The third book of the *Pistis Sophia* contains a giant laundry list of dogmas for practicing Gnostics.

There is virtually no solid evidence for a pre-Christian Gnosticism. This has been proven again and again, but is one of the biggest sticking-points. This isn't to say that there absolutely was not a pre-Christian Gnosticism, but literally no evidence exists that this is the case.

These are just a few examples. Just about every valued notion about Gnosticism held prior to the discovery of the Nag Hammadi Library has been exploded in recent years. Even the automatic assumption that many have that Mary Magdalene was Jesus's favorite has been called into question in a paper called 'Rethinking the Gnostic Mary' by Prof. Stephen Shoemaker, which rather convincingly suggests that the Mary so often appearing with Jesus in the Gnostic literature is in fact Jesus's mother, Mary of Nazareth, and not Mary Magdalene at all!

just about every valued notion about Gnosticism held prior to the discovery of the Nag Hammadi Library has been exploded in recent years

My point isn't that these conclusions must be wholeheartedly embraced by modern Gnostics. My point is simply that modern Gnostic movements must acknowledge that they are *modern* Gnostic movements, with innovations for our *modern* society, which is fine. They must become comfortable with the idea that knowing history and embracing scholarship is not a bad thing, even when scholarship comes to a different conclusion than you.

Many original Gnostics were likely very literate people, with a high regard for scholastics. Denying historical truths due to sentimentalism, romanticism or a desire for rebellion may feel good, but will only harm contemporary Gnosticism in the long run. If we want to be taken seriously instead of viewed as a bunch of people playing at church (and I include myself in this), Contemporary Gnostics need to check and cite their sources, keep up on the research, and underline their differences with historical Gnostics.

Religious innovation is a good thing. If historical Gnostics didn't actually focus on Mary Magdalene, but your group does, that's fine, as long as you're honest with the history. As an example, I, personally, think that in many cases understanding gnosis as more of an enlightenment experience is fine in our contemporary society, but I'm also careful to underscore that the original Gnostics very likely saw it differently. There's nothing wrong with that; it doesn't detract from your path to embrace history. Ignoring scholarship because your 'personal gnosis' tells you that the Gnostics did this or that thing isn't just dishonest, its antithetical to what our forebears sought since the very beginning: a true comprehension of the inbreaking of the Pleroma into the World of Forms.

And another thing: appeals to ignorance are unimpressive. I don't trust a priest who doesn't have interest in actual scholastic studies. If you're a Gnostic Priest and don't have an interest in Gnostic historical studies, you're establishing a 'sola scriptura' of experience. Fundamentalist claims that the Bible is the only authority, who pride themselves on anti-intellectualism and polemicize against historical research that contradicts the literal word of the Bible make just as much sense as the Gnostic Priest who claims that myth trumps history and practicing Gnostic sacramental ritual gets them a free pass to ignore scholastic work. How many times have I heard this from Gnostic priests? 'Oh, that's all well and good, but my experience trumps all of this, so I can safely ignore it.'

Now, I used to hold this attitude, so I can

understand it completely. But I can tell you this: when I started looking into the history with an open mind, that open mind was consistently blown. The visions it gave me about what contemporary Gnosticism can be, just based on the actual history, by being honest about the tradition instead of basing it on séances, still get me really excited. The conscious decision on my part to start ignoring the Frekes and Gandys of the world (who do have their value for some, but not for **serious** students of Gnosticism) and instead to start reading articles from scholarly journals and listening to people who have studied this stuff in the original Coptic was one of the best decisions I've ever made.

What it comes down to for me is this: a stringent embrace of historical honesty is the only thing that separates a valid modern Gnostic view from the UFO cultishness of Samael Aon Weor and John Lash, or the moronic pseudo-gnosticism of Sylvia Browne. Traditions based on the 19th Century Gnostic Revival of Jules Doinel and his motley crew are based on séances and Ouija board sessions, and historically inaccurate descriptions of channeled Cathar Bishops. This doesn't make them wrong or invalid, but it does mean they have the same burden of proof as Weor and crew if they want to be taken seriously.

The desire to take care of those in need/do charitable works/help those in distress is absolutely admirable, laudable, etc., but the same desires can be found in Scientology. What is it that distinguishes these desires in Gnosticism from these desires in Scientology? Gnosis. What is the foundation of the establishment of the Gnostic tradition? Real, actual history as opposed to stuff made up by L. Ron Hubbard.

No one is saying that historical Gnosticism should be reconstructed. Quite the opposite; many of the ancient 'Gnostics' had some pretty odious practices. All that's being asked for is a

little honesty — a little, 'We're not doing exactly what they were doing,' an admission that there really is scant evidence to support the idea that the Cathars were Gnostic (they weren't) but we honor them anyhow because they were amazing people. Instead, when these things are taken as automatic attacks by those of us interested in historical honesty, it comes across as fundamentalism.

What embracing historical honesty can give you is far more profound than what it takes away. Disinterest in historical honesty, or writing off scholasticism because sacramental practice or 'doing good things' somehow means you don't have to worry about it, just comes across as intellectual laziness. What contemporary Gnosticism needs is Sophia and the Logos. Sophia is Wisdom: feminine, intuitive, mythic, beautiful. The Logos is the Word: masculine, intellectual, scholarly/historical, often ugly. It's so focused on Sophia right now that the Logos isn't getting its say, and that's a real potential tragedy.

> *Sophia is Wisdom: feminine, intuitive, mythic, beautiful. The Logos is the Word: masculine, intellectual, scholarly/historical, often ugly*

Andrew Phillip Smith

Into the Bridal Chamber:

Blasphemy: Making Sacred Images into Sacred Cows

This year, for no apparent practical or popular purpose, a new blasphemy law was passed in the Republic of Ireland by the Dáil, the Irish parliament. I will briefly outline the political process by which and for which the bill was passed, but I am more interested in the nature of blasphemy itself, its relationship to free speech and whether it is really important. Ireland already has a blasphemy law, and this is required by its constitution (which has a substantial religious content, beginning, 'In the Name of the Most Holy Trinity, from Whom is all authority and to Whom, as our final end, all actions both of men and States must be referred'; the blasphemy provision comes straight after the guarantee of free speech!) but in 1999, in the last case of blasphemy to be tried, the judge determined that under current law it was impossible to determine 'of what the offence of blasphemy consists'.[1]

This was surely a neat and modern solution. Ireland had its blasphemy law, as required, yet nobody could be prosecuted for it—entirely appropriate in what is now quite a secular country. Catholicism still holds its place in the heart of the Irish people, anchored there by long periods of British Protestant oppression, yet the sex abuse scandals, the authoritarianism of post-independence Irish Catholicism and the general secularisation of western Europe have had their effect. There was no substantial movement of genuine concern over blasphemy, no Catholic leaders urging for stricter blasphemy provisions, no moral campaigners. Sure enough, Ireland has had a bit more religion-based censorship than much of the western world (Monty Python's Life of Brian was banned, so was Madonna

picture book Sex; the list of hundreds of books and periodicals still on the list include such disparate publications *How to Drive Your Man Wild in Bed*; *Abortion: Right or Wrong?*; *Best Detective Cases*; and a magazine called *Anus*.)

As an advocate of free speech I became interested in the bill and even found myself attending a meeting of Atheist Ireland, though I missed the earlier fireworks caused by the attendance of a prominent right-wing Catholic journalist. (I should add that while I'm not really a theist, I'm certainly not an atheist in the common sense of the word; neither am I an atheist-hater, my poem in this issue is intended to be humorous.). The bill that was eventually passed (by a vote of 23 to 22) was extremely vague in its definition of blasphemy. ('a person publishes or utters blasphemous matter if (a) he or she publishes or utters matter that is grossly abusive or insulting in relation to matters held sacred by any religion, thereby causing outrage among a substantial number of the adherents of that religion, and (b) he or she intends, by the publication or utterance of the matter concerned, to cause such outrage') and had an extra clause tacked onto the end at the last minute with the intention of denying an appeal to the blasphemy law by controversial groups such as the Scientologists. Probably the government are hoping that the law will be filed away, no one will bring up a case, and that is the last that we will ever hear about it.

Atheist Ireland wanted to issue some kind of blasphemous statement or image as a test challenge to the law once it is in effect. They had trouble deciding what the statement should be, and how to publish it. Atheist Ireland wished to record attendees proclaiming that they blasphemed the holy spirit, reasoning that, since Matt. 12:31-32 and parallels describes this as the only unforgivable sin, it's a worthy form of blasphemy. Strangely, I was a bit squeamish at doing this, since I interpret the Holy Spirit in this saying as referring to one's own spiritual possibilities. However, I have no objection to anyone else blaspheming the Holy Spirit, recording and broadcasting it.

How about an image of Jesus on the cross with an erection? Few people with any kind of Christian background can hear that suggestion without at least drawing breath for a moment. I believe I owe the concept to a record cover by the anarchist punk band Crass, though I have been unable to trace it. There have been other images of an aroused Jesus. A one foot high statue of a very traditional Jesus, of the good shepherd not the crucified variety, with a disproportionate and crudely- fashioned erect penis by Terence Koh caused controversy when it was exhibited at the Baltic Centre for Contemporary Art in Gateshead, in the north of England.[2] The March 2006 issue of the Student Insurgent, a student newspaper at University of Oregon featured a picture of a brightly coloured Christ with a snaky red penis entitled, straightforwardly, *Jesus With Erection*.[3] Photographer Andres Serrano's 1987 photo *Piss Christ* settled for a crucifix in a bottle of the artist's urine. There is undoubtedly something teenage and obvious about these works, yet they are still unsettling.

Ironically, the notion of an erect Jesus may be biologically sound, as crucifixion may actually result in an erection, because of asphyxiation. Apparently there a few examples of this depicted in sixteenth Flemish art, when the understanding of anatomy was developing swiftly.[5]

I find this very interesting. What seemed to be the most shocking example of blasphemy

that I was willing to entertain publicly (and it certainly shocked me as a teenager) turns out to be historically feasible and to have pious associations in at least one period. A number of medieval churches boasted the foreskin of Jesus as a holy relic. The eighteenth-century Moravian sect visualised Christ's side wound as a vagina and saw the spear as a phallic object. Clearly, what may be blasphemous to certain Christians at a certain time is acceptable to others. Blasphemy is relative.

Why would opponents of religion, or anyone else, wish to blaspheme? There can certainly be a destructive element, and it's common for disaffected ex-religionists to insult the traditions in which they were brought up. But religions have set themselves up for this. Sacred images are easy targets when they have been made into sacred cows. I believe that free speech overrides any niceties of religious power.

It may not be pleasant for believers to have their sacred images defiled, but there is some potential benefit in it for the believer. Idolatry is a common pitfall in religion, and what better antidote to it could there be than in having one's idols blasphemed?

Idolatry is a common pitfall in religion, and what better antidote to it could there be than in having one's idols blasphemed?

Religious practitioners could even facilitate this themselves. Perhaps all religions should set aside one day a year on which all sacred images are to be blasphemed, ridiculed and generally assaulted and insulted. Display that statue of Jesus with an erection, lewd tableaux of the pope with a bare arse, frolicking disciples and the sexual triumph of Mary Magdalene.

Arguably, Protestants have already discarded or downgraded the importance of religious iconography, so perhaps they could imprison their ministers naked in the stocks and pelt them with rotten eggs, or burn stacks of Bibles on the bonfire. Similarly for Muslims with the Qur'an and Islamic symbols—those Danish cartoons might come in handy after all. Gurus and occult paraphernalia would not be exempt. The very next day, everything could be put back in place and all could go back to normal. I am of course being a little facetious in my exaggeration, but I do feel that there is an important point here. Recognise the temporal quality of your religious iconography. If you meet Buddha on the road, kill him.

Where should the line be drawn, if it should be drawn anywhere? Simple courtesy is a good principle—when individuals meet, it's important to have a basic respect for the other's position, but discussion . But in the public arena, different rules apply and, with very few exceptions, which are to do with the direct incitement of violence and the use of harmful acts (such as child sex) to produce the art in the first place, free speech should be tolerated absolutely. Blasphemy is not necessarily motivated by hatred of others, but is part of an interaction with tradition. Images and concepts do not retain a positive power indefinitely and last millennium's revolutionary insight might be today's justification for oppression. Sacred images are human creations. The crucified Jesus is the work of artists, Muhammad the work of writers.

If the Irish blasphemy law were taken seriously we might find that many popular works of the last century are candidates for banning—even the Da Vinci Code might be banned. (This might be no bad thing in itself, but we have to respect Dan Brown's right to free speech.) Many Gnostic texts are technically blasphemous. Yaldabaoth in the place of Yahweh in the garden, Jesus laughing on the cross, Simon of Cyrene crucified in the place of Jesus. Religions, though they are keen to attack blasphemy against their own traditions, tend to blaspheme each other. Dante places Muhammad in the hell of the schismatics (making the recent Muhammad cartoons seem particularly a feeble cause for Islamic rage.) The Qur'an states that Jesus didn't die on the cross; in some copies of the Talmud, Jesus is boiled in shit. Perhaps the Inferno should be removed from Irish bookshops.

Surely it is best to have an attitude to one's religion that does not require a rigid identification with arbitrary images. If one's religion is true or meaningful or useful or valuable, blasphemy is of no account whatsoever. The mainstream religions are big enough to take it.

NOTES

1 There was widespread coverage on the new blasphemy law in the Irish and British press. Search for 'ireland blasphemy' in Google News for several articles. Justification for the new law, which was bundled with a reform to the Irish libel laws, is entirely based on constitutional issues.

2 See http://www.dailymail.co.uk/news/article-505880/Controversial-statue-Jesus-erection-offends-gallery-visitors.html

3 'Jesus With Erection' has a Wikipedia article all to itself, http://en.wikipedia.org/wiki/Jesus_with_erection

4 Ditto *Piss Christ*, http://en.wikipedia.org/wiki/Piss_Christ

5 Roland Mushat Frye, review of The Sexuality of Christ in Renaissance Art and in Modern Oblivion by Leo Steinberg in *Theology Today*, http://theologytoday.ptsem.edu/apr1985/v42-1-bookreview6.htm

Book Reviews

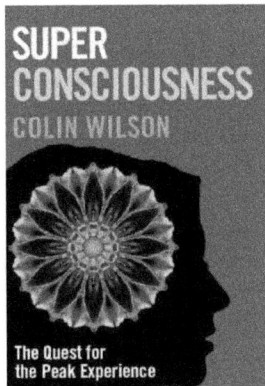

Super Consciousness: The Quest for the Peak Experience, **Colin Wilson, Paperback, Watkins Publishing 218pp, £10.99**

The author tells us in the foreword that most of his 75 years of life have been devoted to a search for what might be called 'the mechanisms of the Peak Experience', and that this present book can be regarded as a kind of DIY manual on how to achieve it. 'Peak Experiences' are what psychologist Abraham Maslow calls those moments of ecstasy when one seems to transcend normal consciousness, when one is granted a 'bird's eye view' of life instead of the 'worm's eye view' we normally have. Others have given it different names. For Maurice Bucke at the beginning of the twentieth century it was 'cosmic consciousness', and for mystics throughout the ages it has been called 'unitive consciousness'. For Proust such experiences were *moments bienheureux*, when, as Chesterton puts it, we feel like recipients of 'absurd good news'.

It has almost always been assumed that such experiences come unbidden, that we can't induce them, and even the great mystics, who enjoy elevated states of consciousness more routinely than the rest of us, would attribute them to grace rather than to effort or to technique. Maslow himself is quoted by Wilson as saying that there is no infallible method of inducing them, and that 'they come when they want to, and go when they want to' (pages 8-9).

But Wilson disagrees, and thinks that we can learn how to experience 'power consciousness' almost at will. Maslow, he claims, is inconsistent. He assumes that such states are beyond our control, and yet he tells us that when people talk about their experiences with others they begin to have them regularly. If sharing such experiences with others increases their frequency, then perhaps there are other techniques that one can employ to bring them about. In the final chapter of the book, Wilson outlines the methods that he has found to be effective and I won't give the game away by telling you what they are here. Suffice it to say that they are simple exercises in concentration, and it is quite possible that every one of us has employed them at some time or another and experienced a consequent elevation of consciousness without realising it, or perhaps, without capitalising upon it.

It takes Wilson a long time to get to this final chapter, but his preparatory material is never boring. He takes a long look at the pessimistic philosophers and writers of the last couple of hundred years, and particularly at the Irish playwright Samuel Beckett, whose work seems to epitomise existential powerlessness and to encourage a sense of defeat which is the very antithesis of 'power consciousness'. Such writers and thinkers, says Wilson, would have us believe that the world is an accident, that human life is pointless, and while we think like them, moments of clarity, optimism and insight will elude us.

With characteristic and breathtaking audacity, Wilson gives a brief outline of history in about eight pages (chapter 9), and chapter twelve reviews the history of philosophy from Descartes to Wittgenstein, just to show how we have been led into an intellectual cul-de-sac but materialist thinkers. The brevity of such chapters and Wilson's tendency to make jaw-dropping generalisations ('neurosis is a form of self-hypnosis', 'now it so happens that we can give the exact date for the birth of musical romanticism, over two centuries ago') will raise a few eyebrows among academics, but Wilson writes with clarity and wit, sprinkling even the more difficult passages with amusing and informative anecdotes, and explaining in a sentence or two the basic ideas of men like Hegel, Schopenhauer, Nietzsche, Hume, and Wittgenstein.

I enjoyed this book, as I have enjoyed everything I've read by Colin Wilson. Few writers can make a work of spiritual philosophy into a page turner. It's a good read and, for the most part, an easy read. What's more, if you succeed with Wilson's methods of achieving peak experiences, the book will be worth much more than the few pounds you paid for it.

Bill Darlison

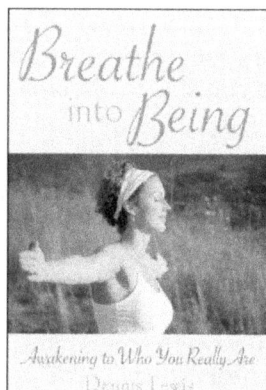

Breathe into Being: Awakening to Who You Really Are, Dennis Lewis, Quest Books, 115pp, $16.95/£14.99

I believe it's a sign of spiritual health and maturity that, as you get older, you start to see things much more simply. Many unnecessary things fall away, and the lens through which you see the world becomes far less cluttered than it was during the frantic search for meaning of your previous decades. Life becomes a kind of distillation of all you have learned, a distillation down to its essential ingredients.

At least, that is how I see it. So I tend to look for spiritual guidance and instruction that has a simple message and practice. For that reason alone, I knew I was going to find Dennis Lewis' new book, 'Breathe into Being,' a valuable addition to my spiritual library.

I've had a long interest in the use of following the breath for developing mindfulness, and Dennis Lewis' work is one of the clearest and most practical expositions of this powerful tool for awakening. Lewis' CV, and authority, is impressive, to say the least. He is a graduate of three grand schools of consciousness: the Gurdjieff Work under Lord John Pentland, Advaita Vedanta under Jean Klein, and Taoism under Mantak Chia. Lewis' approach is a skilful distillation of these three fruitful paths to awakening, with a powerful simplicity and great depth.

In Lewis' own words, there are few, if any contemporary books that 'explore the depths to which breathing itself, natural breathing, is a portal to presence, an ever-present gateway to awakening to and being what you really are.' There are no lengthy and learned treatises here, but a rich tapestry of around 70 micro-chapters. It is more like a workbook, which Lewis says comes closer to how he actually teaches in a workshop setting. Each chapter contains a specific practice, and there were many unique exercises that I had not seen before which I immediately incorporated into my daily practice.

Many of these exercises are effective methods for healing tension, undoing the physical and emotional knots and blocks that impede thee free flow of energy in what Lewis calls 'this amazing temple of awareness' called the human body.

However, the main focus of these practices is developing non-attachment, or non-identification, gently disengaging our identity away from the ego or personality, and releasing it into that wider ground of being that we are.

Lewis' practices of simply following the breath are effective tools for generating mindfulness and presence, the space in which we can discover the truth about ourselves and the world. They are wonderful exercises for developing that most valuable of spiritual commodities: attention.

'The key is simply to be present, to pay attention without any expectation or judgement, to what is happening as you read and practice and live. And it is to realise that *being* this presence, along with whatever appears within its field of illumination, is the very miracle and meaning for which you have been searching. (*Breathe into Being* p.8)

Leonardo Da Vinci once said that simplicity is the ultimate sophistication. *Breathe into Being* is one of the most sophisticated guides to awakening I have read.

Tony Cartledge

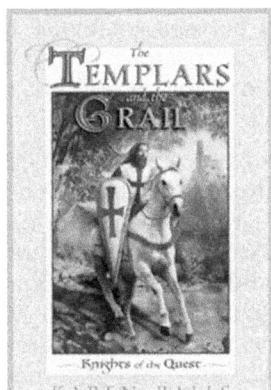

***The Templars and the Grail: Knights of the Quest*, Karen Rails, Quest Books, 320pp, $22.95/£22**

Who were the Knights Templars? Were they an esoteric sect possessed of great secrets, or just a bunch of medieval merchant bankers (Cockney rhyming slang intentional.) Books on the Templars tend to polarize between the two views, either being fully-fledged works of alternative history, with all the unorthodoxy, fascinating possibilities and dubious scholarship that implies, or solid histories of stolid warrior-monks, decent fellows who would always honour a cheque.

This slim book manages to include both views. The first half of this book is a fairly straightforward and careful account of the Templars that draws on standard scholarly resources. It's a nice, readable summary of what we know of the Templars, sketched out in a little over some 100 pages, covering their nature, origins, organisation and beliefs and downfall. There are plenty of conundrums and disagreement even among mainstream historians.

The second part is also a careful summary, but here the subject is the more speculative alternative historical research. Alternative history flourishes in the absence of reliable resources, and in areas of research that are somehow seen as unrespectable by academic historians. The loss of the Templars' archive means that there is much that we do not know about this influential group. After all, if we can't be certain of what was going on, then why not be a little more extravagant, more speculative, a little more romantic? Rails' particular strength is that she never mocks these unorthodox reconstructions and conjectures, neither does she resort to a mere tradition history of the post-Templar myths. Rather, she investigates the claims and shows what is feasible and what is pure speculation. Her survey covers the question of what secret (treasure or otherwise) the knights may have uncovered beneath the Temple Mount, whether the Templars had a connection with Oak Island, Nova Scotia, and whether at the end of the fourteenth century, Prince Henry Sinclair established Templar colonies in the New World. I was, however, disappointed to see no discussion of Baphomet, the idolatrous head alleged to be worshipped by the Templars.

All in all, this book is a wonderful brief introduction to the Templars of fact and speculation and an excellent guide to either hemisphere of Templar research.

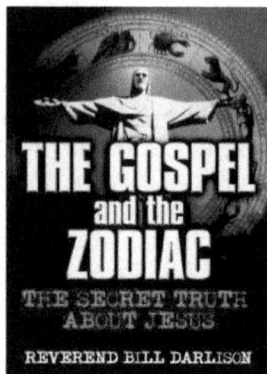

The Gospel and the Zodiac, **Bill Darlison, Gerald Duckworth and Co, 256pp £16.99/$14.95**

The Gospel and the Zodiac by Bill Darlison explores the astrological foundations of the Gospel of Mark from the perspective of a Unitarian minister. Darlison considers the possibility that the writer of Mark was well-versed in astrology, and that he deliberately defied the convention of the other synoptic gospels in order to lay out the life of Jesus on the cyclical map of the Zodiac. This approach, Darlison says, answers many of the questions that scholars have puzzled over for ages, by putting it in context of the wheel of the Zodiac. Further, while some might think that this astrological framework takes away from the gospel, 'the annual journey of the sun through the zodiac is a natural symbol for all journeys and, in particular, for the life-journey of the human being.' Darlison shows that we, like Jesus, can follow this pattern, making this symbolic journey in what ultimately is a spiritual transformation.

The book includes a few introductory chapters (to set the astrological scene), and then one chapter per Zodiac sign, and finally a few appendices, mostly notable of which includes Darlison's own translation of the Gospel of Mark (which he admittedly did to avoid infringing any copyright upon existing translations). This translation is very similar to other modern ones, barring the odd word or two or a few differences in structure of verse. It's not exactly essential to the book, but it's a nice addition, as anyone wishing to read the quotes that Darlison gives to support his work might want to check them in context to see if they really live up to the claim. I suggest reading multiple modern translations, however, in order to ensure a less biased view of this gospel.

The main twelve chapters dealing with the Zodiac signs are where we really get into the heart of the matter. Darlison has divided the Gospel of Mark into what he views are its distinct astrological segments, which he then explores in some detail in the relevant Zodiac chapter. Some material slots in easily, while other pieces seem a little forced, but all in all these sections make for an intriguing and revealing read. The link between the names of some of the stars in the constellations and similar wording used in Mark (often giving supporting versions from the other gospels, which, Darlison argues, don't have the astrological cycle, but retain the astrological symbolism better than Mark) is particularly intriguing, and every so often you'll come across something that ties up so well you have a hard time believing it could be any other way.

While I'm not entirely sold on everything that Darlison postulates, I was very impressed with this book. It's clear that Darlison has done a lot of astrological study, and his background as a minister gives him an edge on reading the gospels in their original tongue (and thus allowing him to point out better approximations for transliterated words). He shares a lot in this book, allowing it to become somewhat of a reference for anyone wishing to explore the topic, as I found myself dipping in and out to reread certain passages that I found intriguing.

Although I am biased in favour of astrology (in its deep, complex form – not the pop-culture astrology of modern magazines, which Darlison likewise dismisses), I've tried to keep as objective a mindset while reading this book as possible. However, that hasn't stopped me from coming to the conclusion that yes, there is astrology in the Bible, and even the most fundamentalist anti-occult party will have a hard time denying it; it has also helped me to come to the conclusion that the gospel writers were not just aware of astrology, but did actively utilise it in their texts, even if merely to add to the impact of their symbolism. While I will not go so far as to say that the texts were deliberately and systematically planned in an astrological framework (after all, there are many more layers to them than that), I find it hard to deny that astrological symbolism and motifs are readily apparent in the texts (the most striking and obvious of which is the frequent Piscean fish symbolism of Christ, correlating with the entry into the Age of Pisces in c. 2000 CE). If you have an interest in either astrology or biblical studies, this is a text to add to your shelf. It doesn't answer all the questions, but it certainly raises a few new and important ones, and will easily expand the knowledge of most people who read it.

Dean Wilson

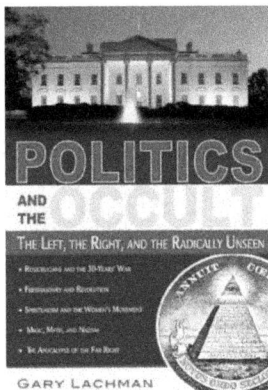

***Politics and the Occult: The Left, the Right and the Radically Unseen* by Gary Lachmann, Quest Books, 336pp, $19.95/£18.99**

Occultism has been a persistent presence in western society throughout the ages, but ever since the European Enlightenment it has been marginalized. Yet great figures, from Newton through to Goethe and Jung have continued to hold occult interests alongside their more respectable studies. Occultism has permeated science, literature, music and the other arts and semi- or pseudo-occult organisations such as the Freemasons have had influence in the highest layers of society. So it should be no surprise that there have been occult influences and associates on all sides of the political endeavour, on both the left and right wings, to use that clumsy terminology.

This is primarily a history of occult movements as they relate to politics—indeed, it covers most of the major western occult movements since the Renaissance and doubles as a selective history of western esotericism. Occasionally the amount of background material that Lachman must provide on the history of the occult groups (small societies and individuals are the essence of this story) swamps the political background, but to be fait, there is really no other way to do it.

Lachmann traces the beginning of western occult association with politics to the early (and invisible) Rosicrucian movement and its influence on Frederick V of Bohemia and James I of England. Along the way he takes in freemasonry, synarchy (supposedly the opposite of anarchy), Theosophy, with Annie Besant's support for Indian independence (and surprising associations between Blavatsky and Garibaldi), and the Nazis of course.

There are surprises throughout. For instance, I hadn't realised that the Romanian academic Ioan Culianu (Couliano in the Italian spelling), author of the excellent The Tree of Gnosis, was murdered with a shot to the back of the head. His story is part of a complex of fascist-leaning European occultism centred around Julius Evola, that takes in René Schwaller de Lubicz, René Guenon and Mircea Eliade.

This is an excellent study, and it will be the standard work on the subject. The overall picture perhaps lacks cohesion, as Lachmann has been careful not to draw false positives from his study. I was left with a feeling that the occult and politics don't share any essential nature, any more that do art and politics or the occult and agriculture, for instance, rather we simply see the intersection of the two, as in a Venn diagram. In the final chapter, Lachman regrets the banality of the modern world, but concludes that the diversity of culture and relative freedoms that we experience are preferable to untenable, authoritarian spiritual utopias like synarchism. It is a moving conclusion, and I wholeheartedly agree with him.

Andrew Phillip Smith

Kiss of Death: The True History of the Gospel of Judas, Tobias Churton, Watkins Publishing, £10.99 /$19.95

When the Gospel of Judas was released at Easter 2006 it caused a scene in the media, flooding newspapers and television stations, exciting some, while unsettling others. However, while the material itself was presented, and various reactions given, there was little said about the unearthing of this work, which is a rather intriguing tale in and of itself. *Kiss of Death*, by Tobias Churton, was primarily written for this purpose, giving the history of the Gospel, along with a summary of the ideas presented in the Gospel (now disputed by a number of scholars), a look at the reaction it got (which most of us know about, given it was not all that long ago), and an appraisal of the character of Judas as a whole, whether he is the ultimate saint or the ultimate sinner.

The early parts of the book are intriguing, filled with the kind of suspense one might find in a thriller or a conspiracy novel. Churton is careful to play up this style in the first chapter of the book (dealing with the history around the discovery and publication of the Gospel), with references to 'the plot', 'characters', and other such fictional devices. This makes for some interesting reading, as well as exposing some little known facts about how the Gospel was treated before its publication. Churton also employs throughout the text a fairly down to earth writing style, a somewhat conversationalist tone that some readers may find appealing: 'Peter was to be, so to speak, Chief Bouncer at Club Jesus.'

Unfortunately Churton's style is also mingled with a number of his personal judgements about various matters, which tend to mar the academic quality of the work. An example of this is when Churton gives a crude comparison of archaeology to grave-robbing: 'If it was *your* grave, would you care who had broken in? *Rest in peace*? You'll be lucky! Of course, many people today probably don't think the dead are in a poisition to care about anything.' Not only is this sentiment entirely irrelevant to the subject matter of the book itself, but its high moral tone is somewhat hypocritical, given the fact that Churton would have been unable to write this book had it not been for the 'grave-robbing' that resulted in the Gospel of Judas being released.

Another example of this is 'Science is for scientists, truth is for sale. The more you pay, the more you get.' I don't really see where this kind of thing has a place in a work dealing with the history of the Gospel of Judas.

If the above was not bad enough, Churton frequently makes irrelevant references to pop culture events, such as: 'the 15 leather-bound codices [...] had been unearthed a few months after the first atom bombs exploded in Japan in 1945, but were not punlished in an edition suitable for the general public until the Sex Pistols sang *God Save the Queen* 32 years later.' Why he could not have simply used the dates alone like most other scholars would have done is beyond me; after all, does someone wanting to know more about the Gospel of Judas really need to know anything about World War II or what songs the Sex Pistols sang? Another example: 'darkness and stale air would envelop [the codex] as menacingly as the flames that embraced Rosebud at the climax of *Citizen Kane*.'

The book is also fairly sparse in references, with a mere handful of them provided at the back of the book. While this allows for the style to be less dry than other academic texts on the matter, its scholarly value is also undermined. For example, at several points he references something indirectly, such as 'One contributor to an internet blogging site has referred to...'. We are never told who the contributor is, what the blog link is, when it was accessed, or given any kind of reference to find this information.

One of the biggest issues with the book, however, and one that Churton cannot really be blamed for, is the fact that the entire translation and interpretation of the Gospel of Judas has, since its initiation publication, been disputed by a number of respected scholars, all of whom suggest that the Gospel does not display Judas in quite as favourable a light as we have been led to believe (one such translation, by Jesse Folks, can be found in Issue 1 of *The Gnostic*). Given that Churton has devoted most of his book to supporting the idea that Judas is really a hero figure (and it is very clear that he does), it makes the entire book open to question. If Judas was not this vilified hero, then Churton's views merely represent an appraisal of the initial perception of the Gospel, not where it stands today. Given this I can see very limited appeal in this book for recent readers who have already been exposed to multiple viewpoints on the matter, and the only real value of the book is in the initial chapter on the discovery and publication of the Gospel.

Dean Wilson

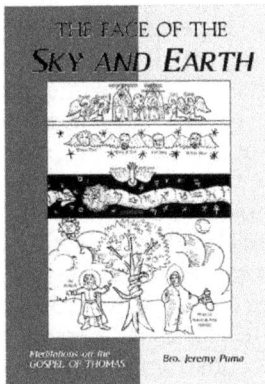

The Face of the Sky and Earth by Jeremy Puma, Jeremy Puma, 271pp, $16.95

Jeremy Puma has positioned himself at the intersection of the modern Gnostic ecclesiastical movement and modern academic scholarship in an online community known as the *Palm Tree Garden*. He makes use of that vantage and his own illustrative idiosyncratic style to produce a great introductory work for individuals interested in cracking some of the puzzling and impenetrable passages of the *Gospel of Thomas*.

Since the *Gospel of Thomas* is a sayings gospel containing a disparate collection of often unrelated phrases, Jeremy separates these out into a collection of short essays that parse and decode metaphors that at times puzzle the modern reader. He makes appropriate connections to New Testament and non-canonical sources and fills in gaps that the original hearers of these words would have understood with ease.

The charm of Jeremy Puma's *The Face of the Sky and Earth* comes from the humorous ways that he breaks down the most complex ideas of the ancient Gnostics without bogging the reader down in the minutiae of ancient cosmological systems. For example, he explains such philosophical conundrums as spacetime, the 'one and the many' and the immanence of God by way of a metaphor involving an infinite block of swiss cheese complete with holes.

This is a very approachable introduction to the *Gospel of Thomas*. It provides a general reader with many of the necessary semiotic codes of the ancient Gnostics required to get beyond first base with a text that can read more like a series of Zen koans than a traditional gospel to the average reader. Beyond that, one is introduced to Jeremy Puma's delicate mental balancing act as he combines his experience of the contemporary moment with an abiding love for the wisdom contained in this most amazing collection of phrases that just may be our closest link to the words of Jesus.

Scott Finch

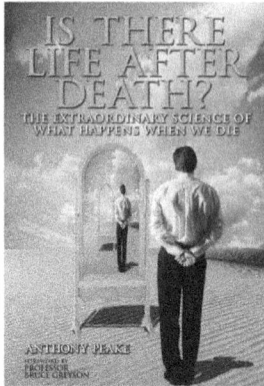

Is There Life After Death?, Anthony Peake, Arcturus Publishing, 416pp, £6.99/$9.99

The Daemon: A Guide to Your Extraordinary Secret Self, Anthony Peake, Arcturus Publishing, 336pp, £9.99

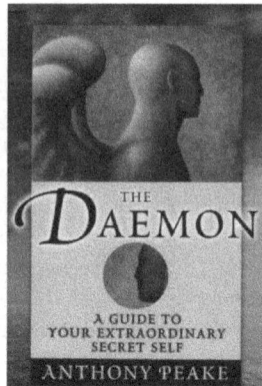

Eternal recurrence is an ancient concept, often confused with reincarnation. In its purest form, it posits that we live a succession of more or less identical lives. When we die we are reborn as the same person at the same time, in the same location, to the same parents, in the same historical setting. Variations on this idea may be found in Dionysian mystery religion, Ovid, possibly in the church father Origen, perhaps in Shakespeare and in modern times in the works of Nietzsche (and hence the twentieth century philosophers Heidegger and Derrida), and P.D. Ouspensky and his associates.

Now writer Anthony Peake has revived and updated the idea as part of the all-encompassing framework of his Cheating the Ferryman theory, as described in his recent books *Is There Life After Death* (*ITLAD*) and *The Daemon*. Peake bases his ideas on modern science, principally quantum physics, neurology and experimental psychology, but finds evidence of his approach in ancient mysticism and anecdotal evidence. The focal point of his theory is his assertion that the human mind is actually a dyad consisting of two separate entities, located in the left and right brain hemispheres respectively, which he terms the Eidolon and the Daemon. *ITLAD* focuses on the scientific evidence for parallel worlds (the Many Worlds theory), déjà vu, Near Death Experience (NDE) and neuroscience, particularly split brain experiments, pulling all of these together into a theory of survival after death (or rather, just before death) in an internal and eternal repetition of the life that has just been experienced. Eternal recurrence, while central to his theory, occupies a single chapter of the first book. (In personal correspondence, Peake told me that he had originally included more material on Ouspensky and Rodney Collin, but the editor had felt that this strayed too far off the beaten track, and the material was cut.)

Peake argues that just before death the brain is flooded with a cocktail of neurochemicals similar to those that cause Temporal Lobe Epilepsy. The dying person experiences time dilation, and other phenomena associated with NDE, including a split between the Daemon consciousness and the everyday Eidolon consciousness. The Eidolon relives the entire life in real-time while the Daemon observes it. The Daemon has experienced this life previously, and hence, when contact with the Daemon is occasionally established, psychological/paranormal phenomena like déjà vu or precognition are experienced, because the Daemon really has seen it all before. When this second life comes to an end, the same thing happens again and the life replays again, in a shorter period of time. Peake makes use of Zeno's Paradox to show that the life can recur again and again in shorter periods of time. This 'recursive recurrence' is hence a kind of immortality. The theory is extraordinarily elegant and encompasses all sort of phenomena. Peake argues us that the world we perceive is actually a virtual reality construct based on the energy and particles out there in the 'objective world'. Peake has been doing further work on his theory, particularly to reduce the solipsistic element, which is certainly the biggest barrier I have to accepting the theory as a whole.

Peake refers to some fascinating anecdotal and

experimental evidence. My favourite is a young man who wished to be put into a light hypnotic trance by the psychologist Milton Erickson. He found himself on a hillside in a perfectly real environment looking at a six-year-old boy on a hill. He quickly realised that this boy was himself and observed his own progress through life in real time all the way until he attended university and volunteered to be hypnotised by Milton Erickson. This is linked by Peake to the famous drowning-man-whose-life-repeats-before-his-eyes of the Near Death Experience.

In *The Daemon* he moves away somewhat from the quantum physics and neurology and examines, for instance, concepts within Gnosticism. *The Daemon* moves on to examine the nature of the dual consciousness and pulls in a good deal more material from religious tradition. The first couple of chapters reiterate the neurological basis of *ITLAD* and, it must be said, its first 100 pages or so are highly repetitive of *ITLAD*. Peake's theory is so broad that he could have come at it from many angles—the first book could have had as its primary theme eternal recurrence, precognition, parallel worlds, synchronicity or the nature of perception.

I am not particularly scientifically minded, but I love the grand and strange ideas of modern physics though I can only really appreciate them via popular science. In *ITLAD*, Peake uses scientific research (though some of it is quite speculative) as the basis for his ideas, but his conclusions go far beyond this. One may have expected that his ideas are unlikely to be taken too seriously by the scientific establishment, but the foreword is written by Dr Jason W. Brown, Clinical Professor of Neurology at NYU, and other open-minded scientists seem to be interested. It would be interesting to see if Peake could devise experiments by which his hypotheses could be tested.

Peake makes good use of the *Hymn of the Pearl*, the beautiful Gnostic story found inserted in the text of the *Acts of Thomas*. The hymn concerns the descent of a prince into Egypt, where he must quest to retrieve a pearl before he can return to his home country and be united with the Robe of Glory. The text is characterised by its overlapping imagery (see my *Gnostic Writings on the Soul: Annotated & Explained* for a translation and commentary) and Peake easily fits the younger and older brothers and other facets of the story into his Eidolon/Daemon scheme.

He interprets the parable of the ass and the millstone in the *Gospel of Philip* as referring to eternal recurrence. The mysterious 'images' in the *Gospel of Thomas* and the *Gospel of Philip* are seen as referring to the Eidolon (though the Coptic original is the Greek loanword EIKON.) Mani's twin is understood to be the Daemon, and in the *Book of Thomas*, Jesus is interpreted as the Daemon and Thomas ('twin') as the Eidolon. An entire chapter of the second book is devoted to the experiences of Philip K. Dick. Peake draws a brief comparison between Mani's experiences and those of Philip Dick. As a young man at the beginning of his writing career, Dick saw what he believed to be a future-self doppleganger, which in Peake's scheme are visual representations of the Daemon. 1974 experiences mirror many of the characteristics of Peake's Daemon concept. There are several errors in Peake's description of the Gnostics, which is unfortunate as whenever I have been able to check the scientific material he uses, I have found his accounts to be accurate. Worst is 'pleorama' instead of Pleroma. At first I had thought this an intentional neologism, but it's a straightforward error, and one that Peake has been keen to correct after publication. The Gnostics didn't actually use the terms Eidolon and Daemon, though Peake gives interesting examples of the word in, for example, Epictetus and Plotinus.

In Gnostic literature, the Gnostic soul-spirit dichotomy is clearly expressed in some texts but very much a below the surface presence in others. The binary soul has been explored, in an unorthodox Christian context, by Peter Novak in his books *The Division of Consciousness* and *The Lost Secret of Death*, but with nowhere near as much clarity.

I found Peake's attempt to limit the extent of precognition unconvincing. He argues (from the examples of Nostradamus, Robert Nixon and Mother Shipton) that precognition is only possible if the predicted events occur within the prophet's own lifetime. Obviously, this is essential for his idea that the Daemon has experienced the Eidolon's life before, and hence may inform the Eidolon of what will occur. Thus, precognition beyond the time of the prophet's death would be impossible, at least for Peake's proposed mechanism. However, I didn't find his examples of seemingly accurate prophecy all that convincing. It is, however, an interesting take on the subject.

Peake bases his study of the Daemon on brain science. Thus, his best examples of individual contact with the inner Daemon rest on illness-induced abnormal psychology, particularly Temporal Lobe Epilepsy. (Well, it's nice to have epilepsy restored to its semi-divine status.) He suggests, as have others before him, that Socrates' Daemon, the inner voice that informed him when he was about to make a wrong decision derives from epilepsy. Socrates' occasional strange habit of standing motionless for shorter or longer periods of time is interpreted as a *petit mal* epileptic seizure . The same is claimed of Joan of Arc and her inner voices. In *The Daemon* Peake reveals that he has suffered from migraines, the initial symptoms of which (including déjà vu) resemble the perception-altering aspects of the aura that precedes temporal lobe epileptic seizures. Additionally he describes the coincidences and a precognitive dream which led him to write his first book.

I found myself wondering whether the Daemon actually a higher self, or merely an older, more experienced version of the Eidolon? Spiritual traditions place the higher self on a different level to the everyday self, but the focus on abnormal brain conditions and psychopathology somewhat undermines the Daemon's claim to really be any kind of transcendent self . However, Peake does acknowledge that the Daemon is a higher self, and believes that it is important to make contact with one's own Daemon, and appeals to the Gnostics and other esoteric religion as examples of people who understood the importance of the Daemon and had developed methods of contacting their own Daemons. Again, it seems that Peake's extension of his theory in collaboration with Karl LeMarks may cover some of these objections.

These are fascinating books. Peake also has a talent for promoting his ideas which resonate with all sorts of disciplines and subject areas. Expect to hear a lot more about the Daemon and Eidolon in the future.

Andrew Phillip Smith

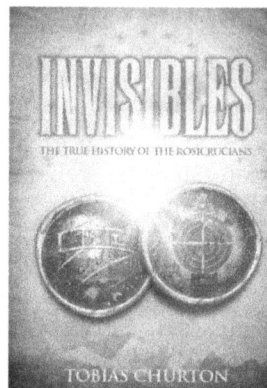

Invisibles: The True History of the Rosicrucians, Tobias Churton, Lewis, 496pp, £19.99

Following the various strands of the Rosicrucian movement from the seemingly fictional beginnings of the group in a 1614 pamphlet to the possible Rosicrucian influence on the twentieth-century Prieuré de Sion debacle, Churton provides the definitive guide to their history and influence. But be warned, this is not an easy read. Churton's prose style is dense and discursive and each stage of the story is described in considerable detail. Along the way we encounter many of the familiar movements of occultism plus figures as diverse as Francis Bacon, Percy Bysshe Shelley, Fabre d'Olivet and neo-Gnostic and neo-Templar Fabré-Palaprat. Churton even reminisces over his acquaintance Hans Jonas, who believed that modern Gnostic churches were 'cheap'. This is an entertaining and excellent guide. If you are an afficianado of the Rosicrucians it is essential; if not, I would advise dipping into it from time to time rather than attempting the whole feast in a single session.

Alan Craddock

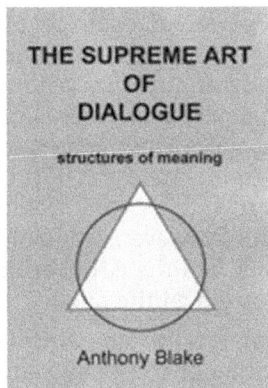

The Supreme Art of Dialogue, Anthony Blake, Duversity Publications, 305pp, £15/$30

This is a book with a hole in the middle. The hole at the heart of the book is the actual practice of dialogue, which is simply of a group of people speaking together as equals, a phenomenon which is surprisingly rare. Blake sees dialogue as an extraordinary event that allows new meaning to emerge. In the introduction, the author explains that 'attempts to find a neat linear order came to nothing, as did the writing of many versions in which topics were separated. The only recourse was to cycle through perspectives many times.'

The result is a difficult but fascinating book which examines the practice of dialogue from a multitude of perspectives, drawing on physics psychology, philosophy and spirituality, primarily Gurdjieff/Bennett influenced. the barely chartered territory lying somewhere between contemporary physics and ancient mysticism.' (p.256). I really would have appreciated more anecdotal evidence, perhaps even brief transcripts of productive dialogue sessions with comments. Yet it may be that transcripts would not trult represent a dialogue session.

Blake draws on practical and theoretical research into dialogue done by the physicist David Bohm, psychologist Patrick de Mare, psychotherapy research such as that done by Bion, J.G. Bennett's Systematics, and other disciplines.

Dialogue can encompass contradictions and accept contradictory points of view, a temporary higher group mind emerging among the participants. It may be seen as a bridge between the conscious and unconscious.

Frankly, I found the book bewildering, at least for the first half, yet fascinating. It's the sort of work from which ten further books could be produced. Almost every page introduces some new theory, another little known discipline, or some sentence pregnant with meaning. Somewhere around half the way through something clicked in me, and I just began to accept the format of the book, and I began to appreciate it.

Blake investigates the nature of meaning itself. He points out 'With the demise of organized religion and the embrace of all-encompassing belief systems based on authority and custom, we have been cast adrift. People are suffering from meaning-sickness... Humans are not rational animals as Aristotle claimed, but are meaning-making animals.' (p. 55)

The book attempts to develop the theory of the practice, but throughout one is continually straining to understand the practice. Fortunately, halfway through the book I experienced two dialogue sessions of around 35 people convened by the author. (The occasion was a week long Gurdjieff-Bennett seminar at which Blake was unexpectedly present for three days.)

The dialogue sessions weren't quite revelatory but I could feel that there's something going on there. I found it very easy to speak at the first session and had a sense that I could say anything and it didn't matter—and I've only previously been comfortable speaking to a large group when I've prepared thoroughly. There were chains of association, which at one point turned into a succession of people speaking in turn in different languages. There was much discussion of the purpose of the session—we were given little in the way of explanation. Some people heartily disliked the utterly freeform approach and said so. I was very tired at the second one and didn't contribute, but I was pleased that the main topic of that one wasn't the dialogue process itself. In these sessions we were told that we were learning how to speak to each other.

A thorough glossary helps with the extensive

jargon used in the book—trialogue and tetralogue, ILM, LogoVisual Technology, median groups—plus a good deal of terms from Bennett and Gurdjieff that I already had some familiarity with.

Blake sees the dialogue process as almost magical and sees it as an entirely new phenomenon that may have major implications for mankind, offering a new way of interaction and thinking for the entirely new and dangerous situations in which humanity now finds itself. There is certainly something very important to be explored here.

Andrew Phillip Smith

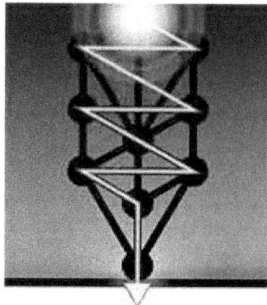

The Kabbalah Experience Review by Dean F. Wilson

The Qabalah (or Kabbalah, if you prefer) has provided a mystical and magical method, tradition, and language for humanity for at least a millenium, if not two, but if the Qabalist was not directly initiated into its mysteries then it can prove an impenetrable system for beginners. A variety of books aimed at Hermeticists embracing the Qabalah have arrived over the years, primarily inspired by Dion Fortune's *The Mystical Qabalah*. Naomi Ozaniec's *The Kabbalah Experience* is one such attempt at making the Qabalistic mysteries a little easier to understand, which it succeeds in doing, albeit at the expense of losing much of the complexity and depth that the Qabalah has to offer.

The book itself numbers some 450 pages and 'provides the core curriculum in the House of Life', a modern Mystery School that the author runs. I cannot help but think that the book could have been 50 to 100 pages shorter if the

numerous quotations (which are primarily used for convention to open each section of a chapter) and the sections entitled 'evocation' (which read rather poorly and simply reiterate what has been said in the previous pages, albeit in a somewhat fictional voice) had been axed. At times it feels as though the inclusion of these was intended as 'filler', to buff out the book a little; it does not need this, however, as it would still be a fairly thick book had the editor tuned into the Sephirah of Geburah a little more.

The format of the book is fairly standard and somewhat derivative, with a chapter devoted to each Sephirah and each Path. However, unlike most books which start at Kether and list the Sephiroth in order before commencing into the Paths, this one starts at Malkuth and jumps then into the Thirty-Second Path of Tav. The reason for this is that it follows the route the Qabalist uses to ascend the Tree. The book is sold as a 'practical guide', and the above structuring taps into this, as do a number of visualisations, meditations, and questions for contemplation. Ozaniec terms some of these *Exercitia Spiritualia*, which comes off as a little pretentious, but the aim is to get the reader to do something as opposed to merely reading.

Unfortunately some of the excercises themselves lack depth, and there is far less of practical use given in the book than is suggested by the sub-title. For example, it lacks any teachings on gematria, talismans, or ceremonial magic, the latter two of which are generally classified as 'the practical Qabalah', and thus the book ends up being primarily for reading, with a bit of meditation on the principles explored therein. This can, of course, prove useful for absolute beginners or those who might not want to explore the more magical elements of the system, but it is definitely not for anyone who already knows a thing or two about the Qabalah.

There is also too much focus on Eastern ideas and principles, which seems to be a trend. The fact that Western teachings cannot be explained in their own right without referencing Eastern ones does not reflect very well on us, but in many ways I think it is because we have not really tried. A new student of the Qabalah will have enough to learn trying to seperate his Malkuth from his Tiphareth (or reunite them, as is actually the case) without needing to learn all about Shiva, Shakti, Boddhisattva, and other Eastern concepts. Some people who already know these Eastern teachings may find it easier to relate one to the other, but for those who are unaccustomed, it simply means having to learn two systems rather than the one the book is supposed to be about.

The chapters dealing with the Paths between the Sephiroth are also surpringly lacking in detail on the Hebrew letters on which those Paths are based, to the extent that many of the chapters only mention them as part of the *Exercitia Spiritualia*, where it says 'Take the Following as Subjects for Meditation' along with 'The Letter Mem' (or other Hebrew letter). Perhaps this was to keep the book at a basic level, or perhaps the author herself is not that familiar with them, but they are a pivotal element of the Paths, and the latter cannot be understood without them. Indeed, the Tarot cards are mentioned, and a picture of each is given from the Rider-Waite deck, but the Hebrew letters which play such a vital role for the Paths and the Tarot cards are suspiciously missing, and when they do show up on a very rare occasion little more than a line is given to cover them.

The Kabbalah Experience is a bit too dependent on its sources, such as *The Mystical Qabalah*, and thus it fails to offer anything new to those who have already ready a book or two on the subject. For a complete newcomer it may offer an easy-to-digest introduction, but I could only really recommend it as a stepping stone to other texts, many of which have been around for a number of decades.

Dean Wilson

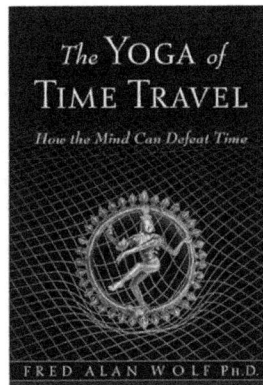

The Yoga of Time Travel: How the Mind Can Defeat Time, Fred Alan Wolf, Quest, 258pp, $19.95/ £17.50.

Can the peculiar notions of the effects of time described by contemporary physics be reconciled with the mystical view of time presented in ancient spiritual traditions? Fred Alan Wolf is a popular physics writer who has also delved into spirituality—Indian tradition, particularly 'mind yoga' appears to be his speciality, though he gives a nod to native Australian Dreamtime too. (Unfortunately, he also appeared in the somewhat awful film, What the Bleep Do We Know?) His approach is to discuss time travel and suggest a practical mind-based method of doing it. Does he teach the reader how to transport herself into the past or future? Well, of course he doesn't, and ultimately his suggested discipline of 'surrendering egoistic patterns' by focusing and defocusing the ego barely resembles any recognisable form of time travel—it's hardly a Tardis.

Wolf describes how possibility waves can travel backwards and forwards in tine. When they meet, they square to become probability curves which actualise the physical reality of our universe. Hence, the present is always implicitly linked to the past and the future. Wold distinguishes between an essential self that lies outside of time, in the realm of possibilities, and the personal ego, which exists as a result of the probability curves. Meditation and other spiritual disciplines allow one to access the timeless and spaceless realms of possibility. From this vantage point, the errors of the past can be psychologically forgiven and the future can be renewed. It's a fascinating approach, which involves a considerable amount of physics in its development.

The book's final destination is therefore not quite what the reader expects—we arrive at a location that is a little foreign, perhaps a little barren, which does not resemble the place we had imagined at all. However, the journey along the way is the whole point of this book. Wolf leads us through the understanding of time given by modern physics, giving us an exhilarating ride, passing through the breathtaking scenery of quantum physics. If anything, the modern physics-based concepts of time are more bizarre and more counter-intuitive than anything that has appeared in the entire history of religion and spirituality. I'm sure that I still haven't quite grasped his ultimate point, despite the final chapter summarising all the previous stages of his exploration, but I'm sure I'll come to understand it. In time.

Alan Craddock

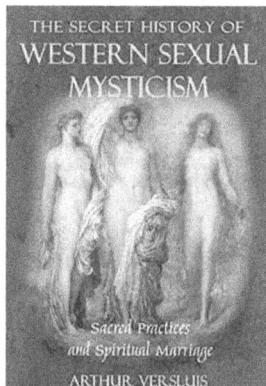

The Secret History of Western Sexual Mysticism, **Arthur Versluis, Destiny Books, 176pp, $14.95.**

William Blake's Sexual Path to Spiritual Vision, **Marsha Keith Schuchard, Inner Traditions, 416pp, $19.95.**

For many people the idea of sexual mysticism was something that appeared in the West with the Hippy movement and Tantric Sex practices. Each of these books in its way opens the readers eyes to the multiplicity of ways in which these practices have long been present in western culture.

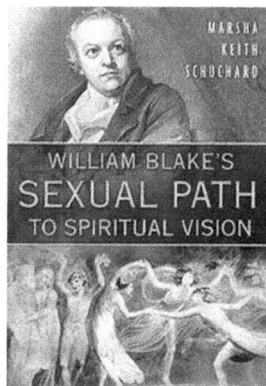

Arthur Versluis' book covers evidence from Historic Europe, meaning Greece (some very interesting interpretations of erotic images) and Christendom. Marsha Keith Schuchard's book goes into much more depth about a much shorter period of time—the world in which Blake grew up and lived (late 18th to early 19th century).

The secret history of Western Sexual Mysticism is a short book— just 145 pages— and it covers a lot of ground, so it may be churlish of me to say that it leaves out some bits. It certainly brings a number of interesting areas to light. It is fascinating to read about the early Christian practice (also early condemned) of virgines subintroductae where men and women slept together without intercourse. He believes this is a true example of a bringing of human sexual nature 'onto the path'— to use Buddhist language. The idea being that one can 'channel' sexual energy and use it to actualise one's highest possibilities. As Versluis puts it, ' given that we are born sexual beings, is it not possible that we might benefit from incorporating and transmuting our sexual nature, just as we may transmute the rest of our daily lives?' Orthodox Christianity found it safer to condemn sexual activity or at least assign it to an area of life foreign from and antipathetical to spirituality.

My main criticism of the book is that seems to me somewhat woolly on the subject of what 'sexual mysticism' actually is; there is a great readiness to assume common practices in situations where we really don't know much. One of a number of characteristics he lists as being typical of groups that practised sexual mysticism is they 'prefer the wilderness to urban society'. Surely many esoteric 'groups' do this whatever their practices are? I feel he has his own preconception of the practices involved and sees the pattern where he will.

I also felt he shied away from any mention of abuses that might happen (and have happened) in the context of such beliefs. One justification for such would be to avoid the prurient fascination of such topics, and he does mention the danger of sexual mysticism in his summing up—but very briefly—and yet it seems a little self serving to ignore so much.

And yet finally his construct is pretty compelling as a workable interpretation: 'Sexual union becomes sexual mysticism not when two individuals join, but when each lover becomes for the other an opening into the transcendence of I and thou, an entry into a new dimension beyond selfhood' 'Sexual union is potentially conducive to such an experience (a kind of gnosis) because in it a man can become an archetypal man encountering an archetypal woman: angel or god unites with angel or god.' And he draws the connection that many artists have seen between harvesting this energy and creative / artistic activity.

Marsha Keith Schuchard's book goes into a great deal more depth, but then it's a bigger book 340-odd pages plus notes and it covers a far shorter period of time, concentrating on the period of William Blake's lifetime and that of his parents.

Most fascinating of all for me was to understand more of the background from which he arose; he's no longer a figure standing on his own.

Ms Schuchard has been able to find out more about his mother's connection with the Moravian church—there is documentary evidence of her membership of the church in Fetter Lane in London with her first husband (she was a widow when she married Blake's father) and possibly members of Blake's father's family. And not only that, but their membership was during the so-called 'Sifting Time' a time of dramatic extremes connected with the influence of Count Nicolaus von Zinzendorf.

For them, sex was sacred, sacramental; whilst this gave a great emphasis on the pleasures of sex (The married Choir were 'to teach sexual procedures and practices to newly wedded

brothers and sisters' and in one of their hymns a wife says 'when my dear husband /lets his oil sizzle in me/.... this grace is sacrament'), it also meant that masturbation or illicit sex was a major sin. But the group was understanding of temptation and advised the young to sublimate by focussing on Jesus' 'holy covenant slit' envisioning Christ's side wound as a kind of vulva.

Zinzendorf fully believed that the worshipper should experience a sexual state he was inspired by reading about Hasidim who 'deliberately give themselves erections during prayer according to the commandment of Rabbi Baal Shem... who said to them that just as one who engages in intercourse with an impotent organ cannot give birth, so one should be potent at the time of prayer, it is necessary to unite with the Shekinah [the Feminine aspect of God]. It is therefore necessary to move back and forth as in the act of intercourse'

For me the most interesting parts of the book are how it shows the influence of Moravian thinking on Blake's upbringing. Even though Blake's mother was no longer part of the Fetter Lane community after she remarried in 1752, she would seem to have been still deeply under the influence of Zinzendorf's thinking.

Zinzendorf had firmly believed in the capacity of children to have visions and, having been such a child himself, in encouraging it; in home schooling under the influence of the mother; in having one's life enriched with as much art, music, poetry as possible (in contrast to the Dissenters of his time to which group Blake's parents are usually said to have belonged); and, in a very modern twist, in the possibility of influencing a child while still in utero by means of music and such like.

Much of the rest of the book could be described as a narrative of Blake's marriage, his search for a mate, his marriage to Catherine, his apparent sexual dissatisfaction and looking for a solution in all the myriad sexual theories of his time and the apparent resolution of that search and how all these themes can be seen in many of his writings and images, reflecting at each stage of his life how he visualised his experiences. It appears that at one point in the marriage Blake considered options such as taking a second wife, due to waning desire and the strong feeling that, in order to be creatively and spiritually at his peak, he needed to be able to be consistently experiencing extended sexual peaks. The blame for this tended to be pretty clearly laid on the wife, a situation that Catherine Blake may not have always been equal to. It certainly does seem likely that the Blakes practised (and mastered?) some form of Tantric sex.

We wade through a veritable sea of theories and wild beliefs, such a sexual 'therapy' involving a couple paying to receive electrical stimulation during coitus which apparently provided prolonged ecstasy. It was a revolutionary time; for many the revolution that was imminent was in the nature of humanity. Marsh Keith Schuchard's book brings to light much that was hidden by the dust of 'respectability' that tends to settle on the past.

Food for Thought

How is poetry born in us? There is, I think, some commerce between the outer and an inner being. Some character in aspiration determines the character of inspiration. In our meditation we are all consciously or unconsciously votaries of the Holy Breath. Our meditation is sacrifice and some one of its tongues of intellectual fire descends upon us. St Paul says there are diversities of powers but they all spring from the same Breath. To one may come the discerning of spirits, to another speaking with tongues, which I interpret to have, among others, these meanings, poetry, music, eloquence.'

AE (George Russell)

The medieval mind ignored the facts of the physical world and so produced a society that was all cathedrals and no sanitation. The modern mind ignores the values of the spiritual world and so has produced a society that is all sanitation and no cathedrals.

John Anthony West

They who can give up essential liberty to obtain a little temporary safety, deserve neither liberty nor safety.

Benjamin Franklin

The leaning of sophists towards the bypaths of apocrypha is a constant quantity.

James Joyce, Ulysses

Watch your thoughts; they become your words.

Watch your words; they become your actions.

Watch your actions; they become your habits.

Watch your habits; they become your character.

Watch your character for it will become your destiny.

If I am not for myself, who will be for me?

If I am only for myself, what am I?

And if not now, when?

Rabbi Hillel

Not all sins are forgiven, but only those committed involuntarily and out of ignorance.

Basilides

There can be no clear cut division between salvation and damnation, between life and death… No man can be perfectly saved—no man can be completely lost.

J.G. Bennett

The Bible is literature, not dogma.

George Santana

Biographies

Anthony Blake was born 1939 in Bristol where he also studied Physics and met David Bohm, followed by studies in the history and philosophy of science at Cambridge. He became deeply involved in the Fourth Way activities of John Bennett, a leading exponent of Gurdjieff's ideas, and worked with him over many years, including educational research. He has published several books including *A Seminar on Time*, *The Intelligent Enneagram* and the recent *The Supreme Art of Dialogue*, dialogue being one of his passions. He lives in Scotland and has six children.

Anthony Cartledge is the author of *Planetary Types: The Science of Celestial Influence*. He has published articles with WellBeing International, Conscious Living and other magazines and web sites within the alternative fields. He is a features writer and sub-editor for his local newspaper and lives in Queensland, Australia.

Mae **Arthur Craddock** yn byw yng Ngororau Cymru ymhlith defaid a chreigiau. Mewn gwirionedd, ffugenw'r golygydd yw.

Miguel Conner is the author of the novel *Queen of Darkness* and host of the Internet radio show *Aeon Byte*, formerly *Coffee, Cigarettes and Gnosis*.

April D. DeConick is the Isla Carroll and Percy E. Turner Professor of Biblical Studies at Rice University. Her interests include early Jewish and Christian mysticism, and Gnosticism. She is the author of many books and articles including *The Thirteenth Apostle, The Original Gospel of Thomas in Translation, Recovering the Original Gospel of Thomas, and Voices of the Mystics*.

Bill Darlison is the senior minister of Dublin Unitarian Church. He trained in Rome for the Catholic priesthood, but left before ordination and became a Unitarian in 1988. He has been a student of astrology for over forty years and is interested in the influence of astrology on early Christian thought and practice. He is the author of *The Gospel and the Zodiac: The Secret Truth about Jesus*, and *The Shortest Distance: 101 Stories from the World's Spiritual Traditions*.

Tessa B. Dick, the fifth and last wife of Philip K. Dick, has been writing since childhood and became a published writer in 1969 with an article in *Alive!* magazine. After 12 years of teaching English and communications at Chapman University, she has retired to a mountain cabin where she writes the stories that have filled her imagination for many years. Her novel *The Owl in Daylight* and her memoir of Philip K. Dick, *Remembering Firebright*, are available at Amazon.

Scott Finch received his BFA from Louisiana State University in 1994 and his MFA from the Tyler School of Art at Temple University in 1996. Finch has exhibited at galleries across the United States and in Europe. He has been featured by the Critic's Choice Exhibition at the Dallas Visual Art Center, the Fleisher Art Challenge at the Fleisher Art Memorial in Philadelphia, and the Gulf South Regional Artists Exhibition at Bridge For Contemporary Art in New Orleans.

Tessa Finn is a native of Dublin, Ireland. A sculptress and ex-poet who writes books reviews at the rate of three words a day, much of her spare time is spent in esoteric sexual practice. Her favourite foods are mashed potatoes and eggs, her favoruite drink gin and tonic.

Mark Holwager completed his Bachelor of Arts degree in Religious Studies at DePauw University in 2008, focusing on congruent practices shared by many religious traditions and *The Prisoner* related appreciation constituents. He is currently a legal assistant in Beech Grove, Indiana with plans to begin law school in the fall of 2010.

Will Parker is a writer and researcher, with a particular interest in the literature and history of Medieval Wales. His book, *The Four Branches of the Mabinogi*, was published by Bardic Press in 2005.

Anthony Peake is the author of *Is There Life after Death? — The Extraordinary Science Of What Happens When You Die* which has sold over 30,000 copies world-wide and *The Daemon — A Guide to Your Extraordinary Secret Self* . He studied Sociology and History at the University of Warwick and at the London School of Economics, and is a professional member of the Scientific & Medical Network, the International Association of Near-Death Studies and the Institute of Noetic Sciences. His *Cheating The Ferryman* theory has been described as one of the most provocative and innovative ideas of recent years. He has a very active website forum which can be viewed at www.anthonypeake.com/forum.

Eugene Poliakov was born after the Orthodox Christmas 1958 in St. Petersburg (formerly Leningrad). Graduated (1974) from Lyceum 239 (see Wikipedia) and subsequently from Technical University in St. Petersburg (1981). He holds a degree equivalent to an M.Sc. in solid state physics and currently deals with non-uniform time frames of reference (www.physicoschronos.org). He has presented his scientific ideas at several international events.

Jeremy Puma has been a student of Gnosticism for over 15 years. He is one of the founding members of the Palm Tree Garden Gnostic community, an online collective of Gnostics from many different traditions, and the Gnostic Order of Allogenes, a collective of independent Gnostic practitioners. Jeremy is the author of a number of books on the theory and practice of Gnosticism in the twenty-first century, all of which can be found online at www.lulu.com/eleleth. He currently maintains two websites at waygnostic.wordpress.com and gnostichealing.wordpress.com. Jeremy lives in Seattle, WA with a lovely lady and two brown dogs.

Robert Lawrence Seitz is a self-taught multi-media artist living in Los Angeles, California. He is currently working as a metalsmith, creating fine jewelry and sculptural objects with bronze, silver, gold and precious stones. He is also writing a science-fiction novel which incorporates mystic themes. As a talismonger, he is in the process of introducing jewelry which include Gnostic symbols, and welcomes custom inquiries in any scale. His work is on display through his website, www.rseitz.com.

Andrew Phillip Smith is the editor of *The Gnostic* and author of *A Dictionary of Gnosticism*, *The Gnostics: History, Tradition, Scriptures, Influence*, *The Gospel of Philip: Annotated & Explained*, *The Lost Sayings of Jesus: Annotated & Explained*, and *Gnostic Writings on the Soul: Annotated & Explained*.

Luc Valentine is a writer who lives in the southeastern United States and is a student of Gnosticism. He has a bachelor's degree in Liberal Arts with majors in history and English and is an administrator of The Palm Tree Garden, a contemporary Gnostic website. His blog, at www.gnosticchristian.org will premier in late September.

Colin Wilson is the author of over 100 books, from *The Outsider* to *Super Consciousness*. His interests include philosophy, psychology, the paranormal, criminology and ancient civilizations.

Dean F. Wilson was born in Dublin, Ireland, where he currently resides. He's a practising Gnostic and ceremonial magician, and author of fiction and non-fiction. More info can be found at: http://www.protosmythos.org.

Valarie Ziegler has taught at DePauw University since 1995, giving courses on Christianity and on religion in American culture, plus a religion and film class on *The Prisoner*. She is the author of three books, *The Advocates of Peace in Antebellum America; Eve and Adam: Jewish, Christian, and Muslim Readings on Genesis and Gender; Diva Julia: The Public Romance and Private Agony of Julia Ward Howe* and is working on *American Edens*, a study of Adam and Eve in American popular culture co-written with Linda Schearing of Gonzaga University.

Also Available from Bardic Press

Boyhood With Gurdjieff; Gurdjieff Remembered; Balanced Man
by Fritz Peters (not available in the USA)

My Father Gurdjieff
Nicholas de Val

New Nightingale, New Rose: Poems From the Divan of Hafiz
translated by Richard Le Gallienne

The Quatrains of Omar Khayyam:
Three Translations of the Rubaiyat
*translated by Edward Fitzgerald, Justin McCarthy
and Richard Le Gallienne*

Door of the Bloved: Ghazals of Hafiz
translated by Justin McCarthy

The Gospel of Thomas and Christian Wisdom
Stevan Davies

The Four Branches of the Mabinogi
Will Parker

Christ In Islam
James Robson

Don't Forget: P.D. Ouspensly's Life of Self-Remembering
Bob Hunter

Songs of Sorrow and Joy
Ashford Brown

Planetary Types: The Science of Celestial Influence
Tony Cartledge

Visit our website at www.bardic-press.com
email us at info@bardic-press.com

Lightning Source UK Ltd.
Milton Keynes UK
UKHW051544180822
407492UK00009B/824

9 781906 834050